Routledge
Taylor & Francis Group

NEW YORK AND LONDON

www.routledgesw.com

Alice Lieberman, The University of Kansas, Series Editor

An authentic breakthrough in social work education ...

New Directions in Social Work is an innovative, integrated series of texts, website, and interactive case studies for generalist courses in the social work curriculum at both undergraduate and graduate levels. Instructors will find everything they need to build a comprehensive course that allows students to meet course outcomes, with these unique features:

- All texts, interactive cases, and test materials are **linked to the 2015 CSWE Policy and Accreditation Standards (EPAS).**
- **One web portal with easy access** for instructors and students from any computer—no codes, no CDs, no restrictions. Go to www.routledgesw. com and discover.
- **The series is flexible and can be easily adapted for use in online distance-learning courses as well as hybrid and bricks-and-mortar courses.**
- Each text and the website can be used **individually** or as an **entire series** to meet the needs of any social work program.

TITLES IN THE SERIES

Social Work and Social Welfare: An Invitation, Fourth Edition by Marla Berg-Weger

Human Behavior in the Social Environment, Fourth Edition by Anissa Taun Rogers

Research for Effective Social Work Practice, Fourth Edition by Judy L. Krysik and Jerry Finn

Social Policy for Effective Practice: A Strengths Approach, Third Edition by Rosemary K. Chapin

The Practice of Generalist Social Work, Third Edition by Julie Birkenmaier, Marla Berg-Weger, and Martha P. Dewees

Social Work and Social Welfare

An Invitation

Fourth Edition

by Marla Berg-Weger,
Saint Louis University

In this book and companion custom website you will find:

- An emphasis on a **strengths-based perspective** and attention to diversity, social environment, theory and theoretical frameworks, levels of social work practice, and an array of fields of practice.
- The histories of social welfare and the social work profession presented as the **intertwined phenomena that they are.**
- A profile of the **contemporary landscape of the society in which social workers practice.**
- Social work practice within the framework of **planned change, encompassing: engagement, assessment, intervention, and evaluation and termination.**
- The opportunity to **hear from social work practitioners working in eight diverse and challenging practice settings.**
- Six unique, in-depth, interactive, easy-to-access cases, which students can easily reach from *any* computer, provide a **"learning by doing" format unavailable with any other text(s).** Your students will have an advantage unlike any other they will experience in their social work training.
- A wealth of **instructor-only resources** also available at www.routledgesw.com/intro provide: **full-text readings** that link to the concepts presented in each of the chapters; a complete bank of objective and essay-type **test items, all linked to current CSWE EPAS standards; PowerPoint presentations** to help students master key concepts; annotated **links to a treasure trove of social work assets on the internet**; and a forum inviting all instructors using texts in the series to communicate with each other, and share ideas to improve teaching and learning.

Social Work and Social Welfare

An Invitation

Fourth Edition

by Marla Berg-Weger,
Saint Louis University

Routledge
Taylor & Francis Group

NEW YORK AND LONDON

Fourth edition published 2016
by Routledge 711 Third Avenue, New York, NY 10017

And by Routledge
2 Park Square, Milton Park, Abingdon, Oxon OX14 4RN

Routledge is an imprint of the Taylor & Francis Group, an informa business
© 2016 Taylor & Francis

First edition published 2005 by McGraw-Hill

Second and third edition published 2010 and 2013 by Routledge

Library of Congress Cataloging in Publication Data
Berg-Weger, Marla
   Social work and social welfare : an invitation / by Marla Berg-Weger. -- Fourth Edition.
      pages cm. -- (New directions in social work)
   Revised edition of the author's Social work and social welfare, 2013.
   1. Social service--United States. 2. Poor--Services for--United States. I. Title.
   HV91.B384 2015
   361.30973--dc23   2015022248

Typeset in ITC Berkeley Oldstyle Std by
Servis Filmsetting Ltd, Stockport, Cheshire

Brief Contents

Contents

CHAPTER 12 *The Social Work Profession* 566

Preface

MAJOR CHANGES TO THE FOURTH EDITION

Like the previous editions of *Social Work and Social Welfare: An Invitation,* this edition introduces students to the knowledge, skills, and values that are essential for working with individuals, families, groups, organizations, communities, and public policy in a variety of practice settings. The fourth edition provides an up-to-date profile of the world in which today's social workers practice—with updated demographic, statistical, legislative, policy, and research information; sensitive discussions of contemporary ethical issues; and new profiles of social workers and first-person narratives from social workers in a variety of fields. The call to become engaged in some of society's most challenging issues is clearer than in previous editions.

For the new editions of all five books in the *New Directions in Social Work* series, each addressing a foundational course in the social work curriculum, the publisher has created a brand-new, uniquely distinctive teaching strategy that revolves around the print book but offers much more than the traditional text experience. Quick Guides within the text offer students guidance for their field experiences. The series website, www.routledgesw.com, leads to custom websites coordinated with each book in the series and offers a variety of features to support instructors as you integrate the many facets of an education in social work.

At www.routledgesw.com/intro, the site for this particular book, you will find a wealth of resources to help you create a dynamic, experiential introduction to social work for your students:

- Companion readings linked to key concepts in each chapter, along with questions to encourage further thought and discussion.
- Six interactive fictional cases (one of them new with publication of the fourth edition) with accompanying exercises that bring to life the concepts covered in the book, readings, and classroom discussions.
- A bank of exam questions (both objective and open-ended).

- PowerPoint presentations, which can serve as a starting point for class discussions.
- Sample syllabi demonstrating how the text and website, when used together through the course, satisfy the 2015 Council on Social Work Educational Policy and Accreditation Standards (EPAS).
- Quick Guides from the books offered online for students to copy and take into the field for guidance.
- Annotated links to a treasure trove of articles and other readings, videos, and internet sites.
- An online forum inviting all instructors using the books in the series to share ideas to improve teaching and learning.

ORGANIZATION OF THE BOOK

Social Work and Social Welfare: An Invitation introduces students to the profession they are considering for their life's work. From a strengths-based perspective, students will be provided with a comprehensive overview of the major areas relevant for social work practice, including diversity, social environment, theory and theoretical frameworks, levels of social work practice, and an array of fields of practice. Presented as the intertwined phenomena that they are, the histories of social welfare and the social work profession are presented to help the student gain insight into the context of the social work profession. *Social Work and Social Welfare* offers a profile of the contemporary landscape of the world and the society in which social workers practice within the concept of planned change, encompassing engagement, assessment, intervention, and evaluation and termination. Students have the opportunity to read first-hand accounts of social work practice in an array of diverse and challenging practice settings and gain insights into the future of the social work profession.

The following paragraphs briefly introduce each of the chapters included in this book, with emphasis on the updated content.

Chapter 1

A Glimpse into the World of Social Work begins by grounding the students in a definition of social work, the ways that social workers help people, the people with whom social workers work, and the places where social workers practice. Information is provided on the three social work degree options available. Current demographic and employment data for the social work profession is presented. In this first chapter, students are introduced to a fictitious social worker named Emily. Throughout each chapter of the book, Emily's experiences as a social work student and later a practitioner provide insights into the rewards and challenges of a career in social work that are addressed in that chapter.

Chapter 2

History of Social Work and Social Welfare enables student readers to understand and appreciate the historical backdrop of the social welfare system and the profession of social work that has produced the systems and profession that exist today. The dynamics of history as it impacts social work and social welfare is emphasized in this chapter. Profiles are provided that highlight the careers of individuals whose contributions have advanced the social work profession. Information is provided on social work leaders and historical perspectives on the African American, disability, and LGBT communities. The section on 21st-century social work has been updated to reflect the economic and social strains of the past few years and current day issues.

Chapter 3

U.S. Poverty and the Implications for Social Work provides students with both a historical and a contemporary look at U.S. and international poverty and the programs aimed at alleviating poverty within our society. As economic philosophy and status are ever-changing, this chapter provides an up-to-date exploration of the current status of those persons living in poverty, the effectiveness of the legislation and programs that are intended to improve the quality of their lives, income inequality, and the importance of social workers having in-depth understanding of the policies that impact the lives of those being served.

Chapter 4

The Social Work Environment is, in fact, the global environment in which modern-day social workers live and practice. This chapter focuses on helping students understand the social forces and realities of changes that influence our society within such issues as race and ethnicity, global issues, and social justice. The dynamics of oppression and discrimination have a new emphasis. Within the context of the political, economic, and social environments that impact life for the client systems served by social workers, current information is provided on issues such as race, ethnicity, age, gender, income (socioeconomic class), sexual orientation, and religion. Current realities of life in the United States are discussed, including the recent economic recession and ensuing recovery period, unemployment, income inequality, the wealth gap, health care challenges, immigration issues, and the new face of poverty.

Chapter 5

Diversity in Social Work Practice introduces the students to key areas of social work practice that will impact virtually every dimension of their lives as social workers. With an emphasis on self-awareness, students are challenged to consider the evolution of their own views on persons who may be different from themselves, whether on the basis of race, ethnicity, culture, age, sex and gender, sexual orientation, socioeconomic class, physical ability, religion, or lifestyle. Framed within theoretical perspectives for understanding diversity, students are offered an overview of the skills required to be a culturally competent social work practitioner. The expanded discussion of intersectionality of race, class, and gender lends insight into the area of diversity. Cultural competence is emphasized along with U.S. trends regarding racial tensions and the status of affirmative action.

Chapter 6

While challenging for the beginning social work student, **Values and Ethics in Social Work Practice** are introduced in this chapter as the foundation that guides social work practice. Using value and ethical dilemmas that challenge social workers, students have multiple opportunities throughout the chapter to consider the origins of their own value and ethical beliefs and to apply them to situations in which they will likely find themselves as they develop as practitioners. The commitment of the social work profession to advocating for ethical practices is emphasized. The National Association of Social Workers *Code of Ethics* (2008) is discussed with an historical and current context. A section on ethical issues related to technology in social work practice has been added to the fourth edition.

Chapter 7

Social Work Perspectives and Methods conceptualizes generalist social work practice within the levels of practice with individuals and families, groups, and organizations, communities, and public policy. Students are introduced to a range of theoretical frameworks that guide social workers as they practice, including systems theory, the strengths-based perspective, and a model for solution-focused interventions. An expanded discussion of the role of theory and evidence-based practice focuses on practice perspectives. Content has been added on critical reflection and the foundation of knowledge underlying the helping process. The chapter ends with a discussion of the integration of social work theory in practice settings.

Chapter 8

Fields of Social Work Practice provides students with up-to-date perspectives on social work practice in the second decade of the 21st century. Thirteen social workers share their experiences in 12 different practice settings, including health and mental health, criminal justice, school, public health, and rural settings; and practice with children and families, immigrants and refugees, military veterans and families, older adults, persons with addictions, and persons with disabilities. It is a lengthy chapter, but through the "voices" of actual social workers, it gives students real-life insight into social work practice. This chapter also serves as an introduction to the following three chapters, in which levels of social work practice are explored, and may provide material for review and discussion throughout the next three chapters.

Chapter 9

Social Work Practice with Individuals and Families is the first of the levels of practice to be presented. Students are exposed to the concepts of planned change. They will learn about the phases of the social work intervention, including engagement, assessment, intervention, and evaluation and termination. Linked to the EPAS, these areas of practice help students gain insights into the knowledge and skills required for competency-based social work practice. Students will become familiar with the effective social work practice behaviors they will need as they practice at all levels with a new focus on interviewing and clinical skills and examples depicting these approaches.

Chapter 10

Social Work Practice with Groups continues the students' exposure to the facets of generalist social work practice. Students are presented with four models of group-level practice. Building on the foundation of social work practice with individuals and families, group-level practice emphasizes the concepts of engagement, assessment, intervention, and evaluation as they are applied at the group level of social work practice. Added areas of content include social justice within group work and using motivational interviewing and solution-focused approach in group interventions.

Chapter 11

Social Work Practice with Organizations and Communities, and Public Policy uses the insights gained about practice at the individual, family, and group levels to expand students' awareness of social work practice areas. In the fourth edition, policy practice is presented to students as a career opportunity as well as a critical part of any area of practice; macro-level practice and global practice discussions are expanded.

Chapter 12

The Social Work Profession brings to a close this introduction to the social work profession. Trends in social work employment opportunities are included along with up-to-date information on salaries. A key part of the discussion is how various current issues—health care, population aging, developments in child welfare, rapidly advancing technology, use of avatars in work with ado-lescents, animal-assisted therapy, financial literacy, disasters and crises, and globalization—are likely to affect social work in the near future. Students are provided with various resources to help direct their interests as they continue their careers.

INTERACTIVE CASES

The website www.routledgesw.com/cases presents six unique, in-depth, inter-active, fictional cases with dynamic characters and real-life situations. One of them—the Brickville case—is entirely new to this edition of the series. Your students can easily access the cases from any computer. The cases provide a "learn-ing by doing" format unavailable with any other book, and the experience will be unlike any other your students will experience in their social work training.

Each of the interactive cases uses text, graphics, and video to help students learn about engagement, assessment, intervention, and evaluation and termi-nation at multiple levels of social work practice. The "My Notebook" feature allows students to take and save notes, type in written responses to tasks, and

share their work with classmates and instructors by e-mail. Through these
interactive cases, you can integrate the readings and classroom discussions:

The Sanchez Family: Systems, Strengths, and Stressors

The 10 individuals in this extended Latino family have numerous strengths
but are faced with a variety of challenges. Students will have the opportunity
to experience the phases of the social work intervention, grapple with ethical
dilemmas, and identify strategies for addressing issues of diversity.

Riverton: A Community Conundrum

Riverton is a small Midwest city in which the social worker lives and works. The
social worker identifies an issue that presents her community with a challenge.
Students and instructors can work together to develop strategies for engaging,
assessing, and intervening with the citizens of the social worker's neighborhood.

Carla Washburn: Loss, Aging, and Social Support

Students will get to know Carla Washburn, an older African American woman
who finds herself living alone after the loss of her grandson and in considerable
pain from a recent accident. In this case, less complex than the Sanchez family
case, students can apply their growing knowledge of gerontology and exercise
the skills of culturally competent practice at the individual, family, and group
levels.

RAINN

Based on the first online hotline for delivering sexual assault services, this interactive case includes a variety of exercises to enable students to gain knowledge
and skills related to the provision of services to persons in crisis. With a focus
on social work practice at all levels, exercises provide insight into program
services and evaluation, interactions with volunteers and clients, and research.

Hudson City: An Urban Community Affected by Disaster

A natural disaster in the form of Hurricane Diane has hit Hudson City, a
large metropolitan area on the northeastern coast of the United States. This

interactive case will provide students with insights into the complexities of experiencing a disaster, including the phases of the human response to disaster and the social work role in responding to natural disasters.

Brickville

The Brickville community is undergoing a transition due to plans that are underway for a major community re-development plan. This interactive case will provide students with the opportunity to learn about macro-level practice within the larger community. Students will also be introduced to the Stone family who have lived in Brickville for several generations and are now experiencing challenges related to the re-development efforts as well as a decades-old family crisis.

I have written this book with the hope that it will provide your students and you not only with an enticing introduction to our profession but also with deep insight into the knowledge, skills, and values that are required for a competent and effective social work practitioner. The multiple options for supporting your teaching of this content are intended to help you address the diverse range of student learning styles and needs. The design of this book and the instructor support materials optimize the experiential approach to the introductory course in social work. I hope this book and the support materials will be of help to you and your students as they embark on their journey toward social work practice.

ACKNOWLEDGMENTS

I would like to extend my appreciation to the many social workers who helped this book to become a reality. To Alice Lieberman and the other authors of this book series, Rosemary Chapin, Anissa Rogers, Judy Krysik, Jerry Finn, Julie Birkenmaier, and Marty Dewees, I thank you for your continued vision, support, and feedback through this enriching and invigorating process. To my colleagues at Saint Louis University, Sabrina Tyuse, Sue Tebb, and Shannon Cooper-Sadlo, I appreciate your willingness to provide resources, review chapters, and serve as a sounding board for my ideas. To the practitioners who contributed their "voices from the field," I am grateful for your willingness to share the stories of your professional journeys. To the social workers and other professionals who agreed to be profiled in this edition, thank you for your willingness to allow us to have a glimpse into your lives. Thank you to Kristina Roselle and Daniel Stewart for your help with this edition. Thanks to the reviewers who provided feedback for the fourth edition:

Jessica Friedrichs, Carlow University
Keri Boer, Montreat College
Shannon Mokoro, Salem State University
Allison Sinanan, Stockton University
Megan Stright, Boise State Univeristy
Linda Wells-Glover, University of Missouri–St. Louis
Jessica Donahue-Dioh, Xavier University
Lisa Hosack, Grove City College
Gailerd Swisegood, College of the Sequoias
Richard Blake, Seton Hall University
Renee Bowman Daniel, Daemen College
Elissa D. Giffords, Long Island University
Pamela Bowers, University of Texas at Arlington
Blanca Ramos, University at Albany
Stephen Monroe Tomczak, Southern Connecticut State University
Clarence Williams, Grambling State University
Nancy Anderson, Warner University
Catherine Phillips, Lakehead University
Lara Vanderhoof, Tabor College
Kristen Humphrey, Pittsburgh State University

To the staff of Routledge, Taylor & Francis, thank you for believing in the potential of this book series.

About the Author

Marla Berg-Weger is a professor in the School of Social Work at Saint Louis University, Missouri, where she also serves as the Executive Director, Geriatric Education Center and is a past Director of Field Education. Dr. Berg-Weger has been a social worker for over three decades and holds social work degrees at the bachelor's, master's, and doctoral levels. Her social work practice experience includes public social welfare services, domestic violence services, mental health, and gerontological and health care social work. Her research and writing focus on social work practice and gerontological social work, particularly in the areas of family caregiving, dementia care, and older adult mobility. With Julie Birkenmaier, she co-authored the textbook *The Practicum Companion for Social Work: Integrating Class and Field Work*. With Birkenmaier and Marty Dewees, she co-authored another book in this series, *Contemporary Social Work Practice*. She is the past president and secretary of the Association of Gerontology in Social Work. She serves as the Managing Editor of the *Journal of Gerontological Social Work*. She is a Fellow in the Gerontological Society of America.

LEARNING OBJECTIVES

After reading this chapter, you should be able to:

1. Define social work.
2. Describe the range and areas in which social workers practice.
3. Describe populations with whom social workers work.
4. Discuss the educational path to becoming a social worker.

EPAS COMPETENCY

1. Demonstrate Ethical and Professional Behavior

A GLIMPSE INTO THE WORLD OF SOCIAL WORK

Source: Shutterstock/Iakov Filimonov

"Social work is a career you can't leave at the office. You are committed to facilitating change in people's lives and the environment in which they live. You often work with, or on behalf of, individuals who have difficult problems and lack the resources with which to cope. It can be inspiring to see your clients help themselves out of a crisis using skills you helped them find within themselves."

As we begin to explore the profession of social work, keep in mind these words, written by an MSW student (Walton, 1996, p. 63). Her words not only capture her enthusiasm for her new profession, but they also provide a sense of the work that social workers do.

■ ■ ■ ■ ■

Ask social workers what drew them to the profession, and you will hear one common message: They liked the idea that their work would help to better people's lives. In one study, the primary reasons social workers cited for entering the profession were their desires: (1) to help others; (2) to advocate for the disadvantaged; and (3) to provide mental health services (Whitaker, 2008, p. 4). Although many might have considered a different helping profession, such as psychology, sociology, teaching, or a health profession (i.e., medicine, nursing, or occupation/physical/speech therapy), in the end they chose social work because the mission and goals of the profession and our commitment to social justice resonate with their own personal goals and aspirations. As you will learn throughout this book, social work is unique among the helping professions because of its broad scope of concern, social justice-oriented core values, professional commitment to social and economic justice, and dedication to bringing about meaningful change.

Social work and other helping professions share many of the same methods and goals, and the social work profession has integrated theories and knowledge from a wide array of sources, including education, economics, sociology, psychology, medicine, law, philosophy, political science, and anthropology (Drake, 2014, p. 2). For example, from psychology, social workers have learned to understand the impact of emotional and psychological factors on the individual. From sociology, we have gained insight into different populations. From the health-related professions (e.g., medicine, nursing, and allied health professions), we have learned about the relationships between biological functioning and physical health, and how these factors impact biopsychosocialspiritual well-being. The health professions also emphasize the value of the interprofessional team approach, an approach that is essential to social workers in virtually every practice setting.

While aspects of social work and other helping professions certainly overlap, social work is distinctive in a number of ways (see Exhibit 1.1). As social work scholar, Reamer (2013a), posits: "Social work is unique among the human service professions in its sustained commitment to the enlightened view concerning the need to focus simultaneously on individual well-being (practice) and broader structural and environmental issues that must be addressed to enhance individual well-being (policy)" (p. 122). The social work profession emphasizes a strengths-based, holistic, or interpersonal perspective, as opposed to the other helping professions, which focus more on the individual (intrapersonal) perspective. The National Association of

Social Workers (NASW), the professional organization for the social work profession, issued a policy statement supporting "the promotion of social work as a distinctly different profession from other human service disciplines (such as counseling, clinical psychology, nursing, marriage and family therapy, and so forth) as it focuses on [both] the intra- and inter-personal aspects of clients' lives" (2012–2014c, p. 80). Social workers consider their clients' social environments—their families, homes, places of work, states of physical and mental health, and communities, and they take into account clients' interactions with those environments. Perhaps the most important distinction between social work and other helping professions is social work's emphasis on social justice and advocacy for those society oppresses or discriminates against. Although social workers often provide services in a community-based agency setting, the profession also strives to influence policy-makers through advocating for resources and justice for such social conditions as homelessness, hunger, teen pregnancy, poverty, health and economic disparities, and discrimination.

Poverty
Having inadequate money or means of subsistence.

This chapter will provide a broad overview of the field of social work. In the following chapters, a more detailed picture will emerge of the history of social work and the social welfare system, the scope and methods of social work practice, and the knowledge, skills, and values that you need to learn to be a competent and effective social worker.

Discrimination
Bias perpetrated by one individual or group over another individual or group due to race, ethnicity, gender, religion, age, sexual orientation, mental and physical conditions, class, and lifestyle.

DEFINITIONS OF SOCIAL WORK

Accurate and comprehensive definitions of social work require an expansive view of the profession and the positions social workers hold. As you may already know, schools, hospitals, ambulatory care clinics, mental health facilities, older adult service programs, schools, and children's residential settings are just some of the helping institutions that employ social workers. You may not know, however, that social workers also handle issues involving mortgages, estate planning, and financial exploitation for banks; facilitate employee assistance programs for large corporations; help bring about awareness of society and culture in work with theater groups and museums; organize groups within community gardens to raise their food for both personal and commercial use; work with active duty, veterans, retirees, and their families in military and veteran programs; provide crisis intervention, mediation, and negotiations at police stations; and work with individuals and communities on issues related to emigration, health and service access, and financial stability for international organizations, both in their own countries and in other countries. Social work professionals work with people in all segments of our global society, from the disenfranchised and devalued who live in poverty to those in the middle and upper socioeconomic segments of their communities. They work with the

EXHIBIT 1.1

Comparison of Helping Professions

Discipline[1]	Similarities to Social Work	Differences with Social Work
Psychology	(1) Both are practice professions. (2) At the graduate level, both train practitioners to provide psychotherapy (for social work, MSW; for psychology, PhD). (3) Psychologists and social workers may work in the same settings with the same clients.	(1) Psychology focuses on persons' internal issues as the source of a problem. Social work focuses on sources of issues as they relate to the person *within* his or her environment (PIE). (2) Psychology focuses on the individual as the target of the intervention. Social work interventions target the individual and those in his/her environment. (3) Psychologists administer and interpret psychological tests. Social workers are typically not trained in this area of practice. (4) In some states, psychologists can prescribe medications. Social workers cannot. (5) For psychologists, clinical practice often requires a PhD. For social workers, clinical practice sometimes requires an MSW, though in many states social workers are licensed to practice as BSWs.
Sociology	(1) Both are interested in the patterns of behaviors of people.	(1) Unlike sociology, social work is a practice profession. Sociology is a social science that considers the population, often in the context of communities.
Health Professions (nursing and medicine, in particular)	(1) Both are practice professions. (2) Both recognize the influence of health on overall well-being. (3) Both work in community/ hospital settings with the same patients. (4) Both have generalist and specialist areas of expertise.	(1) Health professions often focus primarily on physical health issues, while social work assessments routinely include biological, psychological, social, and spiritual perspectives and factors. (2) While health professionals may be aware of available community resources, social workers are experts at identifying and making use of those resources. (3) Physicians and some nurses can prescribe medications. Social workers cannot.

Marriage and Family Counseling	(1) Both are practice professions.	(1) Like psychologists, counselors focus primarily on the individual as the source of the problem.
	(2) At the graduate level, both train practitioners to provide psychotherapy.	(2) Counselors are not typically trained in community practice (e.g., advocacy, organizing, etc.). Social work training emphasizes competence at the individual, family, *and* community levels.
	(3) Both have licensing and certification requirements.	
	(4) Both marriage and family counselors and social workers can conduct clinical practice with a master's degree.	
	(5) Neither marriage and family counselors nor social workers can prescribe medications.	

[1]Additional sources used here include: Ginsburg, 2001; Peck, 1999.

young and the old, with the healthy and the sick, with people from diverse cultures and backgrounds—including immigrants and refugees, and with survivors of disasters and traumatic experiences. Many people are attracted to the social work profession because of this diversity and because of the activist, social change elements of social work.

How do social workers define such a broad field in a comprehensive, meaningful way? Professional definitions of social work have evolved over time in response to the culture, political climate, events, and societal norms of the country or culture in which social work is practiced. After decades spent striving to hone the most accurate definition for the social work profession, this 1973 definition developed by the National Association of Social Work (NASW) begins to capture the essence of the profession as a profession committed to helping people at all levels when social work was defined as the "professional activity of helping individuals, groups, or communities to restore their capacity for social functioning and creating societal conditions favorable to that goal" (NASW, 1973, p. 4). This definition includes four basic goals for the profession:

1. linking people to resources;
2. providing direct services to individuals, families, and groups;

Refugee
Person who seeks refuge from danger or persecution in her or his home country.

3. helping communities or groups provide or improve social and health services; and
4. participating in relevant legislative processes (pp. 4–5).

As the profession has continued to expand and change, so has its self-definition. While later definitions included more detail and a focus for empowerment practice, the following definition was first included in the profession's 1996 NASW *Code of Ethics* and remains relevant today:

> The primary mission of the social work profession is to enhance human well-being and help meet the basic human needs of all people, with particular attention to the needs and empowerment of people who are vulnerable, oppressed, and living in poverty. A historical and defining feature of social work is the profession's focus on individual well-being in a social context and the well-being of society. Fundamental to social work is attention to the environmental forces that create, contribute to, and address problems in living.
> (NASW, 2008)

In addition to a focus on empowering groups that are vulnerable and oppressed, this definition of the practice of social work emphasizes a number of the concepts that will be highlighted in this textbook, including a systemic approach to working with people and attention to the influences that one's environment can have on the individual's situation, resources, and perspectives.

As our world has become more globalized, so has the social work profession. While social work has been practiced around the world for centuries, social workers are just beginning to understand globalization's impact on the profession. As Cree (2013b) notes, "[I]n spite of the differences across countries, work settings and even job titles, there is a level at which shared knowledge and values underpin professional practice in social work" (p. 215). Despite there being similarities across countries and cultures in philosophy, goals, and commitment to social justice, social workers, regardless of where or with whom they practice, need to be aware of issues, values, theories, and approaches that are outside the scope of their own familiar culture and community. As a starting point toward gaining global awareness and competency, let us consider the definition of social work from the International Federation of Social Work (www.ifsw.org) in which you will note similarities and differences in focus:

> Social work is a practice-based profession and an academic discipline that promotes social change and development, social cohesion, and the empowerment and liberation of people. Principles of social justice, human rights, collective responsibility and respect for diversities are central to social work.

Muslim Children

Source: iStock/Distinctive Images

> Underpinned by theories of social work, social sciences, humanities and indigenous knowledge, social work engages people and structures to address life challenges and enhance wellbeing.

As you can see, the internationally focused definition of social work emphasizes respect for diversity and the knowledge of the persons and groups who live in that country/region, and change at the highest levels while continuing to stress the importance of social justice, human rights, and the individual. The global definition can be applied at different multiple levels, from local, regional, to national. All three of these definitions suggest that, whether social workers work with clients in their own neighborhood, community, state, or country, or even internationally, directly with people, or through taking action to change society, the goal of social work is to help people become empowered in order to optimize their abilities and quality of life. The openness and flexibility of these definitions enable social workers to respond to the ever-changing and evolving needs within their communities, regardless of where they work. The populations, health crises, social and economic conditions, and ethical dilemmas with which social workers are engaged may vary, but the work transcends time and individual circumstance because of its all-encompassing nature. Before we move on in our preliminary introduction to the social work profession, take a moment to review these three definitions. What similarities and differences do you detect? How might these definitions be similar to or different from your previous perspectives on the profession? How do these definitions differ from those of other helping professions?

THE PRACTICE OF SOCIAL WORK

Consider the experiences of a midcareer social worker named Emily. Like many of her professional counterparts, Emily has worked in a number of different social work positions and settings. Early in her career, following completion of her baccalaureate degree in social work (BSW), she worked in her state's public welfare system in several different practice areas, ranging from child and adult protective services, to home-based services for older adults and persons with visual impairments, to outreach work in a domestic violence program. Later, Emily obtained a graduate degree in social work (MSW), and over the years she has held social work positions in a mental health center, home health agency, hospital, and primary care medical outpatient clinic.

One of the things that Emily has found especially rewarding about her chosen profession is the variety of experiences her social work degrees have enabled her to have. When she worked in a program that serves persons who have experienced intimate partner violence, for instance, she responded to calls from law enforcement and hospital emergency rooms where women had gone after being battered by their partners. Emily would meet clients at the hospital and assess their current situation, abuse history, safety needs, and resources. She would then arrange housing for the woman and her children either at a shelter or at a safe house. During the client's stay in alternate housing, Emily would work with her to explore her options and help her make long-term plans. Sometimes, this effort involved helping the woman leave her partner for a new life, but other times it meant watching her return to the relationship. In these cases, Emily always worked out a safety plan with the woman in case the violence ever occurred again. Emily used a number of social work skills in this position including crisis intervention, interviewing, **assessment***, information sharing and referral, brokering,* **intervention** *planning,* **evaluation***,* **termination***, and documentation.*

At the mental health center, Emily conducted intake assessments for persons requesting therapy services. She met with those persons for an hour-long assessment of their presenting concern, social situation, and mental health status. After completing this assessment, she compiled an assessment report and recommended a treatment plan. In this role, Emily used a slightly different set of social work skills including assessment, diagnosis, preparation of documentation, and crisis intervention.

As a social worker in an acute care inpatient hospital setting, Emily provided services to patients and their families at the medical staff's request. She often assisted the patient and her or his family in making discharge plans. This process could include helping to access and navigate the complexities of the health care system, arranging for financial assistance, home health or hospice services, rehabilitation, community-based or residential care, medications,

Assessment
A component of the planned change effort in which the social worker collaborates with the client system to obtain information that provides the foundation for developing a plan of intervention.

Intervention
A component of the planned change effort in which the social worker and the client system develop and implement a plan of action to achieve the mutually agreed-upon goals.

Evaluation
A component of the planned change effort in which the social worker and the client system assess the progress and success of the planned change effort.

Termination
A component of the planned change effort in which the social worker ends the planned change relationship.

medical equipment, and possible relocation. Emily also provided support to families when a patient died. While on call for the social work department, she covered the emergency room, which required her to be ready to handle just about any emergency care situation ranging from pediatric to geriatric, physical or mental health to routine illness to life-threatening crises. Her crisis intervention skills clearly were a major asset here.

Because social work training provides a core set of knowledge and skills that can be applied in a variety of settings with a diverse population, Emily has been able to work in a number of challenging but rewarding positions: investigating adult and child abuse and neglect, working with women who have experienced intimate partner violence and their children, conducting assessments for therapy in a mental health center, arranging discharge plans for hospitalized patients, and providing therapy for persons experiencing conditions such as depression, a new medical diagnosis, or family and relationship problems. Emily has enjoyed a broad and diverse career made possible by her social work degrees. While she thrives on the opportunity to work with different types of people who are experiencing different life situations, the various positions have not been without challenges. Confronting social injustices and inequities, bureaucratic complexities, and stressful, intense situations are all part of Emily's professional experience. Her training in crisis intervention, advocacy, self-care, and the importance of utilizing supervision and consultation have been just a few of the skills that have enabled her to meet the challenges. Emily enjoys being able to help people survive and thrive through difficult life experiences.

As you can see, Emily has had a number of professional experiences that have helped to shape her perspective on the practitioner that she has become. Being able to use her social work knowledge and skills to move into new positions and face challenges as they arise have enabled Emily to enjoy a gratifying career in which she has worked with diverse populations. As you can see, there are many ways to practice social work.

What Social Workers Do

To begin our exploration into learning what social workers do, let us first gain insight into the numbers of professional social workers and the settings in which they practice. While over 800,000 people in the U.S. self-identify as social workers, only approximately 650,000 of those employed as social workers in 2012 were professionally educated as social workers (U.S. Department of Labor, Bureau of Labor Statistics (BLS), 2014b). Of social workers who practice with children, families, and in school settings, over half (56%) work in health, social service, educational, or faith-based settings, while the remainder work in publicly funded organizations (BLS, 2014b). Those social workers employed by health care organizations primarily work in hospitals and ambulatory and residential settings (BLS, 2014b). To learn more about the presence of social workers in each U.S. state, visit HIPAASpace at: www.hipaaspace.com/Medical.Statistics/Healthcare. Professionals.Availability/104100000X.

Most social workers work directly with individuals, couples, families, and small groups (Whitaker & Arrington, 2008). In fact, most social workers who responded to an NASW workforce survey self-reported that they provide services in the areas of mental health (35%), physical health (14%), family/children's services (11%), schools (6%), adolescent programs (5%), or addiction treatment (4%)—all of which are types of direct practice (i.e., delivering services directly to individuals, families, and groups) (NASW, 2007). Note that these areas of practice may be housed within different types of organizations. For instance, a social worker providing mental health services may work in an out-patient clinic, in-patient mental health facility, or be in private practice. See Exhibit 1.2 for a visual depiction of these categories. Social workers in the United States provide more mental health and therapy services than professionals in any other discipline, including psychologists and counselors (for more information, visit: www.socialworkers.org/pressroom/features/general/profession.asp).

Direct practice
Social work with individuals, couples, families, and small groups. *see also* **group work; individual and family social work practice.**

In fact, social workers provide more than 60% of all mental health services, and there are 200,000 more clinically trained social workers in the U.S. than psychiatrists, psychologists, and psychiatric nurses combined (NASW, n.d.). In this field of practice, social workers engage primarily in direct social work practice through the provision of crisis intervention and counseling services to individuals, families, and groups experiencing difficulty coping with a life crisis or transition, such as a relationship problem, unemployment, trauma, death or injury, divorce, or illness.

A social worker's training extends beyond the individual and family level of practice. While the majority of social workers spend much of their time providing direct services to individuals and families, a survey of licensed social workers reports that most social workers spend at least a portion of their time on activities that go beyond their direct practice responsibilities (Center for Health Workforce Studies (CHWS) & Center for Workforce Studies (CWS), 2006). Supervising and teaching social work students are the most frequently mentioned secondary areas of work. A significant number of social work professionals are also engaged, in whole or in part, in supervisory, administrative, research, and fund-raising activities for the agencies and organizations in which they work.

Social workers often initiate new social programs because they have been in the field and are able to see where needs exist. This experience helps social

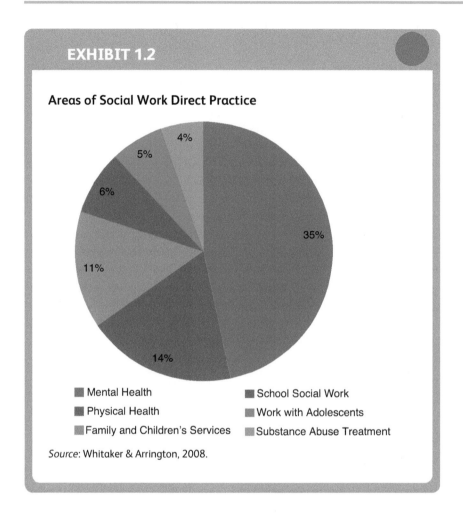

EXHIBIT 1.2

Areas of Social Work Direct Practice

- 4%
- 5%
- 6%
- 11%
- 35%
- 14%

Legend:
- Mental Health
- Physical Health
- Family and Children's Services
- School Social Work
- Work with Adolescents
- Substance Abuse Treatment

Source: Whitaker & Arrington, 2008.

workers understand and influence social policies. Social workers can share real-life stories with legislators to help them understand the effects of their votes on constituents. In fact, hundreds of social workers serve their communities and states as elected officials, including nine Members of Congress (NASW, 2013a).

Social workers' training prepares them to work with any population in any situation or setting. Social workers are employed in a broad range of areas and specializations (Barker, 2014; Hopps & Lowe, 2008; NASW, 2009):

■ Case management. Social workers conduct needs assessment and referrals, provide information and referrals, and access resources in social casework as a part of the skill set needed for case management (e.g., helping individuals and families improve personal and social functioning by referring them to education, training, employment, and personal growth services).

Case management
A method of social work practice in which the social worker conducts needs assessments, provides information and referral and enables client systems to access resources. *see* **social casework**.

Child welfare
Public or private social service and residential programs aimed at the protection and welfare of children who are being abused, neglected, or exploited.

■ Child welfare and youth services encompass working with child abuse and neglect, adoption, child custody, kinship care, criminal justice, and family services.

■ Planning and facilitating transitions. For example, a social worker in a health care setting provides crisis intervention, information, resources, counseling, and planning for health care transitions both in the in-patient or out-patient setting.

■ Addressing social, emotional, and economic issues. For instance, in schools, social workers work with students and their families on emotional, social, and economic concerns to enable those students and their families to focus on the student's education.

Clinical social work
A field of practice in which the social worker counsels individuals, families, and groups in settings such as hospitals, schools, mental health facilities, and private practices.

■ Clinical social work. Clinical social workers provide services for individuals of all ages, families, and groups in settings such as hospitals, schools, mental health facilities, behavioral health services, and private practices by assessing, diagnosing, and treating mental health and emotional conditions. Social workers also intervene domestically and internationally in emergency and disaster services, with immigrants and refugees, military service members, veterans, and their families, employment programs, and in cases of environmental justice (unsafe living and working environments).

Administration and management
A field of practice in which the social worker supervises programs and people.

■ Administration and management. Program planning and development and supervision of programs and staff are tasks of the organizational-level social worker.

■ Advocacy and influencing policy. With a primary focus on advocacy (often in the form of lobbying) for underserved populations, social workers use engage in research, planning, to develop, implement, and evaluate legislation and social policies and programs in order to promote social justice.

Community organization
A method of social work that involves working with groups and communities to identify conditions and develop strategies to address community-level conditions.

■ Community organization. Working with groups and communities to identify conditions and develop strategies to address them. For example, coordinating and working with governmental, private, civic, religious, business, and trade organizations to establish community awareness and response programs can help combat social problems.

Social policy research
A method of social work practice that involves analyzing conditions, programs, and policies and conducting and studying research in an effort to improve the social service system.

■ Social policy research/analysis. Analyzing conditions, programs, and policies and conducting research in an effort to improve the social service system. Research can be utilized to improve resources, social programs, and health services and to encourage communities and organizations to be responsive to identified needs.

Social workers deliver services through the use of planned change interventions (e.g., a structured, organized approach to developing and implementing a social work intervention) that involve four phases:

1. Engagement
2. Assessment
3. Intervention
4. Evaluation and termination

(Council on Social Work Education (CSWE),
2008 (updated August 2015))

These phases are a part of each competency-based practice approach that incorporates the knowledge, skills, and values inherent in and unique to the social work profession. As specified in the *Educational Policy and Accreditation Standards* of the CSWE (2015, p. 6):

> Competency-based education rests upon a shared view of the nature of competence in professional practice. Social work competence is the ability to integrate and apply social work knowledge, values, and skills to practice situations in a purposeful, intentional, and professional manner to promote human and community well-being. EPAS recognizes a holistic view of competence; that is, the demonstration of competence is informed by knowledge, values, skills, and cognitive and affective processes that include the social worker's critical thinking, affective reactions, and exercise of judgment in regard to unique practice situations. Overall professional competence is multi-dimensional and composed of interrelated competencies. An individual social worker's competence is seen as developmental and dynamic, changing over time in relation to continuous learning.

Each of the four phases of planned change intervention will be explored in greater depth throughout this book.

Social workers play a wide range of professional roles, and their practices differ based on the theories and approaches relevant to the communities and cultures in which they work. As Cree (2013a) noted, no one task is specific to the social work profession; instead, each social worker's experiences are individualized and unique, making the profession "greater than the sum of its individual parts" (p. 4). Read in Exhibit 1.3 the words of one social work student who sees the magnificence, diversity, and gratification of the social work profession. While social work is a gratifying profession, the challenges cannot be dismissed; however, for many, there is gratification in overcoming the challenges both for oneself and the client system.

The Populations Social Workers Serve

Whether you are planning to become a social worker or will be working in another profession, it is important to understand that many social work clients

EXHIBIT 1.3

The Magnificence of the Social Work Profession

How magnificent this profession is,
It gives you satisfaction, pain and euphoria.
The profession itself talks about the history of equality and fairness among society.
It allows you to believe in a world that could reach a utopia.
How magnificent this profession is,
It recruits people with the courage to fight for what they believe is real.
It gives people the tools to change the world and reach the stars with dignity and ethical principles.
It trains people to be sensitive and rational.
And it gives people the chance to fight a battle of oppression and despair.
How magnificent this profession is,
It speaks a language that can be understood regardless of your culture, your dialect, your race or any
    other characteristic.
It speaks with symbols that are spread around the globe and ensure the welfare of the people.
How magnificent this profession is,
It unifies people despite their religious beliefs or spiritual bonds.
It cooperates with humanity regardless of their God or their holy book.
The profession emerged from love and compassion; the same love and compassion that made
    possible the creation of religions around the world.
How magnificent this profession is,
With its holistic perspective and comprehensive coverage it allows people to become transformed
    into one being.
It demonstrates that brotherhood, honesty and collaboration can be reached.
It confirms the idea that we all came from the same blood line and that we are bonded forever in this
    life.
The struggle is always there.
The challenge is always present.
Frustration is part of the process of the profession.
However, the social work vocation is the only one that can assure you of a true experience of
    happiness.
When you help people and you make a genuine change in the society, you are able to experience a
    thrill of satisfaction.
When you fight for abolishing pain and despair, you are able to feel alive and content.
When you practice the social work profession, you do not stop being a social worker when you leave
    your workplace.
You live and die for the things that you consider important.
You live and die for enhancing humanity and renovating society.

Claudia Marcela Hernandez Palacio

Reprinted with permission from *The New Social Worker. Source:* Claudia Marcela Hernandez Palacio, 2014. Available at:
www.socialworker.com/extras/creative-work/the-magnificence-of-the-social-work-profession/

are struggling to function within their personal worlds. Exhibit 1.4 provides some insight into the range of people who might find themselves in need of a social worker's services. Fortunately, most people have strengths on which they can draw, and helping to activate those strengths is the social worker's specialty.

From the beginnings of the profession, social workers have worked both one-on-one and at the organizational and community level with persons facing discrimination because of ethnic background, race, gender, ability, sexual orientation, or age, and with those experiencing life crises, or physical or mental health or cognitive challenges. Often working with people who are struggling with life's most significant challenges, social workers help clients to address issues of: "poverty, discrimination, abuse, addiction, physical illness, divorce, loss, unemployment, educational problems, disability, and mental illness. They help prevent crises and counsel individuals, families, and

Race
Human characteristics identified by physical traits (e.g., skin color or hair texture), geography (e.g., place or origin), or culture.

EXHIBIT 1.4

Who Needs a Social Worker?

You'll Need a Social Worker When ...

When you come into the world too soon

When you can't find anyone to play with

When you are left home alone

When you hate the new baby

When you don't think your teacher likes you

When you are bullied

When you don't want your mommy and daddy to divorce

When you miss your big brother

When you don't like how the neighbor touches you

When you get into fights at school

When you don't make the team

When your best friend moves away

When you get poor grades

When you always fight with your siblings

When your friends pressure you to get high

When you can't adjust to the move

When you can't talk to your parents

When you want to quit school

When your friends don't like you anymore

When you didn't want this baby

When you feel like running away

When your friend swallows an overdose

When you are the only one that thinks you're fat

When you can't find someone who speaks your language

When you can't forget the assault

When you can't decide on a career

When your family pressures you to marry

When your boss is hitting on you

When you can't stick to a budget

When you want to adopt

When you wonder if you are drinking too much

When you can't find good day care

When you think you are neglecting your kids

When you are hated because of who you are

When you lose your baby

When your community has gang problems

When your kids want to live with your ex

When your partner is unfaithful

When you want to meet your birthparent

When your disabled child needs friends

When your step-kids hate you

When your mother won't speak to you

When you can't face moving again

When your spouse wants a divorce

When you want to be a foster parent

When your city officials don't respond

When your best friend has panic attacks

When you find drugs in your son's room

When your job is eliminated

When your mother-in-law wants to move in

When your neighborhood needs a community center

When you find there is no joy in your life

When your car accident destroys your career

When you sponsor a refugee family

When your legislature passes a bad law

When your brother won't help care for dad

When your partner has a mid-life crisis

When you are stressed by menopause

When your mom gets Alzheimer's

When you are caring for parents and children

When you want to change careers

When you lose your home in a fire

When you are angry all the time

When your nest really empties

When your partner insists you retire

When you can't afford respite care

When you can't find a job and you're 60

When your kids demand that you move in with them

When your daughter suddenly dies

When you are scared about living alone

When you can't drive any more

When your children ignore your medical decisions

When your retirement check won't pay the bills

When you learn you have a terminal illness

When you need a nursing home

Life's Challenges—Social Workers Are There For You!

Source: © 2001, Darlene Lynch & Robert Vernon. For free distribution information visit: http://lhsmedia.biz.

communities to cope more effectively with the stresses of everyday life" (NASW, n.d.). The scope of practice and service boundaries for social workers has expanded throughout history and continues to expand to respond to the ever-changing array of societal needs around the world. Today, for example, social workers assist people who have lost their jobs, health benefits, or homes and military veterans and their families dealing with posttraumatic stress disorder and readjusting to civilian life. Read below to learn about an experience that Emily had as a relatively new social worker in the community working with older adults.

As an adult services social worker in a public welfare agency, Emily started off one typical day by making a home visit to Mrs. H., a 70-year-old widow with no family. Mrs. H. lived alone in a small house that Emily could see was not clean or well maintained. Mrs. H.'s minister referred her to Emily's agency because he was concerned about her well-being. Mrs. H. was visually impaired due to glaucoma, and had severe arthritis and insulin-dependent diabetes. She had been trying to cover up her increasing debilitation by isolating herself and not participating in her usual social activities. To some observers these issues may have seemed like insurmountable problems, and the only reasonable response might have seemed, at first contact, to be placing Mrs. H. in a nursing home.

Mrs. H. desperately wanted to continue living independently. She was financially independent, and she had a small circle of caring people, such as her minister and neighbors, who provided social support. Through Emily's psychosocialspiritual assessment (i.e., assessment of the psychological, social, and spiritual aspects of the client's situation), which included family, financial, mobility, spiritual, and health information, she concluded that Mrs. H. was a candidate for a number of social services: homemaker/chore (help with house-keeping tasks), home health services (nursing assistance to monitor her dia-betes), services for persons with visual impairments (a rehabilitation teacher to help her adjust to her visual impairment), transportation services, and tel-ephone reassurance services (a daily telephone check-in service). With the help of these services, Emily's ongoing case management, and a willingness to build on her strengths, Mrs. H. remained independent and functional until her death 10 years later.

As you can see, Emily gathered critical information by conducting an assessment focused on seeing Mrs. H. within the environment in which she lives. By asking about strengths, resources, and links to the community, Emily was able to collaborate with Mrs. H. to develop and implement a plan that enabled Mrs. H. to reach her goal of remaining in her own home and living independently.

Where Social Workers Work

Emily's social work degrees and experience have enabled her to change positions within the social work field throughout her career. Her social work training pre-pared her to work with varied groups of people—children, families, older adults, and persons with disabilities or persistent physical or mental illness—in direct practice. Her knowledge and skills have also enabled her to facilitate groups and to work in administration and education. Emily values what she has learned working in each of these settings.

Nevertheless, over the course of her career, Emily has developed prefer-ences based on her strengths and passions. Emily's social work experience began with a community service learning assignment in her introductory social work course. She found an opportunity at a senior residential complex, helping older adults. Once she had earned her undergraduate degree in social work, Emily secured a position in the public social service sector. Emily developed an extensive knowledge of the public welfare system that helped her get into graduate school and find work in a shelter program for abused women and their children. Interviewers were impressed with her experiences in public welfare and domestic violence when she applied for a position at a mental health center.

Although each work setting offered a unique experience and enabled her to develop her knowledge, skills, and professional values, Emily found that her personality was better suited to some settings than others. For example, she learned that she enjoys working in an agency in which she is among a large group of co-workers with whom she can interact on a daily basis, and that she likes to work with clients with whom she can develop and maintain ongoing relationships.

Like Emily, most social workers gain experience in multiple settings, which may include:

- Organizations that primarily provide social services.
- Host settings, or secondary organizations, such as schools, correctional facilities, or health care facilities.
- Voluntary nonprofit agencies, both faith-based and sectarian.
- Governmental or public agencies.

Although some social workers are independent therapists in private practices, most work for an organization.

Within these broad types of social work settings, practicing social workers most often specialize in the areas described in Exhibit 1.5 (BLS, 2014b). The most frequent specialization, family and child service agencies, includes child welfare agencies, health and mental health agencies, and elementary and secondary schools. A visit to the NASW website (socialworkers.org) provides an illuminating listing of areas in which social workers may be employed, including schools, hospitals, mental health clinics, senior centers, elected office, private practices, prisons, military installations, veterans programs, corporations, and in numerous public and private agencies that serve individuals and families in need. Social workers often specialize in one or more of the practice areas listed in Exhibit 1.6.

Between one-half and two-thirds of all social workers are employed in the private social service sector (BLS, 2014b; Whitaker & Arrington, 2008). A majority work in nonprofit settings such as social service agencies, hospitals, residential care facilities, home health agencies, health centers, and criminal justice programs. Boards of directors administer these privately-funded agencies, and they reinvest their profits in the programs to enhance service delivery. These agencies raise funds through individual and corporate donations, grants, fundraisers, and public sector contracts. In addition, an increasing number of

EXHIBIT 1.5

Social Work Employment

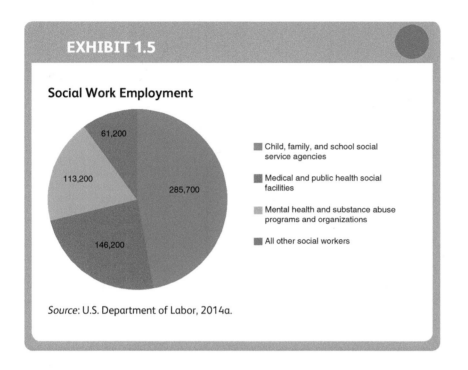

- Child, family, and school social service agencies
- Medical and public health social facilities
- Mental health and substance abuse programs and organizations
- All other social workers

Source: U.S. Department of Labor, 2014a.

social workers (over one-quarter) work in for-profit settings such as private schools and corporations (for example, in employee assistance programs) (Whitaker & Arrington, 2008). The private social service delivery system in the United States consists of approximately 94,700 organizations—75,700 (two-thirds) serve individuals and families; 9,500 provide food, housing, and other relief services; and 9,500 focus on vocational rehabilitation (BLS, 2010a).

Although a majority of social workers secure jobs in the private sector, many social workers also find employment in public and government settings. In these settings, social workers manage cases and determine eligibility for a wide range of services, including physical and mental health, social services, child welfare, housing, education, and corrections (BLS, 2010a). The overwhelming majority of social workers in the public sector are employed at the state and local level, with a smaller number working in federal programs. Of all persons employed in state and local agencies, approximately 6% are engaged in community and social services areas (BLS, 2010a). These publicly-funded local, state, and federal settings include state-funded public welfare/human service departments; mental health agencies; child welfare agencies; housing programs; veterans' and military programs; local, state, and federal court/justice systems; public schools; hospitals; and policy-making organizations.

EXHIBIT 1.6

Areas of Social Work Practice

Mental health therapy
Rural social work
Family preservation services
Genetics
School violence
Institutional care
Developmental disabilities
Community mental health
Veterans services
Policy development
HIV/AIDS
Gerontology services
Alzheimer 's disease and other dementias
Housing assistance
Disaster relief
Adoption and foster care
Homeless family assistance
Hospital social work
Hospice and palliative care
Chronic pain
International social work

Employee assistance
Child abuse and neglect
Parent education
School alternative programs
Community-based services
Addictions prevention and treatment
Public welfare
Military social work
Child welfare services
Eating disorders
Crisis intervention
Depression
Outpatient treatment
Advocacy, consulting, and planning
Private practice (e.g., clinical or consultation)
Domestic violence
Family planning
Difficulties in school
In-home services
Criminal justice
Employment services

PATHS TO BECOMING A SOCIAL WORKER

When Emily married shortly after graduating from high school, she had no way of knowing that domestic violence would occur in her marriage. When it did, Emily ended the marriage relatively quickly. With her family's support, she headed off to college. She had no idea what her major would be, but her past life experiences came to influence her studies.

It was in a psychology course Emily took to fulfill her university's general education requirement that Emily was first intrigued by the idea of trying to understand the ways people think and behave. Among her friends, she was often the person in whom others confided—maybe because she was a good listener? Next, Emily took additional general education courses in sociology and anthropology. She was drawn to the idea of thinking about people within the context of their societies, but she also liked the possibility of being able to help people.

One of Emily's instructors commented that she seemed to enjoy these classes, and he asked if Emily had considered social work. Emily had never met a social worker, but she began to investigate her college's social work program. Emily went on to get her bachelor's and master's degrees in social work, and she has since worked in a variety of settings, some of them involving domestic violence. Because of her training as a professional social worker, Emily recognizes the importance of exploring her own life experience in relation to her professional work, and she has continued to do just that throughout her career.

Emily's path to becoming a social worker is unique to her as yours will be to you, but in several ways it is a typical one. Many social workers are attracted to the profession out of a desire to help people, through their interest in a psychology or sociology course, or because of past personal experiences. In Emily's case, all three played a part. Her psychology course helped her connect with one of her strengths—an interest in helping people. Her personal experience as a survivor of intimate partner violence made her aware that people sometimes need to ask for and receive assistance and helped her tap into a reservoir of empathy she could draw on to help others. Having survived a violent relationship, Emily also learned the importance of processing and talking with others about your experience before embarking on a career in the helping professions. She knew she could not bring her own unresolved feelings into the helping relationship.

You might wonder why Emily decided to major in social work instead of psychology or sociology. Had it not been for that insightful faculty member, Emily would likely have graduated with a psychology degree. Research shows that faculty members who teach introductory courses can often be extremely influential when it comes to which majors students select (Chambliss & Takacs, 2014). Those instructors who provide a caring and inspirational presentation of the social work profession can help students to see new possibilities for themselves.

Having a degree in psychology would likely have taken Emily down a different career path. She might have gone on to complete a graduate degree in psychology, in which case her work might have focused primarily on psychological testing. If she had gone on to earn a doctorate in clinical psychology, she might have gone into private practice, research, or academic life. Psychology can sometimes overlap with social work, but there are differences, too. With a master's degree in social work and a clinical credential (state license), Emily is qualified to become a therapist. In psychology, she would need a doctorate.

There is no one path to becoming a social worker. However, some common patterns emerge among the paths most social workers take to join the profession, including (Cree, 2013a):

- Childhood and family background—Many social workers were brought up to value caring for others, have had positive experiences with a helping professional, or come from a dysfunctional family that experienced crisis.
- Educational or work experiences—Often future social workers are exposed to the profession through coursework, volunteer service, or paid employment.
- The influence of significant individuals—A teacher, family member, friend, or helping professional may plant the seeds of a student's interest in social work.
- The value-base of social work—Many are drawn to the commitment to social justice that is at the core of the social work profession.

Consider for a moment those persons or experiences that may influence your choice of major and future career.

SOCIAL WORK EDUCATION

To practice social work, social workers need the proper training and credentials. Only a person who has earned a bachelor's or master's degree from a college or university social work program accredited by the CSWE can provide professional social work services. NASW has issued a policy statement that conveys the importance of reserving the title of social worker for persons who hold social work degrees (NASW, 2012–2014c) and actively lobbies state legislatures to uphold that policy. In fact, many states have passed title protection legislation stipulating that only persons with social work degrees from CSWE-accredited programs may refer to themselves as social workers. In addition, all states have enacted legislation that enables degreed social work practitioners from CSWE-accredited programs to obtain a license or certification to practice social work. The specifics of these laws vary from state to state and by area of practice.

Institutions in the United States grant three types of social work degrees:

Bachelor of Social Work (BSW)
A generalist practice degree

Master of Social Work (MSW)
Advanced practice social work degree

1. Bachelor of Social Work (BSW) prepares the graduate for generalist social work professional practice.
2. Master of Social Work (MSW) prepares the graduate for advanced professional practice in a specific area of concentration.
3. Doctorate of Philosophy in Social Work (Ph.D. or DSW) is typically considered a research-oriented degree with a focus on preparing the graduate for a teaching, research, and/or administrative career. However, several programs offer a doctorate degree in social work that emphasizes clinical practice.

In the 1970s, the number of practicing MSW-level social workers was not adequate to fill the positions the War on Poverty programs of the 1960s had created. As a result, the BSW degree was introduced with a curriculum developed to expose students to a wide range of content areas to prepare them for practice in the community (Sheafor, 2014). While it is unusual for an undergraduate degree to emerge after the graduate degree, the societal demand for persons to work in the anti-poverty programs created a need for direct service workers, thus the BSW degree was created. Despite incentives being offered by the Department of Health and Welfare (federal agency overseeing the War on Poverty programs), not everyone was supportive of the creation of the BSW degree. Some MSWs feared that the BSW-trained social worker would be incapable of working with the complexities of client situations and entry of BSWs on the scene could be viewed as a denigration of the MSW degree, roles, reputation, and ability to be hired (Sheafor, 2014).

BSW programs include a liberal arts background to provide students with basic knowledge and skills that are useful in social work practice, including an appreciation for scientific methods and historical developments; effective communication and critical thinking skills; awareness of the human condition and the contribution of the arts to society; openness to diversity, difference, and improvability; and knowledge of human biological function. For their elective coursework, many undergraduate social work students gravitate to courses that will strengthen their knowledge of human behavior (i.e., psychology) or the political and legal systems as they related to social policy development. A growing number of BSW students seek fluency in a second language, such as Spanish or American Sign Language (ASL).

As our society becomes increasingly diverse, multiple language skills and knowledge of global issues are becoming more important within the social work profession. In response to the ever-changing global landscape, the social work profession has recognized the need for practitioners to have knowledge and skills to serve an international population, whether in the domestic or international arena. Through coursework, service learning, field practicum, and study abroad experiences, social work programs are expanding in scope to include exploration of the way in which social work and social welfare programs are delivered around the world. Gaining knowledge of issues and cultures outside one's home country can prompt one to question their assumptions and stereotypes and gain understanding of the ways in which people have been oppressed, even by the student's own country (Lalayants, Doel, & Kachkachishvili, 2013). In addition to the traditional strategies for enhancing your global knowledge, consider the possibilities of using social media to develop linkages with students in other countries to engage in discussions regarding social work in each country (Lalayants et al., 2013). See Exhibit 1.7 to learn about one social worker's international experiences and the impact on her life.

EXHIBIT 1.7

"Don't be a Passenger in Your Education. Grab the Steering Wheel"

When Rachel Barth was an undergraduate student, she became involved with her university's Newman Catholic Center and participated in a student-led group that raised funds for community-run projects in Haiti. Rachel made her first trip to Haiti with the students on a 10-day immersion experience to meet Haitians working on the projects and to continue to build relationships and community. In one of the three communities her group visited, Rachel learned about a religious order that provided services (e.g., children's programs and micro-financing programs) and offered two volunteer opportunities—a summer program and a year-long experience. Rachel returned to Haiti for a summer to work with children aged 8-12 years old in a summer camp. Later, Rachel again returned to Haiti with her new husband to complete the year-long service experience. Upon their arrival, they began taking language courses six days/week to learn the national language, Haitian Creole. While they were learning the language, they painted houses, worked in a shelter for the homeless, and spent time getting to know the members of the community. During their year of service, Rachel and her husband learned about a nutrition program in Haiti, Meds and Foods for Kids, operated by an American organization that provided enriched food to children. To determine if their community could benefit from this program, they conducted a community needs assessment by assessing child malnutrition at a health clinic (measuring arm circumference of children aged 6 months–5 years). Their assessment determined that the children of the community were experiencing malnutrition so they moved forward to bring the program to their community. For the remainder of their year of service, they worked to provide ongoing assessment and follow-up with the children and their families and helped to train clinic staff to assess and treat malnutrition.

When Rachel returned to the U.S., she began an MSW program. She was able to return once again to Haiti, this time for a practicum in which she conducted a research project to evaluate the micro-financing project administered by the religious order. The religious community wanted information on the borrowers, the ways the loans were being used, the repayment rates, and the barriers to repayment. Rachel spent a summer interviewing current and former recipients of the micro-loans and prepared a report for the religious community. To learn more about Rachel's research project, see Barth, Birkenmaier, & Berg-Weger (2014).

Rachel describes her international experiences as fantastic and challenging. She experienced true hospitality and felt welcomed by the Haitians who were open about talking with her about their dreams. Adjusting to the culture, particularly the work culture (slower paced than U.S. work styles) is critical to having a positive and effective experience. For social work students interested in gaining international experiences, she encourages them to be proactive in taking advantage of or creating opportunities to study and work in another country. She offers these insights on her experience: "Reflect and think critically about what you want to do and how you want to do it. There are lots of ways to work internationally. Learn about the community and remember, you are a foreigner. It is easy to think we know more than they do, but we don't. We need to listen to them. They are the experts on their lives." To read more about Rachel's experience, see Barth, Birkenmaier, & Berg-Weger (2014).

Within the BSW program, an array of courses in the major cover the areas CSWE identifies as essential competencies for the professional social worker (CSWE, 2008, updated 2015) (see Quick Guide #1.1). Specifically, social work majors complete coursework in human behavior in the social environment, social welfare history/policy, practice-focused courses for working with individuals, families, groups, communities and organizations, diversity, research, and field practicum.

QUICK GUIDE #1.1 COMPETENCIES FOR PROFESSIONAL SOCIAL WORKERS (COUNCIL ON SOCIAL WORK EDUCATION)

Competency 1: Demonstrate Ethical and Professional Behavior

Competency 2: Engage Diversity and Difference in Practice

Competency 3: Advance Human Rights and Social, Economic, and Environmental Justice

Competency 4: Engage In Practice-informed Research and Research-informed Practice

Competency 5: Engage in Policy Practice

Competency 6: Engage with Individuals, Families, Groups, Organizations, and Communities

Competency 7: Assess Individuals, Families, Groups, Organizations, and Communities

Competency 8: Intervene with Individuals, Families, Groups, Organizations, and Communities

Competency 9: Evaluate Practice with Individuals, Families, Groups, Organizations, and Communities

Source: Council on Social Work Education, 2015. Available at: http://www.cswe.org/ Accreditation/EPASRevision.aspx.

Among the helping professions, social work is the leader in preparing graduates with a bachelor's degree to work effectively in social services. The BSW permits such direct and quick entry into professional practice for three reasons:

1. Students in BSW programs are required to participate in two or three service-learning experiences in a health or social service agency, educational institution, or advocacy program.

2. BSW programs are accredited by a professional body—the Council on Social Work Education (CSWE).
3. The BSW degree provides graduates with the education required to obtain licensing or certification (Hopps et al., 2008).

One NASW survey asked practicing social workers to indicate their highest degree completed; only 12% indicated that the BSW was their highest degree completed, while nearly 80% indicated that they possessed an MSW degree (NASW Center for Workforce Studies, 2005). BSW and MSW programs differ in terms of content, program objectives, and the depth, breadth, and specificity of knowledge and skills they impart (CSWE, 2015). In further delineating the differences between the expertise of BSW-level and MSW-level social workers, Sheafor (2014) notes that BSW practitioners are typically better equipped than MSW social workers to perform tasks in the areas of risk assessment, protective services, case planning and maintenance, service connection, tangible service provision, and dispute resolution (Sheafor, 2014, p. 204). MSW practitioners, on the other hand, are trained more often for group work, individual/family treatment, and staff supervision (p. 204). Sheafor also points out practice areas that are the two levels of social work practitioners routinely share: interprofessional helping, professional development, staff deployment and information exchange, organization maintenance, community delivery system knowledge, and program, research, and policy development (p. 204).

Social workers with BSWs and MSWs often work together in the same setting and with the same client systems, but functioning at different levels and performing different tasks. For example, a BSW in an organization may be responsible for intake assessments, determining eligibility for services, and case management, while an MSW may have clinical, administrative, and supervisory duties. In some organizations, the lines between BSW and MSW duties may blur or overlap. In some rural or small communities, for example, due to a shortage of available MSWs, baccalaureate-level social workers may function in positions that might typically be held by an MSW in a more urban area. For example, social workers in schools and hospitals in urban areas usually hold an MSW degree, but in a small community, these positions may be held by a BSW. In other settings, MSWs may engage in assessment and case management along with a BSW colleague (e.g., community-based agencies working with persons with chronic mental illness or care/treatment facilities).

Emily worked in a domestic violence program at different stages of her career. At the BSW level, Emily worked directly with women and children, helping them gain admittance to a safe-house program and to obtain legal, financial, health, and mental health services. Once she had earned her MSW, Emily possessed a

skill set that qualified her to provide mental health treatment for the women and
children in the shelter.

Emily's path to becoming an MSW included earning the BSW degree first, gaining several years practice experience, and then returning to school to complete her MSW. Because she held a BSW degree from a CSWE-accredited social work program, she received credit toward her MSW degree, thus taking only three semesters for the MSW degree. Other paths include direct admission into an MSW from a BSW program. There have been an emergence of "five-year" programs in which BSW students are provisionally admitted to the MSW program during their junior year and begin taking MSW coursework during the senior year. Another path is to complete an undergraduate degree in an area other than social work and then apply for admission to an MSW program. See Exhibit 1.8 to learn about one social worker's journey through social work.

EXHIBIT 1.8

Camille: "My Calling...."

My name is Camille Haberman, and I am a Licensed Clinical Social Worker. I work for the Austin, Texas Police Department (APD) as a Victim Services Counselor. APD's Victim Services Division was one of the first in the nation to offer advocacy and support services to crime victims from counselors employed within the law enforcement agency. Traditionally, these services were provided by community nonprofit agencies. Victim Services Counselors work with crime victims and people impacted by trauma on the streets, with patrol officers, and in investigative units, with detectives. I have worked for APD for fifteen years, initially in the Child Abuse Unit. I am currently assigned to the Sex Crimes Unit, working closely with the detectives who investigate sexual offenses against adult victims.

After graduating with my MSW, with a concentration in Children and Families, I began my career at a domestic violence shelter, working in the Children's Program, providing individual therapy and support groups with children who had witnessed domestic violence and sexual assault, and often experienced abuse directly. Although I felt that I had a meaningful impact on these children's lives, I was frustrated that the abusers who sent them into shelter were rarely held accountable for their crimes at least in that small town, at the time. I began to fantasize about a job where I could do the counseling that I loved but play some role in the justice system. I saw an ad for a Victim Services Counselor in the Child Abuse Unit of the Austin Police Department, interviewed for the job, and was hired. I had found "my calling."

After working in the Child Abuse Unit for six years, my wise supervisor suggested to me that we explore my career and ways in which I could broaden my skills. She recognized, as I could not, that

I was burning out. Many social work positions involve exposure to trauma and the risk that such exposure poses to the social worker, but I believe daily witnessing of child abuse can be especially demoralizing. I began to work with other investigative units and different crime types, eventually discovering my next passion, to work with adult sexual assault victims. I provide support to victims of sexual assault during the course of an investigation which usually entails numerous phone, in-person (at the APD, school, or work) client contacts. I help the victim understand the investigative process, the criminal justice system, and her rights as a crime victim. Aspects of the investigative process are particularly anxiety-producing for victims (e.g., giving a formal statement to a detective, viewing a photo array to identify the person who has harmed her). I am present during these investigative steps to provide support and crisis counseling. With the victim, I explore the impact of the sexual assault, thoughts and feelings about the assault, and her coping. I educate on common trauma reactions, facilitate coping skills, identify support systems, and make referrals to longer-term counseling as appropriate. I conduct assessment with the victim about her strengths and needs, and her history with other crises. I make referrals to outside agencies when indicated and often advocate for the client with these other agencies and organizations, as well as within the police department. In short, I hope to contribute to a victim's recovery from a profoundly violating experience, help her to regain her voice and to access resources for her continued recovery process.

As a side note, I use the term "victim" throughout this essay and the pronouns she/her. Clearly, there are male victims of sexual assault, but the vast majority of victims with whom I interact are female, thus the feminine pronouns. There is legitimate debate among those who work in this field about the appropriate term to use for someone who has been sexually assaulted. Many believe that we show the most respect to a person's experience and her resiliency by calling her "a survivor." I understand this argument and am awed by a person's capacity to overcome a sexual assault, but believe that survivorship is a state that a person progresses toward slowly. It takes time and hard work and is painful. I believe that by **not** acknowledging that a person has been hurt, has been **a victim**, we minimize the devastating impact of rape. I work in a law enforcement agency in which those involved are labelled as victims, witnesses, and suspects. So my use of the word victim derives from my own beliefs about recovery, but also from my work culture.

I both love and hate my job, so want to elaborate about both its rewards and challenges. I am fascinated by human nature and find it interesting to hear a person's story, what has gone before, how she came to this place, and what this event means to her. I am daily amazed by our resiliency. I could not work in this field if I did not have an abiding faith in resiliency as I hear about another person's trauma and see the struggle after. Many victims find ways to cope, to reconstruct their lives, and often, to grow and become "more" through the process. I am honored that victims allow me to witness this process. When I think about helping a victim, I think in terms of witnessing. As a less experienced social worker, I frequently felt anxious when trying to determine what I should **DO** to help a client. I imagined there were magical words or steps that would fix the problem. The truth is that I do my best work by simply being present with a victim, listening to what this experience means to her and acknowledging that there is no quick fix. I feel great satisfaction when a victim feels she was "heard."

I enjoy the multidisciplinary aspect of my job. I collaborate daily with law enforcement, prosecutors, community advocates, and Sexual Assault Nurse Examiners (SANEs). Our different professions mean we offer varying skill sets and perspectives, but it sometimes means that we argue, vehemently. This collaborative approach represents the best practice in terms of serving victims, and it is rewarding to be part of a team, working toward a common goal.

I have discussed the honor I feel that victims are willing to share with me their most private and painful emotions during a dark period in their lives. It *is* an honor and one of the most rewarding aspects of my work, but also a risk. As a student, I learned about secondary traumatization (vicarious trauma), but I did not appreciate its depth until working in the field. It is not just that I hear a victim's despair, see her tears and sometimes bruises and scratches every day, but it is the knowledge that there are people in our world who are capable of doing these horrible things to others. Exposure to multiple traumas can make a person vulnerable to sexual assault, youth, old age, mental health challenges, physical and cognitive disabilities, addiction, prostitution, and homelessness. These are the issues that I confront and they are well beyond the scope of my work (or individual abilities). It is impossible to face some of the saddest aspects of the human condition, and to feel somewhat helpless in combatting them, and to not be affected. My view of the world is not the same as when I graduated with my MSW. There is probably less hope and more distrust than when I was 25 years old. Fortunately, my organization and leadership recognize these risks and are supportive in terms of self-care and accessing resources to cope with the impact of our work. I know that social work programs now place more emphasis on self-care or perhaps I was dismissive of the need back then. In any case, I would not trade my profession or my job, but I have come to recognize there is a cost and I could have been more proactive in my self-care efforts.

Also challenging are societal attitudes toward sexual assault. Many people have this "Hollywood version" of sexual assault, in which a terrifying stranger jumps out from a dark alley and brutally rapes his victim, who screams and fights then immediately reports to the police. That is not how most sexual assaults happen. Most of the time, a person is raped by someone she knows and probably trusted. It often occurs when she is intoxicated and less able to perceive the risk or to extricate herself from the situation once she realizes what is happening to her. There is almost always fear and rarely physical violence and a victim may be afraid to report the assault, blaming herself for "getting that drunk" or not reacting the way she thought that she should, wondering if she caused it in some way. I expect to hear statements of self-blame from sexual assault victims and to explore those statements with her. It is disheartening that society blames the victim, focusing on her behavior and vulnerabilities instead of the perpetrator's actions. These beliefs are so pervasive that I do not talk about my work in my personal life as I will inevitably hear something like, "Well, what did she expect would happen after she went home with him after meeting him at a bar?" It makes me sigh; it makes me exhausted.

I would like to share education prepared me for this work. I learned that the greatest predictor of a "successful" intervention with a client is the quality of the relationship between that client and social worker. I think daily about the importance of building rapport with a client. As I student, I learned and practiced relational skills, to convey respect and empathy, to probe, explore, clarify, paraphrase, be genuine, and employ the ever-elusive "professional use of self." While I was confused for years about this last concept, I learned it means finding a way to apply your education and experience while still being yourself. At this point in my career, I wouldn't know how *not* to do that!

As simplistic as it sounds, we assume these skills come naturally because we are social creatures. That is not the case. The deliberate attention to relational skills was an important part of my development as a social worker. The theories I learned prepared me as well as I apply theories related to crisis intervention, mental health and feminist theories of rape. I like to think I practice my own form of narrative therapy in talking to a victim about her life story, the chapter in which I play a role, and what her continuing narrative can look like.

While I value my education, I have learned more from my experience in the field and from my clients. Before I worked for APD, I probably held the same expectation as others in our society that a sexual assault victim would **of course** report it to the police. I have learned from victims there are multiple reasons that a victim may not report, most based on fear. A primary reason victims, even children who are abused, do not report to police or disclose to someone they know is fear of not being believed. It is a sad statement about our society that an outcry of sexual abuse or assault is so often met with disbelief that it would hinder a victim's willingness to ask for the help and support she desperately needs. I do not understand our skepticism when it comes to sexual assault outcries. Perhaps we do not want to confront this ugly aspect of human nature. It is frightening to face that there are predators among us, callous to others' rights, the most basic of which is to control what happens to one's own body. It is especially frightening when the alleged perpetrator is charming and likeable, the boy next door. Maybe it is easier to disbelieve the outcry than to admit the dangers around us. Victims also fear judgment about those vulnerabilities. They are afraid of being judged for the decisions they made before the sexual assault, whether that was getting drunk or high, trusting someone that they recently met, expecting that their partner would respect their willingness to participate in some kinds of contact but not others, etc. If they have a mental illness, they have already been called "crazy" by someone in their lives and may fear judgment about this issue as well. Victims fear the criminal justice system itself—the humiliation of a forensic medical examination, demands of multiple interviews in which the rape is re-visited, and threat of being cross-examined by a zealous defense attorney during testimony (another piece of the Hollywood version of sexual assault). Victims are overwhelmed and making a decision about whether they can handle the prospect of this daunting process at exactly that moment when their inner resources are depleted. They often feel unsure if they can handle the next thirty minutes. We have made significant strides in responding more sensitively and respectfully to sexual assault victims, but our process remains tedious and difficult, often referred to as "re-traumatizing." These are just some of the legitimate barriers that prevent a victim from reporting a sexual assault. I wonder that any victim would make a report, considering what may ensue after! I have stand-by questions when talking to a victim and trying to gain insight into her world. I ask about her thought process when deciding to call police and what made her choose to do it. Victims tell me that they made the report because it was the "right" thing to do, and they want him to know that what he did is not acceptable. Invariably, this is followed with a comment that maybe this investigation will prevent the suspect from raping someone else. What incredible bravery! It touches me that victims are usually motivated by a desire to save others from hurt and a sense of justice that goes beyond their own experiences. I have learned courage from the clients I have served, and I am humbled and inspired.

A memorable woman comes to mind as I write about courage. In 2008, I met a sexual assault victim named Candace. The initial report read that Candace had come home after working a night shift at a local music venue. As she was walking home from a convenience store near her home, she encountered a man with a T-shirt wrapped around his face. Only his eyes and cheek bones were clearly defined. This image disturbs me. She must have known in that moment that she was in trouble because he was hiding his face! Before she could react, he struck her on the head and knocked her unconscious. When she regained consciousness, he was raping her.

A few days later, Candace came to the Sex Crimes Unit. She was bruised and complained of pounding in her head (where she had received stitches). Despite her physical pain, she was anxious to proceed with the investigation and wanted to do everything she could to help catch the offender. She had already contacted the neighborhood newsletter in order to notify the community of the danger. Candace was "a trooper" during a long and emotionally painful interview. She was receptive to my role, and we spent time talking about the assault and its impact. She later met with a composite artist to generate a sketch of the suspect. During that session, Candace glanced at the sketch, gasped, and stated, "Oh my God!" Her eyes welled up with tears. She made some suggestions for minor changes, but soon was overwhelmed and indicated that she could not continue the session, as the image was eliciting such strong emotional reactions.

Throughout my contacts with Candace, she consistently voiced concerns for community safety. She felt that she had not been as alert that night as she usually was, feeling comfortable in her quiet and "safe" neighborhood, and she wanted to warn other women to be cautious. She even met with a reporter to talk about her experience and to get her message out. Candace was task-centered and practical in the first days after the assault, which is not uncommon. It was not until weeks later that she called me and stated that the initial "shock" had passed, and she was now "beginning to unravel." She described panic attacks, generalized anxiety and feelings of anger. She was worried about her ability to maintain a healthy and intimate relationship with a man she was dating. She had accessed therapy and was developing coping strategies, but she was struggling.

I hesitate to share Candace's story because a brutal attack by a stranger is so uncommon and I do not want to reinforce the Hollywood myth. The truth is that the brutality is part of what makes this case so memorable for me. It is also unsolved. There is DNA evidence that links this perpetrator to another unsolved sexual assault. Candace was devastated when she learned this.

The case, this woman's story, stands out in my memory for a more positive reason though. Candace, at the age of 39, quit her job and went back to school. She recently graduated with her bachelors in Social Work and received a Social Work Student of the Year award. She has applied for graduate school at my alma mater. She works with girls with disabilities and GENaustin, both centered on female empowerment. She volunteers at a local college to raise awareness about sexual assault and has a trip planned to Central America to serve victims of domestic violence, sexual abuse, and trafficking. It has been six years since the night of the rape, and Candace still maintains contact with me and the detective, periodically checking in to see if there have been any new leads and to let us know how and what she is doing.

I learned in school that the Chinese character for crisis is also the character for opportunity. Candace endured a terrible event, but she grew from it and found a passion and a new life direction as a result. When I wrote to her to ensure she was comfortable with my writing about her, she told me that she was honored and encouraged me to "put it out there!" I am honored to have known her and welcome her to our profession. For me, she personifies resilience.

I have described my experiences with sexual assault victims, but I work with other crime types as well. A powerful memory relates to Brenda whose daughter was murdered. When Brenda reported her daughter missing in June 2012, I was asked to call her by the Sergeant of the Missing Persons Unit because she called in daily and was distressed. When I first called her, she was very frustrated. She did not feel the police department was doing enough to find her daughter. I do not think she believed I could be helpful to her unless I was going to somehow make that happen. Brenda's daughter, Margo, was an addict and prostituted herself to support her addiction. Brenda believed that Margo was forgotten and uncared for and our conversation that first day involved my validating her fears and frustrations but assuring her that Margo's case was important. We frequently talked by telephone and eventually met in person. Brenda told me she went to the area of town where Margo met customers and stood on corners, holding up a sign and a photo of Margo in hope of learning what happened to her. She asked gas station clerks, homeless individuals, and other prostitutes about Margo. Brenda was 65 years old. She told her employer that she could not take any shifts until her daughter was found.

As the days and weeks passed, Brenda grew suspicious of a man with whom Margo had developed a relationship. She confronted this man, who claimed he did not know where Margo was. Brenda would call me to talk about what she had learned, all of which we relayed to detectives. She told me about Margo's younger life, about her sweet nature, sense of humor, and the tragedy of her addiction. Brenda loved her daughter, and the stress of the situation was affecting her physically and psychologically. I remember well the shift that occurred at some point, when Brenda acknowledged aloud that she knew that her daughter was dead. She could not bear that Margo was "out there" in the Texas summer heat. She just wanted her to be found so that she could lay Margo to rest.

One Saturday morning in late August, I was at home and heard a news brief that a badly decomposed body had been found in a park and police were on the scene. I had this sinking feeling and an absolute conviction that "they found Margo." I was worried that Brenda would see this same coverage but be unable to get any answers. I contacted my supervisor, the Missing Persons detective and the Homicide Unit. I learned that Brenda had been notified that a body was found, but it would take some time for an identification to occur. I called Brenda then, and we talked about how excruciating it was for her to wait. It *was* Margo, and the homicide detectives soon elicited a confession from the paramour that Brenda had suspected for weeks. Charges were filed against him, and I began to transition Brenda to my counterpart in the District Attorney's Office who would continue to provide her with support and information through the prosecution. Brenda called me after the first time that they talked by telephone. She told me that she wanted *me* to keep the case, and explained that the Victim Assistance Counselor called Margo by her given name (Margo was her nickname) and did not seem to know anything about her. I reminded Brenda it took me time to learn about Margo and asked her to be patient. A year later, that same Victim Assistance Counselor updated me on the trial and Brenda. At 5:15 pm on a Thursday evening, I went to the courthouse to sit with Brenda and her family to listen to closing arguments. The man was convicted of manslaughter rather than murder. A few months later, Brenda called me. She joked that I would never get rid of her. She had been thinking about her own health and really, her own death. She wondered what would become after she (Brenda). She had decided that she wanted to bury the ashes and asked for my assistance in coordinating this with the Crime Victims' Compensation fund. I attended that burial ceremony on the second anniversary of Margo's death. Brenda was surrounded by relatives (she is the matriarch of a large family) and friends, and I think I may have stuck out a little. Even so, I was encouraged to sit next to Brenda in the front row. It was so meaningful to me to be there, and I think it was for Brenda, too. It was coming full circle, from the beginning to the end.

I share this story as it illustrates my earlier point about the power of "witnessing," or being present with a victim through their trauma. I was not able to find Margo, bring her back, or deliver a guilty verdict but I was able to stand by Brenda through this journey and I trust that I helped her bear the grief. I am honored by that opportunity.

FIELD EXPERIENCES

Whichever level of social work education you might pursue, you can expect the theory you learn in the classroom to be integrated into a practice-focused field experience. Field education experience is the signature pedagogy of social work programs, promoting the application of the knowledge, skills, and values of the profession. BSW students are required to complete at least 400 hours of supervised practice in a social work setting; MSW students must complete at least 900 hours. Leaders in the field feel strongly that aspiring social workers should be mentored and supervised by practicing social work professionals in the settings in which social work services are delivered. This training socializes social work graduates into the profession so that they enter the workforce prepared to work competently, effectively, and ethically with clients facing real challenges.

Actual experience in the field is invaluable. In fact, one of the best strategies for confirming whether or not social work is the right profession for you is to gain exposure through a volunteer or service-learning experience (service-learning experience are typically tied to an academic course and include formal reflection on the experience). Whether or not you have previously engaged in community service, now is an excellent time to work with and observe social workers as they perform their professional responsibilities. Seek out a population or setting that interests you, and try to imagine yourself as a social work professional in that setting. If you are not required to engage in a community service or service-learning project as part of your introductory coursework, do it anyway. Take advantage of the opportunity to challenge yourself and determine if the social work profession is for you. Ensuring that you incorporate self-reflection into your service and volunteer experiences is an important skill to develop for the social work profession. Self-reflection includes putting your thoughts about an experience into written or verbal form for the purpose of assessing and processing your feelings, strengths, and areas for growth.

Community service provides valuable experience, but it also serves many other purposes, including (Dale, 2001):

- Helping you identify your goals and interests, and helping you steer clear of areas that do not interest you.
- Enhancing your résumé, future marketability, and social work network.
- Building self-confidence and guiding your career direction.

Most social service agencies welcome—and actually rely on—the contributions of volunteers. Here are some ways you can learn about service opportunities in your community:

- Consult with social work faculty members, the field education department, or your academic advisor.
- Contact your state's NASW chapter office for possible linkages to agencies.
- Contact your local United Way to obtain a list of funded social and health service agencies that are seeking volunteers.
- Check your university's community service or volunteer clearinghouse office.

There are an array of other resources that can help you to learn more about the profession of social work. A few of these resources include:

- www.beasocialworker.org/. This NASW-sponsored website provides information and connections to help you explore social work as a career option for you.
- http://careers.socialworkers.org/explore/. NASW provides information on positions, educational requirements, school loan foregiveness, and professional credentials.
- https://www.socialworkers.org/students/. In the student section of the NASW website, you can find information to aid your campus to career journey.
- www.socialworkers.org/. Check out Trending Topics in Practice on the NASW website to learn more about specific areas of social work practice.

After you have reviewed the information on one or more of these sites, reflect on new information that you now have about the social work profession.

Like Emily, you may find yourself drawn to the profession of social work. If you do, like Emily, you will find that every bit of experience helps. In each of the jobs in which Emily has worked, she has used the skills she learned during her training and in previous jobs. Each job led to the next, and each new job built on the last. As you are gaining knowledge of the social work profession and skills for working with people, you can begin to reflect on the strengths that you possess that will be an asset to you as a helping professional.

CONCLUSION

This chapter has introduced the social work profession, its definitions, areas in which social workers practice, the education required to become a social worker, and the distinctions between practice areas for social workers with different levels of education. Social work is a broad and diverse profession that encompasses multiple practice areas and educational requirements (Sheafor, 2014). You may have entered this course with stereotypical ideas about the social work profession (e.g., social workers only "steal babies and hand out food stamps"). It is the intent of this book not only to dispel those myths, but also to introduce you to the varied and exciting world of social work and to the types of work social workers do with individuals, families, communities, and organizations using a multitude of skills and practice methods. As you have already begun to learn, social workers help individuals and families in crisis, but social work also spans many other service areas. For example, social workers help groups of people to become better parents, help neighborhoods to enhance residents' safety, and help communities to influence legislation that will improve the services available to them. Once you have reached the end of this book, you may find that you will see social work in a new and different light.

The remaining chapters will explore the development of the social welfare system in the U.S. and the rich history of the social work profession, current challenges that influence social work, areas of practice, diversity and cultural competence, values and ethics, theoretical frameworks for guiding practice, fields or areas of practice (terms are used interchangeably), and the possibilities for the future of the social work profession. As you will learn in subsequent chapters, the social work profession exists and evolves in response to both "internal and external forces that give rise to this contextual profession" (Hopps & Lowe, 2008, p. 37).

Does social work sound like the right career for you? Check out the top 10 reasons for being a social worker in Exhibit 1.9 for some insight into a profession whose mission is to address the social and economic inequalities that exist in our society, to be agents of change striving to make the world a better place, and to perform meaningful work that helps others.

EXHIBIT 1.9

Top Ten Reasons for Being a Social Worker

10. Help People
9. Do What Counts
8. Practice Your Principles
7. Foster Success Stories
6. Match Skills with Life's Challenges

5. Change the Future
4. Make the World a Better Place
3. Satisfaction Guaranteed
2. World-Class Peers
1. Career of Champions

Source: National Association of Social Workers, n.d.

MAIN POINTS

- Social work is a helping profession that provides the opportunity to work with individuals, families, groups, organizations, and communities. Over a half-million people in the United States are degreed and practicing social workers.

- Other professions, such as psychology and sociology, have contributed to the knowledge base that informs social work, but the social work profession has its own unique values, skills, and practices.

- Social workers act as agents of change by providing a wide array of services such as counseling, advocacy, case management, education, prevention, support, crisis intervention, domestic and international social and community development, and program development.

- Social workers work with persons throughout all areas of society, including children, adolescents, and adults experiencing life changes or crises; persons who are struggling with illness, disability, addiction, or homelessness; persons who are victims of oppression, discrimination, or social injustice; and persons who have survived a disaster, including immigrants and refugees.

- Social workers work in a variety of settings, including schools; hospitals; ambulatory care centers; mental health facilities; addiction treatment programs; advocacy programs; residential facilities for children, youth, persons who are homeless, and older adults; planning and community development organizations; and governmental institutions.

■ Social workers can obtain degrees at the bachelor's, master's, and doctoral levels. The NASW and the CSWE have defined the criteria for competence in a degreed social worker.

■ There are many paths to becoming a social worker. One can directly enter an MSW program upon graduating from a BSW program, or gain work experience between completion of the BSW degree and entry into an MSW program, or enter an MSW program with an undergraduate degree other than social work.

■ All CSWE-accredited social work programs require students to complete several hundred hours of social work field practicum. Getting hands-on experience prepares the graduate to enter the professional world ready to practice.

EXERCISES

1. Visit one of the following websites to obtain information about the social work profession and reflect in writing on the information you review:
   a. NASW: www.naswdc.org or www.socialworkers.org. Click on "State Chapters" to get information about NASW programs in your state, including student resources. You may also want to check out the NASW Twitter feed at www.twitter.com/nasw. Consider reviewing the General and Issue Fact Sheets that are available at the NASW Press Room (www.socialworkers.org/pressroom/features/genfactSheets.asp) and the Occupational Profiles available through the NASW Center for Workforce Studies to learn about social work employment options (http://workforce.socialworkers.org/whatsnew.asp#profiles).
   b. CSWE: www.cswe.org. Review information regarding the accreditation process and the many resources CSWE provides.
2. In a small group discussion or in writing, reflect on the following social work-related issues:
   a. your understanding of the social work profession as you begin this social work course;
   b. the role that social workers play in our society, both globally and domestically;
   c. the meaning of social work for you and for those individuals that social workers serve.
3. In a personal written reflection, describe yourself (character, traits, and values) in terms of the ways in which you perceive the world and human nature. Then, reflect on a time that you asked for help. Discuss how these qualities and experiences may impact your professional work.

4. Meet the Sanchez family. Go to: www.routledgesw.com/caseStudies and click on the Sanchez family case. Read the introduction to the case, and explore how you can use the interactive program. Click each button to familiarize yourself with the presentation of information, the questions and tasks, and the Case Study Tools. Go to the Engage tab, and complete Tasks 1 and 2 to understand better the needs of the Sanchez family. You may use My Notebook to reflect on the roles that a social worker can play: describe the types of things a social work professional might be able to do to help the Sanchez family.

5. Review the RAINN National Sexual Assault Online hotline case. Go to: www.routledgesw.com/caseStudies and click on RAINN. Read the introduction to the organization, and explore how you can use the interactive program. Click each button to familiarize yourself with the presentation of information, the questions and tasks, and the Case Study Tools. After reviewing the information on the two client scenarios, Sarah and Alan, respond to the following:

    a. Summarize your concerns about each of the clients.

    b. Discuss the ways in which RAINN may prove to be a helpful resource for both clients.

6. This exercise introduces the Brickville community, some of its current and former residents, and the professionals who work there. Go to www. routledgesw.com/caseStudies and click on Brickville. After reviewing the Introduction, Real Estate Development Plan, Sources of Conflict, and You, the Social Worker and viewing the Town Map, respond to the following questions (in a small group in class or as an individual writing assignment):

    a. What are your initial impressions about this community?

    b. What are the primary issues that need to be addressed to promote the wellbeing of the community?

    c. What role(s) might the social worker play in the Brickville community?

HISTORY OF SOCIAL WORK AND SOCIAL WELFARE

Source: The Social Welfare History Project

Social work
The professional activity of helping individuals, groups, or communities to enhance or restore their capacity for social functioning and creating societal conditions favorable to this goal.

Social welfare
System that helps people meet their basic needs in order to maintain stability and social and economic justice within society.

Settlement house
A facility based in a geographically bound neighborhood whose purpose is to provide a center for the "neighbors" to come together for educational, social, and cultural activities. Settlement houses also provided social services and financial assistance. The settlement house movement is based on the concept that: (1) social change can occur; (2) social class distinctions can be narrowed through information and education; and (3) change can come only when social workers immerse themselves into their clients' community.

The exact beginnings and origins of the profession of social work and the social welfare system are somewhat difficult to determine due to lack of documentation, but ample evidence throughout history suggests that what has come to be recognized as social work has been in existence for thousands of years. Modern social work of the past century grew out of the humanitarian work of persons, often affiliated with religious institutions, who provided tangible goods and services to the sick and the poor. As you will learn in this chapter, this "charity" work evolved over the centuries to include the provision of mental health services, community organization and development work, and advocacy for oppressed, disenfranchised groups. The histories of social work and the social welfare system are inextricably linked—as one evolves, so does the other. This is due in large part to the fact that the social workers who helped to mold the social work profession have also been instrumental in developing social welfare programs, systems, policies, and laws. This chapter will provide an integrated overview of the histories of both the social work profession and the social programs that serve those with whom social workers work. An appreciation of their simultaneous development provides valuable insight into the current states of the social work profession and the social welfare system as well as lessons for the future.

Imagine what it was like to be one of the pioneers who practiced social work before it had a name. What would it have been like to pursue social work before much of society acknowledged the idea that we should care for all our citizens? Imagine that you are in 17th-century England trying to help poor families obtain enough food to eat; in 18th-century America trying to gain support to open that first orphanage; in 19th-century America working in one of the settlement houses helping immigrants adjust to their new home. In the 20th century, social work was finally identified as a profession, and it expanded to work for school desegregation and the elimination of domestic violence. In the 21st century, social work continues to address new challenges in the same areas and in additional areas of need. The mission of social work remains to heed the "call to help the poor, the destitute, and the disenfranchised of a rapidly changing societal order. It continues today still pursuing that quest, perhaps with some occasional deviations of direction from the original spirit" (McNutt & Floersch, 2008, p. 138).

Although the terms social work and social welfare are often used interchangeably, and though their histories have evolved in a parallel fashion, the two are not the same. However, both the social work profession and the social welfare system developed along with and in spite of the industrial growth experienced in the 19th and 20th centuries in the U.S. (McNutt & Floersch, 2008).

As you learned in Chapter 1, social work is a professional practice that involves helping individuals, groups, and communities. In contrast, social

welfare is a formalized and often legislated system of public and private programs aimed at creating social and economic justice for the residents of a
community, state, or country and has been administered at all levels from the
local to state to federal. Social welfare services and programs have been part of
society for centuries, and they provide the cornerstone for the emergence and
development of the social work profession.

The discussion that follows will chronicle both the history of social
welfare programs and services in which many social workers are active and
the history of the social work profession. The chapter will then provide an
overview of the issues related to development of social work practice and education. Along with a number of historical accounts of social work and social
welfare history, the chapter relies in particular on three informative references:
National Association of Social Workers (NASW)'s *Milestones in the Development
of Social Work and Social Welfare* (1998), the 20th edition of Mizrahi and Davis's
Encyclopedia of Social Work (2008), and the History of Social Work (available at:
www.historyofsocialwork.org).

DEVELOPMENT OF SOCIAL SERVICES AND THE SOCIAL WELFARE SYSTEM

The Religious Roots of Social Work

The roots of the social work profession lie within the religious community.
For many centuries, the provision of charity (or alms) was entirely within the
purview of religious groups. As early as 1200 BCE, religious leaders urged
Jews to help the poor of their communities. Historical Jewish documents
describe charitable services that resemble modern-day mediation and casework (Senkowsky, 1996). For examples of the influence of religious doctrine
on modern-day social services, see Exhibit 2.1. It is important to note that followers of many faiths—including many of the Judeo-Christian, Muslim, and
Confucian traditions—have historically championed the needs and rights of
those living in poverty or those experiencing discrimination or oppression.
Historical documents suggests that charity, social justice, and social reform
were incorporated into the tenets and practices of many of the faith traditions. For example, Muslims are encouraged to contribute 2.5% of their annual
income to support those living in poverty, a practice known as *zakah*, as an act
of social justice and redistribution of wealth (Leighninger, 2008). Also in the
name of social justice, the Old Testament urges individuals to care for those
unable to care for themselves (Leighninger, 2008).

In the 1st century CE, Christian leaders selected seven Jewish deacons
to see to the needs of enslaved Jews. One of these seven men, Stephen, was

Poverty
Having inadequate money or
means of subsistence.

Discrimination
Bias perpetrated by one
individual or group over another
individual or group due to race,
ethnicity, gender, religion, age,
sexual orientation, mental and
physical conditions, class, and
lifestyle.

Oppression
The restriction by one group
over an individual or another
group in the areas of activities,
access to resources or ability to
exercise their rights.

particularly effective in this mission. Along with his six peers, he collected food and money for distribution to the "needy." These activities were not particularly innovative; however, designating specific persons to do the work *was* innovative. Stephen is widely considered to be the "first" social worker. Many people commended Stephen for his work, but the leaders of Jerusalem did not support his efforts. He was tried by the High Court of the Great Temple and executed by the religious leadership for his values and beliefs (Marson & MacLeod, 1996).

Beginning in the 14th century, social changes in Europe began to transform attitudes toward the poor and the provision of charity. The feudal system of paying for services with land was beginning to shift to a more wage-based economic and social system, and increased trade within towns and cities created

---

EXHIBIT 2.1

Early Cornerstones of Modern-Day Social Services

- 1750 BCE—In a code of justice, King Hammurabi of Babylonia decrees that his subjects must help others in times of need.
- 1200 BCE—Jewish faith embraces the tenet of helping the poor and those in need.
- 500 BCE— The concept of philanthropy identified in Greece (i.e., acts of love for humanity) is incorporated into daily life as people begin donating money for the good of others.
- 300 BCE—Followers of Confucian philosophy promote the belief that humans are obligated to help those in need.
- Circa 43 BCE—Cicero, a Roman statesman, decreed that humans are social animals who should "cooperate with and assist his fellow men" and that it is "better to give than to receive."
- 30 CE—The teachings of Christ focus on helping others.
- 313 CE— Christian churches use the money converts have donated to help the poor.
- 400-787 CE—"Hospitals" are established in India to care for those who are disabled or homeless. This movement expands into Europe, being first developed in France and later in Italy, with staffing provided by the religious community.
- 650 CE—Islamic beliefs specify that taxes be directed to help the poor.
- 1100 CE—Catholic canon law mandates that the rich have legal and moral obligations to help the poor.

Sources: Leighninger, 2008; NASW, 1998.

a new middle class (Reid, 1995). In 1349, England established the Statute of Labourers to distinguish between the "worthy" and the "unworthy" poor. Under this law, only older adults and persons with disabilities were deemed worthy to receive charity.

Two centuries later, the Henrician Poor Law of 1536 expanded this concept. King Henry VIII of England created even more restrictive categories of persons eligible to receive aid. He also developed government regulations for the collection and disbursement of mandatory donations (taxes) from the general citizenry. One effect of this law was to transfer the responsibility for charity from the church to the state. Together, the Statute of Labourers and the Henrician Poor Law established the precedent for public social services and provided the framework for the enactment of the Poor Laws of 1601.

Elizabethan Poor Laws of 1601

The passage of the Elizabethan Poor Laws of 1601, during the reign of Queen Elizabeth I, was a defining point in the history of social services and the eventual development of a social welfare system. These English laws are thought to have defined the social service and welfare delivery system for the next 300 years and even into our modern-day society. Many historical accounts of the development of the social work profession actually begin with the institution of these history-making laws.

Advancing the philosophy of Henry VIII toward caring for persons in need, the Poor Laws of 1601 sought to place responsibility for charity in the government's hands and to categorize levels of charity based on worthiness. The Poor Laws employed the concept of mandatory local taxation to fund social and financial assistance (Corbett, 2008). Public assistance was provided to persons deemed eligible in three distinct categories:

1. Monetary help for persons living in poverty who were deemed unemployable (older adults and persons with disabilities).
2. Work for persons of limited income who were neither older nor disabled.
3. Apprenticeships for orphaned and dependent children.

In order to receive assistance, adult recipients were often required to live in residential institutions known as workhouses, poorhouses, or almshouses, and children were often required to live in orphanages. Known as "indoor relief," this practice continued well into the 19th century, and in some areas of Europe and the United States, workhouses or poor farms could be found into the mid-20th century. While the almshouses were often harsh and unwelcoming environments, the staff members were responsible for identifying those in need of

Poor Laws
Also known as the Elizabethan Poor Laws of 1601, these laws employed the concept of mandatory taxation to fund social and financial assistance. Public assistance was provided to persons deemed eligible in three distinct categories: (1) monetary help for poor people who were deemed unemployable (i.e., older persons and persons with disabilities); (2) work for poor people who were not elderly or disabled; and (3) apprenticeships for orphaned/dependent children.

Indoor relief
Requirement for adults to live in residential institutions known as workhouses, poorhouses, or almshouses, and for children to live in orphanages.

help, food, and shelter—functioning in roles that would later become known as early social work (Leighninger, 2008).

The Poor Laws arose during a time of profound change in the European social and political climate. Due to what were called the Enclosure Laws, an increasing number of persons were denied the right to farmland and were thus displaced from rural areas. This resulted in increased unemployment and homelessness and led to the creation of the Poor Laws. These laws were an attempt to do the following:

■ Extricate the church from the delivery of social services.
■ Eliminate begging and criminal behavior.
■ Centralize assistance within the government.
■ Standardize the types and amounts of assistance provided for the growing working class.

The Poor Laws made a significant, long-term policy impact by creating a clear-cut distinction between persons deemed *worthy* or *unworthy* of receiving assistance. Persons determined to be unworthy of aid were expected to be responsible for themselves, their families, and their situations. This belief is at the core of the current debate regarding funding for social programs. The Poor Laws also represent a clear shift away from private-sector (that is, religious institutions') involvement in social service to government responsibility for the poor. This controversy over private versus public responsibility still continues today.

Social Services in the 17th and 18th Centuries

The basic principles of the English Poor Laws had a profound effect on social services in Europe and, later, in North America. During the 17th and 18th centuries, social services expanded in scope and reach primarily in England and Europe and later into North America.

Despite the Poor Laws-era movement toward government-provided services, some religious organizations still play a voluntary role in providing social services. For example, in the early 1600s, Father Vincent de Paul founded charity and religious organizations in France that established formalized structures for providing food, clothing, and financial support for persons in need. The St. Vincent de Paul Society operated solely on voluntary contributions from parishioners, a model that prevails in the social service delivery system today. You might recognize the name, as the Society itself is still active in many communities.

Also during the 1600s, the concept of a Protestant work ethic was gaining popularity in England and other parts of Europe. This philosophical belief system and way of life emphasizes self-discipline and frugality and has had a significant influence on societal attitudes toward the poor around the world. Many people now believe that all persons, through hard work and self-discipline, should be able to care for themselves at all times without requiring or requesting help from others. Such thinking often translates into opposition to funding for social service programs and sadly, the voices of the opposition are often more powerful than the voices of those in need.

Protestant work ethic
A belief system and "way-of life" philosophy that emphasizes self-discipline and frugality and has had a significant influence on societal attitudes toward the poor.

Further efforts in 17th-century England to restrict the poor's access to aid took the form of the 1662 Law of Settlement, which stipulated that aid was based on one's place of residence. It is not clear if the intent of this law was to discourage aid recipients from moving to other areas where they might find work, but that was the outcome (Reid, 1995).

Meanwhile, British colonists in North America began formulating social welfare policy fashioned after the English Poor Laws. By 1657, Boston was home to the first private social welfare agency in the American colonies, the Scots' Charitable Society. In the same year, New York was the site for the first almshouse in the colonies, with others following soon thereafter in Plymouth, Massachusetts (1658) and Boston (1660). In 1727, the Ursuline Sisters in the French colony of New Orleans opened the first residential facility for orphans, and in 1773 the first psychiatric institution was established in Williamsburg, Virginia. Most of these newly created organizations were private and often religiously affiliated. Even as the colonists focused on expanding into new territory, establishing themselves in a new world, and grappling with the issue of colonization versus independence, they were devising plans to care for those living with poverty, health problems, and other disadvantages.

Soon after gaining independence from England, the government of the United States made its first major efforts to create public social and health services. A government-funded orphanage opened in Charleston, South Carolina, in 1790, and in 1798 a legislative act aimed at creating a health care system for merchant seamen established the U.S. Public Health Service. The Public Health Service still exists today to provide health care and mental health services to underserved populations around the world, to prevent and control disease, and to conduct research.

Although the primary focus of most of the charitable programs of this era was to alleviate poverty by providing financial aid, they also established the importance of addressing other aspects of an individual's life in order to facilitate a move out of poverty. During this era, a shift occurred in terms of the provision of indoor relief. While the methods would later be viewed as less than benevolent, persons living in poverty were initially forced to leave their communities, but were later sent to almshouses as life in the poorhouses was considered cheaper than financial assistance, character-building, and a deterrent to asking for help (Leighninger, 2008). The shift toward helping those living in poverty to gain economic stability planted the seed for modern-day social casework and clinical treatment. American colonists built a social system literally from the ground up, and that system became institutionalized as the country gained independence from England. However, moving forward the belief in public responsibility for social and health services among American citizens would wax and wane—and it continues to be a source of controversy well into the 21st century.

The 19th Century, a Defining Era for Social Work and Social Welfare in the United States

The 1800s were a boom time for the development of social welfare programs and the social work profession, particularly in the United States, where public and private agencies and organizations were established to address the country's growing social problems. During this century, the United States experienced substantial geographic and population growth. In addition, with rising immigration, the population became increasingly diverse. Following the Civil War, the United States underwent periods of economic depression, and the time was ripe for the formation of a more organized system of social service delivery. With the growth of the social service system came a dawning awareness that qualified and trained persons were needed to provide these services and to work with the increasingly diverse population.

Exhibit 2.2 highlights some of the advancements made in the burgeoning U.S. social services system during this period. Perhaps most important among them was the emerging belief that certain groups within our population need help to make their voices heard. The new United States was taking a more humane view of its citizens living in poverty than it previously had.

Children, ethnic and racial minorities, widows and children of war veterans, persons with mental illnesses, and people devastated by disasters are just a few of the groups whose voices are often not heard by the majority of society. Nineteenth-century advocates faced considerable adversity as they defended the rights of these marginalized groups. They often risked their reputations, safety, and personal finances to start programs to enhance the quality of life for these groups. Ida B. Wells-Barnett was one such pioneer. She championed the rights and needs of the African American community and performed an instrumental role in the founding of what became the National Association for the Advancement of Colored People (NAACP). To learn more about Ms. Wells-Barnett, visit: www.biography.com/people/ida-b-wells-9527635#synopsis.

EXHIBIT 2.2

19th-Century Advances in Social Services

- 1812—Societies for the Prevention of Pauperism are founded in New York, Baltimore, and Philadelphia to provide aid to those suffering as a result of the War of 1812.
- 1817—The first Society for the Prevention of Pauperism in the U.S. was founded in New York City.
- 1824—The U.S. Federal Government establishes the Bureau of Indian Affairs. The House of Refuge, the first state-funded program for "juvenile delinquents" is established.
- 1835—Boston follows New York City by establishing the Society for the Prevention of Pauperism, the forerunner of the Charity Organization Society (COS) movement.
- 1836—Boston passes child labor laws.
- 1841—Dorothea Dix (1802–1887) conducts the first investigations of services in the U.S. provided to the "insane." Dix goes on to help create 32 state and federal hospitals for persons with mental illness.
- 1845—The first U.S. public mental health facility (or "asylum") opens in Trenton, New Jersey.
- 1853—Children's Aid Society (CAS) (still in existence in many states today) is organized in New York by a group of social reformers and clergy led by Reverend Charles Loring Brace.
- 1863— Massachusetts establishes the first oversight organization for social services programs in the U.S.
- 1865—A partnership between the federal government and private philanthropies creates the Freedmen' s Bureau, the first federal welfare entity to help freed slaves secure education, protection from abuse and violence, and prospects for the future (ceased services in 1872).
- 1868—Public monies are used to pay "foster" families to house children in Boston (New York followed in 1875).
- 1870—A forerunner to the modern-day long-term care facility, the Home for Aged and Infirm Hebrews of New York City, is established.
- 1877—Society for the Prevention of Cruelty to Children is organized in New York. The first COS begins serving clients in Buffalo.
- 1880—The Salvation Army, founded in 1878 in England, expands to the United States.
- 1886—First U.S. Settlement House opens in New York.
- 1889—Hull House opens in Chicago.
- 1896—Providence, Rhode Island, offers public education to the "mentally deficient."

Source: Corbett, B.S. 2008.

Although many authorities held that indoor relief was the best way to provide aid, "outdoor relief," the provision of services outside an institutional setting, gained prominence. This paradigm shift led to the founding of two important movements. The settlement house and Charity Organization Society (COS) movements, similar in intent but different in function, changed the nature of social service delivery and are credited with spawning the social

Outdoor relief
The provision of services outside an institutional setting.

Dorothea Dix

Dorothea Lynde Dix first worked as a teacher but later focused her attention on improving conditions for persons living in prisons and almshouses. An ardent advocate for legislative change, Dix lobbied in the United States and abroad to gain support for public and private funds for hospitals to house persons with hearing loss and mental illness.

Source: J.K.Quam, 2008b.
Photo: Corbis.

Charity Organization Society (COS)
The movement was based on the belief that the person was responsible for his or her own difficulties but could be rehabilitated through individual sessions with a "friendly visitor" as opposed to a financial handout.

work profession. Both movements placed great value on the American ideals of individualism and personal freedom—even if neither movement was always compatible with the prevailing individualistic stance of the era. That is to say that both of these movements were committed to offering help to those who were in need and did not allow the individualistic philosophy to prevent persons receiving help. Despite the contradictions, settlement houses and charity organizations became the cornerstone of the American social service delivery system and the foundation for the social work profession.

The Settlement House Movement A settlement house is a facility based in a geographically bound neighborhood whose purpose is to provide a center for neighbors to come together for educational, social, and cultural activities. Settlement houses also provide social services typically in the form of goods, services, crisis intervention, and ongoing social support as well as financial assistance. A key belief of this movement is that the social structure and society overall are responsible for the problems of individuals. The settlement house

Ida Wells-Barnett

Ida B. Wells-Barnett (1862–1931), born in Mississippi to parents who were slaves, was able to attend high school and college and then work as a teacher. Her teaching career ended when she was fired for drawing attention to the poor school conditions for Black children. She turned her passion and talents for social justice to a career in journalism where she was able to raise awareness about her community. Her newspaper in Memphis was burned by a mob in 1892. Undaunted, Wells-Barnett went on a crusade for justice for Black men and women through her work with the Negro Fellowship League, Anti-Lynching Bureau of the National Afro-American Council (which later became the National Association for the Advancement of Colored People (NAACP)), and the Alpha Suffrage Club of Chicago.

Source: Peebles-Wilkins, 2008.
Photo: Getty Images.

idea is based on three key concepts: (1) social change can occur; (2) spreading information and providing education can help narrow social class distinctions; and (3) settlement house workers can only facilitate change when they immerse themselves in their clients' community (Blank, 1998). Simply stated, settlement houses are an attempt by socially-minded persons to engage in "friendship with the poor through sharing their lives" (Kendall, 2000, p. 16).

The first settlement house, Toynbee Hall, opened in London in 1884, and not long after the settlement house model spread across England and the United States. Just two years later, the first American settlement house opened in New York under the leadership of a former resident of Toynbee Hall, Stanley Coit. By the early 20th century, the number of settlement houses in the United States had grown to over 400 (Hopps et al., 2008). Jane Addams and her colleagues established the best-known U.S. settlement house, Hull House, in Chicago in 1889. Sadly, after several years of financial challenges, the 120-year-old Hull House Association closed its doors on January 27, 2012. The Hull House Museum on the campus of the University of Illinois-Chicago provides visitors the opportunity to walk through the dining room, view artifacts of the movement, and envision what it would have been like in the pioneering days of Jane Addams. For more information on Hull House, visit: www.uic.edu/jaddams/hull/hull_house.html. Denise E. Dedman reflects on the continuing impact

Jane Addams
Widely considered the originator of social work in the United States, Jane Addams (1860–1935) opened Chicago's Hull House in 1889.

Group work (mezzo-level practice)
A method of social work practice in which the social worker works with a client system comprised of multiple persons to develop a planned change effort that meets the needs of the group.

Social action
A method of social work practice with organizations and communities in which the planned change effort is focused on addressing issues of social injustice.

of Hull House in her firsthand account of visits to the Hull House Museum (Exhibit 2.3).

Originally intended to serve the growing immigrant population, the early settlement houses used a variety of intervention strategies, including group work and social action, to educate and socialize residents in the American culture of the time (Blank, 1998). Innovative programs included a nursery,

---

EXHIBIT 2.3

Connecting with Hull House
Denise E. Dedman

I've had the privilege of escorting several groups of social work students to visit the Hull House museum in Chicago, home to Jane Addams and dozens of other social reformers. Many don't realize that Hull House is where the social activists lived as well as worked. This settlement house began with Addams and Ellen Gates Starr, and expanded as more women and men joined their work and study. Eventually, their community grew to include a 13-building complex that occupied an entire block on Halsted Street in Chicago. They had gyms, theatres, and libraries that served the public, but the apartments were for the activists and visiting scholars.

Upton Sinclair lived at Hull House while researching *The Jungle*. John Dewey, Paul Kellogg, and Susan B. Anthony visited. Activists who lived there were involved in a variety of projects: Florence Kelley and Julia Lathrop both pioneered work in child welfare that helped end child labor and created juvenile justice programs; the Abbott sisters were social researchers and professors; and Alice Hamilton, one of the first female physicians, researched occupational hazards including toxins and dangerous work processes.

Most of the buildings are now gone. In the 1960s, the whole neighborhood was razed to make room for the University of Illinois-Chicago. Tremendous effort was made to save Hull House and the residents' dining hall, adjacent to UIC. Because of the success of that effort, we are fortunate to still be able to visit these historic landmarks to this day.

Sitting in the residents' dining hall is an amazing experience. We sit at the tables and realize that pioneer social workers had dinner there every night. It's so powerful to hear my students say, "Florence Kelly maybe was sitting here talking youth and factories. Alice Hamilton may have been sitting next to her, talking about occupational hazards to factory workers." In the dining room, the synergy of such dialogue, the sharing and blending of their individual work, can easily be imagined.

Amazing stuff came about, yet it was dinnertime discussion. In this commonplace act, through interest in each other's daily lives, they strengthened their commitment to reform. In this exchange over dinner, they could talk about their individual successes, and inspired by the little achievements they made, they motivated each other to reach further, resulting in decades of progressive social change.

When the students go upstairs to Jane Addams' small bedroom and see that it was really her only personal space—it was not *her* mansion, she had one small private area—they're shocked, and they gain an idea of the commitment of the residents to a greater social cause. Though Addams and other residents ate well, had lovely furnishings, and were surrounded by art and beautiful gardens, it was far from the luxurious homes of the wealthy. They had a very modest lifestyle, living next to their neighbors—the people of the immigrant ghetto.

The 120-year-old Hull House Association went bankrupt and closed [in 2012], and many thought that meant the end of Hull House, the museum. Fortunately, it didn't. The association had moved from the neighborhood long ago, but the museum is still there, a part of the UIC campus. That Hull House still stands is a mark of its ability to connect us to the lives, dreams, and work of a group of social reformers.

I feel renewed each time I go. Hull House is there, inspiring me still. I can share this with my students, and they are part of that synergy. The students return to their various field placements, coming together for seminar each week, and we are still building that community of social workers supporting each other in very hard but meaningful work.

Additional Reading

Addams, J. (1912). *Twenty Years at Hull House*. New York: The Macmillan Company. Retrieved from http://digital.library.upenn.edu/women/addams/hullhouse/hullhouse.html.

Simkin, J. (2013). *Hull House*. Retrieved from: www.spartacus.schoolnet.co.uk/USAhullhouse.htm.

Thayer, K. (2012). *Hull House Closing Friday. Chicago Tribune*. Retrieved from: http://articles. chicagotribune.com/2012-01-25/news/ct-met-hull-house-20120126_1_child-care-union-contract-employees.

University of Illinois-Chicago College of Architecture & Arts. (2009). *Hull House Museum*. Retrieved from: www.uic.edu/jaddams/hull/hull_house.html.

Source: Reprinted with permission from The New Social Worker. Denise E. Dedman, 2014. Available at: www.social-worker.com/feature-articles/practice/connecting-with-hull-house/

kindergarten, a club for working girls, a free labor bureau, a meeting space for political groups, and a visiting nurse service (Leighninger, 2008, p. 13). Jane Addams described her approach to the settlement house movement this way:

Teaching in a Settlement requires distinct methods, for it is true of people who have been allowed to remain undeveloped and whose facilities are inert and sterile, that they cannot take their learning heavily. It has to be diffused in a social atmosphere, information must be held in solution, in a medium of

Jane Addams

Widely considered the originator of social work in the United States, Jane Addams (1860–1935) opened Chicago's Hull House in 1889. Partnering with Ellen Gates, Addams established Hull House after visiting the original settlement house, Toynbee Hall, in London. Ever the activist, Addams fought for improved sanitary conditions in Chicago and, as a result, was appointed neighborhood sanitation inspector.

Many organizations had their roots among the activism of Hull House. One example is the organization that later became the Children's Bureau. Quaker and staunch pacifist, Jane Addams' contributions go far beyond the work of Hull House. She was a community organizer, peace advocate, 1931 co-winner of the Nobel Peace Prize, and one of only two social workers inducted into the Hall of Fame of Great Americans. In 1909, Addams was elected president of the National Conference of Charities and Correction (later to be called National Council on Social Welfare), the first woman to hold this post. A prolific writer, Addams' works include six books on her life and her views. Addams' dedication to the issue of world peace resulted in her active involvement in a number of peace organizations, including the Women's Peace Party, the National Progressive Party, and the Women's International League for Peace and Freedom. She accomplished all of this despite the fact that as a woman she did not acquire the right to vote until 1920.

Source: Barker, 2014; Corbett, 2008; Hopps et al., 2008; NASW, 1998; L. Quam, 2008.
Photo: Getty.

fellowship and good will . . . It is needed to say that a Settlement is a protest against a restricted view of education.

(Urban Experience in Chicago, available at http://uic.edu/jaddams/hull/urbanexp/contents. htm). To read more about Jane Addams, visit the History of Social Work at: www. historyofsocialwork.org.

Settlement house workers are thought by many to have been at the forefront of the social work profession's long history in social justice, social action, and policy practice. They were typically young, mostly female, well-educated adults interested in social issues and the arts. Because settlement house workers chose to live in the same neighborhoods as those with whom they worked, they could not ignore mounting social concerns like living and sanitary conditions, housing, child care, education, and worker exploitation. Thus, settlement house workers became frequent instigators of controversial and much-needed social change and advocated for marginalized groups. They helped to develop juvenile courts, mothers' pensions, child labor laws, and workplace protec-tions (McNutt & Floersch, 2008, p. 3), and instituted training programs aimed at the settlement house workers that would later become a component of the social work profession.

The leaders of the Settlement House movement epitomized the Progressive Era goals of promoting social justice; solving urban infrastructure problems; and improving living, working, and education systems for recent immigrants and those persons living in poverty. However, some scholars contend that Settlement House leadership failed to give the plight of the African American community the attention it required (Hopps et al., 2008). While Settlement Houses were being established throughout the country, African Americans and, in some cases, Whites living in southern states were excluded mainly based on societal discrimination versus the beliefs of the Settlement House workers (Hopps et al., 2008). Three leaders of the African American community—all women—took matters into their own hands and helped to establish Settlement Houses in Chicago, Illinois, in 1910 for African Americans moving north (Ida B. Wells-Barnett); outside Tuskegee, Alabama, during the early years of the 20th century (Margaret Washington); and Atlanta, Georgia, in 1911 (Lugenia Burns Hope) (Hopps et al., 2008). Lugenia Burns Hope was also the founder of the first social welfare organization for African American women (Leighninger, 2008).

Contemporary incarnations of settlement houses differ in many ways from their 19th-century predecessors. Neighborhood-based community centers like Grace Hill Settlement House in St. Louis, Missouri (Exhibit 2.4) that provide a wide array of goods and services, including food and clothing, health care, after-school and summer recreation, crisis intervention, and counseling, have replaced those original centers where idealistic, youthful volunteers lived among the residents and endeavored to teach them arts and literature. However, the ideal upon which settlement houses were founded, that change is most effective if it comes from within the community itself, still guides com-munity centers.

Charity Organization Society (COS) While settlement houses were improv-ing life for immigrants and influencing the formation of social welfare ser-vices in the United States, another movement that would impact the future of social work got underway with the formation of the first Charity Organization Societies (COS). With its roots in early 19th-century Scotland and created by Reverend Thomas Chalmers, the early COS movement was parish-based and was viewed as a mechanism for addressing poverty by providing financial help and character-building aid (Leighninger, 2008). The London-based Society for Organising Charitable Relief and Repressing Mendacity provided the frame-work for the first North American COS in Buffalo, New York, in 1877.

Progressive Era
The 1890s and early 1900s were a time of significant reform in far-ranging areas such as women's rights (specifically suffrage), health care and social service programs, education, and political practices, ethical, occupational and consumer safety, child and social welfare laws, environmental preservation, and socialization for immigrants.

EXHIBIT 2.4

Grace Hill Settlement House

Grace Hill Settlement House, located in St. Louis, Missouri, can trace its origins to the town leaders' 1844 decision to donate land for a church. Grace Episcopal Church was built in a mostly Episcopal neighborhood. As wealthier residents moved out, the neighborhood became home to a middle-class and then a low-income population, including many recent immigrants. In response, Grace Episcopal Church founded the Holy Cross Mission in 1903 to meet the neighborhood's changing needs.

To expand their mission into the delivery of health care services, the Episcopal Diocese opened the Holy Cross Dispensary in a nearby location in 1906. In 1914, Holy Cross Mission was incorporated. In 1923, the organization joined with the Community Fund (now United Way) to provide kindergarten, health clinics, recreation, and classes in crafts, dance, athletics, and music. From 1938 to 1944, Grace Hill gained recognition as a settlement house and began accepting African Americans and replacing religious staff with social workers. By 1965, Grace Hill had established its first Head Start program for preschool education. Shortly thereafter, Grace Hill, in consultation with neighborhood residents, started to offer a meal program for older adults and developed a 10-year neighborhood improvement plan that resulted in the construction of low-cost apartments and the rehabilitation of existing housing stock.

By the 1980s, the agency had expanded its philosophy to involve neighborhood residents in the development of training programs, forums, a resource bank, self-help groups, and communication centers. Keeping the settlement house model alive, Grace Hill now provides child and older adult care, housing for low-income persons and families, self-help, job skills training, and community and economic development.

The Charity Society Movement held the moral belief that while each person is responsible for his or her own difficulties, he or she can be rehabilitated in individual sessions with a "friendly visitor" rather than through financial handouts (Brieland, 1995). Friendly visitors were the early COS workers, who believed that extending friendship and sympathy would enable persons living in poverty to feel better about themselves and to rise out of poverty, took "not alms but a friend" as their motto (Kendall, 2000). Four organizing principles guided each COS: (1) detailed investigation of applicants; (2) a central system of registration to avoid duplication; (3) cooperation between the various relief agencies; and (4) extensive use of volunteers in the roles of "friendly visitors" (Corbett, 2008, p. 7). The concept of a charitable service in which workers did not live with those they served spread quickly throughout the U.S.; by 1892, 92 such societies were in operation (Brieland, 1995).

Friendly visitor
Early Charity Organization Society workers, who believed that extending friendship and sympathy would enable persons living in poverty to feel better about themselves and to rise out of poverty.

The first COS workers were primarily middle-class women who voluntarily ventured into poor neighborhoods in order to share their wisdom and advice on what they considered good and moral living. These "friendly visitors" were the predecessors of modern-day social workers. COS volunteers performed individual assessments and registered those "worthy" of receiving charity and, ultimately, of securing employment and legal services (Brieland, 1995).

Although the COS movement has been criticized by later leaders within the social work profession as shortsighted and judgmental, and this negative attitude about the COS movement became a pervasive part of social work for many decades, these well-intentioned volunteers laid the groundwork for advances in the social work profession, including social casework and the establishment of family and children's service agencies. Despite the individualistic and conservative explanations offered for the causes of poverty and challenges in recruiting adequate numbers of volunteer friendly visitors, the COS model was quickly and enthusiastically embraced throughout 19th- and 20th-century America (Leighninger, 2008). The COS movement's systemic and organized approach introduced the concept of "scientific charity" to the service delivery system, professionalizing and bureaucratizing the social work profession (Hopps et al., 2008).

The Settlement House and COS movements were key to the evolution of the social work profession, enabling society to move forward in its treatment of persons experiencing challenges such as poverty, abuse, and oppression. The Settlement House and COS innovations enabled social workers to begin developing approaches to social casework, group work, community development, social planning, social action, mental health treatment, and even the beginnings of social work research. Exhibit 2.5 summarizes the contributions of these two movements.

In what ways have attitudes changed since the inception of these two service delivery systems—and in what ways have they stayed the same?

EXHIBIT 2.5

Contributions of the Settlement House and Charity Society Movements

	SETTLEMENT HOUSE MOVEMENT	CHARITY SOCIETY MOVEMENT
Central Vision	Reform systems and environment	Provide relief for clients
Contributions to Social Work Profession	Introduced practice of assessing and understanding the conditions and cultures in which clients live	Introduced (or instituted) assessment of each individual's situation
	Acknowledged the impact of environmental conditions on quality of life	First tailored interventions specific to the individual
	Established goal of achieving client empowerment through education, information, and group work	Recognized that money alone does not always facilitate change

Source: Hopps et al. 2008.

Social Services in the 20th Century

The first two decades of the 1900s were a time of economic prosperity. The country emerged from the depression of the late 1800s and with economic prosperity comes decreased rates of poverty. Leaders in the social service movement had the opportunity to focus on coordinating services and organizing coalitions to enhance service delivery. Socially and politically, the 1890s and early 1900s, known as the Progressive Era, were a time of significant reform in far-ranging areas such as women's rights (specifically suffrage), health care and social service programs, education, political practices that were more transparent and ethical, occupational and consumer safety, child and social welfare laws, environmental preservation, and socialization for immigrants. The United States was in a period of rapid transition during the early years of the 20th century, in part due to immigration and shifts from agrarian to urban life, which led the Progressives to advocate for improved working, housing, and infrastructure (e.g., sanitation) conditions (Leighninger, 2008). The leaders of the Progressive Movement successfully advocated for changes in social insurance, government regulation, and the professionalization of helping professions (Reid, 1995, p. 2212).

By this time, social work was established as a profession that responds to current economic, political, and social events and trends. The Progressives, a group of social and political activists that included Jane Addams, started a national conversation about the need to establish a federal infrastructure for financial assistance, public health interventions, and social work professionalization that would concretize the delivery of social services for many years to come (Reid, 1995).

At the same time, the COS movement continued to grow and evolve. Often considered one of the architects of the social work profession, COS administrator Mary Richmond (see Exhibit 2.6) and her colleague, Frances McLean, worked together to strengthen the COS organizational structure and approach. In 1911, McLean oversaw the development of the National Association of Societies for Organizing Charity (which became the Family Welfare Association of America in 1930), while Richmond focused on developing casework as a social work intervention practice (Hopps et al., 2008).

Though social workers played a role in founding the Progressive Era-born National Urban League, Children's Bureau (first headed by Hull House alumna, Julia Lathrop), and the Child Welfare League of America, how those organizations influenced social work may not be readily apparent. The endorsement by governmental agencies of child welfare and the merging of smaller groups into larger ones strengthened the position and voice of those committed to serving the poor. Because of social workers' tireless, demonstrated commitment to child welfare—as evidenced through the work of the Children's Bureau and the Child Welfare League of America—they cemented the public's perception that social workers are the experts and leaders in child advocacy and child welfare work. As a result of social workers' continuous vigilance in advocating for child welfare, social workers have become identified as the profession with the commitment and expertise to assess and intervene with children who are in need of care (Briar-Lawson, 2014). Despite an effort by federal and state governments to deprofessionalize (i.e., hire nondegreed social workers) the child welfare workforce, the Children's Bureau has funded the National Child Welfare Workforce Institute through 2018 (Briar-Lawson, 2014).

During this period, the social work profession expanded to meet the needs of soldiers serving in World War I. In response to mental health crises in the field, the American Red Cross deployed social workers to the front (Hopps et al., 2008). Social workers also provided counseling, guidance, information, and support for families back at home.

In the early 20th century, social workers actively championed policies and programming to benefit workers, women, and children. In 1911, Wisconsin was the first state to successfully pass workers' compensation legislation, and within 10 years most states had followed suit.

The Mothers' Pensions program that provided assistance for women and children was launched in 1911 by the Illinois State legislature and initially administered by the Cook County (Chicago) Juvenile Court (Goodwin, n.d.). Recipients of the Mothers' Pensions were typically Caucasian widowed mothers. Though it was modeled after traditional charity programs that focused on moral reform and offered minimal financial benefits, the Mother's Pensions program was the first nationwide public program that attempted to destigmatize and provide financial assistance to women who were rearing families on their own (Seccombe, 1999).

Before the 1920s, most social service organizations relied largely on wealthy benefactors. After World War I, Community Chests, fundraising efforts rooted in nationwide War Chest programs and predicated on the belief that citizens at all socioeconomic levels should support their neighbors in need, took over that primary funding role (Hopps et al., 2008). These programs supported private social service agencies throughout the 1920s, but the Great Depression of the 1930s forced nearly one-third of all Community Chests to close down (Hopps et al., 2008).

The early 20th century also saw the emergence of dedicated social service departments within medical institutions. The term "psychiatric social worker" was first used in Boston in 1914, and the Massachusetts General Hospital was the first medical facility in the United States to establish in 1914 a department to serve patients' social and psychiatric needs headed by an early graduate of a social work program, Ida Maude Cannon (Massachusetts General Hospital, n.d.). Soon, over 100 U.S. hospitals had established similar social service units.

Developments During the Depression and the New Deal The stock market crash of 1929 sent the country spiraling downward into an economic and social depression that would last through the next decade. The Great Depression of the 1930s was a time of suffering and unrest. In the early years of the Depression, President Herbert Hoover attempted to shift responsibility for social services to the states and private agencies. His strategy's success was short-lived as increasing poverty meant decreasing charitable donations (Hopps et al., 2008). Nevertheless, social workers rose to the occasion.

When Franklin D. Roosevelt, a Democrat, was elected to the presidency in 1932, nearly one-third of Americans were living in poverty. Manufacturing and agriculture had been devastated, and the breadlines were long and getting longer. Roosevelt took aggressive measures to address the country's troubles. When he appointed social worker Frances Perkins to serve as Secretary of Labor, she became the first woman in the U.S. Cabinet and is credited with writing the recommendations that resulted in the passage of the Social Security Act in 1935. His administration instituted a sweeping set of

Signing of Social Security Act

President Franklin Delano Roosevelt signed the Social Security Act of 1935.

Source: Getty Images.

Frances Perkins (1882–1965)

Frances Perkins earned a master's degree in social work from Columbia University in 1910 and went on to have an illustrious career as an administrator, leader, and author. She served in a number of leadership roles, including the New York Consumer's League, New York Committee on Safety, New York State Factory Commission, New York Council of Organizations for War Services, Council on Immigrant Education, and New York State Industrial Board. She then became U.S. Secretary of Labor, the first appointment of a woman to the U.S. Cabinet. Following her service as the Secretary of Labor, she spent her final working years on the U.S. Civil Service Commission.

Source: J.K.Quam, 2008c.
Photo: Getty Images.

New Deal
A set of reforms to relieve poverty in the Depression era, brought about by Franklin D. Roosevelt.

Social Security Act
Legislation in 1935 that granted benefits to a range of recipients who were in need.

Temporary Assistance to Needy Families (TANF)
Government program of social welfare that provides cash assistance to poor women and children; established by the 1996 Personal Responsibility and Work Opportunity Reconciliation Act (PROWRA). TANF provides monthly cash assistance to eligible low-income families with children under age.

programs, collectively called the New Deal, that would have a lasting effect on our society.

Since the early 1900s, members of the progressive movement had campaigned for legislation to alleviate the poverty of older adults, widows and widowers, the unemployed, persons with disabilities, and dependent children. Their efforts led to the passage of the Social Security Act of 1935, which became the foundation of our current public welfare and retirement systems. Roosevelt appointed social worker Jane M. Hoey to direct the Federal Bureau of Public Assistance, the entity that oversaw distribution of aid in accordance with the Act.

In addition to ensuring retirement income for older adults, the Social Security Act resulted in later decades in the development of public assistance programs to provide health care, employment services, transportation, and child day care for persons living in poverty and/or with disabilities which will be discussed later in this chapter. This initial legislation also established the basis of public assistance for impoverished women and children (known as Aid to Dependent Children, then Aid to Families with Dependent Children—AFDC, and now Temporary Assistance to Needy Families (TANF)). The Social Security Act and other New Deal reforms affirmed the federal government's role in the administration of social services. The development of public (cash) assistance for single female-headed families would later serve U.S. society well, because these structures and programs were already in place when the country faced times of economic crisis.

Interestingly, many in the social work profession raised concerns about the passage of the Social Security Act of 1935. While Social Security and other New Deal programs provided greater access to services for more persons in need, the programs shifted service delivery away from the private sector and into the public sector and perpetuated certain forms of discrimination, primarily racial and economic (Bowles & Hopps, 2014). In order to receive benefits, one had to have a "legitimate" work record, a requirement that excluded many African Americans and economically disadvantaged individuals whose work histories were erratic and often unrecorded.

The New Deal instituted a number of social and economic programs including:

■ *Federal Emergency Relief Administration (FERA)*: Headed by social worker Harry Hopkins, FERA established a system of state grants to provide financial assistance to persons who were unemployed. FERA later became the Works Progress Administration (WPA), an agency that created jobs for over 8 million people from 1935 to 1943 in such diverse areas as the construction of roads and bridges and the development of cultural programs. To read more about Hopkins, see the profile included in this chapter.

■ *Civilian Conservation Corps (CCC):* From 1933 to 1942 the CCC worked to conserve and develop the nation's natural resources, while creating jobs for unemployed men.

■ *National Youth Administration (NYA):* Out of concern for ensuring that the country's high school and college students be able to complete their education, the NYA provided funding for part-time employment so that the youth could continue their education while providing support for their families.

Developments During World War II and the 1950s World War II had a significant impact on both U.S economic recovery and the social work profession. The mental health programs social workers developed and administered to military personnel during the war led to the creation of the nationwide, community-based mental health system that remains the basis for the provision of mental health services in the United States (Reid, 1995). During the latter half of the 1940s, social welfare efforts focused on aiding returning veterans, 1 million of whom used the 1944 GI Bill of Rights to acquire a college education and purchase homes. The emphasis on mental health services created more employment opportunities for social workers.

In 1946, the group now known as the Baby Boomer generation made its debut. The Boomers ushered in the economically robust, politically conservative 1950s. Historically, Republican presidential administrations in prosperous times have devoted little attention (or funding) to the social service community; the 1950s are a prime example of that historical pattern.

Baby Boomer
Persons born between 1946 and 1964.

One noteworthy development did occur in 1953 when Republican President Dwight D. Eisenhower's administration created the cabinet-level Department of Health, Education, and Welfare (HEW). Reminiscent of the New Deal programs, the creation of HEW was an acknowledgment by the federal government that the well-being of all people in the United States was a high priority. This department—which in 1979 was divided into the Department of Health and Human Services and the Department of Education—continues to be instrumental in formulating and administering virtually every federally-funded social welfare program in existence in this country.

Social work practice during the 1940s and into the 1950s focused on individual and family casework. In keeping with the profession's whole-person focus, social workers viewed clients within the contexts of the environments in which they lived. However, at that time social work training did not emphasize culturally-oriented practice approaches. Interventions tended to be Eurocentric and did not attend to individual and family economic, racial, ethnic, religious, and cultural backgrounds, often ignoring the fact that "cultural values, economics, and public policy are inextricably linked aspects of the human experience" (Bowles & Hopps, 2014, p. 7). Because cultural sensitivity

Harry Hopkins (1890–1946)

Known best for his work during the New Deal era, social worker Harry Hopkins led the newly created Federal Emergency Relief Administration (FERA). Committed to the social work profession early on, Hopkins had first worked with boys at a New York settlement house and later for the Bureau of Family Rehabilitation and Relief. Appointed by then New York Governor Franklin D. Roosevelt, Hopkins served as the executive director of the Temporary Emergency Relief Administration. Having gained the respect of the future president, Hopkins went on to serve Roosevelt in the Works Progress Administration and as the Secretary of Commerce.

Source: Longres, 2008a.
Photo: Getty Images .

appeared lacking during this era, Bowles and Hopps (2014) go on to state that the social work profession "was confronted to think back to its founding mission and concern for the real poor" (p. 5).

Developments During the 1960s and 1970s The 1960s was a tumultuous decade on many fronts. In 1960, the nation elected a Democratic president, John F. Kennedy. The Civil Rights Movement was heating up. The war in Vietnam would soon take center stage, bringing with it civil unrest here at home. A revolutionary youth movement was challenging older generations. Many young people opposed the Vietnam War and military service in general, participated in the sexual revolution, and experimented with illicit drugs.

From the social work perspective, the 1960s were an interesting time, indeed. As our society was changing, so too was the social work profession. Due to the creation of a number of social programs, advances in civil rights, and the willingness of U.S. citizens to confront injustices (racial, economic, and gender issues, in particular) in a public way, many social workers feel that the 1960s was one of the most significant times for the profession. Increased government spending on expanded social programs during the 1960s led social workers to become the primary providers of mental health services by the end of the decade—a distinction that continues to present day. Social work developments of the 1960s still impact social work practice and education in the 21st century, particularly in the realm of politically-oriented community and social action, social planning, and clinical treatment approaches (Hopps et al., 2008).

The Kennedy administration established the Peace Corps in 1961 and encouraged Congress to pass the Community Mental Health Center Act in 1963. While the initial momentum for changes that significantly impacted the social service system as well as the social work profession can be traced to the Kennedy administration, it was Kennedy's successor, Democrat Lyndon B. Johnson, who oversaw passage of the Civil Rights Act of 1964 as well as the Economic Opportunity Act of 1964—an array of social welfare legislation known collectively as the Great Society. The last of the Baby Boomers were born in 1964, at the dawn of this major shift in social welfare policy, signaling the end of one era and affirming the eminence of a new one.

Great Society
Domestic programs initiated by President Johnson to eliminate poverty and racial injustice in the 1960s.

Designed to build on the Roosevelt administration's "welfare-oriented" initiatives that of the 1930s, Johnson's efforts specifically focused on creating safety nets for those living in poverty and on improving racial dynamics, particularly in inner cities (Terrell, 2010). The War on Poverty was a "unique anti-poverty experiment . . . that powerfully influenced the character of community policy-making and administration in subsequent decades" (Terrell, 2010, p. 1061). Although some critics consider Johnson's War on Poverty and the Great Society to have been a failure, the 1964 legislation was responsible for the creation of numerous social programs, many of which still exist in some form today, including Job Corps, Head Start, Volunteers in Service to America (VISTA—the domestic version of the Peace Corps, now a partner with AmeriCorps), and the Neighborhood Youth Corps. Critics of these innovations point to the current levels of persons living in poverty (46.5 million persons live in poverty in the U.S. in 2014 (Urban Institute, 2014), as evidence of the failure of these programs to eradicate poverty. Proponents of War on Poverty efforts contend that the programs were responsible for decreasing poverty levels, and that erosion of such programs resulted in corresponding increases in the number of persons struggling to survive (Rank, 2008). Although halted due to increasing program costs and the escalating war in Vietnam, the War on Poverty produced two significant outcomes the long-term consequences of which are with us today: (1) for the first time it gave more people, particularly those with low incomes and persons of color, a voice in policy-making activities; and (2) it formed service delivery partnerships between public and private institutions (Terrell, 2010).

Five major social programs enacted during the Great Society have enhanced—and perhaps saved—the lives of the people they serve and, as many contend, have decreased the number of persons living in poverty:

1. *Food Stamp Act (now referred to as Supplemental Nutrition Assistance Program (SNAP))*: This Department of Agriculture program, enacted in 1964, provides food assistance to people living on limited incomes.

2. *Medicare:* Passed in 1965, this national social insurance program provides health insurance for older adults and younger persons experiencing a disability.
3. *Medicaid:* Also passed in 1965, Medicaid supplies health insurance for those who receive public welfare benefits.
4. *Older Americans Act:* This nationwide system of community-based services for older adults was created in 1965.
5. *Elementary and Secondary Education Act:* In 1965, the Elementary and Secondary Education Act directed federal funding for the first time in history toward the goal of providing students in public school systems with an array of services and support.

The Civil Rights Act of 1964 represents one of the most significant strides in the history of U.S. legislation aimed specifically at protecting the rights of more Americans. This legislation provides protection against discrimination based on race, color, religion, or national origin, and it led to the desegregation of public schools and more equal employment opportunities (Pollard, 2008). Numerous laws have since been enacted to protect the civil rights of many specific underrepresented and oppressed groups, including persons with disabilities; the gay, lesbian, bisexual, and transgender community; and immigrants and refugees. Social workers have always been, and will continue to be, on the front lines of these activities, ensuring that every person's voice is heard.

Although perhaps not as glamorous or revolutionary as the 1960s, the 1970s was a decade of progress in social services. The emphasis in the 1970s on the provision of "hard" services (i.e., goods, services, resources, etc.) versus "soft" services (i.e., counseling, mental health treatment, etc.) diminished social work employment opportunities somewhat during this time (Hopps et al., 2008). As a cost-savings measure, a certain amount of deprofessionalization of the social work profession occurred during the 1970s—that is, positions previously held by degreed social workers were re-classified so that non-social workers and non-degreed workers could be hired at lesser salaries (Hopps et al., 2008).

Despite the ultimate downfall of Richard M. Nixon and his Republican administration and his criticism of the Great Society initiatives, a significant number of programs were created under his leadership. Though Nixon's administration held the traditional Republican stance against endorsing "charity," it did support work incentives (Reid, 1995). The social welfare laws passed during the administrations of Nixon and his successor, Gerald Ford, described below, had far-reaching effects on social service delivery.

■   *Supplemental Security Income (SSI):* In 1972, SSI made additional benefits available to older persons and people with disabilities whose income was still well below poverty standards.

- *Comprehensive Employment and Training Act (CETA):* This 1974 program provided educational and job opportunities for persons of limited income.
- *Child Abuse Prevention and Treatment Act:* Enacted in 1974, this measure created a comprehensive approach to the prevention, investigation, and treatment of child abuse, and it was expanded in 1978 to address inadequacies of the adoption system.
- *Education for All Handicapped Children Act:* This 1975 legislation required all public schools to provide children with disabilities educational experiences that are comparable to those available to children without such disabilities.
- *Title XX amendment to the Social Security Act:* In 1975, this act provided funds for the purchase of social services, training, and housing for persons who qualified based on their income.

Developments During the 1980s and 1990s Those in the social work community do not typically view the 1980s with favor. The administrations of Ronald Reagan and George H.W. Bush followed the traditional Republican pattern of decreased spending on domestic and social programs. Guided by "Reaganomics", the federal government attempted to reduce federal responsibility for social services by awarding block grants to states (Hopps et al., 2008). Moreover, conservatives within the federal government did not hold social workers in high regard during this era, but instead saw them as "misguided philanthropists, harming poor people" (Hopps et al., 2008, p. 163).

Specifically, two legislative acts passed during Reagan's first term severely decreased public social service funding: the Omnibus Budget Reconciliation Act (OBRA) of 1981 and the Tax Equity and Fiscal Responsibility Act of 1982. OBRA gave more authority and less funding to states for the administration of public assistance programs. Further, OBRA made it more difficult for those living in poverty to benefit from services, as states could individually determine eligibility and access. The 1982 law reduced Medicare, Medicaid, AFDC, SSI, and unemployment funding.

Continuing in his predecessor's footsteps, George H.W. Bush advocated for increased privatization of the social service system based on a belief that public funds should not be used for social welfare. Enacted in 1988, the Family Support Act was an attempt to positively impact the welfare system by providing improved employment and training programs, child support enforcement, and child care services. Bush later signed into law the landmark 1990 Americans with Disabilities Act. Ironically, some argue the Reagan and George H.W. Bush administrations' attempts to disempower the social welfare system resulted in a strengthening of sorts. Increased funding and management options at the state level and a renewed interest by the general public in the nonprofit sector helped bring the attention of the general public to the need for a centralized social service system (Reid, 1995).

President Bill Clinton's campaign platform in the early 1990s was designed to redirect the public's attention to domestic issues. Clinton's presidency focused on reviewing and revamping a number of domestic programs. His administration took on such intractable social issues as health care, family health and wellbeing issues, abortion, discrimination against gays and lesbians in the military, welfare reform, and distressed communities (Green & Haines, 2002). With a Republican-controlled Congress, the effort to embrace universal health care failed. Yet the Clinton administration made efforts to revitalize the economy, increasing the minimum wage to $5.15/hour, creating new jobs, and eliminating the budget deficit despite fierce opposition from the "Conservative Opportunity Society's" Contract with America. Spearheaded by Newt Gingrich, the Contract with America aimed to decrease public welfare funding and change the public assistance system that had been in place for decades, thus penalizing families economically if they needed/utilized assistance by terminating benefits (Hopps et al., 2008). This adversarial relationship resulted in persons moving from "welfare poverty" to "employment poverty" (i.e., former public assistance recipients went to work but in low-paying positions with minimal benefits) (Leighninger, 2008, p. 22).

The most significant social welfare legislation of the 1990s addressed welfare reform and community development. The 1996 Personal Responsibility and Work Opportunity Reconciliation Act (PRWORA) became law, replacing Aid to Families with Dependent Children with Temporary Assistance for Needy Families (TANF). TANF continues to provide cash assistance to low-income women and their children, but with greater restrictions, mandated work requirements, and a 5-year lifetime cap on the receipt of benefits. Proponents believe that the welfare-to-work programs TANF created have brought about positive changes because they limited the length of time that families could receive benefits and placed the emphasis on moving recipients into the workforce and off of public assistance, while others (mostly those on the front lines) feel they have been a deterrent to getting out of poverty. Many former welfare recipients secured jobs during the prosperous 1990s, but critics questioned whether this trend could be sustained in weaker economic times (Green & Haines, 2002). In addition, many persons working full-time in minimum wage jobs still lived in poverty and lacked health care and other basic resources.

The 1990s saw an array of new legislation aimed at protecting the rights of certain populations and ensuring access to services. Passed in 1990 during the presidency of George H.W. Bush, the Americans with Disabilities Act guarantees persons with disabilities access to public facilities and protection from employment discrimination. The Mental Health Parity Act (1996) mandates that insurance companies must provide coverage for mental health services as well as physical health services.

In spite of the Clinton administration's efforts, critics question whether real change occurred and, if so, who benefited from that change. For example, the military publicly addressed homosexuality for the first time when it instituted the "Don't Ask, Don't Tell" policy. The gay and lesbian movement viewed this policy, which meant that the military could not officially inquire about a service member's sexual orientation and that service members could not offer that information, as a setback—not as progress. This policy was only reversed when President Obama signed the repeal in 2010.

Social Services in the 21st Century and Beyond

The first president of the new millennium was a Republican who stated in his campaign platform that he did not support increased public funding for social programs. In fact, one of George W. Bush's early efforts in this area was to make federal monies available to faith-based social services instead of public social service agencies. Faith-based social service providers are those that explicitly identify with a religious tradition or are affiliated with a religious organization or community, but whose services are not necessarily religious in content (Crisp, 2014, p. 11). There were many who opposed this initiative, claiming that the federal government was attempting to save money and shirk its ethical responsibility to provide adequate funding for social services.

In many ways, Bush's approach grew out of the agenda promoted by his father, George H.W. Bush, who launched the 1,000 Points of Light project to showcase private-sector agencies who were delivering programs to meet the needs not then being met by public sector welfare programs. Though their approaches were similar, George W. Bush's philosophy was framed as "compassionate conservatism," which played out tragically in the aftermath of Hurricane Katrina when needed goods and services were slow to arrive to the affected area (Bowles & Hopps, 2014). Compassionate conservatism is a political concept of government supporting social services but not being the primary provider of them, leaving that instead to privately funded entities. Through George W. Bush's two presidential terms, the privatization of social services steadily increased as government responsibility for funding social services steadily decreased. The 2005 Deficit Reduction Act, passed to offset the budget shortfalls that tax cuts, the Iraq War, and natural disasters like Hurricane Katrina had created, tightened funds for many social services (Hopps et al., 2008).

The economic crisis that began in 2008 made sweeping changes both challenging and necessary. Due to the burst of the escalating housing "bubble" in

2006, the value and pricing of real estate began a dramatic and rapid downturn which then forced the financial community into an economic crisis. Thought to be the worst economic depression since the Great Depression of the 1930s, the economic crisis saw unprecedented numbers of mortgage foreclosures and the highest rates of unemployment in decades.

With the election of Barack Obama, the first non-white president in U.S. history, the 2008 presidential elections marked a dramatic shift on several levels. Obama's candidacy focused on turning the country's economic, educational, and social tides. Within his first month in office, the new president's historic economic stimulus package endeavored to stabilize the economy by creating new jobs. Early in his administration, Obama also made a commitment to tackle other areas of crisis within our country, including housing, education, and social services. He fulfilled his promise through the introduction of the "Affordable Care Act (ACA)," the repeal of "Don't Ask, Don't Tell", increases in aid and employment opportunities for veterans and their families, extensions of unemployment benefits, and programs for persons in danger of losing their homes due to foreclosure. Another important gain made during Obama's first term was the latest update of the Individuals with Disabilities Education Act (IDEA). Originally established as the Education for All Handicapped Children Act of 1975, the Individuals with Disabilities Education Act (IDEA), was put in place in 2010 and provides services for children with disabilities who attend public schools.

In Obama's second term, his administration continued to focus primarily on domestic issues, including equality for LGBTQ citizens, gun control, income equality, and access to health care. The administration made strides in certain areas, but challenges persist in others. For the persons and groups social workers serve, some important developments include the following:

- Despite initial challenges with the ACA-initiated Health Exchange website, the number of previously uninsured Americans has decreased 22.3% (Long et al., 2015).
- Particularly during Obama's second term, the number of new jobs has increased, while unemployment continues to decline.
- Applications for food stamps continue to decrease.
- Troops are being withdrawn from Afghanistan.
- The Supreme Court ruled the Defense of Marriage Act (legislation enacted in 1996 that grants states the right to refuse recognition of same-sex marriages performed in other states) unconstitutional, thus paving the way for the Supreme Court ruling in June 2015 allowing same-sex marriage.
- The shootings of African Americans Trayvon Martin, Michael Brown, and other young African American men have stirred tremendous unrest and are indicators of ongoing discrimination, racial profiling, socioeconomic

diversity, gun control, community relations, and educational and economic inequities—all of which are issues relevant to social work.

While these events have served or may eventually serve to improve clients' and patients' lives, there are sadly a number of societal challenges that continue to loom on the horizon. Personal income is not keeping up with inflation. Individual and government debt continues to climb. Despite alarming statistics and a number of recent tragedies, gun control does not appear to be a priority for many Americans; gun production and sales are increasing, and pro-gun legislation has been introduced and/or passed in many states. Gun violence affects our entire society and social workers often work with the victims and their families. As the next presidential election approaches, what will the campaign issues be? Although historical trends can be a guide, we cannot know for certain what will happen in the coming years. We can predict, however, which issues among the current social, economic, and political challenges that confront our social service system will affect future social work practice. A sampling of the most pressing issues that will affect social workers and their clients includes: welfare reforms; changing population and family demographics; restricted access to benefits (e.g., persons living in poverty, older adults, and LGBTQ persons); an aging society; the need for greater understanding of global issues; improving services to active duty military and veterans and their families, including administrative changes and resignations among the leadership of the Veterans Administration Medical Centers, with the intended aim of making significant improvements in veterans' access to Veterans Administration health and mental health services; expanding college access; unemployment rates (particularly among young adults); immigration issues, particularly related to the 60,000 children who entered the U.S. without appropriate documentation in 2013–2014 (President Obama requested $4 billion in aid for this group) and the implications of the economic crisis and, as some believe, partial recovery on all citizens (minority groups, in particular). These challenges are all expected to test social workers' skills.

Ongoing Challenges Facing Government Leaders and Social Workers

Observations culled from current research indicate that today's social workers must be prepared to confront challenges related to the following:

■ Approximately two-thirds of our population will use public assistance benefits at some point in their adult lives (Rank & Hirschl, 2002). In fact, over any three-year period, approximately one-third of Americans spent at least two months living in poverty (DeNavas-Walt, Proctor, & Smith, 2013). More federal funding is needed to support welfare-to-work programs, particularly for single, female-headed households.

■ Both domestically and internationally, the population will continue to trend older, creating new challenges for older adults, their families, and their societies in such areas as access to health care, housing, transportation, and adequate financial stability.

■ Immigrants and refugees face multiple challenges. They are at higher risk than the general population of living in poverty, and this is particularly true for those who enter the United States as undocumented persons especially if they are unaccompanied children who are not identified as being eligible for the Special Immigrant Juvenile Visa or asylum. Continued anti-immigrant sentiment in some areas of the country sometimes leads to racial/ethnic profiling, arrests, discrimination in the legal system, and prosecutions.

PROFESSIONAL SOCIAL WORK EDUCATION AND PRACTICE: A HISTORICAL PERSPECTIVE

Though the social work profession has been evolving for centuries, it was only in the late 1800s and early 1900s that the term "social work" came into use and social work education became a formal discipline. In a sense, the first social work education occurred in the early settlement houses, which served as "social laboratories" for university students. A charity organization worker in England, Octavia Hill, is credited with introducing in the late 1800s, group discussions by caseworkers in which they could offer support and consultation to one another regarding their client situations. Thus some social work training originated "in the field" and not at university. To read more about Octavia Hill, visit: www.historyofsocialwork.org.

Despite not being based within a university setting, social work training was beginning to be formalized. It was only in the 1930s, with the introduction of an accreditation process for the MSW degree that required that social workers be trained in institutions of higher education, and with the establishment of a professional organization, the American Association of Social Workers, that social work earned full recognition as a profession (Sheafor, 2014). Educator Simon Patten first used the term social work in 1900 to refer to the work of both friendly visitors and settlement house workers. Patten and Mary Richmond could not agree on whether or not this new profession should be focused on advocacy or serving individuals. Jeffrey Brackett, Director of

Source: Getty Images.

Octavia Hill (1838–1912)

A little-known charity organization worker from an upper-middle-class English family, Octavia Hill entered the "charity" world by working with young girls in a toy-making project under the guidance of her mentor, social reformer John Ruskin. Hill soon became aware of the appalling conditions in which the girls lived.

By 1869, she had moved from the toy project into recruiting and training other volunteers to help improve housing for low-income persons. These female volunteers, known as housing estate managers, collected rents and engaged in individual work that would later be known as social casework.

Hill's contribution to the development of the social work profession around the world is that she trained the volunteers to work with tenants on an individual basis in a caring, respectful manner, affirming their dignity and autonomy—the cornerstone of what we now know as social work. In fact, Hill's group discussions about cases, facilitated by a mentor, were the origins of organized social work training. Hill is also credited with establishing an organization that became the model for the Charity Organization Society movement.

the Boston School of Social Work contributed to the clarification of the focus of social work by pointing out that social work had to be distinguished from sociology (Calhoun, 2007; Crocker, 2006).

This bit of social work trivia indicates that the emergence of the profession coincided with the growth of these two movements during the late 1800s. The volunteers prominent in these early movements were motivated to "address the 'social question,' the paradox of increasing poverty in an increasingly productive economy" and recognized the need to develop their voluntary efforts into an occupation and then into a profession, even if that profession was viewed by the public and the policy-makers as informal, fragmented, and destined to provide charity and improve the moral and physical lives of the recipients (Hopps et al., 2008, p. 1). As Porter R. Lee, President of the National Conference on Social Work said at a 1929 conference: "social work 'once a cause' had become a function of a well-ordered society" (Hopps et al., 2008, p. 159).

Educating Social Workers

As in England, U.S. social work training emerged from the COS and settlement house movements, taking the form of apprenticeships and in-house training. The leadership of the burgeoning profession quickly determined that more formal training was needed. By 1893, they had issued a call for "formal education in applied philanthropy" because the "on-the-job" training offered within the agency setting did not adequately instill important principles and theory (Leighninger, 2000, pp. 1–2). In 1894, the first social welfare textbook, *American Charities*, was published. Two decades later, in 1917, Mary Richmond developed the book *Social Diagnosis*, which became the primary textbook for the emerging profession. To learn more about Mary Richmond and to read *Social Diagnosis* and more of her work, visit: www.historyofsocialwork.org.

The idea of formalized social work training quickly gained appeal throughout the United States. These early educational ventures were agency-based, but with agency personnel's input they moved quickly and increasingly into university settings (Frumkin & Lloyd, 1995). Many Americans believed that the early British approach was more advanced than U.S. methods because British training was entirely university-based. Many English social workers, however, considered the slower-developing American system—with its independent schools of social work heavily influenced by community agencies—to be superior to their university-based system (Kendall, 2000).

A program founded in 1895 at the Chicago School of Social Economics is widely considered to be the first social work training program in the United States. By 1903, the program was known as the Chicago School of Civics and Philanthropy (which later became the University of Chicago School of Social Service Administration) and was offering a year-long training program. Mary Richmond and her COS colleagues were instrumental in founding the New York Summer School of Applied Philanthropy in 1898 where one of the graduates, George Haynes, later established the first social work program for Africans Americans at Fisk University in 1903 (Leighninger, 2008). By 1918, seventeen social work training programs had been established (Frumkin & Lloyd, 1995)—an average of one new program per year. Most programs emphasized a casework curriculum, thus carving out a niche for clinical social work. Despite the rapid growth of educational endeavors, however, the profession was still in its infancy, and it was generally unorganized and fragmented.

Abraham Flexner, an educator with the General Education Board of New York City, but not a social worker, made a major contribution to the growth of the social work profession. His 1915 critique resulted in some of the most important advancements in the profession's history. Flexner's report states that a profession must:

■ Involve intellectual operations with large responsibility (i.e., develop its own methodologies).

■ Derive raw material from science and learning and apply it to a practical and definite end.

■ Possess educationally communicable techniques.

■ Have self-organization.

■ Be altruistic in motivation.

Flexner recognized that social work at the time possessed character, practicality, a tendency toward self-organization, and altruism, but he stated that it was not yet a profession due to deficits in individual responsibility and educationally communicable techniques (Syers, 2008).

Social work professionals of the time rallied in an effort to strengthen the profession. Social work training programs became more formalized, and social workers began to conduct their own research and generate their own theories. Finally, the profession began to articulate its own methods of practice and focused on organizing social workers into a professional group. One response to Flexner's concerns, Mary Richmond's 1917 book, *Social Diagnosis*, outlined assessment techniques for use with clients (Exhibit 2.6). These early efforts to organize and deliver social work training emphasized educating students for types of practice (e.g., advocacy or casework) as opposed to practice in general (Watkins & Holmes, 2008).

By 1917, seventeen of the social work education programs that were in operation in the United States and Canada had come together to establish the Association of Training Schools for Professional Social Work. Reorganizing later, the group became known as the American Association of Schools of Social Work (AASSW). In 1952, the AASSW joined forces with the National Association of Schools of Social Administration to become the Council on Social Work Education (CSWE)—the organization that now accredits bachelor and master of social work programs. In 1955, seven previously separate professional social work organizations joined to form one national organization that could represent the interests of the profession, the National Association of Social Workers.

With the advent of the Great Society programs and the dramatic societal changes of the 1960s, the world of social work education experienced change as well. The infusion of federal funding enabled persons of color to earn social work degrees. Their increased numbers changed the demographics of social work programs and underscored the lack of relevant curriculum and diverse faculty in many schools (Bowles & Hopps, 2014). Schools of social work responded by hiring faculty who were persons of color and developing curricula that included content on non-White populations, poverty, and oppression.

EXHIBIT 2.6

Mary Richmond (1861–1928)

The "foremother" of American professional social work, Mary Richmond (1861–1928) was a social activist who wrote prolifically on social issues. Richmond started out as a treasurer for a Maryland Charity Organization Society and also served as a friendly visitor.

In 1897, Richmond, then secretary of the Charity Organization Society of Baltimore, delivered a speech at the National Conference of Charities and Corrections in which she said: "we owe it to those who shall come after us that they shall be spared the groping and blundering by which we have acquired our own stock of experience." Richmond argued that workers needed training as "relief and child-saving agents" with "shoulder-to-shoulder contact which makes cooperation natural and inevitable" (p. 181). She went on to state that theory and practice should be concurrent, with students beginning in a general area of study and moving into a specialization—the model still used as the basis of social work education today. Richmond's 1922 definition of social casework set the stage for the future of social work practice: "those processes which develop personality through adjustments consciously effected, individual by individual, between men and their social environment."

Richmond echoed Massachusetts community activist Anna Dawes' earlier call for the formalized training of "charity" workers, but that call was not heeded until 1898 when the New York School of Philanthropy (now the Columbia University School of Social Work) offered a 6-week summer school session that became a 2-year program in 1910. Richmond went on to become a faculty member in this program.

She is best known for her 1917 book, *Social Diagnosis*, in which she compiled her own lectures with interdisciplinary reading. This book became the primary text used by early social work educators. Interestingly, Richmond debated with Simon Patten (who coined the use of the title "social worker") on whether social workers should focus on working with individuals or serving as advocates.

Source: Barker, R.C. 2014.

EXPANDING PROFESSIONAL BOUNDARIES AND PRACTICE

As social work education was coming into its own as a formal discipline in the late 19th and early 20th centuries, social work practitioners and educators were also striving to "develop expertise in understanding the behavior of individuals in their social, political, and economic contexts" (Hopps et al., 2008; McNutt & Floersch 2008, p. 146). With this framework, professional social work was gaining recognition in three fields of practice: medical social work, psychiatric social work, and child welfare. In 1905, the first hospital social work department was organized at Massachusetts General Hospital, and just two years later, the same institution offered psychiatric social work services. The title "psychiatric social worker" came into use in 1914.

In the realm of child welfare services, a variety of practices were emerging. Social workers were being trained in mental health diagnosis at the same time that juvenile court systems were being established to address juvenile crime and delinquency (Brieland, 1995). Social workers were also making their presence felt in public school systems, where they worked with children whose home lives were dysfunctional. These areas remain a central part of social work today.

In the early years the profession focused on developing knowledge and skills for working with individuals and families. Since then, other concepts and areas of practice have emerged. By the 1930s, group work and community organizing were gaining recognition as areas of practice (Hopps et al., 2008). The years since the 1960s have seen an expansion of these areas as well as the introduction of generalist practice, ecological and systems theory, and, most recently, evidence-based practice (McNutt & Floersch, 2008). As you will learn throughout this book, each of these areas has found its place in contemporary social work practice.

In 1977, the journal *Social Work* devoted a special issue to defining, describing, and discussing conceptual frameworks pertinent to social work practice at that time. This effort to refine further the definition of the profession of social work addressed issues such as the mission, objectives, professional oversight, knowledge and skills, and educational implications associated with the profession (Minahan, 1981). This special issue generated such attention that a second special issue appeared in 1981. This second effort to frame social work as a strong profession included a working statement on the purpose of social work and a list of its objectives. The complete statement, reproduced in Quick Guide #2.1, is a point from which to build a collective understanding of the social work profession.

The period from the 1960s through the 1980s was one of expanded thinking and practice for the social work profession. Throughout the history of the profession, social workers have worked with persons and groups who are vulnerable and oppressed, but it was not until the 1960s that both society and the profession engaged in direct efforts to alleviate the suffering of specific groups that had longstanding experiences with social injustice, including persons of color, women, and the LGBTQ and disabled communities. One of the ways in which the social work profession has advocated is through the formal issuance every two years of policy statements in National Association of Social Work publications, *Social Work Speaks* (2012–2014) that serve as advocacy on behalf of vulnerable populations.

Social work activists were and continue to be on the forefront of movements

QUICK GUIDE #2.1 WORKING STATEMENT ON THE PURPOSE, PRINCIPLES, AND OBJECTIVES OF THE SOCIAL WORK PROFESSION

The purpose of social work is to promote or restore a mutually beneficial interaction between individuals and society in order to improve the quality of life for everyone. Social workers hold the following beliefs:

✓ The environment (social, physical, and organizational) should provide the opportunity and resources for the maximum realization of the potential and aspirations of all individuals, and should provide for their common human needs and for the alleviation of distress and suffering.
✓ Individuals should contribute as effectively as they can to their own well-being and to the social welfare of others in their immediate environment as well as to the collective society.
✓ Transactions between individuals and others in their environment should enhance the dignity, individuality, and self-determination of everyone. People should be treated humanely and with justice.
✓ Clients of social workers may be an individual, a family, a group, a community, or an organization.

Social workers focus on person-and-environment in interaction. To carry out their purpose, they work with people to achieve the following objectives:

✓ Help people enlarge their competence and increase their problem-solving and coping abilities.
✓ Help people obtain resources.
✓ Make organizations responsive to people.
✓ Facilitate interaction between individuals and others in their environment.
✓ Influence interactions between organizations and institutions.
✓ Influence social and environmental policy.

Source: Minahan, 1981, p. 6.

to advocate for vulnerable populations and championed a new understanding of these groups and their needs. For example, within the disability community, two NASW Pioneers, Ruby Morton Gourdine and John Pardeck, have helped to bring attention to the needs of persons with disabilities. Gourdine's long career has been dedicated to ensuring the rights and needs of children are being met. She has worked tirelessly for decades to help school social workers enhance their abilities to work with children with disabilities (www.naswfoundation.org/pioneers/RubyGourdine.htm). John T. Pardeck helped the profession and the public and private sectors understand the 1990 Americans with Disabilities Act (ADA) as well contributed to our knowledge base through his role as the founding editor of the *Journal of Social Work Education in Disability and Rehabilitation.*

There have been a number of social workers whose work in their communities, their research, and their teaching have brought attention to the needs of the LGBTQ community. NASW Social Work Pioneer William Meezan of Fordham University published the only research methodology book that focuses on the LGBTQ population. Michael LaSala, Rutgers University, has contributed to our understanding of LGBTQ issues in families, couples, youth, and intergenerational relationships, to highlight a sampling of his work. Arlene Lev, founder and director of the Sexual Orientation and Gender Identity Project, has written and lectured extensively on issues of gay parenting and transgender emergence.

Progress did not occur without its challenges. For example, critics viewed the second wave feminist movement of this period as a white-focused initiative that failed to recognize the experiences of women of color (Bowles & Hopps, 2014). During this time, the African American community called for social work education and services more responsive to the needs of African American individuals, families, and communities. The National Association of Black Social Workers was formed in 1968 and successfully advocated for increased numbers of persons of African ancestry within social work organizations. While some have criticized the social work profession for being slow to change, the profession did change, improving social work education and practice to keep up with the issues occurring within society (Bowles & Hopps, 2014).

The professionalization of social work continued during this era, with the creation of a number of professional associations. See Exhibit 2.7 for some of the highlights of the profession's organizational efforts.

The issue of the mission of the social work profession and whether or not contemporary practitioners continue to fulfill that original mission is one that has sparked controversy in recent decades. As this chapter has highlighted, the roots of the social work mission and profession lie in the social justice-focused settlement house model that aimed at working with vulnerable populations. Today, the majority of social work practice is not grounded in the settlement house or mission-based approach in which social workers live and work within the community they serve. Instead, much social work practice today is built on a model in which clients/patients come to the social worker, and the work is primarily focused on helping individuals and families rather than seeking community-level change. Challenges also continue regarding the meaning of "just." One school of thought suggests that justice is retributive (i.e., restitution for

EXHIBIT 2.7

The Professionalization of Social Work

- 1898—New York Charity Organization Society offers the first social work training course. This later becomes the Columbia University School of Social Work.
- 1905—Massachusetts General Hospital establishes a social services department.
- 1917—Social workers organize for the first time in the National Social Workers Exchange, which later becomes the American Association of Social Workers.
- 1924—The Atlanta School of Social Work establishes the first social work program for African Americans.
- 1934—Puerto Rico passes social work regulation for the first time.
- 1937—The American Association of Schools of Social Work (AASSW) determines that the 2-year Master of Social Work degree will be required to perform professional social services.
- 1952—The AASSW and the National Association of Schools of Social Administration merge to form the Council on Social Work Education (CSWE), which becomes the accrediting body for social work education.
- 1955—Seven social work organizations merge to establish the National Association of Social Workers (NASW).
- 1962—NASW creates the first social work credential, the Academy of Certified Social Workers (ACSW). Prior to the introduction of state licensure laws in most states, the ACSW was the primary credential for social workers, and it is still widely recognized today.
- 1962—NASW passes the first professional *Code of Ethics* (later revised in 1990, 1996, 1999, and 2008).
- 1969—NASW, which had previously welcomed only master-level social workers, invites baccalaureate social workers to join.
- 1979—The American Association of State Social Work Boards (AASSWB) is established to coordinate state licensure of social workers.
- 1983—CSWE officially recognizes the Bachelor of Social Work (BSW) degree as the first level of social work education.
- 1987—NASW publishes the first social work dictionary compiled by Barker.
- 1991—NASW establishes the Academy of Certified Baccalaureate Social Workers (ACBSW).
- 1998—The social work profession celebrates its first century.
- 2000—By this date, every U.S. state has social work licensure or certification.
- 2005—Comprised of 400+ social work leaders, the first Social Work Congress meets and develops 12 imperatives for the future of the social work profession.
- 2008—CSWE develops the Educational Policy and Accreditation Standards (EPAS) to emphasize a competency-based social work education in baccalaureate and master's programs.
- 2009—Volunteer programs (including Americorps) are expanded by the Edward M. Kennedy Serve America Act with new programs added, including Clean Energy Corps, Education Corps, Healthy Future Corps, and Veterans Service Corps.
- 2010—Patient Protection and Affordable Care Act (known as ACA) is signed into law by President Obama aimed at creating near universal access to health care for Americans.
- 2012—U.S. Supreme Court supports the Act with a 5–4 vote.

harm done), while others believe it to be distributive (i.e., access to resources) (Hugman, 2012). Both have merit in today's society.

Mission-based social work focuses on providing services in a specific geographic or symbolic community and those services have meaning for the community, and the practitioners possess a knowledge base for working with that particular community (Chatterjee & Fauble, 2008). The 1994 book by social work scholars Specht and Courtney, *Unfaithful Angels: How Social Work Has Abandoned its Mission,* charges the social work profession with forsaking the community-focused mission in favor of clinical social work with individuals, families, and groups, thus leaving behind the original foundation on which the social work profession was built (i.e., to help those persons who are vulnerable, oppressed or living in poverty).

Much like the critique of the social work profession that Abraham Flexner offered in 1915, Specht and Courtney's book has spurred social workers to look inwardly, to seek to re-connect with the profession's original mission, and to envision ways in which to stay true to that mission while expanding the original scope of social work practice. Though the profession has been criticized as too broad in scope and too narrow in depth of expertise, and though social workers still struggle to maintain a commitment to social justice, the drive to develop new knowledge and competencies in order to respond to constant social changes persists (Hopps et al., 2008; McNutt & Floersch, 2008). Chatterjee and Fauble (2008) suggest strategies for safeguarding against abandonment of the original social work mission, such as locating person-based interventions within the communities in which service recipients live, incorporating advocacy and policy work into direct services and engaging clients in addressing issues of social justice and oppression, ensuring an empowerment-focused approach to client interventions so that the client may engage in their own intervention (e.g., moving from a medical to a recovery model of treatment), and involving communities in the process of service delivery (e.g., engaging community members with new immigrants and refugees).

You have learned that some believe the social work profession may have abandoned its mission. How do you describe the current mission of the social work profession? Does it encompass working with individuals and families? If so, how? If you do not believe it does, how can change occur?

LEADERS IN THE DEVELOPMENT OF THE SOCIAL WORK PROFESSION

It would be impossible to highlight the accomplishments of all of the people who have contributed to the past, present, and future of the social work profession.

One effort, the NASW Foundation Social Work Pioneers program, honors the achievements of many of these role models, not all of whom are well known, but who have made significant contributions through service, teaching, writing, research, program development, administration, or legislation. The Social Work Pioneers publicly recognizes those social workers—past and present—who "have explored new territories and built outposts for human services on many frontiers" (NASW Foundation, n.d.). To learn more about these leaders and innovators, visit: www.naswfoundation.org/pioneers/default.asp.

Thousands of other social workers have helped to improve society. What can we learn from them? How can their work help to inform our understanding of social work and improve our practice? In Exhibit 2.8 one social worker relates how she turned to the profession's innovators to find her own niche in the profession. In her essay, Sonya Hunte (2014) turns to three of the exemplars of the social work profession: Jane Addams, Whitney M. Young, Jr., and Dorothy Height. You can read about all three at the NASW Social Work Pioneers website. To learn more about Young's life as a teacher, scholar, Director of the Urban League, and about her role in the War on Poverty, visit: www.socialworkers.org/whitneyyoung/. To read more about Dorothy Height, civil rights activist, leader, and memoirist, visit: www.ncnw.org/about/height.htm.

While not every social worker receives public accolades for his or her work, every social work practitioner does have a place in the profession's history. What events, persons, or trends in the history of social work resonate with you as you journey down the path to find your niche?

WHERE WE HAVE COME FROM AND WHERE WE ARE GOING

The history of social work and social welfare is thought to have begun more than 3,000 years ago with the concept that the profession has a moral obligation to help others. Throughout the centuries, those early hints of altruism have blossomed. However, the social work profession as we know it did not come into existence until the 19th century, out of a need to respond to the "social question" of the time, specifically, how could poverty and social need exist in a country of prosperity (Hopps et al., 2008)? In just over 100 years, the definition of a social worker has evolved from "anyone involved in activities with a social purpose" (Kendall, 2000, p. 93) to a professional who completes one or more degrees from an accredited social work program and who is engaged in a theory- and evidence-based practice of helping others to optimize their potential in life. As a profession, social work has moved from a belief system that blamed individuals for creating their own pauperism to an understanding that environmental conditions lead to poverty and other societal challenges, including access

EXHIBIT 2.8

Social Work Professional Discovery: Find Your Niche
Sonya Hunte

Social work is a life call to serve society's most marginalized people and communities. The profession varies as much as the needs of the people it serves. Like many social workers, I began with a burning desire to help people. The desire began at age 11, after seeing the devastation that crack cocaine caused in my childhood community. Over time, the desire to help others blossomed and became fine-tuned. Here are a few short tips for discovering your social work specialty.

- *What is my niche?* Helping those in a broken system of poverty and its implications can be tiring. Whenever you attempt to pull apart the causes of a client or community's crisis, other major issues emerge. For example, tackling affordable housing isn't just about housing itself, but about public education, livable wages, transportation access, healthcare, and overall economic development. Even social workers cannot be all things to all people. It is more effective to become an expert in one area. Over the past thirteen years in the profession, I learned to work hard at finding a niche within the field. Finding an area of specialty that connects your reason for joining the profession and strengthens your greatest talents is ideal.
- *How did social work icons do it?* I tapped into the work of social work icons for a clue on how to find my own life's work within a very broad profession. For some reason, I took a liking to figures like Jane Addams, Whitney M. Young, Jr., and Dorothy I. Height. These social workers were instrumental in creating social programs to lift people out of poverty, using the power of the pen to communicate the plight of the poor to elected officials, and developing social work leaders through national organizations with statewide chapter presence. Learning of their social program expansions, legislative impact, and leadership development efforts helped me to place myself within the larger context of the work and profession.
- *How long is this process?* Finding your specialty is not a one-year or five-year event. The process is continual. Your moment of clarity may come while working at an internship, with a particular family, on a unique program, or while watching a documentary about a specific issue. It is like trying out different fitness activities until you discover what produces the best results. My niche of administrating education programs for at-risk youth came after years of working in child welfare, juvenile justice, and now public education. I was working with the same population of at-risk youth but providing a different service. In the last few years, I developed a love for creating programs for, writing policies for, and applying funding to improve academic outcomes for at-risk/homeless youth populations.
- *Social workers are great but are not super heroes.* The desire to help others can be tiring when not properly channeled. There is no exact formula for finding your social work niche. The work toward finding a niche or becoming an expert in one area may prove effective for your target population and you. Find a way to connect your reason for joining the profession with your talents. Look to social work icons for perspective and direction. Be patient in this process for it will yield positive results for the profession and the people and communities you serve.

Source: Reprinted with permission from *The New Social Worker*. Sonya Hunte, 2014. Available at: www.socialworker.com/feature-articles/practice/social-work-professional-discovery-find-your-niche/.

to health and educational resources, safe living conditions, violence, mortality, and morbidity. In addition, both social action and individual casework are now recognized parts of the profession (Kendall, 2000). The profession faces two primary challenges moving forward. Many social workers entered the profession during the 1960s and 1970s, and large numbers of those Baby Boomers have retired and will continue to retire. In addition the age of social workers entering the profession is rising. In the face of these circumstances, can recruitment and retention of social work practitioners and educators keep up with the changing demographics of the coming decades (Hopps et al., 2008)?

Social work education has also evolved from informal apprenticeships to a three-level, accredited professional competency-based education built on a framework of knowledge, skills, and values aimed at preparing ethically-grounded social workers to be committed agents of change. While Flexner's 1915 report may have spurred the profession into a critical review of its educational and practice models, it is the work of many educators and practitioners that has kept the field of social work abreast of society's needs. Despite skepticism from within the profession itself and from the social service community, visionary social work educators and scholars in the 1970s moved forward with the creation of the baccalaureate social work degree to respond to societal needs for a generalist practitioner to work on the front lines of the War on Poverty program. Clearly, their efforts were a success, as there are now over 500 CSWE-accredited BSW programs in the U.S. (CSWE, 2015; Sheafor, 2014).

A 2008 overview of social work education noted that its focus is, and should be, strengthening accountability to clients, specifically by developing key competencies for students and practitioners (particularly in the area of multiculturalism—the ability to work with diverse populations), determining appropriate outcomes for education and interventions, and evaluating our practice (Hoffman et al., 2008; Hopps et al., 2008). To remain on the cutting edge of human service education and delivery, members of the social work profession continuously review educational programs and explore ways to make them more available and effective. Providing distance education programs in alternative formats and venues is just one example. Social work's long and rich history helps will to guide social workers as the profession continues to develop now and into the future.

Former NASW President, Elizabeth Clark, articulated well the possibilities for the future of social work when she made the following statement in *A Broader Vision for the Social Work Profession* (Clark, 2009, pp. 10–11):

> As a profession, we have the capacity to prevent hopelessness, to restore hope, and to change society for the better. We have the potential—the social work potential—to make a great difference. However, to do so, we must collectively craft a bolder and broader vision—a vision of social work for today that will

carry us into the future. We need to recognize how essential and important our profession is, and that there is a crucial need for social workers today. This is the time to redouble our efforts and expand our horizons. Instead of complaining about cuts in services, we need to formulate viable solutions. Instead of criticizing others, we need to assume leadership roles. Instead of worrying about encroachment, we need to foster collaboration. Instead of yearning for the past, we must craft the future.

CONCLUSION

This chapter has described the history of social welfare and the social work profession, and has highlighted the many innovative and courageous women and men who helped shape the profession that is so integral to our modern-day society. Their stories provide meaningful context for understanding the values and ethics of the profession, the fields of practice in which social workers engage, and some of the skills needed to be a competent professional social worker.

Developments in social work and social welfare are always linked to the events of the time. There are, however, four particular eras in American history that have had especially significant influence on the way in which the social work profession has evolved: (1) the post-Civil War era during which large numbers of widows, orphans, disabled veterans, and former slaves migrated to northern states; (2) the Great Depression of the 1930s during which millions lived in abject poverty and social service delivery shifted from the private to the public sector; (3) the 1960s, a time when our country experienced dramatic social and political changes and that shed significant light on social programs and groups that had been living with oppression; and (4) the "conservative revolt" of the 1980s Reagan and Bush administrations when funding for domestic programs was slashed (Hopps et al., 2008).

As social workers respond to the changing needs of the individuals, families, groups, communities, and organizations that they serve, they constantly develop new knowledge and skills. To be effective practitioners, social workers must be acutely aware of the constant changes that occur in economic, political, and social policies, both in the domestic and international sectors, while at the same time adhering to our professional values and ethics.

Social workers have long been committed to perceiving clients within the context of the environments in which they live and to interventions targeted at individuals, families, groups, communities, and societies. The social work profession was founded on the desire to address the needs of people who are impacted by a changing environment, a mission that continues to guide social workers today. While definitions of the social work profession have evolved over time, the commitment to social justice and social change has never wavered.

MAIN POINTS

■ Social welfare is the system of programs and services that respond to social and economic needs and injustices. The first organized attempt at mandating the provision of social services was the 1349 Statute of Labourers that designated categories of need in England.

■ The Elizabethan Poor Laws of 1601 established an approach to the delivery of financial and social aid that continues today. Intended to transfer the authority for charity from the church to the government, standardize aid programs, and decrease criminal activity, these laws dictated that public aid could be given to the unemployable, but that the employable must work and children who were orphaned or dependent would serve as apprentices.

■ The U.S. social service system has its roots in the British system of settlement houses and charity organizations. In the settlement house movement, young well-educated adults lived and worked in poor neighborhoods to help improve living conditions; in the charity organization movement, caseworkers focused on helping individuals overcome their problems.

■ The 20th century saw the formalization of the social work profession and growth in the social service delivery system. The Depression of the 1930s prompted a shift of services from the private to the public sector. The civil unrest of the 1960s and 1970s prompted new social initiatives to address issues of poverty and the needs of women, minority groups, children, and older adults.

■ Demographic changes in the 21st century are creating a society with widening economic gaps and an older, more diverse population with greater social, economic, and physical needs.

■ For over a century, social work education has continued to change in response to societal needs. Flexner's critical 1915 report helped solidify social work as a profession.

EXERCISES

1. Go to the Sanchez family interactive case (www.routledgesw.com/caseStudies). You will note from Celia Sanchez's history that Celia makes use of the food bank at her church to feed her family. Along with many groups in the faith community, the Catholic Church has a long and venerable history of caring for the poor in its communities. Identify a faith-based organization and a publicly funded agency in your community that both offer services to persons with limited incomes, and read their mission statements and lists of programs and services. Briefly describe each organization

in terms of mission, services provided, and service eligibility. Discuss the ways in which their mission and focus differ and how they are the same.

2. Select one of the concerns or needs identified in the Sanchez family case (www.routledgesw.com/caseStudies). Citing examples from this chapter, speculate on the ways that the concern or need would have been addressed in different eras.

3. Review the case file for Hector Sanchez (www.routledgesw.com/caseStudies). Note that Hector was given amnesty under a 1986 federal amnesty program. Conduct an online search to learn about the history and current policies associated with federal amnesty programs.

4. Familiarize yourself with the Carla Washburn interactive case at www.routledgesw.com/caseStudies. You will note that the social worker is employed by the Area Agency on Aging (AAA). The AAA was established through the Older Americans Act. Develop a brief report on the history and current focus of the Older Americans Act, specifically as it relates to the Area Agency on Aging. Identify those services the AAA provides that Mrs. Washburn could receive.

5. Go to the RAINN interactive case at www.routledgesw.com/caseStudies. After familiarizing yourself with the history of the development of RAINN, research the history of services to victims of sexual assault at the federal level or in your state or local community.

6. Go to the History of Social Work website, located at: www.historyofsocialwork.org/eng/index.php. Click on Overview. Select three individuals or items that helped to shape the social work profession. After reviewing the summaries of each of your three selections, provide a synopsis of the contributions of the individual or issue to the social work profession and identify the implications of the contributions for present-day social welfare and social work.

7. Go to the History of Social Work website, located at: www.historyofsocialwork.org/eng/index.php. Click on and complete the quiz. You will find the biographical summaries provided in the Overview section to be a helpful resource in responding to quiz items.

8. Go to the Brickville case at www.routledgesw.com/caseStudies. Review the history and background of the Brickville community, including the real estate development plan, social worker's role, and sources of conflict. In class discussion, small groups, or in a written assignment, reflect on the ways in which Brickville would be approached from a Settlement House versus Charity Organization Society framework.

9. To gain a more in-depth perspective on life in a poor house, read "The Flight of Betsey Lane" by Sarah Orne Jewett, found at: www.classicreader.com/book/3308/1/ and provide a written or in-class reflection on this short story.

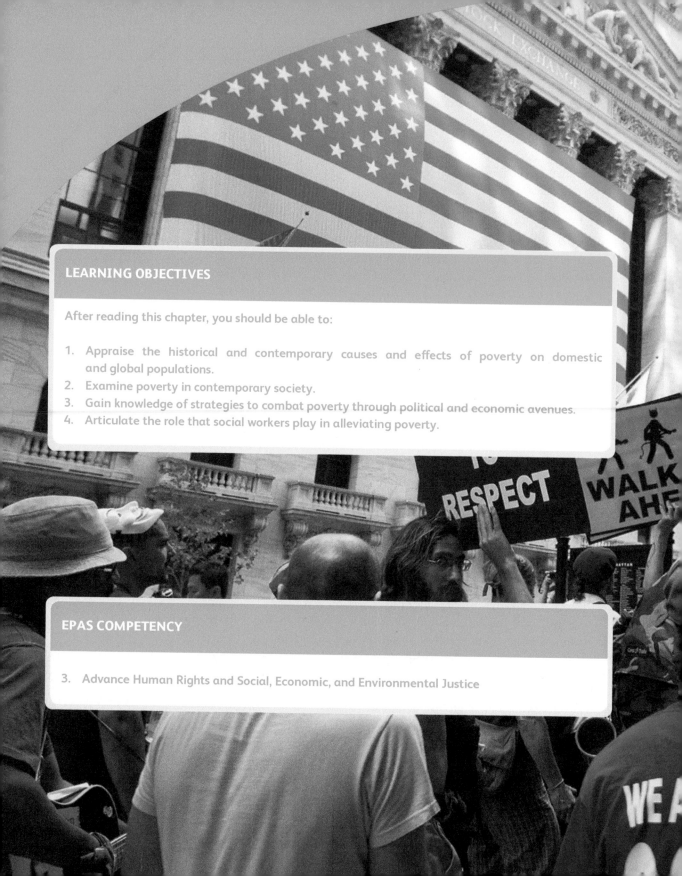

LEARNING OBJECTIVES

After reading this chapter, you should be able to:

1. Appraise the historical and contemporary causes and effects of poverty on domestic and global populations.
2. Examine poverty in contemporary society.
3. Gain knowledge of strategies to combat poverty through political and economic avenues.
4. Articulate the role that social workers play in alleviating poverty.

EPAS COMPETENCY

3. Advance Human Rights and Social, Economic, and Environmental Justice

U.S. POVERTY AND THE IMPLICATIONS FOR SOCIAL WORK

Source: Shutterstock/Glynnis Jones

How did I get to be eighty

> *And*
>> *Never*
>>> *Get over*
>>>> *Being*
>>>>> *Poor?*
> *When I was little*
> *I was poor.*
>> *But playing*
>> *And*
>>> *Dreaming*
>>> *Kept some of the pain*
>>> *Of*
>>>> *Being poor*
>>>>> *Away*
>> *And my folks*
>> *Kept*
>>>>> *Lots of the worries from me.*
> *When I was a teenager*
> *I just knew I'd marry a good man*
>> *With work*
>> *And*
>>> *Things would be all right.*
> *And I did.*
> *But he was poor, too.*

> *Work was steady for a while,*
>> *But so were the children.*

> *There were good days*
>> *And warm times*
> *But there were lots of times*
> *When his work died off*

> *And*
>> *His worrying*
>>> *Brought pain.*
> *He worked any kind of job*
>> *In*
>>> *Any kind of weather*
>>>> *Till*
>>> *The fever got him*

And
    The Lord took him
       And I had to go to welfare.
Then
      They cut that—some.

Reverend,
    Do people born poor?
      Have
    To stay that way—always?
Ain't there any other way—
        Even when we get to be eighty?
Does "poor" always have to be
    A
      Life sentence?

From *If . . . A Big Word With the Poor* by
Donald C. Bakely, Faith & Life Press,
Newton, Kansas. Used by permission.

This poem, composed by social activist Don Bakely, focuses on the plight of an impoverished 80-year-old woman. Nearly forty years after its publication, the issues it raises continue to plague our society. The woman who is the subject of this poem contacted Bakely for help one Thanksgiving Day because she was out of food and fuel. His powerful words move us because they address lifelong poverty, what it's like to be an older adult and poor, and the inadequacy of the public welfare system. His words also capture the hope and resilience this woman continued to have throughout her life—characteristics we do not usually associate with chronic poverty and advanced age.

The social issues the poem raises serve as a starting point for a discussion of the needs of many persons in our society and the approaches that have been devised by governmental and social service organizations to address those needs. It is critical that all social workers understand poverty, public assistance programs, and related social services. This chapter covers the origins of poverty, the ways in which the public and private sectors have attempted to minimize poverty and its effects, and the social worker's role in optimizing clients' capacities within a context of poverty.

DIMENSIONS OF POVERTY

Before she decided to become a social worker, Emily had little knowledge of and no personal experience with poverty. She knew there were people in the world and in her community who lived in poverty, but she did not think about their situations, so the situations were not real for her. She had no insight into the realities of living in poverty. She had heard people say that poor people could escape poverty simply by "pulling themselves up by their bootstraps." Not being sure about the truth of that adage, Emily found herself wondering why so many people become impoverished and whether it was a matter of their work ethic.

Emily first encountered persons living in poverty while doing community service for her introductory social work course. She believed that, as a social worker, she needed to learn about the lives of persons living in poverty. Therefore, she opted to complete her service learning experience at Oasis House, a shelter for families who are homeless. There, she began to gain insight into the sources of poverty and the ways in which living in poverty affects people. As she worked with children on their homework, they shared with her stories about having their utilities cut off, being hungry, getting evicted, and living in the car—all because a parent was laid off from her or his job. Emily learned that poverty is not simple or just, and that it is not caused by a lack of motivation or work ethic. Rather, poverty is a complicated phenomenon with many contributing factors and that it has many faces that range from young children to older adults.

Many people have opinions about what it means to be poor, who is poor and how they became poor, and what keeps people in poverty, but those opinions are often not fact-based. The definition of poverty, profiles of those who live in poverty, and the causes of poverty have been and continue to be emotional and value-laden issues with which our society struggles in the political, social, religious, and public and private social service arenas.

What Is Poverty?

In short, poverty exists when a person has inadequate financial resources or means of subsistence to meet basic needs (Barker, 2014). Stated more poignantly:

> Poverty is hunger. Poverty is lack of shelter. Poverty is being sick and not being able to see a doctor. Poverty is not being able to go to school and not knowing how to read. Poverty is not having a job, is fear for the future, living one day at a time. Poverty is losing a child to illness brought about by unclean water. Poverty is powerlessness, lack of representation and freedom.

(Worldbank Group, 2003)

The quantification of poverty was first documented in 1795 when the English government subsidized wages that fell below a designated level. In this program, known as the Speenhamland system, the amount of the subsidy was based on a predetermined amount (i.e., the current price of bread and the number of members in the family) (Barker, 2014).

It was not until 1964 that the U.S. federal government devised the poverty line as an official measure of poverty. The poverty line is the minimum income level, as defined by the federal government, at which a family or individual can meet their basic needs. The measure was originally based on research from 1955 that suggested that people spend one-third of their post-tax income on food (Sherraden, 1990). For what was known as the Thrifty Food Plan, the government calculated the poverty line by identifying the amount needed for the minimum subsistence diet and then multiplying that number by three. Based on this formula, in 2015, a family of four living in the contiguous United States with a total household income of $23,834/ year ($1,986/month) or less meets the poverty guidelines (U.S. Department of Commerce, Bureau of the Census, 2014). The economic recession (known as the "Great Recession") that began in 2008 resulted in the second highest number of persons living in poverty since the mid-1960s (Trisi, Sherman, & Broaddus, 2011). Moreover, the number of persons living in deep poverty (annual income less than $6,000) whose incomes were below the halfway mark of the poverty line (e.g., an annual income for a family of four of $11,917 or less) was the highest in recorded history (6.7% of the U.S. population) (Trisi et al., 2011). Those persons experiencing deep poverty have not been employed in the past twelve months and often face multiple, chronic challenges, including addiction, homelessness, disabilities, and chronic illness (Lei, 2013). In 2014, the number of children living in poverty who then became homeless was at a 15-year high, with 1 in 30 children experiencing homelessness (Bassuk, DeCandia, Beach, & Berman, 2014). Much like adult homelessness, child homelessness can be attributed to poverty, lack of affordable housing, racial disparities related to education, employment, and health care, lingering effects of the Great Recession, single parenting, and traumatic events (e.g., domestic violence) (Bassuke et al., 2014). While the economy appears to be recovering, not all sectors of society are experiencing rapid improvement. Recovery has been slow due to lack of job growth and policies that have not supported economic expansion (e.g., budget decreases, particularly in unemployment insurance benefits, and tax cuts for those at the highest income levels) (Sherman, Trisi, & Broaddus, 2014). In 2013, poverty rates fell significantly for the first time since pre-recession years, but as of 2014 estimates suggested that it would be 2017 before these rates would be at pre-recession levels (Sherman et al., 2014). Poverty rates decreased most for children, those in deep poverty, foreign-born persons, persons living outside metropolitan areas, Hispanics, and families, but not for other groups, including the working poor (DeNavas-Walt & Proctor, 2014; Sherman et al., 2014). In 2014, the poverty rate for those persons who were working but whose

Poverty line
The amount calculated at the federal government level that establishes the minimal income needed for a person or family or individual to maintain basic needs.

Deep poverty
A measure of level of poverty used in the U.S. indicating the state of people with an annual income of less than $6,000, whose incomes were below the halfway mark of the poverty line.

incomes remained below the poverty line was the highest (15.8%) since 1987. What are possible solutions? According to Sherman and colleagues (2014), increasing jobs, reinstating Recovery Act funding, and counting SNAP benefits as income are just three potential remedies that could have a significant impact.

Many consider the poverty line, as it is currently calculated, to be an inadequate measure of poverty. Current spending patterns differ dramatically from the spending patterns of 1964. Today's families spend a smaller percentage of their income on food and a much larger percentage on transportation, housing, and medical care. Moreover, poverty is measured on income before taxes are deducted, and some nonmonetary supports (such as food stamps, a government program to supplement income through food purchases) can be considered a part of income. Thus, welfare rights advocates consider strictly economic measures of poverty, which are still used, to be outdated. They lobby instead for the Supplemental Poverty Measure (SPM) to be the primary measure of poverty. The SPM includes noncash benefits, expenses such as taxes, health care costs, and work; shifting family configurations; and cost of living based on geographic location. Many social workers think that poverty can best be understood in social, political, economic, and emotional terms. Economically, "absolute" poverty occurs when an individual's income is less than the amount needed to obtain the minimal necessities for living. On an emotional level, "relative" poverty is the perception that the assets of an individual or family do not afford them the average standard of living of the community in which they reside, but that if compared to others in an area with greater levels of poverty, their assets might not be considered poverty-level (Barker, 2014). Both types of poverty are real, and both can be devastating for the individual and the family.

Who Are the Poor?

Many people believe in the stereotype that the poor are non-White, unemployed, single mothers with lots of children who subsist on welfare and who are homeless or live in dilapidated housing in "bad" (i.e., low socioeconomic, crime-ridden) areas. Most unfortunate is the widespread myth that people who live in poverty are lazy and unmotivated to change their situations. The reality is that many people living in poverty are employed, have two or fewer children, are exceptional money managers, and are very motivated to move out of poverty and do within a short period of time. In reality, four-fifths of Americans will receive public assistance or experience near-poverty or unemployment at some point in their lives (Rank, 2013).

The 21st century, particularly the years since the economic recession of 2008, saw the rise of the "new face of poverty." This new face of poverty

Food stamps
Administered by the Department of Agriculture, this social program (renamed Supplemental Nutrition Assistance Program in 2008) provides a means for eligible persons to supplement their income through the purchasing of food items.

Supplemental Poverty Measure (SPM)
A measure of poverty that includes noncash benefits, expenses (e.g., taxes and health care), family make-up, and geographically-related cost of living.

Absolute poverty
State when an individual's income is less than the amount needed to obtain the minimal necessities for living.

Relative poverty
The perception that the assets of an individual or family do not afford them the average standard of living of the community in which they reside, but that if compared to others in an area with greater levels of poverty, their assets might not be considered poverty-level.

includes women, children, persons of color, and older adults being represented at higher rates than in the past. As the U.S. population becomes more
diverse, so do the "faces" of those living in or near poverty. In 2013, 14.5% of
individual Americans, or 45.3 million people, were living in poverty. That is
about 1 in 7 Americans (DeNavas & Proctor, 2014).

As Exhibit 3.1 shows, the percentage and number of Americans living
in poverty fluctuates. Earlier in this century, the greatest increases in poverty
occurred in mid-western and southern states and among immigrants (Rank &
Hirschl, 2001a; Sherman, Greenstein, & Parrott, 2008), but in the most recent
Census analyses, the highest numbers of persons living in poverty were primarily in the southern United States (averages at or more than 16% in 22 states
and Puerto Rico (45.4%)) (DeNavas & Proctor, 2014).

At-Risk Groups While the numbers of those living in poverty have decreased
since the period immediately following the 2008 economic crisis, some groups
in the U.S. are still at-risk for experiencing poverty. Although many stereotypes
about poverty are unfounded, the reality is that certain groups are especially
vulnerable:

EXHIBIT 3.1

Incidence of Family Poverty in the United States Since the 1980s

Year	All Races	White	Black	Asian and Pacific Islanders	Hispanic
1980	13	10.2	32.5	N/A*	25.7
1985	14	11.4	31.3	N/A*	29.0
1990	13.5	10.7	31.9	12.2	28.1
1995	13.8	11.2	29.3	14.6	30.3
2000	11.3	9.5	22.5	9.9	21.5
2005	12.6	10.6	24.9	11.1	21.8
2010	11.7	11.7	20.8	18.1	30.7
2013	12.4	10.1	25.7	8.1	22.3

*Data not available.

Sources: DeNavas-Walt & Proctor, 2014; DeNavas-Walt et al., 2011; U.S. Census Bureau, 2012; Statistical Abstracts.

- *Women* are disproportionately represented among those living in poverty, particularly when they are the single heads of households. Overall, one in six adult females in the United States lives below the poverty line (DeNavas & Proctor, 2014). Among female-headed households, 30.6% lived in poverty in 2013 (down from 32.5% in 2009) (DeNavas & Proctor, 2014). For those female-headed households located in higher-income geographic areas, the poverty rate was 14%, while those in lower economic regions experienced poverty rates as high as 46% (Bishaw, 2011). Adult women of all ages are at risk for living in poverty, with 15.3% of women aged 18–64 (compared to 11.8% of males) and 11.6% of women aged 65 and over living in poverty (compared to 6.8% of males) (DeNavas & Proctor, 2014). Non-White women are at the greatest risk for poverty among all groups, with approximately 25% of Hispanic, African American, and Alaska Native/American Indian women living in poverty (U.S. Department of Health and Human Services Health Resources and Services Administration, 2013).

- *Racial and ethnic minorities.* Being African American and having limited education places one at higher risk for poverty (Rank, 2004, 2008). In 2013, 27.2% of African Americans and 23.5% of Hispanics/Latinos were reported to have incomes below the poverty line as compared to 9.6% of non-Hispanic whites (DeNavas & Proctor, 2014).

- *High school dropouts.* By age 75, 98% of African American women and 96% of African American men with less than a high school education will have spent at least 1 year of their lives living in poverty, compared to 65% of white women and 74% of white men lacking a high school diploma (Rank, 2004; Rank & Hirschl, 2001b).

- *Children.* Approximately 20% of all children in the United States live in poverty (DeNavas-Walt et al., 2014). Approximately 31% of children have a parent who lacks secure employment. The number of children whose parent lacks secure employment ranges from 22% (Asian American) to 49% (African American and American Indian) (Annie E. Casey Foundation, 2014). Children, who make up nearly one-quarter of the U.S. population, have the highest levels of poverty of any age group. Approximately one-third of U.S. children live in poverty (DeNavas-Walt et al., 2014). In fact, one-half of American children are in a family that receives food stamps (Rank, 2013). African American, American Indian/ Native Alaskan, and Hispanic children are more likely (39.6%, 36.8%, and 33.7%, respectively) to live in poverty than their white and Asian counterparts (Children's Defense Fund, 2014).

- *Lesbian, Gay, Bisexual, and Transgender Persons.* Due to discrimination, LGBT individuals, couples, and families are more likely to experience poverty than their heterosexual counterparts. Twenty percent of LGBT individuals earn under $12,000/year, compared with 17% of heterosexual persons (Lavers, 2014). State of residence can also impact LGBT poverty— those couples living in a state with legalized same-sex marriage are more likely to earn less or to live in poverty (Lavers, 2014).

■ *Older adults.* Approximately 9.5% of older adults have incomes below the poverty line (DeNavas-Walt et al., 2014). When measured using the SPM, the rate of older adult poverty rises to 14.8%, primarily because of high out-of-pocket healthcare expenditures (AoA, 2013). After age 65, 60% of Americans will have incomes below the poverty level for at least one year, two-thirds will require assistance from at least one form of a social welfare or "social safety net" program (publicly funded programs that prevent people from falling below the poverty line) such as Medicaid, food stamps, and cash assistance, and 40% will use one or more of these programs for a total of five years over their working years (Rank, 2004).

Social safety net
A publicly funded program that prevents people from falling below the poverty line, such as Medicaid, food stamps, and cash assistance.

■ *Individuals with physical or mental disabilities and those who live in economically disadvantaged areas* are also at increased risk of long-term poverty (Rank, 2008). These risks are magnified if an individual with a disability is a child. Poverty of this type may continue through multiple generations. Experiencing poverty as a child places an individual at greater risk for experiencing poverty in adulthood (Fass, Dinan, & Aratani, 2009). Clearly, age influences one's risk for experiencing poverty, with the risk being greatest during one's 20s, 60s, and 70s, and the risk being least during one's 40s and 50s as these are the prime earning years (Sandoval, Rank, & Hirschl, 2009).

Safety net programs like the ones listed below allow millions of children to leave poverty behind (Children's Defense Fund, 2014):

■ Tax credits prevent 9 million children from living in poverty.
■ Earned Income Tax Credit (EITC) and Child Tax Credit eliminates poverty for 5.3 million children.
■ SNAP keeps 2.2 million children from living in poverty.
■ Social Security enables 1.5 million children to live above the poverty line.
■ Housing subsidies help 1 million children out of poverty.

While there are some new faces among those living in poverty, families headed by single women, particularly in the non-Caucasian community, disproportionately continue to experience economic struggles, even when the mother is employed outside the home. The majority of single mothers *are* employed (67.8%), but their unemployment rates still surpass those of the general population (Albelda, 2012). Despite the fact that employment rates and wages for single mothers have both increased in recent years, today many of these families are living on resources that are comparable to what an average family lived on in the 1990s. Many women are employed, but frequently in low-paying jobs without consistent schedules and benefits (e.g., health insurance, vacation, and sick leave) that do not enable them to move out of poverty or near-poverty (Albelda, 2012).

Patient Protection Act
Health insurance coverage for Americans, including those with pre-existing conditions.

There has been some relief. In 2010, the Patient Protection **and Affordable Act** (known as the Affordable Care Act (ACA)) expanded health insurance coverage to a much greater number of Americans, including those with pre-existing conditions. This legislation is a beginning, but will not by itself eliminate poverty. The ACA is aimed at ensuring "quality, affordable health care for all Americans," which includes improving health care access, quality, and efficiency, and expanding illness prevention and workforce resources (Responsible Reform for the Middle Class, 2010, p. 1). The components of ACA are consistent with the social work values of benefits parity, education, outreach, prevention, screening and treatment, and cultural competency (Harriman & Blount, 2014). Specific areas of focus include coverage for persons not previously able to obtain access and services through: expansion of Medicaid eligibility to 138% of the poverty line, coverage for young adults, particularly those aging out of the foster care system, and Medicare recipients (Collins, 2014).

Affordable Care Act (ACA)
see Patient Protection Act.

By mid-2015, the ACA resulted in a 42.5% decrease in the number of uninsured persons in all age, sex, and race and ethnicity groups (Long et al., 2015). In particular, many more low-middle-income adults, those with historically low rates of insurance coverage (young adults, males, and minority adults), and residents of those states that also expanded Medicaid benefits, are now insured. In fact, in states that expanded Medicaid coverage, the number of uninsured persons has decreased 52.5% and 30.6% in states that have no expanded Medicaid (Long et al., 2015).

Living wage
Minimum amount needed to maintain a standard of living that exceeds the poverty line.

Providing full-time, living wage (an amount that enables the individual to maintain a standard of living consistent with the local economy) employment opportunities and ensuring that those positions include benefits (i.e., health care coverage) to support workers are two interventions that can make a difference. To achieve these necessary changes, social workers can advocate for policy and regulatory changes. To learn more about poverty-related legislation and to examine legislators' voting records, visit the Sargent Shriver National Poverty Law Center website at: www.povertylaw.org/.

Working poor
A person who is employed, but whose income from employment falls below the poverty line because the employment is part-time or low paying.

Working poor employment is no guarantee that a person will escape poverty. The working poor are defined as "persons who spent at least 27 weeks in the labor force (working or looking for work), but whose incomes still fell below the official poverty level" (U.S. Department of Labor, Bureau of Statistics (BLS), 2014c, p. 1). In 2012, 7.3% of employed persons in the U.S. experienced poverty, but that number increased to 16.6% if the person was employed only part-time (DeNavas-Walt et al., 2013). The percentage of the population considered to be working poor has climbed steadily in recent years, from 5.1% (2006) to 7.0% (2009) to 7.1% (2012) (BLS, 2014c). Persons more likely to be categorized as "working poor" are female, African and Hispanic Americans, those lacking a high school diploma, families with children under the age of 18, female-headed households, and those working in the service industry (BLS, 2014c). The total income for a family of four in which one member is earning minimum wage still falls nearly $9,000 under the poverty line. A wage earner would have to earn $11.64/hour ($4.39 above the current federal minimum wage) for 40 hours/week, 50 weeks/year to reach the federal poverty line (Annie E. Casey Foundation, 2014). Clearly, working full-time in a minimum-wage position does not raise a family above the poverty line.

Consider the situation for the family of four represented in Exhibit 3.2. The "breadwinner" is working full-time at a minimum wage job. If $23,834 is the federal poverty line for a family of four, this family would be considered to have an adequate total income, but would still probably struggle to make ends meet. However, that income includes earned income tax credit (EITC), child tax credits, and food stamps (now called the Supplemental Nutrition Assistance Program (SNAP)). Without those benefits, the family's

EXHIBIT 3.2

Profile of the "Working Poor"

Source of income	Amount ($)
Annual income from full-time employment at $7.25/hour	14,372.40
Plus tax credit	5,370.00
Food Stamps (SNAP)	10,740.00*
Total Annual Income	30,282.00

*SNAP benefits vary by state. The amount presented here is based on benefits in Missouri.

Sources: IRS Tax Credit Calculator:
http://apps.irs.gov/app/eitc2013/CalculateAgiExpense.do
Missouri SNAP Calculator: https://dssapp3.dss.mo.gov/fseligibilitytool/Results.aspx

QUICK GUIDE #3.1 CALCULATING A HOUSEHOLD'S MONTHLY SNAP BENEFITS

Consider a family of three with one full-time, minimum-wage worker, two children, dependent care costs of $81 a month, and shelter costs of $858 per month.

✓ Step 1—Gross Income: The federal minimum wage is currently $7.25 per hour. Full-time. Work at this level yields monthly earnings of $1,256.

✓ Step 2—Net Income for Shelter Deduction: From the gross monthly earnings of $1,256, subtract the standard deduction for a three-person household ($155), the earnings deduction (20% of $1,256, or $251), and the childcare deduction ($81). The result is $769 (Countable Income A).

✓ Step 3—Shelter Deduction: From the shelter costs of $858, subtract half of Countable Income A (half of $769 is $384) for a result of $474.

✓ Step 4—Net Income: Subtract the shelter deduction ($474) from Countable Income A ($769) for a result of $295.

✓ Step 5—Family's Expected Contribution Towards Food: 30 percent of the household's net income ($295) is $89.

✓ Step 6—SNAP Benefit: The maximum benefit in 2015 for a family of three is $511. The maximum benefit minus the household contribution ($511 minus $89) equals $422. The family's monthly SNAP benefit is $422.

Source: Center on Budget and Policy Priorities, 2014a, p. 5.

income would be approximately $1,000 above the poverty line (adapted from Furman & Parrott, 2007). See Quick Guide #3.1 to learn how to calculate SNAP benefits.

The wage earner in this example is making $7.25 per hour, the federal minimum wage as of July 2009. While the median hourly wage in the United States is $16.876, a minimum wage of approximately $11.00 per hour would enable this family to live above the poverty line. Although five states do not have any minimum wage, 23 states and the District of Columbia have enacted laws that require minimum wages above the federal standard, 18 states have minimum wage laws equal to the federal standard, three states are below the federal level, and one state repealed its minimum wage requirement. The highest minimum wage in the country is $9.50 per hour in Washington, D.C.

(National Conference of State Legislatures, 2014). The purchasing power of the federal minimum wage has decreased by nearly one-third in the last 40 years (National Law Project, 2012).

Lifetime Chances of Temporarily Living in Poverty People who do not consider themselves to be among the poor may nevertheless live in poverty at some point in their lives. Due to employment instability, lower wages, weakened safety net, lack of access to health insurance, and increasing personal debt, the risk of living in poverty has increased steadily since the late 1970s, despite the fact that the overall length of time spent living in poverty has decreased (Sandoval et al., 2009). Approximately 40% of all Americans will live in poverty for at least one year, and 54% will live in near poverty (i.e., 100–125% below the federal poverty line (Hokayem & Heggeness, 2014)) at some point between the ages of 25 and 60 (Rank, 2013). By the age of 70, over half of U.S. citizens will have lived in poverty at some point during their lives (Exhibit 3.3), and over half will have received food stamps (Rank, 2004). Prior to the most recent economic recession, many of these individuals and families were living in the middle-income category, but were forced to utilize food pantries in order to make mortgage payments to avoid losing their homes. Not only are African Americans more likely than U.S. Caucasians to live in poverty, but they are also less likely to own a home, accumulate assets, or reach a level of financial affluence (Rank, 2009). In fact, over 90% of African Americans will experience poverty at some point in their lives, while only 13% will reach financial affluence.

Near poverty
State of living 100–125% below the federal poverty line.

Individuals and families can transition in and out of poverty. Poverty is typically short-term (fewer than three years and often one to two years), as is the time it takes for applicants to receive public assistance benefits (Rank, 2013; U.S. Department of Health and Human Services, 2012), but can be chronic, lasting for years or across generations. Those living in poverty for briefer periods of time can also move in and out of poverty depending on their life circumstance. For example, a person may be laid off from her or his job or have a short-term disability. Recent immigrants may also fall into this category. Individuals in these situations may receive public assistance until they are able to rejoin the labor force.

Income Inequality

Defined as the gap between incomes of those persons at the top of the economic range and those in the lower and middle income brackets, **income inequality** is a primary threat to economic stabilization in the U.S. Coinciding with the end of the era of shared prosperity which existed in the mid-20th century, the

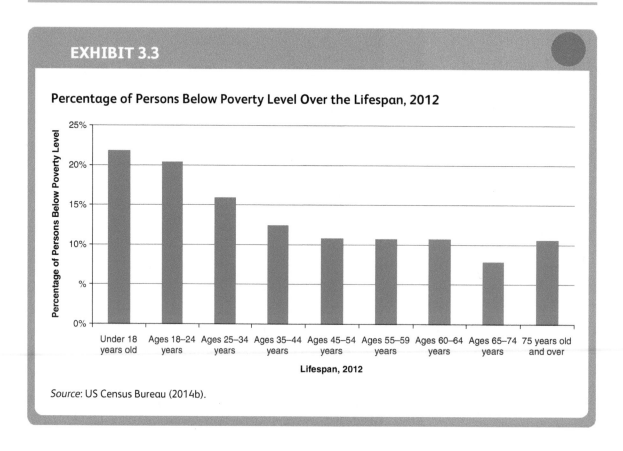

EXHIBIT 3.3

Percentage of Persons Below Poverty Level Over the Lifespan, 2012

Source: US Census Bureau (2014b).

Gini Index
A measure of income distribution and inequality at the national level.

income gap began to widen during the 1970s and continues to grow (Stone et al., 2014). The Gini Index measures income distribution and inequality at the national level. On a 0 (perfect equality) to 1 (perfect inequality) scale, a country's score is based on the net income of its residents (Investopedia, n.d.). The U.S. Gini Index in 2013 was 0.476, signifying a moderate but worrisome level of income inequality (DeNavas-Walt et al., 2013). Exhibit 3.4 provides a visual depiction of income inequality in the U.S.

The following statistics are but a sampling of the abundant evidence of widespread income disparity (Mishel, Bivens, Gould, & Shierholz, 2012):

- 1% of the U.S. population receives 17.2% of all income.
- 1% of the U.S. population holds 35.4% of all wealth.
- The top 10% of the population holds 77% of all wealth.
- From the late 1970s through the first decade of the 21st century, the earnings of the top 1% increased 156%, while the bottom 90% experienced only a 17% increase.

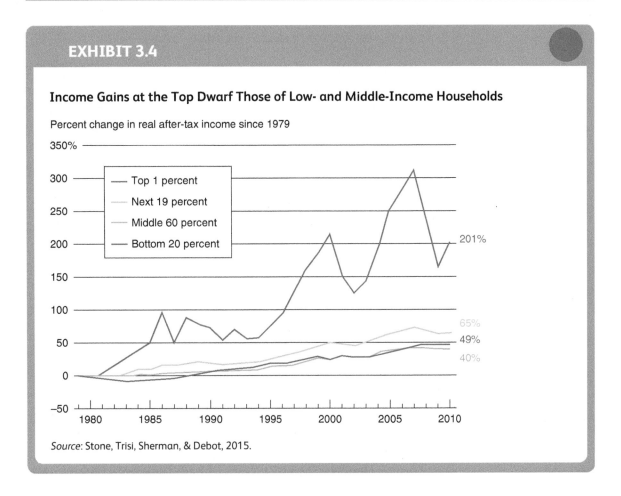

EXHIBIT 3.4

Income Gains at the Top Dwarf Those of Low- and Middle-Income Households

Percent change in real after-tax income since 1979

Source: Stone, Trisi, Sherman, & Debot, 2015.

When the average salary of top chief executive officers (CEOs) is 400 times greater than the average American worker's salary, it's not hard to argue that we have a misguided set of priorities, which have led to significant income inequality (Rank, 2014). When a country's economy is strong (i.e., when unemployment, poverty rates, and welfare program usage decreases), income inequality is greater, but lessens (along with economic insecurity and poverty) when the tax-supported safety net and social welfare programs are in place (Lens & Garfinkel, 2012).

Examples from other countries illustrate ways in which policies have lessened income inequalities. For example, Sweden, Finland, and Norway have implemented economic policies that provide greater support for education and health care. As a result, the quality of these services surpasses that found in the U.S., where recent economic policy decisions appear to favor those who have the greatest wealth (Stiglitz, 2014). Stiglitz attributes the lack of U.S. success in addressing income inequity to an ideology that manifests in revolving door or economic and political inequalities. Specifically, the post-World War II ideological premise in which the government requires less regulation depletes the funding for safety net programs, thus providing decreased funding for persons in need. Income inequalities in the 21st century are a reality that impacts a significant segment of our global society. Current U.S. inequalities and economic policies deny benefits to those with lower incomes, persons of color, women, and children, in particular (Parrott, 2014). What are the solutions? Lens & Garfinkel (2012) suggest the following policy-related remedies for reducing income inequality:

- Employment at a living wage.
- Secure and stable housing.
- Access to health care.
- Parental support (e.g., child care assistance).
- Effective and efficient social welfare system.

What Causes Poverty?

The causes of poverty are among the most controversial issues in U.S. society today. Most Americans hold one of two beliefs about the causes of poverty: (1) the individual is responsible; or (2) societal structure is responsible. The discussion that follows examines both arguments.

Individual Differences Even before the Charity Organization Society movement, some people believed that individuals are solely responsible for their own inability to earn an adequate income to meet their basic needs. This philosophy, which is referred by some as "blaming the victim," is rooted in the belief that all individuals can and should be self-sufficient and should not require any outside assistance for themselves or their families. This belief is consistent with the popular national narrative that contends that anyone can be rich if they work hard enough. A related belief is that persons living in poverty differ from mainstream Americans in their behaviors and attitudes regarding work and in their motivation, that they engage in poor decision-making, and that these differences explain their poverty when, in fact, persons living in poverty are essentially the same as those in the mainstream in all of these areas (Rank, 2013). This belief system presents an ongoing challenge for those who advocate for the poor, particularly when funding decisions are at stake. Voters and policy-makers who adhere to the "pull yourself up by your bootstraps" philosophy are typically less supportive of spending tax dollars on programs to combat poverty. These views often fall neatly along political lines and can become a debate between the philosophy of "pulling yourself up by your bootstraps" and one in which society is obligated to help and support its members. What does seem to play a significant role in determining one's earning potential? Research findings consistently confirm that "human capital," such as parental income or one's education, health, and accumulated wealth, have a clear impact (Rank, 2008).

Social Structure The predominant alternate view places the responsibility for poverty on societal structures. Much like the founders of the settlement house movement, people who hold this view believe that external factors outside an individual's control may make that individual vulnerable to a life of poverty. In the United States, being female, non-White, disabled, elderly or very young, or being born into poverty—all characteristics over which a person has no control—may reduce opportunities in life, including career. Other factors over which a person has little control that may affect his or her socioeconomic status include domestic violence; institutional oppression; discrimination based on disability or social class; or growing up in an economically disadvantaged neighborhood with poor-quality schools, few mentors/role models, or little opportunity for higher education.

That is not to say that our social system prevents disadvantaged individuals from finding any work. Rather, structural vulnerability occurs when the safety net, already weak in the U.S. when compared to other developed countries, does not fill the gap between earnings and need (e.g., opportunities for employment that provides a living wage, health and child care, and housing) (Rank, 2013). Many individuals who live in poverty do work, but their earnings—even coupled with social and financial support—are not sufficient to maintain an adequate standard of living. In fact, persons living in or near poverty in the U.S. consistently experience greater difficulty moving out of poverty than persons living in or near poverty in other developed countries (Rank, 2014). Persons experiencing poverty or near-poverty in the U.S. cannot achieve financial stability when the only jobs available to them pay poverty-level wages and do not offer adequate benefits or the possibility for advancement. Even in economic boom times, there is no guarantee that individuals who lack a high school diploma and/or higher education, or specialized training, will be able to access good jobs.

Rank (2006; 2013) offers an alternative paradigm for understanding poverty from a structural perspective:

> **Structural vulnerability**
> The state when the safety net does not fill the gap between earnings and need, e.g., opportunities for employment that provides a living wage, health and child care, and housing.

■ Poverty occurs when economic and political structures, not the individual, fail.

■ Over a lifetime, many people move in and out of poverty, often following the loss or reduction of employment, health problems, or a change in family status.

- Poverty creates deprivation that goes beyond income to include quality of life, health, and opportunities.
- Poverty is an injustice because it can be prevented.
- Poverty affects everyone through creating problems in the areas of health, education, and crime.

As one of the countries with the highest rates of poverty in the western industrialized sector, the U.S. needs a new vision, specifically one that does not focus on the way in which the wealthy are treated, but one that invests in all persons (Rank, 2014). Viewing poverty as a societal issue moves the discussion away from holding the individual responsible for both the cause and the solution and makes all citizens responsible.

A recent 14-year study found that social work students believe the causes of poverty are structural and that poverty can only be eliminated through societal change. Further, a majority of social work students believe that those living in poverty are the best determiners of their own lives (Clark, 2007). While these findings are largely attitudinal, they highlight the possibility that a focus of an intervention could be targeted at the intersection of both ability and opportunity.

CHALLENGES AND BARRIERS TO MOVING OUT OF POVERTY

Living in poverty can become chronic and cyclical for those individuals who begin their lives in poverty. Throughout their lives they may move in and out of poverty, particularly with changes in employment or partner status, health, and child care status. Consider the following:

- Recall the older woman in the poem at the beginning of the chapter. She was born into poverty, without adequate opportunities for health care, education, or career choices. She may not have completed high school. She and her husband worked in a series of low-paying jobs that did not offer opportunities for upward mobility or even stability and certainly not for saving for their old age or their children's education. Her children grew up in this environment of deprivation and limited choices, and became another generation who will rear their children in poverty. Thus, the cycle continues.
- Consider the lifelong struggles of a teenage girl who experiences an unplanned pregnancy and applies for public assistance as a single parent. Because of her pregnancy, she may not be able to complete high school or pursue higher education. If she obtains full-time employment, she will

lose the financial assistance she receives from the government or other agencies for child care. Even with her salary, she may be unable to pay for child care and other basic needs. If her car breaks down, she may not be able to afford the repairs. Without a car, she could lose her job due to absenteeism and may be forced to reapply for public assistance. Thus, the cycle continues.

▪ Consider a woman who married at a young age and had several children. Her husband insisted that her job was to take care of the children, so she did not work outside the home. His occasional violent outbursts devolved into physical abuse, and the woman decided she and the children had to leave. She sought safety for herself and the children in a shelter for survivors of intimate partner violence, applied for public assistance, and filed for divorce. The court ordered her husband to pay child support, but his payments were erratic at best. Because the woman had never held a full-time job, she had no work history or discernible skills to market to potential employers. She found a few minimum-wage jobs, but she was always the first worker to be laid off. Even when she was able to survive without public assistance, she could never move herself out of poverty. Thus, the cycle continues.

▪ Imagine the man who dropped out of high school and has struggled throughout life to "make ends meet." In an ill-advised effort to gain economic stability, he becomes involved in drug trafficking, which lands him in prison. While in prison, his wife divorces him and is awarded child support for their two children, which, of course, he is unable to pay. As a paroled felon, he finds it difficult to secure employment, cannot obtain credit, and must return to prison for not paying child support. Thus, the cycle continues.

These are just four examples of the challenges that perpetuate the cycle of poverty. These are the types of people who benefit most from an expanded safety net and social work services. Social workers can help people living in poverty to receive services to help meet their basic needs and can work toward changing society to alleviate poverty. The section that follows will review different approaches to addressing poverty in the United States.

APPROACHES TO POVERTY REDUCTION: SOCIAL WELFARE

The best strategy for addressing poverty has long been the subject of heated debate in the United States. Strategies for raising individual and family incomes above the poverty line stir controversy because tax dollars are the primary funding source for public assistance programs. On one side of the public debate, there are those who contend that providing a safety net for those living in poverty discourages work and rewards laziness. Whether and how to help persons living in poverty are value-laden and emotional decisions, and all U.S. taxpayers have a vested interest in how their money is spent.

The group with the greatest interest in the ways in which public funds are spent is the persons who are themselves living in poverty. Unfortunately, this group often has the least influence over decisions affecting their well-being. Very few lobbyists speak for those living in poverty, and their resources are limited compared to those of many other advocacy groups. For these reasons, their views are underrepresented in the decision-making process. Social workers as a group also share a keen interest in social welfare programs. It is much easier for social workers to fulfill their mission to empower if they have adequate funding and the support to do so.

Before reviewing the poverty reduction strategies that have been employed in the United States and around the globe, it is important to understand the philosophies that underpin those strategies. As Rank noted (2006): "How we view poverty is critical to guiding how we will address it. Part of America's ineffectiveness in reducing poverty during the past three decades stems from a skewed and incorrect perception of impoverishment" (p. 19).

Definitions and Connotations of "Social Welfare"

In its literal interpretation, the word *welfare* means "physical health, emotional comfort, and economic security" (Barker, 2014). However, in the context of our discussion, **welfare** is a societal effort to help people achieve and maintain physical, emotional, and financial well-being.

Since the early 1900s, when social services were being formalized in the United States, the term welfare has come to have a negative connotation for some and has become synonymous with poverty and the public assistance programs that provide cash assistance to single mothers and their children. However, the term welfare, if taken in its literal sense, is a public program designed to promote the physical, emotional, and financial well-being of recipients. For example, welfare also comes in the form of corporate and realty investor tax benefits, corporate bailouts, home mortgage deductions, tax abatements for home ownership in economically depressed areas, and farm and low-income housing development subsidies. These benefits and subsidies are dollars that otherwise would be paid in taxes, and contribute to the amount of public funds available to meet public needs in our communities and at the federal level.

The term social welfare has also taken on a dual meaning. Social welfare describes a group's level of emotional, physical, and economic stability.

However, social welfare also refers to our country's system of programs, benefits, and services that supports those in need of financial, social, and health care support. The term public welfare, often used synonymously with public assistance, also refers to the policies that a country develops to provide for the well-being of its citizens.

Public welfare
A system of programs, benefits, and services that support those in need of financial, social, and health care support. Also referred to as social welfare or public assistance. *see* social welfare.

Social welfare programs are guided by **social policy**, the government rules and regulations used to develop and guide practices and procedures related to social issues. These policies guide social workers' practice. Social policies address programs in education, health, criminal justice, and social welfare, but are aimed at creating resources to meet the basic needs of society. Social work is inextricably linked to the social policies (perhaps even dependent on the policies) that underlie the funding, insurance reimbursements, and authority to enact, implement, and oversee the programs.

Social policies can be of two types: residual and institutional. Residual social policies address a social need that is specific to a population and that persists regardless of the policies' effectiveness or ineffectiveness. Services for women who are pregnant and persons with disabilities are examples of programs that result from residual social policies. In contrast, institutional social policies address universal social needs. Social Security, which provides retirement insurance for all older adults who have invested at the required level in that system, is an example of an institutional social policy.

Residual social policy
Policy that addresses a population-specific social need.

Institutional social policy
Policy that addresses a social need that is universal to a population.

A subset of social policies, social welfare policies, allocate financial, social, and health resources to health and social service organizations. Social workers' activities are impacted by social policies, in general, and social welfare policies, in particular.

Social welfare policy
A type of social policy that addresses the allocation of governmental resources designated for the provision of health and social services.

The social welfare system in the United States is adapted from the English model. For a country founded on the principles of independence and autonomy, it is not surprising that the basis of the welfare system is "competitive individualism and the validity of market-based economics" (Hopps & Collins, 1995, p. 2268). The historical review that follows targets the important events that led to the creation of our contemporary programmatic approaches to social needs.

Social Welfare in the 17th–19th Centuries

Social service-related areas in the United States made considerable progress in first two centuries of the country's history, though much of that progress occurred strictly in the private sector. Before 1862, all government-provided welfare benefits were administered at the local, rather than the federal, level, but a comprehensive national response was needed to address the widespread disability and death suffered due to the Civil War. In 1862, the federal government enacted legislation to provide pensions for Union soldiers and their dependents or survivors in the event of a soldier's death (Albelda, Folbre, & the Center for Popular Economics, 1996). The Civil War triggered other public assistance programs, including the Freedmen's Bureau, which provided help for freed slaves from 1865 to 1872, and the 1890 Dependent and Disability Act that awarded pensions to all veterans who served in the Union army.

SLEEPING ARRANGEMENTS IN SHILOH SHELTER, NEW YORK.
Source: iStock/duncan 1890

Social Welfare in the 20th Century

During the late 19th and early 20th centuries, alongside the settlement house and Charity Organization Society movements, public programs emerged to combat the effects of the economic depression that had beset the country in the 1890s. Many of these programs were initiated at the state level and spread from state to state. The lack of a comprehensive approach marginalized groups such as orphaned or fatherless children and older adults.

In 1909, a White House Conference on Children recommended that children should remain with their parents whenever possible (Albelda et al., 1996). As a result, public funds were shifted toward providing services in homes rather than in institutions. One law that reflected this new approach was the 1921 Sheppard-Towner Act, the first federal program to fund maternal and child health care for low-income women and children, thought by many to be the forerunner to modern-day public assistance Temporary Assistance to Needy Families (TANF) program for single women and their children.

New Deal Welfare Reforms The extreme deprivation of the Great Depression of the 1930s—nearly one-third of the workforce was unemployed at its height—called for a strong, comprehensive federal response. To alleviate the suffering of millions of Americans, the administration of Franklin Roosevelt created a number of public welfare programs. Under the umbrella of Roosevelt's New Deal, a number of welfare programs were established, including the Social Security Act of 1935 (see Exhibit 3.5). Social Security was particularly important as it was an innovative strategy for creating retirement income that was based on contributions made by the individual worker during her or his years of employment.

Most New Deal interventions were repealed or discontinued following the Depression. Programs developed to address crisis situations are typically intended to last only until the crisis is alleviated. Of the New Deal programs, Social Security is the exception. It created a comprehensive system for providing an income for older adults and later for the children of deceased workers and workers who suffered disabilities. The program has continued to have appeal as many view it as participatory (based on their individual contributions) and not a government "welfare" program.

Social Welfare from World War II Through the 1970s Social welfare programs established during the economically prosperous late 1940s were primarily aimed at war veterans and their dependents and survivors (although it is doubtful whether many people considered these programs to be welfare).

EXHIBIT 3.5

A Sampling of New Deal Programs

- *Federal Emergency Relief Act (FERA) 1933* provided temporary financial support to unemployed persons.
- *Civilian Conservation Corps (CCC) 1933* was an early federally funded employment program that became the forerunner to the Job Corps program of the 1960s.
- *Social Security Act 1935* provided assistance to fatherless families through the Aid to Families with Dependent Children (AFDC) program. AFDC became the cornerstone of the public response to poor families and remained essentially unchanged until the 1990s.
- *Works Progress Administration (WPA) 1935* was aimed at creating employment opportunities and employed 8 million workers in the building of parks, bridges, and roads.

Civilian Conservation Corps

Tree-planting crews within the
Civilian Conservation Corps
(CCC), one of the New Deal social
welfare programs, are believed to
have planted some 3 billion trees
between 1933 and 1942. The CCC
not only put unemployed young
men to work but also helped to
mitigate forest degradation and
soil erosion, as in the Dust Bowl
states; preserve and improve
watersheds; and build recreational
facilities such as well-appointed
campgrounds.

Source: Getty Images.

Economic prosperity in the U.S. continued into the 1950s, with moderate growth in the development of social welfare programs. The Social Security
Act was expanded in 1950 to include benefits for low-income children and
the disabled. The U.S. Housing Act of 1954 prompted urban renewal projects
across the country. In 1953, President Dwight D. Eisenhower established the
Department of Health, Education, and Welfare, a cabinet-level department to
oversee funding and programs in these three areas.

From a public welfare standpoint, the 1960s were a boom time. The
Economic Opportunity Act of 1964, a part of Lyndon Johnson's War on
Poverty, established many new programs. The Act funded training and community action programs such as the Job Corps, which provided employment
training for youth; Volunteers in Service to America (VISTA), which sent volunteers into poor neighborhoods; community action programs, community-
based antipoverty programs; and Head Start, the program still in place today
that provides early childhood development services to low-income families.
The Older Americans Act of 1965, which dispersed funds to communities to
develop programs for older adults, and the food stamps program both grew
out of the War on Poverty. While some have questioned the impact of many
of these programs, decades of data show that the benefits of one program,
Head Start, clearly outweigh the cost of delivering the program in the areas of
educational attainment, earnings, and decreased arrests (Society for Research
in Child Development (SRCD), 2013).

Despite the new programs being created to decrease the numbers of
persons receiving public assistance in the 1960s, the welfare rolls increased

in both size and composition. Increasingly, Aid to Families with Dependent Children (AFDC) recipient families were headed by single mothers and families of color. Opponents of welfare programs called for making benefits more restrictive and requiring welfare recipients to work based on the assumption that these rules would motivate recipients to propel themselves out of poverty by gaining employment.

Aid to Families with Dependent Children (AFDC) Former government cash assistance program for women with minor children

In an effort to respond to the criticisms of public assistance programs, Congress established the Work Incentive Program to provide training, job placement, child care, and transportation. However, the program failed due to lack of adequate funding.

After the string of new programs in the 1960s, few new programs appeared in the 1970s. Rather, adjustments were made to existing programs. For example, the 1975 Title XX amendment to the Social Security Act provided additional funding for personal social services for low-income persons, including services to promote economic independence (for example, employment training and placement), child and elder abuse and neglect prevention, and community-based services to prevent institutionalization of older adults and persons with disabilities.

One notable exception is the Supplemental Security Income (SSI) program, established in 1972. This publicly funded program provides financial assistance for persons who are older, visually impaired, or have disabilities and live on limited incomes. Unlike Social Security, SSI assistance is based not on previous employment, but on current income.

Following the demise of the Nixon administration, Presidents Ford and Carter endeavored to continue the "welfare revolution" begun in the 1960s but had only moderate success. Social welfare program funding increased, and the number of individuals receiving welfare benefits decreased. Proponents of the work-ethic school of thought believed that these programs were making the poor more dependent on public assistance rather than lifting them out of poverty (Reid, 1995). The "revolution" as such ended with the election of Ronald Reagan in 1980.

Social Welfare in the 1980s and 1990s Much like the Nixon administration, the Reagan and George H.W. Bush administrations of the 1980s and early 1990s focused on a supply-side economics approach known as "Reaganomics." They designed tax policies to benefit corporations and citizens at the highest socioeconomic levels, and the prosperity those groups enjoyed was supposed to "trickle down" to the middle and lower socioeconomic levels. Both administrations subscribed to the philosophy that welfare should be a private business handled by nonprofit organizations, not a public responsibility. To implement this philosophy, Reagan proposed, and Congress passed, the 1981 Omnibus Budget Reconciliation Act (OBRA), which eliminated public-service jobs, decreased benefits for low-income workers and AFDC recipients, and granted states the authority to distribute resources (Albelda et al., 1996). The Family Support Act of 1988 required recipients to seek employment to move themselves to self-sufficiency and made access to the welfare system more punitive and restrictive by limiting eligibility to a five-year lifetime cap. Issues such as children living in poverty, homelessness, and AIDS took a backseat to support for corporate America and military spending (Segal, 2007). Many critics contend that the policies adopted by the Reagan and Bush administrations constituted a significant setback and that these policies encouraged anti-welfare sentiments and increased tensions between the social service and political communities (Hopps et al., 2008).

The 1990s brought a renewed focus on public responsibility for social needs. Clinton's election strategies focused on returning the nation's attention to domestic issues, specifically, health and education. Congress passed several laws that had economic implications for impoverished families, people with disabilities, and minority populations. For example, the Americans with Disabilities Act (1990), the Family and Medical Leave Act (1993), the Brady Handgun Violence Prevention Act (1993), and the Violent Crime Control and Law Enforcement Act (1994) were all aimed at enhancing the quality of life and, in many cases economic well-being of large groups of Americans (Segal, 2007).

The tides soon shifted again, however. Republican Congressmen Newt Gingrich and Richard Armey drafted the Contract with America, which their party introduced in 1994. The Contract was an effort by political conservatives to reverse the more liberal social welfare policies of earlier decades (for example, Lyndon Johnson's Great Society programs). Responding to the economic recession that was occurring during the 1990s and the increased number of people living in poverty, welfare which previously was available to families until the youngest child was 18 years old was politically reconceptualized as temporary (five-year limit) and states' control over allocations was strengthened (Gibelman, 2005).

In 1996 the Clinton administration agreed to support the Personal Responsibility and Work Opportunity Reconciliation Act (PRWORA), which replaced AFDC with Temporary Assistance to Needy Families (TANF). The PRWORA was intended to decrease dependence on welfare and, because the federal government would fund TANF through block grants to the states and would not provide a uniform set of guidelines, the PRWORA authorized each state to determine: (1) the ways that funds would be allocated and the amounts that would be awarded; (2) time limits for cash assistance; and (3) eligibility requirements for Medicaid (MA) health coverage. States that did not comply with general federal regulations regarding the restrictions for receiving TANF benefits risked losing funding. One condition of the PRWORA is a five-year

Medicaid (MA)
Health care coverage available to some recipients of the eligibility-based programs (TANF, SSI, and SSD).

lifetime cap on public assistance benefits. In addition, TANF recipients are required to be engaged in a work-related activity for at least 30 hours per week.

As a program for reducing poverty, the PRWORA was not a success. The number of children living in deep poverty actually rose between 1996 and 2006 (Sherman & Trisi, 2014), sparking significant concern as deprivation early in life can result in delayed development, poor health, and chronic illness (Lei, 2013). Though the Clinton administration made few strides in social welfare, it has generally been viewed as more supportive than its predecessors of the social work profession and those people the social welfare systems serves (Gibelman, 2005). Nevertheless, welfare reform required the social work profession to reconceptualize program delivery. Exhibit 3.6 provides a timeline of social welfare programs during the 20th and 21st centuries.

Social Welfare in the 21st Century The 2000 election of George W. Bush ushered in decreased public funding for social welfare programs and a renewed shift from public to private responsibility for meeting societal needs. In fact, the first executive act of the new President was to create the White House Office of Faith-Based and Community Initiatives. A commitment to "compassionate conservatism" and a supply-side economic philosophy meant decreased governmental support and fewer resources for social welfare programs (Gibelman, 2005; Hopps et al., 2008).

The 2006 elections brought a change of legislative leadership as the Democrats gained control of Congress. This shift resulted in the enactment of a voluntary prescription drug plan through Medicare (2006) and legislation to raise the minimum wage from $5.15 to $7.25 by 2009.

During the first decade of this century, concern was mounting for the well-being of TANF recipients who would have difficulty gaining and maintaining employment. Welfare rights advocates lobbied state legislatures to reauthorize TANF benefits. While the Deficit Reduction Act of 2005 did just that, it also placed more stringent requirements on states and, ultimately, the recipients themselves (Hagen & Lawrence, 2008). The Final Rules of TANF went into effect in 2008 with a loosening of the activities that "count" as work. Critics, however, remain unconvinced that TANF requirements are sensitive to employment barriers for all TANF recipients, particularly those with disabilities (Schott, 2008). Opponents of TANF continue to view it as its work requirements and inflexible time limits as coercive and its focus on the labor force as opposed to human capital as shortsighted (Hagen & Lawrence, 2008). Some critics object to the assumption that poverty is a temporary situation that can be rectified by a stable national and global economy (National Association of Social Workers, 2009–2012). Other critics point out that TANF recipients have been unable to obtain employment with wages high enough to lift them out of poverty.

EXHIBIT 3.6

20th and 21st Century Advances in Social Welfare

- 1910—Workers' Compensation legislation passes
- 1911— Mothers' Pensions programs are established in Illinois (by 1934, 46 states had initiated statewide programs to support mothers and children)
- 1914—The term "psychiatric social worker" is introduced in Boston
- 1836—Child labor laws are passed in Boston
- 1935—The Franklin D. Roosevelt administration passes the Social Security Act to address the Depression-era needs of older adults, widowed persons, the unemployed, persons with disabilities, and dependent children
- 1944—GI Bill of Rights legislation enables returning veterans to purchase homes and attain college educations
- 1953—Department of Health, Education, and Welfare (HEW) is established (name changed to Department of Health and Human Services in 1979)
- 1961—The Kennedy administration creates the Peace Corps
- 1963—Community Mental Health Center Act
- 1964—Civil Rights Act and Economic Opportunity Act
- 1964–1965—War on Poverty and Great Society programs include Job Corps, Head Start, and VISTA (1964); Food Stamp Act (1964); Medicare and Medicaid (1965); Older Americans Act (1965); and Elementary and Secondary Education Act (1965)
- 1972—Supplemental Security Income provides stipends for older adults and persons with disabilities whose financial means are the most limited
- 1974—The Child Abuse Prevention and Treatment Act formalizes intervention in cases of child abuse and neglect
- 1975—Title XX services are established as an amendment to the Social Security Act, enabling purchase of income-based social, training, and housing services
- 1988—The Family Support Act aims to strengthen programming for children and families in employment, training, and child support and care
- 1990—The landmark Americans with Disabilities Act ensures access and equity for persons with disabilities
- 1996—As part of welfare reform, the Personal Responsibility and Work Opportunity Reconciliation Act (PRWORA) creates Temporary Assistance to Needy Families (TANF), replacing Assistance to Families with Dependent Children
- 1996—The Mental Health Parity Act expands insurance coverage to include mental health services
- 1999—The "Ticket to Work Act" allows persons with disabilities to retain their Medicaid and Medicare eligibility while working
- 2002—The "No Child Left Behind Act" aims to reform the education system by improving educator accountability for student performance
- 2003—The "Medicare Prescription Drug, Improvement, and Modernization Act" attempts to help persons receiving Medicare pay for their prescription medications
- 2008—The Mental Health Parity and Addiction Equity Act (MHPAEA) mandates that coverage for mental health service be comparable to physical health coverage
- 2009—The "American Recovery and Reinvestment Act" (ARRA) attempts to stimulate the

lagging economy through federal tax incentives for employers, expansion of unemployment and health care benefits, and grants for home purchases, education, research, and energy
- 2010—"The Patient Protection and Affordable Care Act" (ACA) provides greater access to health care coverage
- 2014—As part of the ACA, Medicaid eligibility is expanded to include persons at or below 138% of the federal poverty line (in 24 states and the District of Columbia) and the marketplace for health insurance is opened for enrollment.

Sources: Barker, 2014; Corbett, 2008; Long et al., 2014; NASW, 1998.

Increasing dissatisfaction with governmental spending priorities became a factor during the campaign of Barack Obama, whose platform of social and economic reform became appealing to voters. Entering office in the throes of a major economic crisis, one of President Obama's first concerns was to stabilize the economy. After unemployment rates hovered near 10% for an extended period of time, the U.S. Department of Labor Bureau of Labor Statistics (2012) reported a lower rate of 8.3% at the beginning of 2012. At any point in time, unemployment hits those on the lowest end of the socioeconomic spectrum hardest (e.g., high unemployment rates for underrepresented groups). To revitalize the economy, Obama introduced the American Recovery and Reinvestment Act (ARRA) within his first month in office. Aimed at restabilizing the nation's economy, the Economic Stimulus Bill infused $840 billion into the economy to strengthen the infrastructure, support state and local governments, provide tax assistance, and invest in health care, energy, the environment, and education (Council on Social Work Education, 2009).

Homeless People

Source: iStock/andipantz

Reports suggest that the ARRA was, in fact, successful in staving off the most dire of the consequences of the economic recession with an estimated 0.7 million to 3.6 million individuals finding employment as a result of the initiative (Leachman & Mai, 2011). These and other safety-net programs kept many out of poverty, including recipients of unemployment insurance (3.2 million), Social Security (20.3 million), SNAP (3.9 million), and EITC (5.4 million) (Trisi et al., 2011). In fact, from 2000 to 2009, poverty among SNAP recipients decreased by 4.4%, and lessened the depth and severity of poverty even more. Depth of poverty decreased by 10.3% overall and 15.5% for children, while the severity of poverty declined 13.2% overall and 21.3% for children (Tiehen, Jolliffe, & Gundersen, 2012, p. 1). In addition, the ARRA expanded the Child Tax Credit, bolstered educational and health programs, weatherized federal buildings and private homes, strengthened road and bridge infrastructure, and provided increased support for scientific research and technology advancements (Recovery Act, 2012). To learn more about ongoing recovery initiatives, visit: www.recovery.gov.

Since 2009, social welfare programming has taken a back seat to concerns over the state of the economy. The priorities of the presidential administration were, not surprisingly, focused on the budget. Though public assistance benefits had not even kept up with inflation, because of federal austerity policies and the sequestration of 2013, a number of federal social and health-related programs were reduced. Many states followed suit, enacting major cuts in TANF that decreased by one-third the number of families eligible to receive benefits, decreased the lifetime cap on eligibility, and decreased support for working families (Schott & Pavetti, 2011). With the median TANF benefit at $429/month, family income stalled at 27% of the poverty level. The addition of the food stamp (SNAP) benefit, that level still only reached 68% of the poverty line (Schott & Pavetti, 2011).

To meaningfully address poverty in contemporary society, noted scholar in the area of poverty, Rank (2006), offers a model that allows people to live a life without poverty. The model rests on five assumptions: (1) poverty is a result of structural failings; (2) poverty is a conditional state that people can move in and out of; (3) poverty creates deprivation in multiple areas (e.g., health, education, and employment); (4) poverty is an injustice; and (5) poverty affects and undermines all of us. Rank outlines the following steps to operationalize this approach:

- Ensure a minimum wage that enables individuals and families to work full-time and to expect to live above the poverty line.
- Better utilize the taxation system to support low-income persons through EITC and other tax credits.

- Ensure that basic goods and services—education, health care, affordable housing and child care—are available to all.
- Create a culture and structure for developing individual assets through Individual Development Accounts (IDA), a matched savings plan to support low-income persons to accumulate savings (see Quick Guide #3.2).

Individual Development Account (IDA)
Savings are matched for use in home purchase, business startup, or education expenses.

QUICK GUIDE #3.2 CURRENT U.S. SOCIAL WELFARE PROGRAMS

✓ **Social Security:** Retirement income (based on amount "invested") for all workers who have paid into the system during their years of employment. Provides income to survivors (spouses and children) of deceased workers and to workers who become disabled if they have worked long enough to qualify.

✓ **Medicare:** National social insurance program that provides health insurance for older adults and younger persons experiencing a disability.

✓ **Temporary Assistance to Needy Families (TANF):** Monthly cash assistance to eligible low-income families with children under age 18. Within the first 2 years of receiving benefits, TANF recipients who are able-bodied must be engaged in work or work-related activities (for example, job training or seeking) or lose benefits. Over a lifetime, an individual can not receive benefits for a total of more than 5 years.

✓ **Social Security Disability (SSD):** Cash assistance for persons deemed unable to work for at least 1 year for reasons of physical or mental disability. Not available to workers who become disabled due to drug or alcohol addiction.

✓ **Supplemental Security Income (SSI):** Cash assistance for low-income adults, older adults, and persons with disabilities or visual challenges who meet income and health standards.

✓ **Medicaid (MA):** Health coverage available to some recipients of eligibility-based programs (TANF, SSI, and SSD). May also be provided to Social Security recipients who are eligible based on need.

✓ **Supplemental Nutrition Assistance Program (SNAP):** Formerly known as food stamps, now an electronic card that can be used to purchase food items. Provided as an income supplement to low-income individuals and families.

✓ **Women, Infants, and Children (WIC):** Eligibility-based benefits for mothers and their children, aimed at enhancing physical health. Can be used to purchase certain foods.

✓ **General Assistance (GA):** Sometimes called general relief. Small, short-term cash benefits for low-income adults who do not qualify for any other cash assistance programs. Currently not available in most states.

✓ **Earned Income Tax Credit (EITC):** Refundable tax credit for low-income ($36,000–$49,000 annual income) workers paying federal taxes (additional tax credits available in some states). Benefits based on number of children and total household income.

✓ **Head Start:** Child development program for low-income children, which includes preschool, health, and nutrition programs.

✓ **Individual Development Account (IDA):** Matching funds available to low-income savers. Funds can be used for financing a home or business, education, or other investments that will help the individual achieve economic well-being. Funded by nonprofit organizations, with legislative support from the federal government and a majority of states.

Although antipoverty programs come and go with the political tides, a core group of programs have weathered multiple political and economic storms. Those programs (e.g., Head Start) that have been able to establish a base of evidence to support their effectiveness have been more sustainable. Quick Guide #3.2 lists some of the enduring programs with which social workers need to be familiar.

SOCIAL WORK AND THE CHANGING APPROACHES TO POVERTY

The social work profession can and does play a significant role in efforts to reduce poverty. Social workers who help students finish high school, work in addictions treatment, aid elders, or support a survivor of intimate partner violence are likely, in fact, working to prevent or reduce poverty (Mason, 2014). As a profession committed to social justice for all persons, social workers must view issues of poverty and income inequality through a socially just lens. Rank (2014) identifies four areas of justice interpretation that relate to any discussion of poverty:

- Entitlement and protection of rights—there should be a basic financial floor and minimum standard of living for all people.
- Equality of opportunities—everyone should be able to achieve a "level playing field" (e.g., education).

- Balance—an individual's financial status should reflect both personal effort *and* background.
- Deservedness—one's prior efforts, actions, and talents determine to what degree she or he deserves to be successful.

One of the roles of an effective social worker is to facilitate access to all the resources for which clients are eligible. In order to do so, the social worker must also have a grounding in the issues related to these programs, their missions, and their limitations. At the policy level, social workers can advocate for changes that will strengthen income security programs by testifying, gathering data and client stories, and disseminating information through newspapers, blogs, and other media outlets (Lens & Garfinkel, 2012). Understanding social welfare philosophy and programming outside of one's country of origin and/or practice can also be an asset when working with clients who have emigrated from another country. What follows are three examples of approaches to poverty reduction that can benefit social workers.

Consider the social worker who is helping a family locate in-home services to avoid placing their family member suffering from early-onset dementia in a long-term care facility. The social worker must have a working knowledge of relevant social welfare programs, such as Social Security Disability, Medicare, Medicaid, and SSI, and must remain up-to-date on the ever-changing policies, eligibility requirements, application protocols, and benefits associated with these programs. The American Association of Retired Persons (AARP) has developed Social Security State Quick Fact Sheets, accessible at: www.aarp.org/work/social-security/info-01-2014/2014-social-security-quick-fact-sheets.html, which are a great resource for social workers who want to become more familiar with these programs.

Consider the social worker whose clients are financially at-risk, experiencing a financial crisis, or in the midst of a life transition (e.g., marriage, divorce, or illness). The social worker can best serve these clients by having knowledge of financial management issues in order to help the client access appropriate financial resources and services (Collins & Birkenmaier, 2013). All clients can benefit from becoming financially literate through financial socialization, education, guidance, and financial inclusion (i.e., access to banks, financial institutions, and services) that are appropriate, accessible, affordable, financially attractive, and easy to use (Sherraden, 2013).

Social workers can benefit from knowledge about poverty reduction approaches around the globe. As a social worker, you are likely to encounter clients who have received benefits in other countries or who are immigrating to or emigrating from another country. Social workers can also benefit from learning about other countries' successful efforts to alleviate poverty. We can gain insight into our own system of anti-poverty programs by examining approaches being used in other countries. Current strategies that are making strides in reducing poverty across the world include (World Bank, 2013b):

- community-driven development programs in which community members control planning and investments;
- increasing educational opportunities, particularly for girls, such as the schools established by Oprah Winfrey in South Africa;
- expanding the use of environmentally sustainable energy sources and implementing safer water and sanitation practices;
- increasing agricultural production to reduce hunger and food crises through such non-governmental organization (NGO) programs as micro-lending in Central and Latin America;
- establishing microfinancing programs (e.g., loans, savings, money transfer, and micro-insurance) to promote entrepeneurship and asset building (strategies that include savings, consumption, and development of long-term care resources such as individual development accounts, child development accounts, elimination of asset limits for public benefit eligibility, and emphasis on saving money versus purchasing on credit) (Shanks, 2012). For one example, check out www.kiva.org.
- strengthening safety net programs through provision of cash transfers when families meet requirements such as healthcare and school attendance;
- improving transportation infrastructures to increase access, efficiency, and safety;
- promoting governmental accountability through transparency and civic engagement.

Asset building
Strategies that include savings, consumption, and development of long-term care resources such as individual development accounts, child development accounts, elimination of asset limits for public benefit eligibility, and emphasis on saving money versus purchasing on credit.

It is instructive to compare U.S. approaches to poverty reduction to the approaches peer countries (i.e., those with similar gross domestic products (GDP)) employ. For example, at 15.7%, the U.S. has the highest rate of relative poverty (income below half of household-size-adjusted median income) among industrialized nations (Mishel et al., 2012). The factors that differentiate the U.S. from its peer countries relate to resource allocation. Specifically, the U.S. ranks near the bottom when compared to other industrialized countries in the area of social expenditures—16.2% of GDP compared to a 21.3% average in most peer countries. The U.S. also trails peer countries in supporting anti-poverty programs when the country experiences economic or labor deficits (Mishel et al., 2012). Exhibit 3.7 depicts the status of poverty in the U.S. in relationship to peer countries.

While peer countries have strengthened their safety nets, the U.S. safety net has weakened just as the income inequality gap in the U.S. has increased. The success of programs in peer countries around the world suggests that we

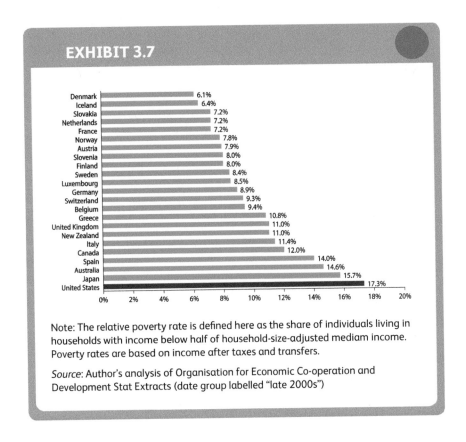

EXHIBIT 3.7

Note: The relative poverty rate is defined here as the share of individuals living in households with income below half of household-size-adjusted mediam income. Poverty rates are based on income after taxes and transfers.

Source: Author's analysis of Organisation for Economic Co-operation and Development Stat Extracts (date group labelled "late 2000s")

need a stronger safety net coupled with full employment policies (Mishel et al., 2012).

Sentiments regarding public welfare resources and programs are complex and closely linked to political, economic, religious, and social trends in the U.S. and abroad. What are the implications of these ever-shifting views for the social work profession? Social and economic needs inevitably prompt a societal and political response. This response, in turn, determines the amount of money that politicians, bureaucrats, private foundations, and individual donors will spend. The availability of funding determines the extent to which social workers can provide social work services. Let us consider three areas in which social work practice is affected by current societal and political trends: (1) public child welfare; (2) food insecurity (lack of access to enough food to live an active, healthy life) (Coleman-Jensen, Gregory, & Singh, 2014); and (3) services for persons experiencing mental illness.

The public child welfare system is a classic example of this sequence of events. When the political climate is unfavorable for public social services,

Food insecurity
Nutritional deficiency due to inadequate types and quantities of food.

funding is decreased, and the number of social work positions is lowered. Although the demand for social work services may remain high, there is not enough funding to meet it. The result is fewer social workers with larger caseloads. During these times, politicians often suggest that the private sector should fill the gap. While such an approach may appeal to taxpayers, the private sector is typically dependent on donations, grants, and government contracts as the primary form of revenue, which can present challenges to maintaining stable operations. Social workers can become involved by documenting impact of funding decisions and engaging in advocacy and fundraising efforts.

A startling 14.3% of persons living in the United States in 2013 suffered from "food insecurity," with 5.6% of the 14.3% experiencing severe food insecurity (Coleman-Jensen et al., 2014). Moreover, over one-fifth of children in the United States are defined as being food-insecure. Insufficient nutrition can negatively impact a child's physical health, school performance, and psychosocial stability (Feeding America, 2012). Social workers can address this concern in several ways: (1) ensure that clients access relevant programs for which they are eligible (e.g., SNAP, Women, Infants, and Children, school breakfast and lunch, and summer feeding programs); (2) advocate for appropriate funding for public programs such as SNAP; (3) work to improve overall participation rates and access to available food programs; and (4) advocate for additional resources for nongovernmental food programs to reach those families that are not eligible for public programs (SRCD, 2011b). To learn more about food insecurity in the U.S., see the interactive map at Feeding America: http://feedingamerica.org/hunger-in-america/hunger-studies/map-the-meal-gap.aspx.

Another example of how societal trends affect social work is the treatment of persons with mental illness. Research indicates that persons experiencing mental illness, specifically personality disorders, utilize social welfare programs and services at higher levels than other groups (Vaughn et al., 2009). Current funding for prevention and treatment programs for those experiencing mental illness is inconsistent, and making prevention and treatment programming a funding priority could, in fact, reduce the burden on the public welfare system.

There will always be a role for social workers in the administration and evaluation of anti-poverty programs regardless of the political, social, and economic climates. However, social workers' jobs may become more or less challenging depending on the political climate, the state of the economy, and the prevailing sentiments regarding safety-net programs in general and social welfare programs in particular. Regardless of the area of social work in which you specialize, you are responsible for staying current with the myriad changes social welfare programs undergo every year. Your understanding of these ever-changing policies and programs is key to your ability to be an effective social work practitioner and advocate for your clients. Your knowledge may prevent your client from becoming homeless or unemployed, may enable your client to gain access to public assistance or employment or disability benefits, or may help the client access health or educational programs. Social workers should have a clear understanding of the eligibility criteria for social welfare programs. Exhibit 3.8 offers one social worker's personal journey from receiving public assistance to teaching human services.

In a policy statement, the National Association of Social Workers (2012–2014p) calls for social workers to advocate for an array of poverty-reduction policies and plans, regardless of climate, some of which include:

- Work to create safety net programs such as comprehensive child support for all single custodial parents, universal health care, meaningful employment and training, education, increases in EITC, and a living wage.
- Help persons living in poverty to build personal and financial assets through programs such as individual development accounts.
- Enable those persons living in poverty to integrate work, education, and family life. Promote services that focus on the underlying economic causes of poverty, including factors such as domestic violence, sexual abuse, mental health issues, substance abuse, and literacy problems (pp. 353–354).

EXHIBIT 3.8

What a Waste My Life Would Have Been If I Had Not Become a Social Worker

Angela Roffle was born in 1959 at four pounds to a 10th grade African American mother. Four years later, she had a sister. Because she was 4 pounds at birth, her childhood was plagued with health issues. She spent time in the hospital and even had her leg broken so that it could grow stronger. With this beginning, Angela's journey could have been very different from the one you are about to read ...

Because her mother did not have a high school diploma or training, her ability to earn an adequate income for her family was limited. What was not limited, however, was her mother's commitment to ensuring that her daughter had a quality education. Along with her parents and extended family members, some who were former sharecroppers, Angela's mother read to and with her daughters, took them to the library, exposed them to culture, including ballet classes, and talked with them about getting an education so they could better themselves.

Angela started public school at age four. By first grade, her mother and grandparents felt the public school was not meeting Angela's needs, and, wanting a better educational experience for her, they sent her to Catholic School. There she was labeled as having a behavioral disorder, but the staff psychologist suggested she may have been bored and perhaps needed more stimulation. An eighth grade teacher suggested to Angela's family that a private, Catholic college preparatory school might be the answer, telling them, "Notre Dame saved my life." Despite there being very little diversity at her new school (she was one of twelve African Americans in the school), she grew and thrived—meeting people from all over the world, re-directing her energy into advocating for causes about which she was passionate even participating in civil rights demonstrations. During high school, Angela convinced her mother to complete her GED. Her mother went on to complete community college and received a scholarship to a private Jesuit university. When Angela was 19, her mother died of breast cancer.

Angela was grieving and had no direction. "I lost my mind." Her son was born when Angela was 21 and her twin daughters were born nine years later, the elder of the two with a seizure disorder that kept her in the hospital for 18 of her first 24 months of life. Angela never stopped going to college, taking a class here and there. She tried to work, but one employer told her that if she left to care for her daughter, she would be fired. At that time, Angela received public assistance, food stamps, and subsidized housing. Because the food stamps did not stretch through the month, she used a food pantry. It was a food pantry worker who referred Angela to the Reform Organization for Welfare (ROWEL), a welfare rights advocacy organization. Angela felt a connection with ROWEL and began volunteering to advocate for and educate others about the needs of people living in poverty. With the help of a supportive caseworker at the Division of Family Services, Angela (whose welfare benefits were reduced when she tried to go to college) went back to college and majored in urban planning.

Angela credits a chance meeting with social worker and faculty member Dr. Susan Tebb with helping to define and shape the next chapter of her life. After Angela gave a presentation to a social work class, Dr. Tebb told Angela she would make a good social worker. Angela's response: "Did you not hear what I just said? I hate social workers. I've dealt with them my whole life. They don't listen or care." Dr. Tebb replied, "Oh, no, you are a social worker."

Then one day she was watching a TV movie, *Mandela*, and was shocked to learn that Winnie Mandela was a social worker. She began talking with others and eventually contacted Dr. Tebb, letting her know that maybe she would like to try social work ... She took one course, and the rest, as they say, is history. Angela went on to complete her BSW and MSW degrees. She has worked at a range of agencies with different populations (children, youth, and older adults) doing case management, administration, lobbying, grant writing, and program development, but one theme is consistent throughout her career—she is committed to advocacy whether at the individual, organizational, state, or national levels. Angela now teaches in a human services program at a community college. She is considering the next chapter of her life—which may involve working with youth and women in Rwanda.

In reflecting on her life and her career, Angela shares these thoughts:

- *On Diversity*: If it's not within the realm of your life experience, it's hard for you to imagine. It can be right in front of you, but if it's not *your* experience, you can't understand it.
- *On the Social Work Profession*: Social work is not for everyone. It's a calling. The scope of the work we do is so broad. You can work in one area and then move on to another area. I haven't gotten rich, but it's the most rewarding career I can imagine. When I die, I will know I had a career where I could make a difference.
- *On Social Work Practice*: The best tool you bring to the helping situation is yourself. Deal with your own issues—if the social worker is not healthy, she can't help her clients. Be honest with yourself—you cannot work with everyone. Know your strengths and your limitations, and deal with them. If you don't, you can hurt people. Remember, do no harm. Keep yourself healthy. Take care of yourself first and be able to say no. Be creative—when a tool or a resource isn't working, create a new one!

Like many social work students, Emily questioned the value of studying the history of social welfare and learning about the numerous and complex government programs. After all, she just wanted to help people, and spending time reading about policies had nothing to do with helping people, or did it? One day at Oasis House, Emily and her social work supervisor, John, met with one of the shelter's residents, Tonya. Tonya and her two children had fled from her violent husband. Tonya's TANF and Medicaid benefits were being terminated because she was not currently employed full-time. Instead, she was enrolled in a full-time licensed practical nurse program and completing her clinical training at a skilled nursing facility. She had only 3 months until graduation, and her only income was the public assistance she received. In addition, Tonya had to make frequent medical visits related to her older child's cerebral palsy. She had held several part-time jobs while enrolled in the licensed practical nurse program, but she either had to quit or was fired from each due to absenteeism because of her child's hospitalization and medical appointments.

In his role as an advocate, John telephoned Tonya's income maintenance caseworker to request that Tonya be scheduled for a hearing at which she could request a work waiver to continue to receive benefits while she completed her training. He also requested that the agency allow him to accompany Tonya to the hearing and to present photographs verifying that she was a survivor of domestic violence. As a result of John's knowledge of Tonya's rights and of government benefits, Tonya obtained a waiver to allow her to finish training. John also helped Tonya apply for SSI for her child.

Through her experience with Tonya and John, Emily learned how important it is for social workers to be knowledgeable about policies and programs so that they can advocate for people in need.

CONCLUSION

The start of the 21st century provides a convenient vantage point from which to look back on the past, particularly on the fifty years since the War on Poverty, and forward to the future of social welfare programs in the U.S. Overall rates of poverty have decreased since the 1960s, due in large part to increased educational attainment, female employment, and lower birth rates (Parrott, 2014). Even so, social workers are still in demand to serve many who face challenges including income inequality; racial discrimination; education, health care and employment disparities; and child poverty; and safety net policies continue to lag behind those in other developed countries (Parrott, 2014).

While both public and private entities deliver social services, the majority of funding comes from government sources. That funding is a political issue thus making it periodically at risk because some members of our society continue to explain poverty and need as being individually based.

The need for a social safety net only grows during economic crises like the Global Financial Crisis of 2007–2008, and the question is whether our society can change from an individualistic perspective to one that focuses on the community to help those in need. When a middle-class wage earner is laid off, the family's home is lost to foreclosure, and they have no health insurance coverage, suddenly they are living below the poverty line. Although social welfare policy and subsequent programs may change to strengthen the safety net, there is also a possibility that the dynamics of political, social, and economic factors will not stretch far enough to relieve this family's need—much less the need of the chronically poor.

Practicing social workers need to understand the historical roots of contemporary social welfare philosophy and programs. Social workers' knowledge, skills, and values give them useful insights into the systemic impact of poverty on those with whom they work.

To help people achieve economic stability, social workers can also advocate for policy changes in areas such as TANF, health care and insurance, the minimum wage, tax structures, and educational benefits. But you cannot advocate for your position unless you understand the varied positions of others. Social workers have long been at the forefront of advocacy efforts, and they will continue to use their knowledge of systems, organizations, and communities to advocate for and with others to alleviate poverty.

Even in this era of uncertainty, another of Don Bakely's poems captures a sense of optimism and hope:

> When I was a kid,
>> I looked to the day when
>> I would stop dreaming those wild hopes
> and
>>> I'd be old enough
>>>> to make real life
>>>>> out of
>>>>>> unreal dreams.
> But I still catch myself
>>> hanging onto dreams—
>> and I'm forty.
> Sometimes I catch myself thinking
>> maybe today
>>> a big, beautiful car is going to pull up out front
>>> and
>>>> the rich man is going to get out
>>>> and say,
> "I heard about you,
>> that
>>> you are a good man
>>> and work hard
>>> and love your kids
>>>> and are down on your luck.
> Here's a check.
> Come by the office. I've got a good job for a man like you.
> By the way, keep the car.
>> I see you need one.
>> I'll catch a cab back."

Of course,
　　　　he never comes.
I really know
　　he
　　　　　never
　　　　　　　will.

But, see,
　　　　with poor folks
　　　　　　even wild hopes
　　　　　　　are
　　　　　　　　　hopes worth thinking.
　　　　　　　　　　Kind of fun, in fact.

Then, too
　　　if we can't have some glimmer
　　　　　in
　　　　　　　tomorrow
　　　even a
　　　　long-shot,
　　　　never-happen
　　　　　glimmer.
Then each today
　　is always
　　　　only
　　　　　　darkness.

Source: Excerpt from "The family of poor: Part three," *from If . . . A Big Word With the Poor* by Don Bakely, Faith & Life Press, Newton, Kansas. Used with permission.

MAIN POINTS

- ■ Poverty—not having enough money to maintain a basic standard of living—is a complex political, economic, and social issue.
- ■ Poverty touches many groups beyond the stereotypical homeless sleeping in doorways or pushing shopping carts on the downtown streets of a city; those groups at highest risk for living in poverty are women, persons of color, high school dropouts, older adults, and children (who cannot work).
- ■ The causes of poverty continue to be hotly debated. Some people believe that the individual is responsible for her or his economic plight, while

others believe that external factors (such as employment opportunities and economic conditions) place people at risk for living in poverty.

■ Poverty can be short-term; it can be episodic when an individual is working but cannot earn enough money to move out of poverty; or it can be chronic, when an individual cannot emerge from poverty over a long term.

■ Understanding both the literal meanings and societal connotations of terms such as welfare, public assistance, and social policy helps in understanding society's perception of poverty.

■ Societal responses to poverty tend to reflect the current political climate, with conservative political administrations restricting social programs and more liberal administrations expanding social programs.

■ A variety of federal, state, and local government agencies are involved in the administration of social welfare programs.

■ Social welfare programs fall into two categories: universal (Social Security and Medicare), and selective (for example, TANF, SSI, and SNAP). Social workers are responsible for being familiar with these programs and staying current with the myriad changes made every year.

EXERCISES

1. Respond to the following questions:
   a. What is poverty?
   b. What causes poverty?
   c. How do we end poverty?
   Then interview friends, family members, co-workers, and/or others and ask them the same three questions. You may also ask your interviewees about their definitions of and attitudes toward "welfare." Reflect on the similarities and differences in their responses and the way in which their definitions and attitudes compare with the definitions described in this chapter.

2. As you learned from this chapter, Tonya is a single mother with two children. Her son, William, is three years old and her daughter, Ava, is six years old. Develop a budget that would be required for Tonya and her two children to live for 1 month. You may want to have a calculator available to help you in this exercise.
   This budget should not reflect a luxurious lifestyle or a life at bare minimum, but rather should show what you believe are essentials for living and their costs for 1 month. For each basic human need, enter an amount that you think is a true monthly cost regardless of who would pay for it. For example, the cost of food will be the same if the family receives food stamps or not. In actuality, the family may not have the resources to

purchase that amount of food, but it is still a cost. As you are creating this budget, identify your reasons for deriving that particular amount.

Once you have developed a picture of Tonya's needs for one month, you can compare your amounts with the actual amounts required if this family lived in your state by calculating a family budget at the Economic Policy Institute Basic Family Budget Calculator at: www.epi.org/resources/budget/.

As you progress with this exploration, consider Tonya's situation from two different perspectives. First, assume that Tonya and her children receive TANF benefits and compare your budget with the amounts of benefits that they will receive. Second, consider the scenario in which Tonya is employed full-time in a minimum-wage job. Decide if she receives health/dental benefits for herself and/or her children. In order to make these comparisons, you will need information on living costs in your community. Questions to consider as you complete this exercise:

a.   What information do you need to know to be able to develop a monthly budget?

b.   What categories of expenses would a single mother with two children have during the month?

c.   What is the amount of TANF your state provides for a mother and two children?

3.   As you have learned from the Sanchez family interactive case (go to www.routledgesw.com/caseStudies), the family has struggled financially throughout the years. As part of his belief system that he should provide for his family, Hector has prevented the family from taking advantage of many of the resources available to them. Complete the following two exercises:

a.   Using the information provided in this chapter, along with information from your state government, identify benefits that may be appropriate for various members of the Sanchez family. You may use resources in the community in which you reside or where your social work program is located.

b.   Reflect on the reasons that Hector may feel resistance to using social services. Additionally, reflect on how you think Hector and the members of his family may feel in the client role.

4.   Review the case file for Junior Sanchez in the Sanchez family interactive case (www.routledgesw.com/caseStudies). Answer Junior's Critical Thinking Questions.

5.   To test your knowledge of poverty, complete the Poverty Quiz located at: www.povertyusa.org/poverty-resources/quiz/. Upon completion of the quiz, write a reflection describing your thoughts and feelings regarding your level of knowledge, reaction to the new information you gained, and the relationship to the social work profession.

6. Go to www.routledgesw.com/caseStudies and familiarize yourself with the case entitled, "Hudson City: An Urban Community Affected by Disaster." Click on Engage to review the details of the case. Natural disasters often affect individuals and families in negative ways, but the impact on persons of limited resources can be particularly devastating as they may not have adequate insurance coverage, financial savings, or a support network that can help in significant ways. Additionally, when disasters strike, many individuals lose their employment when businesses are affected. Utilizing the information included in the Hudson City case, this chapter, and online sources, develop a list of resources that may be of value to an individual or family who has experienced a disaster. From your research, identify those services and resources that are based on means testing (i.e., based on income).

7. Social workers must be aware of poverty and its related issues in the U.S. and around the world. To learn more about living in poverty, visit one of the following three interactive websites:

   ■ Global Poverty Project: www.live58.org/survive125/.
   ■ Spent: http://playspent.org/.
   ■ Feeding America: http://feedingamerica.org/hunger-in-america/ hunger-facts/quiz.aspx.

After completing one or more of the interactive exercises, reflect in writing on the choices you made, the rationale for your choices, and what you may have done differently.

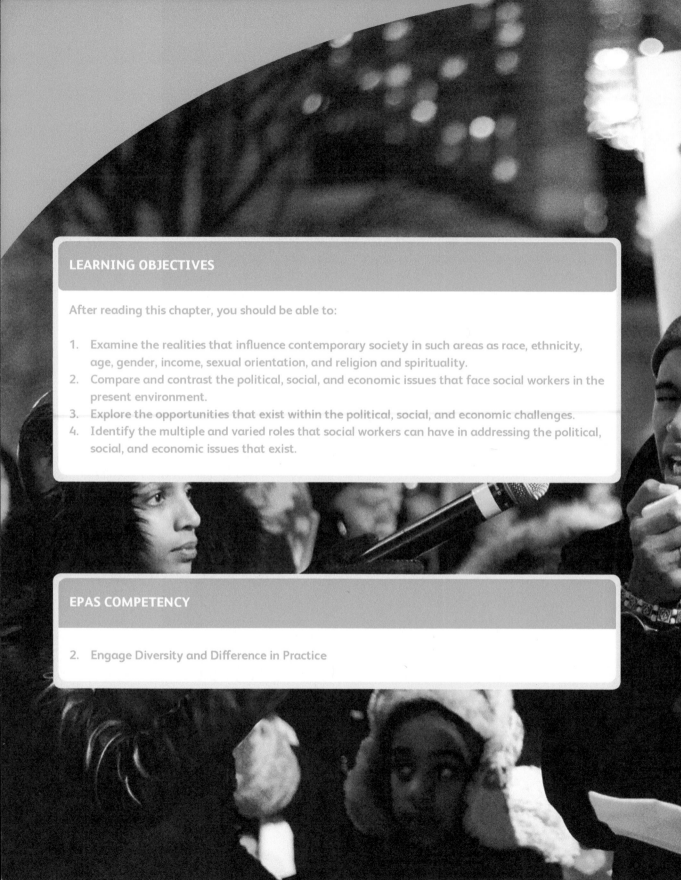

THE SOCIAL WORK ENVIRONMENT

Source: Shutterstock/nisarqmedia.com

T he social work profession's helping mission places it in the center of people's lives and the societal issues that influence them. Therefore, social workers must be knowledgeable about the makeup of society in general and the populations who use social workers' services in particular. Social work "is created within a political, social, cultural, and economic matrix that shapes the assumptions of practice, the problems that practice must deal with and the preferred outcomes of practice" (McNutt & Floersch, 2008, p. 4:138). Fortunately, the political, economic, and sociocultural issues facing the persons social workers serve are also opportunities for growth and social change. This chapter will discuss the diversity of the U.S. and global population and then examine the challenges that confront social workers in contemporary society.

CHANGING POPULATION PROFILES

As of 2014, the world is comprised of over 7.3 billion people, over 325 million of whom live in the United States. The world population is slated to surpass 9 billion by 2044, while the U.S. population is expected to reach 400 million by 2039. In fact, by 2050, the world population will increase 38% overall, but the population of children will increase by only 10% (Kochhar, 2014). The significance of this trend means there will be fewer future contributors to the economy. A new American is born every 8 seconds, one dies every 13 seconds, and one immigrates to the U.S. every 40 seconds, which results in an overall population increase of one person every 15 seconds (U.S. Census Bureau, 2015). The period from 1990 to 2000 saw the largest population growth (32.7 million people) of any 10-year period in U.S. history, with the largest growth occurring in the western states and metropolitan areas. During the next decade (2000–2010), the United States experienced a smaller rate of growth more comparable to that of the 1980s at 9.7%. As with the growth of the 1990s, the population increased mostly in the southern and western regions of the country (Mackun & Wilson, 2011). While impacted by environmental, political, and social changes, the world population typically grows at a rate of 1.5–2% per year. Twenty-first-century world population growth is anticipated to slow due to trends toward waiting longer to marry and have children.

While overall population growth is expected to decrease, population distribution, growth areas, and the average age of the world's population are expected to change. The majority of the world's people live in developing countries, and a number of these countries (e.g., Sub-Saharan Africa) are experiencing increases in fertility rates while struggling with economic, health, government, and poverty crises (Williamson, 2010). By 2050, Nigeria is expected to become the third most populated country in the world, surpassing the U.S. (Kochhar, 2014). India and China will remain the two most populous countries, with India growing more quickly than China, while the populations of Japan, Russia, and Germany will all decrease by as much as 10% (Kochhar, 2014).

Overall, the world's population is aging. By mid-century, the following age-related changes are expected (Kochhar, 2014):

- the number of persons age 65 and older is expected to triple, reaching 1.5 billion worldwide;
- the majority of residents of Japan, South Korea, and Germany will be 50+ years old;
- most of the world will have populations in which more persons will be over 65 than under 15 years of age;
- workers in developed countries will have more persons to support, while workers in some developing countries will have fewer dependents.

The world population as a whole is incredibly diverse in terms of race or ethnicity, age, sex or gender, income level, religion, and a variety of other factors. Some societies, such as North Korea, are relatively uniform (at least as far as race/ethnicity, income level, and religion are concerned). Others, like the United States, are quite diverse. The global profile is not only shifting toward an older population, but also toward a non-Caucasian one, and this impacts the world's economic, political, health care, and migratory realities (Williamson, 2010). In fact, recent demographic shifts (changes in the makeup of the population) have made the U.S. population more diverse than ever before.

Demographic shifts
Changes in the makeup of the population.

Social workers' clients reflect this diversity, although some groups have fewer opportunities and resources than others and thus may be overrepresented. In addition, government policies are not always supportive of all these segments of the population, making it necessary for social workers to lobby specifically for particular groups.

To highlight the diversity of the U.S. population, this chapter uses data from a number of sources, including: U.S. Census Bureau reports (2010 census data), *Women's Health USA 2013* (U.S. Department of Health and Human Services Health Resources and Services Administration, Maternal and Child Health Bureau, 2013), and *Income, Poverty, and Health Insurance Coverage in the United States: 2013*. The discussion focuses on five demographic characteristics: race and ethnicity, age, gender, income, and religion. Exhibit 4.1 highlights some of the major changes the U.S. Census Bureau (2014) predicts will occur by 2060.

EXHIBIT 4.1

The U.S. Census Bureau predicts the following changes by the year 2060

- The U.S. population will be 420.3 million, up from 325 million in 2015 and 400 million in 2051.
- Fifty-seven percent of the population will be persons of color, up from approximately 37% in 2015, with notable growth occurring among young people.
  - The proportion of Hispanics in the population will double to 1 in 3 persons, up from approximately 1 in 6 persons.
  - The African American population will increase from 13% to 15%.
  - The numbers of Asian Americans will increase from 5% to 8%.
  - The non-Hispanic white population will peak in 2024 at approximately 200 million (66% of the population) but will then decrease by 20 million by 2060 (46% of the population).
  - The American Indian and Alaska Native population will increase from 4 million to 6.3 million (going from 1.2% of the population to 1.5%).
  - The Native Hawaiian and Other Pacific Islanders population will double from 706,000 to 1.4 million.
  - Those persons identifying as two or more races will more than triple, going from 7.5 million to 26.7 million.
- About 67% of the child population will be children of color, up from 44% in 2010.
- The children/youth population will actually decrease from 23.5% to 21.2% of the population.
- About 92 million Americans will be 65 years or older, up from 43.1 million, making 1 in 5 persons age 65 or greater. By 2056, this group will outnumber those under 18 years of age.
- About 18 million Americans will be 85 years or older, up from 5.9 million, making them 4.3% of the population.

Source: U.S. Census Bureau, 2010.

Changes in Race and Ethnicity in the U.S.

Exhibit 4.2 illustrates changes in the racial and ethnic makeup of the United States population from 2000 to 2013. The United States is becoming more and more racially and ethnically diverse. From 1995 to 2050, the U.S. population is expected to increase by 50% overall, with the largest growth occurring in Hispanic/Latino and Asian populations, primarily due to immigration. Racial and ethnic diversity is increasing, particularly among older adults, in general, and older adults of color, in particular. One reason for this trend is that persons of color are gaining better access to health care and are therefore living longer than they have in the past. At the same time, birth rates among this group are expected to remain constant.

The U.S. is currently the most popular destination in the world for immigrants (Pew Research Center Hispanic Trends Project, 2013). Approximately

EXHIBIT 4.2

U.S. Population Changes by Race, 2000–2013

Racial Group	Percent of Population in 2000	Percent of Population in 2010	Percent of Population in 2013
One Race			
White, not Hispanic	69.1	63.7	62.6
Hispanic or Latino	12.5	16.3	17.1
Black or African American	12.3	12.6	13.2
American Indian and Alaska Native	0.9	0.9	1.2
Asian	3.6	4.8	5.3
Native Hawaiian and Other Pacific Islander	0.1	0.2	0.2
Two or More Races	2.4	2.9	2.4

Source: U.S. Census Bureau, 2014e.

40 million people currently living in the U.S. (13% of the total population) were born in other countries. Nearly half of those have become U.S. citizens, while over 11 million are not approved to live or work in this country (Congressional Budget Office (CBO), 2013). Immigration has always been a part of the American story, and in recent years immigration has surged. Thirty percent of U.S. foreign-born residents immigrated to the U.S. between 2000 and 2009, with 46% of immigrants being of Hispanic or Latino origin (Nwosu, Batalova, & Auclair, 2014).

One consequence of this increased diversity is that the U.S. population will include greater numbers of people whose first language is not English and who identify with more than one racial or ethnic group. Over 6,000 languages exist across the globe, and nearly 400 of them are represented within the U.S. population, largely because of immigration. Eight-five percent of U.S. residents speak a language other than English at home, with the greatest numbers residing in six states: Texas, California, Illinois, Nebraska, New Mexico, and Nevada (Gambino, Acosta, & Grieco, 2014). English fluency is lowest for those residents from Mexico, China, El Salvador, Vietnam, Cuba, and Korea (Gambino et al., 2014).

Another outcome of America's increasing diversity is an increase in interracial marriages, which were once illegal in many states. Today, one in six (15%) marriages in the U.S. include spouses from different races (Wang, 2012).

Over 1.7 million persons became naturalized citizens or lawful permanent residents (LPRs) of the United States in 2013 (Lee & Foreman, 2014; Monger & Yankay, 2014)—a number that will rise to an annual rate of over 2 million by 2050. These numbers do not include those persons who are in the United States in an undocumented status. Nearly 70,000 of those immigrants are refugees (persons who seek refuge from danger or persecution in their home country) who were resettled in the United States in 2013 alone (U.S. Department of State, Bureau of Population, Refugees, and Migration (PRM), 2014).

Increased racial and ethnic diversity requires that social workers develop greater cultural competency. Clients whose experiences, perspectives, cultural heritage, language, values, and traditions are so different have different needs. To learn more about the social work response to immigration and refugee resettlement and make use of resources for working with immigrants and refugees, visit the NASW site: www.naswdc.org/practice/intl/issues/immigration.asp.

The Aging Population

The population is becoming not only more racially and ethnically diverse, but also older, as Exhibit 4.3 shows. Currently, the U.S. median age is 37.6 years (36.3 for males and 39 for females), and it is expected to increase to 41 years by 2050 (Central Intelligence Agency, 2013–2014; Kochhar, 2014). Worldwide, the current median age is 29 years and will grow to 36 years by 2050 (Kochhar, 2014). Significantly, a greater percentage of the population of persons of color falls within the under-18 category, whereas whites make up the largest percentage of older adults. Based on current demographic projections, by 2030 more than 40% of the total U.S. population will be either under age 17 (21%) or over age 65 (22%). As children and older adults tend to be the most vulnerable segments of the population, such increases will result in a greater need for social work competence in working with these groups. While more males are born than females, females outrank males over the course of the lifespan, making older women particularly vulnerable (Howden & Meyer, 2011).

Life expectancy in the U.S. is currently 79 years for all groups. Exhibit 4.4 provides an overview of expected longevity for various population groups within the U.S. Longevity is on the increase for all groups; by 2050, life expectancy is projected to be as high as 83.9 years overall, although still lower for persons of color and males. The fastest-growing segment of the population will be those over 85—this group will reach 19 million in 2050. A small but rapidly growing group are the 55,000 persons who are currently 100 years or

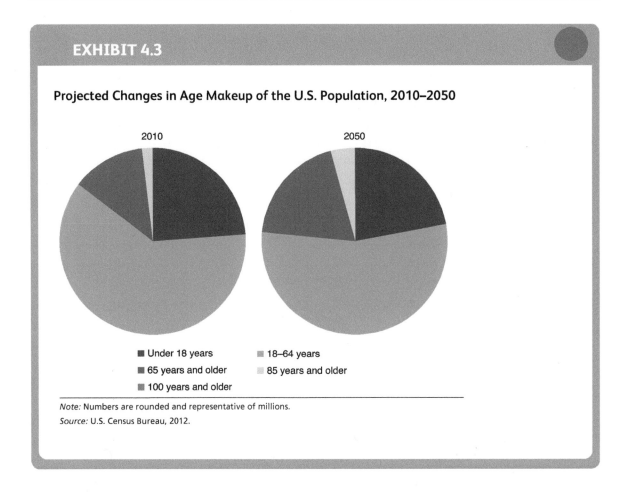

EXHIBIT 4.3

Projected Changes in Age Makeup of the U.S. Population, 2010–2050

2010   2050

- Under 18 years   ■ 18–64 years
- 65 years and older   ■ 85 years and older
- 100 years and older

Note: Numbers are rounded and representative of millions.
Source: U.S. Census Bureau, 2012.

older. Centenarians are largely female and widowed and have an increased risk of experiencing poverty (17% compared to 9% for their younger counterparts) (Kincel, 2014).

Median incomes are not keeping up with longer lifespans. Median incomes for older Americans have decreased, with nearly one in ten older adults living below the poverty line (Administration on Aging, 2013). Many older adults have exhausted their savings and are now living on limited resources.

Social workers need the skills to work with clients of all ages, particularly in multigenerational family situations. More (over 500,000 in 2013) older adults are rearing their grandchildren when parents are unavailable for a variety of reasons, including substance abuse, incarceration, and divorce. Current trends suggest that multigenerational families will become more common. More older adults will live in retirement communities, assisted living facilities, and long-term care facilities, which will give social workers many opportunities to work with older adults.

EXHIBIT 4.4

Current Life Expectancy of U.S. Population

	All Persons	Females	Males
All Racial Groups	78.6	81.2	76.0
White Non-Hispanic	78.7	81.2	76.2
African American	74.3	77.6	70.7
Hispanic	83.5	86.2	80.6
Asian American	87.3	89.7	84.6
Native American	75.1	78.1	72.0

Source: USA Life Expectancy, www.worldlifeexpectancy.com/usa/life-expectancy

Trends in Gender Ratios

Though the male population grew more than the female population between the 2000 and 2010 Censuses (9.9% and 9.5%, respectively), today women make up nearly 51% of the U.S. population. Men outnumber women until age 24, but for the 65-and-older segment, women make up 58% of the population. By age 85, women outnumber men by two to one. Exhibit 4.5 depicts gender ratio changes by age. As men age, mortality begins to increase, initially due to professional and recreational activities and later due to chronic fatal illnesses such as heart disease and cancer. These patterns are expected to continue. Exhibit 4.5 also depicts the ways in which age and sex distribution will change by 2050.

Social workers need to be increasingly aware of the issues that confront the growing population of older women. Compared to older men, older women are more likely to live alone, to have lower incomes, to experience more chronic health problems, and to assume more caregiving responsibilities (for example, for spouses or grandchildren). With the changes that have occurred in recent decades regarding women's roles in society, social workers also need to be preparing proactively for the new generations of older women who have participated in the workforce for most of their lives. This new and emerging group of older women may differ from their predecessors as they may have greater financial independence, fewer children, be unavailable to serve as family caregivers as they are still employed, and have different expectations for their older adult years. Consider the profile of successful aging (Exhibit 4.6) in which Mrs. B. continues to embrace her life.

EXHIBIT 4.5

Age and Sex Distribution in the United States (numbers are rounded)

Gender/Age	2015	2050
Females	163 million	223 million
Under 18 years	42 million	49 million
18–64 years	96 million	124 million
65 years and older	27 million	48 million
85 years and older	4 million	11 million
100 years and older	64,000	429,000
Males	159 million	215 million
Under 18 years	42 million	51 million
18–64 years	95 million	124 million
65 years and older	21 million	40 million
85 years and older	2 million	7 million
100 years and older	14,000	172,000

Source for 2050 projections: U.S. Census Bureau, 2011.

Source for 2015 data: Bureau of Census (2014g). Resident Population Projections by Sex and Age: 2015 to 2050 (Quinquennially, as of July 1) ProQuest Statistical Abstract of the U.S. 2014 Online Edition. Retrieved from http://statabs.proquest.com/sa/abstract.html?table-no=9&acc-no=C7095-1.1&year=2014&z=CC7ACAA06FB0D0A70E958C EE142E529C0CF1C839

Increasing Income Inequality

In 2013, the median household income for all Americans was $52,250 per year, up slightly from $51,915 in 2012. Black Americans made an average of $34,598 per year while Hispanics made $40,963, non-Hispanic whites earned $58,270, and Asian Americans earned $67,065 per year (DeNavas-Walt & Proctor, 2014). Incomes varied considerably across states, from a high of $72,483 per year in Maryland to a low of $37,963 per year in Mississippi (Noss, 2014).

Over the past 30 years, as the population has increased, the number of persons living in poverty has climbed steadily and is now at an all time high of 48.8 million persons or 20.6% of the population. One of the most

EXHIBIT 4.6

A Profile of Aging Successfully

Mrs. B is an 85-year-old retired executive from the banking industry. She had been married and had two sons, one of whom she lost at birth. Starting before she retired, Mrs. B. has been planning to age successfully. After serving as a caregiver for nine years for her mother who was in a long-term care facility, she knew that she had to plan for her own aging in the areas of housing, stimulating activities, and physical and emotional well-being. After retiring, she moved across country to live near her son and his family.

Being deliberate about the home in which she wanted to age-in-place, Mrs. B. spent over a year looking for just the right home to purchase. She "wants to feel at home" in a community that is comfortable, safe, and accessible where she can live for many years. She finds a roomy one-level condo within a short drive to all the necessities and amenities she needs. Moving again is not something she wants to do. She considers the aging possibilities that could force her to move and explores her options.

Upon arriving in her new home, Mrs. B. begins her search for activities that will keep her mentally and socially engaged. She searches until she finds the right combination of activities that feel comfortable. Along her journey, she takes classes, including dance and computers, connects with an older adult group, serves as a research assistant to a university professor with whom she works on three projects, helps start a wellness partners program, trains to be a support person for other older adults working on a change in their lives, and tutors third graders for several years. Though she never developed strong art skills before, she enjoys taking a sketching class. When she needs a new challenge, she embraces new activities. Currently, she is teaching English as a Second Language to a group of Chinese residents, volunteering for a state representative, serving as a volunteer and advisor for two university faculty members doing research on older adults, and while writing her biography, is delving into her own family history.

Mrs. B. shares these insights on aging: "I had to first anticipate what it means to get older and what I wanted my life to be when these changes came. What do you want to do and how will it affect you? Some things are scary. The physical changes aren't always pleasant and some people aren't respectful or patient with older adults. I look around at people and measure if I'm ok. I feel fortunate to be able to do what I am doing. That includes new experiences as well as what I have always done, just not as fast. I feel fortunate to be doing what I do."

Mrs. B. hopes younger people will be respectful of older adults. "They need to know an older adult is still actively living and for that, they need to be respected."

significant impacts of the Great Recession on the current social work environment is the increase in both the number and percentage of people living in poverty. On a hopeful note, poverty appears to have leveled out since 2012 in most states—with the exception of New Jersey, New Mexico, and Washington, and decreases in New Hampshire and Wyoming (Bishaw & Fontenot, 2014). The southern region of the U.S. continues to have the most persons living in poverty (16.1%), compared with 14.7% in the West, 12.9% in the Midwest, and 12.7% in the Northeast (DeNavas-Walt & Proctor, 2014).

As Exhibit 4.7 shows, the poverty rate for the non-Hispanic white population is now approximately 12.3%, while rates for African Americans and persons of Hispanic/Latino origin are over 27% and 25%, respectively, with the rate of poverty for African Americans remaining level (DeNavas Walt & Proctor, 2014). Only Asian Americans did not experience an increased rate of poverty. For those U.S. residents who immigrated to this country, 18% live below the poverty line, ranging from a high of 22.8% for non-citizens to 12.7% for naturalized citizens.

Income inequality continues to remain at record high levels, with the incomes of the top one percent of households rising 31% in 2015, while the incomes of the other 99% of households increased only 0.4% (Center on Budget & Policy Priorities (CBPP), 2014c). The per capita income of those living in poverty has remained unchanged over the past two decades, resulting in a decreasing income share for the poor and a widening gap between rich and poor (Buss, 2010). Overall median household incomes held steady from 2012 to 2013 but still remain 8% lower than in 2007, the year before the Great Recession, and 8.7% lower than in 1999 (DeNavas-Walt & Proctor, 2014). Consider aggregated 2013 household incomes by breaking them down into quintiles (DeNavas-Walt & Proctor, 2014):

Lowest quintile: $20,900 or less
Second quintile: $20,901–$40,187

EXHIBIT 4.7

Changes in U.S. Poverty Rate by Race/Ethnicity

Race/Ethnicity	2010	2012	Percent Change
Total	15.1	15	−0.10
White	13	12.7	−0.30
Black	27.4	27.2	−0.20
Asian/Pacific Islander	12.2	11.7	−0.50
Hispanic	26.5	25.6	−0.90

Source: U.S. Census Bureau, 2014d.

Third quintile:	$40,188–$65,501
Fourth quintile:	$65,502–$105,911
Top 5%:	$196,000 or more

Upon examination, the significance of these numbers becomes apparent. Families at the 50th percentile earn 8.7% less than they would have in 1999, and persons at the 10th percentile earn 14.3% less than they would have in 1999, but the income inequality ratio when comparing persons at the 90th and 10th percentiles has increased 16.2% since 1999 (DeNavas-Walt & Proctor, 2014). This means that the rich are continuing to accumulate wealth at high levels while middle- and lower-income households are losing ground.

Despite the fact that the Great Recession negatively impacted U.S. citizens at all economic levels, the small elite at the highest levels did not experience the same devastation as the majority of the population. Exhibit 4.8 provides a more detailed look. To place the gap into perspective, the richest 20% of the population receive 51% of all household income, while the remaining 80% receive a total of 49%.

A related issue is the "wealth gap." Wealth is the accumulation of financial resources. Two people may be earning the same income, but if one owns a home and has a 401(k), that person has more wealth than the other. Wealth often reflects the passing-along of property and financial resources from one generation to the next. A financial setback, such as the loss of a home due to foreclosure, may affect a family's wealth for generations. As Exhibit 4.9 shows, the bottom 90% of Americans have a much smaller share of national wealth than of national income.

A longer-term trend has been a discrepancy in the poverty rates between women and men. Over 15% of women and 13% of men currently live in poverty (DeNavas-Walt & Proctor, 2014). One reason for the discrepancy is that, despite the 1963 passage of the Equal Pay Act, women's incomes still lag behind their male counterparts (U.S. Census Bureau News, 2014). Interestingly, overall incomes for women have risen 5% since 1963, bringing the female-to-male earnings ratio to an all-time high of 0.78.3 (women earn 78.3 cents for every dollar men earn). While the "wage gap" (determined by dividing annual earnings for women by their male counterparts) has closed somewhat since the 1960s, discrepancies among racial and ethnic groups persist. From 2012 to 2013, earnings for all women rose 2.1%, with Hispanic women earning 4.8% more than other groups, but Asian women's earnings decreased 6.5% and African American and Caucasian women's earnings experienced no improvement (Institute for Women's Policy Research, 2014).

Despite some gains for women, the trend over the past few decades has been toward the "feminization" of poverty. Higher divorce rates and more households headed by single women have contributed to this trend. Poverty rates in female-headed households with no second wage earner are 30.6%

Wage gap
Difference between the wages of women and men.

EXHIBIT 4.8

The Growing Income Gap in the U.S.

Income Inequality Remained at Record Levels in 2012

Share of Household income, 1967 and 2012

Legend: 1967 | 2012

	Bottom 20 Percent	Second 20 Percent	Middle 20 Percent	Fourth 20 Percent	Top 20 Percent	Top 5 Percent
1967	4.0	10.8	17.3	24.2	43.6	17.2
2012	3.2	8.3	14.4	23.0	51.0	22.3

Source: U.S. Census Bureau

Center on Budget and Policy Priorities | cbpp.org

Source: Trisi, 2014a.

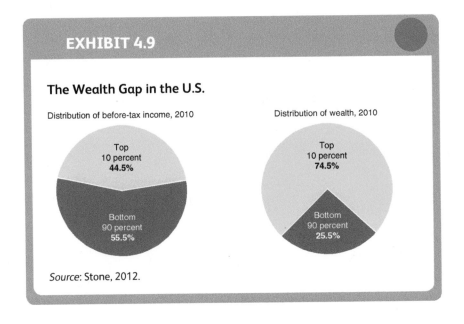

EXHIBIT 4.9

The Wealth Gap in the U.S.

Distribution of before-tax income, 2010

Top 10 percent 44.5%
Bottom 90 percent 55.5%

Distribution of wealth, 2010

Top 10 percent 74.5%
Bottom 90 percent 25.5%

Source: Stone, 2012.

while poverty rates for male-headed households with no second wage earner are 15.9% (DeNavas-Walt & Proctor, 2014).

Social workers can help to close that gap by addressing the structural causes of poverty and lobbying to increase women's and other at-risk group's opportunities for education, health coverage, child care, and employment that provides a living wage (National Association of Social Workers (NASW), 2012–2014j). When poverty rates increase, more people will need assistance with finances, health care, employment, job training, food, housing, utilities, transportation, and child care. In addition, family crises and violence often increase when families experience stress. Social workers need the skills to work with diverse families in crisis.

Trends in Religious Affiliation

At the beginning of the 21st century, approximately 1,600 different religions and denominations are being practiced in the United States. Almost half of those have been established in the past 40 years (Mindell, 2007). Conducted each decade, the U.S. Religion Census cites that nearly half of U.S. residents report membership in a religious institution (Briggs, 2012). The majority of those individuals practice a form of Christianity, but non-Christian-based (e.g., Judaism, Islam, Buddhism, and Hinduism) and nondenominational/independent religious institutions are increasing. Recently, membership appears to be decreasing among mainline religious organizations (i.e., approximately 13% decrease for Protestant and 1% for Catholic) (Briggs, 2012) but increasing by one-third for non-Christian groups and nondenominational churches (now the third largest religious group in the United States) (Briggs, 2012). Although people who self-identify as Muslim are a small percentage, their number, and the number of people who self-identify as members of other religions, is increasing. Increases in membership reported include Islam—109%; Buddhism—170%; Hinduism—237%. A portion of this change can be attributed to increases in immigration from the Middle East and Asia. Exhibit 4.10 depicts this growth.

Conflicts and attitudes toward religious and ethnic traditions are cause for great concern around the world. A recent Pew Research Center (Pew Research Global Attitudes Project, 2014c) finding cites religious and ethnic hatred as one of the top three threats to the world as reported by countries in four regions: Middle East (#1), United States and Africa (#2, tie), and Europe (#3). What role can the social work profession play in addressing this concern?

As a facet of being culturally competent, social workers need to be aware of their own religious and spiritual beliefs as well as those of others. They can then effectively incorporate spirituality into their practice and promote religious and spiritual acceptance and understanding. For example, having an inclusive

EXHIBIT 4.10

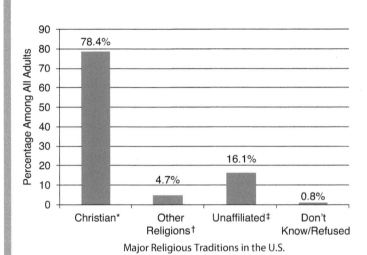

* Includes: Protestant, Catholic, Mormon, Jehovah's Witness, Orthodox and Other Christian.

† Includes: Jewish, Buddhist, Muslim, Hindu, and other world religions.

‡ Athiest, Agnostic, Unaffiliated.

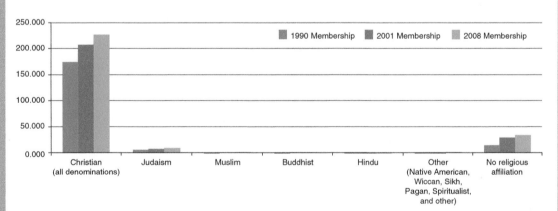

Religious Affiliation in the United States

Source: Pew Forum on Religion and Public Life (2008). U.S. religious landscape survey. Religious affiliation: Diverse and dynamic. Washington, D.C: Pew Forum on Religion and Public Life. Available at: http://religions.pewforum.org/pdf/report-religious-landscape-study-full.pdf; U.S. Census Bureau, 2011.

definition of spirituality such as the one that follows can be useful in conducting intake interviews and ongoing encounters with clients (Senreich, 2013):

> Spirituality refers to a human being's subjective relationship (cognitive, emotional, and intuitive) to what is unknowable about existence, and how a person integrates that relationship into a perspective about the universe, the world, others, self-moral values, and one's sense of meaning (p. 553).

With our skills in building on strengths, cultural competency, and coalition building, social workers are well positioned to engage in and promote dialogue to find common ground.

Because the population is aging and religious affiliation increases with age, social workers benefit from sensitivity to the roles religion and spirituality play in the lives of older adults. Regardless of the client's age, gender, race, ethnicity, or culture, integrating religious and spiritual information into the information-gathering, assessment, and intervention processes can expand a social worker's perspective on the client's situation and potentially provide helpful resources. Additionally, linking to religious and faith-based organizations may provide inroads into marginalized communities that would otherwise be difficult to reach (Crisp, 2014).

OPPRESSION AND DISCRIMINATION

Oppression
The restriction by one group over an individual or another group in the areas of activities, access to resources or ability to exercise their rights.

The groups social work practitioners serve face persistent oppression and discrimination. Oppression is an ongoing "set of policies, practices, traditions, norms, definitions, and explanations (discourses), which function to systematically exploit one social group to the benefit of another social group" (Sensoy & DiAngelo, 2012, p. 39). Oppression occurs when a group or groups within a society control or repress the actions or beliefs of other individuals, groups, and/or institutions. Young (2012) poignantly describes the five faces of oppression as:

- Exploitation of women and racial and ethnic minority groups through the absence of recognition of valued work;
- Marginalization of racial and ethnic groups, older adults, the unemployed, youth, single mothers with children, persons with disabilities, and Native Americans through policies that prevent participation and inclusion;
- Powerlessness which occurs when individuals or groups "lack authority, status, and sense of self" (p. 332);
- Cultural imperialism which enables the dominant group culture to become the norm; and
- Violence, which can take the form of harassment, intimidation, or physical attacks.

Oppression is formalized and overt when it is built into societal structures and systems, as in the historical treatment of gay, lesbian, bisexual, and transgender persons in society. However, it can also be informal and covert, such as the continued mistreatment of these groups despite the passage of hate crimes legislation. While oppression can take the form of systemic domination or exploitation of other societies, peoples, and resources or of one's fellow citizens, the outcome is always "social injustice, manifested in multidimensional, socially structured inequalities" (Gil, 2012, p. 24).

In contrast, discrimination is the *behavior* that expresses a bias toward an individual or group based on characteristics such as race, ethnicity, gender, religion, age, sexual orientation, mental and physical conditions, class, or lifestyle (Barker, 2014). Along with prejudice, discriminatory behaviors manifest on the individual level (Sensoy & DiAngelo, 2012). Both oppression and discrimination involve actions, and in both cases an individual or group exerts power over a less-powerful group, often through force, violence, or restriction of resources with oppression being more overarching and systemic than discrimination (Van Soest, 2008). In sum, oppression can be thought of as (Sensoy & DiAngelo, 2012, p. 39):

Prejudice and Discrimination + Power = Oppression

To better understand the significance of this statement, consider the situation in which those persons or groups who wield power in economic, political, and social areas also hold (and act on) attitudes and beliefs that are discriminatory against one or more groups. When these two situations come together, systemic or institutionalized oppression can occur.

In spite of the fact that many people come to the United States to escape oppression and discrimination in their homelands, U.S. history has been fraught with devastating and longstanding examples of both. Persons of color, women, homosexual, transsexual, or transgender persons, persons living with a disability, and many immigrant, refugee, and religious groups have been mistreated. If such treatment goes unchallenged, both the oppressed and the oppressors may rationalize oppression and discrimination, and therefore perpetuate these behaviors. For example, both the oppressed and the oppressors may come to believe that those in power are, in fact, superior to or acting to protect those being oppressed (Van Soest, 2008).

Regardless of its form, all oppression has the following characteristics (Van Soest, 2008, p. 323):

1. Those viewed as "normal, mainstream, or traditional" are perceived to have power, and those who are seen as "abnormal, eccentric, or radical" are perceived as lesser or subordinate to the groups who possess power.
2. Violence or the threat of violence is at the root of oppressive acts.

3. The oppression persists because it is institutionalized—that is, it is built into the policies and practices of institutions.
4. Oppression becomes a part of the fabric of the oppressing group, and those being oppressed become devalued or invisible.

Oppression is thus a deep-seated and persistent element of the social world. To exist, oppression must be (Sensoy & DiAngelo, 2012):

■ historically sustained by passing from one generation to the next (e.g., oppression of women, African Americans, and religious minority groups);
■ ideologically integrated into a society's policies and practices (e.g., banning interracial and same-sex marriage);
■ institutionally adopted through the passage of legislation and regulations (e.g., prohibiting same-sex relationships and marriage); and
■ culturally accepted through unspoken and unconscious perpetuation of oppressive beliefs and actions (e.g., women's work is not as valued as men's).

The Social Work *Code of Ethics* (NASW, 2008) calls for social workers to work to fight oppression. As Martin Luther King Jr. said: "Injustice anywhere is a threat to justice everywhere" (King, 1963).

CYCLE OF OPPRESSION

Oppression is self-perpetuating. The cycle of oppression is a three-step process:

1. Everyone is born into a social group. Oppression develops when we absorb stereotypes, misinformation, biased history, and missing facts about both our own groups and other social groups.
2. We are socialized by people we know, respect, trust, and love to follow certain rules about how to be, think, and behave. The misinformation we receive about other groups is reinforced by the people and entities within our individual environments.
3. Continued socialization then becomes internalized, and we come to accept societal values. The oppressed begin to believe the dominant culture's stereotypes, resulting in the inability to distinguish truth from misinformation.

Each phase of the cycle of oppression can elicit one or more of the following reactions from both oppressors and the oppressed:

■ *Emotional reaction:* The emotions that one feels about oppressive attitudes and behaviors may include anger, guilt, sadness, confusion, and aliena-tion. The individual must determine how to act on one or a combination of these emotional responses.

- *Internalization:* Emotions rooted in stereotypes can evolve into attitudes and behaviors that may then become part of a person's mindset. The person may then act on these attitudes at either a conscious or unconscious level. Internalized dominance allows one to rationalize her or his privilege as natural and earned and justifies the perpetuation of superiority (Sensoy & DiAngelo, 2012).
- *Collusion:* Individuals may simply accept the oppression they encounter and thus act in ways that perpetuate the cycle of oppression.
- *Dissonance:* When the emotions, attitudes, and behaviors that occur through socialization come up against contrary evidence about a group, individuals often respond by examining and exploring their feelings about the oppression they have observed, which can result in a newfound understanding of the oppression experienced.

As this list of reactions implies, the only way to break the cycle of oppression is to confront stereotypes, prejudices, and discriminatory or submissive tendencies. Strategies for promoting social justice practices and behaviors may include legal mandates and changing social interactions (Society for Research in Child Development, 2011a). There will always be diversity and difference, so we must learn to understand, accept, and value diversity. Social workers have a lead role to play in breaking the cycle.

Social Work and Oppression

Throughout the history of the profession, social workers have played an active role in working to eliminate social injustices that arise from oppression and discrimination. They have helped vulnerable groups organize, as in the case of welfare rights organizations, and they have advocated for change in the legislative arena at both federal and state levels. Social workers have lobbied and, in some cases, sought elected office to work for justice for victims of domestic violence and hate crimes. They have campaigned for access to housing and public facilities for older adults and for persons with disabilities.

As they work to reduce oppression and discrimination, social workers abide by the following principles:

- People are not born with prejudice; they learn it—and can unlearn it.
- We all make assumptions about others, which can lead either to prejudicial attitudes and discriminatory behaviors or to cultural insight and appreciation for diversity.
- Devaluation and disempowerment are preconditions for prejudice and oppression.

■ All people have prejudices, but not all people can enforce their attitudes through institutions and systems of power.

■ Discrimination and oppression create real problems for oppressed groups.

■ Those who are not oppressed enjoy a privilege that is a social and economic (or political) benefit.

■ Assigning guilt and blame for discrimination and oppression immobilize individuals and groups; social workers must focus instead on issues and solutions.

As a profession, we are obligated to deal with the privilege and oppression present in our own and our clients' lives. We can listen to the experiences of our clients, and be willing to take action to eliminate oppression and discrimination (Johnson, 2013). To do so, we must recognize that privilege is typically so internalized that those with privilege do not realize they have it (Sensoy & DiAngelo, 2012). As you review the following statements (Sensoy & DiAngelo, 2012, pp. 74–75), determine if you have experienced or observed them and reflect on the impact of the statements on the social work profession:

■ "If we haven't personally discriminated, we are not benefitting."

■ "If we can't feel our social and institutional power, we don't have it."

■ "If a minority person is in charge, there is no oppression."

■ "If we are oppressed in one social group membership, we can't be privileged in another."

Consider the situation that Kristina, a BSW who worked in a homeless prevention agency, faced one day when a refugee from Sudan came to her agency for help. Her agency provided clients with rent support, food, clothing, and assistance procuring identification and documentation. The client reported that he was addicted to alcohol and had no current documentation. Kristina was having a challenging day and struggling to engage with the client, and reports that she was likely not attentive or actively listening. The client confronted her about her seeming lack of interest in his situation. They were able to have an open and honest dialogue and went on to develop a productive working relationship in which Kristina was able to help the client meet his goals. In reflecting on this experience, Kristina realized that she was contributing to the oppressive and discriminatory experiences of her client who had fled his home country out of fear of persecution. She gained insight into the importance of listening to her client, meeting him where he was, accepting his words, and being honest, open, and empathetic.

Kristina's experience is emblematic of the importance of critical reflection and of being open to acknowledging that even as a helping professional with the best of intentions, we can exhibit privilege and perpetuate oppressive

EXHIBIT 4.11

Group Identities Across Relations of Power

Minoritized/Target Group	Oppression	Dominant/Agent Group
Persons of Color	Racism	White
Working-Class/Persons living in poverty	Classism	Persons of middle and upper socioeconomic classes
Women	Sexism	Men
Transgender Persons	Cis-genderism	Heteronormativity
Persons who are lesbian, gay, bisexual, and two-spirited	Heterosexism	Heterosexuals
Persons who are Muslim, Buddhists, Jewish, Hindu, and other non-Christian groups	Religious oppression and anti-Semitism	Christians
Persons with disabilities	Ableism	Able-bodied
Immigrants (perceived) and indigenous persons	Nationalism	Citizens (perceived)

Adapted from: Sensoy & DeAngelo, 2012, p. 42.

practices. Exhibit 4.11 provides examples of institutional, political, and cultural oppression.

Social Work and Social Justice

When faced with social injustice, what is the social worker's ethical obligation? The profession's *Code of Ethics* (2008) charges us to strive for finding a socially just solution. Social justice must be viewed within the context of a society's history, traditions, and institutions (Reisch, Ife, & Weil, 2013). Gil (2012) contends that just societies promote equality, liberty, individuality, cooperation, and a collectivity orientation (or mutualism) and through advocating for socially just policies and practices, social workers can help to ensure that resources are distributed with the goal of equality for everyone. Such advocacy can be done on the individual level (e.g., fighting for one family's landlord to test and treat their home for lead paint which is a serious health hazard for children) to the group level (e.g., serving as the voice for a group of transgender teens who want gender-neutral bathrooms in their school or want to be able to use the bathrooms of the gender with which they identify) to the community level (e.g., standing with residents of Ferguson, Missouri, as they protest racial discrimination) to the global level (e.g., calling for attention to the physical, emotional, and sexual violence perpetrated upon children and youth that results in tens of thousands of deaths each year in many developing countries). In each example, the social worker can be more effective using a client-centered approach that embraces social justice. Allowing clients to describe their perception of the issue and desired solution, building on clients' strengths and resources, and acknowledging that social justice may mean different things to different people are three strategies for helping clients gain justice (Hodge, 2010). You can use evidence-based research and social media to advocate for justice; bring public attention to the issues by speaking out in person, through writing in news outlets, and by providing testimony; and help the client voice concerns to those who need to hear them.

Anti-oppressive social work practice is a logical extension of the ethical mandate to achieve social justice for our clients. Anti-oppressive practice is a social change orientation focused on client empowerment (Dominelli, 2012). It is grounded in a commitment to clients' resilience and social activism based on a belief in human rights and citizenship; views individuals as agents of change in their own lives and values their uniqueness; addresses structural inequities, dominance, and the need to redistribute resources; and supports holistic and innovative interventions (p. 331). To practice in an anti-oppressive manner, social workers can engage in the following types of professional activities (Dominelli, 2012):

- Take individual and collective action to address inequities within organizations and communities.
- Proactively form and participate in alliances and mobilize people and communities to address structural inequities at personal, institutional, and sociocultural levels.
- Anticipate the risks and controversies inherent in politically-charged issues.
- Conduct research to understand the issues.
- Educate people about inequities.
- Foster egalitarian social relationships and partnerships to promote empowerment (pp. 338–339).

Now that you understand the role social workers play in combating oppression and advocating for social justice, consider some of the political, economic, and social challenges and opportunities that confront society and, in particular, the social work profession. Social workers need specialized knowledge and skills to practice competently in an ever-changing society. Current demographic changes present both challenges and opportunities for social work practice. Social workers must be aware of these changes so they can respond to the needs of diverse client groups.

CHALLENGES AND OPPORTUNITIES FACING SOCIAL WORKERS

Emily began to notice that the domestic violence shelter program where she worked served an increasing number of women whose first language was not English and who frequently had limited English-speaking skills. The community was experiencing an overall increase in refugees and immigrants from Eastern Europe, Russia, African and Middle Eastern countries, and Spanish-speaking countries. The women in the shelter were being identified primarily through hospital emergency rooms where they were seeking emergency medical treatment.

Emily and her co-workers realized that their understanding of domestic violence within other cultures was limited. They also recognized that program staff and volunteers spoke only English and therefore had to rely on the women's family members (often their children, who were more proficient in English) or the on-call interpreters engaged by the hospitals. Without regular interpreters, it was difficult for Emily to establish rapport, gather information, and develop supportive and helpful interventions with this client group. Consequently, Emily and her co-workers became increasingly concerned that their agency and other agencies that provided services to victims of intimate partner violence and their children were not effectively serving non-English-speaking clients. Having identified this gap in the service delivery system, the shelter staff developed a twofold plan to enhance services. This plan included gaining increased knowledge of the clients' cultures and creating a pool of volunteer interpreters. Having more competence working with a diverse population and ready access to an interpreter who is not related to the client or based at the hospital enabled the staff to develop more accurate and appropriate assessment and intervention plans for clients.

As you have learned, social work practice is often shaped by current political, economic, and social philosophies, ideologies, and events. Changes bring new and controversial issues for social workers, but social work's "values and mission ... anchor the profession in the sea of change" (Allen-Meares, 2000, p. 179). In order to see opportunities for affecting change in political, economic, and social environments, social workers must gain insight into the ultimate outcomes being sought, that is, needs of the community to achieve the desired well-being needs. Once identified, these goals can then be incorporated into the social work intervention. Quick Guide 4.1 provides an overview of community well-being within these three environments.

QUICK GUIDE #4.1 CONCEPTUALIZING COMMUNITY WELL-BEING

Political Well-Being:

✓ All people should have freedom to associate, speak, vote, and participate in the governments that make policy for them.

✓ As noted in the Ethics in Social Work, Statement of Principles, "Social workers should promote the full involvement and participation of people using their services in ways that enable them to be empowered in all aspects of decisions and actions affecting their lives" (IFSW & IASSW, 2004, p. 2).

Economic Well-Being:

✓ Economic systems—the production, distribution, and consumption of commodities and services— should include opportunities for paid and unpaid work and asset development.

✓ Livelihoods encompass the striving people do for themselves, their families, and their communities. A wide variety of livelihoods should be available to encourage creative, artistic, esthetic, and inventive endeavors. Livelihood opportunities should not exclude differently abled people.

✓ Wages should be sufficient to meet a family's needs for shelter, food, health care, transportation, and continuing or higher education.

✓ Economic well-being requires equitable economic and exchange systems as well as information systems and infrastructure. Exchange and financial systems, the reciprocal placed on particular commodities and services, must be transparent and fair.

✓ Degradation to the environment as well as cleanup costs and the costs of rehabilitation that result from damage to health should be included in production costs. Overconsumption should be recognized as a danger to individuals as well as to the planet.

✓ Measures such as Gross National Product (GNP) and Gross National Income (GNI) are deficient for measuring well-being. The costs of war, violence, prisons, and deaths due to poverty should be subtracted from well-being measures whereas uncompensated contributions such as child rearing and volunteer work should be added.

Social Well-Being:

✓ All people should have access to the supports and opportunities provided by social institutions and relationships. In other words, everyone should have access to supportive families or surrogate families, neighborhoods, and communities.

✓ Everyone—women and men, girls and boys—should have the opportunity to engage in education, recreation, cultural organizations, spiritual and religious institutions, and political organizations.

✓ Families, neighborhoods, and communities must have supportive health, welfare, education, security (i.e., basic human needs), and policy-making organizations to help them invest in their children and future generations.

Source: Gamble, 2012 (first introduced in Gamble & Weil, 2010 and adapted by Gamble, 2011).

Political Environment

Because funding for social services is often a volatile and controversial political issue, the political climate in the United States has always had a significant impact on the social work profession. As you read in Chapters 2 and 3, the political climate of the early part of this century shifted in a more conservative direction, resulting in decreased political and financial support for many social service programs and resources. The end of the 20th century, much like its beginning, was known as a "period of increasing political tension," with issues of race, culture, diversity, civil rights, immigration, religion, abortion, gun control, and nontraditional families at the forefront of the political scene (Austin, 1997, p. 398). With a shift toward an antigovernment sentiment, the 21st century began with much the same antisocial service sentiment, but experienced some glimmers of hope with the enactment of the Economic Stimulus and Affordable Care Act initiatives. Because the issues with which practitioners work have long been "politicized," social workers cannot view their work as apolitical.

The 2008 election of Barack Obama signaled a shift in the political climate and, optimistically, a commitment to bipartisan collaboration aimed at enhancing the quality of life for Americans, particularly those in need. For example, the passage of the American Recovery and Reinvestment Act of 2009 (known as the economic stimulus package) was a result of a cooperative effort on the part of politicians from both parties in the House of Representatives, the Senate, the Obama transition team, and the newly appointed administration (Council on Social Work Education, 2009).

The 2008 elections provided considerable hope for those working in the social service arena. President Obama's campaign agenda and his economic stimulus package and health care reform were evidence of the administration's strong commitment to strengthening not only the economy but also the social infrastructure of our society. The economic stimulus package allocated hundreds of millions of dollars for services for health, children and families, older adults, Native Americans, education, persons with disabilities, employment, and housing. Elements of the economic stimulus package, like the infusion of new funds into Temporary Assistance to Needy Families (TANF), employment and educational programs, unemployment insurance, child care and support, Supplemental Nutrition Assistance Program, emergency shelter, and tax credit programs—Child Tax (up to $1,000/child) and Making Work Pay ($400/worker), specifically focused on those with low and moderate incomes (CBPP, 2009). The new and expanded initiatives resulted in keeping 6.9 million persons above the poverty line: tax credit—3.1 million; unemployment insurance—3.4 million; and SNAP—1.0 million (numbers reflect multiple programs/person) (Sherman, 2014). The initial optimism that surrounded the Obama administration quickly gave way, however, to unpleasant political and economic realities. The economic recession, bipartisan divisions, and mounting concerns about the federal budget became the focus of the political environment.

The 2010 passage of the Affordable Care Act (ACA) renewed optimism among health and social service providers. While it is still too early to determine the full impact of the ACA, to date some encouraging outcomes include: reduced medication costs for Medicare recipients; expansion of prevention services for persons of all ages; health care coverage through parents' policies for young adults until age 26; Medicaid expansion (although not all states have opted in); improved communication regarding benefits and processes; a health insurance marketplace in place in all states, with stipulations against discrimination based on pre-existing conditions or gender; and higher Medicare taxes for the country's highest wage earners.

Challenges in the Political Environment From the early days of the social work profession, social workers have initiated change by working inside the political system (Reisch, 2000). Reisch (1997, p. 90) challenges the profession to consider the following:

> We have long operated under the illusion that compassion alone will produce change. Although compassion motivates some people to act and think differently, it is insufficient to transform the deep-rooted institutional indifference of our society.

In the midst of political and economic turbulence, the continuation of many social service programs requires social workers to integrate their work with individuals, families, groups, organizations, and communities, and political activism to ensure that adequate funding and resources continue to be available for those services.

Conservative political trends early in the 21st century have had considerable impact on social policy. The century began with a large-scale transfer of policy making from the national to state level, creating widespread inequities in the way that individual states administer social policies and programs (Schneider, 2002). Additionally, the government is increasingly contracting outside agencies to provide services. While such policy decisions may be intended to drive efficiency and lower costs, social workers can monitor to ensure such policies are socially just. Using evidence-based critical thinking skills, social workers can analyze and organize the facts, develop informed positions, and advocate for socially just policies to best serve client systems (Colby, 2008). Another recent political development has been the rise of hyper-partisanship. The U.S. is more politically polarized than it has been in over twenty years, resulting in a doubling of those persons who identify as consistently conservative or liberal in their political ideologies (i.e., fewer commonalities between Republicans and Democratic Party members) (Pew Research Center for the People & the Press, 2014). The hyper-partisan political environment has created an ongoing debate and dissension regarding the funding of health, education, and social service programming, oftentimes resulting in the decrease or cessation of needed funding. Energy assistance, reproductive health services (specifically, through Planned Parenthood), housing, Medicaid, and Supplemental Security Income (SSI) programs are just some of the threatened programs. In his 2012 State of the Union address, President Obama called for change in this era of hyper-partisanship:

> We need to end the notion that the two parties must be locked in a perpetual campaign of mutual destruction; that politics is about clinging to rigid ideologies instead of building consensus around common-sense ideas.

Then, in his 2014 State of the Union Address, Obama called upon Congress to see 2014 as a "year of action" in which to address such issues as income inequality, minimum wage, health care coverage, immigration reform, and education. However, resolution or even progress on each of these issues has been stymied due to partisan opposition. For example, Obama's charges to Congress to raise the minimum wage, support health care reform, pass immigration reform, and fund educational initiatives all face opposition from legislators, primarily members of the Republican Party.

While Obama's words are considered by many to be motivational, change in this longstanding partisan climate will be slow to occur. Social workers engaged on the frontlines of the social service delivery system can strive to meet the President's challenges by advocating for their clients at local and agency, state, national, and international levels. Social workers are well positioned to document and draw attention to how political decisions can impede their clients' ability to achieve and maintain economic stability, much less progress to a higher level of economic security.

Within the global political environment there exists an array of global issues of particular concern to social workers. The following such issues have reached crisis proportions: widespread poverty; immigration, migration, and displacement trends; devastatingly acute and chronic health issues (e.g., HIV/AIDS and Ebola); food insecurities leading to malnutrition and illness; trade issues; religious-motivated discrimination and violence; violence against women and children; terrorism; and government corruption.

Social workers in international and domestic settings witness the impact of widespread world poverty, rising AIDS and malnutrition-related deaths in developing countries, and increasing military and government corruption that hinders productivity and equality, international support, and credibility. Lack of access to adequate food, health care, education, and government protection have motivated many to leave their home countries. The "Arab Spring" (the recent wave of political demonstrations in the Middle East), civil wars around the globe, increases in extreme poverty in Sub-Saharan Africa, and the continued criminalization of homosexuality in 78 countries (seven of which have the death penalty for those convicted) have led to decreased access to the basic services needed to survive, and many individuals and families have fled their homes out of fear for their lives, often to live in refugee camps lacking adequate support and stability.

In 2013, for the first time in history, a total of 51.2 million persons, half of them under the age of 18, were forcibly displaced from their home countries due to persecution, conflict, violence, and/or human rights violations (United Nations High Commissioner for Refugees (UNHCR), 2014). The highest number of persons fled from Afghanistan, Syrian Arab Republic, and Somalia, and most fled to Pakistan, Islamic Republic of Iran, Lebanon, Jordan, and Turkey (UNHCR, 2014). For these many individuals and families living with instability, the possibilities for experiencing continued poverty, violence, and physical and mental health problems abound.

While the U.S. is a country founded by immigrants, over time our policies and attitudes toward immigration have become less welcoming. The general population is sharply divided on the issue (Pew Research Center Hispanic Trends Project, 2013). Those who support liberal immigration policies see benefits for the immigrants themselves and value the economic contributions and increased diversity that immigrants provide. Opponents posit that immigrants over-use U.S. healthcare, education, and welfare systems, placing a burden on these systems without contributing to them (Ali & Hartman, 2015). Immigrants face considerable challenges when migrating to a new country, regardless of their destination. They may face discrimination, racial and ethnic tension, dilemmas regarding assimilation, and, in the most extreme situations, human trafficking (Ali & Hartman, 2015). While these issues are not typically a high priority for presidential administrations, in November 2014, President Obama announced significant executive actions related to immigration policy. With an emphasis on preserving and reuniting families, the President's proposed plans focused on prevention of parental and child deportations, developing priority levels for handling immigrant detainees, increasing resources for border security, and easing eligibility requirements for Green Cards.

Consider the increasing crisis of Latino children and youth from Central America who risk their lives to flee gang violence, the drug trade, and poverty, entering the U.S. illegally at a rate that more than doubled from 2013 to 2014 (over 60,000 children and youth), often to join family members with the optimistic belief they will not be deported (Krogstad, 2014). President Obama has described the crisis as an "urgent situation," but the U.S. response has been politicized and divided. Unaccompanied children entering the U.S. is just one example of one of the areas in which social workers are ethically obligated to "work with the causalities of globalization; with those whose movement in time and space is limited in some way, by age or gender, class or caste, imprisonment or infirmity" (Cree, 2013b, p. 216). For up-to-date information on immigration and migration, visit the International Organization for Migration at: www.iom.int/cms/en/sites/iom/home.html.

Opportunities in the Political Environment Using our grounding in the strengths-based and empowerment perspectives, social workers can seize opportunities to engage with and influence political decision-makers both inside and outside the U.S. Social workers can effect political change through both education and participation. Throughout history, social workers have strived to make client systems, community residents, organizational staff, and policy-makers aware of how political systems render social services inadequate to meet the needs of people (Reisch, 1997). Social workers have long engaged in the electoral advocacy and lobbying process, becoming candidates for political office, encouraging candidates to support issues that are important to their clients, supporting candidates who may be excluded from political office due to the exorbitant costs of contemporary political campaigns, and working to promote government monitoring of the social service delivery system (Reisch, 2000).

NASW has a longstanding commitment to helping social workers be involved in political activity. Political Action for Candidate Election (PACE) endorses and financially supports national, state, and local candidates from any party whose political platforms are consistent with the NASW agenda. To learn more about PACE and the candidates it supports, visit the NASW website at: www.socialworkers.org/pace/default.asp.

PACE-endorsed Edolphus "Ed" Towns, a Democratic Congressman and social worker from New York introduced legislation to enact the Dorothy I. Height and Whitney M. Young Jr. Social Work Reinvestment Act, and worked with 53 Congressional colleagues to launch the Congressional Social Work Caucus. This bi-partisan congressional caucus (i.e., a political group or meeting focused on a specific issue) has the following objectives (www.socialwork reinvestment.org):

- Initiate and support legislation to address the unique challenges and opportunities for professional social workers.
- Monitor and evaluate programs and legislation designed to assist and support individuals, families, and communities at all income levels who are coping with economic, social, and health problems, particularly those with limited resources.

■ Provide Congressional staff members with educational tools and resources directed toward improving the social work profession and the people social workers serve.

■ Assist in education and awareness efforts on the breadth and scope of the social work profession.

At the inaugural event of the Caucus held on World Social Work Day 2011, Congressman Towns shared these inspiring words:

> I am excited about the possibilities for our newly created Congressional Social Work Caucus. This Caucus will provide a platform in the House of Representatives where social workers' voices can be heard, social workers' concerns can be addressed and social work's best and brightest can serve their fellow Americans in meaningful ways. Whitney M. Young spoke many times about how important it is for social workers to tell our story. We want to have a stronger voice in the national conversation about what needs to be done to strengthen families, protect the elderly, and make sure children have the opportunity to prosper. The Congressional Social Work Caucus plans to host a series of public briefings this year to explore the impact professional social workers have on health care, mental health, aging, and child protection outcomes. We want to educate legislators, their staffs, and the public on issues that challenge the social work profession.

To learn more about the work of Congressman Towns and the Caucus, visit the Social Work Reinvestment Initiative website at: www.socialworkreinvestment.org.

Social workers can embrace opportunities to influence political decision making through a variety of strategies, including working to increase voter registration and participation, advocating for legislation that supports clients and services, and getting involved in the political process through campaigning, joining PACE or other groups and coalitions working for policy change, and even running for political office. For example, following the tragic police-involved shooting of Michael Brown in Ferguson, Missouri, social workers have worked with community groups to register voters, particularly in the African American community. Increasing voter participation is one strategy to begin to address some of the concerns raised in the aftermath of the shooting regarding lack of representation within city government. Many social workers organize client groups to engage in advocacy efforts at local, state, and federal levels. Strengthening the role of social work in the public sector can help political leaders understand better the needs of client systems and the groups with whom we work. Such understanding is critical when social workers advocate for policy changes. Social workers have been on the front lines of the campaign to pass legislation for same-sex marriage, to seek justice for the tens of thousands of children crossing into the U.S. without documentation, and to advocate for the ethical use of drugs not yet approved for use to treat victims of the Ebola virus in Africa.

The ever-changing relationship between the social work profession and the political environment can be both frustrating and exhilarating, but the relationship is worth tending. For example, in 2011, the Occupy Movement raised awareness of the wealth gap in the United States and provided social workers with an opportunity to engage in the political process. The Occupiers challenged the leadership of our country to invest in ecological reforms, electoral changes, and changes to the American infrastructure (Mason, 2012, p. 3). The Occupiers inspired similar strategies (staging peaceful demonstrations) to address social injustices at the local, state, national, and international levels.

Occupy Movement

Source: iStock/Richmatts

As a voting public, we must demand that our elected officials examine economic inequalities, particularly the causes of poverty and its economic and social realities. Policy change begins with a public discussion. We can, for example, advocate for policies that promote gender equality in terms of resources, roles, and power relations and recognize both women and men share in unpaid family caregiving responsibilities (Daly, 2012). As an example, recall the strategic efforts employed by the suffragettes in gaining the right to vote. Beginning at the grassroots level, the issue of women's suffrage was brought into the public arena by women organizing and advocating for change.

Understanding the impact of global events on social work practice can enable social workers to better serve increasingly diverse client systems. Supporting political efforts to increase international aid efforts combatting poverty and hunger, improving access to health care, and eliminating government corruption are all strategies consistent with the values of the social work profession. The 2014 report entitled *Global Agenda for Social Work and Social Development: First Report–Promoting Social and Economic Equalities* identifies an opportunity for social workers to advocate for social justice at the global level. Compiled by a multinational group of social workers from the International Association of Schools of Social Work (IASSW), the International Council on Social Welfare (ICSW), and the International Federation of Social Workers (IFSW), the report draws attention to evidence-based findings about inequality, including:

- *People cannot be developed by others:* Our frontline experience teaches us that to escape from poverty and oppressive situations, people need to be actively involved in their own futures.
- *The cornerstone of a thriving economy is a stable, well-resourced, and educated community:* Though governments often argue that they cannot afford to invest in community, social work experience plainly indicates that investing in community stimulates entrepreneurship, skill development, cultural innovations, and business growth and widens opportunities for young people, men, and women.
- *Equitable societies support their citizens' happiness and well-being:* Severe inequalities in distribution of wealth cause social instability, crime, and health problems, negatively affecting everyone.
- *When people have a collective voice, they are better able to advocate for their rights and participate in decision-making processes, which enhances their well-being* (pp. 11–12).

Social workers are acting at the individual and family level to help unaccompanied children and youth entering the U.S. from other countries (primarily from Honduras, El Salvador, Guatemala, and other parts of Central America) find pro bono legal services, adjust to their living situation, get enrolled in school, and meet their other immediate needs (Malai, 2014). Social workers use their knowledge of immigrant cultures, the barriers immigrants face, and the gap between the public perception of immigrants and the realities of immigration to advocate for immigration-friendly policies and practices (Elliott & Segal, 2012). Through the 2014 *Social Justice Brief: Unaccompanied Migrant Children: Overview & Recommendations,* NASW supports the following recommendations of The First Focus Campaign for Children to Congress and the Obama administration:

■ Adopt a "best interest of the child" standard for addressing the needs of unaccompanied children.

■ Increase funding to meet the needs of unaccompanied children when they are detained and to see to their ongoing care in the community, including legal, medical, mental health, and educational services, reunification efforts, and home studies.

■ Establish effective and cost-efficient alternatives to family detention centers.

■ Strengthen screening and due process mechanisms for children and youth.

■ Ensure that temporary U.S. Customs and Border Patrol (CBP) facilities where children are detained meet humanitarian standards.

Social workers have many opportunities to engage the various political systems. Consider volunteering for political candidates who share your goals, joining PACE, running for political office, testifying before state or national legislatures, or joining in a peaceful demonstration.

Economic Environment

The economy is inextricably linked to the political climate and has a powerful influence on the social work profession. To practice effectively, social workers need to understand how the U.S. and global economies relate to daily work with clients. For example, the overall employment opportunities in a community, which can be tied to the economic health of the region, will affect a social worker's efforts to help people trying to secure jobs.

The U.S. economy in recent years has benefited only those who were already quite wealthy, while creating difficulties for most people. Widespread social and economic inequities (the rich becoming richer, the poor becoming poorer, and the middle class disappearing) have increased poverty rates for persons of color, children, women, immigrants, and older adults. The severe economic downturn that began in 2007–2008 and continued into 2012 led many employers to lay off workers, consolidate jobs, use temporary workers who do not receive costly employee benefits, and move companies out of the country to less expensive work environments. Employment instability, particularly in periods of economic recession, typically results in increased unemployment and underemployment (e.g., more temporary workers and individuals working at lower-level positions) and forced employees to be more flexible, to give up assumptions about long-term commitments from employers, and to be prepared for longer durations of unemployment (Hollister, 2011). Men working in the private sector were hit particularly hard, while employment stability for women remained largely unchanged (likely due to the increased number of women in the workforce) (Hollister, 2011). These trends mean social workers will encounter more persons with greater economic needs, individuals seeking employment for longer periods of time, families who have lost their homes due to foreclosures, families living apart due to employment and/ or homelessness, and individuals and families who have never previously utilized social services. The U.S. economy in the beginning of the second decade of the 21st century unfortunately continued this historical trend.

The economy began its slow recovery in June 2009. Unemployment, underemployment, poverty, and foreclosure rates have all lessened thanks, in large part, to the economic stimulation and affordable care act initiatives. Over 10 million jobs have been restored or added, lowering the unemployment rate from its 2010 high of 10% to 5.9% in 2014 and 5.1% in 2015 (Center for Budget Policy & Priorities (CBPP), 2014b). At the height of the recession, there were seven unemployed persons for every open position. This number has now dropped to two persons for every opening. The Gross Domestic Product (GDP) (i.e., value of goods and services produced) has steadily been increasing as well and has been aided by the economic stimulus initiative.

Challenges in the Economic Environment Despite the economic upturn, challenges continue to confront U.S. and global economies. As noted in Chapter 3, persons experiencing extreme poverty and portions of those in the middle class have not enjoyed the levels of relief that other groups, particularly those at the highest socioeconomic levels, have experienced. Globalization, the shift from a manufacturing economy to a service-oriented one, and an upsurge in technology, have meant dramatic changes for the U.S. population, and for the middle class in particular (Leicht & Fitzgerald, 2014, p. 5). Where long-term employment was once considered the norm, most people now work at a job for 1–2 years. Employee loyalty is no longer rewarded as it once was, and, with economic instability, the rules of marriage, family life, home ownership, saving for children's education and the future, and planning for retirement, are now less certain (Leicht & Fitzgerald, 2014). Poverty, once thought to be an urban issue, has become a suburban challenge as well. Consider, for instance, the demographic and economic shift that occurred in Ferguson, Missouri, a shift that many people view as an antecedent to the events of the summer and fall of 2014 that began when African American teen, Michael Brown, was fatally wounded after being shot by a police officer. In 2000, Ferguson's racial make-up was approximately half White and half African American, with 5% unemployment. Within a decade, two-thirds of Ferguson residents were African American, and the unemployment rate had risen to 13% (Nicks, 2014). The Great Recession hit hard in communities like Ferguson, causing residents to become poorer. The community, including businesses and social services, were left with increasing economic and political strife.

Economic turbulence has pervasive and challenging implications for social work practice, both domestically and abroad. It seriously affects both the lives of clients and the social worker's ability to provide services and promote economic stability. An unstable economy can generate financial, social, and emotional difficulties for all citizens, but especially for those who are economically vulnerable. Women and persons of color may be particularly vulnerable, as these two groups often have the least stable employment histories and are the first to be laid off in times of economic hardship. Many U.S. military veterans returning from overseas deployments face challenges adjusting to civilian life, securing employment, and reintegrating into their families and communities. In 2012, President Obama initiated a plan, Veterans Job Corps, to create more jobs specifically targeted at military veterans. This program will employ post-9/11 veterans in conservation-related jobs, building roads and levees, and in the country's fire and law enforcement departments.

Even in a recovering economic period, social workers whose agencies experience downsizing as a result of decreased funding and fewer private contributions often face larger caseloads and thus have less time to devote to each client. An increased emphasis on cost-effectiveness in social service delivery can result in fewer resources being allocated to clients. Because of the recent economic recession, the majority of state governments decreased state budgets, many to pre-recession level—cuts averaged 10% (adjusting for inflation) (Leachman, Williams, & Johnson, 2011). The majority of states that cut public funding targeted pre-kindergarten through post-secondary education, health care-related programs that primarily impacted persons living on limited incomes, and public welfare programs (Leachman et al., 2011).

In the current period of economic recovery, there are some reasons for optimism. More people are employed, have health care coverage, and are experiencing the benefits of the safety net. According to the Supplemental Poverty Measure (SPM), the safety net provided some economic relief to 39 million persons, 8 million of whom are children (Trisi, 2014b). The safety net programs that provided the greatest benefit include Social Security, rent subsidies, SNAP, and Earned Income Tax Credit. Such programs make up a larger portion of the U.S. safety net than they did 50 years ago, providing support for the need to continue these programs (Trisi, 2014b). By providing a larger portion of the safety net, these programs effectively enable a greater number of individuals and families to avoid falling below the poverty line or to gain economic stability to rise above the poverty line. Earnings also make a difference in a nation's ability to achieve economic stability. During 2014, 13 states raised the minimum wages and the initial results look promising—real wages have increased along with employment (Hart-Landsberg, 2014).

A nation's economic policy and the extent of government involvement in employment play an important role in determining the availability of different types of employment and the salaries paid (NASW, 2009–2012). In the years immediately prior to 2008, there were signs that the economic policy of the previous administration was not working. Unemployment rates for those with limited income and education levels, food stamp applications, and the numbers of those living in deep poverty all rose. Weakened safety nets in the form of inadequate unemployment insurance (despite unemployment benefits being extended to 96 weeks) and limited cash assistance for families who are poor made the Great Recession doubly challenging (Parrott, 2008). At the outset of the recession, analysts speculated that the number of people, including children, living in poverty would increase. These predictions have turned out to be correct. While the number of children living in the United States increased only 3% from 2000 to 2009, the number of children living in poverty increased 18%, and over 40% of children were living in economically struggling families compared to 23.5% of children living in poverty in 2014 (Annie E. Casey Foundation, 2011; 2014). The 2014 Casey Foundation report emphasizes that children growing up in poverty experience problems in a multitude of areas, including school, behavior, and health, and, over the course of their lives, they attain lower levels of education and earn less.

Despite the fact that the national debt is the lowest it has been since 2007, concerns persist regarding our ability to implement and improve—even to continue—social welfare programs. The austerity measures that helped to lower the national debt and jumpstart the economy are, in part, why funding has not yet flowed back into social welfare programs.

Globally, governments have invested in safety net programs, helping to reduce the number of persons living in poverty, but significant challenges remain. Levels of extreme poverty are still high in a number of developing and emerging countries, with a higher concentration in Sub-Saharan Africa (World Bank, 2013a). Many people believe that economic policies favoring the wealthy and failing to provide employment and educational opportunities create income inequalities, one of the greatest challenges facing the world today (Pew Research Global Attitudes Project, 2014a). In fact, many feel that achieving economic stability is outside of their control.

Economic globalization can potentially have negative effects in developed and emerging countries, including (Reisch, 2013):

- exploitation of natural resources;
- production and distribution of illegal drugs;
- abuse of women and children through prostitution, international sex trafficking, and commercial exploitation;
- unpaid debts from developed countries to emerging nations;
- worldwide economic slowdowns resulting in unemployment and underemployment;

- increasing immigration and migration costs;
- ongoing civil and international conflicts;
- rise of social and political instability in developing countries (pp. 59–60).

Opportunities in the Economic Environment To understand and participate in the economic process, social workers must develop a working knowledge of economics and the role they play in the practice of social work. Understanding economic trends and implications can improve the social worker's ability to serve and advocate for social service resources. Armed with knowledge of social work and economics, social workers can influence the economic system by advocating for economic justice—"an ideal condition in which all members of society have the same opportunities to obtain material resources necessary to survive and fulfill their human potentials" (Barker, 2014, p. 135).

Economic justice
All persons are able to have the resources needed to survive.

Within any country, efforts to promote economic justice are rooted in a nation's willingness to invest in its people. Strategies that have proven effective in progressing toward economic stability, particularly for persons living in poverty, include: social protection or safety net programs that involve cash transfers; asset-building programs that emphasize saving and accumulating assets (e.g., home, business, education, and retirement plan); and microfinancing initiatives that provide financial services to persons who do not have access to traditional institutions (Chowa, De Vera Masa, Sherraden, & Weil, 2013, pp. 616–617). Delving deeper into social development strategies that can help societies achieve economic justice, Midgley (2012) offers these additional suggestions:

- Invest in human and social capital and support childcare, preschool, literacy, job training, lifelong learning, nutrition, and health care initiatives, and participation in community activities.
- Establish public-private partnerships to create more employment opportunities, including self-employment through micro-enterprise.
- Enact legislation and policies that do not perpetuate institutional inequalities by discriminating against women, racial and ethnic minority groups, persons with disabilities, and older adults.
- Develop cost-effective programs using evidence-based practice models, outcome evaluations, and cost-benefit analyses.

Developing and promoting policies are effective mechanisms for affecting economic change. The first legislation enacted by the Obama administration in 2009, the Lilly Ledbetter Fair Pay Act is one example of a U.S.-based political intervention aimed at remedying an economic injustice. This law holds employers responsible for wage discrimination. To promote economic justice on a larger scale, specific policy-related strategies have been proposed but not fully realized within the U.S., including (CBPP, 2014c):

- Tax code reforms to enable low- and middle-income persons to pay a lower portion of their income taxes. Currently, these two groups pay a higher portion of their incomes in taxes than do those with the highest incomes.
- Strengthen safety net supports for low-income families by expanding childcare, job training, transportation, and health insurance.
- Raise, and index, the minimum wage to bring it in line with 21st century economics. At present, the purchasing power of the federal minimum wage is 22% lower than it was in the 1960s.

We can also call for employers to pay a living wage (the amount needed to ensure the a person/family does not fall below the poverty line) to promote self-sufficiency, which can, in turn, decrease the need for a number of safety net services such as financial assistance, housing, and health care. Community-based advocates across the country have calculated that amount to be an hourly wage ranging from approximately $7.00 to $12.00 an hour, with many advocating for at least $8.20 an hour in most areas of the country. To learn more about the amount that is considered to be a living wage in your state, county, and city, visit the "Living Wage Calculator" at: http://livingwage.mit.edu/. The Calculator also provides information on poverty and minimum wages, taking into consideration the cost of living in a particular region.

During times of economic challenge, social workers have the opportunity and an obligation to develop and learn new practice methods to meet client needs (McNutt & Floersch, 2008). Whether practicing within one's home country or internationally, one social work approach is community practice (practice focused on social change within communities and organizations) which embraces the social work principles of self-determination, social justice, and democratic participation (Reisch, 2013). Social workers can advocate with policy-makers to increase opportunities for employment, education, and tax credits and allocations for food, housing, and cash assistance—all areas that can buffer the impact of economic instability (Parrott, 2008). For example, in the recent economic downturn, social workers advocated such large-scale economic changes as the expiration of tax cuts for the wealthy, retaining workers' rights, and sustaining the role of government in social programs, particularly safety net programs. With many in our country consistently calling for decreased spending for safety net programs, social workers can attest to the fact that such programs are not just helpful, but necessary for many of those our agencies serve. In 2013, nearly half (49.2%) of U.S. households received some form of government help, up from 37% in 1998 (U.S. Census Bureau Newsroom, 2013).

Social workers can express their multicultural vision by bringing to light the failures of economic policies that separate and isolate ethnic groups.

Community practice
Practice focused on social change within communities and organizations.

Advocating for interventions that address issues of foreclosure prevention, health care inequities and coverage, and financial and educational interventions is key to tackling some of our current economic struggles, particularly as they relate to children (Annie E. Casey Foundation, 2011). Educating others regarding the relationships among economic instability, financial literacy, decreased resources, and social stressors such as chemical dependency and addiction, domestic violence, child/older adult abuse and neglect, and mental illness is another strategy for positively impacting clients' lives. With our skills for empowerment and resource mobilization, social workers are well positioned to advocate for economic justice, whether in the area of safety net programs, saving through individual development accounts, creating access to home ownership, or optimizing financial capacity.

Social workers have the opportunity to work at multiple levels of practice to promote economic justice. At the micro level, we can empower people to be financially literate and help them to manage such potential economic challenges as credit card debt, rent-to-own/lease arrangements, and poor savings habits, while at the macro level, we can collectively advocate for employers to reward long-term service through tax credits and pension plans, strengthen families' economic bases by valuing all forms of work, and acknowledge that income inequalities do exist and make it difficult for people to feel connected to society and to have faith in the economic system (Leicht & Fitzgerald, 2014).

Social Environment

Inequality and social justice are continuing themes for social work practice and social policy, and socially just ends must be achieved through socially just means (Reisch et al., 2013). Social work values and ethics inform every professional social worker's social justice efforts. Socially just practice strategies embrace a number of important concepts, including: human rights within all cultural, national, and class boundaries; use of mediating structures and processes; working with different organizational and institutional contexts and fields of practice; identity and group memberships as an influence in people's lives; and the dynamic nature of change and power (Reisch et al., 2013, p. 99).

A number of major social issues face the clients social workers serve, including the aging of the U.S. population, access to sufficient health care, lack of upward mobility, housing inadequacies, reintegration of military veterans, substance abuse, intolerance in the form of hate crimes and bullying, and the need for increased knowledge of multicultural issues. The political and economic environments of recent years have introduced uncertainty into social life in the U.S. and in other countries. Not only politicians and public officials are affected by the hardening of political positions: families and neighbors are

Gay pride

Source: iStock/Marilyn Nieves

finding themselves at odds over issues of social policy, such as reproductive rights and responsibilities (sometimes referred to as "sexual politics") and the role of government in people's lives. In addition, budgetary problems in government, organizations, and households are creating anxieties about spending priorities and economic mobility or lack thereof. Political and economic realities have created considerable uncertainty and have led to changes in the way we live and relate to one another and the priorities we establish.

Challenges in the Social Environment While the social environment is always in flux, current economic and political turbulence presents social workers with several new and unique challenges. Anticipated growth in the population of persons of color, especially younger persons of color, and older adults in the U.S. population over the next several decades will impact society economically, politically, and socially. As the second largest cohort in U.S. history, the Baby Boomers have made a significant mark on society. By 2029, this generation will have reached age 65, and 65+ year-olds will account for over 20% of the U.S. population. By 2056, this group will be larger than the under 18-year-old segment of the population (Colby & Ortman, 2014). Similar trends are expected at the global level, with 65+ year-olds constituting 8% of the world population in 2015 and 16% by 2050 (Pew Research Center Global Attitudes Project, 2014b). For a comparison of the aging of the U.S. and global populations, visit the interactive graph at: www.census.gov/prod/2014pubs/p25-1141.pdf.

As the older population is growing, the young population is changing as well. The segment of the U.S. population under the age of 15 is shrinking and becoming more racially and ethnically diverse. This "generational race gap" means there are fewer workers contributing tax dollars to the government-funded benefit programs that serve older adults. As they age, the younger generation will set the agenda for economic and social support programs, and if the two generations do not perceive a connection to each other, the tension and lack of support could become critical (Meckler, 2014).

Projections suggest that health care needs, particularly for persons of color and older adults, will increase, but that available resources will decrease. For example, Social Security benefits rose 1.7% in 2015 (approximately $20/month/person). It was the third consecutive year that the increase did not keep up with inflation, particularly in the area of health care costs. With Social Security as the primary source of income for millions of older adults, an increasing number of elders will be teetering at the edge of poverty. A major expense for many older adults is long-term care. While the percentage of older adults living in skilled care facilities has decreased slightly, the number of older adults living in long-term residential care facilities (e.g., retirement communities and assisted living facilities) is on the rise, requiring considerable increases in both financial support and staff trained in gerontological care.

While the number of persons and families with access to health care coverage grew in the early years of the 21st century, those numbers slid again with the economic recession. However, in the years of recovery following the recession, the number of people who have health care coverage through private or employer-based plans has risen to 64.2%, while coverage through government programs is at 34.4%, and the number of persons with no health coverage has dropped to 13.4% from the recent 2010 high of 15.5% (Smith & Medalia, 2014). Due to the implementation of the Affordable Care Act and the upturn in hiring, the numbers of persons without health care coverage have decreased somewhat. However, workplace downsizing; use of part-time, temporary, and contract workers (who typically do not have employee benefits); and the growth of the "working poor" have tempered these improvements.

Another effect of the recent turbulence in the U.S. economy has been an increase in the number of persons lacking adequate housing. One example is the increase in household "doubling up" (i.e., having at least one additional adult living in the household who is not a spouse or partner). Eighteen percent of households are now multi-generational, with increases particularly among young adult children living with parents—currently at the rate of one in four—due to employment losses and low-paying jobs (likely due to lower educational attainment or education that does not adequately prepare one with skills for the workforce) (Fry, 2014).

Mortgage defaults and foreclosure rates skyrocketed during the recession, causing record numbers of families to lose their homes. Many of these families were forced to rent or to move in with family or friends, and some even became homeless. Since the recovery began, foreclosure rates have slowed, but fewer young adults have been able to buy their own homes. Home ownership among young adults fell from 38% to 31% in the past decade (Fry, 2013). It is virtually impossible to improve one's economic standing when what limited resources a family has are used up securing basic needs. Without stable employment, health care coverage, and/or housing, it becomes a challenge to maintain, and virtually impossible to achieve, any level of upward mobility. Families with inadequate housing face frequent relocations, which can have a negative effect on the economic, emotional, and educational stability of children. Social workers' clients may be experiencing the effects of housing inadequacies even if that is not the primary reason they are receiving services.

Social workers serving military and veteran populations are experiencing increased numbers of clients and are often seeing more cases of posttraumatic stress disorders and more severe injuries. Social workers in many settings—not just those programs and agencies whose primary mission is to serve the military and veterans—must be prepared to work with this population and their family members. Increased numbers of veterans are seeking services in mental health facilities, domestic violence programs, child welfare, educational and employment programs, programs serving the homeless population, and substance abuse treatment facilities. Social workers are obligated to gain knowledge and skills for working with veterans and their families so they may understand better the experiences and the appropriate and effective interventions that will best serve our returning soldiers and their families.

While certainly not a new social problem, substance abuse continues to be a significant challenge for our society and the social work profession, in particular. Approximately 9% of adults living in the United States have substance abuse addiction (Substance Abuse and Mental Health Services Administration (SAMHSA), 2014). Oftentimes, an addiction co-occurs with a mental illness. Over 3% of adults in the U.S. struggle with a mental illness as well as an addiction (SAMHSA, 2014). Over one-third of youths (ages 12–17) who report experiencing major depression also report abusing drugs and/or alcohol. While these numbers affect a staggering number of individuals, that is only part of the full picture. Substance abusers are members of families, employees, and friends and their addictions negatively and profoundly impact many who care about and depend on them. Social workers in essentially every setting are confronted on a regular basis with the challenges of addiction; therefore, they must be competent to address the issues, for both the substance abuser and for her/his support network.

As our society becomes more diverse, it stands to reason that we should be more accepting of others. While this statement is true for the most part and we, as a society, have made many strides in our treatment of one another, there are glaring and tragic exceptions. In 2012, the Federal Bureau of Investigation received reports from over 5,796 victims of 6,718 incidents of hate crimes based on race (48%), religion (19%), or sexual orientation (19.6%) (FBI, 2013). While the real number of hate crimes is decreasing, online harassment and cyberbullying are on the rise. Forty percent of persons surveyed report they have experienced some form of online harassment, including offensive names, intentional embarrassment, physical threats, stalking, or sexual harassment (Duggan, 2014). Not surprisingly, 70% of those affected are 18–29 years old, and 60% of all harassment is ignored (Duggan, 2014). We have to assume that the vast majority of incidents go unreported. It is likely those cases that are not elevated to the level of law enforcement that present to social work practitioners.

A final area for this discussion is the continuing challenges of racism. As one of the multiple forms of discrimination, racism will be discussed further in Chapter 5, but is included in this overview because it is a major challenge in the social environment that social workers face as we commit ourselves to social justice and culturally competent practice. Racism can be perpetuated through overt acts such as harassment, physical violence, or damage to property, but also through more subtle acts such as blaming the victim or using offensive or non-inclusive language. All forms of racism make explicit the belief that the group being discriminated against is inferior to the dominant group (Appleby, 2011).

Racism
Discrimination or oppression based on an individual or group's race.

While some strides have been made within the U.S. to achieve racial equality, racism still exists. The protests following the police shooting of Michael Brown in Ferguson, Missouri, in August 2014 drew national and international attention to this reality. Longstanding gaps remain between Caucasians and persons of color, particularly African Americans, in unemployment rates, income and wealth, and educational achievements (Irwin, Miller, & Sanger-Katz, 2014). Children and adults of color are over-represented in social services caseloads, foster care and criminal justice systems, persons living in poverty, and those without access to adequate health care. Moreover, persons of color are under-represented in executive and managerial positions, institutions of higher education, elected offices, and health care and social service professions. Social workers will work with many persons of color, but the majority of social workers are White. Our challenge is to commit to being culturally competent and to recognize that this is a process that will continue throughout our careers.

Each of the social issues described in this section can lead to a host of social, physical, and mental health issues that present for social work intervention including decreased social relationships, which in turn can result in increased isolation, morale problems, and reduced productivity. Increases in single-parent (mostly female and many persons of color) households will result in greater financial and social service needs. Related to increases in single-parent households, decreases in average household incomes will lead to more households, particularly those with children, being considered "poor." Social workers must identify the opportunities for intervention in each of these areas and develop the skill set and cultural competence to practice effectively in any and all of these areas.

Opportunities in the Social Environment Social workers have the knowledge, skills, values, and vantage point for creating changes in the health and social service systems to address conditions in the social environment. Let us consider the opportunities that exist in each of the areas of social environment challenges previously discussed.

In anticipation of working with older adults, their families, and care networks, social workers can ensure they understand and can intervene in physical, emotional, economic, and political areas that impact the lives of older adults, particularly those older adults who are vulnerable and at-risk for living in poverty, being abused, neglected, or exploited, or do not have adequate access to quality health care. Specific strategies that social workers can employ to advocate for older adults, particularly related to economic challenges, include (Herman, 2014):

- Debunk the myths of aging by ensuring that you have accurate information about older adult issues and you are committed to sharing non-ageist information with others.
- Strengthen intergenerational alliances through collaborations to leverage resources.
- Facilitate access to resources by being aware of community resources, conducting accurate, comprehensive, and ongoing assessments of the needs of older adults and their care partners, and aiding clients in gaining access to available resources.
- Advocate for policy change through organizations committed to justice for older adults, such as NASW, Alzheimer's Association, AARP, and others (pp. 3–4).

Opportunities exist for social workers to help all clients, regardless of age, access needed or health care resources. The National Culturally and Linguistically Appropriate Services (CLAS) Standards is a good place to begin your understanding of health equality. Developed by the U.S. Department of Health and Human Services, the CLAS Standards can guide professionals in establishing a goal for health equality and cultural competence in health care for all ages

(Webb, 2013). Beyond upholding these standards, social workers can learn about the policies and regulations regarding health care benefits, commit to helping clients navigate the various health care systems, and advocate for laws and policies that will help clients gain access to needed resources with the least complication possible.

Within the areas of upward mobility and having access to adequate housing, social workers can grasp opportunities to become financially literate and competent themselves. As social workers learn about financial resources and strategies, they can work with clients directly or refer them to appropriate resources and can advocate for legislation, policies, and funding to help clients obtain credit counseling services, gain access to banking and credit institutions, learn about savings and asset development opportunities (e.g., individual development accounts, micro-financing programs, etc.), advocate for themselves in situations of potential financial exploitation, and in some cases become homeowners.

While their areas of practice, agency mission, and client caseload may not be directed specifically at serving groups like older adults, military veterans, persons experiencing an addiction, or survivors of hate crimes or bullying, the reality is that most social workers will encounter at some point in their career persons struggling with one or more of these issues. The issues affecting these persons also affect their partners and families, and many issues occur in tandem, not in isolation. For example, many persons with mental illness have a co-occurring addiction. A client seeking services to help her children adjust to a divorce may be the victim of online harassment or may have a family member diagnosed with posttraumatic stress disorder and may bring the concerns to you for help. Social workers must develop at least a basic understanding of the issues these populations face so they can support the families and partners, refer to appropriate resources, services, and benefits, and advocate for socially just policies and practices.

The social work profession provides leadership in achieving racial equity and justice (i.e., a society in which one's race does not influence the way in which a person is identified or treated). In 2014, the Social Work Policy Institute convened a think tank on racial equity with the goal of defining racism as a systemic issue, creating actionable competencies to guide the profession, and developing best practices for planning, executing, and measuring the reduction and eventual elimination of racial inequity. Using the definition of racial equity developed by the Center for Assessment and Policy Development (n.d.), the think tank considered racial equity to be the "condition that would be achieved if one's racial identity no longer predicted, in a statistical sense, how one fares" (Social Work Policy Institute, 2014, p. 2). Moreover, racial equity includes the elimination of policies, practices, attitudes, and cultural messages that reinforce differential outcomes by race or fail to eliminate them (p. 2).

Racial equity
A society in which one's race does not influence the way in which a person is identified or treated.

The think tank issued an Action Brief calling on the social work profession to embrace the following recommendations (Social Work Policy Institute, 2014):

- Be explicit about race and racism and the social work professions—all social work practice should be viewed through a racial equity lens.
- Impact social work education—social workers must be exposed to antiracist curricula, and be trained to confront "color-blindness" and to advocate for racial equity in all areas of practice.
- Build opportunities to develop, engage, and strengthen leadership of color; through multiple strategies, strive to empower social workers of color to share power.
- Ensure availability of professional development for social workers to acquire the core competencies to combat institutional racism—social workers must gain knowledge and skills to understand and fight against the widespread, negative impact of racism and its relationship to poverty, classism, and oppression.
- Engage NASW as a leader in undoing racism—through the provision of education, tools, advocacy, and funding to support racial equity, NASW can continue to be on the forefront of the fight against individual and institutional racism.

Such a framework provides social workers with an opportunity to develop competencies to confront racism by recognizing that racism exists and must be addressed if it is to end. Being able to perceive oppression and discrimination through the words, experiences, social realities, vulnerabilities, and internalization of stigma of those individuals and groups being oppressed can help the social worker to facilitate an intervention that helps the client avoid oppressive barriers (Appleby, 2011; Colon, Appleby, & Hamilton, 2011; Howe & Hamilton, 2011).

In order to competently address the challenges in the current social environment, there are multiple areas in which social workers have had and continue to have the opportunity to engage in change, including:

- We must first consider the demographic makeup of the profession itself. The social work profession continues to be comprised primarily of white female practitioners. This profile does not adequately reflect the population of the United States or the clients we serve, and the profession must strive to recruit a workforce that encompasses greater ethnic, racial, and gender diversity so that we may better serve our clients through service delivery and advocacy (NASW Center for Workforce Studies, n.d.).

■ The profession has made a significant commitment to preparing its members for culturally competent practice through the development of the 2007 *Indicators for the Achievement of the NASW Standards for Cultural Competence in Social Work Practice*. The Standards promote the concept of being well trained, and receiving ongoing professional development in working with and advocating for diversity is considered essential for all social work professionals. Through cultural competence, we have an opportunity to gain insight into our clients' lives.

■ Social workers can advocate for legislative actions that will address the current social issues that impact clients, whether in the areas of reducing poverty, confronting racial/ethnic intolerance, improving access and services for specific client groups, or creating mortgage foreclosure prevention programs. Social workers have the opportunity to help the voices of our clients be heard. Facilitating the passage of legislation to create legal regulations, programs and policies, and interventions is one way to strengthen the social service delivery system and enhance the quality of the lives of those we serve.

■ Social workers must be aware of the needs of specific populations. Regardless of where they work, social workers will serve diverse people with a range of needs. Social work practitioners should have a level of comfort and competence in order to address the issues of persons who are older, veterans, homeless, struggling with addictions and financial issues, or who have been victims of discrimination, bias, crime, or oppression.

■ Becoming more globally sophisticated helps social workers intervene successfully with the increasing numbers of clients who live in or have emigrated from other countries. Social workers may engage in self-assessment and expansion of global awareness as well as develop knowledge and skills related to cultural norms, beliefs, behaviors, language, values, culture, and policies (Hoffman et al., 2008).

■ Social workers can create more ethnically sensitive social service and health care programs that focus on localized community building. Such efforts can help to develop services for diverse and changing client populations and can help improve coordination and communication among agencies in the social service delivery system. Clients must often travel to multiple agencies in varying locations to complete applications for services.

Although the future of the social service delivery system seems fraught with challenges, and many social workers currently have diminished resources with which to respond to these challenges, the profession can look to its strengths. The social work profession has always worked to build and strengthen the system for those who count—clients and their communities. Social workers will

be participants in shaping the future "to ensure that people's lives are characterized by human dignity and social inclusion with economic security access to
education and health care, affordable housing and services to meet needs arising
from daily living, social work may have to articulate more clearly, and then
deliver research-informed and evidenced intervention that ensure social protection" (Preston-Shoot & Höjer, 2012, p. 262). To learn about one social worker's
heroic efforts to help others, read about Sister Jean Abbott in Exhibit 4.12.

EXHIBIT 4.12

"If anybody comes to you hungry ... you treat them as if they were a king"

These words from her father were a motivating force in the life of Sister Jean Abbott, MSW and
founder and former clinical director of the Center for Survivors of Torture and War Trauma, an
agency that provides individual and group therapy for refugees who have experienced violence in
their home countries, often in the form of torture. Sr. Jean's journey from her working-class upbringing to her commitment to creating a safe and healing place for survivors took her to Central America
and back to St. Louis where she learned of the atrocities that humans can inflict on one another.
After working as an elementary school teacher, Sr. Jean became a community organizer, a calling
that took her first to Nicaragua with Witness for Peace and then to Guatemala with Peace Brigades
where she helped organize groups to speak out against violence and corruption. When the Catholic
Church was no longer able to protect her, she was eventually deported for political reasons. Upon
her return to the U.S., she felt a strong commitment to help those refugees who found their way
out of their war-torn countries. She opened a sanctuary house for persons from Guatemala and El
Salvador where she provided shelter and assistance with asylum applications and employment and
had a back-up plan should she be arrested. She made one return trip to Guatemala to rescue the
daughter of one of the women she sheltered and was nearly arrested, but was saved by the girl's
sudden nosebleed. She closed the sanctuary but continued to provide shelter to refugees, this time
from African countries being ravaged by war.

   Sr. Jean began to realize that refugees who were survivors of torture were struggling to adapt
to new lives in America. She could find little research or guidance for working with this population,
so took a position working with children who had experienced abuse so that she could learn how
to help. Armed with a strong commitment and knowledge of the power of healing, Sr. Jean opened
the Center for Survivors of Torture and War Trauma in 1997. The original staff of two has grown
now to eight and the nonprofit agency is one of 21 U.S. member agencies of the International
Rehabilitation Council for Torture Victims.

   In 2010, with the hiring of an administrator, Sr. Jean returned to providing therapy and developing programs for the Center. Through their work with over 9,000 survivors, Sr. Jean and the staff

have learned that an effective intervention has to fit the unique needs and culture of their diverse client population because "different cultures store trauma differently ... the result of trauma is to align it with a body part or physical ailment" (p. 158). For example, tai chi and yoga have proved effective with Bosnian refugees while art and storytelling is a successful approach with refugees from Afghanistan. Body-oriented therapy (e.g., dance, healing touch) brings together the mind and body and enables the client to feel a sense of control, connect with their inner self, and heal from the inside out. Sr. Jean measures her agency's effectiveness by the survivors' stories and their small personal successes (for instance, sitting through a fireworks show without having flashbacks). "They were treated so cruelly, and if we treat them with grace and love, we can replace some of that with them" (p. 159). Sr. Jean is no longer at the helm of the agency she founded and believes that the greatest success a social worker can have is to work themselves out of a job and she has done just that. She is devoting her time to training people in Uganda who are offering trauma care to the northern Ugandan community.

Source: Excerpted from: Curley & Tebb (2010) and interview transcripts and interviews with Susan Tebb and Kristin Bulin, current Executive Director of the Center for Survivors of Torture and War Trauma.

Emily and her co-workers were concerned about communicating effectively with the increasing number of women appearing in emergency rooms who did not speak English. They saw this situation as an opportunity to assess their own cultural competence and the need for interpreters, to develop an in-service training program for staff, to determine the availability of interpreting resources, and to develop a network of interpreters who could supportively and accurately translate for this client population during times of crisis.

In addition to seeking out training to enhance their knowledge and skills for working with this population, the staff conducted interviews with agencies that typically provided services to victims of domestic violence—public welfare, health care organizations, schools, mental health agencies, and housing programs— to determine their needs and resources for translation services. Following this assessment, Emily's agency contacted other agencies and organizations that had access to the ethnic communities that spoke the languages of the women who were being abused. The staff created a database of volunteer interpreters who spoke a variety of languages, and they sent the list to all the organizations with which they worked that provided services to victims of domestic violence.

As a result of having identified the need for additional training and a new service, Emily and her co-workers became aware of the need for yet further change to support their non-English speaking clients better. Through the coalition that was formed to address the need for interpreters, the group engaged in legislative advocacy at the state level with the aim of seeking legislation that would enable the creation of interpreter services throughout the state.

CONCLUSION

Social work in today's world is a call to justice. As social work is a profession that functions within the context of the larger society, social work practitioners must have a comprehensive understanding of the political, economic, and social environment in which their clients live. We must understand the inequities over the life course specifically in the areas of health, nutrition, education, and employment and incorporate those insights into the processes of assessment and intervention. Our position on the frontlines of social issues obligates us to draw attention to the political, economic, and social environments with decision and policy makers.

The projections related to shifts in the U.S. and international demographic profile included in this chapter give you insights into the knowledge and skills you will need to practice social work in the coming decades. You have seen how understanding diverse racial and ethnic groups and their languages and cultures, the needs of older adults and their families and caregivers, and the impact of religious and spiritual beliefs on behavior will be critical in the coming years. These are just a sampling of the competencies needed for effective social work practice.

Social workers must also be vigilant in their efforts to maintain up-to-date knowledge of the political, economic, and social issues that impact their work and their clients' lives. Social work is built on the premise that we can respond to societal needs; therefore, it is our "capacity to change that gives hope for the profession's future" (Kindle, 2006, p. 17). It is for this reason that social work students must take coursework in such areas as economics, political science, and philosophy along with sociology and psychology. Regardless of the path that you pursue in your social work career, responding to contemporary societal issues and advocating for social and economic justice and participating in the political process are going to be a part of virtually every social worker's professional life.

MAIN POINTS

- The demographic profile of the United States is becoming more diverse. Effective social work professionals need to be aware of demographic trends and to develop the knowledge and skills to work with diverse client systems.
- The largest population growth in U.S. history occurred between 1990 and 2000, with the biggest increases in the Hispanic/Latino and Asian populations. The following decade (2000–2010) saw a decreased growth in the population and the current decade continues to see our society aging.

■ By 2030, nearly one-fourth of the U.S. population will be 65 years or older, with the fastest-growing segment of the older-adult population being in the 85 and older group. Women make up the majority in this age group, and social workers will need to be aware of gender-related issues.

■ Religious diversity is increasing and in some cases means increased religious discrimination.

■ Social workers remain advocates of social and economic justice while working with individuals and groups that continue to experience discrimination and oppression.

■ Both challenges and opportunities exist for the social work profession, specifically within the context of political, economic, and social changes.

■ The political and economic environments, which are fraught with contentious issues and hard choices, are making the social environment more difficult.

■ The social work profession has an obligation not only to serve clients but also to advocate for more helpful programs and more equitable policies.

EXERCISES

1. Using the Sanchez family interactive case (www.routledgesw.com/caseStudies), answer the following:
   a. What political, economic, and social issues are present in this case?
   b. Identify the information from the case that helped you to determine the political, economic, and social issues.
   c. Select one of the policy areas identified and examine the evolution of that issue throughout the case. Identify the relevant societal, economic, political, or religious implications of the policy.
   d. Hector may be laid off from his job at the construction company. Reflect on the implications for Hector and his family if he were to be laid off. What benefits will he/they be eligible to receive? What strengths does Hector possess that will enable him to obtain employment? What barriers exist that may present challenges for Hector in obtaining employment?

2. Understanding the environment in which social workers practice can be complex. Go to the Riverton interactive case at www.routledgesw.com/caseStudies. Upon familiarizing yourself with the community, particularly the Alvadora neighborhood, choose a social, political, or economic perspective and respond to the following:
   a. Describe the community from the perspective that you have chosen.
   b. What are the issues and challenges that exist within the Alvadora neighborhood?

    c.   Describe your perspective on the reasons for the presence of the issues and challenges you identified.

    d.   Within the perspective that you have selected, identify the opportunities for the Alvadora community.

3.   Go to the RAINN interactive case at www.routledgesw.com/caseStudies and take the virtual tour of the RAINN organization. Investigate the resources in your community/region that are available for survivors of sexual assault and molestation. Reflect on your thoughts regarding the benefits and drawbacks of an online versus community-based resource.

4.   In an attempt to gain insight into the societal and legal protection for gay, lesbian, bisexual, and transgender individuals, search the web to identify a city or municipality in your state that includes sexual orientation in its city or municipal codes. Write a reflection paper on the number of communities that have included protection for sexual orientation. Are you surprised by your findings?

5.   From a recent issue of your local newspaper, identify key political, economic, and social issues. Reflect on your thoughts regarding whether these issues are consistent with social work concerns.

6.   Describe the socioeconomic class with which you identify and respond to the following:

    a.   Do you believe your socioeconomic class influences your attitudes toward others in society?

    b.   Do you believe your socioeconomic class influences your behaviors and life choices?

    c.   If so, how? If not, explain.

7.   The Brickville community is one that is undergoing a transition. Go to www.routledgesw.com/caseStudies. Click on Engage, select and review Real Estate Development, and respond to the three critical thinking questions. After completing the engagement phase, click on Assess and respond to the three community-level critical thinking questions.

8.   To better understand your perspectives on achieving success within the context of global realities, complete the Global Opportunity Quiz, located at: www.pewglobal.org/2014/10/09/emerging-and-developing-economies-much-more-optimistic-than-rich-countries-about-the-future/. Write a reflection paper on the rationale for your selections and compare your perspectives to those for other countries (located at the end of the quiz).

After reading this chapter, you should be able to:

1. Examine your self-awareness of attitudes, beliefs, and behaviors of your own culture and cultures with whom you were be working as a social work professional.
2. Review and integrate information regarding diversity within the U.S. and internationally.
3. Delve into issues of intersectionality of race, class, and gender and gain an understanding of the ways in which they impact social work practice.
4. Demonstrate knowledge and skills of cultural competence in social work practice.

2. Engage Diversity and Difference in Practice

DIVERSITY IN SOCIAL WORK PRACTICE

Globalization
Worldwide movement related to
economic and cultural activity.

A s a result of increased globalization (i.e., worldwide movement related to economic and cultural activity) (Barker, 2014), enhanced communication, greater access to transportation, and the broadened awareness that comes with those developments, the world in which social workers function has expanded. The population of the United States has become more diverse or varied in the areas of race, ethnicity, culture, age, and sexual orientation. Diversity has affected every facet of social work practice throughout the history of the profession. Responding to diversity means recognizing that different people have different needs, and social workers must be prepared to tailor their practices to respect differences and to meet many different needs, some of which will be with persons who have experienced discrimination and oppression. From its earliest days, the social work profession has worked with the "marginalized, oppressed, and excluded population in any given society, and therefore has always included guidelines for working with such populations" (Garran & Rozas, 2013, p. 97).

Diversity
Variety in the areas of race,
ethnicity, culture, age, and
sexual orientation.

Since practitioners work with the entire spectrum of society, they must possess knowledge, skills, and values to work effectively with all people, whether they are similar to or different from themselves and to be inspired by them. The social work profession's commitment to social justice and emphasis on culturally competent education help social workers to address diversity in assessments and interventions while staying focused on the larger socio-political-structural factors impacting clients (Garran & Rozas, 2013, p. 98). For example, the social worker who learns about her clients' culture before she meets with them is demonstrating culturally competent practice. CSWE accreditation standards for social work education programs require that students acquire the knowledge and skills necessary to demonstrate their understanding and appreciation of diversity. Specifically, the curriculum guidelines mandate that social workers engage diversity and difference in practice, as follows:

> Social workers understand how diversity and difference characterize and shape the human experience and are critical to the formation of identity. The dimensions of diversity are understood as the intersectionality of multiple factors including but not limited to age, class, color, culture, disability and ability, ethnicity, gender, gender identity and expression, immigration status, marital status, political ideology, race, religion/spirituality, sex, sexual orientation, and tribal sovereign status. Social workers understand that, as a consequence of difference, a person's life experiences may include oppression, poverty, marginalization, and alienation as well as privilege, power, and acclaim. Social workers also understand the forms and mechanisms of oppression and discrimination and recognize the extent to which a culture's structures and values, including social, economic, political, and cultural exclusions, may oppress, marginalize, alienate, or create privilege and power. Social workers:

- apply and communicate understanding of the importance of diversity and difference in shaping life experiences in practice at the micro, mezzo, and macro levels;
- present themselves as learners and engage clients and constituencies as experts of their own experiences; and
- apply self-awareness and self-regulation to manage the influence of personal biases and values in working with diverse clients (p. 7).

Effective practice requires social workers to learn continually about other cultures, ethnic groups, communities, countries, and the many aspects of our diverse society. The first step in becoming a social worker who can effectively serve a wide range of clients is to embrace cultural competence as a vital social work skill. Culturally competent social workers understand the need to address diversity and examine their own self- awareness and experiences related to interacting with persons who are different from themselves. Moreover, culturally competent practitioners "seek to promote the understanding, acceptance, and appreciation of cultural differences" in order to address social justice as it relates to the intersection of power and inequities (Garran & Rozas, 2013, p. 100).

Cultural competence
Interactions with persons with respect and value of the individual's culture, race, ethnicity, religion, sexual orientation, age, and other factors that make them unique.

Standards for culturally competent social work practice define cultural competence as:

the process by which individuals and systems respond respectfully and effectively to people of all cultures, languages, classes, races, ethnic backgrounds, religions, and other diversity factors in a manner that recognizes, affirms, and values the worth of individuals, families, and communities, and protects and preserves the dignity of each.

(National Association of Social Workers (NASW), 2007, p. 11)

Achieving linguistic competence is also critical. Linguistically competent individuals and organizations are committed to communicating in ways that everyone can understand. For instance, engaging an interpreter, assigning a social worker proficient in the client's language, and learning correct pronunciations of clients' names and preferred forms of address are strategies to demonstrate linguistic competence. Organizational strategies that promote linguistic competence include employing a multicultural (persons who represent a variety of cultures and traditions) staff and spoken and sign language interpreters, offering multilingual written and electronic materials, and providing information in a way that is sensitive to a diverse audience (Goode & Jones, 2006). The NASW's policy statement on cultural and linguistic competence in the social work profession (2012–2014b) calls upon social workers to view language

Linguistic competence
Demonstrations of communication skills that are applicable to a range of diverse populations.

as one expression of an individual's culture and to promote and support the "implementation of cultural and linguistic competence at three intersecting levels: the individual, institutional, and societal" (p. 74).

This chapter explores the importance of diversity to the social work profession and the roles that language plays, both positive and negative. The chapter also reviews the particular areas of diversity that have presented challenges for social workers and introduces the social work practice skills necessary for working effectively with diverse client systems.

DIVERSITY AS A COMPONENT OF SOCIAL WORK EDUCATION

One of Emily's child protective service cases provided her with a new perspective on the meaning of culture and family. Emily was assigned to investigate the alleged neglect of Shanté, a 6-year-old African American child who lived with her mother, Jerilyn. Shanté had missed a number of days of school and often came to school unkempt and hungry. During her investigation, Emily learned that Jerilyn had sustained a traumatic brain injury during a car accident several years earlier and was now living with a physical and cognitive disability. Until recently, the two had lived with Jerilyn's mother, who had been the primary caregiver for both Jerilyn and Shanté, but the mother had recently died following a stroke. Recognizing that she was unable to care for Shanté, Jerilyn agreed to award custody to her sister, Roberta. Roberta lived in the house next door to Jerilyn and Shanté.

Emily initiated the process to bring the case before the family court system. The case went to court to finalize the custody arrangement, and during Roberta's testimony, she revealed she was not Jerilyn's biological sister. The two women had been lifelong friends and belonged to the same church, one whose members referred to one another with the honorifics of "sister" and "brother." Emily had assumed that sister meant a familial connection because her cultural experiences had not included in-depth knowledge of the African American culture or the religion the two women practiced. This experience taught Emily some valuable lessons about making assumptions, particularly when working with persons whose ethnic and religious cultures are different from her own. Ultimately, Roberta was awarded custody of Shanté, who was well cared for and saw her mother on a daily basis.

In the United States and other multicultural societies, social workers must not only be open to working with diverse populations, but they must work toward gaining knowledge about the history, beliefs, family structure, religion, dress, food, and lifestyles of the groups with whom they are likely to interact. As the social work world continues to become more multinational, social workers can gain valuable insights from exploring the methods social workers employ in different places around the world. Even within the western world, there are a number of similarities but differences do exist. For example, most European countries, Canada, Australia, and the U.S. have strong national identities but, due to shifting demographic profiles, are home to peoples of increasingly diverse norms and values (Sundar, Sylvestre, & Bassi, 2012). Social workers in these areas of the globe strive to approach diversity from anti-racism, anti-oppression, and cultural competence perspectives (Sundar et al., 2012). In these developed regions, the social work profession is relatively well developed but still has considerable variation in the way in which practice is approached. Each of these areas has increasingly diverse populations and are confronted with poverty, discrimination, and inequalities. For example, social workers across a number of European countries are collaborating on anti-oppression models, while social workers in Australia and New Zealand are working on models of practice that are culturally appropriate for the Indigenous communities (Pawar, 2012).

Anti Racism

Source: iStock/VLIET

In other regions of the world, the social work profession is challenged by widespread poverty, health crises, and civil wars and violence. In Africa, social workers are working to develop Afro-centric models of practice and social development initiatives that will address the economic, health, and political challenges (Pawar, 2012). There is considerable wealth in Middle Eastern countries, but the social work professions in that region are confronted with political and religious unrest, displacement, and changing demographics, while in Latin and South America, poverty and marginalization are on the rise as is concern for children, older adults, and women (Pawar, 2012). While social workers around the world face different issues and are in different stages of development as a profession, there is an opportunity to be mutual sharers and learners in what has become an interdependent world (Pawar, 2012, p. 2102).

Mexican Border

Source: iStock/Patrick Poendl

The NASW *Code of Ethics* (2008) calls for social workers to respect the inherent dignity and worth of a person, to be sensitive to cultural and ethnic diversity, and to work toward ending discrimination, oppression, poverty, and social injustice. The *Code* further directs social workers to understand human behavior within a cultural context. In 2008, language was added to the *Code* that urges social workers to respect and protect gender identity and immigrant status as well. The *Code* thus binds all social workers to practice without discrimination.

Though the majority of social workers and social work students in the U.S. are Caucasian, over 40% of social workers providing direct services work with a caseload that is largely non-Caucasian. See Exhibit 5.1 for a profile of the race and ethnicity of clients served by social workers in the U.S. Because the majority of social workers serve a racially and ethnically diverse group of clients, it is imperative that social workers possess knowledge of multiple cultures and their values and that they have the skills to work with individuals and groups from those cultures.

Having knowledge of different persons and groups is only one step in the journey toward becoming culturally competent. Developing an understanding on one's own social identity is another critical step. Our social identity encompasses not only our lived experiences, circumstances, and how we view and categorize ourselves, but also incorporates the complexities of the history and power structures of the community(ies) or group(s) of which we are members (Garran & Rozas, 2013, pp. 99–100).

Social identity
Our lived experiences, circumstances, and how we view and categorize ourselves, and the complexities of the history and power structures of the community or group of which we are members.

NASW membership has committed to a set of Standards for Cultural Competence in Social Work Practice that go beyond the *Code of Ethics*. Culturally competent practice requires more than knowing about diversity; it requires the ability and skills to take action (Simmons, Diaz, Jackson, & Takahashi, 2008). In 2007, as an acknowledgment of this premise, the profession expanded those

EXHIBIT 5.1

Race and Ethnicity of Persons Served by Social Workers

Clients	Any Clients (%)	Greater than 51% of Clients (%)
Non-Hispanic White	99	59
Black/African American	85	10
Hispanic/Latino	77	5
Asian/Pacific Islander	49	1
Native American/Alaska Native	39	1

Source: Center for Health Workforce Studies (CHWS) & NASW Center for Workforce Studies (NASW CWS) (2006).

standards to include indicators for demonstrating the achievement of cultural competence (see Quick Guide #5.1).

In sum, cultural competence is the ability to examine your own attitudes, beliefs, and values and to gain knowledge and skills that will enable you to adapt your practice to the unique needs of all individuals, families, groups, and organizations. Being culturally competent "can mean the difference between a person making it or falling through the cracks" (NASW, n.d.a). For instance, if a social worker lacks awareness of a client's cultural traditions and/or asks the

QUICK GUIDE #5.1 STANDARDS AND INDICATORS OF CULTURALLY COMPETENT SOCIAL WORK PRACTICE

Standard	Interpretation	Indicators
Ethics and values	Within the context of the client system's culture, the profession's values mandate that social workers respect the individual and her or his right to self-determination, and confront any ethical dilemmas that result from conflicts.	Knowledge of the NASW Code of Ethics and social justice and human rights principles. Ability to recognize and describe areas of conflict and accommodation in values. Awareness of differences and strengths.
Self-awareness	Culturally competent social workers are responsible for being aware of their own cultural identities as well as "knowing and acknowledging how fears, ignorance, and the 'isms' have influenced their attitudes, beliefs, and feelings."	Examine and describe cultural and social heritage and identities, beliefs, and impacts. Display ability to change attitudes and beliefs and increase comfort. Demonstrate understanding of limitations. Work with others to enhance self-awareness.
Cross-cultural knowledge	Securing baseline and ongoing knowledge of cultures other than one's own is an expected component of culturally competent practice.	Gain knowledge of: client groups, dominant and nondominant groups, privilege, and interactions of cultural systems.
Cross-cultural skills	Because culturally effective social workers intervene with a wide range of people who are different from them, they must remain open to learning and applying new knowledge and skills.	Gain skills to communicate, interact, assess, intervene, and advocate with diverse groups. Effectively use clients' natural supports.

Service delivery	Interacting with co-workers, agencies, and the community to maintain awareness of cultural diversity and to ensure the provision of culturally competent services is critical to effective practice.	Utilize formal and informal community resources. Advocate for and help to build culturally competent services.
Empowerment and advocacy	Within the context of the client system's culture, social workers advocate for and with client systems to promote consciousness raising, client empowerment, and social change.	Advocate for culturally respectful policies. Utilize appropriate methods and interventions. Be aware of own values and their impact on client systems.
Diverse workforce	Social workers advocate for maintaining the diversity of the social service delivery system.	Advocate for and support a diverse workforce that reflects the needs of the client systems being served.
Professional education	Social workers advocate for culturally-focused education and training for the social work profession.	Advocate for and participate in education to ensure culturally competent knowledge, skills, and values.
Language diversity	Social workers are obligated to provide services in a linguistically competent manner.	Advocate for and implement use of culturally competent written, electronic, and verbal communications.
Cross-cultural leadership	The profession is committed to sharing its values and ethics with others.	Social work leaders model cultural competence through interactions, communications, policies, and hiring.

Source: Adapted from NASW, 2007.

client to act in a way that is inconsistent with a belief or tradition, the client may refuse to accept services or to work with that social worker, resulting in the client not being optimally served. It is important to note that cultural competence extends beyond racial and ethnic differences to include gender, sexual orientation, socioeconomic status, place of origin, religious affiliation, and any other aspects of diversity.

SELF-AWARENESS: AN EXPLORATION

Think of a time when you felt you stood out or were a minority in a group. What emotions does that memory evoke? Why did you feel different—was it race, gender, age, economic level, religion, sexual orientation, or maybe your dress or speech? What was the outcome of that situation? Getting in touch with the experience and feelings of being different can help you develop empathy for others and for their experiences of difference.

Raising your self-awareness about issues of diversity, oppression, discrimination, and social justice is critical for effective social work practice, and it can be exhilarating and liberating to learn more about your own culture and heritage and the values and beliefs you have absorbed from your own lived experience and history. At the same time, however, delving into your own culture, your place in society, and the impact of your behavior on others can be a painful process, as you may discover biases about which you were unaware.

Bias
Positive or negative perception of an individual or group based on stereotypes.

To understand the meaning of social justice and the injustices clients experience, it is important to identify the ways in which you knowingly or unknowingly, in your speech and actions, discriminate against other persons or groups. While this will not enable you to understand the specific injustices that your clients may be experiencing, increasing your self-awareness about your own behaviors can help you to develop more culturally competent skills. You may come to terms with your own biases (we all have them) or with times that you or those around you have engaged in or supported disrespectful or hurtful behaviors. Recognizing these facts will likely be uncomfortable, but it is an important step toward achieving cultural awareness and sensitivity and, ultimately, cultural competence.

How do you differ from those around you? How that has impacted your life? What roles have power and privilege (or lack thereof) played in shaping the person you have become? Understanding these elements of your personal identity provides valuable insight into how differences, power, and privilege affect your clients, and how they might manifest themselves in your interactions with clients, groups, organizations, co-workers, family, and friends (Garran & Rozas, 2013). To identify issues related to your own culture and experiences, consider the questions posed in Exhibit 5.1. Compare your culture to other cultures by identifying the similarities and differences in language to describe your group and other groups, values, assumptions, and traditions, for example.

Consider the suggestions below to expand your range of experience and broaden your perspectives on other cultures in your quest for cultural competence. Each of these experiences will be most educational and meaningful if you are with other people with whom you can compare observations and feelings.

- Seek out interactions with persons or groups who are different from you. For instance, engage someone you see on a regular basis but have never talked with one-on-one.
- Attend international and cultural festivals, celebrations, awareness raising events, museums, or arts events, and ask questions about the group or

QUICK GUIDE #5.2 SELF-AWARENESS OF CULTURAL IDENTITY

Who are you?

With which racial, ethnic, religious, gender, age, social class, and sexual orientation groups do you identify?

Into which of these groups were you born, and which have you joined since birth?

What unique characteristics do your affiliations have that other groups do not?

What do you like about your culture(s)? What do you not like about your culture(s)?

Have you ever experienced discrimination as a result of your affiliation with one or more of the cultures to which you belong?

What was the nature of that discrimination?

Consider your perspective on other groups. What assumptions do you have? What language/terms do you use? What actions do you take?

What assumptions do others have about you? What language/terms do others use to refer to you? What actions do others take toward you?

culture. It is ideal to attend an event with someone familiar with that group, culture, or heritage.

■ Read a magazine or newspaper targeted to a specific group with whom you are not familiar.

■ Attend a service in a religious institution that is new to you. This experience will be even more meaningful if you attend the service with a member of that religious group.

■ Read a book or view a movie that portrays a culture with which you are not familiar.

- Watch a television show or movie in a language other than your first language or one that portrays a culture with which you are not familiar.
- Visit a restaurant or eat food that is new to you (or better yet, organize a potluck gathering in which people bring food of their culture).
- Identify a controversial issue that is currently plaguing society or your community that has cultural implications, and identify your thoughts and feelings about the issues. Talk with others, seek out information from credible sources on the issues, and reflect on strategies for resolving the dilemma on the individual, community, or societal level.
- Observe the conversations of others: Do they use discriminatory language (e.g., slang or stereotypical descriptions), make inappropriate jokes, or engage in offensive behaviors? If so, what is your response (or lack of response)? Do you keep quiet, and if so, why?
- Volunteer with an age or a cultural group with whom you have little experience. Senior centers, skilled nursing facilities/adult day centers, child-care centers, and programs for persons who are developmentally disabled, new to this country, or experiencing poverty or homelessness are all good choices.

Moving out of your "comfort zone" to have new experiences is a positive step toward understanding more about yourself, your cultural origins, and other people. It also serves to expand your comfort zone so that you can work more effectively with those who are different from you. Maintaining culturally competence is a lifelong endeavor that has professional and personal benefits as it enables us to better understand ourselves and others, work through life's day-to-day and major challenges, build confidence in our ability to effectively interact with others, and lessen fears of the unknown.

THEORY THAT HELPS US UNDERSTAND DIVERSITY AND SOCIAL JUSTICE

Competent social workers understand diversity issues from multiple perspectives, and they use their knowledge and skills to incorporate issues of social identity(ies), power, and privilege into ongoing advocacy for social justice through the implementation of just policies and practices (Garran & Rozas, 2013). Having explored these issues from historical and demographic perspectives in earlier chapters, we will now consider working with diverse populations from social justice and theoretical perspectives.

The social work profession is deeply committed to ensuring social justice for *all* persons—a distinctly unique mission among helping professions—and social justice concepts guide social work practice in an increasingly diverse population. When asked to articulate the ways in which they understand and practice social justice, a group of social workers described social justice using such terms as "fairness", "equal rights and opportunity", "social responsibility", "resource redistribution", and "decent standards of living," all of which are consistent with the values and ethical practices of the social work profession (Olson, Reid, Threadgill-Goldson, Riffe, & Ryan, 2013, p. 38). Moreover, respondents felt obligated as social workers to advocate for policies to support this definition of social justice. As criminal justice scholar Norman White (2011) states: "social justice is not a concept to be defined, it is an action to be taken." These words guide social workers to create a more just society in which all people, particularly our clients, can survive and thrive. For example, social workers can organize a group of parents to lobby state legislators to protest Medicaid cuts that will result in their children with disabilities losing healthcare benefits.

Many of the clients and groups social workers serve experience oppression and discrimination. Social justice theory guides social workers to view clients' lived experiences of oppression as a hierarchical dynamic in which one group dominates or disempowers another group (Bell, 2013). Guided by this theory, social workers can view the oppression clients experience as "a fusion of institutional and systemic discrimination (e.g., racial profiling), personal bias, bigotry, and social prejudice in a complex web of relationships and structures that shade most aspects of life in our society" (Bell, 2013, p. 22). Understanding the ways in which oppressive acts and practices compromise clients' rights and capacities can provide the social worker with insights into the cultural, social, economic, and educational experiences that come together to shape clients' lives. Using culturally competent knowledge and skills, social workers can incorporate clients' history of oppression into their assessment and intervention planning. For example, knowing that your client is a refugee and survivor of torture who is experiencing posttraumatic stress disorder (PTSD) and is fearful of government authorities and law enforcement can provide insight into her reluctance to engage with you or in a social work relationship. Alternatively, consider the client who was laid off from his executive-level position and has been unable to obtain comparable employment for the past three years. He presents to you for assistance as he is depressed and experiencing a financial crisis. Understanding the life change that he has undergone is significant to the helping process.

The ecological perspective and its strengths-based approach are the primary theoretical framework guiding social work practice. This perspective sensitizes social workers to the need to consider cultural information. For example, along with lived experiences of oppression and discrimination, culturally competent social workers note clients' differing home environments and family cultures, and they identify culturally-related strengths within these

Social justice theory
Viewing clients' lived experiences of oppression as a hierarchical dynamic in which one group dominates or disempowers another group.

environments. These strengths can then be incorporated into an empowering intervention process.

The ecological perspective and its focus on strengths-based practice guides social workers as they provide services to and recommend policies for all clients, but it is particularly helpful to social workers working with clients and groups whose cultural experiences are different from their own. As you come to appreciate the ways in which theory can help you engage, assess, intervene, and evaluate, focus on the language and challenges of multicultural social work practice.

Ecological Perspective

Ecological perspective
A theoretical framework in which the individual is viewed within the context of the environment in which she/he lives.

The ecological perspective (a.k.a. the person-in-environment perspective) is a longstanding theoretical approach to social work practice that views the client within the context of the environment in which he or she lives (Germain & Gitterman, 1980). The concept of "environment" includes family, work, religion, culture, and life events (for example, developmental issues and life milestones and transitions). This perspective directs the social worker to consider each aspect of the client's history and lived experiences, including those with discrimination and oppression, when establishing rapport, conducting an assessment, and developing an intervention plan with the client. The ecological approach emphasizes the fact that clients' past and present life experiences, as well as the larger society in which they live, including social structures, policies, and societal beliefs and actions, influence their own beliefs, emotions, behaviors, and interactions. Within each client encounter, the social worker must be aware of the influence of cultural factors such as race, ethnicity, place of origin, age, gender, social class, religion, and sexual orientation. Culturally competent practitioners incorporate any and all societal, cultural, and personal influences that impact the client's experience.

A fundamental component of the ecological perspective is recognition of the impact oppression has on the client's life experiences. For example, imagine you are a social worker working with a client who is Native American and you are not Native American yourself. Our society has oppressed Native Americans for centuries, unjustly allocating resources, education, and employment. Native Americans have been victims of exploitation, abuse, segregation, open hostilities, and violence. In working with the client, you would be remiss if you did not consider the historical, political, and societal issues related to Native American life, both in general and for particular tribes. Clients who have experienced institutionalized oppression are likely to feel powerlessness and mistrustful, particularly when dealing with members of the oppressing group. The *Code of Ethics* (2008) binds social workers not only to oppose such oppression, but to understand its origins and impact, to actively advocate against it, and to develop interventions to combat it (Van Soest, 2008).

In building rapport, the culturally competent social worker actively seeks knowledge of the client's experiences of discrimination and strives to understand the client's values, beliefs, and cultural practices. All of these things impact the client's perspective and interactions with her or his environment. Such sensitivity conveys to the client the social worker's respect for the client's cultural heritage and experience. For example, the social worker assigned to work with a Native American family can be more culturally effective if she or he is prepared with knowledge about that client's tribal affiliation, history, traditions, and current issues, and has reflected on her or his own experiences, education, and beliefs about Native American culture.

Strengths-Based Perspective

Embedded within the ecological perspective, the strengths-based perspective views the client's cultural experiences and beliefs as strengths on which the client can build. This is particularly important for culturally competent social work practice (Saleebey, 2006). Using a strengths-based approach, the social worker builds a relationship with the client based on the client's lived experiences, thus demonstrating respect for the client's culture, lifestyle, and right to self-determination. Viewing cultural diversity issues from the perspective of the client environment provides the social worker with valuable context for understanding the stressors a client is experiencing and the positive and negative coping strategies a client may be using. It also helps the social worker build rapport and trust with clients and contributes to the development of culturally appropriate intervention plans.

Strengths-based perspective
A social work practice approach that recognizes the person and her/his cultural experiences and beliefs as an asset on which to develop a plan for change.

Too often in the past, practitioners dismissed culture, ethnicity, religion and spirituality, and sexual orientation as irrelevant, deficient, or an area for change, rather than as an asset or resource in problem solving. For example, homosexuality was considered a mental illness in the *Diagnostic and Statistical Manual* (the reference for diagnostic criteria for mental health providers) until 1978. Incorporating the client's cultural characteristics and lived experiences into the intervention strategy as a strength is consistent with the social work value of respecting each individual's uniqueness and worth. Applying the knowledge and skills of the strengths-based perspective along with those of culturally competent practice, social workers can promote a just, multicultural environment.

Consider a scenario in which you are a social worker working with an older Jewish woman who, as a child following World War II, immigrated to this country from Europe. She is a widow and a retired teacher who lives alone and has no immediate family nearby. Since the death of her husband, she has become withdrawn and feels useless, and you are concerned that she is depressed. While conducting an assessment, you learn that she is a survivor of the Holocaust and concentration camps. You help her to see her life experiences as a resource for educating others about the atrocities committed during the Holocaust, and you arrange for her to join a speaker's bureau for the local Jewish Community Center. She travels to schools to share her story with children, most of whom have never met a Holocaust survivor as their numbers are rapidly decreasing. Her depression dissipates; she is now feeling useful because she is using her skills as a teacher and her life experiences as a survivor.

While oppression and discrimination are certainly not positives, a client's negative and likely painful experience can be an opportunity for growth. Utilizing the strengths perspective, a social worker can help reframe past experiences so the client can identify ways in which she or he endured and grew, helping the client to view her- or himself as a competent person who has the capacity to achieve goals. This shift in outlook can be immensely empowering for clients. For a person with a long history of experiencing discrimination and oppression, the collaboration, empowerment, and access to resources that the strengths-based approach makes possible may be uplifting first-time experiences.

THE "ISMS"

"ism"
A suffix that, when added to a word that describes an individual or group, signifies discrimination or prejudice (e.g., racism, sexism, or ageism).

Throughout history, social workers have been on the forefront of challenging certain ever-present "isms" —doctrines, causes, or theories that motivate behavior. Within the social work context, the suffix, "ism," is a set of ideologies and prejudgments that are typically viewed with negative connotations (Barker, 2014, p. 227). Although "isms" can be positive or neutral belief systems (for example, patriotism or romanticism), to social workers they typically connote negative attitudes or beliefs regarding a specific population. The "isms" that social workers most frequently encounter are racism, ageism, sexism, classism, ableism, heterosexism, and religious discrimination.

Intersectionality
When the multiple dimensions of diversity (e.g., race, class, gender, and sexual orientation) and issues of power, privilege, and institutional practices meet, typically in a situation involving discrimination or oppression for the person or group involved.

Once a person identifies an individual as a member of a vulnerable group, that person tends to view that individual predominantly in terms of her or his membership in that group. For example, many people see a person with a physical disability and ignore that person's other traits, strengths, qualities, roles, or other group memberships, such as being outgoing, loyal, a parent, a teacher, or an employee. As you read the following sections, keep in mind that each group is made up of individuals who are also members of other groups. Each person is so much more than her or his race, age, gender, social class, abilities, sexual orientation, or religious affiliation. Intersectionality occurs when the multiple dimensions of diversity (e.g., race, class, gender, and sexual orientation) and issues of power, privilege, and institutional practices meet, typically in a situation involving discrimination or oppression for the person or group involved. This concept helps us gain insight into the fact that diversity encompasses a complex range of issues, not just one, and they come together to create the lived experience. Social workers must be aware of intersectionality as their clients may be subjected to discrimination based on, for example, sexual orientation and the fact that many states do not recognize same-sex marriage.

The following discussion is not intended to be an all-inclusive examination of "isms," but rather a sampling of those that social workers routinely encounter. Awareness and knowledge of these isms are part of becoming a culturally competent social worker. Because the demographic characteristics of the United States are always changing, it is important for social workers in the U.S. to keep abreast of changing attitudes and preferences among the population as a whole and among their clients in particular.

Racism

Probably the most common "ism" challenging the U.S. today is racism, the categorization and stereotyping of groups based on racial characteristics or ethnic origins. Throughout the country's history, racism has permeated essentially every aspect of U.S. society. Racism continues to exist on multiple levels, and in the United States it has manifested as: individual, cultural, institutional, and systemic ways in which groups historically or currently defined as White have a distinct advantage over groups historically or currently defined as non-White (African, Asian, Hispanic, Native American, etc.).

Race is not a genetic phenomenon, but is in fact a social construct borne out of centuries of human interactions that are the result of the social and historical controversies that have occurred (Sisneros, Stakeman, Joyner, & Schmitz, 2008). Because "race" is such an emotionally-charged word, many scholars and practitioners are choosing more and more to instead focus on "ethnicity" and "ethnic origin" to place greater emphasis on ethnic/national origin (Hall & Lindsey, 2014). Whether on a personal, institutional, or societal level, racism is defined as the belief, or actions taken based on the belief, that one group is superior to (an)other group(s) based solely on race. Racism is actualized when a racist person or group exerts control through the distribution of resources, power, and/or privilege which can include language, actions, violating civil rights, and denying access to services (Sisneros et al., 2008). Exhibit 5.2 presents many of the terms that social workers must be able to use correctly when discussing racism.

EXHIBIT 5.2

Terminology Related to Race and Ethnicity

- Accommodation: A dominant group's efforts to enable another group to live more comfortably within society, for example, offering printed materials in multiple languages to make it possible for persons whose first language is not English to read them.
- Acculturation: A process in which one cultural group borrows or adopts the values, beliefs, and behaviors of another culture.
- Assimilation: Adoption of the dominant group's cultural practices (including values, norms, and behaviors) by another group, for example, the "Americanization" of refugees who immigrate to the United States
- Bias (prejudicial): Positive or negative prejudgments or attitudes toward a person, group, or idea, typically based on misperceptions and not on fact or evidence.
- Color: Despite political, social, and emotional connotations, literally, the pigmentation of a person's skin.
- Culture: Social construct encompassing such traits as race, ethnicity, and group membership; defined by the many characteristics and components a group possesses, such as values, beliefs, religious and political tenets, rituals and other behaviors, and artifacts; and used in interacting, communicating, and interpreting information (Okun et al., 1999).
- Ethnicity: Aspect of one's identity characterized by national origin, culture, race, language, and religious beliefs and practices.
- Ethnocentrism: Belief that one's culture is the norm (and thus, typically, superior) and that other cultures with different practices or beliefs are therefore outside the norm (Okun et al., 1999).
- Integration: Bringing together of diverse groups as equals in such institutions as public schools, the military, and the workplace.
- Marginalization: Subordination of individuals or groups who possess less power; due to the perpetuation of stereotypes and oppression.
- Multicultural competence (multiculturalism): Practice of understanding, recognizing, and respecting the cultural values, beliefs, and behaviors of others.
- Pluralism: Belief that all groups have value; a basis for understanding the way members of a society interact with one another and with the environments in which they live (Logan, 2003).
- Race: "Sociopolitical, not a biological, constructor, one that is created and reinforced by social and institutional norms and practice, individual attitudes, and behaviors" (Castañeda & Zúñiga, 2013, p. 58). The 2010 Census uses five racial categories to describe the U.S. population:
  - White—origins in Europe, the Middle East, or North Africa.
  - Black or African American—origins in any of the black racial groups of Africa.
  - American Indian or Alaska Native—origins in any of the original peoples of North, Central, or South America; maintains tribal affiliation or community attachment.
  - Asian—origins in any of the original peoples of the Far East, Southeast Asia, or the Indian subcontinent, including Cambodia, China, India, Japan, Korea, Malaysia, Pakistan, the Philippines Islands, Thailand, and Vietnam.
  - Native Hawaiian or Other Pacific Islander—origins in any of the original peoples of Hawaii, Guam, Samoa, or other Pacific Islands.

- ■ Segregation: Racial and religious segregation—the separation of one group from other groups; institutionalized racial and religious segregation are currently unlawful, but many other forms of segregation, whether institutionalized or informal in both public and private organizations, are not.
- ■ Social class: An individual's or group's standing in a social hierarchy based on characteristics such as income, status, and education.
- ■ Stereotype: Assumption that a person possesses the same characteristics as all other individuals within his or her group.

In the most visible manifestation of racism, a majority or dominant culture segregates, isolates, and disempowers a minority or less powerful group of people based on racial difference. In the United States, the majority of the population has historically been Caucasian, but, as demographic trends indicate, population ratios are changing. However, that demographic change has not yet resulted in significant shifting of racist attitudes in the U.S. (NASW, 2012–2014l). Change is slow to occur because racism can be learned from previous generations and it takes time for people to internalize different attitudes and behaviors. Racism is built on three faulty assumptions which have helped to perpetuate racist attitudes: (1) biological race equates to categorizations of people; (2) categorizations are linked to culture and individual characteristics (e.g., personality and intellect); and (3) categorizations logically promote a hierarchical system of superiority of one race over another (Sisneros et al., 2008). For example, anti-immigrant sentiment, which is often based on racism, continues to exist in areas such as access to social services, education, employment, and housing. Consider the immigrant family who moves into a new community and experiences racist remarks and vandalism. Whether it is perpetrated at a conscious or subconscious level, racism has consequences for both the dominators and the oppressed (Bell, 2013). As the demographic make-up of the U.S. continues to change, the Caucasian population will no longer be the majority of the population, but discrimination (including racism) is often the product of power and control of resources, not actual numbers. Racism is perpetuated through a passing on of cultural messages that translate into beliefs and actions (Sisneros et al., 2008). The social work profession can continue to work to educate and confront racism as it occurs.

Many hoped and believed legislative attacks on expressions of racism would eliminate those expressions, at least within institutions. The heroism of the civil rights movement and passage of affirmative action legislation have succeeded in bringing an end to several forms of overt institutional racism. Tensions still exist between those who advocate for color-blindness (i.e., race should not be a factor) and those who seek increased race consciousness— which often falls down political party lines with the Republican Party becoming more conservative and White and the Democrats being more liberal and non-White (Omi & Winant, 2015). Omi and Winant (2015) contend that "race has served as a fundamental organizing principle of injustice in the United States—one that has influenced the definition of rights and privileges, the distribution of resources, and the ideologies and practices of subordination and oppression" (p. 263). What does this mean for the social work practitioner? How can we, individually or collectively, hope to make a difference? Omi and Winant (2015) encourage us to maintain our focus on the interruption of racism by promoting anti-racism in the workplace, schools, politics, families, culture, and, in fact, in every interaction we have (p. 266). For example, we can draw attention to acts of racism through letters to the editor of newspapers, confronting racist language, or reporting acts of workplace or school racism.

In simple terms, racism is often manifested as prejudice plus power, a common phrase in the field. Combining the concepts of prejudice and power points out the mechanisms by which racism leads to different consequences for different groups. For example, if an employer has certain assumptions about an employee based on the employee's race or ethnicity and the employer treats the employee different from other employees, this is prejudice plus power. The use of power to extend prejudice has allowed racism to recreate itself generation after generation, such that systems that perpetuate racial inequity no longer need racist actors or to explicitly promote racial differences in opportunities, outcomes, and consequences to maintain those differences (Racial Equity Tools, n.d.: www.racialequitytools.org/glossary#racism).

Institutional Racism Racism perpetuated at the institutional level includes cultural and systemic racism and refers to discrimination against persons of color in accessing resources such as employment, education, financial assistance and credit, organizational membership, and home ownership. Institutional racism is "those policies, practices, or procedures embedded in bureaucratic structures that systematically lead to unequal outcomes for people of color" (Barker, 2014, p. 218).

As with all forms of discrimination, institutional racism can be difficult to change for a host of reasons, including such factors as:

Institutional racism
Abuse or mistreatment propogated by a person or group that knowingly promotes the discrimination of another person or group.

- Institutional racism is typically longstanding and entrenched.
- Affected individuals do not feel empowered to effect change.
- Institutions are slow to change (due to the need for system-wide policies and practices to be modified which, in some cases, requires legislative mandates).
- Institutional racism is usually complex as it involves policy and practice changes at multiple levels.
- Society often reinforces it (Diller, 2015, pp. 67–68).

Discriminating against a group (e.g., African Americans or Hispanic Americans) in mortgage lending to prevent that group from establishing ownership in certain communities is one example of institutional racism.

Individual Racism In contrast to institutional racism, individual racism is abuse or mistreatment propagated by a person or group that knowingly or unknowingly promotes the discrimination of another person or group. In other words, there is an attempt to exert power over another person through preventing access to resources or showing a lack of respect through racist language or actions. For example, the uttering of a racial slur by one person to another is individual racism.

Individual racism
Abuse or mistreatment propagated by a person or group that knowingly or unknowingly promotes the discrimination of another person or group.

Historical Approaches to Diversity Over the past 50 years, U.S. society has dramatically modified its definitions of and approaches to race-related issues. During the mid-20th century, a "melting pot" approach that emphasized sameness among the races aimed to create a society in which all cultures become blended into a single culture without the distinctions of diversity. While this approach was largely viewed as well-intentioned, the goal of blending all cultures without sacrificing individual traditions was not successful. One might speculate that the lack of success underscores the role that power plays in shaping a dominant culture. Not all segments of society embraced such an approach; for example, those U.S. states that enforced segregation, and many members of minority racial and ethnic groups, such as Latinos/Latinas, Asian Americans, and African Americans, wanted to retain elements of their own cultural identity. Then, during the late 1950s and 1960s, support grew for an approach that embraced a "world of difference" focused on racial uniqueness. Still others within the civil rights movement advocated for total racial integration.

Melting pot
An approach that emphasized sameness among the races aimed to create a society in which all cultures become blended into a single culture without the distinctions of diversity.

In the 1970s and 1980s a multiculturalist movement emerged that valued individual ethnicities. This perspective met with intense intellectual and political opposition from persons and groups that wanted to maintain racial separateness which essentially was an attempt to devalue groups who were different from those who opposing the perspective. For some, this view again shifted during the 1990s to a pluralistic conceptualization that viewed society as a collection of groups of distinctive ethnic origin, cultural patterns, and relationships.

Multiculturalism
The practice of embracing and honoring the values, beliefs, and culture of others.

The NASW's 2012–2014 policy statement articulates the social work profession's goal to promote an "inclusive, multicultural society in which racial, ethnic, class, sexual orientation, age, physical and mental ability, religion and spirituality, gender and other cultural and social identifies are valued and respected" (NASW, 2012–2014l, p. 285). In the second decade of the 21st century, the social work profession continues to refine its approach to gaining cultural competence. This is guided by an ethnocultural framework

Pluralism
Individual and group differences are held in esteem by all members of a society without discrimination or prejudice.

Ethnoculturalism
An approach that recognizes that culture shapes us.

that recognizes that culture shapes us and that the social worker's competence evolves when he or she provides the client with the opportunity to develop a narrative that tells the story of her or his lived experience (Kohli, Huber, & Faul, 2010). An ethnocultural approach builds on the strengths-based perspective and conveys to the client that her or his culture is valued and will be incorporated into the helping process. To this end, NASW has developed a policy statement that calls for human service programs to work to preserve cultural and linguistic diversity through policies, printed materials, and services (NASW, 2012–2014g). Through the 2014 Achieving Racial Equity Action Brief issued by the Social Work Policy Institute (SWPI), social workers are called upon to develop competencies to combat institutional racism, including:

- Understanding that people are poor because they lack power (resources, decision-making, law, land, etc.), not because they lack programs.
- Understanding how social programs maintain poverty and institutional structures that limit access to wealth.
- Asserting that the social work profession focuses on well-being and social justice:
  - Consider anti-racism to be how social workers "do" social justice—it's not outside the work we do—it should not be a separate subject, but rather a lens.
  - Use the *Code of Ethics* (NASW, 2008) to speak to anti-racism.
- Recognizing that racism is the glue that holds classism/poverty together and is maintained through structures and systems of racial inequity.
- Identifying and interrupting color-blind racial ideology.
- Working to understand that it is essential to develop authentic relationships to create and maintain human boundaries—with individuals and communities and across systems.
- Understanding that racism has negative impact on all races.
- Fighting injustice due to:
  - Lack of access to resources and opportunities.
  - Disinvestment.
  - Intertwining of racism and poverty which have both structural and systemic dynamics.
  - Continued existence of racism, even when no longer poor.
  - Manipulation of poor Whites using racism, for example, poor Whites vote on race (p. 18).

Racial issues can evoke intense emotional reactions and having a set of competencies such as the ones described here to guide your practice can help you to maintain a professional and socially just approach. Most people have been either a victim or perpetrator of racist thoughts or behaviors, and many people have been both at one time or another. Some students, both White students and students of color, report being uncomfortable in a classroom in which racism is discussed because of shame related to the behaviors of their racial group, anger regarding the treatment of persons of color, or resentment toward students who have not experienced discrimination (those seen as having "White privilege"). However, when students agree to create a safe environment in which issues, and not people, are confronted, they can initiate stimulating and meaningful discussions. As long as we remain open to expanding our cultural awareness and sensitivity, the social work classroom, service learning site, and field experience can be excellent environments in which to learn and develop cultural competence. To learn more about strategies for achieving racial equity, visit: www.racialequitytools.org/home. A westernized approach known as critical multiculturalism, goes beyond race to include education on culture, oppression, multiple identities, power, whiteness and privilege, historical context, and social change (Daniel, 2008).

Multiculturalism
The practice of embracing and honoring the values, beliefs, and culture of others.

The status of racial justice and racial equity in the second decade of the 21st century remains controversial and is, as yet, undetermined in specific terms of progress made. With changing demographics and continued covert and overt displays of racism, we still have a long way to go to become a racially equitable society. While considerable strides have been made by society and the social work profession in recent years to eradicate racism, events like the 2014 police shooting of 19-year-old Michael Brown in Ferguson, Missouri (a predominantly African American suburb of St. Louis) remind us that we must continue our efforts (Blank, 2006). The shooting and killing of Brown, an unarmed African American, by a White police officer sparked demonstrations, looting, and violence. Journalists were detained and threatened, the FBI became involved, and President Obama made a special statement calling for peace and resolution. On a possible hopeful note, the incident also instigated community-wide and nationwide conversations. The recommendations made in a 2015 U.S. Department of Justice report on the Ferguson Police Department draw attention to the need for change, including:

1. Implement a Robust System of True Community Policing
2. Focus Stop, Search, Ticketing and Arrest Practices on Community Protection
3. Increase Tracking, Review, and Analysis of FPD Stop, Search, Ticketing and Arrest Practices
4. Change Force Use, Reporting, Review, and Response to Encourage De-Escalation and the Use of the Minimal Force Necessary in a Situation
5. Implement Policies and Training to Improve Interactions with Vulnerable People

6. Change Response to Students to Avoid Criminalizing Youth While Maintaining a Learning Environment
7. Implement Measures to Reduce Bias and Its Impact on Police Behavior
8. Improve and Increase Training Generally
9. Increase Civilian Involvement in Police Decision Making
10. Improve Officer Supervision
11. Recruiting, Hiring, and Promotion
12. Develop Mechanisms to More Effectively Respond to Allegations of Officer Misconduct
13. Publicly Share Information about the Nature and Impact of Police Activities

What are your thoughts on the DOJ recommendations and ways we can address and prevent these ongoing challenges?

Social workers can confront racism in many ways. The most obvious strategies include advocacy, education, and, sometimes, mediation (for example, serving as an agent to promote effective communication). To be effective in any of these areas, social workers must be willing to recognize areas in which their own knowledge and skills are lacking. Social workers must always be mindful of implementing assessments and interventions in ways that take into consideration the race, ethnicity, culture, and social identity of each client, along with the roles power and privilege play in a client's relationships (Garran & Rozas, 2013; Golden, 2008). Social workers may confront racial injustices at any and all levels and areas of practice, and must all consider their individual, personal, and professional role is in promoting racial equity and justice.

Ageism

When most people hear the term *ageism,* they immediately think of the mistreatment of older adults. In fact, ageism refers to discrimination based on *any* age. The two groups most at risk for age bias and discrimination are children and older adults as their "voices" are often not heard or respected. Being on the two ends of the age spectrum places these groups in vulnerable positions regarding access to resources. Moreover—and perhaps even worse—the two groups are sometimes pitted against each other when resources are allocated.

The sheer number of older persons has risen across the world and will continue to rise dramatically. Increasingly, they are making their collective voices heard, in part because they have become highly organized through groups like the American Association of Retired Persons (AARP), and in part because they advocate for legislation and vote in ways that benefit seniors and promote their rights. Even so, older adults continue to need support from social workers and other advocates to ensure that their voices are heard at the legislative level, within the health care and social service systems, and within their communities.

While older adults have made their voices heard, children and youth must depend on adults to champion their causes. Children and youth have been overlooked in terms of funding for health and education, in particular. Federal and state budgets have been consistently decreased for health care coverage (e.g., Medicaid) and public school resources. Oftentimes, those groups who advocate for the rights and needs of children and youth are non-profit, grassroots organizations that are not well resourced themselves. These groups are in competition with lobbying efforts that are better funded and more influential.

If you are reading this book, you have experience being on the youthful end of the age spectrum. You may have experienced ageism in a variety of situations from being closely watched in a store (fearing that you will shop lift) or not taken seriously by those older than you. However, most of us have yet to experience life as an older adult. Therefore, we rely on our perceptions of older adults, which may be biased and stereotypical. In one study of social work students' perceptions of themselves at age 75, most students expected that they would have health and memory problems, but that they would still be attractive, valued, and active (Kane, 2008). To better understand the needs of older adults you will encounter in your social work practice, consider how you see yourself as you age. What will you look, feel, and act like as an older adult? What will your life be like when you are 65, 75, and 85 years old? While you are limited in your ability to actually know what your life will be like as you age, engaging in an exercise to imagine yourself as an older adult can help you to build empathy for the social and physical experiences you may encounter.

Consider the experience of one of Emily's classmates, Elizabeth. Elizabeth was in Emily's introductory social work class. She entered the social work program with the sole intent of working with young children. Elizabeth had hoped to complete her required service learning experience at a crisis center for children, but she was unable to complete her hours at this site because the center did not have any more volunteer slots available that semester. It was late in the semester, and Elizabeth worried that she would have difficulty fulfilling the course requirement. The course instructor suggested that Elizabeth team up with Emily at the senior residential complex, because that program was in need of volunteers. While she followed through with the instructor's suggestion, Elizabeth was certain she would absolutely hate it. She had very little experience being in the company of older adults and had never been comfortable with them. Initially, she felt awkward and ill at ease at the senior complex, particularly when helping with events where the residents gathered. Over the course of the volunteer experience, and with the help of the on-site staff and the older adults themselves, Elizabeth gradually began to feel more comfortable in the setting, and, in fact, she decided to expand her career plans to include working with intergenerational programs that serve both children and older adults.

Dealing effectively with ageism begins on a personal level. Conduct an inventory of your ageist experiences:

- Have you ever purchased a greeting card that lamented the fact that a person was "over the hill?"
- Have you ever been dismissed or discounted by someone because you were too young or too old to understand something?
- Have you heard or made stereotypical remarks about the driving abilities of either younger or older persons?
- Have you ever referred to a person's age in a derogatory manner—"geezer" or "baby," for instance?

Social workers are obligated, as a part of any diversity self-awareness campaign, to check themselves and society as a whole on issues of ageism. All social work practitioners are ethically bound to acquire knowledge and skills that will enable them to be effective in working with persons of any age, and the best way to begin that process is to gain experience with persons at both ends of the age spectrum. Children's and aging service agencies welcome volunteers to spend time with clients or participants. When we develop personal connections and relationships with others, we typically find that any stereotypes we may have held begin to melt away.

Sexism and Women's Issues

Sexism
the belief that one gender is superior to another.

Sexism is typically defined as the belief that one gender is superior to another. However, a more expansive perspective speaks to the impact of that belief. Sisneros and colleagues (2008) suggest that sexism is not just the belief of superiority, but the preferential treatment of males over females and the misogyny (hatred of females and femininity) that results in the oppression of persons who are female, fender variant, transgender, gay, lesbian, and bisexual (p. 55). Based on this concept, sexism occurs when women are discriminated against because they are women. While sexism or gender bias is usually male-to-female, men can be the victims of sexism as well. Consider the online interactive case (www.routledgesw.com/caseStudies) in which Hector Sanchez disapproves of his son's desire to cook, which he considers "unmanly." Despite the fact that men can be the targets of sexist acts, the most oppressive discrimination based on sexism in our society is directed toward women, which will be the focus of the discussion that follows.

Historically, institutionally enforced sexism has oppressed women in many aspects of life. At various times women could not own property, vote, run for public office, or divorce their husbands, and they were prevented entering many professions. For example, less than a century ago, women were granted the right to vote. Although the U.S. has made considerable strides toward improving the status of women, significant gender-based inequities remain around the world. In parts of the world, women are being oppressed for expressing their independence, speaking out for women's rights, and challenging the traditional restrictions placed on them.

In the U.S., where progress has been achieved, women continue to face such challenges as:

- Women continue to earn less than men for the same work.
- Women are still in the minority in most traditionally male-dominated professions (such as medicine and engineering), and when women achieve a major presence within a professional discipline, the salaries of both men and women tend to decrease.
- The majority of persons who are victims of violence or living in poverty continue to be women, and many families living in poverty are female-headed households.
- Among the older adult population, women and particularly women of color are most at-risk economically.
- Women are less frequently elected to public office and continue to be in the minority of leaders in companies, organizations, and government.
- Women are stilled viewed at the primary caregiver of family members.

Although equal employment and sexual and gender harassment policies have legislated equality for women, some would argue that institutional sexism, while illegal, persists but appears to have gone "underground." For example, when both genders continue to make sexist remarks, particularly in the areas of domestic violence (e.g., "I wonder what she did to set him off?") and sexual violence (e.g., "There is no such thing as date rape), clothing (e.g., "Look how she was dressed"), and behaviors (e.g., "What did she expect being out late at night?"). When women engage in traditionally male activities, they may be criticized, particularly when the women excel in the activity. The goal should, in fact, be to eliminate sexual designations for any kind of activities—there are no longer "traditional" male or female activities or professions. When males are told they "throw like a girl," should not wear pink, or watch "chick flicks," these comments constrict men and contribute to misogyny and perhaps even violence against both genders. Women continue to function as the primary caregivers for the family, even when they work full-time outside the home. The question we have to ask is: are women continuing to provide the majority of care to family members because they are expected to, they want to, or are not being supported by other members of the family in the caregiving responsibilities?

An interplay of characteristics multiplies many women's vulnerability to discrimination and oppression (Worden, 2011). Consider the female client who is also a woman of color, a religious minority, or economically disadvantaged, and the way in which those factors impact her life experience and self-perception. Each person is unique and complex, and traits cannot be considered in isolation. Sexism is further complicated when race, ethnicity, class, and/or national origin are a part of the scenario; these factors cannot be viewed separately. Moreover, race cannot be considered without factoring in gender, class, and sexual orientation (Sisneros et al., 2008).

Social workers have an ethical responsibility to address issues of gender equality. Sexism can be institutionalized, systemic, and interpersonal, thus disadvantaging women at the structural and emotional levels (Worden, 2011). Gender can impact employment; public assistance programs; education; physical, emotional, and mental health; and global gender issues. In the 2012–2014 policy statement, NASW calls for equity and social and economic justice in these areas (NASW, 2012–2014p). Social workers can endeavor to prevent sex discrimination by dispelling stereotypes and myths about the sexes. Stereotypes about both men and women contribute to sexism from all sides and promote harm to persons of both sexes. Social workers can also empower clients by informing them that they do not have to let a sexual assault go unreported or remain in a physically, psychologically, or sexually violent relationship. At the organizational level, social workers can advocate for the completion of a gender audit—a review of an organization's policies and practices to assess the level of gender equality in an organization's staffing, programming, and evaluation processes (NASW, n.d. available at: www.socialworkers.org/practice/intl/definitions.asp).

Gender audit
a review of an organization's policies and practices to assess the level of gender equality in an organization's staffing, programming, and evaluation processes.

At the policy level, social workers can act to ensure that policies promote gender equity. Every social worker can write letters to the media when women are portrayed unfairly, stereotypically, or as inferior to men, petition government leaders and offices, educate and organize in their communities, and boycott businesses. What activities might you undertake to combat sexism?

Classism

Although some philosophers have claimed that the United States should be a classless society, in reality our society has distinct classes that have evolved over time and that hold class-related values, expectations, beliefs, and lead class-based lifestyles (Okun, Fried & Okun, 1999). Classism, or discrimination based on social class, can occur as a result of occupational status (for example, blue collar or white collar), educational achievement (for example, high school diploma or college graduate), or income (for example, working class or middle class). Despite the seemingly clear class distinctions that we presume to have in the U.S., most Americans self-identify as being in the middle socioeconomic class even when their incomes are higher or lower than the income designations (Sisneros et al., 2008). For example, the Occupy Movement was aimed at drawing attention to the fact that the wealth gap continues to widen.

Like other prejudices, prejudiced views lead to the unfair labeling of the members of different social classes. Some believe that people can earn membership in higher socioeconomic classes if they are willing to work hard—the idea of pulling oneself up by one's bootstraps. Those who accept that idea tend to characterize people on the lower end of the economic continuum as lacking ambition. Such thinking may lead to person to have racist, sexist, or ableist attitudes (i.e., that African American woman is poor, therefore, women and African Americans are unmotivated). This combination of characteristics, intersectionality, places this woman at significant risk for discrimination and oppression, but she has the potential to identify and mobilize her strengths and resources to establish and reach her goals. Too often, persons at risk for discrimination and oppression are unable to navigate the socioeconomic ladder because their opportunities to achieve economic success may be limited and the challenges overwhelming (Sisneros et al., 2008). In essence, one can subscribe to the "pull yourself up by your bootstraps" philosophy, but the reality may be that having a willingness to work hard may not be adequate to overcome the obstacles that some people face.

As Chapter 4 showed, the distinctions between the richest and the poorest in our society continue to become more extreme. With an increasingly small percentage of the population controlling the overwhelming majority of resources and the shrinking of the middle socioeconomic class (despite self-identifications increasing as people view being middle-class as being "normal" and acceptable), those on the lowest end of the economic spectrum have less and less opportunity to positively affect their financial status. As a great percentage of the wealth is held by a small minority of the population, the government employing austerity measures to curtail funding, and the U.S. still being in a period of economic recovery, those living on limited incomes have fewer avenues to economic stability.

As you conduct your diversity self-assessment, consider your personal experiences with and views on socioeconomic class. How have the messages you have received throughout your life regarding social class and income affected your views and attitudes? Ask yourself the following:

■ Have you ever thought about the socioeconomic class into which you were born? What was your family's socioeconomic status at the time of your birth?

■ Are you still a member of that same socioeconomic class? If you have changed socioeconomic class, how did that occur? How has that shift changed your life?

■ What does membership in your socioeconomic class, or any other socioeconomic class, mean in terms of a person's education, resources, opportunities, place of residence, and employment?

■ Have you been a victim of classist remarks, or (try to be honest here) have you made classist remarks?

■ Do you perceive a difference between those students whose parents/family pay for college and those students who must take out loans?

As with all the isms, the social worker's role in combating classism is often one of advocacy and education. Countering the "bootstrap" myth, empowering people to reach their optimal functioning and quality of life, and confronting classist language are just three anti-classism activities in which social workers can engage proactively.

Ableism

Ableism
Discrimination against individuals who have neurological/intellectual/cognitive, emotional, and/or physical functioning disabilities.

Ableism is discrimination against individuals who have neurological/intellectual/cognitive, emotional, and/or physical functioning disabilities. Disabilities can be perceptual, illness-related, physical, developmental, psychiatric, psychological, mobility-related, or environmental (for example, severe allergies, exposure to toxins, etc.). That is, one can be born with a cognitive or physical disability (e.g., Down Syndrome) or one can experience it later in life (e.g., depression, brain injury, or visual impairment). Disabilities are generally categorized into four groupings: (1) sensory (e.g., hearing or vision impairments); (2) mental/intellectual (e.g., developmental disabilities, mental illness, and dementias); (3) learning/cognitive disabilities (e.g., speech and attention deficits disorders); and (4) physical disabilities (e.g., spinal cord injury) (Sisneros et al., 2008). Overall, approximately 19% of the U.S. population currently experience a disability (U.S. Census Bureau Newsroom, 2012). The number of children identified as having documented disabilities has risen to 8% of all children (Houtrow, Larson, Olson, Newacheck, & Halfon, 2014). This is an increase from past reports that is likely due to heightened awareness and diagnosis, particularly in the areas of neurodevelopmental and mental health (e.g., autism and attention disorders), with the largest increases occurring among children from wealthier families (Houtrow et al., 2014).

Unfortunately, U.S. society has oppressed disabled populations for centuries, from using discriminatory language to refer to people with disabilities, to failing to provide access to schools and public buildings, to the tendency to "warehouse" people with disabilities in separate institutions and schools. Such oppression has had a dehumanizing effect on many disabled persons, as they have often been stigmatized, socially isolated, marginalized, and even exploited. Disabled persons have historically been denied adequate support for education, employment, housing, transportation, access to services, resources, physical spaces, and beneficial policies (Sisneros et al., 2008).

Many in our country will experience a disability within our lifetimes. In fact, one in four persons will experience a disability after the age of 20 years (U.S. Social Security Administration, 2013). However, it was only in the 1970s that policy-makers began addressing the problems of the disabled and that the public became more aware of and sensitive to their needs. This recent shift is due, in large part, to a shift in theoretical views on disability from an applied medical/ deficit model focused on labeling, diagnosis, and treatment, to a social model focused on the environment, social structures, values, and providing support services (Sisneros et al., 2008, p. 70). Since persons with disabilities and their families led the grassroots disabilities rights movement of the 1970s, Congress has passed over a dozen major legislative acts addressing the needs of the disabled (NASW, 2012–2014i). In particular, two legislative mandates, the Rehabilitation Act of 1973 and the Americans with Disabilities Act of 1990, established institutional mandates and support for the civil rights of, and supportive accommodations and services for, persons with a wide range of disabilities. Despite this significant progress at the policy and institutional levels, discrimination against persons with disabilities still occurs, often in a more covert manner.

Accommodation
Efforts of one group to make changes to enable another group to live within society.

Throughout history, society has used and misused a variety of terms to describe people with various disabilities. Think for a moment of all the disability-related terms you have heard or used throughout your lifetime. Exhibit 5.3 lists some common terms and provides alternative language, or "words with dignity," that are less likely to offend persons with different abilities. There is still some disagreement regarding these terms—some disability advocates challenge the use of some of them, contending that disabilities are a form of diversity, not a pathology (Mackelprang, Patchner, DeWeaver, Clute, & Sullivan, 2008). Generally, using person-first language is considered most appropriate; for example, saying, "he is a person with a disability," instead of "he is a disabled man." This practice can and should be extended broadly (e.g., a person who is homeless versus a homeless man).

Person-first language
Language in which the person is noted first followed by the situation or condition (e.g., "person with a disability" instead of "disabled person").

In striving to eradicate ableism, the social work profession has long championed equity, respect, and physical accommodation. Although our society has made strides in many areas affecting people with disabilities—particularly in improving education, accessibility, employment, and benefits, social workers

EXHIBIT 5.3

Substitutes for Ableist Terms

WORDS WITH DIGNITY	AVOID THESE WORDS
Person with a disability, disabled	Cripple, handicapped, handicap, invalid (literally, invalid means "to weak")
Person who has, person with (e.g. person who has cerebral palsy)	Victim, afflicted with (e.g. victim of cerebral palsy)
Uses a wheelchair	Restricted, confined to a wheelchair, wheelchair bound (the chair enables mobility; without the chair, the person is confined to bed)
Non-disabled	Normal (referring to nondisabled persons as "normal" insinuates that people with disabilities are abnormal)
Deaf, does not voice for themselves, nonvocal	Deaf mute, deaf and dumb
Disabled since birth, born with	Birth defect
Psychiatric history, psychiatric disability, emotional disorder, mental illness	Crazy, insane, lunatic, mental patient, wacko
Epilepsy, seizures	Fits
Learning disability, mental retardation, developmental delay, ADD/ADHD	Slow, retarded, lazy, stupid, underachiever

Other terms which should be avoided because they have negative connotations and tend to evoke pity and fear include: abnormal, burden, condition, deformed, differently abled, disfigured, handi-capable, imbecile, incapacitated, madman, maimed, manic, moron, palsied, pathetic, physically challenged, pitiful, poor, spastic, stricken with, suffer, tragedy, unfortunate, and victim.

Preferred terminology: blind (no visual capability), legally blind, low vision (some visual capability), hard of hearing (some hearing capability), hearing loss, hemiplegia (paralysis of one side of the body), paraplegia (loss of function in the lower body only), quadriplegia (paralysis of both arms and legs), residual limb (post-amputation of a limb).

Source: Paraquad, n.d.

continue to tackle the challenge to draw attention to the abilities and strengths of persons with different abilities. Identifying and advocating for persons with disabilities require ongoing effort.

Keep in mind the following principles when working with individuals with disabilities (Mackelprang & Salsgiver, 2009, pp. 436–438):

- All people are capable or potentially capable.
- Disability does not imply dysfunction; persons with disabilities do not need to be "fixed" in order to function in society.
- Disabilities are a social construct, and interventions therefore must target the political barriers that exist within the environment, prevalent attitudes, and public policy. Persons with disabilities have experienced societal responses and challenges related to living with a disability.
- Persons with disabilities should be viewed as unique, not dysfunctional.
- Persons with disabilities have a right to self-determination.

Social workers are ethically obligated to be on the cutting edge of services, resources, and advocacy for persons with disabilities. They must combat both the use of inappropriate language and discrimination in the provision of services. Finally, they should fight to ensure the rights of any person with a disability. To learn about one social worker who epitomizes social work's mission to dispel the myths of living with a disability, read about John Foppe, MSW in Exhibit 5.4.

Heterosexism and Homophobia

Heterosexism, the belief that heterosexuality is the only acceptable form of sexual orientation, exists at all levels of our society and is perpetuated formally and informally. Homophobia is overt hostility toward anyone who is not hetereosexual. Both heterosexism and homophobia emerge from sexism, which promotes traditional and rigidly defined gender role expectations (Sisneros et al., 2008). Rather than viewing sexual orientation as a part of an individual's identify, many people continue to view a nonheterosexual orientation as a choice or preference, a defect, or a perversion and therefore see it as "curable." Not long ago, heterosexist beliefs barred lesbians, gay men, bisexuals, and transgender persons (persons whose gender identity is counter to their presumed biological sex) (LGBTQ) from employment in many areas, from legally marrying, from adopting children as a single parent or couple, from receiving partner benefits, from openly serving in the military, and from making legal and medical decisions for their partners. Heterosexist individuals and groups have committed hate crimes against the LGBTQ community ranging from verbal harassment to physical assaults, "or gay bashing," and even murder. Recall the 1998 case of Matthew Shepherd, the University of Wyoming student who was lured by two men who had posed as gay allegedly to rob him but instead tortured and murdered him because he was gay. This act of hatred brought public awareness to the heterosexism that existed in the country. As a result, the Matthew Shepherd and James Byrd, Jr. Hate

Heterosexism
The belief that heterosexuality is the only acceptable form of sexual orientation, exists at all levels of our society and is perpetuated formally and informally.

Homophobia
Overt hostility toward anyone who is not heterosexual.

EXHIBIT 5.4

What's Your Excuse? Making the Most of What You Have

Meet social worker, motivational speaker, agency director, husband, father, and .... a person society would label as having a disability, John Foppe. Below is an excerpt from John's biographical statement describing his life. To learn more about John, visit his website at: www.johnfoppe.com/ or view his TedX talk at: www.youtube.com/watch?v=FnaYjOtLzXs.

Born without arms, John Foppe understands firsthand the difficult gaps between envisioning an outcome and achieving it. He once led a miserable, dependent, and limited existence. At 10 years old, for example, he couldn't put his own pants on. Today, he operates his own company, travels the world, runs a large nonprofit agency, and he is a husband and father.

John has learned that a person's ability to do something is not dependent on having all sorts of ability, time, and money. Instead, making something happen has more to do with one's personal sense of value and ability to cast a vision.

In the field as part of his master's degree in social work, John saw this scenario play out repeatedly. To his surprise, he discovered that many people subconsciously substitute personal improvement with systems to support their perceived limitations. As an advisor and speaker, John also witnessed this resistant mindset operate in all sort of companies. He repeatedly heard leaders complain about how difficult is to motivate their people.

John has addressed this common performance challenge through years of research, clinical study and field testing, which ultimately led to the discovery of the primary cause of failed vision execution. In light of this important, personally-significant discovery, he has developed a variety of solutions to help individuals and leaders overcome their exasperation and translate their visions into outcomes.

John's career in motivation began when his compelling story and methods caught the attention of the legendary Zig Ziglar, who broke his long-standing rule of promoting from within and recruited and mentored John.

In 1995, John launched a successful corporate motivation business, Visionary Velocity Worldwide (www.johnfoppe.com/index.htm), that has taken him to over 25 countries, pro-football organizations like the Miami Dolphins, and to Fortune 500 clients such as Boeing, GE, and State Farm and international companies such as Fortis, ST Microelectronics, and UniCredit.

He is the author of *What's Your Excuse? Making the Most of What You Have* (2002), which has been translated into six foreign languages.

In 1993, the U. S. Junior Chamber of Commerce (Jaycees) recognized John as one of the "Ten Outstanding Young Americans." With this prestigious award, the Jaycees proudly spot young leaders before they achieve their greatest accomplishment.

In the nonprofit world, John has put his leadership and motivation skills to work helping the less fortunate by earning a master's degree in social work from Saint Louis University and serving as the Executive Director of the Society of St. Vincent De Paul–St. Louis Council.

In 2013, he received an honorary doctorate in Humanities and Public Service from Saint Louis University.

Today, John resides in his native town of Breese, Illinois, with his wife, Christine, and daughter, Faith Teresa.

While the sight of how he tackles life with his toes will amaze you, once you hear his message, you will not be looking at him—you will be looking at yourself!

Reprinted with permission from John Foppe, MSW. Photo from http://www.johnfoppe.com/ pressphotos.htm

Crimes Prevention Act was signed into law by President Obama in 2009. While increased awareness and enactment of legislation is progress toward eliminating hate crimes, there continues to be anti-gay sentiment. Because of the overwhelming biases that have historically prevailed in our society, members of these groups have often been highly reluctant to disclose their sexual orientation in any but the safest places, often not even "coming out" to their families, co-workers, or some friends.

In recent years the gay rights movement in the United States has made significant progress. The 2012 Census counted 639,440 same-sex U.S. households (333,646 were female households and 305,794 were male households) (U.S. Census Bureau, 2012a). This number has increased from 605,472 in 2011 (U.S. Census Bureau Fertility and Family Statistics Branch, 2013). That some states and employers now recognize same-sex marriages and the rights of same-sex partners is one example of that progress. At the beginning of this century, no state granted marriage licenses to same-sex couples, but by 2015, the Supreme Court ruled that prohibiting same-sex marriages is a violation of the U.S. Constitution (Procon.org, 2015). See Exhibit 5.5 for a timeline of U.S. legislation related to same-sex marriage. As of 2014, locations in twenty countries around the world have legalized same-sex marriage (Pew Research Religion and Public Life Project, 2014a). In 2011, the U.S. military policy of "don't ask, don't tell" ended when President Obama worked with the military to reverse the policy, thus making the burden of being identified as homosexual less onerous for members of the military.

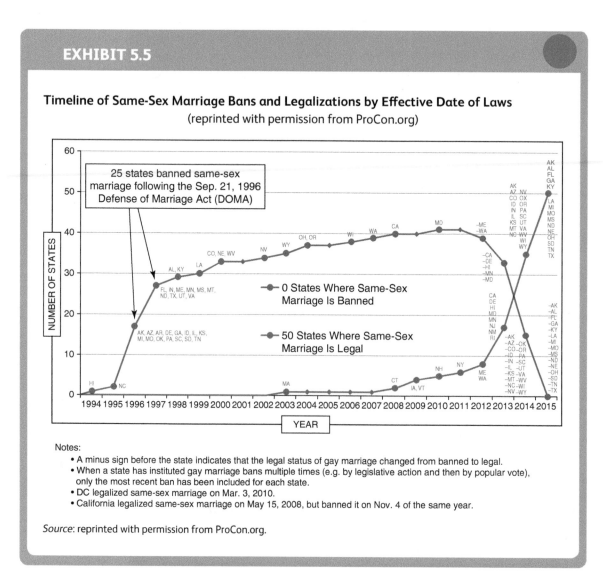

EXHIBIT 5.5

Timeline of Same-Sex Marriage Bans and Legalizations by Effective Date of Laws
(reprinted with permission from ProCon.org)

Notes:
- A minus sign before the state indicates that the legal status of gay marriage changed from banned to legal.
- When a state has instituted gay marriage bans multiple times (e.g. by legislative action and then by popular vote), only the most recent ban has been included for each state.
- DC legalized same-sex marriage on Mar. 3, 2010.
- California legalized same-sex marriage on May 15, 2008, but banned it on Nov. 4 of the same year.

Source: reprinted with permission from ProCon.org.

Despite these gains, there are still areas in which members of the LGBTQ community face discrimination. Members of the LGBTQ community, particularly LGBTQ families, continue to face restricted access to the health and social service system. Approximately two million children in the United States are being reared by LGBTQ parents, but in many parts of the country, LGBTQ couples are still barred from adopting children or becoming foster parents (Movement Advancement Project (MAP), Family Equality Council (FEC) and Center for American Progress (CAP), 2011, p.2). LGBTQ families also experience startling health disparities, including:

- *Inadequate access to health insurance*—employers are not required to provide benefits to same sex partners and their children, and in cases where coverage is available, it may be at a higher cost or include restrictions.
- *Restrictions on caregiving and medical decision-making*—For example, LGBTQ employees may not be granted leave under the Family Medical Leave Act to care for a partner, or a non-biologic parent may not be permitted access to medical information on her or his child.
- *Unwelcoming health care environments*—LGBTQ families may find that health care providers are judgmental regarding their family arrangement.
- *Increased health disparities*—Risks to well-being include limited access to care and increased incidence of HIV/AIDs and other chronic diseases (e.g., diabetes, obesity, and arthritis) due to the health education/literacy, lack of screening, prevention, and diagnostic evaluations.

Another example of intersectionality is the multiple obstacles that impede access to health and social service resources for LGBTQ families of color. In addition to the difficulties any LGBTQ family experiences accessing health insurance and care, LGBTQ families of color often face the following:

- Poverty (32% compared to 7% for White heterosexual married couples).
- Poorer health due to risk factors associated with race or ethnicity (obesity, cancer, diabetes, and HIV/AIDS).
- Feeling unwelcome in school and religious institutions.
- Impeded access to safety net programs (e.g., cash assistance and support for food, housing, health insurance, child care, and education).
- Perceived lack of visibility and support from society (MAP, FEC, & CAP, 2012).

These problems can be further exacerbated for LGBTQ couples who immigrated to the U.S., as immigrants are ineligible for many public programs. LGBTQ families of color do report receiving greater support from their families than do White LGBTQ families, and more LGBTQ couples of color have children and serve as foster parents. Still, LGBTQ families of color often struggle to prosper in U.S. society.

Talking about sexuality, in general, is awkward for many of us, but a lack of knowledge, fear of offending, deep-rooted religious beliefs, or even fears about our own sexuality can make talking about homosexuality and homophobia in particular difficult. A social work course might be the first time some students engage in a discussion about sexuality in which homosexuality is not framed as deviant. Social work classrooms can be a safe place to share thoughts and feelings about working with issues of sexual orientation.

Two separate NASW policy statements take a stand against LGBTQ discrimination and prejudice in areas such as inheritance, insurance, marriage, child custody, employment, credit, immigration, health and mental health services, and education (NASW, 2012–2014h, o). To become culturally competent in order to intervene successfully with LGBTQ clients, social workers must trained to understand the historical, political, social, and religious issues that surround the oppression the LGBTQ community has faced. To that end, NASW (2013c) has partnered with the Substance Abuse and Mental Health Services Administration to develop a series of educational resource materials with information to support social workers and allies working with children and youth who are lesbian, gay, bisexual, transgender, questioning, intersex, and/or two-spirit (LGBTQI2-S) and their families. To view this and other professional resources, visit www.socialworkers.org/diversity/new/lgbt.asp.

Adhering to the values of the social work profession, social workers promote a "celebration of the strengths of this largely invisible minority," not just an acceptance or tolerance of it (Boes & van Wormer, 2015, p. 1032). In the interest of maintaining these values and working effectively with persons of different sexual orientations, social workers must also (Gates, 2006):

- Learn and use appropriate language (see Quick Guide #5.3 for appropriate terminology).
- Be open to understanding sexual and gender differences.
- See beyond the person's sexual orientation to view her or him as a whole person, for whom sexual orientation is one of many defining traits.
- Advocate for all organization to ensure LGBTQ-inclusive language and materials in their policies and eligibility criteria (e.g., list "partner" on intake forms or allow the person to write in gender pronoun preference).
- Advocate for equality and respect in legislation, policies, service delivery, and practices for these groups.

As with those affected by other isms, the discrimination and oppression members of the LGBTQ community experience rarely occurs in isolation. A gay man may be discriminated again because he is gay, but he may also experience discrimination, even from some members of the gay community, because he is African American. Consider Dan's personal narrative in Exhibit 5.6. Dan's experience as a transgender male currently in transition is a complex one.

QUICK GUIDE #5.3 LGBTQ DEFINITIONS: A PRIMER

✓ Sex is assigned at birth based on our external, physical bodies. Are our genitals clearly male or female? Additional sex markers include our chromosomes and our internal and external reproductive organs. Some people also use the term sexed bodies to describe our physical sex. When considering the definition of sex, keep the following in mind:

    ✓ People often use the terms male or female to describe physical sex. As intersex children can attest, though, a person's biology is not always so clearly one way or the other.

    ✓ People often conflate the term sex with the term gender. While sex and gender may align for a majority of people, for some they are not the same.

✓ Intersex children are born with chromosomal and/or reproductive differences. They may have an extra or missing chromosome, have some elements of both male and female reproductive systems (for example, one testicle and one ovary), or have genitals that do not appear clearly male or clearly female at birth.

✓ Gender is a social status associated with the sex a person is assigned at birth based on societal conventions regarding gender expectations. Gender may or may not be consistent with a person's anatomical sexual identifiers.

✓ Gender Identity is an inner psychological sense of oneself as a man or a woman, as both, as neither, or non-gender specific. This term refers to the gender with which one identifies regardless of one's assigned sex at birth.

✓ Gender Expression is the communication of gender through behaviors (e.g., our style , mannerisms, speech patterns, etc.) and aspects of appearance (e.g., clothing, hair, accessories, etc.) culturally associated with a particular gender. Societal definitions of gender influence these communications.

✓ Gender Dysphoria are clinical symptoms of excessive discomfort, confusion, pain, and anguish from feeling an incongruity with the gender assigned to one at birth. Gender dysphoric young people often suppress and hide these feelings from others. Not all transgender youths or adults experience gender dysphoria.

✓ Transgender: An umbrella term that describes people whose gender identity or gender expression differs from expectations associated with the sex assigned to them at birth. This term may be used to describe pre-operative transsexuals, post-operative transsexuals, non-operative transsexuals, cross-dressers, androgynous people, gender benders (person who does not acknowledge traditional gender roles and expectations), drag kings, and drag queens. Transgender people may be heterosexual, bisexual, gay, lesbian, or asexual. Gender variance in children may forecast a same-sex sexual orientation or transgenderism (with or without gender dysphoria), or may simply indicate variance in gender expression.

✓ A transgender woman or transgender girl, also sometimes referred to as a male-to-female or MTF transgender person, is someone who identifies as female but was assigned "male" at birth. Conversely, a transgender man or transgender boy, also sometimes referred to as a female-to-male or FTM transgender person, is someone who identifies as male but was assigned "female" at birth. Transgender people express their gender and identities in diverse ways, including:

    ✓ Crossdressing: Crossdressers occasionally dress in clothing more common to another gender for relaxation; catharsis; sexual pleasure; to express more feminine or masculine sides of themselves; and for any other number of reasons. Many crossdressers report that they are not interested in transitioning to a different gender.

✓ Presenting as Transsexuals. Transsexuals are people whose gender identity does not match expectations associated with the sex assigned to them at birth. Transsexuals may or may not opt to transition to another sex via medical treatments and may or may not live full-time in the gender expression congruous with their identity. For those individuals who are interested in sex reassignment, medical treatment may be financially impossible since it is rarely covered by insurance. Often, people who are able to live consistent with their gender identity full-time will opt for some form of hormonal therapy to support a congruent gender expression.

✓ Presenting as Genderqueer. Genderqueers are people who identify not as male or female, but as in-between or beyond the binary. Genderqueer youths are more likely to reject the idea that there are only two genders.

✓ Gender Identity Disorder: A strong, persistent desire to be the opposite sex, as well as a persistent discomfort about one's anatomical sex or a sense of inappropriateness in the gender role corresponding to one's anatomical sex. Gender Identity Disorder was eliminated from the American Psychiatric Association's Diagnostic and Statistical Manual for Mental Disorders (DSM-V) and replaced with Gender Dysphoria. Some people oppose classification of transgender identity as a disorder, while others recognize the advantages of having explicit standards of health care for transgender individuals. NASW National Committee on LG Issues recommends that DSM-IV no longer include Gender Identity Disorder as a mental health diagnosis. For more information: www.socialworkers.org/diversity/new/lgbtq/51810.asp).

✓ Sexual Orientation: A person's emotional, romantic, and erotic attraction to others, for the most part and over a period of time, is that person's sexual orientation. It exists on a continuum of feelings and attractions, and is not necessarily congruent with behavior. In understanding sexual orientation, note that most youths in early adolescence have a wide and confusing range of feelings. This is totally normal.

Sexual behavior and sexual orientation are not the same thing. Most people, for example, know to whom they are attracted long before they act on those attractions. Some LGBTQ youths may act out sexually with the opposite sex to hide or deny their same-sex feelings. Some youths may engage in same-sex behavior when their underlying attractions are predominantly toward the opposite sex while others may feel an attraction to a person of the opposite sex at particular times in their lives or feel pressured by peers to display feelings for one or the other sexes.

Some of the terms used to describe sexual orientation include:

✓ Heterosexual, Straight: People who are predominantly attracted to people of a different sex.

✓ Homosexual, Gay, Lesbian, Same Gender Loving, Two Spirit: People who are predominantly attracted to people of the same gender. The term Same Gender Loving emerged in the late 1980s and may be used most often by persons of color; Two Spirit emerged from First People or Native Americans Traditions and has in various contexts been used to describe people who have same-sex attractions and people who take on cross-gendered roles within the community.

✓ Bisexual: People who are attracted to members of the same and other genders. Note that individuals may vary in the degree to which they are attracted to other or the same genders.

    ✓   Pansexual: People who are attracted to persons of any gender.

    ✓   Asexual: People who are not sexually attracted to others.

    ✓   Questioning: Some youths identify as questioning when they are unsure of where their primary attractions lie.

    ✓   Cisgender or Cissexual: People whose gender assignment, body, and identity match.

✓ LGBTQ: This is an acronym that stands for Lesbian, Gay, Bisexual, Transgender, and Questioning/Queer.

✓ Heterosexism: The institutionalized assumption that everyone should be heterosexual, and that heterosexuality is inherently superior to and preferable to homosexuality or bisexuality.

✓ Homophobia-Biphobia-Transphobia: The irrational fear or hatred of, aversion to, or discrimination against, homosexual, bisexual, or transgender people and behavior.

✓ Internalized Homophobia-Biphobia-Transphobia: The experience of shame, aversion, and self-hatred in reaction to one's own attractions or gender identity.

Other terms which may be in use in your community might include: Not-Straight, Queer, and Non-Labeling.

EXHIBIT 5.6

Just Because You Know One Transgender Person Doesn't Mean You Know All Transgender Persons

Daniel Stewart knew when he was four or five years old that he did not feel like a girl. His self-identity and physical characteristics just did not fit the gender role expectations for being female. Until puberty, he was able to live a generally gender-neutral life except when it came to stereotypically "girl" things like dance class and wearing dresses. By the time he was in middle school and he and his peers were experiencing puberty, he began to feel his body was betraying him. His internal discomfort turned into depression and feelings of being ostracized because he was not comfortable doing the things his female friends were doing. He tried to tell himself that not all girls were feminine and that it was okay to enjoy doing more male-oriented activities and to have male friends, but he cried when he had his first menstrual period and felt that every menstrual cycle thereafter was like a slap in the face. He could not avoid the reality of his feelings.

Dan decided to cope with his feelings by self-identifying as a lesbian. He perceived this option as more acceptable than coming out as transgender (a person who transitions from female to male). People saw him as female, and he was attracted to girls. So, by default, he identified as a lesbian—at least he had put a label on his feelings which he expressed to others, but not his family at this point.

Growing up in a traditional Hispanic family, gender roles were very important, and Daniel periodically dealt with backlash because he did not conform to the perception his family had of appropriate feminine behaviour. By age 14, Dan had self-identified as transgender but did not have any plans to come out or medically transition. He lived in a politically and religiously conservative area without access to services for transgender persons—he did not see living as a transgender man as achievable. Fear of disapproval and abandonment, and a lack of positive transgender role models played a role in his thinking at this point.

At 18, Dan came out as a lesbian to his conservative Hispanic family and had several long-term lesbian relationships. Though coming out relieved some of the burden of hiding his gender identity, he did not feel pride in being lesbian. He did not see himself as a woman attracted to someone of the same gender. However, due to his circumstances (lack of resources, support, etc.) he did not feel safe or able to "come out" as transgender. In order to cope, Dan began educating himself about options available to those who wish to transition. But he knew that he could not come out as transgender until he was completely independent from his family. At 23, Dan publicly identified himself as transgender and began to socially transition (i.e., going by a male name and using male pronouns).

Because Dan had not shared his feelings about his struggle with his gender identity and being transgender with many people, some were shocked, even his friends in the gay community. He continued to be vigilant about sharing his feelings because he did not want to jeopardize his situation as he had other priorities (school and financial stability) and wanted to plan his transition to ensure it came at the right time. When he began identifying as transgender, Dan was in a lesbian relationship and planned to be married.

At age 24, Dan began the medical transition process to live as a man. In order for his health insurance to cover the hormone therapy, he was required to complete six months of therapy with a credentialed mental health professional with expertise in gender issues and to obtain a letter confirming that he had been diagnosed with gender dysphoria and that he was of sound mind to take the next step in the process. Next he needed to be evaluated by an endocrinologist or other qualified physician to determine his hormone levels. With the physician's approval, hormone replacement therapy could begin. Since Dan identifies as male but was born female, he began taking testosterone. He will continue hormone replacement therapy via weekly intramuscular injections for the rest of his life. In addition to taking testosterone, transgender men may also seek surgery in order to fully match their body with their mind. These surgeries, such as "top (e.g. bilateral mastectomy)" or "bottom (genital reconstruction)" surgery, are usually not covered by insurance. Therefore, Dan, like many transgender individuals, raised funds to pay out of pocket for his hormones and "top surgery." Though Dan had "top surgery" and takes testosterone, he wishes to emphasize that each transgender persons' experience is different. For Dan, taking testosterone and surgery are crucial to fully expressing his gender. For other transmen, that is not always the case.

Dan has legally changed his name and is uncertain if he will change his gender marker on his driver's license—that requires a court hearing, a physician's letter of approval, and more money. He worries that once his identifying documents state "male" it will be more difficult to obtain coverage for "gendered" services such as gynecological care.

Dan recently married his long-term partner and she has come to accept his transition because she understands how difficult it has been for him to present himself as someone he is not. She has begun to understand the roots of his depression, has seen the positive changes in him that the transition has brought, and is happy for him.

In reflecting on his journey, Dan notes that every transgender experience is different because gender expression is as varied among the transgender community as it is in the population as a whole. He realizes that he has to accept his transition as a journey and give thought to the possibilities and challenges that may be yet to come. He could lack the resources to fully achieve his goals. He may lose relationships, housing, or employment, and he will spend a significant amount of money so that the world can see him as the person he knows he is. Conversely, he is now free to be himself, to be more authentic and present, and to be more confident than he has ever felt in his life.

As his appearance has changed and his voice has deepened, he has noticed that people respond differently to him. He receives more respect from males than he did as a lesbian. His relationships with females are also changing. At times, he feels that barriers have arisen and that women question his intentions toward them. His relationship with his family has been both positive and challenging. His father has remained supportive, while his mother does not recognize his true gender identity as male in transition.

Dan recognizes how privileged he is to be able to transition into the person he is and wants to share his story to help educate others, particularly professionals, about what it means to be a transgender man. While there has been great progress for transgender persons, Dan believes the "T" in LGBTQ is often forgotten and misunderstood—"we just are not on people's radar." Dan offers this advice for professionals working with the transgender community:

- Do not make assumptions about a person's gender. Assumptions can lead to mis-gendering someone, which can be uncomfortable and unsafe. To be more sensitive, helping professionals can ask the person the preferred name/pronoun, provide gender options beyond the binary (male/female) on forms, and use gender-neutral language.
- Respect a person's preferred pronouns and name regardless of your own personal view.
- If someone identifies as transgender, do not "out" that person to others.
- Gender and sexuality are not the same thing—just as with every other group, transgender persons can fall anywhere on the sexuality spectrum.
- Transgender persons can transition in different ways. How a person transitions is often dictated by available time, resources, access, and support. Transgender persons may undergo no medical transition, low dose hormones, and/or multiple types of surgical procedures. A transgender person can stop her or his transition at any stage, which can often make it challenging to identify someone as transgender.
- Do not ask questions for which you do not need answers, and do not ask anything you would not want to be asked yourself. Respect the same boundaries you would with anyone.
- Given that only 8% of people say they know a transgender person, an individual going through the transition process may not have a large or helpful in-person support network. Social media is a great resource for the transgender community.
- Provide a welcoming and culturally competent helping environment; transgender persons often avoid seeking health and social services because there are few supportive, knowledgeable, and non-judgmental professionals in most communities. Understand that being transgender is a risk, but a risk that someone going through transition believes is worth taking. Be supportive of that.

Religionism and Religious Discrimination

Religionism
Religious zeal or the belief that religions other than one's own are inferior.

Religious oppression and discrimination have existed for thousands of years in virtually every country in the world, largely because of religionism (religious zeal or the belief that religions other than one's own are inferior). Discrimination against people practicing a variety of religions has taken and continues to take many forms, both formal and informal, including segregation; restricted educational, employment, political, and social opportunities; and even torture and killing. The Holocaust, which targeted primarily people of the Jewish faith, is the most notorious example of religionism in the recent past, but sadly there continue to be ongoing and tragic examples of religious discrimination around the world. The ongoing religious conflicts that exist in Middle Eastern and African countries in which persons are persecuted, tortured, and killed for their religious practices are realities in the 21st century. In 2012, global religious hostilities were at a six-year high, with 33% of 198 countries studied experiencing high levels of religious-focused hostilities (up from 29% in 2011 and 20% in 2007) (Pew Research Religion and Public Life Project, 2014). The greatest increases in hostilities occurred in the Middle East, Northern Africa, and some areas of Asia-Pacific. In these conflicts, individuals and groups who perceive a threat to the majority faith have abused religious minorities; threatened and used violence to force people to comply with religious norms; harassed women regarding religious dress; incited mob violence; and carried out religion-related terrorism (Pew Research Religion and Public Life Project, 2014b). Members of the groups being threatened have, on occasion, responded with violence as well in order to protect their traditions. What do you think these findings mean for the social work profession in the U.S. and around the world?

Despite the constitutional guarantee of freedom of religion and a religiously diverse population, the United States is far from being free of religious segregation and discrimination. For example, the events of September 11, 2001, prompted a rash of discrimination directed toward Muslims, many of whom had been born in the U.S. or had lived in the U.S. for many years. Although many Muslim leaders vehemently criticized the actions of the Muslim terrorists who led the attack, Muslims in the United States have been subjected to physical, verbal, and written assaults, threats against their lives, and damage to their businesses, homes, and religious institutions. Muslims are one example of a group that has become "racialized," that is, a group whose members identify themselves primarily by their religious affiliation as opposed to their race or ethnicity (Adams & Joshi, 2013, p. 233). This attitude has served as a reminder for the need to separate religion from political, ideological, and cultural conflicts.

Racialized
a state where a group identify themselves primarily by their religious affiliation as opposed to their race or ethnicity.

Celebrate Difference

Source: iStock/aimintang

Although religion has always been a part of the lives of many of the people social workers serve, religion has not always been addressed in mainstream social work education and practice. Another strong American value, secularism (broadly, the separation of church and state), has led many social workers in both private and public organizations to avoid the topics of religion and spirituality, with the positive goal of reducing discrimination based on religion and respecting client privacy. In recent years as the profession has committed to the goal of cultural competence, social workers have recognized the important roles that religion and spirituality play in some of their clients' lives. Religion and spirituality can contribute to a persons' beliefs, self-perspective, and behaviors. Religious beliefs can be sources of self-worth for clients, can provide the strength to overcome helplessness, and can encourage liberation and social transformation (Knitter, 2010). Consequently, social workers have begun to incorporate clients' religious beliefs into their assessments and intervention plans. Along with knowledge of biological, sociological, cultural, and psychological development across the lifespan, knowledge of spiritual development is now required content in CSWE-accredited programs.

Secularism
Seperation of church and state.

The social work profession recognizes that the "faith life" of a client can be an important component of the social worker-client relationship. Considering the client's religious and spiritual beliefs within the context of the strengths-based perspective can enable both the client and the social worker to use these aspects of the client's life in a positive way (Casio, 2012). Exploring, supporting,

Gay Wedding

Source: iStock/Ed Stock

and connecting the client's spiritual beliefs and faith life can lead to a more effective intervention strategy. We have always been a multireligious society but have more recently begun to recognize religious diversity. Social workers must not only acknowledge clients' values and beliefs, but also engage those beliefs, values, and convictions in the social work intervention (Knitter, 2010, p. 260). For example, when working with persons dealing with death and dying issues, the client's faith beliefs can provide a valuable coping resource. As the profession continues to integrate faith beliefs into social work practice, social workers explore issues of religion and spirituality on both personal and professional levels. On the personal level, the social worker can clarify her or his own religious and spiritual values and beliefs to ensure that she or he does not attempt to impose those beliefs on the client. Although social workers cannot possibly be knowledgeable about all of the world's religions, they are professionally bound to consider each client's faith life as part of the client's environment and to learn the influence of faith, religion, and spirituality on that client.

Intersectionality

Social work clients' experiences with "isms" often combine multiple and complex types of oppression and discrimination. These intersecting dynamics can influence numerous aspects of clients' lives, but they do not need to be overwhelming. Social workers need to be aware of intersections between religion and ethnicity, class, gender, and nationalism in clients' lives and of the impact those intersections have on the individuals and groups involved

(Adams & Joshi, 2013). We must also recognize the role that power and privilege (or lack of) plays in the intersections of discrimination and oppression (Garran & Rozas, 2013). If an individual or group has experienced discrimination or oppression, there can be a reluctance to building trust with a helping professional or engage in planning for an intervention. P.H. Collins (2013) offers the following strategies for creating social change by acknowledging and incorporating intersectionality into the social work intervention:

- Acknowledge that personal experiences with power and privilege (regardless of the nature of those experiences) can contribute to challenges relating to others, but are a part of who we are.
- Look for common experiences that cut across boundaries and differences to promote feelings of empathy toward others.
- Develop empathy for individuals and groups by assuming responsibility for your own actions and acknowledge the feelings and responses clients have developed as a result of their experiences. Building empathy for others is an essential part of becoming a knowledgeable and culturally competent social work practitioner.

Intersectionality is a complex and challenging concept. Society has a tendency to view an individual or group for that characteristic that is being viewed in only one context (i.e., race, ethnicity, gender, sexual orientation) when, in fact, all humans are members of multiple groups and may be experiencing discrimination and oppression in more than one category. Social workers must view the client as a whole person whose life is multi-faceted and encompasses a number of characteristics and qualities. To read an example of intersecting "isms" when one is an older LGBTQ adult, read the reflections of one social work activist and advocate for the LGBTQ community (Exhibit 5.7).

THE CULTURALLY COMPETENT SOCIAL WORKER

When she worked in the domestic violence program, Emily encountered a particularly challenging cultural dilemma involving ethnicity, religion, and gender issues. At a neighbor's urging, Huang, a young woman with limited English who had recently immigrated from South Asia, sought protection at the shelter. When presented with the option of pursuing an Order of Protection through the court system, Huang stated that a legal order would have little to no influence with her husband. She told Emily and the staff that the only person who could help influence her husband would be the local leader of her faith community. She believed that her husband would be more responsive to the faith leader's rule than to a court judge.

EXHIBIT 5.7

"We Have to Change the Face of Services for LGBTQ Elders ..."

Sherrill Wayland is a social worker on the front lines of advocacy for older adults who are lesbian, gay, bisexual, transgender, and questioning. She is Manager of National Projects for SAGE National and former Executive Director of SAGE Metro St. Louis (www.sageusa.org/), a not-for-profit organization committed to enhancing quality of life for LGBT older adults through service, advocacy, and community awareness. What follows are Sherrill's thoughts on how far the older LGBTQ community has come and on the challenges they still face accessing needed health and social services. Sherrill also touches on the role the social work profession plays in this community and relates her personal experiences with the continued lack of societal awareness regarding LGBT needs.

- The Gains—In the six years that Sherrill served as the Executive Director of SAGE Metro St. Louis (now SAGE of PROMO Fund), the LGBTQ community in general and older LGBTQ adults in particular have made a number of policy and service gains. For the first time, the Department of Health and Human Services (HHS) and the Administration on Aging (AoA) have come together to fund a National Resource Center on LGBT Aging (to learn more, visit: http://lgbtagingcenter.org/), a "game-changer" in securing recognition for the older LGBTQ community.
- The Ongoing Challenges—Despite gains in securing recognition, beneficial policies and funding, improved marriage laws, and increased societal awareness, challenges persist, particularly in the area of equal access to health and social services. As Sherrill notes, "Policy does not guarantee implementation"—legislation may be passed, but new policies cannot be implemented without necessary funding, and changing attitudes and providing training takes time. Sherrill and other activists who advocate for older LGBTQ adults view this lag as a time to build relationships that will create welcoming environments for older adults and ensure that services for older adults will not be segregated. "We have to monitor and ensure that policies are, in fact, implemented."
- ACA Impact—The Affordable Care Act (ACA) has provided additional support for those with whom SAGE works, particularly through its first-time mandate for non-discrimination on

the basis of sexual orientation and gender identity (particularly for transgender persons) in health care and insurance—a boon for the LGBTQ community, which has historically suffered a number of health disparities, in part due to a lack of access to health care. In the past many older LGBTQ adults did not seek out health care because they feared judgment and discrimination. Now activists are reaching out to the health care system to help providers become culturally competent and welcoming of LGBTQ patients, particularly those who are older adults.

Other ACA-related gains for the older LGBT population include:

- HHS has lifted the ban on Medicare-covered service for transgender-related health care.
- ACA requires cultural competency training for health care systems (implementation still in progress).
- ACA requires that health care providers create standards of care for serving LGBTQ patients.
- A Presidential memorandum grants LGBTQ patients and partners visitation rights in all hospitals that receive Medicare and Medicaid funding.
- A U.S. Department of Labor ruling states that married LGBTQ spouses are eligible for leave under the Family Medical Leave Act (FMLA). The FMLA ruling is important as it allows both parents in same-sex families to have access to their children even if one is not a legal guardian or biological/adoptive parent.

The social service delivery system is changing as well. Sherrill has seen increased awareness of LGBT issues at the both individual and organizational level. Several states now require staff in social service organizations to be trained in LGBTQ cultural competence. Agencies are beginning to acknowledge their LGBTQ older adult clients (when Sherrill started training six years ago, most agencies claimed they had no LGBT clients), and they are seeking out SAGE cultural competence training. As Sherrill says, "The climate is changing."

- Social Work Role—NASW's *Code of Ethics* (2008) obliges social workers to endeavor to end the marginalization of persons in the community and to ensure that services are open and welcoming to all. According to this mandate, social workers must take the lead inside organizations in order to prevent discrimination. Sherrill credits social workers with helping to bring about progress for LGBT older adults, but urges the need for diligent advocacy—"It's up to us to ensure policies and practices are implemented. We must do outreach into a community that has largely been invisible and marginalized. LGBT older adults are five times less likely (than heterosexual older adults) to seek services due to fear."

An Eye-Opening Experience ...

At age 43, Sherrill found herself reaching out to the health and social service community for the first time in over a decade. During that time, she had been too afraid of experiencing discrimination to seek out healthcare for herself. As a result, she was a self-described "picture of health disparities," a smoker who had had no preventive care for the past fifteen years, when she found a 10 cm mass in her breast. Out of fear and denial, she waited four days to see a physician. To her relief, the health care system welcomed her, and she did not suffer any overt discrimination, but one part of her experience did make her realize how much education and increased awareness is still needed.

When Sherrill arrived for one of her medical appointments, the receptionist asked her to provide an emergency contact. Sherrill gave her partner's name and number, and the receptionist asked, "Don't you have a family member we can contact?" Sherrill again provided her partner's information, but the receptionist persisted until finally Sherrill acquiesced and provided her mother's name and number. In reflecting on this experience, Sherrill realized that though she was an advocate and activist for LGBT rights, at that moment, she was a scared and vulnerable patient. She also realized that this exchange would not have occurred had she been a married heterosexual woman. As Sherrill puts it, "This was a huge wake-up call. I have to personally make changes. I have to advocate for myself. What does that look like?"

The epilogue to this lived experience is that the physician's office responded positively. When Sherrill related this experience to her physician's office, they responded positively and proactively, assuring her that they would address the receptionist's actions. Sherrill's experience inspired a local playwright to write the play, "Are You Married?" which has been produced and performed on several stages, including St. Louis and New York (to learn about the playwright, visit her at: www.uppityco. com/aboutjoan.html).

Sherrill closed her reflection by saying that she takes a lifespan approach—healthy young adults make healthy elders. "We have to stop the cycle of people not feeling safe at an early age. As we look at health disparities, we get diseases like cancer not because we're gay, but because we have not had preventive care because we were afraid and because we have had unhealthy strategies for coping, like abusing alcohol, tobacco, drugs, and food."

Training Resource: Building Respect for LGBT Older Adults—six-module training available at: http://lgbtagingcenter.org/training/buildingRespect.cfm

In this situation, Emily was required to conduct an assessment, offer the services of the domestic violence program, explore options for Huang's safety, and, if Huang agreed to it, develop an intervention plan. Because she was unfamiliar with Huang's religion and customs, Emily was uncertain how to proceed. She consulted with her supervisor, and together they contacted Huang's religious leader, who then intervened on her behalf.

Consider for a moment the cultural competency skills Emily needed to use to respond to this situation:

- Willingness to seek out knowledge of the client's faith beliefs, traditions, and values.
- Ability to communicate with a reluctant person in crisis through an interpreter.
- Ability to relate to a client whose values and religious beliefs differed dramatically from Emily's own.
- Willingness to affirm the client's right to self-determination.

As Emily's experience shows, culturally competent practice requires multiple skill types: cognitive (knowledge of the client's cultural background and associated issues), affective (emotional), and behavioral (language and communication skills) (Schlesinger & Devore, 1995). An effective practitioner possesses strong command of all of these skills, and adheres to the idea that cultural competence is a lifelong learning process that is both challenging and rewarding. You may feel anxious about the process of becoming culturally competent. You likely have a lot to learn as gaining cultural competence is a lifelong endeavor, you will probably make some mistakes, you will need to examine your existing beliefs, and all of this work may take an emotional toll (Diller, 2015). First suggested by Tervalon and Murray-García (1998), cultural humility is a related skill that can aid in your development of cultural competency. Cultural humility is being able to tell the client you do not know something but are willing to seek out information and resources. Rest assured that, while these fears are legitimate, the journey will be worth the effort if you are honest and realistic about your feelings and beliefs and make a commitment achieving cultural competence.

A multiculturalist approach to social work is based on the premises that cultural reality is socially constructed and unique to each individual, each person's worldview has value, people experience multiple cultural realities, and the role of the social worker is to identify client strengths so the client may be empowered to overcome painful experiences (Kohli et al., 2010, p. 266). The skills critical to this approach—awareness of culturally-related beliefs, values, practices, language (e.g., terms), and communication strategies—are not specific to any particular group, because diversity within client populations does not lend itself to a "cookbook" approach to social work practice (Colon et al., 2011; Congress, 2015; Dunn, 2002).

Cultural Awareness

Achieving increased self-awareness and knowledge of your own identity are the first steps to becoming culturally aware. Consider incorporating the following concepts and strategies into your practice:

- Every social worker–client relationship is a cross-cultural experience in that each person brings a distinct cultural background to every interaction.
- Cultural characteristics and differences can be a valuable resource in the helping process.
- There is as much diversity within a culture as there is between cultures; do not assume anything about a client based solely on her or his membership in a particular group.
- If you and your client share membership in a cultural group, do not assume

that you have anything else in common. Likewise, do not assume that you have nothing in common with a client whose cultural background differs from your own.

■ Recognize that the client with whom you work may be uncomfortable with your cultural differences.

■ Stay in touch with your own beliefs—your biases and any feelings of comfort or discomfort.

■ Before you encounter a client or situation, identify the knowledge and skills that you may need. For instance, do you need to arrange for an interpreter, do you need to obtain information on religious practices, or do you need to ensure that the meeting location is accessible for the client(s)?

■ If you need an interpreter, try to find someone other than the client's child or another family member to provide interpretation unless it is uniquely appropriate or necessary. It is best to have an objective interpreter not related to the client to avoid the possibility of bias or influence being infused into the encounter and mis-representing the information being provided.

■ Approach each assessment from a cultural diversity perspective. Take into account a client's place of origin, reason for relocation (if applicable), language(s) spoken, and beliefs about health, illness, family, holidays, religion, education, and work. The culturagram (Congress, 2015) is one tool you can use to conduct a culturally focused assessment. Designed as a strategy for engaging and assessing the experience of immigrant families, the culturagram highlights a family's past and current experiences, values, and strengths, beliefs and practices, and providing information that can be central to developing effective interventions. See Exhibit 5.8 for more information on the culturagram.

■ Monitor your communication style and the ways in which your verbal and nonverbal behaviors could be interpreted. For example, do you speak too quickly to be clearly understood by a person who is just learning English? Are you uncomfortable when people you do not know well get physically close to you?

■ Demonstrate cultural humility and know that you will make mistakes, and be open what the client can teach you about diversity and how she or he can help you learn from your mistakes. When you make a mistake, do not attempt to cover it up. Rather, acknowledge the mistake, and take the opportunity to learn from it.

Culturagram
Tool for assessing a family within the context of their culture.

While each area of diversity requires specialized knowledge and skill, working with clients who identify as being multiracial can be particularly challenging. With approximately 3% of the U.S. population reporting one or more racial categories (Humes, Jones, & Ramirez, 2011), social workers need to

EXHIBIT 5.8

Culturagram

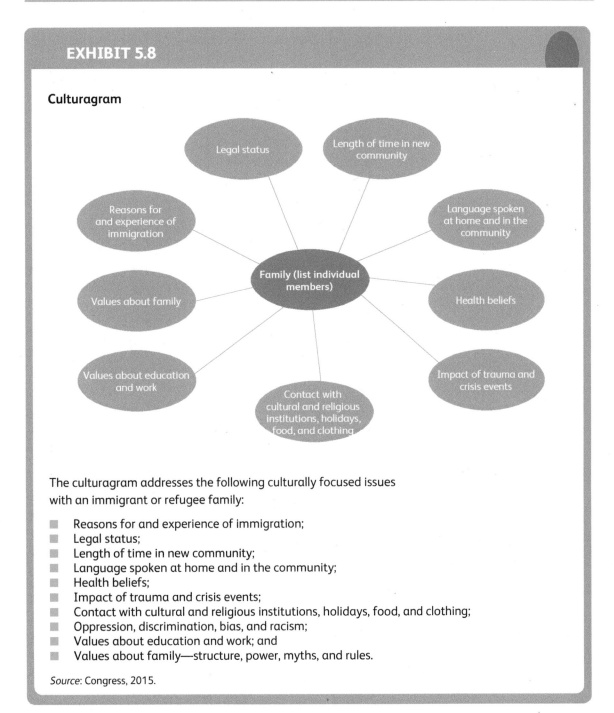

The culturagram addresses the following culturally focused issues with an immigrant or refugee family:

- Reasons for and experience of immigration;
- Legal status;
- Length of time in new community;
- Language spoken at home and in the community;
- Health beliefs;
- Impact of trauma and crisis events;
- Contact with cultural and religious institutions, holidays, food, and clothing;
- Oppression, discrimination, bias, and racism;
- Values about education and work; and
- Values about family—structure, power, myths, and rules.

Source: Congress, 2015.

expand traditional approaches to include multiracial awareness. Sundar and colleagues (2012) suggest that we have not yet achieved complete success as culturally competent practitioners. They write that social workers should see differences not as the end solution, but as the beginning of the conversation. After recognizing differences, they should be incorporated into the social work intervention using a strengths-based. Sundar and colleagues (2012) contend that differences can and should be acknowledged, particularly as they related to culture, power, and oppression, and then worked "through" to move on to other areas of intervention. It is then the responsibility of the social worker to ensure that the differences are not overlooked but, instead, embraced and utilized to reach the client's goals.

Using a culturally-attuned ecological approach, social workers can identify advantages and challenges of a client's multiracial background and help the client connect with her or his multiracial legacy (Jackson & Samuels, 2011). The action continuum in Exhibit 5.9 provides further guidance in developing greater cultural awareness. Where would you place yourself on the continuum now? Where would you like to strive to be on the continuum in the future? What will help you improve?

Language and Communication Skills

Language and communication are particularly important, yet often challenging areas of culturally competent practice. Language is intricately tied to the culture of any group. It is a powerful mechanism for imparting positive and negative messages, and for this reason it can serve both to perpetuate oppression and discrimination and to demonstrate respect and sensitivity. Therefore, it is crucial that social workers use appropriate and culturally sensitive language and communication whenever they refer to or speak to any group.

Usually, there are many ways to say the same thing, but the group you are addressing will prefer one way over others. Using the language a group prefers helps create a safe environment for the client that fosters trust and builds rapport. Although slang may be acceptable in certain settings, it is difficult to use slang appropriately, and its use is easily misinterpreted. Slang terms change, they may have regional connotations, and people view them in different ways. More mainstream language is a safer option.

Effective multicultural practitioners communicate sensitively with diverse groups. When in doubt regarding the most appropriate language to use, obtain more information. Ask other members of the cultural group with whom you are working or other professionals who have worked with that group to serve as cultural guides. In cases in which you have established a rapport, you may ask the client for help in understanding appropriate language. Be particularly

EXHIBIT 5.9

Action Continuum: From Discrimination to Respect

Discrimination Phase:

1.

Actively Participates

a. Tells "ism" jokes

b. Excludes those that don't fit traditional roles or norms

c. Engages in verbal and physical harassment

d. Works for anti-civil rights legislation

2.

Denies or Ignores

a. Inaction

b. Unwilling or unable to understand

3.

Recognizes, but no action

a. Recognizing does not result in action or response

b. Colludes with dominance

c. Lacks knowledge about specific action to take

4.

Educates self

a. Takes steps to learn more Listens, observes, and reads

b. Begins to move out of one's comfort zone

Respect Phase:

5.

Recognizes and interrupts cycle of oppression

a. Takes action

b. Begins to make changes in own attitudes and behaviors

6.

Questions and Dialogues

a. Attempts to begin educating others

b. Engages others in dialogue

7.

Supports and Encourages

a. Supports prejudice reduction strategies and activities

b. Supports and encourages others to take risks

8.

Confronts and counters racist behavior and structure

a. Active in identifying manifestation of "ism"

b. Works for social change and justice

c. Continues to monitor own attitudes and behaviors

d. Cultivates cross-cultural partnerships

e. Engages in verbal and physical harassment

f. Works for anti-civil rights legislation

Source: Adapted from NCCJ St. Louis.

careful to open each new encounter by introducing yourself by name and title, referring to adult clients using a respectful and culturally appropriate honorific (for example, Mr., Mrs., or Ms.), and clarifying the pronunciation of the client's name and address. Then inquire about the client's culture, specifically how the client prefers to refer to the group in which she or he is a member (for example, Indian versus Native American).

Here are further suggestions for communicating sensitively:

- Balance the use of professional language and language that is familiar to the client. Clients may misunderstand or be offended by professional jargon (particularly medical or legal terminology or acronyms), slang, or colloquialisms.

- Be genuine in your use of language and style of communication; do not try to use words or exhibit behaviors with which you are not familiar.

- Be aware of the meanings different cultures attach to certain nonverbal behaviors. These meanings may be assigned or interpreted based on traditions with which you may be unfamiliar, and their use may result in misunderstandings (Okun et al., 1999). For example, in some cultures, eye contact is considered an invitation to continue speaking, and in others it may be seen as a sign of sexual interest, aggression, respect, or disrespect. Similarly, silence and various facial and physical expressions convey different messages, ranging from discomfort to anger to respect, depending on an individual's culture. Different degrees of personal space and physical touch may be interpreted as intimacy, aggression, or dominance based on cultural definitions.

- Be sensitive to and aware of a person's culture, but do not discuss it unless it is relevant to the situation. For example, a disability or sexual orientation may not be pertinent to your encounter. Therefore, there is no need to focus the professional relationship on that aspect of the person's life.

- To avoid labeling, remember to use person-first language, which refers first to the person and then to the situation (for example, "person with a disability" instead of "disabled person" or "person from the Middle East" rather than "Middle Easterner").

- At the beginning of the helping relationship, check with a person whose culture is different from your own to ensure that she or he has understood what you have said or meant. Ask the person to repeat her or his understanding of the content of the conversation. This strategy will prevent you from assuming that you are being understood simply because the person nods in assent.

- If you are unsure of the meaning of a word, phrase, or behavior a client uses, ask the client in a nonjudgmental, nonpatronizing way to explain the meaning.

CONCLUSION

William M. Chace (1989) offers this perspective on diversity:

> Diversity is generally understood and embraced, is not casual liberal toler-ance of anything and everything not yourself. It is not polite accommodation. Instead, diversity is, in action, the sometimes painful awareness that other people, other races, other voices, other habits of mind, have as much integrity of being, as much claim upon the world, as you do. No one has an obligation greater than your own to change, or yield, or to assimilate into the mass. The irreconcilable is as much a part of social life as the congenial. Being strong in life is being strong amid differences while accepting the fact that your own self can be a considerable imposition upon everyone you meet. I urge you to con-sider your own oddity before you are troubled or offended by that of others. And I urge you, amid all the differences present to the eye and mind, to reach out and create the bonds that will sustain the commonwealth that will protect us all. We are meant to be together.

Like other aspects of social work practice, cultural competence requires that you continually seek out knowledge, skills, and self-insights. No one can be an expert in all areas of diversity, but social workers must strive to acquire as much information as possible about the populations they serve. When you engage in culturally competent practice, you proactively endeavor to understand other cultures. Each client has a rich and often-fascinating cultural history and has much to teach a social worker who views that background as a strength.

MAIN POINTS

- Being a culturally competent social work practitioner is working respect-fully and effectively with all persons. Your beliefs and values about your own culture and the cultures of others affect your practice. To achieve cultural competence it is important to routinely examine those values and beliefs and to continually strive to learn more about those who differ from you.
- Within the context of oppression and social justice, two theoretical frameworks, the ecological and strengths-based perspectives, help social workers understand and work with clients different from themselves.
- Understanding "isms" and the dimensions of intersectionality many people face can help social workers be more sensitive to people of different races, ages, sexual orientations, and abilities.
- Language and communication in all forms play a major role in both the oppression of and the work of building respect for diverse groups.

EXERCISES

1. Review the case file for Vicki Sanchez at www.routledgesw.com/caseStudies. Answer the Critical Thinking Questions related to Vicki's case. Next, review the case file for Hector Sanchez and answer the Critical Thinking Questions related to his case.

2. Using the Sanchez family case, imagine that you are a social worker newly assigned to work with Hector and Celia on the adoption of their grandson, Joey. Based on your own cultural heritage, select a description from the general list below:

   ■ You are not of Hispanic or Latino origin and have had little experience with this population.

   ■ You are not of Hispanic or Latino origin, but have had some experience with the Hispanic population and have limited Spanish-speaking skills.

   ■ Your ethnic background is of Latino origin, but you have not lived in or near a Latino community.

   ■ Your ethnic and cultural background is Latino. You speak fluent Spanish and your upbringing is similar to that of the Sanchez children.

   Having identified your personal characteristics relative to the Sanchez family, consider the following social work skill issues:

   a. What differences might you encounter?

   b. What similarities might you encounter?

   c. What are your feelings and beliefs about working with the Sanchez family, including stereotypes, biases, feelings of familiarity, or anxiety?

   d. Given your knowledge of the Latino culture (or lack thereof), what information or skills do you need to acquire before meeting with the Sanchez family?

   e. How might you respond if you make a cultural mistake (speak or behave in such a way that you offend the person(s))?

   f. How might you ask the Sanchez family to help you in establishing a rapport?

   g. Who or what resource can help you prepare for your meeting with the Sanchez family?

   h. If you do not speak Spanish, how will you communicate with Celia? If you are bilingual, will you speak in Spanish or English? How will you determine which is appropriate?

3. Using the Carla Washburn interactive case (www.routledgesw.com/caseStudies), write a narrative description of Mrs. Washburn and her

current situation. Review your narrative for any evidence of ageist terms or attitudes. If you find any evidence of ageism, rewrite your description to remove it. Lastly, write a brief reflection on this experience (i.e., in what ways were you ageist, what are the origins of your ageist attitudes, etc.).

4. In order to understand better the origins of your thoughts, feelings, and stereotypes about the diverse range of persons in our society, consider each of the social groups listed in Exhibit 5.10 and the sources of your information about each group. List the specific information you gained from each of the sources in the two categories on the right of the table.

5. Consider an experience that you have had with diversity at any point in your life. This experience may be one in which you were the recipient or perpetrator of discrimination or oppression, or an experience in which you felt uncomfortable due to your lack of familiarity with a situation or person(s). After you have identified the experience, write a narrative that includes the following:

   a. A description of the experience.

   b. What was uncomfortable, awkward, or painful about this situation?

   c. Which of the "isms" is relevant to this situation? Why?

   d. How did you respond to the experience?

   e. If you were to encounter this situation again, would you respond differently? Why? How?

   f. How might this experience influence your future professional life?

   Now that you have completed this portion of the exercise, stop and read the narrative that you have written and answer these questions:

   g. Did writing your narrative teach you anything new about yourself?

   h. Have you changed since this experience with diversity? How?

   i. What would you say to someone else who has had this experience?

   j. What culturally competent skills did you use to respond to the situation? If you were to encounter this situation again, which culturally competent skills would you use?

   You have begun the lifelong journey of self-reflection essential for culturally competent social work practice. You can repeat this exercise as you encounter future issues of diversity.

6. To gain further insight into beliefs and biases, respond to the following:

   a. What do you think when you see an older adult in a wheelchair?

   b. How do you react when you encounter someone with an intellectual disability (for example, an older person with dementia, an individual with a traumatic brain injury, etc.)?

   c. When you are on public transportation and you are sitting next to a person with a developmental disability or a possible mental illness, how do you react? What are your feelings in this situation?

d. How do you react when you encounter a person with Down syndrome?

e. How do you react when you see two persons of the same gender walking down the street holding hands?

f. Can you think of situations that have made you feel uncomfortable because of a person's differences from you or from those with whom you interact most frequently?

Once you have considered your responses to the above questions, identify the culturally competent skills that you feel you possess. How did you gain these skills? What cultural competence skills do you lack?

7. Personal reflection: Identify an event or situation related to diversity (racial, ethnic, religious, economic, gender, age, sexual orientation) that has challenged you. Describe your response, how you might respond differently in the future, and how this experience may impact your professional work.

8. Visit the Brickville interactive case (www.routledgesw.com/caseStudies) and review the History and Background, Demographics of Current Community Residents, Real Estate Development Plan, Source of Conflict, and the Community Reaction to the Plan. After familiarizing yourself with Brickville, develop a diversity analysis in which you identify real and potential areas of discrimination and oppression, including any "isms" that you note. After you complete the analysis, reflect on ways a social worker could address those areas of discrimination and oppression (Exhibit 5.10).

EXHIBIT 5.10

Things I Have Learned About Diverse Groups

SOCIAL GROUP	LEARNED FROM FAMILY, TEACHERS, AND FRIENDS	LEARNED FROM MEDIA*
African Americans		
American Indians		
Asian Americans		
European Americans		
Hawaiians and Pacific Islanders		
Hispanics and Latino Americans		
Persons of dual racial heritage		
Men		
Women		
Young adults		
Older adults		
Persons with disabilities		
Persons who are economically disadvantaged		
Persons who are affluent		
Persons who are gay, lesbian, bisexual, or transgender		
Persons who practice religions other than my own		
Muslim Americans		
Other†		

* Media can include television, radio, internet, magazines, and advertisements.

† Fill in other groups you have learned about.

Source: Adapted from the National Conference for Community and Justice—St. Louis Region.

VALUES AND ETHICS IN SOCIAL WORK PRACTICE

While completing the community service requirement for a social work course at Oasis House, a shelter for persons who are homeless, Emily faced a difficult situation. Emily had developed a special bond with one of the residents, Lorinda, a single mother with two young children. Lorinda and Emily were the same age and had many similar interests. They had both been on their high school track teams and had competed in the same events. During one of their frequent conversations, Lorinda asked Emily for money. She told Emily that she needed the money so her boyfriend could take a bus back home. He had gone to another city hoping to find work so he could earn money and send for Lorinda and the children, but he had not found a job and had no money for the trip back. Lorinda assured Emily that she would repay the money as soon as she and her boyfriend found jobs.

Emily did not know what to do. She liked Lorinda and wanted to help her, but was not sure that she should lend Lorinda her own money. What would you do in this situation?

Ethical dilemma
A situation in which a person's ethical position, based on personal values, contradicts that of other persons or the choice being faced.

Lorinda's request presented Emily with an ethical dilemma, a commonplace occurrence in the social work profession in which a social worker "must choose between two or more relevant, but contradictory, ethical directives, or when every alternative results in an undesirable outcome for one or more persons" (Dolgoff, Loewenberg, & Harrington, 2012, p. 10). A social worker faces an ethical dilemma when a situation presents a conflict between at least two personal or professional ethical principles and standards. Challenges in the client's life might arise in connection to the birth of a child; loss of a loved one; natural disasters; child or older adult abuse, neglect, or exploitation; mental or physical illness; financial or housing needs; discrimination; or domestic violence. Such value-laden issues create the potential for an ethical dilemma to occur because the social worker may have to involve authorities, challenge the client's choices, or confront an injustice. As will be discussed in more detail later in this chapter, the ethical standard for social work practice that is relevant in the situation in which Lorinda asked Emily for money is conflict of interest, specifically, the potential for creating a dual relationship between the social worker and the client. By interacting with a client on a personal level (i.e., loaning her money), Emily potentially engages in a dual relationship with Lorinda that can potentially lead to exploitation or harm of the client.

The value systems and ethical practices of the social worker, the client, the agency, and society as a whole impact each social work intervention and its outcome. This chapter focuses on those values and ethics and the ways in which they relate to social work practice. The chapter begins by defining some important terms, highlighting the importance of values and ethics to competent social work practice, and considering the National Association of Social Workers (NASW) *Code of Ethics* (2008). You will have an opportunity to examine your own values, to explore the ethical implications of technology and social media, and.to apply social work values and ethics to challenging social work practice problems.

SOCIAL WORK'S COMMITMENT TO VALUES AND ETHICS

National events determine our ideals, as much as our ideals determine national events.

—Jane Addams

Values are a system of beliefs, principles, and traditions that guide behaviors and practices. You might also think of values as the ideals by which a person or group lives. For example, the social work profession believes that all people have a right to access the resources needed to optimize their quality of life. Values are important because they are deeply ingrained in each of us and significantly impact our encounters with individuals and with society as a whole. To paraphrase Jane Addams, our values shape society and society shapes our values. Take, for example, the events of September 11, 2001. The U.S. response to the bombings that killed thousands was not only influenced by America's values on nationality and patriotism, but also impacted the way in which the U.S. has addressed the threat of terrorism.

Values
An individual or group's customs, beliefs, and behaviors.

Ethics, on the other hand, are: "a system of moral principles and perceptions about right versus wrong and the resulting philosophy of conduct that is practiced by an individual, group, profession, or culture" (Barker, 2014, p. 146). Professional ethics are a critical part of the social work profession as they provide the moral compass for social work practice. You can think of values as the inner beliefs underlying ethics, which are the guidelines for appropriate action and behavior. Much like the discussion of "isms" in Chapter 5, values are beliefs versus the manifestation of those beliefs and how and whether we act in accordance with those beliefs. Each of us possesses a personal value system (i.e., beliefs) that informs and shapes how we interact with the world around us (i.e., our ethical standards and behaviors). Our intellect and emotions dictate our value systems, and we put those values into practice when our attitudes, words, behaviors, and practices adhere to the ethical standards and responsibilities that align with those values. As we develop into social work practitioners, we adopt the values of the profession and commit to complying with the ethical standards the profession has established and endorsed.

Ethics
The behaviors of an individual or group based on the value system to which the individual or group is committed.

Values and ethics are different but closely related and interdependent in terms of social work practice. For example, social work ethics dictate that social work practitioners advocate for marginalized groups because of the value the social work profession places on ensuring access to resources for all clients. Social workers advocate for all of their clients—including families living on limited incomes, immigrants, LGBTQ clients, and clients with disabilities—so that they may all have better access to resources.

Values and ethical issues play a part in every client-social worker interaction. The role of the social worker may be to advocate for a client's rights, to help the client access information and resources, or to assist the client in enhancing her or his quality of life. At this level, a competent social work practitioner is aware of relevant values and ethical issues that may be present in the client situation and the implications of those values and ethics on the social work intervention. For example, social workers may advocate for the ethical use and distribution of public benefits to those individuals and families in need. A number of states continue to cut Temporary Assistance to Needy Families benefits, resulting in hundreds of thousands of individuals losing their access to those benefits. Social workers can advocate with state legislatures to try to prevent those decreases in state spending for children and families living in or near poverty. As another example, some people in the U.S., including some lawmakers, are adamantly opposed to allowing undocumented workers or immigrant children to enter the country or access services. Social workers can advocate at the agency, local, state, and national levels to try to secure admittance and access to resources for these groups.

When approaching an ethical dilemma or value conflict, social workers must first understand the value systems of all involved: themselves, clients, the agency they work for, the social work profession, and the larger society or societies in which they work and/or their clients live. Although social workers are not expected to *share* them, they are ethically bound to *respect* the value systems of their clients. In fact, experiencing "gaps" from time to time between your values and those of your clients is common and unavoidable (Dolgoff et al., 2012, p. 109). The social worker does not attempt to change the client by imposing her or his values on the client, but instead strives to understand and respect the client's values. Being aware of a client's value system can help social workers avoid using inappropriate language or behavior that would amount to unknowingly discriminating against the client. For example, if you were aware that your female client was married to a same-sex partner, you would not ask about her husband. Moreover, it helps social workers to understand the client's decision-making processes, choices and behaviors, and patterns of functioning or dysfunction.

VALUES IN SOCIAL WORK

Just as every client with whom a social worker interacts is different, each conflict of values is unique. Therefore, no one response is appropriate or effective for all conflicts. Instead, social workers must be mindful of each client's values as well as the ethical implications of the social worker-client relationship.

The social work profession looks at values from a number of different perspectives. The historical perspective describes the values of the profession as they have evolved in response to changes in the political, economic, and social environment. According to this perspective, the profession's values have moved through five phases (Reamer, 2009; 2014):

1. *The Morality Period* In the late-19th century, the client's morals were of primary interest, and social workers focused on helping clients adjust to align their morals with societal expectations.

2. *The Values Period* From the early- to mid-20th century, social workers focused less on morality and more on social reform and the profession's development of core values (i.e., those professional values on which the mission of the social work profession was established), intervention approaches, strategies and techniques, and education and training. The beginnings of the modern-day social work code of ethics surfaced during this period with the passage of the first Code in 1947. In response to the events of the 1960s, social work values shifted toward promoting social justice, equal rights, and reform of societal systems that impact client's lives (e.g., welfare and public assistance systems).

   Core values
   Specified by the NASW *Code of Ethics*, beliefs and practices of the profession that include service, social justice, dignity and worth of person, importance of human relationships, integrity, and competence.

3. *The Ethical Theory and Decision-Making Period* In the late-20th century, social work emphasized the application of professional ethics, developing guidelines and protocols for responding to specific ethical dilemmas that emerged with controversial advances in health care such as euthanasia, organ transplants, psychopharmacological treatments, and test-tube babies.

4. *The Ethical Standards and Risk Management Period* In the early years of this century, the profession recognized professional conduct and malpractice as real and complex issues and instituted sweeping changes to the profession's *Code of Ethics* (NASW, 2008).

5. *The Digital Period* In the 21st century, the profession has concentrated on the impact of technology, the Internet, and social media on the delivery of ethical social work services. The capacity to practice social work by providing information, referral, crisis intervention, and social services online; by video, telephone, or mobile device; and through the use of avatars has presented the profession with a myriad of ethical questions and challenges concerning confidentiality, informed consent, privacy, and maintaining professional boundaries with the client.

Through this evolution the profession has established a core set of values, processes for ethical practice, and guidelines for protecting clients. In the early years of the 21st century, social workers' professional ethics still incorporate aspects of the Ethical Theory and Decision-Making Period and, by necessity, elements of the Risk Management perspective related to malpractice as well as technology. Ethically-based theoretical frameworks and the NASW *Code of Ethics* (2008) continue to guide professional practice. Social workers are obligated to adhere to ethical standards that will provide legal safeguards for both our clients and ourselves.

More than a century of focus on professional values and ethics has highlighted the complex nature of social work. Social work operates at the intersection of multiple levels of stakeholders, each with its own interests, and social workers must be knowledgeable about the values of stakeholders at each level. Dolgoff and associates delineate values by level of involvement (2012):

- *Individual or personal values:* the values of one person.
- *Group values:* the values of groups within society (for example, religious and ethnic groups).
- *Societal values:* the primary values of the larger social system.
- *Professional values:* the values of a specific discipline or professional group.

Social workers inevitably face value conflicts from time to time. Having a conceptual basis for understanding their own values and the values of clients, society, and the profession provides social workers with a starting point for successfully resolving those conflicts.

Value Conflicts

After graduating with her BSW degree, Emily's landed her first social work job at the adult social service unit of a multiservice public community agency. When she interviewed for the position, she was told she would be working as a case manager helping older adults maintain their independent living situations.

At first, Emily enjoyed her work, but after three years the agency reorganized so that all workers took on "generic" duties, handling both child and adult services. Emily was sometimes assigned child protection cases for which she investigated allegations of abuse and neglect, testified in court, and often recommended that a child be placed in foster care and sometimes even that parental rights be terminated. For the first time in her career, Emily felt conflicted regarding her role as a social worker. She felt that working with children and their parents was out of her scope of expertise and that her lack of experience and interest in working with this population hampered her ability to serve clients' best interests.

Value conflict
One's values are incongruent with the value system of another.

Emily experienced a value conflict—a situation in which a social worker's values (or "shoulds") clash with the value system of a client, agency, co-worker, or society in general. In this case, Emily's dilemma was the result of her adherence to both the social work value and ethical principle of practicing only in her areas of competence. She felt that being asked to work with children and families at that point without training was outside the scope of her practice competence.

Value conflicts present themselves in many different forms and may have no easy, clear, or even acceptable resolution. While you cannot anticipate all the potential conflicts you will encounter, you can prepare yourself to grapple with those conflicts when they do arise by developing a set of response skills and a support network to help you process information and weigh your options.

An important aspect of practicing ethically is to be prepared for the inevitability that conflicts will occur. When personal and professional values conflict in practice situations, as they will from time to time, social workers are obligated to set aside personal desires and to apply professional values and ethics in the interest of serving the client (Comartin & Gonzáles-Prendes, 2011). Consider the client who is seeking services to end her addiction to substances. She expresses the desire to be "clean and sober" but has been unsuccessful in her past attempts to sustain her goal of abstinence. The client agrees to participate in treatment which includes a commitment not to use drugs and to consent to regular drug testing. While, on the surface, this situation does not appear to be a potential value conflict for the social worker. The conditions of receiving services are clearly stated and the client has agreed to abide by the conditions or be terminated from the program for violations. However, value conflicts potentially exist in every social worker–client relationship. Utilizing this example, here is one plan for dealing with value conflicts that could occur in this case scenario (Dolgoff et al., 2012, p. 109):

1. Identify the conflicting values and consider the impact of the conflict on your client and yourself, e.g., my client is not complying with her treatment plan to remain clean and sober. I believe that she will function better and will be better able to benefit from the social work intervention if she is not using drugs.

2. If possible, frame the problem so that the value conflict is not relevant, e.g., I am ethically bound to allow my client her right to self-determination and to refrain from imposing my values on clients.

3. Clarify the connection between the value differences and the explanation the client has presented to you, e.g., my value system does not support the use of illegal substances and the client acknowledges she is using illegal drugs, but does not feel the power to stop.

4. Begin the intervention by addressing issues that do not include the value conflict, e.g., my client has stated she wants to stop abusing substances

and gain control of her life again, my agency provides services to clients who are struggling with addiction, and my client is asking for help.

5. Engage in a discussion with the client regarding the conflict so you can make a joint decision to determine if your differences will negatively affect the working relationship, e.g., I can let my client know about my concerns regarding her substance use and abuse and my observations regarding its impact on her ability to reach her desired goals. I can tell her that I may not be able to provide services if she continues to use drugs.

6. Determine if you can continue to work with the client or if you should refer the client to another professional e.g., I can negotiate a "clean and sober" contract with the client that clarifies both of our responsibilities and the consequences should either of us violate the contract.

First and foremost, clients always have the right to self-determination. In virtually every situation, a clients' choices have consequences that can potentially result in positive or negative outcomes. In the example above, the client can choose to continue her substance use in spite of her stated goals. Having entered into a "clean and sober" contract with the client can help her to prioritize her goals and subsequent actions and serve as a reminder of her desired goals. As the social worker, you may not agree with her choices, but they are hers to make, and your role is to provide options and to support her right to choose. The exception to this approach is if the client is considered a danger to herself or others. If this occurs, as a social worker, you are ethically and legally obligated to intervene.

The following sections describe some of the different types of value conflicts you may encounter as a social work professional.

Job-Related Value Conflicts Emily's conflict described earlier in this chapter is one example of a situation in which a social worker's value system came into conflict with the duties that she or he was expected to perform which she perceived to be outside her scope of competence. In every social worker–client relationship, there is a power differential in place as the social worker may have control or influence over resources or access to services. In Emily's situation, the potential exists for her to have significant influence over the clients' lives (e.g., recommend removal of children from their parents' care and possible termination of parental rights). Given the enormity of this responsibility, Emily was conflicted because she lacked confidence in her ability to competently perform her assigned duties and feared that she would not act in the best interests of the child.

While value conflicts can occur in any setting or client situation, social workers should be particularly aware of the risk for value conflicts in settings in which clients are vulnerable and/or mandated for services, including the public welfare system, the criminal justice system, an incarceration facility, a residential care facility, or an agency to which clients are mandated for social work services by the judicial, legal, or educational system or by an employer. Social workers working in host settings (organizations such as schools, hospitals, or the court system whose primary service is not social work) can find that their values are in conflict with those of their employer. While all professionals who work in these settings serve the client or patient population, the values of the host setting may conflict with those of the social worker.

Value conflicts can also arise when social workers find themselves in the role of an authority or "pseudo-cop" (Baldino, 2000, p. 25). Pseudo-cop social workers may be torn, for example, between their duty to comply with court directives and their obligation to support their client. Social workers who find themselves in such a dilemma can benefit from observing and consulting with other social workers who have dealt with similar experiences in similar settings.

A co-worker's unethical or impaired or compromised behavior may also create value conflicts. Consider a scenario in which you learn that a co-worker's drug or alcohol use is beginning to interfere with his ability to do his job, or one in which a co-worker defames or discriminates against clients and other co-workers. What is your personal and professional obligation in these situations? Is it acceptable to just look the other way? Should you confront the co-worker or report your suspicions to a supervisor? As a social work professional, you must grapple with the conflict between your personal loyalty to a co-worker and your professional standards for ethical behavior (NASW, 2008).

Value Conflicts Related to Religion or Spirituality Beliefs You may have been drawn to the social work profession out of a sense of religious or spiritual calling or obligation or as a result of experiences related to your religious or spiritual beliefs. Faith-based organizations that espouse a religious mission and philosophy are one big employer of social work practitioners. Ideally, social workers employed by religious organizations will work with clients and colleagues who share their religious or spiritual beliefs. In reality, though, religious differences are common, even in situations in which a social worker and a client or colleague share the same faith. If a social worker's religious beliefs conflict with those of her client or the agency for which she works, that can impede the worker's ability to do her job. For example, a social worker who is pro-life may be assigned to work with a client who is seeking an abortion or the social worker who identifies as a feminist practitioner who is asked to work with a woman who is being physically abused by her husband but her religious beliefs dictate that she serve her husband and not question or protest his actions. Although social workers are trained to maintain emotional objectivity, when dealing with issues related to religious beliefs and practices, the social worker's experiences and awareness of the beliefs of those whose religion differs from their own may be an asset.

Learning about and respecting the client's religious and faith beliefs and traditions is only the first step in incorporating them into the social work intervention. The next step is to actually engage the client's faith into the helping process and appreciate the power that one's beliefs can have on the intervention (Knitter, 2010). For example, consider a situation in which a client appears resistant to the professional's suggestions for intervention. If the social worker is familiar with the client's religious or spiritual beliefs, she or he is more likely to understand when the client's lack of cooperation is not resistance at all, but rather an expression of the client's religious beliefs, which may make it impossible for the client to comply or there could be a possibility that the client is, in fact, reluctant to engage in the helping process and they are citing religious beliefs out of avoidance (Knitter, 2010; Williams & Smolak, 2007). Regardless of the reasons, the social worker can address the client's religious beliefs with the client to better understand the role that faith plays in the client's life. Understanding, for instance, that a particular client's sense of self-worth is directly linked to her or his faith beliefs can guide a social worker to focus an intervention on helping the client connect or re-connect with her or his religious identity (Knitter, 2010).

Value Conflicts Concerning the Distribution of Resources The social work profession values each person's right to access the resources necessary for optimal quality of life. Although society as a whole generally supports this value, there is much disagreement over how to distribute these limited resources.

For example, many people believe that persons living in poverty do not deserve a "handout," but that they should instead work "like the rest of us" to earn their living. People who hold this view often support political candidates who oppose funding for public and social welfare programs that help the poor. Social work students may struggle with this particular issue; the values to which they have been exposed in their families and/or their communities may conflict with the value systems they encounter as they learn about the profession.

The Social Worker's Values

Although social work education emphasizes maintaining a nonjudgmental and objective perspective, in reality you cannot simply "check your values at the door." Your value system reflects the influences of the family and community who reared you; your friends and peers; your educational, religious, spiritual, social, and professional background; and your formal social work training. You bring your value system into each and every social work situation. Before you can strategize for understanding and working with the value systems of clients, agencies, groups, communities, and society, you must first consider your own value system, its origins, and the implications of your values for your life and your future practice.

Throughout the history of the social work profession, some social workers have espoused the views that social work practice should be value-free and that values should not affect social work practice (Dolgoff et al., 2012). Over time, however, most social workers have recognized that personal, group, and societal values do unavoidably influence their work, and that social work professionals need strategies that enable them to explore and clarify their own values and the profession's values and to acquire ethically competent social work skills.

To develop an appreciation of and respect for values and their impact on ethical behavior, it is helpful to engage in values clarification, the process of exploring your own values and comparing them to the values of others (Barker, 2014). Clarifying your values does not necessarily mean changing them. In fact, critically examining different perspectives may deepen your commitment to your existing values. Sometimes, however, exposure to new and different ideas and information may expand or alter your views. Values clarification does carry some risk—exposing yourself to views and value systems that may differ from your own can threaten your personal status quo. A professional social worker needs to be willing to take that risk in the interest of honoring her or his commitment to developing self-awareness. Without some level of resolution or clarity by the social worker of her or his own values and beliefs, the client may be negatively impacted (Comartin & Gonzáles-Prendes, 2011).

Values clarification
Self-exploration and assessment of one's belief system with the goal of developing a respect for others' values..

One could argue that attaining a social work degree is, in fact, an ongoing exercise in values clarification. As a social work student, you will find discussions with faculty and fellow students, readings, assignments, and field experiences will constantly challenge your value system. You can begin the values clarification process by engaging in casual conversations about issues that arise in your classes. Although you may not always be comfortable sharing your personal views and listening to the views of others, it is important to begin opening yourself up to these kinds of discussions during your training so that you will be more comfortable with them once you become a practitioner. As you progress through your career, you will eventually develop a strategy that will enable you to comfortably approach these situations. Valutis and colleagues (2011) report that learning about and clarifying values and ethical beliefs is related to one's age as opposed to academic class standing; that is, a student may be a freshman in college yet have life experiences or chronological age that has enabled her or him to clarify values and ethical beliefs. Therefore strategies for promoting effective learning and practice include being proactive in learning about the range of others' values and planning to engage in learning throughout one's career. Utilizing your support system of colleagues, supervisors, and mentors can aid in exploring and clarifying your values and processing values conflicts.

To engage in values clarification in discussions with others, ask yourself these questions:

- What do I think about this issue?
- What are the origins of my values on this issue?
- What are the other person's values on this issue? Are our values similar or different? In what ways? If they are different, does this difference create a dilemma for me or for the two of us?

ETHICS IN SOCIAL WORK

Action indeed is the sole medium of expression for ethics.

—Jane Addams

As you read this book, do you question why the social work profession, guided by the National Association of Social Workers and the *Code of Ethics* (2008), perceives the need to dictate and guide appropriate professional behavior? After all, don't people usually choose social work for altruistic reasons? If so, why do social workers need a formal document to guide and monitor practice? As social workers' roles have become increasingly complex, so has the potential for ethical dilemmas, malpractice, and legal liability. When faced with multiple alternatives, directions, or potential contradictions of ethical principles, formal ethical guidelines can help social workers establish an intervention that serves the best interests of the client and the client's system in a manner consistent with present-day cultural demands which are ever-changing (Dolgoff et al., 2012).

Code of ethics
A professional group's articulation of its values, ethical standards, and expected behaviors of its members..

Many professions have developed a standardized approach, or a code of ethics, to guide competent and effective practice. By definition, a code of ethics is a set of specific guidelines for appropriate and expected professional behaviors based on the profession's values and ethical standards.

In the 1960s and 1970s, the social work profession first began developing a formal code of ethics to guide professional practice. Changes affecting the clients social workers serve, such as advances in medicine (i.e., treatments, technology, and disease awareness), electronic technology, global awareness, resource management, and the social work mission, prompted this development (Reamer, 2008b). Of the several codes aimed at promoting ethical social work practice, the NASW *Code of Ethics* is the most prominent. Other social work organizations have developed codes of ethics similar in intent to the NASW's, but tailored to their specific organizational mission and membership. For example, the *Code of Ethics* of the National Association of Black Social Workers (NABSW) prescribes a commitment to "protect the security of the Black community, and to serve as advocates to relieve suffering of Black people by any means necessary" (NABSW, n.d.). The International Federation of Social Work (IFSW), an organization whose mission is to strive for "social justice, human rights, and social development through the promotion of social work best practice models and the facilitation of international cooperation" (IFSW, n.d.), has also established a set of ethical principles emphasizing human rights, human dignity, and social justice (IFSW, 2012). To view the IFSW document along with the individualized codes of ethics of over twenty countries, visit: http://ifsw.org/policies/statement-of-ethical-principles/. These codified set of statements are the profession's attempt to publicly share our profession, its mission, principles, and practices but must continue to evolve and change as our society undergoes transitions (Reamer, 2012). For example, as society has become more aware of the need for protecting individuals' rights and privacy, the NASW *Code of Ethics* (2008) was updated to reflect the social worker's role in respecting the client's right to self-determination, maintaining confidentiality in written and verbal form, appropriately transferring information.

Even a well-developed, professionally binding code has its limitations. Standards set forth in codes are, by necessity, broad in nature and leave particular situations open to interpretation. Nevertheless, the NASW code remains the best resource a social worker can consult when faced with an ethical dilemma.

The NASW *Code of Ethics*

The NASW Delegate Assembly, a body of NASW members elected by their state chapters, meets once every three years to debate and vote on NASW policies, including the *Code of Ethics*. The initial NASW *Code of Ethics*, accepted in 1960, emphasized the primacy of professional responsibility over personal interests, the client's right to privacy, the obligation to serve during public emergencies, and the duty to contribute to the knowledge of the profession (Reamer, 2008a). Recognizing that social work changes as society changes, NASW has revised the *Code* several times, most recently in 1999 and 2008. The current version builds on earlier versions. Today's longer *Code*, with its more sophisticated legal terminology, reflects social work's increasing professionalization and its responsiveness to society's ever-changing needs. Specifically, the newest *Code* includes resources social workers can use to navigate ethical dilemmas, with particular emphasis on ethical and social work practice, theory and decision-making, research, laws, agency policies, and related codes (Reamer, 2014, p. 171). This version of the *Code* acknowledges that: (1) conflicts are inherent within the document itself when individual client situations are considered as well as within organizations and practice; and (2) when conflicts surface, seeking counsel from experienced colleagues is appropriate and encouraged (Reamer, 2014). To view the current version of the NASW *Code of Ethics* (2008) in English and Spanish, and to see earlier versions of the document, go to: www.socialworkers.org/pubs/code/code.asp. Notice how earlier versions of the document were more moralistically-focused and instinctually-oriented, and how the guidelines developed over time to become a more complex set of ideals and standards aimed at guiding, monitoring, and promoting social work as a profession (Reamer, 2012). For an overview of the history of the NASW *Code of Ethics*, see Exhibit 6.1.

EXHIBIT 6.1

History of the National Association of Social Work Code of Ethics

1960: The Original NASW Code of Ethics

- NASW's Delegate Assembly approved the first edition of the NASW *Code of Ethics* on October 13, 1960.
- It defined the social work profession and the responsibilities of the social worker.
- It outlined fourteen responsibilities for social workers.

1967: The First Revision Addresses Non-Discrimination

- NASW members first revised the original *Code* in 1967, when they added a principle to address non-discrimination.

1979: The Second Revision Re-Conceives the Code

- This significant revision added six sections of standards, consisting of 82 new principles and a new preamble.
- Set forth principles related to social workers' ethical responsibility to their clients, colleagues, employers and employing organizations, the social work profession, and society.
- Introduced the idea of the Code as a tool for the enforcement of ethical practices among social workers in their everyday conduct.

The 1990s: More Changes

■ In 1990, NASW members modified the *Code* following a U.S. Federal Trade Commission inquiry. This revision focused on principles related to soliciting clients, fee setting, and accepting compensation for referrals.

■ In 1993, NASW members added five new principles related to social worker impairment and dual relationships.

■ The last major revision of the NASW *Code of Ethics* occurred in 1996. The revision came in response to developments in health care, litigations, and public perceptions, and accounted for ethical issues not addressed in the 1979 *Code*.

■ A minor 1999 revision clarified the circumstances in which social workers may need to disclose confidential information without a client's consent.

2006: Ethics Summit

■ In 2006, NASW hosted a Social Work Ethics Summit to examine the continuing relevance of the Code. This summit was co-sponsored by the NASW Legal Defense Fund, the Social Work Ethics and Law Institute, and the Wicher's Fund.

■ The Summit convened a small group of social workers representing diverse practice specialties, academia, research, licensing and regulatory boards, and attorneys to examine the 1999 *Code of Ethics*.

■ Summit participants did not see a pressing need to revise the *Code*, but they did recommend a renewed focus on the development of ethics education resources to facilitate the proper interpretation and application of the *Code*.

2008: Revisions Bolster Non-Discrimination Standards

The most recent revision, in 2008, incorporated language related to sexual orientation, gender identity, and immigration status into existing non-discrimination standards.

Source: NASW History of the Social Work *Code of Ethics*, available at: http://www.socialworkers.org/nasw/ethics/ethicshistory.asp.

While the NASW *Code of Ethics* (2008) has evolved and changed throughout history as society has evolved and changed, several themes emerge to suggest the way in which the *Code of Ethics* (2008) can and should be used. Social work ethics scholar, Reamer (2012), poses the following uses of the *Code of Ethics* (2008):

■ Articulate social work's principal mission, values, and ethical principles.
■ Guide social workers and employers in addressing ethical issues.
■ Delineate standards for ethical practice.
■ Protect consumers from incompetent practice.

- Provide a mechanism for the social work profession to govern itself.
- Protect social workers from ethical complaints and litigation (pp. 306–307).

How the *Code* is Organized The NASW *Code of Ethics* addresses a broad range of important—and sometimes controversial—behaviors and practices. It is separated into four sections: preamble, purpose, values and ethical principles, and ethical standards.

The preamble outlines the mission and core values (i.e., those beliefs that serve as the basis of the profession's purpose and perspective) of the social work profession. The 2008 *Code of Ethics* states:

- The mission of the social work profession is to enhance human well-being and help meet the basic human needs of all people, with particular attention to the needs and empowerment of people who are vulnerable, oppressed, and living in poverty.
- A historic and defining feature of social work is the profession's focus on individual well-being in a social context and the well-being of society.
- Fundamental to social work is attention to the environmental forces that create, contribute to, and address problems in living.
- Social workers promote social justice and social change with and on behalf of clients. "Clients" is used inclusively to refer to individuals, families, groups, organizations, and communities.
- Social workers are sensitive to cultural and ethnic diversity and strive to end discrimination, oppression, poverty, and other forms of social injustice.
- Social work activities may be in the form of direct practice, community organizing, supervision, consultation, administration, advocacy, social and political action, policy development and implementation, education, research, and evaluation.
- Social workers seek to enhance the capacity of people to address their own needs.
- Social workers also seek to promote the responsiveness of organizations, communities, and other social institutions to individuals' needs and social problems.
- Social work's six core values are service, social justice, dignity and worth of the person, importance of human relationships, integrity, and competence.

Following the preamble, the second section outlines the six purposes of the *Code*:

1. Identify core values on which social work's mission is based.
2. Summarize broad ethical principles that reflect the profession's core values and serve as the basis for a set of specific ethical standards to guide social work practice.

3. Help social workers identify relevant considerations when professional obligations conflict or ethical uncertainties arise.
4. Provide ethical standards to which the general public can hold the social work profession accountable.
5. Socialize practitioners new to the field to social work's mission, values, ethical principles, and ethical standards.
6. Articulate standards that the social work profession itself can use to assess whether social workers have engaged in unethical conduct.

The statement of ethical principles, the third section (see Quick Guide #6.1), is based on the six core values identified in the preamble. These ethical principles are the "ideals to which all social workers should aspire" (NASW, 2008). Theses ethical principles provide the basis for the standards that follow (Reamer, 2014). The principles and their annotations guide social work practice in the face of ethically challenging situations.

The final part of the *Code* lists six areas of social workers' ethical responsibilities:

1. Clients.
2. Colleagues.
3. Practice settings.
4. Professionalism.
5. Social work profession.
6. Larger society.

QUICK GUIDE #6.1 ETHICAL PRINCIPLES BASED ON CORE SOCIAL WORK VALUES

CORE SOCIAL WORK VALUES	SOCIAL WORK ETHICAL PRINCIPLES
Service	Help people in need and address social conditions and concerns.
Social justice	Challenge social injustice.
Dignity and worth of the person	Respect the inherent dignity and worth of the person.
Importance of human relationships	Recognize the central importance of human relationships.
Integrity	Behave in a trustworthy manner.
Competence	Practice within areas of competence, and develop and enhance professional expertise.

Source: Dolgoff et al., 2012, pp. 79–80

Considered to be the essence and substance of the *Code of Ethics* (and, one could argue, the social work profession itself), these six standards stipulate social workers' 155 specific ethical responsibilities (see Exhibit 6.2 for a summary of these ethical concerns). The standards are intended to guide the conduct of social work professionals and to serve as the basis for evaluating possible *Code* violations. The language in this section varies from the prescriptive (narrow

EXHIBIT 6.2

Ethical Concerns for Social Workers

Ethical concerns with clients
- Client's right to self-determination
- Client's decision-making capacity
- Informed consent for sharing information
- Competence of social work professional
- Appreciation of diversity
- Conflicts of interest
- Privacy and confidentiality
- Access to records
- Sexual relationships and harassment
- Physical contact
- Derogatory language
- Interruption/termination of services
- Payment for services

Ethical concerns with colleagues
- Confidentiality
- Interdisciplinary collaboration and consultation
- Disputes involving colleagues
- Referral for services
- Sexual relationships and sexual harassment
- Impairment or incompetence of colleagues
- Unethical conduct of colleagues

Ethical concerns with practice settings
- Supervision and administration
- Education and training
- Performance evaluation
- Confidentiality and completeness of client records
- Client billing
- Continuing education

- Commitment of social worker to employers
- Labor management disputes

Ethical concerns with professionalism
- Practice that is ethical, competent, fair, and honest
- Interference of private conduct with professional responsibilities
- Dishonesty, fraud, and deception
- Impairment of ability
- Misrepresentation
- Solicitations
- Failure to acknowledge colleagues' contributions
- Discrimination

Ethical concerns with social work profession
- Commitment to the entirety of the social work community
- Integrity of the profession
- Evaluation and research

Ethical concerns with larger society
- Social welfare
- Public participation
- Public emergencies
- Social and political action

and directive in focus) to the proscriptive (reactionary and conservative) to the aspirational (focused on achievement of ideals) to the enforceable (actions for which one must be accountable) (Strom-Gottfried, 2015). The apparent contradictions within the *Code* reflect the complexities of social work practice in contemporary society with its contradictory values, ethics, behaviors, needs, and expectations. Despite the document's directive nature, its occasionally imprecise language leaves the standards somewhat open to interpretation; how a reader understands and applies the standards depends upon his or her frame of reference (Strom-Gottfried, 2015).

A number of themes recur throughout the *Code*. Possibly the most prominent is respect for the client, which appears again and again in standards related to the social worker's commitment to clients and client self-determination. One way social workers demonstrate this respect for the client is by staying committed to ethically responsible and culturally competent practice (NASW, 2007). Another frequent theme is the social worker's responsibility to uphold the integrity of the profession, as evidenced by those standards that address the ethical responsibility when one has a colleague experiencing an impairment and demonstrating unethical behaviors. The *Code* also articulates the

Self-determination
The belief that the individual or group has the right to make decisions that affect her/himself or the group.

profession's responsibility to society, which translates into advocacy, education, and political action. Buila (2010) notes that the NASW *Code* is unique among professional codes because it proclaims ethical responsibility for social justice, social activism, and confronting the discrimination of specific oppressed populations. Given that social justice and advocating for those being oppressed is at the heart of the social work mission, the profession would be remiss in not making these goals central to the professional *Code of Ethics*. With inequities and inequalities escalating around the globe—particularly income inequalities, religious persecution, and health and educational disparities, the *Code of Ethics* guides social workers and reinforces the obligation to bring attention to the consequences of such injustices.

Application of the *Code of Ethics* The application of social work ethics evolves over time as social problems and issues come into focus. For example, until the 1970s, social workers were not legally required to report incidents of suspected child abuse, neglect, and exploitation. However, as society directed attention to these issues, the social work profession followed suit by mandating reporting. It was not until the latest version that the *Code of Ethics* addressed issues related to contemporary technology. Future versions will likely expand on the role and impact of technology.

Although the *Code of Ethics* is intended as a guide, it also serves as a mechanism for monitoring social workers' competency and professional ethics. In reality, violations are committed typically through two avenues: omission or nonfeasance (i.e., not taking an action specified within the *Code of Ethics* (2008)) and commission or malfeasance (i.e., taking an action the *Code of Ethics* specifically prohibits because that action is deemed unethical or unlawful) (Reamer, 2012; Strom-Gottfried, 2015). A social worker who is aware of a possible violation can report the alleged violation to a state NASW chapter or to the national NASW office. A committee of NASW members will review the complaint and, if the complaint is substantiated, recommend an appropriate response. That response may include corrective action (such as suspension, mandated consultation, or censure), notifying the social worker's state regulatory board, or other public sanction. In every U.S. state, social work licensure or certification requires ethical practice. Social workers who violate the *Code* may face civil malpractice suits or even criminal charges.

Critics of the *Code of Ethics* argue that, to be ethical, social workers need only "practice wisdom" (the knowledge, skills, and values that a social worker collects over the course of a career), instincts, and virtuosity and that being governed by a code is time-consuming, coercive, and a wasted effort (Dolgoff et al., 2009, pp. 34–35). Now that you have reviewed the *Code of Ethics,* do you think it is needed to guide social work practice? Why or why not?

Ethical Dilemmas

During one of her practicum experiences at a mental health center, Emily's field instructor invited her to join two male colleagues to co-lead a group for men who had been perpetrators of intimate partner violence. You will recall from Chapter 1 that Emily is a survivor of past intimate partner violence. She did not share that personal information with her field instructor or her co-workers because she was afraid they would see her as having too much emotional baggage to be effective. Nevertheless, Emily agreed to participate in the group, feeling that she would disappoint her supervisor if she rejected the invitation. She believed she had come to terms with her experience and that because of that experience and her social work training she would bring a valuable perspective.

Unfortunately, Emily's experience was less than successful. Hearing the men in the group rationalize violence against female partners made her extremely uncomfortable. Based on her value system, Emily viewed violence as reprehensible, and her own experience reinforced that view. Emily had become convinced that batterers could not be rehabilitated. She soon realized that she probably had not "put the experience behind her," and she was faced with two potential ethical dilemmas:

- *In her state of discomfort, she was not able to be a competent co-facilitator.*
- *If she left the group, her team would have no positive female role model and co-facilitator.*

Based on what you have learned, were these, in fact, ethical dilemmas?

The agency was strongly committed to having a male/female team lead this group. In an effort to display professionalism, Emily had chosen not to share with her supervisor or her colleagues her past experience, so she was fearful they would think she was hiding this information, which might lead them to question her ethical behavior. Were her personal values impeding her practice obligations? She was especially afraid of how she might react if she continued in the group: Would she "lose it" during a group session? What would you do in Emily's situation: leave, stay, and/or seek help?

An ethical dilemma is most challenging when personal values and professional ethical obligations conflict. Ethical dilemmas require the social worker to engage in a "complex analysis of ethical puzzles where social work's values, duty, and obligations conflict" (Reamer, 2014, p. 164). Most practitioners agree that the "best interests" of the client should take precedence, but your personal values may override your professional duty in some situations. Consider Emily's dilemma, for example. Her personal experience with intimate partner violence made it difficult for her to work with males who had battered their partners. Nevertheless, when she was given the opportunity to co-lead a group of men who had battered a female partner, she felt she could maintain enough emotional objectivity to be an effective co-leader. Clearly, however, her personal experiences and values clouded her objectivity and, possibly, her professional competence. It was important for her to learn that putting personal values aside is not always an easy task. Because of the negative group, she worked to confront her fears during supervisory sessions. With her supervisor's support, Emily was able to come to terms with her feelings and shift her beliefs to allow for the possibility that treatment could effectively rehabilitate men who had battered women in the past. As a result of delving into this personal and professional dilemma in consultation with an experienced supervisor, Emily was eventually able to successfully co-facilitate the group.

In confronting an ethical dilemma, determine whether the situation meets the criteria of a *professional* ethical dilemma. In order to be considered a professional ethical dilemma, three conditions must be met: (1) the social worker is faced with deciding on a course of action; (2) multiple possible courses of action exist; and (3) regardless of the course of action the social worker chooses, one of the profession's ethical principles will be compromised (Allen, 2012, p. 4).

Although the ethical challenges and dilemmas you are likely to encounter in your practice will all have unique characteristics, and though they will change with shifting trends that you cannot plan for or anticipate, a core group of ethical dilemmas transcends eras and social issues. These frequent ethical dilemmas include client rights; cultural and social diversity; client self-determination and professional paternalism; confidentiality, privileged communication, and privacy; informed consent; service delivery; boundary issues, dual relationships and conflicts of interest; recording, reporting, and documentation; supervision; consultation and referral; dishonesty, fraud, and misrepresentation; termination of services; administration; evaluation and research; and social welfare and social action (Reamer, 2012; 2014, p. 175). The ethical challenges presented in the following sections are drawn, in part, from this list. When linked to the social values and ethical principles discussed earlier, these examples provide a context in which to consider appropriate responses to some of the most common practice situations. As you review these challenges, consider your personal value system, your potential responses, and the intersection of the two. You may find that these situations prompt more questions than answers, but keep asking the questions. The key to gaining insight into how best to approach ethical dilemmas is to regularly engage in self-reflection and discussion with others (e.g., co-workers, supervisors, and faculty) to process the issues and your experiences.

Confidentiality, Privileged Communication, and Professional Paternalism

The social worker–client relationship is based on trust. When that trust is threatened or violated, an ethical dilemma may occur. The concepts of confidentiality, privileged communication, and professional paternalism are three areas that are important within social work practice and will be highlighted here.

To establish a trusting relationship, the social worker must respect the client's confidentiality. On the surface this may seem clear-cut, but in practice it can be less so. Defined as refusing to disclose client information without the client's permission, confidentiality may be either absolute or relative. *Absolute confidentiality* means that all information is held in confidence; *relative confidentiality* means that some information may be disclosed. Privileged communication is the explicit agreement between the social worker and the client that the social worker will not share information about the client without the client's permission which is typically made in writing. The social worker has the right to refuse to share client-related information that is deemed confidential (Strom-Gottfried, 2015). For example, if the client shared with the social worker that she or he has engaged in illegal activity, the social worker is not obligated to share that information unless there is a risk of danger to the public.

Professional paternalism occurs when a social worker, often operating with good intentions, makes decisions for the client without her or his consent or awareness (Barker, 2014). Despite the social worker's belief that she or he can envision the correct or best path for the client, the ultimate decision lies with the client and not the social worker. The client always has the right to self-determination.

Because the social work profession places such importance on privacy and confidentiality, two different professional documents—the NASW Policy Statements and the *Code of Ethics*—address these issues (NASW, 2008). The current Policy Statement (NASW, 2012–2014a) on confidentiality and information utilization provides clear guide lines for obtaining, sharing, and using client information. Additionally, because social workers are often privy to considerable and intimate client information, Standard 1.07(a–r) of the NASW *Code of Ethics* addresses privacy and confidentiality in great detail. The standard, derived from the value social work places on viewing each person with dignity and worth, provides guidelines for protecting information related to the client's reasons for receiving services, her or his legal and financial status, and other personal life details.

Legally, clients have relative confidentiality. There are two exceptional situations in which social workers must share some client information:

1. Social workers must report the suspected abuse, neglect, and/or exploitation of children, older adults, and persons with disabilities to appropriate state-level agencies.

Confidentiality
Maintaining client-related information and disclosing only with the permission of the client or the client's guardian.

Privileged communication
The explicit agreement between the social worker and the client that the social worker will not share information about the client without the client's permission which is typically made in writing.

Professional paternalism
When a social worker, often operating with good intentions, makes decisions for the client without her or his consent or awareness.

2. Social workers must report to designated state authorities any cases in which a person threatens harm to him or herself or to others.

Social workers are among the group of professionals mandated by law in every state in the United States to report suspected abuse, neglect, and/or exploitation; therefore, if a social worker reports concern for an individual's safety or well-being to an appropriate state agency, this is considered as an exception to the rule of client confidentiality. Further, the social worker may be in violation of the profession's ethical standards to not report suspected abuse, neglect, or exploitation of others. One other exception to the rule of client confidentiality is when a court order mandates that a social worker provide certain client information. Consider the ethical implications of confidentiality as you read the case vignette in Exhibit 6.3.

EXHIBIT 6.3

Confidentiality: The Case of Julio

Potential Dilemma:

Your agency has no formal policy on serving undocumented persons (individuals who are in the U.S. without appropriate legal standing), and there is controversy among the staff on this issue. Some believe the agency should serve this population; others do not. There is general agreement that the agency should not report undocumented persons to the Immigration and Naturalization Service (INS), but some feel a staff member should notify authorities if there is reason to believe the person may be involved in criminal activities, addicted to alcohol and/or drugs, is abusing a partner, or is earning money illegally.

Sixteen-year-old Julio has come to your agency for help accessing health care. He entered the country without documentation to join his mother, an undocumented worker who moves frequently to avoid detection and deportation, and he was held for several months at a detention center. Upon his release, he learned that his mother had moved again. He does not know where she is, he has no place to live, and he has been supporting himself through prostitution.

Analysis

The ethical issues are two-fold: (1) Are you obligated by agency policy or state mandate to report Julio to the INS for being engaged in prostitution? (2) Do you report Julio to Child Protective Services for being a minor without a guardian? Your agency does not have an official reporting policy and despite the fact he is 16 years old, he may or may not be treated as a traditional minor in many jurisdictions.

The following NASW *Code of Ethics* Standard 107 is applicable in this situation:

(a) Social workers should respect clients' right to privacy. Social workers should not solicit private information from clients unless it is essential to providing services or conducting social work evaluation or research. Once private information is shared, standards of confidentiality apply.

(b) Social workers may disclose confidential information when appropriate with valid consent from a client or a person legally authorized to consent on behalf of a client.

(c) Social workers should protect the confidentiality of all information obtained in the course of professional service, except for compelling professional reasons. The general expectation that social workers will keep information confidential does not apply when disclosure is necessary to prevent serious, foreseeable, and imminent harm to a client or other identifiable person. In all instances, social workers should disclose the least amount of confidential information necessary to achieve the desired purpose; only information that is directly relevant to the purpose for which the disclosure is made should be revealed.

(d) Social workers should inform clients, to the extent possible, about the disclosure of confidential information and the potential consequences, when feasible before the disclosure is made. This applies whether social workers disclose confidential information on the basis of a legal requirement or client consent.

(e) Social workers should discuss with clients and other interested parties the nature of confidentiality and limitations of clients' right to confidentiality. Social workers should review with clients circumstances where confidential information may be requested and where disclosure of confidential information may be legally required. This discussion should occur as soon as possible in the social worker-client relationship and as needed throughout the course of the relationship.

According to the *Code of Ethics*, you are ethically bound to protect your client's right to confidentiality, which suggests that you are not obligated to report him to the INS since your agency does not have a formal mandate to do so. Reporting Julio to the Children Protection Agency, however, is another matter. As a mandated reporter, you are obligated to report a minor without a guardian. The decision to investigate and/or intervene will then rest with the agency.

As a 16-year-old undocumented minor without a home, Julio is in need of shelter, health care, legal services, and assistance locating his mother. You can work with the Child Protection Agency to facilitate Julio's access to these services.

- Consider these questions:
- Is there a gap between agency policy and the NASW *Code of Ethics*?
- If a gap exists, how could and/or should the *Code of Ethics* guide agency policy?

Situations in which a person is a danger to him or herself or to others are particularly complex, in part due to the fact that legal statutes vary from state to state. In *Tarasoff v. Regents of the University of California* (1974, 1976), the Supreme Court of California ruled that mental health professionals, including social workers, have a duty to warn and protect potential victims of violence.

As social workers have expanded their areas of practice over the years, the duty to warn and protect has expanded to include cases involving HIV/AIDS, intimate partner violence, and health care situations (e.g., end-of-life and genetic issues) (Granich, 2012). For example, if a social worker comes to possess information that her or his client intends to physically harm a partner, the social worker is within her or his right to inform the person who may be harmed. In these situations, social workers often find that preserving confidentiality conflicts with the obligation to warn and protect (Granich, 2012).

Familiarity with ethical guidelines and available resources is indispensable when any crisis arises. For example, a client threatens to harm her or himself. Knowing the exact steps you must take to respond to this situation can save a life. Guidelines may include knowledge of state law and agency policy; having a plan/protocol to follow (including prior consultation with appropriate agency personnel) that helps you to assess danger and develop a planned response; understanding documentation requirements; and ensuring your own self-awareness and self-care (Tapp & Payne, 2011). Of critical importance is that social workers assume responsibility for knowing the policies of their agency, laws of their state, and implications for malpractice and licensure. For more information on state laws, review the information on the NASW website at: www.naswdc.org/ldf/legal_issue/2008/200802.asp?back=yes.

For beginning social workers, the responsibility to maintain a client's privacy and confidentiality can seem overwhelming. When do you share or not share client information? What can you write or not write/enter in a client record? What if you accidentally commit a breach of confidence? These are all questions that you should routinely ask yourself. The recommended practices that follow can help you answer these and other questions about maintaining client privacy and confidentiality (adapted from Dunlap & Strom-Gottfried, 1998).

- Be vigilant; take note of your location as you communicate information to or about the client. Keep confidentiality foremost in your mind.
- Protect records in a locked receptacle, and safeguard computer files with a firewall, password, and short-delay screen saver.
- Monitor your ongoing client-related activities by gathering only the information that is relevant to the services being provided.
- Learn and understand laws and agency policies and practices regarding the protection of information.
- Monitor yourself. Consult with your supervisor and colleagues, not with clients or your friends or family.
- Picture yourself as a consumer of your services—how would you like to be treated?

Informed Consent Social workers can share information when a client or legal guardian has granted informed consent in writing. Such consent is needed for the practitioner to share the information contained within client records (e.g., assessment, intervention, and evaluation information) with insurance companies, other providers, and family members (Polowy, Morgan, Bailey, & Gorenberg, 2008). Relative confidentiality exists in these situations. To obtain valid informed consent, a social worker must make the client or the client's guardian aware of the specific information to be shared and the reasons for sharing it, with whom the information will be shared, and the date of expiration that the information can be shared, and the client or the client's guardian must then give written permission to release that information. Most agencies have a standardized informed consent form. The social worker is obligated to ensure that the client is capable of providing informed consent and must assure the client that she or he always reserves the right to refuse to provide consent (Reamer, 2012).

Informed consent
Release of client-related information based on the client having full understanding of and agreement with the disclosure of the information.

Confidentiality Agreement

Source: iStock/aluxum

The Health Insurance Portability and Accountability Act of 1996 (HIPAA) further protects client information (U.S. Department of Health and Human Services, 2004). The HIPAA legislation is designed to protect and enhance the rights of consumers of health care services without compromising their access to or the effectiveness of the provision of services. The law mandates that consumers of health care services have the following rights: to see and obtain copies of their health care records; to be informed in writing about the ways in which health information is used by their health care provider; and to have assurance that their identifiable health information is protected.

Client Self-Determination The social work profession's commitment to each client's right to self-determination stems from the value the profession places on the dignity and worth of each person. A relatively recent content area social work ethics, Standard 1.02 specifies that the social worker is obligated to respect the client's right to make decisions and choices and to determine personal goals. Situations sometimes arise that limit the social worker's ability to fully comply with this obligation. As with confidentiality, when a client threatens physical harm to self or to others, the social worker's ethical and legal obligation to protect the person overrides the client's right to self-determination (Reamer, 2012).

Ethical dilemmas can also occur in non-life-threatening situations in which the social worker feels the client is making a decision that may have a negative or harmful outcome. Consider, for example, the person who resumes drinking or using drugs, returns to a violent relationship, or refuses services even though noncompliance will result in a return to prison. In these situations, the social worker must balance respect for the client's right to self-determination with the obligation to help the client achieve a positive outcome (Dolgoff et al., 2012).

In these difficult situations it is useful to remember that the person's right to self-determination takes precedence whenever possible. Even the client who has not voluntarily come to the social worker for services has the "right" to choose nonparticipation. The social worker's responsibility is to provide the opportunity to identify and examine the consequences of a client's choice. If social workers truly respect and value each client, they must diligently respect the client's right to self-determination. All people have the right to make decisions about their own lives. Review the case vignette in Exhibit 6.4 involving Agnes Holmes and her right to determine her end-of-life care. Upon reviewing the case, how do you think you would respond to the client's request? What legal or ethical basis do you have for your response?

Boundaries
Delineations between the professional and the client system that serve to separate the personal from the professional relationship.

Boundaries and Self-Disclosure The parameters that define your relationship with the client system as a professional one rather than a social one are called boundaries. Boundaries can be difficult to delineate and maintain because clients often share intimate details of their lives, making the relationship seem close and personal. While it may sometimes be difficult to determine whether a particular situation constitutes an infringement of boundaries, there are some lines that the profession explicitly prohibits social workers from crossing. These include sexual relationships with a current or former client, a client's family member, a client's friend, a supervisee, a trainee, a student, or a colleague; friendship, physical contact, or a public meeting with a client or former client (including attending a client's social event); receiving or giving gifts, favors,

EXHIBIT 6.4

Client Right to Self-Determination: The Case of Agnes Holmes

Potential Dilemma

Eighty-three-year-old Agnes Holmes is a patient in the long-term care facility where you work. She had a major cardiovascular accident (i.e., stroke) and is completely paralyzed on her right side. She is cognitively intact, but she needs total care. She does not have a formal advanced care directive, but she has verbally indicated her wishes that all treatments be discontinued, including nutrition (she currently receives nutrition through a feeding tube inserted into her abdomen). Her family has gathered. Her daughter, who has Durable Power of Attorney, wants every possible measure to be taken to save her mother's life. Her grandson is advocating for his grandmother's wishes to be respected. Her sister and brother-in-law are torn—they want to respect Agnes' wishes but feel that withdrawing all care, including life support is too extreme and worry that Agnes is suffering. Agnes and her grandson ask you for your help to convince Agnes' daughter to let her die on her own terms. Agnes feels that "it wasn't supposed to be like this." She is at peace with her decision but does not want her daughter to be upset.

Analysis

The issues in this case are three-fold: (1) Agnes has the right to self-determination but does not have a formal advanced care directive; (2) Agnes gave her daughter Durable Power of Attorney to make health care decisions in the event that Agnes is unable to make those decisions; and (3) you have been asked to advocate with family members on Agnes' behalf.

The following parts of NASW *Code of Ethics* Standards 107 apply in this situation:

1.01 Commitment to Clients

Social workers' primary responsibility is to promote client well-being. In general, clients' interests are primary. However, social workers' responsibility to the larger society or specific legal obligations may on limited occasions supersede the loyalty owed clients, and clients should be so advised. (Examples include when a social worker is required by law to report that a client has abused a child or has threatened to harm self or others.)

1.02 Self-Determination

Social workers respect and promote clients' right to self-determination and assist clients in their efforts to identify and clarify their goals. Social workers may limit clients' right to self-determination when, in the social workers' professional judgment, clients' actions or potential actions pose a serious, foreseeable, and imminent risk to themselves or others.

In this scenario, Agnes is cognitively able to make her own decisions regarding health care; therefore, neither an advanced care directive nor Durable Power of Attorney is needed. Rather than advocating *for* Agnes with her family, you can suggest a family conference and serve as a mediator while Agnes speaks on her own behalf. After hearing Agnes voice her wishes, if her daughter is still insistent on her position, you may help her acknowledge that she is fearful of losing her mother and facilitate a conversation between mother and daughter. As a last resort, you may have to involve the hospital's legal counsel to intervene.

Self-disclosure
The sharing of personal information with a client system.

barter, or money; self-disclosure (the sharing of personal information with a client) to clients; and business relationships with current or former clients (Reamer, 2012, p. 311).

The social worker-client relationship can involve sharing, cooperation, and even mutual regard, but it cannot become a friendship, romance, or business partnership (Strom-Gottfried & Dunlap, 1998). Dual relationships with clients—that is, those that are both personal and professional—present conflicts of interest and are unethical and inappropriate. Standard 1.06 of the *Code of Ethics* addresses conflicts of interest, stating that a social worker must maintain separateness in personal, religious, political, and business areas.

Becoming familiar with the profession's ethical standards as well as agency policies and practices will help you avoid committing ethical infractions related to client-worker boundaries. Conducting periodic reality checks with colleagues and supervisors can also help social workers maintain appropriate boundaries.

Despite taking the best precautions, it is not always possible to maintain proper boundaries. You might encounter a client somewhere outside the social work setting, for example, particularly if you practice in a small community. In those instances, allow the client to acknowledge you first, and if you engage with the client, ensure that you do not discuss the professional relationship during the encounter. Be prepared for the possibility that the client may not choose to acknowledge you at all, or, conversely, that she or he may openly acknowledge you and discuss the reasons why you know each other. In either case, it is the responsibility of the social worker to maintain professional boundaries.

Maintaining boundaries means avoiding most self-disclosure with clients. The *Code of Ethics* states that social workers should not allow their personal issues to interfere with the best interests of the client. Although this does not specifically address the issue of self-disclosure, it implies that social workers should approach self-disclosure with caution and maintain the focus on the client.

A social worker may share personal information with clients with the best of intentions. For example, substance abuse treatment programs may hire individuals who are themselves recovering from chemical dependency or addiction and encourage them to disclose their history of abuse to their clients in order to establish rapport. The social worker may believe that if the client knows that the worker has had similar experiences, the client will be better able to work through the challenge. In cases in which the social worker has a similar life experience to the client, she or he may have knowledge and insight that others who have not had the experiences would not have and be able to operate from a position of deeper understanding. In fact, the social worker's self-disclosure may help achieve that goal. If a client knows that a social worker shares the same experience, that client may see the social worker as more credible or trustworthy, feel that her or his experience is normal, or feel more confident and inspired to change (Reamer, 2001). It is important for the social worker to recognize that her or his experience will not be the same as the client's experience.

In other cases, however, self-disclosure can sabotage the social work intervention. The social worker's disclosure may confuse the client. The client may try to mirror the worker's recovery, or the disclosure may shift the client's attention away from her or his own situation and onto the worker's life (Strom-Gottfried & Dunlap, 1998; Reamer, 2001). Consider Emily's experiences at Oasis House; her self-disclosure prompted the client to feel comfortable asking Emily for money. When working with the group of batterers, would Emily have wanted to share her history as a victim of domestic violence?

Social workers must closely monitor their disclosure of personal information. Some effective strategies for self-monitoring include:

- Learn the agency policy and practice regarding self-disclosure.
- Determine the appropriateness, benefits, and costs of sharing particular information and the client's ability to use that information (Strom-Gottfried & Dunlap, 1998).
- Remember that the social worker's responsibility is to support the client; the social worker and client are not in a reciprocal relationship (i.e., a friendship).
- Consult with colleagues and supervisors regarding their experiences with self-disclosure.

Allocation of Resources, Social Welfare, and Social Action Particularly during challenging economic times, social workers often have too few resources to adequately serve their many clients. A social worker may have to deny an application for assistance because of insufficient funding or lack of space in a shelter or food in the pantry. As clients' first contact in the social welfare system, social workers typically shoulder the burden of informing clients when there are not enough resources to fulfill a request.

Resources are typically allocated on the basis of equal-sized proportions (i.e., all recipients receive the same portion or allocation), a lottery system, or on a competitive basis using financial need or past oppression as the criteria (Reamer, 2001). Frustratingly, there may be little that the social worker can do to influence resource allocations. Nevertheless, social workers have an ethical obligation to take action to promote the fair allocation of resources within the social welfare system. Social workers who work directly with client systems can speak up for those clients, and social workers who occupy supervisory, administrative, and policy positions in public or nonprofit organizations can advocate for the equitable allocation of resources and against discriminatory and oppressive policies. A social worker may approach her or his own agency, another agency, or a particular source of funding to secure resources for individual clients. Social workers can also solicit those who have the power to make funding and policy decisions for greater allocation of resources to groups of clients. Legislative advocacy, political campaigning, community organizing, and speaking out on behalf of clients can help raise awareness of funding inequalities and lead to more positive resolutions in the face of limited resources.

Technology and Social Media Technology has become a part of our daily personal and professional lives and has allowed our society to become more connected and to be better and more quickly informed. It can be hard to imagine what life was like before the advent of technology and social media. What professional ethical implications do these capabilities, which have so rapidly changed the world we live in, present? To date, no legislation or regulatory standards have been enacted to govern the delivery of on-line services but referring to the NASW & ASWB (Association of Social Work Boards) 2005 *Standards for Technology in Social Work Practice* can serve as a grounding in the ethical and practice-related issue when using technology. Social workers are obligated to consider ethical and legal issues related to client privacy, boundaries, self-disclosure, potential ethical dilemmas and violations, and the sharing of information as we use technology and social media. The three main areas in which ethical issues related to the use of technology often arise in social work practice are: (1) using technology to provide services at all levels of social work practice (individuals, families, groups, organizations, and communities); (2) managing your presentation of self through social media; and (3) connecting with clients via social media. Let us explore these areas here.

While not all agencies provide services, including therapy, in an online environment, doing so is certainly not a new or novel approach. Many agencies provide telemental health services which are mental health services delivered not in a face-to-face format, but through email, electronic social networks, chat rooms, and videoconferencing, to name a few. Technology has rapidly become an accepted part of the service delivery system, and many practitioners acknowledge that it can enhance the immediacy and continuity of client contact (Mishna, Bogo, Root, & Fantus, 2014).

But what about delivering services by text or even Twitter? What about cybertherapy, in which clients and professionals interact in a three dimensional environment through avatars (Reamer, 2013b) For the most part, ethical and legal standards have not kept up with the development of these technologies, leaving agencies and individuals unclear on the implications of their professional use (e.g., is a client's privacy protected when they receive mental health services through Skype or is there a risk for dual relationships?) (NASW Legal Defense Fund, 2011–2012). As we progress through the digital age, the social work profession must re-evaluate its core ethical concepts and practices in the context of technological resources and communication methods and the profession's legal vulnerability regarding their use (Reamer, 2013b).

Most of us connect with others through one of many online social networks—Facebook and Twitter are two of the most common. For some, social networking has become a primary way to stay connected with family and friends, to alert the world (which they have "friended") to their latest activities, thoughts, and life accomplishments or disappointments. What happens if those Mardi Gras photos or those comments you posted about your experience that do not show you in your best light make their way to a potential employer, graduate school admissions director, or client? What happens if you post a picture of yourself working with the children at your agency and their parents (who did not give their consent for the photo) see it? These are just two of the infinite number of ethical challenges that can arise in connection with your use of social media.

What about connecting intentionally or unintentionally with clients through a networking site? Is it appropriate to "friend" a current or former client? What happens if a client learns that you have "vented" about your job, or conversely, if you learn that a client has discussed you on her or his network site? The list of potential boundary and privacy violations goes on.

The use of technology and social media varies by agency setting. Many social service organizations use technology to communicate, to educate, and to provide services, promote programs, and advocate for legislation. In an effort to clarify and guide social workers in the appropriate professional use of technology, the Association of Social Work Boards has developed the Model Social Work Practice Act, which includes a section on Electronic Practice (to review the Act, go to: www.aswb.org/wp-content/uploads/2013/10/Model_law.pdf).

Telemental health services
Mental health services delivered not in a face-to-face format, but through email, electronic social networks, chat rooms, and videoconferencing.

As the social work profession grapples with the real and potential ethical and legal dilemmas that stem from the use of always-changing technology and social media, consider the following recommendations from social work scholars (Halabuza, 2014; Mishna et al., 2014; NASW, 2015; Strom-Gottfried, Thomas, & Anderson, 2014):

- To ensure that you are practicing within your scope of competence, be confident that you are fully competent in the use of any technology that you use in your practice.
- Familiarize yourself with or develop organizational policies and/or state laws regarding the use of technology and social media with clients and the public.
- From the outset, clearly articulate to clients your organization's policies regarding communication through technology and social media, with particular attention to issues of informed consent, boundaries and privacy, appropriate content and actions (e.g., it is generally not appropriate to "friend" or "Google" your client or blog/post negative comments about your organization or co-workers), and vulnerabilities of both the worker and client. For example, ensure that your client is aware that their own use of social media can jeopardize their confidentiality and privacy.
- In your personal use of social media, establish and maintain stringent privacy settings where you can—what goes on the internet stays on the internet.
- Give thought to the information and materials you post to social networking sites, particularly as they relate to your professional life.
- Do not access clients' sites without their consent or a valid reason to do so.

What do you think about the use of technology and social media within the social work profession? In your opinion, what is acceptable and what is not acceptable?

VALUES AND ETHICS IN PRACTICE

Social work practitioners must be wary of the potential for value conflicts or ethical dilemmas at all times. No matter how clear, straightforward, or mundane a situation may seem on the surface, social workers cannot trivialize any situation or routinize their interpretations or responses. Instead, social workers adhere to the values that have long guided social work practice. The knowledge and skills developed by social work professionals are deeply rooted in this set of values, which have changed little since they were first introduced. As social work scholar Reamer (2015) offers:

To practice competently, contemporary professionals must have a firm grasp of pertinent issues related to ethical dilemmas and ethical decision-making. This knowledge enhances social workers' ability to protect clients and fulfill social work's critically important, value-based mission.

(p. 148)

Although social workers widely accept the profession's core values and ethical principles, the meanings and implications of those values and principles are open to interpretation, and differing interpretations (Dunlap & Strom-Gottfried, 1998). Therefore, it is important for social workers to be armed with knowledge and skills to aid in applying the values and ethical principles in practice situations. Known as ethical decision-making, this component of social work practice can be defined as: "the process by which social workers engage in an exploration of values—that may be evident in the personal, professional, social and organizational spheres—in order to establish where an ethical dilemma might lie according to what competing principles, and what factors take priority in the weighing up of alternatives" (McAuliffe, 2010, p. 41). Being aware of areas that may be potential ethical dilemmas and identifying and exploring the intricacies and implications of the ethical issues is a critical part of the social work role.

Noted social work scholar Donna McAuliffe (2012) offers the following suggestions for social workers as they engage in ethical decision-making in social work practice:

- Ethical decision-making is a process with many component parts, constructed differently according to one's theoretical and ideological perspective, but commanding rigorous attention to identification of competing ethical principles with a view to resolution of an identified dilemma.
- It is a highly reflective and conscious activity that draws on many sources of information and discards those pieces of information not relevant to the contextual situation at hand, while placing high priority on relevant information that can help inform judgment.
- It is both an individual activity and a collective one, best undertaken by engaging in dialogue with others and working to understand divergent views while seeking consensus on converging views.
- It involves power, and a critical part of an ethical decision-making process is to ensure that power is not misused or abused, and that all those with a vested interest in decision outcomes are involved in some way in the decision-making process.
- It is not about blindly following a prescribed set of instructions (or an ethical code) or steps in a model, but is about personal and professional self-awareness, and the intentional development of an integrated and

consistent set of principles that, in combination with a practice framework, can guide actions.

■ It takes into account and seeks to challenge those structural factors that
   contribute to oppression and social injustice and that result in human
   rights violations.

■ It must be learned from social work practice, and the responsibility for
   this learning lays with the practitioner, who remains accountable for his
   or her conduct, behavior, and actions connected to rights, responsibilities,
   duties, and obligations.

■ It necessitates both knowledge and skills—drawing on ethical theory and
   moral philosophy, law and policy, international conventions and cultural
   world views, ethical codes and standards, research and evidence—to work
   in ways that maximize human potential and opportunity through collaborative partnerships, open communication, respectful dialogue, and
   conduct demonstrating competence, caring, and integrity (p. 324).

To better understand and interpret the ethical principles and standards of
the NASW *Code of Ethics* (2008) and to apply those standards to social work
practice situations, social work theorists and scholars have developed several
tools (also referred to as models or frameworks) for making ethical decisions.
Four of the most common tools: (1) the DECISIONS Approach (NASW Office
of Ethics and Professional Review (NASW OEPR), n.d.); (2) ETHIC–A Model
(Congress, Black, & Strom-Gottfried, 2009); (3) the Six-Question Model
(Strom-Gottfried, 2015); and (4) the Enhanced Ethical Decision-Making
Matrix (D'Aprix, 2005; D'Aprix, Boynton, Carver, & Urso, 2001) are described
below. While each tool is different, all four aim to help social work practitioners organize information, use the profession's ethical principles and standards
to determine a course of action, and ensure that their actions uphold the ideals
and ethics of the profession. In selecting an ethical decision-making model or
framework for your own practice, consider your practice setting and population, the theoretical approach(es) you most often employ, and how much
structure and detail you need in a framework based on your familiarity with
the *Code of Ethics* (NASW, 2008).

Exhibit 6.5 presents all four of the ethical decision-making models discussed here, followed by a case application of one of the models:

■ *The DECISIONS Framework* (NASW OEPR, n.d.) emphasizes the gathering
   of information from all involved parties involved and from the literature,
   considering the impact of your decision, developing a rationale for that
   decision, and providing documentation.

■ *The five-step ETHIC–A Model of decision-making* (Congress, 1999) also
   stresses gathering information and considering the decision's impact, but

EXHIBIT 6.5

Models for Ethical Decision-Making

Ethical Decision-Making Framework: the *DECISIONS Approach*

- Determine the facts.
- Are there any ethical considerations that you need to take into account? If so, what ethical standards apply?
- Determine the personal and moral values involved.
- Impact of Self—how is the social worker influencing this dilemma?
- Who are the stakeholders?
- Review professional literature.
- Other considerations: standards of practice, agency policies, regulatory and/or legal considerations, consultation.
- Be prepared to articulate your decision. Do some critical thinking and be confident.
- Secure and support your decision thorough careful documentation and evaluation of the outcome of your decision.

Source: (NASW Office of Ethics and Professional Review, n.d., www.socialworkers.org/nasw/ethics/resourcesliterature.asp)

ETHIC-A Model

- Examine the issue and the dilemma.
- Think about values—personal, societal, cultural, agency, client, and professional.
- Consider possible scenarios and the consequences of different decisions including the role of advocate.
- Identify who will benefit or be harmed by possible courses of action, and maintain a commitment to protecting the most vulnerable.
- Consult with your supervisor and colleagues about possible ethical choices.
- Advocate within your agency, the social work community, and at the local, state, and national levels.

Source: Congress et al., 2009.

The Six-Question Model

1. Who will be helpful?
2. What are my choices?
3. When have I faced a similar dilemma?
4. Where do ethical and clinical guidelines lead me?
5. Why am I selecting a particular course of action?
6. How should I enact my decision?

Source: Strom-Gottfried, 2015.

Ethical Decision-Making: Identifying the Issues

Questions to Identify Ethical Issues	Basis for Question
1. What are the interventions and ethical issues that make it difficult to choose a course of action?	Worker is able to address all potential ethical issues to be addressed. Worker determines if any *Code of Ethics* standards or laws are involved.
2. What are my viewpoints on these issues?	Worker is able to recognize her/his personal biases and determine any impact those biases may have on client outcomes.
3. Which actions (interventions) might address the practice and ethical issues listed in number 1?	Worker is able to consider all potential alternatives for intervention.
4. What are the potential consequences/ outcomes of these actions?	Worker can conduct a cost-benefit analysis of the potential intervention.
5. How would I prioritize the intervention and ethical issues?	Using the EPS (Ethical Principles Screen), the worker can rank-order priorities.
6. Based on this prioritization, which issues will I address first and which action will address the issue that I will address?	After prioritizing the ethical issues, the worker can prioritize the proposed interventions.
7. Throughout this process, have I consulted with colleagues for their professional opinions?	Worker can benefit from the practice wisdom of other social work professionals.
8. How will I monitor and evaluate the effectiveness of this plan of action?	Ongoing monitoring enables the worker to know when to proceed to the next priority and to assess the status of the dilemma.

Source: D'Aprix et al., 2001.

adds emphasis on exploring options, consultation and advocacy as key components.

- Developed by Congress (1999), *the ETHIC-A Model* is particularly useful in fast-paced practice situations. The Six-Question Model expands on the ETHICS approach to incorporate prior experience, helpful guidelines, and plan development (Strom-Gottfried, 2015).

■ *The Enhanced Ethical Decision-Making Matrix* (D'Aprix, 2005; D'Aprix, Boynton, Carver, & Urso, 2001) expands on the basic premise of the other three models discussed here even further, adding attention to identifying priorities monitoring of change, and evaluating the results of the chosen action. Critical to the process of applying any of these models is to identify the ethical issues involved using the *Code of Ethics.*

Once she or he has identified the ethical issues involved, the social worker can use another tool, called the Ethical Rules Screen (ERS), to decide how to proceed. The ERS comprises the following steps (Dolgoff et al., 2012, pp. 79–80):

1. Examine the *Code of Ethics* (2008) to determine if any *Code* rules apply.
2. If the *Code* does not apply, move on to the Ethical Principles Screen (EPS).

The Ethical Principles Screen (Dolgoff et al., 2012, pp. 79–80) is a mechanism for rank-ordering client-related issues using seven ethical principles. Quick Guide 6.2 lists those seven ethical principles that can be helpful in determining the most ethical way in which to approach a complex situation. Using these seven principles, a social worker can prioritize the ethical questions and determine what issues are most important to address. While each of the seven principles is significant, the principles are listed in order of their perceived importance within the client's life. For example, protecting life is considered to have greater value than preserving confidentiality and, in decision making, anything that would impact the client's life would take precedence over maintaining client confidentiality.

Applying any of these decision-making frameworks does not ensure "easy answers to the tough questions," but these tools provide an approach for devising ethical and thoughtful responses to difficult situations. The models prompt the social worker to ask questions relevant to the ethical dilemma, to organize information, to establish priorities, and to consider the impact of the outcome on all parties involved.

QUICK GUIDE # 6.2 ETHICAL PRINCIPLES SCREEN

Ethical Principle 1: Protection of Life
Ethical Principle 2: Social Justice
Ethical Principle 3: Self-determination, Autonomy, and Freedom
Ethical Principle 4: Least Harm
Ethical Principle 5: Quality of Life
Ethical Principle 6: Privacy and Confidentiality
Ethical Principle 7: Truthfulness and Full Disclosure
Source: Dolgoff et al., 2012, pp. 79–80.

CASE: CATHLEEN'S RIGHT TO PRIVACY AND CONFIDENTIALITY

We have explored a number of issues related to social work values and ethics. Now it's time to apply those concepts and frameworks to an ethical dilemma.

Imagine that you are a social worker at Oasis House, where your supervisor asks you to talk with a new resident, Cathleen. Cathleen told shelter workers that she is 18 and homeless. During your talks with Cathleen, however, she admits that she is really only 15 and has run away from home. She further divulges that she does not want to go home because her mother's live-in boyfriend sexually abused her. She begs you not to share the information about the sexual abuse with anyone or to contact her mother.

As you consider how to handle this situation, you may ask yourself the following:

- Does the adolescent have a legal right to make decisions about her life without parental consent?
- What is your responsibility to Cathleen's parents?
- Would it be appropriate for you to discuss Cathleen's situation with her mother without Cathleen's informed consent?
- If Cathleen is being sexually abused, does she have a right to privacy after she has shared her secret with you?
- Was Cathleen informed that you might not be able to maintain complete confidentiality *before* she confided in you?
- What are the agency's policies and procedures related to sexual abuse and Cathleen's status as a minor and a runaway?

Use one of the decision-making models in Exhibit 6.5 as a guide to analyze this situation. Then review Exhibit 6.6, which examines the general categories of the Ethical Decision-Making Model to present possible ways of categorizing the issues to reach a satisfactory solution. (D'Aprix, 2005; D'Aprix et al., 2001). As you can see, this ethical dilemma poignantly addresses the client's right to protection, self-determination, privacy, and confidentiality. Client self-determination is at the heart of the NASW *Code of Ethics's* (2008) first ethical standard, Social Workers' Ethical Responsibilities to Clients. Having respect for the client is based on the core social work value of "dignity and worth of the person" and the ethical principle to "respect the inherent dignity and worth of the person."

Respecting Cathleen's right to self-determination, privacy, and confidentiality is key to upholding her dignity and worth. You are ethically bound to respect her dignity and worth, behave in a trustworthy manner, and practice with competence. By asking you to keep the alleged abuse in confidence and

EXHIBIT 6.6

Ethical Decision Making: Preserving Privacy and Confidentiality in Cathleen's Case

PRACTICE/ ETHICAL ISSUES	ETHICAL PRINCIPLE(S)	PERSONAL BIASES	ACTION(S) OPTIONS	POTENTIAL CONSEQUENCES/ OUTCOMES	ACTION(S) TAKEN	MONITOR/ EVALUATE EFFECTIVENESS
Client's request to not report sexual abuse.	1) Protection of human life. 6) Privacy and confidentiality.	I think the mother is at fault.	a) Report the abuse to the public agency despite client opposition. b) Work with client to make the report together.	a) Report is made, but client's trust is lost. b) Build trust with client so report can be made.	Jointly work with client to make report.	Check with client at each step to determine her: sexual safety; comfort levels with contacting her mother; feelings about her working relationship with the social worker.
Client's request to not contact her mother.	6) Privacy and confidentiality. 3) Self-determination 1) Commitment to client.	I think her mother must be contacted.	a) By reporting to the public agency, the mother is contacted despite client opposition. b) Trust is built and mother is contacted.	a) Mother is contacted, but client's trust is lost. b) Trust is built and mother is contacted.	Jointly work with client to contact her mother.	

Ethical Principles Screen:
1) Protection of life
2) Equality and inequality
3) Autonomy and freedom
4) Least harm
5) Quality of life
6) Privacy and confidentiality
7) Truthfulness and full disclosure

Source: Adapted from D'Aprix et al., 2001; Dolgoff et al., 2009.

to help with her emancipation, Cathleen is attempting to exercise her right to self-determination, privacy, and confidentiality. However, although you want to maintain her trust, as a social worker you are ethically and legally bound to report the abuse because she is a minor. The ethical dilemma here is clearly between client confidentiality and mandated reporting of suspected abuse. To serve Cathleen best, you must report the suspected sexual abuse to the child welfare agency. At the same time, you must continue to respect her right to self-determination and privacy.

The challenge is to help Cathleen without losing her trust. Exploring her options and the pros and cons associated with those options could help her to feel positive about reporting the abuse. Helping Cathleen to understand that reporting the abuse is part of the helping process can help to maintain her trust.

CONCLUSION

The frequent ethical dilemmas social workers face may seem overwhelming; it is useful to put them in professional perspective and to remember that clarifying your personal values and practicing social work in an ethical manner is a lifelong endeavor. As social workers interact with people in a changing society, new ethical challenges will continue to emerge. The *Code of Ethics* and frameworks for decision making exist to support social workers when they face these challenges. See Exhibit 6.7 to learn about one social worker's insight about the role of values and ethics in her practice.

To practice effectively, social workers must question the ethical implications of their actions in each situation. Although each case is unique, societal expectations and moral rules inform every ethical decision (McAuliffe, 2012). I hope this chapter encourages you to begin to explore your own values and ethics and their origins, and that such an exploration will become an ingrained part of your social work practice. As social work scholar Frederic Reamer has stated:

> I would argue that social workers' preoccupation with professional values and ethics must be the centerpiece of practitioners' education and training. After all, social work is a profession rooted in action, and this action must be anchored in a deep sense of moral mission and ethics.
>
> (Reamer, 2014, p. 176)

MAIN POINTS

■ Social work values are the profession's beliefs about the world that inform professional interactions with clients and communities. Social workers'

EXHIBIT 6.7

"People Around You are Your Greatest Resource"

Kristina Roselle enrolled in an Introduction to Social Work course to explore the possibility of majoring in social work. This course, along with the requirement for service learning (which she completed at a drop-in center for youth transitioning out of the foster care system), inspired her to further explore a career in social work. The hands-on, interactive nature of the work helped her to connect class to experiences with people. She went on to complete more service and practicum experiences at a range of sites, including: an in-patient medical surgery unit, a hospice in the Dominican Republic, and a center for the prevention of homelessness. Her practicum at the homelessness prevention program exposed her to issues of homelessness and people and issues with which she had not previously had experience. She learned that working in a small not-for-profit agency had its ethical challenges in terms of scarce funding and resources, and in turn being unable to provide the services that one hoped could be provided. As a result, she discovered the importance of actively engaging and listening to clients and learned that just being present to an individual in crisis can make a difference.

Following completion of her BSW, Kristina fulfilled a two-year service commitment with L'Arche, an international network of communities for persons with and without disabilities. She lived in a home with adults with varying physical and intellectual disabilities who each had unique strengths and limitations. Through this experience, Kristina learned a great deal about interpersonal relationships, boundaries, and values and ethics when living and working with the people being served. While the challenges that result from living and working in the same environment were present, she witnessed a beautiful, counter-cultural way of life that was filled with joy and growth.

After living in the L'Arche community for two years, Kristina returned to school to pursue an MSW and deepen her understanding of the social systems and challenges that exist. She wanted to gain professional experience that a BSW would not enable her to gain and wanted the trial-and-error opportunities that practicum offers.

In reflecting on her career thus far, Kristina encourages students, when selecting a service or practicum site, to not be afraid to seek opportunities that are outside their comfort zone because that is probably where you will learn the most. Take time to explore various areas of interest and discern what population or issue inspires you, brings you joy, or challenges you to strive for change. "Make a point to connect with people you meet. Social Work is all about networking and building relationships because it is a profession in a constantly changing world."

professional ethics are the manifestations of those values—the codes of action based on those professional values.

- The social work profession is grounded in a commitment to a set of six core values and practicing in accordance with the ethical principles and standards.

■ To practice social work in an ethical manner, awareness and ongoing clarification of your own values and of the profession's code is essential, recognizing that your value stances may change over time in response to changing culture, contemporary norms, and events.

■ Ethical dilemmas can occur in every aspect of social work practice. Social workers are especially likely to face ethical dilemmas in the areas of legal and health care issues, client rights and responsibilities, allocation of resources, and privacy and confidentiality.

■ The NASW *Code of Ethics* (2008) serves as the social work profession's guide for ethical practice. Taking advantage of the practice wisdom of your social work colleagues, consulting the *Code of Ethics,* and familiarizing yourself with the laws, policies, and practices related to your position are three "musts" for being an ethical practitioner.

EXERCISES

1. To prepare yourself for processing ethically related social work issues, go to the interactive cases website for this text at: www.routledgesw.com/ caseStudies. Select from the following cases, click on My Values, and complete the assessment: .
   a. Brickville—After you have responded to the items in My Values, write a reflection about your answers.
   b. RAINN—After you have completed the E-Therapy Attitude Scale, go to the Engage tab and respond to the Critical Thinking Questions, incorporating your experience with the E-Therapy Attitude Scale into your responses.

2. Using the Sanchez family case (www.routledgesw.com/caseStudies), review the case file for Roberto Salazar and answer the accompanying Critical Thinking Questions. Next, click on the Interaction Matrix and examine the interactions between Roberto and the other family members. Summarize your thoughts on the values and ethical implications of Roberto's situation as it relates to the other Sanchez family members.

3. The best method for clarifying your values and developing responses to the inevitable ethical dilemmas that will arise during your social work career is to practice. In this exercise, you can explore the professional values, ask the questions, and apply the ethical principles highlighted in this chapter. Consider the following scenario. Using the Sanchez family interactive case study (www.routledgesw.com/caseStudies), imagine that you are a social worker in a not-for-profit agency that provides crisis services over the telephone and to walk-in clients. Emilia Sanchez, a 24-year-old who is two months pregnant, has telephoned several times. In her last telephone

call, she confided to you that she uses heroin, smokes marijuana, and drinks alcohol daily. You have expressed your concern that her drug and alcohol use may be dangerous for her unborn child, but she does not seem worried. She has also stated that she is unable or unwilling to give up the drugs and alcohol. In this telephone conversation, she told you that she is unsure if she wants to keep "it." You suspect that she has traded sex for drugs and she is not working or attending school. Emilia tells you that her Catholic parents do not know about the pregnancy, and she does not want them to know anything because they will insist she have the baby. Her mother already cares for Emilia's son, Joey, and has two younger children still living at home, and Emilia's father works long hours. They have little money and she does not want to burden them with another mouth to feed. Now use the Enhanced Ethical Decision-Making Model found in Exhibit 6.5 to complete the matrix in Exhibit 6.8.

If your best friend were in Emilia's situation, would your analysis change? If so, in what way?

4. Go to the Riverton interactive case at www.routledgesw.com/caseStudies. The social worker in this case is both a professional working in the community and a resident of the community. Using the information included

EXHIBIT 6.8

MATRIX FOR ETHICAL DECISION MAKING						
PRACTICE/ ETHICAL ISSUE	ETHICAL PRINCIPLES IDENTIFIED IN THE CODE OF ETHICS	PERSONAL BIASES	ACTION(S) OPTIONS	POTENTIAL CONSEQUENCES/ OUTCOMES	ACTION(S) TAKEN	MONITOR/ EVALUATE EFFECTIVENESS
1.						
2.						
3.						

in this chapter, identify the potential ethical implications for this social worker and develop a response to each issue identified.

5. Go to the Carla Washburn interactive case at www.routledgesw.com/caseStudies and consider Mrs. Washburn's right to self-determination. Using the information from this chapter, describe her right to refuse services and health care, specifically responding to the following:

   a. Does Mrs. Washburn have a right to refuse services and treatment?

   b. What is the social worker's role and what are her or his options should the client refuse services or treatment?

   c. Discuss the ethical implications of the client's right to refuse services and treatment.

   d. Cite the section of the NASW *Code of Ethics* (2008) that addresses this issue.

6. Part I: To understand better where your values come from, complete the matrix in Exhibit 6.9:

   a. Identify five values that are important in your life and consider the origins of those values (first and second columns).

EXHIBIT 6.9

PERSONAL VALUE	ORIGINS OF VALUE	BEHAVIOR	RELEVANT SOCIAL WORK VALUE	DILEMMA	NASW *CODE OF ETHICS* STANDARDS
1.					
2.					
3.					
4.					
5.					

b. Think about the ways in which you act on each value (third column). Do you engage in activities or behaviors that enable other people to discern your values on that particular issue, or would other people have no idea about your values?

c. Compare those values to those of the social work profession (fourth column).

d. Finally, consider whether each value has ever created a dilemma for you (fifth column). If so, what was the dilemma, and how did you resolve it?

To help you compare your values with those of the social work profession, the six social work values are listed again below:

- Service
- Social justice
- Dignity and worth of the person
- Importance of human relationships
- Integrity
- Competence

Part II: After you have completed Part I, reflect on your work and consider these questions:

a. What, if anything, did you learn about yourself?

b. What, if anything, did you learn about anyone else?

c. Are you satisfied with the ways in which you act on your value system? If yes, explain the reasons for your satisfaction. If not, what changes can you make?

d. If any of your values created an ethical dilemma for you, were you satisfied with the way in which you handled the dilemma? If yes, explain the reasons for your satisfaction. If not, what could you have done differently?

e. Do you feel your value system is consistent with the values of the social work profession? Cite specific areas of consistency or inconsistency.

f. Which of the social work values is the most important to you?

g. How do you currently exercise this value in your life?

7. When responding to a natural disaster, social workers often face complex value conflicts and ethical dilemmas. To begin the process of clarifying your values related to working with survivors of natural disasters, go to the Hudson City case at www.routledgesw.com/caseStudies and click on My Values. Respond to the questions presented. After answering the questions, refer to the list of six core values of social work presented in this chapter and reflect on the social work practitioner's ethical obligations when working in disaster response.

8. Personal reflection: Identify and write about a value conflict or ethical question you have encountered in your life. Include your thoughts and feelings, your response to the dilemma, and what you might do in the future in a similar situation. Discuss how your values related to this issue may impact your profession.

9. As a in-class group or written assignment, review the following scenarios and (a) determine if the situation is an ethical dilemma; (b) identify the relevant *Code of Ethics* (2008) principle/standard; and (c) provide a rationale for your decision. Practice situations include:

   ■ Purchasing groceries for a client with your own money and not informing your supervisor.
   ■ Friending a client or former client on social media.
   ■ Meeting a former client for lunch or coffee.
   ■ Informing the parents of a 16-year-old that she had an abortion when she asked you not to.
   ■ Informing the parents of an 18-year-old that she had an abortion when she asked you not to.
   ■ Reporting suspected child abuse, neglect, or exploitation to the state agency, knowing that your actions will likely end your relationship with the client.
   ■ Informing your supervisor that an applicant for a position at your agency has a history of battering his partner but has no criminal record. You do not have information about his current relationship, so you do not know if he changed.

SOCIAL WORK PERSPECTIVES AND METHODS

Source: Shutterstock/De Visu

Prior to completing her MSW degree, Emily worked as a generalist practitioner. Her BSW degree provided her with the knowledge and skills to work as a generalist with individuals, families, groups, and communities. In her first job as an adult services social worker in a small multiservice community agency, she used her generalist practice knowledge to intervene on three levels:

■ *At the individual level, she worked with the older adults through a home-maker/chore service program, with persons with visual impairments, and with female recipients of public assistance who were seeking employment. In each of these programs, she also worked with clients' families.*

■ *At the group level, Emily facilitated a support group for persons who had recently lost their vision.*

■ *At the community level, Emily helped a community group develop a tel-ephone reassurance program in which Senior Center volunteers telephoned homebound older adults daily to check on their safety and well-being. Emily helped to oversee this program and to set policy. Through her involvement with the Senior Center group, Emily became part of a community task force that brought together community agencies and older adults for an annual community-wide resource and wellness fair.*

Emily performed at all these levels of social work in just one job. Her varied activities are a good example of the kinds of things social workers do in general-ist practice.

Generalist social work practice
A method of social work practice that encompasses a broad-based set of knowledge, skills, and values that are applied to assessment and intervention with client systems at the individual, family, group, organizational, and community levels.

In generalist social work practice, social workers use broad-based knowl-edge and skills to assess and intervene at multiple levels. This chapter will define and explore the generalist social work education and social work interventions from both theoretical and practice perspectives.

In the section titled the Importance of Human Relationships, the National Association of Social Workers (NASW) 2008 *Code of Ethics* calls on social workers to "strengthen relationships among people in a purposeful effort to promote, restore, maintain, and enhance the well-being of individuals, families, social groups, organizations, and communities." Similarly, the 2008 (updated in 2015) Council on Social Work Education (CSWE) *Educational Policy and Accreditation Standards* requires accredited BSW programs to include content on working with individuals, families, groups, organizations, and communities.

HISTORY OF GENERALIST SOCIAL WORK PRACTICE

Though the concept and practice of providing services to individuals, families, groups, and communities have deep roots in the social work profession, formal generalist practice is a relatively recent development.

The Charity Organization Society, which emphasized the individual, and the settlement house movement, with its emphasis on groups and communities, helped to both unite the profession around the concept of generalist practice and to pave the way for three distinct professional paths: individual casework, group work, and community organization (Hernandez, 2008). The social turmoil of the 1960s and the War on Poverty initiatives prompted the U.S. Department of Health, Education, and Welfare to provide educational and financial incentives to the social work profession to produce the new baccalaureate level of social workers who could function within the new programs at the individual, group, and community levels (Sheafor, 2014). Before this period, the only social work degrees granted were at master's level. This philosophical shift precipitated the development of generalist perspective, but not without some controversy. Some social workers with masters' degrees resisted the idea of a baccalaureate-level social worker, contending that the BSW would be viewed as a demotion of the hard-earned respect that the social work profession had achieved, that young, inexperienced social workers would not have the maturity or life experience to intervene in complex life situations, that the lower-paid BSW would replace the MSW, and that the BSW and MSW curricula would become indistinguishable (Sheafer, 2014).

Interest in a universal approach to social work practice persisted, and the baccalaureate in social work emerged in the 1960s and 1970s. Social work scholars and practitioners eventually agreed that practitioners with BSWs, trained in the generalist perspective, could best perform professional case management services in inner city and rural agencies, and in organizations in the private and public sectors. The generalist practice model provides solid preparation for the graduate social work degree, for which a social worker focuses on one particular area of concentration. Thus, the BSW curriculum prepares generalist practitioners, and the MSW curriculum builds on the generalist perspective to allow social workers to develop more specialized expertise in a particular area.

After decades of debate, a consensus has been reached regarding the definition of generalist social work. In 2007, the Association of Baccalaureate Social Work Program Directors approved the following definition:

Generalist social work practitioners work with individuals, families, groups, communities and organizations in a variety of social work and host settings. Generalist practitioners view clients and client systems from a strengths based perspective in order to recognize, support, and build upon the innate capabilities of all human beings. They use a professional problem solving process to engage, assess, broker services, advocate, counsel, educate, and organize with and on behalf of client and client systems. In addition, generalist practitioners engage in community and organizational development. Finally, generalist practitioners evaluate service outcomes in order to continually improve the provision and quality of services most appropriate to client needs. Generalist social work practice is guided by the NASW *Code of Ethics* (2008) and is committed to improving the well-being of individuals, families, groups, communities and organizations and furthering the goals of social justice.

GENERALIST SOCIAL WORK PRACTICE

What does it mean to be a generalist social work practitioner? Perhaps the greatest strength of the generalist approach is that it facilitates the application of social work skills to different types of situations and allows practitioners to affect social change on multiple levels—structural (e.g., communities and organizations), personal (e.g., individual and family), and group (e.g., groups for support or advocacy). Within generalist practice, the nature of an intervention may be determined by the "size" of the client system. The BSW-level social worker has a broad professional skill set that qualifies her or him to perform case planning and management, protective services, assessment, and service delivery (Sheafor, 2014). Not only can a generalist social work practitioner apply her or his knowledge and skills (i.e., action with a special goal) across contexts, but these skills may also be more transferable across groups and settings than an MSW level practitioner's more specialized skills (Trevithick, 2012).

As you know by now, generalist social work practice takes place at three levels:

1. *Individual and family level:* Interventions on this most basic level involve working one-on-one with individuals and their support networks facing virtually any kind of personal issue. For example, a generalist might work with an older adult and her or his family to develop a post-hospital discharge plan or with a survivor of sexual assault and her or his significant others. Consider the social worker who conducts the home study for a couple seeking to adopt a child. The social worker interviews the couple to determine their motivation and qualifications for adoption, compiles a written assessment, and guides them through the legal adoption process. When working with individuals and families in almost any situation, the social worker can sometimes gain insight into the larger service delivery system. A social worker working with persons of color who routinely experience racial profiling during traffic stops can help those individuals to process and to address the emotional aftermath of their experiences.

2. *Group level:* Social work practice at the group level demands many of the same skills generalists use with individuals. Group-level practice may involve assisting families seeking family therapy, instituting a support group for persons with eating disorders, or providing guidance to a group seeking to eradicate drug problems in their neighborhood. A social worker helping a couple seeking to adopt a child may engage the couple in a support group for adoptive parents. A social worker whose clients have been racially profiled might start a support group or a social action group to address the problem.

3. *Organization and community level:* At this level social work practice involves interventions with large groups, organizations, and communities of all sizes. The practitioner may be engaged in varied activities such as locality or community development (intervention targeted at enhancing living conditions in a specific geographic area or region); analysis and implementation of policy; policy practice, advocacy activities (for example, lobbying, letter writing, or public speaking); and administration (for example, personnel, supervision, budgeting, or grant writing). An adoption social worker might promote legislation to open adoption records for adult adoptees. The social worker dealing with racial profiling issues may choose to initiate or join a community-wide effort to raise awareness and provide education on this issue, particularly to local law enforcement agencies. A social worker might also create a community task force to support legislation that would address issues of racial profiling at the state level.

Generalist social work training enables the social worker to practice ethically and competently at all three levels, and most social work positions require the social worker to function at all three levels at some point. Most generalist practitioners develop a stronger focus on one or two of these areas over the course of their careers, depending on their personal preferences and employment opportunities. For example, you might begin your career working with individuals in direct service, but find later that you have a desire or opportunity to move into social work policy or administration. This is a major benefit of being a social worker: Your knowledge, skills, and values transfer to different populations, settings, and levels of practice.

Each of the three levels of practice is interconnected and somewhat interdependent. Social work knowledge, skills, and practice behaviors identified with working with groups, organizations, and communities are frequently incorporated into practice with individuals and families. For example, such skills as mediation, brokering, program planning, raising funds, and evaluation are typically associated with macro-level practice but are critical to the process of working with individuals and families. The reverse is also true—knowledge and skills used at the individual and family level are a key component of group, organizational, and community practice. For instance, developing rapport is an essential skill for any level of social work practice. A generalist social work practitioner demonstrates competence across multiple levels in various systems.

Many social work professionals contend that there is no better preparation for becoming an MSW student and practitioner than to have worked in the social service delivery system as a BSW generalist practitioner. Generalist experiences provide professional socialization, identity, and maturity, which provide those seeking MSW degrees greater insight into the needs of clients and systems.

GENERALIST SOCIAL WORK SKILLS AND ROLES

Regardless of where or with whom a beginning social worker will intervene, she or he must acquire a basic set of skills. Exhibit 7.1 lists the "100 Skills of the Professional Social Worker" compiled by an executive director of a state NASW chapter. The list is a testament to the breadth of skills in the social work repertoire or "tool kit" that enable generalist social workers to function in a number of roles in a variety of situations.

Some of the most important roles generalist social workers fill include (Association of Baccalaureate Social Work Program Directors, 2007; Barker, 2014):

Broker
A social work role in which the social worker aids the client in obtaining needed resources.

■ *Broker:* The social worker who serves as a broker helps client systems at the individual, group, and organization/community levels to access needed resources. Brokers might help an older adult apply for assistance with his heating bill, work with a group of parents of children with attention deficit hyperactivity disorder to arrange a meeting with the school board to improve school-based services, or coordinate with another social service agency to streamline their application process.

Advocate
A social work role in which the social worker articulates client system needs on behalf of the client system.

■ *Advocate:* In this role, the social worker can voice the needs of a client or group to facilitate a change that will improve their lives. Social workers often strive to impact a positive change in an unjust situation. For example, a social worker might advocate on behalf of a client at an adoption hearing, or she or he could lobby the state legislature to enact laws to address the needs of foster children.

Direct service provider
Social work professional who engages in direct practice with individuals and families.

■ *Direct service provider:* Social workers engaging in direct practice provide services to clients at all levels and in all areas, including one-on-one, family, and group counseling, therapy, and group work. They engage

EXHIBIT 7.1

100 Skills of the Professional Social Worker

Activism
Administration
Adoption
Advocacy
Applied research
Assessment
Basic skills training
Behavior therapy
Brief therapy
Career counseling
Case management
Child advocacy
Client and family conferences
Client and family education
Client screening
Coaching
Coalition building
Cognitive therapy
Community organization
Conflict resolution
Conjoint therapy
Consultation
Continuity of care
Coping skills
Counseling
Crisis intervention
Data collection
Direct practice
Discharge planning
Divorce therapy
Empowerment
Expert witness
Family therapy

Fundraising
Financial counseling
Gestalt therapy
Goal setting
Grant writing
Grass-roots organizing
Group therapy
Health education
Health planning
Home studies
Intake
Independent practice
Information and referral
Interagency collaboration
Interdisciplinary collaboration
Intervention
Interviewing
Legislative advocacy
Life skills education
Lobbying
Mandated reporting
Marital therapy
Mediation
Milieu therapy
Needs assessment
Negotiation
Networking
Outcome evaluation
Outreach
Parent training
Placement
Planning
Policy analysis
Policy development

Post-discharge follow- up
Political action
Prevention
Problem evaluation
Problem- focused therapy
Problem resolution
Program administration
Program planning
Psychosocial assessment
Public relations
Qualitative research
Quantitative research
Rational-emotive therapy
Reality therapy
Recording
Referring
Residential treatment
Resource allocation
Role playing
Service contracting
Service coordination
Short- term therapy
Social action
Social work education
Staff development
Supervision
Support group
Task-centered casework
Teach coping skills
Team player
Termination
Treatment planning
Utilization review

Source: Akin, 1998.

with individuals, families, groups, and organizations/communities to assess needs and develop plans for intervening to achieve desired change. For example, at the individual and family level, a social worker providing direct services might meet with people to provide financial counseling or conduct intake surveys for an organization. At the group level, a social worker might serve as a facilitator for a group of persons experiencing a life change. At the organizational and community level, social workers may collaborate with individuals to develop a plan for improving neighborhood safety.

Case manager
Role for social worker in which the focus is to mobilize the client system to achieve mutually-determined goals.

■ *Case manager:* Some direct service providers serve as case managers. In this role, social workers act as liaisons between clients and the systems needed to meet the goals of each intervention. As a case manager, a social worker may help to develop, coordinate, and mobilize a variety of health, education, and social services. For example, a case manager for a person with severe and persistent mental illness may provide suggestions or referrals regarding resources for housing, mental health, financial, employment, and transportation services for the client. A frequently sought-after job for social workers with BSWs, case managers are on the front lines of social service delivery.

Educator
Social work role of providing information on coping strategies and resources.

■ *Educator:* In the role of educator, a social worker uses a variety of strategies to provide information to clients. In one-on-one encounters, a social worker may convey information on strategies for coping, enhancing well-being, using resources, and identifying alternative behaviors. Social workers can act as role models, or they might engage in more traditional forms of education by making presentations, facilitating groups, or lobbying for change.

Organizer
Social work role utilized when mobilizing resources to meet needs of client system.

■ *Organizer:* Social workers use organizing skills at all levels of practice. Understanding how organizations operate, social workers can mobilize resources to fulfill client needs and goals. At the community level, organizers bring together groups of people to advocate for and facilitate change. Generalist practitioners analyze the strengths and weaknesses of policies and programs and work to influence positive change within those systems.

In addition, generalist social workers may help to maintain service systems (as analysts or supervisors, for example), teach social work students, or conduct evaluation research (e.g., conduct evaluations of programs and services to determine effectiveness of interventions). Generalist social work offers roles for those who prefer to work directly with people and for those who are more comfortable working with systems and social policy.

THEORY IN GENERALIST SOCIAL WORK PRACTICE

The knowledge and skills of the competent generalist practitioner are based on an evidence-based framework known to be effective for the client system in which the social worker has been trained. Empirically tested theoretical frameworks can provide the practicing social worker with a foundation for determining the type and direction of the assessment, intervention, and evaluation of the client relationship. Theory, as it is applied in the social work profession, encompasses both the traditional scientific concept of explanations derived from empirical tests and the more contemporary concept of pragmatism—explanations that emanate from practice (McNutt & Floersch, 2008). Empirical studies provide scientific support for the realities of the systems with which social workers interact. Theory enables the identification of client characteristics, attributes, and power issues, which the social worker then takes into account and translates into an intervention through a series of actions (McNutt & Floersch, 2008).

To be competent and effective practitioners, social workers need to understand how theory informs and guides practice decisions and to integrate theory into their critical thinking process. In social work, theory does the following:

■ Deepens the social worker's understanding of practice situations.
■ Helps the social worker determine which professional knowledge to draw from in order to understand the client system.
■ Guides thinking and action throughout the client system intervention.
■ Facilitates professional communication with everyone involved.
■ Enhances social workers' confidence in their abilities to intervene.
■ Helps define professional identities and boundaries.
■ Promotes professional status.
■ Builds the knowledge base for social work interventions.
■ Contributes to the public problem-solving process (addressing community-level issues).

(Forte, 2014a, pp. 4–8)

Effective social work practice starts with the study of social work theory. To develop an intervention (i.e., to put knowledge, skills, and values into action) that will change a situation, event, thoughts, feelings, or behaviors, social workers must take learned content (i.e., theoretical and factual knowledge often discussed within academic social work courses) and apply it to a practice context within an agency or organizational setting with clients and systems (i.e., practice knowledge) (Trevithick, 2012).

Practice theory
A subset of theory that has been empirically tested for use in the practice setting.

A subset of social work theory, referred to as practice theory, is this pragmatic aspect, specifically targeted at work with individuals, families, and groups (Walsh, 2010). Practice theories are those concepts, theoretical approaches, and frameworks that depict knowledge about people, social systems, and the interactions that occur and provide guidance for the development of goals, interventions, and strategies to be used toward purposeful action (Barker, 2014, p. 331). For example, the social worker can apply systems theory to engage and assess a blended family who is undergoing a significant transition such as a divorce. Gaining insight into the complex relationships that exist within the blended family that will be impacted by a divorce can help the social worker and the family to negotiate present and future relationships as the divorce becomes final. Knowing and being able to understand, interpret, and apply current practice theory enables the social worker to: (1) help predict and explain client behavior; (2) generalize among clients and problem areas; (3) bring order to intervention activities; and (4) identify knowledge gaps about practice situations (Walsh, 2010, p. 4). In recent years, generalist practitioners have generated a number of new practice theories, helping to conceptualize generalist practice as "using an essentially constant set of approaches at multiple levels" (McNutt & Floersch, 2008, p. 140).

Researchers test practice theory in controlled situations so that social workers have empirical evidence that a particular approach is appropriate for specific populations and settings. The result is evidence-based practice (EBP), which combines the results of research with clinical experience, professional ethics, and client needs and preferences to guide the social worker in developing effective client system interventions. EBP is a process in which an evidenced-supported intervention is facilitated in a specific practice situation (Soydan & Palinkas, 2014). EBP is a tool that helps social workers improve the services they deliver by helping them select the most effective approaches (Thyer, 2012). A social worker who embraces EBP seeks out the approaches and interventions that research shows to be most effective.

Evidence-based practice (EBP)
Social work practice that is derived from a theoretical approach that has been empirically tested using rigorous research methodology.

The ability to link theory with practice and to articulate the *who, what, when, where, why, and how* of all interactions and activities in which social workers engage differentiates the professional from the nonprofessional or the paraprofessional. As Forte (2014a) notes: "The use of sound and scientific knowledge adds value to the generalist and specialist social worker and to the profession, and helps distinguish us from amateurs, technicians, volunteers, and other non-professionals" (p. 3). Using a multi-step process, practitioners identify the questions for which they require answers, seek empirical evidence to answer those questions, and then apply selected approaches and evaluate the outcomes (Jenson & Howard, 2008). Social work interventions have not always been theoretically or empirically based (remember from Chapter 2 that Flexner maligned the social work profession for its lack of a theoretical basis), but today social workers use theory and research to guide effective interventions. Of note are the criticisms directed at evidence-based practice which contend that in working in clinical settings with individuals, families, and groups, the social worker's clinical/practice wisdom and the client's perspective are not incorporated into the development of the EBP approach (Simmons, 2012). This criticism remains controversial within the social work profession. EBP advocates emphasize that clinical expertise and judgment are an important component in selecting and implementing EBP interventions (Rubin, 2014). As with any controversy, practitioners must weigh the information with their own values and ethical beliefs to determine their own professional stances.

Over time, each social worker develops a personal theoretical orientation to social work, an "organized set of assumptions, concepts, and propositions used to understand the person interacting in an environment" (Forte, 2014a, pp. 11–12). The development of one's orientation evolves in relation to a number of influences, including family of origin, reference groups, role models, life philosophy, values, and personality style (Forte, 2014a, p. 12). Social work knowledge emanates from multiple sources, including: personal learning/lived experiences, formal teaching and learning, practice experience, and research findings (Trevithick, 2012). A component of one's development of her or his theoretical orientation is the integration of theory into the practice setting. See Exhibit 7.2 for respected British social work scholar and practitioner Pamela Trevithick's comprehensive depiction of the process of integrating theory with practice. Trevithick describes three types of knowledge—theoretical, factual, and practice—which are distinct but interrelated areas of social work practice. Theoretical knowledge encompasses adapted theories (i.e., those theories "borrowed" from other disciplines such as psychology and sociology), role and task theories (i.e., theories that guide the roles, tasks, and purposes of such functions as case management), and practice theories (i.e., knowledge that guides such practice areas as fields and levels of practice, practice approaches, value-based perspectives, and skills and interventions).

The following sections explore several theoretical frameworks that have become hallmarks of the social work profession, particularly within generalist social work practice. As you review the rest of this chapter, keep the practical applications of theory in mind. Theory helps practitioners to (Forte, 2014a):

- explain the causes of a situation;
- classify categories of events and their place in the client's situation;
- predict possible future events;
- describe and organize the details of the client's situation;
- identify actions during the intervention that may change and improve the situation; enable cooperation and collaboration with the client (p. 36).

EXHIBIT 7.2

Integration of Theory into Practice

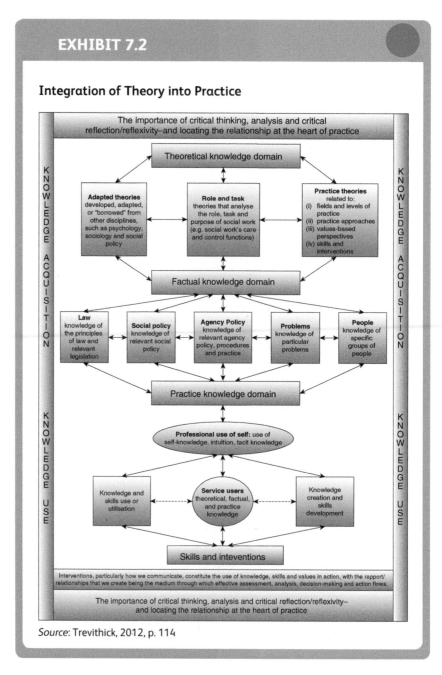

Source: Trevithick, 2012, p. 114

Theory guides practitioners to the appropriate practice methods or approaches. Applying theory to practice situations can be challenging. Effective social workers are well versed in a variety of perspectives so that applying the most appropriate theory becomes a natural part of the service delivery. No one theory can exactly explain or predict human or organizational behavior; day-to-day practice realities present ambiguities, with sometimes-competing theories and guidelines and changing circumstances (McNutt & Floersch, 2008).

Earlier chapters introduced two important social work theories—ecological and strengths perspectives. This chapter examines these in greater detail, particularly within the systems framework along with solution-focused perspective and behavioral, cognitive behavioral, and task-centered approaches. These frameworks, working together and in conjunction with theories drawn from other disciplines, can be helpful in practicing at all levels.

Each social work approach is different, but all reflect commitment to collaborative intervention and person-centered perspective that takes into account the "whole person". Theories inform and guide the social work practitioner, enabling the social worker to combine them as appropriate to better understand the client system. Theories cannot predict behavior or events. Empirically based research supports each approach and referring to that literature can be helpful in developing a theoretical and practice knowledge base.

Systems-Based Perspectives

In Emily's work for a senior homemaker/chore program, she came to appreciate the importance of viewing clients within the context of their complete social and physical environments. A homemaker/chore agency provides in-home services to older adults who are unable to perform the day-to-day tasks required to maintain independent living. The typical client is an older adult with physical health problems who lives alone. Without the support of the program, the individual would likely have to enter a residential long-term care facility.

Marietta, a 78-year-old, widowed, African American woman living alone in a rental house, taught Emily the importance of seeing the "big picture." Marietta's family physician, Dr. Stephens, was concerned about Marietta's ability to care for herself, so he referred her to Emily's agency. Based on her initial assessment of Marietta's situation, Emily was ready to recommend that Marietta be placed in a skilled care facility due to her physical frailty, vision problems, inability to cook or maintain her house, limited income, and apparent lack of social support.

Through her assessment, Emily learned that Marietta's only son had recently died and that she was estranged from her daughter-in-law and adult grandchildren because she believed they had not provided her son with adequate care during his illness. Marietta's daughter lived nearby, but they were frequently in conflict because Marietta believed her daughter should leave her husband, who was abusive to her when he was drinking. Marietta's only living sister suffered from Alzheimer's disease and was also no longer able to care for herself. Marietta told Emily that she did not believe her children or sister would help her, and she refused to consider moving in with any of them.

Upon conducting a more thorough assessment, Emily learned that Marietta did have close ties with her neighbors, church, and several of her nieces and nephews. Although she did need in-home services to continue living independently, she was part of a large, close, and supportive network of caregivers.

Theoretical perspectives that inform and guide contemporary social work practice are rooted in a philosophical commitment to the concept of societal systems (i.e., institutional and organizational entities within a society). Each individual, family, group, organization, or community exists within one or more larger systems with which it interrelates and is often interdependent. The following section provides an overview of various systems-based perspectives.

Societal systems
Institutional and organizational entities within a society.

Person-in-Environment and Ecological Perspectives As noted in Chapter 5, the social work profession has a long history of emphasizing the person-in-environment perspective, now more commonly referred to as the people:environment perspective or P:E perspective, to highlight the interplay between people and their environments (i.e., how people influence their environment and not are just influenced by it). The P:E perspective perceives each individual as an interactive participant in a larger physical, social, communal, historical, religious, physical, cultural, and familial environmental system (Kondrat, 2008, p. 348). The NASW *Standards for Cultural Competence* (2007), the CSWE Educational Policy Statements (CSWE, 2008, updated 2015), and the IFSW (2012) all specifically state that social workers are obligated to consider cultural factors when they use the person-in-environment framework. Had Emily not used the P:E approach with Marietta, she would not have recognized that Marietta was in fact part of a larger, functioning, and supportive system. The person-in-environment perspective has essentially become the guiding idea underlying the helping process.

People: Environment Perspective (P:E)
Perspective that emphasizes the interrelationship between individuals and the environment in which they live.

During the 1950s, social work scholars began urging practitioners to consider the interaction between the individual and the larger world. Expanding the original ecological theory used in the biological sciences to understand the relationships between organisms and their environments, including systems, subsystems, and ongoing interactions and changes, social scientists saw that they could use this theory to organize and understand the voluminous amount of information social workers gathered from their clients (Jack, 2012). While the impact on the social work profession has been profound, with ecological theory serving as the cornerstone of most practice approaches used in the profession today, policy-makers continue to determine eligibility requirements with an eye toward the issues that occur within the individual or family rather than between the individual/family and the environment (Jack, 2012).

A landmark event in this movement occurred in 1973, during an era of heightened interest in the social environment, when social work scholar Carel Germain introduced the ecological perspective for social work (Kondrat, 2008). With its roots in the person-in-environment framework, this perspective contends that the relationship between the individual and her or his social environment determines the individual's life situation. According to the ecological perspective, to understand human behavior, one must examine the interaction between the client system and the larger social and physical environment, rather than looking to the cause of the interaction. For example, understanding the impact of a child's relationships with her family regarding her ability to perform well academically is more important than explaining the cause of specific parent–child interactions. This perspective expands the focus beyond the individuals involved which excludes information about the larger social and physical environment and provides an incomplete picture while the ecological and systemic perspectives emphasize the importance of taking into account that environmental component. Intervention outcomes are the result of client strengths and vulnerabilities intersecting within the context of the client's world (Jack, 2012).

The original ecological model developed by Germain (1973) included ten conceptual components, and eight concepts were added later as the framework evolved (Germain & Gitterman, 1995; Gitterman & Germain, 2008). These 18 concepts are described in Exhibit 7.3. The ecological model emphasizes the importance of helping clients positively interact with their environments by eliminating life stressors. It provides a strategy for identifying the client system; assessing the client's dilemma in terms of strengths, supports, resources, and previous coping and adaptive skills; and intervening with the client with a number of possibilities that could be incorporated into their desired goals. Had Emily not used the ecological perspective to identify and mobilize her client's existing family and community resources, Marietta would not have been able to continue living in her own home.

In order to use the ecological perspective in the holistic, anti-oppression way that it is intended, the social worker should make use of research on person-in-environment approaches and apply the ecological perspective with: (1) a culture of listening—clients will provide information about the environments in which they live, but the social worker must be willing and able to interpret it as such; and (2) attention to social networks—by determining the sources and types of support people receive, the social worker can help identify areas of strength and areas in which more resources are needed (Jack, 2012).

Systems and Ecosystems Theory From a social work perspective, a system can be a physical and/or social entity made up of individuals, families, groups, organizations, and communities—from local to global, and even nations.

System
Can be a physical and/or social entity made up of individuals, families, groups, organizations, and communities—from local to global, and even nations.

EXHIBIT 7.3

Basic Concepts of the Ecological Perspective

ECOLOGICAL CONCEPTS	DESCRIPTION
ORIGINAL MODEL:	
Person–environment fit	The ability of client system to positively engage with the environment—a positive fit suggests the client system has adapted successfully.
Adaptations	To maintain a stable person–environment fit, systems constantly adapt to changing environment.
Life stressors	The person–environment fit may be compromised if the client system is unable to adapt to life crises.
Stress	The individual's response to a life stressor.
Coping measures	To maintain a desired person–environment fit, systems develop methods for adapting to life stresses.
Relatedness	Connections that people make with others in their environment; they serve as resources for adaptations.
Competence	Systems must have the resources to function effectively.
Self-esteem	The person's self-perception influences her/his ability to feel competence.
Self-direction	The client system's ability to feel control over itself impacts self-esteem, competence, and ability to adapt to life stresses.
Habitat and niche	Referring to clients' physical space and place within that space, habitat and niche can determine the client system's well-being.
ADDED CONCEPTS:	
Coercive power	Poverty, "isms," and homelessness are examples of "social pollutions" that inhibit the client system's ability to adapt and fit with the environment.
Exploitative power	Another stressor, exploitative power is the oppression of one group over another.
Life course	Ecologically, the path of a client's life is fluid, changing, and unique.
Individual time	The meaning that the client system attaches to life experiences.
Historical time	The impact of historical and social change on the client system.
Social time	The client system's transitions and life events are a product of social, biological, economic, demographic, and culture factors.
Resilience	Protective factors enable people to thrive in spite of life stressors.
Flexibility	In order to adapt to environmental changes, the network must have the ability to be diverse and responsive.

Sources: Germain & Gitterman, 1995; Gitterman & Germain, 2008.

You have no doubt noticed from your reading so far that the persons or groups social workers serve are considered client systems, and that the term is used interchangeably with clients.

Rooted in theoretical biology, the concept of viewing clients within a systems framework first emerged in the late 1950s and early 1960s and became the major guiding theoretical framework for the social work profession for several decades (Kondrat, 2008). Systems theory evolved from the idea that a system is comprised of multiple components that interact with one another to create an entire entity.

Every social work system is made up of multiple elements, which can be any physical, social, or personal entity that is interactive, and functional. For example, a person may be part of a system of physical elements such as a household, neighborhood, community, city, country, and world. Social elements can include the client system's relationships with persons that make up the environment in which the client lives. A system is composed of the various parts that interact with one another to contribute to the overall functioning of the system, sometimes in a circular and dynamic fashion.

In recent years, social work scholars have incorporated the idea of the ecosystem into general systems theory. The ecosystem perspective emphasizes the shifting and interdependent relationships that the client system has with the surrounding environment (Kondrat, 2008). To function, a system must be dynamic and flexible. A change in one element affects all of the other elements. For example, if an older member of the family is diagnosed with cognitive impairment (e.g., Alzheimer's disease), the family system is changed in terms of interactions, daily routines, frequency of contact, and sometimes the quality or closeness of relationships. Whether the change either positively or negatively affects the system, the system is altered.

Systems Theory Concepts The systems theory framework helps social workers view clients within the context of their interactions with a larger environment and explains human behavior in terms of the reciprocal relationships among the elements in the system. Whereas the ecological model illuminates the relationship between a client system and the environment, systems theory provides a way of understanding the change process that the client system undergoes.

To understand change from a systemic perspective, consider that when one part of a system changes, the entire system must change. For example, when a family member is added or removed from a family system for any reason (e.g., birth, death, marriage, divorce, leaving for college, etc.), the system must change because the addition or loss creates a different configuration of people, relationships, required tasks, and available resources.

Just as organically occurring change can modify a system, a social work intervention can also prompt a system to change. In fact, the mere addition of

Client/client system
The consumer(s) of services provided by the social worker.

Systems theory
A theoretical framework used to guide social work practice that conceptualizes client systems within the context of the environment in which they exist and explains the interactions of the components within the system.

Ecosystem
A component of systems theory, an ecosystem encompasses the relationship among individuals, families, and organizations within the environment in which they exist.

the presence of a social worker as a "change agent" produces a change within the system.

Viewing the person, family, group, or community as a part of a larger system has numerous implications for generalist social work practice:

- The social worker is able to understand the way in which interactions between the client and her or his environment (including the people in the environment) affect the client system.
- The social worker may target multiple system components for intervention.
- The system incorporates the unique qualities of the client, emphasizing the dynamic and changing nature of human interactions by building on the individual's strengths and resources.

No one theoretical approach will explain all situations, but frameworks that view client systems in terms of the environment have prevailed within the social work profession because they are most consistent with social work's values and mission.

Systems Theory in Generalist Practice Now that you are familiar with the intersecting systems-oriented, person-in-environment, ecological, systems, and ecosystems frameworks, let us apply these concepts to generalist social work practice. Due to the universality of these systems-based theories, the concepts can be applied to virtually every level and type of social work relationship.

Ecomap
A tool for assessing individuals, families, groups, and communities that provides a framework for understanding the interrelationships between members of the system.

Social workers use particular tools to assess and intervene in client situations from a systems perspective. One such tool is the ecomap. Developed by Ann Hartman in 1975 as a strategy for systemically assessing individuals and families, the ecomap depicts the type and quality of relationships along with the dynamic nature of those relationships (Hartman, 1978). The ecomap can be used at all levels of social work practice.

An ecomap of Emily's experience with Marietta is presented in Exhibit 7.4. In an ecomap, each component of the client system is identified within a circle. The number and types of components in each person's map will be different as they reflect the individual's current life situation. The quality of relationships is coded using various types of lines. Arrows indicate the flow of energy and resources invested in and derived from each relationship. The social worker and the client can review the ecomap together to identify strengths, stressors, and areas the client would like to target for change. An imbalance of energy either flowing into or out of a relationship may suggest an area for change and help identify the resources needed to achieve that goal. For example, if a college student reports that he is putting considerable energy into his academic work but receiving little gratification in return, the intervention may focus on exploring other majors, evaluating the student for possible depression, or

EXHIBIT 7.4

Ecomap

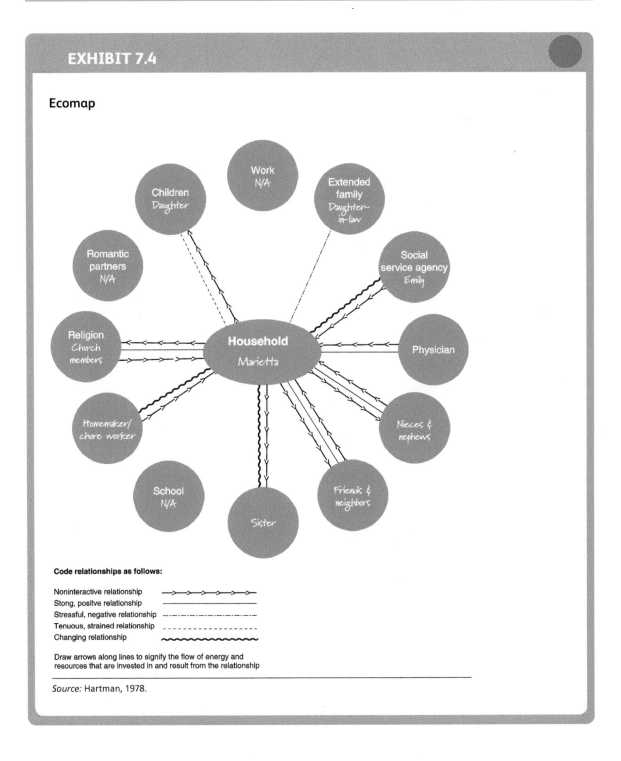

Code relationships as follows:

Noninteractive relationship
Stong, positve relationship
Stressful, negative relationship
Tenuous, strained relationship
Changing relationship

Draw arrows along lines to signify the flow of energy and
resources that are invested in and result from the relationship

Source: Hartman, 1978.

exploring possible changes of school or living situation. This collaborative tool can be used to establish a social work relationship at multiple levels, to monitor change, and to evaluate progress at the termination of the professional relationship. Ecomaps can be completed at different times to provide the client with insight regarding his or her progress toward effecting change. Think about your own ecomap—what would it look like today, next year, or in five years?

An ecomap is useful not only for individual client systems, but also for larger systems (for example, neighborhoods). For an organization, the client would be at the center of the ecomap, surrounded by all the organizations and institutions that are part of its environment. The ecomap clearly identifies links within and outside the larger system.

As the ecomap shows, the relationships in Marietta's life are sources of both support and stress, and several are in a state of change. Marietta's relationships with her nieces and nephews, her neighbors, the members of her church, and her physician are among her strengths. Marietta's relationship with her sister is changing, as her sister's memory is deteriorating due to Alzheimer's disease. Stressors in Marietta's life include her relationships with her estranged daughter-in-law and with her daughter. The new relationships Marietta is developing with Emily and with the homemaker/chore workers have the potential to be sources of social support, but they are still stabilizing. Having the ecomap as an assessment tool helped Emily to identify Marietta's existing resources and strengths and to target areas for intervention.

Strengths-Based and Empowerment Perspectives

While working at a public welfare agency, Emily took her turn at "intake"—seeing walk-in or call-in clients who were in crisis. Sarah, a 16-year-old, came in and explained that she found the agency's address on the Internet. She had her one-day-old daughter with her and told Emily that she had delivered the baby at her friend's house, in the bathroom with only her 16-year-old friend present. Neither Sarah's nor her friend's parents were aware of the birth. The friend's parents were out of town. By Sarah's calculations, the baby was near full-term. Neither Sarah nor the baby had seen a health care provider. Sarah was nursing the baby, and from Emily's quick assessment, the baby appeared to be healthy. Sarah refused to identify the father, but Emily suspected it might be her 21-year-old stepbrother. Sarah's verbal and nonverbal cues raised Emily's suspicions.

Sarah appeared extremely distraught, asserting that she "had to do something with this baby now." However, she was also adamant that she would not involve her parents, or anyone else, in her situation. She reported that she was an above-average student, was active in a service organization, and worked part-time at a fast-food restaurant. She claimed to have dated casually, but denied that she was currently involved in any serious relationship. She informed Emily that her family belonged to a conservative fundamentalist religion, and she feared severe consequences if they discovered that she had become pregnant.

In this case, Emily faced multiple challenges: Sarah, a minor who may have been sexually assaulted by a family member, delivered her own child without benefit of health care and was afraid that her family would find out. However, upon closer examination, there are a number of reasons to have hope for Sarah and her baby. First, Sarah was courageous and resourceful enough to deliver the baby safely (seemingly), to nurse the baby, and to come to Emily's agency for help. She has a supportive friend, attends school and performs well academically, has a job, and is involved in community service. Thus, despite all the challenges Sarah's situation presents, there are strengths on which to build: Sarah has a history of being responsible, she is concerned for the child, and she is asking for help. Concentrating on Sarah's strengths as opposed to her deficiencies is the essence of strengths-based social work practice, or the strengths-based perspective. As noted in Chapter 5, the strengths-based perspective is rooted in the premise that each person has strengths, assets, and resources on which an intervention for change can be built.

The strengths-based perspective only emerged in the profession fairly recently, in the 1980s (Saleebey, 2006). Historically, social workers focused first and foremost on the client system's problems, deficits, and inadequacies. Exhibit 7.5 compares the client-social worker relationship as viewed from a strengths perspective and a deficit perspective (i.e., viewing the client or system from a perspective weaknesses or pathology) (Saleebey, 1996, p. 298).

The shift to a strengths-based perspective was conceived originally as a strategy for working with persons with severe and persistent mental illness. With the shift away from hospitalizing persons with mental illness and treating them instead in the community, the founders of the strengths perspective saw the need to develop new approaches to care (Rapp & Sullivan, 2014). In their history of the strengths-based approach, Rapp and Sullivan (2014) highlight four areas to support the use of the approach which was initially applied in working with persons experiencing mental illness but has since been expanded to working with virtually all areas of social work practice. The four areas for use include: (1) concern over the effectiveness of other current approaches being used with vulnerable populations; (2) by focusing on strengths and naturalistic resources (i.e., supports that exist within the client's system), social work is less dependent upon ever-decreasing social services funding; (3) the continued acceptance and codification of strengths perspectives in practice and policy arenas; and (4) the "hope-inducing" nature of the approach that occurs for both the social worker and the client (p. 139).

EXHIBIT 7.5

Comparison of Deficits and Strengths Models

THE ISSUE	FROM THE DEFICITS PERSPECTIVE	FROM THE STRENGTHS-BASED PERSPECTIVE
The person is . . .	the case, symptoms, and the diagnosis	unique and her/his traits are strengths
The intervention is . . .	problem-focused	possibility-focused
The client's "stories" are . . .	reinterpreted by the expert	a way to know and appreciate the client
The social worker . . .	is skeptical of the client's "stories" and rationalizations	knows the person from the inside out
Childhood trauma . . .	predicts adult pathology	can either weaken or strengthen the client in adulthood
The expert on the client's life is . . .	the social worker	the client
The intervention is determined by . . .	the social worker	the client's aspirations
Possibilities and development are . . .	limited by the client's pathology	opened by the client's possibilities and development
Resources and skills are possessed by . . .	the social worker	the client and the social worker
The focus of the relationship is . . .	symptom reduction	moving, affirming, and strengthening

Source: Adapted from Saleebey, 1996.

The strengths-perspective is a natural outgrowth of both social work's core values and systems-based perspectives because it considers the client's own positive qualities as well as the support that exists within his or her environment. Using a systems framework to understand the environment in which the client system functions and then building on available assets and resources facilitates the change process.

The social work value of recognizing client uniqueness and self-worth is inherently a strengths perspective. The strengths approach is now used in every area in which social workers practice, including working with diverse populations; advocating for social justice; respecting the client system's right to self-determination; and developing interventions for individuals, families, groups, organizations, and communities (Blundo, 2008).

Strengths-Based and Empowerment Concepts One of the founders and ardent proponents of the strengths-based perspective, Dennis Saleebey has emphasized that "possibilities, not problems" are the basis of the strengths-based perspective:

> *Everything* you do as a social worker will be predicated, in some way, on helping to discover and embellish, explore, and exploit clients' strengths and resources in the service of assisting them to achieve their goals, realize their dreams, and shed the irons of their own inhibitions and misgivings, and society's domination. (Saleebey, 2006, p. 1)

Although the strengths approach is relatively simple to comprehend, it can be challenging for both the client system and the social worker in practice. It may be difficult for client systems in crisis or those facing multiple challenges to recognize any strengths in either themselves or their situations. Some clients may be hostile, resistant, or have a history of inappropriate or illegal behavior. However, every client has strengths, and it is important to recognize and reinforce those strengths in areas such as knowledge, resiliency, and goals (Blundo, 2008).

The key to the implementation of the strengths-based perspective in difficult cases is empowerment, or collaborating with the client system and giving the client the power to participate in solving his or her own problems. Jane Addams exhorted her colleagues to "Do things with people, not for them." When you work *with* people and give them some control over creating change, you empower them.

Empowerment
The process of working with a client system to optimize the system's capacity to function and change.

Six basic principles undergird the strengths perspective (also highlighted in Quick Guide #7.1) (Saleebey, 2006, pp. 16–20):

1. *Every individual, group, family, and community has strengths:* To discern client system strengths, a social worker must respect and value the client's "story" and knowledge of her or his situation. For example, one strength of a client suffering from severe clinical depression may be that she or he was able to get out of bed three days this week as opposed to only one day last week.

2. *Trauma and abuse, illness, and struggle may be injurious, but they may also be sources of challenge and opportunity:* Without minimizing the emotional and physical scars that come from a painful or traumatic experience, a social worker can help the client to see that she or he can use an experience

to learn and grow, to move beyond a self-defeating perception of her- or himself as a victim or a failure. Think of a neighborhood in which older adult residents are afraid to leave their homes. A social worker might empower the residents to rally together and organize a community center where they can go and participate in safety.

3. *A social worker must not presume to know the upper limits of a client system's capacity to grow and change, and must take individual, group, and community aspirations seriously:* A social worker can empower client systems to think beyond negative life experiences, disabilities, or challenges, in order to expand the client's perception of her or his own capacities and possibilities. Consider, for example, a middle-aged mother who dropped out of high school and receives public assistance, but who goes on to finish high school, community college, and college to become a social worker.

4. *Social workers best serve clients by collaborating with them:* Respecting clients' knowledge and expertise in their own lives or communities is a crucial step in developing a collaborative and empowering relationship. When a worker and a client collaborate, they combine their strengths and resources, reducing the likelihood of the client's further victimization. For example, consider a situation in which the social worker facilitates a meeting between police and a group of immigrants whose neighborhood is the target of hate crimes to discuss strategies for addressing the problem.

5. *Every environment is full of resources:* Regardless of the apparent level of chaos or the lack of obvious strengths, the strengths-based social worker can identify resources on which to build an intervention plan with the client system. For example, a person who is experiencing homelessness, has an addiction to drugs, and is estranged from his family comes to a program serving military veterans who are homeless. In this situation, the fact that the man has come for help constitutes a strength.

6. *Caring, caretaking, and context are key:* The social work profession is deeply committed to caring for others, helping people care for themselves, and mobilizing communities and societies to care for their members all within the context of the situations and environments in which the clients exist. Because the strengths perspective focuses on helping people recognize their strengths and have hope, it is a natural fit for social work interventions.

Strengths-Based and Empowerment Perspectives in Generalist Practice

Before applying these six principles, the social worker needs to identify strengths that will enable the client system to respond to the situation and the social worker with a sense of empowerment. The social worker must commit to the

> ## QUICK GUIDE #7.1 PRINCIPLES OF CLIENT STRENGTH
>
> 1   Every individual, group, family, and community has strengths.
> 2   Trauma and abuse, illness, and struggle may be injurious, but they may also be sources of challenge and opportunity.
> 3   A social worker must not presume to know the upper limits of a client system's capacity to grow and change, and take individual, group, and community aspirations seriously.
> 4   Social workers best serve clients by collaborating with them.
> 5   Every environment is full of resources.
> 6   Caring, caretaking, and context are key.

notion that a strengths-based approach requires considerable creativity, both on the part of the social worker and the client; it takes creativity to identify strengths, to determine how to use those strengths within the intervention, and to stay focused on those strengths (Sullivan, 2012). The following is a list of topics that a social worker might discuss with a client in order to discover the possibilities that can become realities for the client (Saleebey, 2006, pp. 82–84):

■   Lessons (i.e., information and insights) learned by clients about self, others, and the environment around the client system.
■   Personal qualities, traits, and virtues.
■   Knowledge of the world (e.g., people, supports, community, etc.) that surrounds the client system.
■   Talents the client system possesses.
■   Cultural and personal stories.
■   Resources within the client system (e.g., the client's own pride).
■   Resources within the client system's community (e.g., people and organizations).
■   Spirituality as a source of meaning and hope.

What other discussion topics can you think of—from your own life experiences or those of others—that could help you identify a client system's strengths?

For many clients, this may be the first time a helping professional has prompted them to consider their life stories in terms of the positives and the successes instead of the negatives and the challenges. In this sense, an empowerment-based approach can be a valuable learning experience for both the social worker and the client: "The formula (for learning) is simple: Mobilize clients' strengths (talents, knowledge, capacities, resources) in the service of achieving their goals and visions and the clients will have a better quality of life on their terms" (Saleebey, 2006, p. 1). The strengths-based assessment is a constructive part of the intervention, as the act of bringing the client's attention to past and present strengths in itself improves the client's life (Sullivan, 2012). Clients and social workers alike may initially find it challenging to identify strengths. As a starting point, consider Saleebey's common classes of strengths (2008):

- Personal qualities, traits, and virtues that people possess.
- Knowledge of the world around them.
- Talents people have.
- Cultural and personal stories and lore.
- Community in which people live, including personal, familial, institutional, and organizational involvements.
- Spirituality and its expression (pp. 136–137).

The strengths-based social work intervention can change the client's experience of receiving help from being viewed as an unwelcome experience to a positive one as it is built around the client's strengths, resources, and goals. Framing the client's strengths as both heroic and resilient can often empower the client with a sense of hope and meaning which can be transformed into commitment to action for change (Saleebey, 2008).

A strengths-based assessment of the client's health, employment, education, living situation, and social supports leads to a proactive plan focused on changing behaviors in pursuit of strengths-based, concrete, and achievable goals. The client and social worker collaborate to develop an intervention that emphasizes the mobilization or creation of resources that not only integrate client strengths but also inspire success when these resources are utilized. What better strength is there than success (Sullivan, 2012)?

Motivational interviewing (MI) is a strengths-based, "person-centered counseling style for addressing the common problem of ambivalence about change" (Miller & Rollnick, 2013, p. 29). MI is built on the concepts of empathy and self-efficacy and de-emphasizes resistance and argument. The mnemonic device FRAMES captures the basic elements of MI:

- **F**eedback of personal status relative to norms (i.e., how one's situation compares to societal expectations)
- **R**esponsibility for personal change
- **A**dvising on need for change
- **M**enu of options from which to choose in pursuing change
- **E**mpathetic counselor style
- **S**upport for self-efficacy

(Miller & Rollnick, 2013, p. 375)

MI is often used with clients who confront addictions, high-risk behaviors, and criminal charges. It places the client in charge of change and employs reflective listening, empathy, and the articulation of the pros and cons of change (Corcoran, 2008). Look for further discussion of MI in Chapter 9.

Consider the strategies Emily could use to empower Sarah to take action. Emily may begin by commending Sarah for being responsible, for her concern for the well-being of the baby, and for seeking help for herself and the infant. Acknowledging these strengths is a step toward establishing rapport and building trust so that Sarah views Emily as a partner in resolving a crisis. Emily can then explore with Sarah the options that are desired, realistic, and necessary.

From a legal and ethical perspective, Sarah's parents must be informed about the birth and possible sexual assault. Using an empowerment approach, Emily can help Sarah develop a strategy she can use to feel safe so that she can talk with them. For instance, Emily can offer to be with Sarah when she talks to her parents.

All fifty states have "safe haven" laws that protect parents from prosecution if they leave their newborn child at a designated site (for example, a hospital, police station, or child welfare agency) within a specified amount of time. Emily can assure Sarah that she has legal protection because she brought her child to a designated safe place within the proper timeframe.

Can you think of additional strategies Emily can use to help Sarah feel empowered?

The strengths-based perspective is a widely accepted social work practice approach. Evidence suggests that it is effective for clients dealing with substance abuse and psychiatric disabilities but could be further validated by studying it with other populations (Rapp & Sullivan 2014). Exhibit 7.6 profiles Dennis Saleebey, one of the principal pioneers of the strengths-based perspective.

Solution-Focused Model

While working for a home health agency, Emily was assigned to work with Charlie, a 30-year-old man recently discharged from the hospital after experiencing a gunshot wound. The gunshot resulted in a spinal cord injury that left Charlie a paraplegic (paralyzed from the waist down). When Emily first visited Charlie, he was hostile and refused to discuss any further rehabilitation. Emily suspected that Charlie was frightened and depressed, so she began to talk with him about the aspirations he had as a child. Charlie had wanted to be a minister in his church, but he strayed from that goal when he dropped out of college.

EXHIBIT 7.6

A Social Worker Whose Vision Changed Social Work Practice: A Profile of Dennis Saleebey

Dennis Saleebey was one of the principal developers and promoters of the Strengths Perspective in social work practice. The perspective is now so commonly accepted that it is difficult to believe that it was ever controversial. However, until the strengths model arrived on the scene in the mid-1980s, social work students were taught to focus exclusively on the problems and challenges of their clients, and to figure out how to "fix" them.

Dennis and his colleagues understood that people suffer and face great adversity. However, the model they developed is based on the underlying assumption that, whatever our difficulties may be, we all have resources, skills, knowledge, supports, etc., and that we can use these to shape our lives as we wish. "All humans," Dennis once said, "have the urge to be heroic; to transcend circumstances, to develop one's powers, to overcome adversity, to stand up and be counted."

Before the advent of the strengths-based perspective, social workers did not routinely ask clients to talk about their strengths. Dennis urged social workers to make this part of an ongoing dialogue with clients, in the belief that it is not our problems, deficits, or failures that move us forward, but our skills, our knowledge, and our supports. Saleebey's work had a lasting impact on our profession.

Source: Contributed by: Alice Lieberman, Ph.D., University of Kansas School of Social Welfare.

Through their conversations, Emily helped Charlie to realize that his disability need not prohibit him from returning to college and becoming a minister. Over time, Emily and Charlie reconstructed his conceptions of his abilities, and they developed a plan for working with occupational and physical therapists so that Charlie could reapply to college and achieve his goal of joining the ministry.

In her work with Charlie, Emily employed a solution-focused model in which she (the social worker) helped the client to construct or reconstruct her or his reality or perspective in regard to a challenging life situation. This model grew out of solution-focused brief therapy, in which the professional and the client begin the intervention process by the client defining his or her own desired solution to the problem and strategies for achieving this outcome (de Shazer, 1982; de Shazer et al., 2007). Like advocates for the strengths-based perspective, de Shazer and colleagues believed that a holistic, strengths-based, empowerment approach that focuses on the solutions rather than the problems could make a difference in people's lives (De Jong & Berg, 2013). Their solution-focused model is based on several assumptions: (1) people are the experts about their lives; (2) they are competent and can formulate their own goals and solutions; (3) clients (and not social workers) must establish the change agenda themselves which makes it complementary to strengths-based perspective; and (4) change can only occur when the client takes a different action (De Jong, 2015, p. 269). The solution-focused model is systematic (incorporates the client's system) and pragmatic (interventions that are focused on tasks and activities that will achieve the client's goals) and is intended to help the client experience success by setting and reaching achievable goals and focusing on the positive aspects of the client's life. To those ends, seven basic tenets ground solution-focused interventions:

> **Solution-focused model**
> A theoretical framework for social work practice that enables the social worker and the client system to reconstruct the perception of the current life situation.

- Focus on the future to help the client imagine how things can be different.
- Solutions may or may not be directly linked to the problem and its origins; a solution need not be related to the past.
- Negative perspectives impede solutions when people become mired in trying the same unsuccessful strategies and become frustrated.
- People want to change.
- To avoid undue social worker influence, the social worker approaches the client system without any pre-conceived notions about the situation or its potential resolutions.
- Changing one's language from problem-focused to solution-focused can be a powerful intervention in and of itself.
- Client systems must determine their own priorities and establish their own goals.

(Van Hook, 2014, p. 160)

Solution-Focused Concepts Solution-focused interventions identify client system strengths and use those strengths to improve the client's self-perception.

The essence of the solution-focused model is to build on those areas of a client's life that work well and to help the client accomplish desired and attainable goals (versus striving toward goals the client cannot achieve) (Nichols, 2011). Like the strengths-based approach, the solution-focused method involves collaboration between the social worker and the client (Nichols, 2011). Together, the client and social worker create an intervention plan outlining the specific behavioral tasks the client will undertake to achieve her or his self-determined goal. Typically, the intervention plan can be built upon a client's previous successful experience. The social worker's role is to help clients modify the ways they perceive situations and interact with others.

In her work with Charlie, Emily employed a solution-focused approach. First she listened to Charlie talk about an earlier goal that was important to him—his wish to join the clergy. She then helped him reconnect with those aspirations and recognize strengths he was not even aware he possessed. She and Charlie then collaborated to develop behavioral strategies to accomplish his goals, including sharing with others his desire to became a member of the clergy, researching his educational options, and setting a timeframe for pursuing his goals.

Solution-Focused Model in Generalist Practice Their emphasis on establishing individual goals and behavior change makes solution-focused methods a common choice for social workers working with individuals and families in clinical settings. Exhibit 7.7 lists some types of questions social workers use in solution-focused interventions. As with all social work knowledge and skills, gaining experience—both inside and outside the classroom—is the best way to become a competent solution-focused practitioner (De Jong & Cronkright, 2011).

Consider Angel, who seeks help because of failing grades in academic work. The social worker asks if this is a recent situation, and the student responds that it is. Using a solution-focused approach, the social worker might ask Angel to describe a time when he was earning better grades. Instead of focusing on things that are not going well, the social worker builds on the student's strengths. The social worker continues by asking the student to speculate as to why he was earning better grades before. Maybe Angel responds that his grades were better when he did his homework, asked for help from the teacher, and played fewer video games. In that case, the social worker may say, "So, you made better grades when you completed your homework, asked for help, and played fewer video games." Therein lies the solution; what worked before may very well work again, and the solution comes from the client, not from the social worker.

Although it was primarily developed for use in therapeutic situations, the solution-focused model can be used at all levels of generalist practice. At

EXHIBIT 7.7

Questions for a Solution-Focused Approach

GOAL FORMULATION QUESTIONS
- What will your days be like when you are no longer feeling depressed?
- What would have to be different in your relationship for you to feel satisfied?

MIRACLE QUESTIONS
- What would your life be like if you were able to reach your goal of graduating from college?
- What do you need in order to accomplish the goal of graduating from college, and how can I help you?

EXCEPTION-FINDING QUESTIONS (WHAT WAS IT LIKE WHEN PROBLEMS DID NOT OCCUR?)
- What was your family life like when your parents were not fighting?
- What is it like for the rest of you in the group when Joe is not angry and hostile?

SCALING QUESTIONS (USING A NUMERIC SCALE TO RATE PAST, PRESENT, AND FUTURE STATUS)
- On a scale of 1 to 10, how motivated are you to quit smoking? Where do you need to be to actually quit smoking? What do you need to do to get from 5 to 8?

COPING QUESTIONS
- When you feel like drinking again, what do you do to stop yourself?
- You and your children were homeless last year. What did you do to change that?
- How will you know when things are going well in your life? What will you be doing, who will you be with, and how will you be feeling, thinking, and acting?

WHAT'S BETTER QUESTIONS
- What is better in your life since we last met?
- How is your life better since you started taking your medication?

Source: De Jong, 2015.

the group, organization, and community levels, the social worker can help the client system to agree on specific goals and to recognize the collective strengths and assets that can be mobilized to achieve those goals. In fact, the members may discover combined strengths they have as a group that do not exist on an individual level.

Behavioral and Cognitive Behavioral Approaches

This chapter has highlighted several well-accepted, tried-and-true approaches, all of which can be used in conjunction with one another and/or other theoretical approaches. While other approaches will likely be addressed in future coursework, two additional theories that are important for social work practice are discussed here, including behavioral and cognitive behavioral and task-centered practice. These theoretical approaches are typically integrated into specific client situations that the social worker determines will be most responsive to a specialized approach.

Behavioral and Cognitive Behavioral Theories

Behavioral theory
a theory a person's behaviors provide insight into her or his social and emotional experiences.

Behavioral theory posits that a person's behaviors provide insight into her or his social and emotional experiences. Specifically, our thoughts, emotions, and behaviors are both linked and influence one another and it is our interpretations of these thoughts, emotions, and behaviors that gives meaning to our lives (Nurius & Macy, 2008). Applied behavioral theory evolved out of advances in research on human behavior and led to the development of applied behavior analysis and cognitive behavioral theory (Angell, 2008). Behaviorally-focused interventions are based on the assumption that changing one's thinking can change one's behaviors and mood, making a cognitive behavioral approach well suited to such challenges as depression, anxiety, and addictions. While various behavioral approaches differ in implementation, they share a number of commonalities, including:

- They focus on the client system's desired and valued outcomes.
- Concerns and goals are described in behavioral terms.
- Assessments and interventions are grounded in evidence-based practice approaches.

Applied Behavior Analysis (ABA)
Uses observation of behaviors to develop a behavior modification plan, often using the token system.

- Resources and significant others are key to the assessment and intervention processes as they influence and support behaviors and outcomes.
- Descriptions of concerns, influencing factors, behaviors, goals, and intervention strategies are clearly and behaviorally-oriented.

Dialectical Behavior Therapy (DBT)
An evidence-based practice approach that is used with individuals who engage in self-harming behaviors (e.g., self-cutting and suicidal ideations) along with mood disorders and addictions.

- Evaluation and ongoing maintenance are essential components of the approaches.

(Gambrill, 2012)

Two common approaches, Applied Behavior Analysis (ABA) and Dialectical Behavior Therapy (DBT), have their roots in cognitive and behavioral theory. ABA uses observation of behaviors to develop a behavior modification

Source: iStock/Alina Solovyora–Vincent

plan, often using the token system (e.g., upon completing a task or goal, the client is given a coupon that can be exchanged for a privilege) to reinforce positive, desired behaviors (Angell, 2008). To learn more about ABA, go to: Association for Behavior Analysis International (http://abainternational.org/) or the American Psychological Association's Division 25 (www.apa.org/about/division/div25.aspx). Using aspects of cognitive behavioral theory, DBT is an evidence-based practice approach that is used with individuals who engage in self-harming behaviors (e.g., self-cutting and suicidal ideations) along with mood disorders and addictions. Focused on the validation of client thoughts and feelings dialectical strategies such as emotional regulation and mindfulness, are used to balance and integrate behaviors and change to produce a desired outcome for the client. To learn more about DBT, visit: http://behavioraltech.org/resources/whatisdbt.cfm.

Task-Centered Practice

Developed in the 1970s by Reid and Epstein, Task-Centered Practice (TCP) is a well-established, evidence-based, client-centered social work approach focused on identifying target problems and establishing goals through the use of a collaborative contract that outlines the tasks to be completed by both the client and the social worker (Kelly, 2008). With its focus on concrete goals and tasks, TCP is applicable to settings that emphasize brief interventions (hospitals, private practices, and community mental health centers), behavioral

Task-Centered Practice (TCP)
A well-established, evidence-based, client-centered social work approach focused on identifying target problems and establishing goals through the use of a collaborative contract that outlines the tasks to be completed by both the client and the social worker.

considerations (schools), and resource mobilization (aging service agencies) (Kelly, 2008). To learn more about the concepts of the overall task-centered model, visit: www.task-centered.com.

Integration of Social Work Theory in Practice

Though this chapter has discussed each perspective separately, these theories are not mutually exclusive. Just the opposite is true: They frequently complement one another. The person-in-environment perspective provides the foundation for identifying strengths and for seeing the client system as part of a larger environment. The ecological and systems frameworks influence each other and enable the social worker to compartmentalize the distinctive environmental influences that impact the client's life experiences. Thinking systemically helps the social worker to focus on the client's relationships with other elements within the system.

Moreover, the perspectives clearly flow along a path from more theoretical to more practical. The strengths-based and empowerment perspectives emanate from the ecological and systems models, while solution-focused practice is one application of these influences.

Consider the following case vignette involving Natalie and the theoretical implications of a social work intervention:

Natalie is a 25-year-old Hispanic female seeking mental health services at your agency per her mother's request. Natalie is divorced with no children, and her recent self-identification as a lesbian has led to relationship issues with her mother. When you ask her why her mother wanted her to seek services, Natalie tells you, "We fight all the time. She thinks that there is something wrong with me and that I need to figure myself out. I think she believes that if I go to therapy I won't be gay anymore."

You begin your assessment of Natalie. She is open and engaging. She relays to you a story of abuse she suffered as a child, but says," I went to therapy when I was a kid and that is not the problem. I dealt with it already." Natalie reports various symptoms that have been negatively impacting her for the past three years. She reports periods of anxiety that have lasted up to a month at a time, and which have included racing thoughts and panic attacks. She is unable to identify any triggers for these experiences. She reports that she has periods of time when she has nightmares about her father. She claims that this is a repeating dream and is terrifying to her.

When you probe further into her history she reluctantly reveals that she was sexually abused by her biological father for six years, from the ages of 6–12 years. She does not believe that her mother knew it was happening, and when she told her, her mother left her father and had him prosecuted. Her mother became depressed, and Natalie had to care for herself and her mother for many years. Natalie's father's family did not believe Natalie and accused her of lying. She has had no contact with her father since. Her father was released from prison, and she found out that he has started a new family and has a daughter who is five. She has no contact with her father or half-sister, but states that she worries for her half-sister.

Natalie recently lost her job due to downsizing and is concerned about how she will make it. She reports that she is a strong woman who has "breakdowns." These breakdowns include insomnia, increased anxiety, and agitation, and she becomes consumed with thoughts of her half-sister. She avoids most men and has left the church due to her father's affiliations.

Natalie blames herself for the end of her marriage, stating, "I never should have married him. I was trying to be normal. When he touched me I would feel like I was going to throw up and then I would have a panic attack. He is a good man but he wanted me to be different. I have known for a long time that I am lesbian but I didn't want to accept it. We were only married for three months."

- *What do you think is happening with Natalie?*
- *What else do you want to know?*
- *What are her strengths? Areas of concern?*
- *From a systemic, person-in-environment perspective, what are the primary areas of Natalie's system that have impacted her life?*
- *From a solution-focused perspective, how can Natalie's situation be framed?*

Source: Shannon Cooper-Sadlo, LCSW

These frameworks can also be integrated with other theoretical approaches and disciplines to develop interventions for specific situations spanning the full spectrum of client and system issues in our society. Eclecticism is the practice of using the knowledge and skills derived from multiple theoretical concepts that are most appropriate to the client system, population, or situation at hand. The following is a sampling of the theoretical influences that social work has borrowed from other professional disciplines:

Eclecticism
The application of knowledge and skills that may be derived from multiple theoretical concepts because they are most appropriate to the client system.

- *Sociology* has aided the social work profession in understanding relationships between people and their environments, particularly with regard to class, culture, and inequality issues.
- *Anthropology* has helped social workers to understand the origins and relationships of the wide diversity of groups they serve.

■ *Psychology* has enhanced social workers' insights into human behavior and suggested therapeutic treatment approaches.

■ *Political science* has helped social workers to understand issues related to government, the political process and political environment, and power and control.

■ *Economics* has helped the profession understand the ways in which the economy impacts client systems' living conditions and to develop strategies for effecting change in the economic lives of persons living in poverty.

■ *Biology* has influenced several areas of social work, including human biological functioning and health and disease issues.

As social workers serve such a wide-ranging spectrum of society, they need multiple approaches for use across different populations, situations, and levels of practice. To adopt an eclectic approach, the social worker clearly must be well versed in a number of theoretical perspectives and processes. See Exhibit 7.8 to learn about one social worker's integration of theory with practice and the need to be open to incorporating those approaches that are best suited for the specific client situation.

Regardless of the theoretical orientation and approach(es) you adopt for practice, it is important to engage in the process of critical reflection at each

Critical reflection
Thinking about the helping relationship and the intervention, identifying the learning that has occurred for the social worker as a result of the experience, and considering the way in which this learning will impact future practice.

EXHIBIT 7.8

"The Best Journeys Answer Questions That in the Beginning You Didn't Even Think to Ask."

My name is Amber Elizabeth Rossman, LMSW, and I am Program Manager of HIV Case Management at my nonprofit agency. I did not know that the world was about to make me into a social worker when I started seeking a vocation. Growing up, I found myself involved in environmental preservation groups and human rights campaigns. I was drawn to projects that worked toward social justice, though I didn't know what that meant yet. Grand social change groups like Greenpeace and Amnesty International inspired me. I also looked toward my local heroes, like my parents who always worked for peace and my aunt who was a social worker. As a student, I was provided with experiences through praxis, volunteer experiences, and formal practicum, which led me to my current job (over 15 years later). The experiences led me to opportunities, but it was the mentors along the way that shaped my worldview and instilled in me the urge to grow as a social worker (whether they knew it or not).

Most importantly, it is what I chose to do and how I chose to be open to random opportunities that also helped me grow. I recently saw a movie with a quote that speaks most to this, "the best journeys answer questions that in the beginning you didn't even think to ask." In my limited worldview when I was in college, I was not really sure what was 'out there'. I was most disappointed when I was not assigned to my requested placement for practicum, which I just knew would lead me to my chosen path in social work. I believed the practicum office was standing in my way by not assigning me to my chosen placement. Then I was given the opportunity to interview for a placement that I had not even known existed. I was to serve as a social work case manager for people living with HIV/AIDS.

I accepted the placement in a small free health clinic, though the location was far away from anything I knew and I did not think I could relate to the field instructor. There was a lot of change going on in a tiny clinic that was growing more quickly than its infrastructure. The field instructor was highly distracted on a daily basis, and I found that mishaps shaped my understanding of ethics, boundaries, and self-care. Just as our clients grow with adversity, so do professionals. At the time, my practicum did not seem to be optimal. I loved my clients and the work, yet I struggled with the work objectives and structure of my placement. My field instructor quit mid-year and left me to cover her entire caseload. There were two other social workers. I constantly debated ethical issues with one, while the other was young and fun, but disenchanted with the organization of the department and seeking alternative employment. Though they were both more experienced than me, I still took on the boss's caseload when she left. There are many stories, and many feelings and emotions with which I had to reconcile, but the good news is that I stuck with it. There would have been other, equally as valuable opportunities had I decided to move on to a new career or even practicum.

I came into this job by being pushed to grow and take on opportunities for which I was not ready. It all goes back to my social work mentors. Along the way, I was frustrated by the ill-fitting projects to which I was assigned. I was frustrated that I was not given the particular opportunities that I sought. I didn't know how exactly I wanted to shape my career, yet I felt pulled away when I was given administrative tasks that were not directly related to working with clients. I loved advocacy and the new frontier feel of a career in HIV/AIDS. As it turned out, 1997 was a unique time for the disease. During this time anti-retroviral drugs (AZT) were a huge breakthrough. I was becoming a professional when these medications were starting to fracture the community of patients and clients due to the controversial aspects of them. Anyone who has watched older AIDS documentaries and movies may understand the environment (I highly recommend, *And the Band Played On*).

There are a few major and life-changing times in my career as a social worker that almost made me want to change careers. Each of these times, I felt inadequate as a professional and as a person. Once, the sheer volume of my work was overwhelming—it was only when my position was split into two full-time positions that I realized my stress had less to do with my inadequacies and more to do with the environment in which I was working. At another time early in my career, many of my clients were dying due to complications and due to the effects of the HIV medications, which were still not entirely understood. Although clients trusted our medical system and me, as a social worker, they could not necessarily trust the medications.

I learned firsthand of the power of rapport. I worked hard to build rapport, and was especially proud of the alliances I built with my African American clients, who had deeply rooted distrust of the medical system. I saw a connection between the history of Tuskegee (when African Americans were enrolled in an experiment on the natural progression of syphilis without the informed consent regarding the trial) and that of newly released AIDS drugs, and witnessed firsthand the broken trust and shaken faith as many of these drugs validated my trusting client's worst fears. Because the medications were so new and somewhat experimental, they sometimes seemed to be doing more harm than good. My clients who grew up knowing the horrific realities of Tuskegee were looking through a lens of their negative historical or familial experiences. By trusting service providers who were mostly from a different race, culture, and system, their family members (already stigmatized by the disease) were becoming sicker. It was in this context that I became determined to find ways to be a stronger social worker, to learn from the experiences, biases, realities, and lessons of my client work, and to find the best place for me to further my knowledge of social work.

The opportunities to work for justice, support behavior change, and help the disenfranchised pushed me through times when I was uncertain where I fit in or how much of an impact I could make. It was also during these times that I felt that my BSW was not enough. I needed to grow, and my knowledge was inadequate. That is not to say that a BSW is not enough for this work. Rather, I personally was not a strong undergraduate student. I attended classes without the benefit of the practical knowledge that I gained in a short year of working after graduation. I had the urge to retake classes. I wanted to go back and pay more attention and learn with the benefit of practical experience. The way for me to do that was to earn my MSW.

With all of this love for client work, how did I end up doing administrative social work? Aren't administrative social workers just another level removed from reality and client work? Even at a small agency, I felt a rub of the competition between who did the "real" work—nurses or social workers? Who had the greatest impact on clients' lives? Who did clients need the most? A nurse explained that she felt the pull to use her nursing expertise in an administrative capacity. By working together with direct practitioners, she was able to create change on an organizational level. From her perspective, she served more people (professionals and patients) in this capacity. This was both a challenge and an inspiration for me. As a social worker, I enjoyed projects that served many clients at once. I fell in love with the idea I might be able to develop a standard or program that could help other social workers to support their clients. I thrived in an environment where I could learn from how a project was working in a system and work to make changes to further improve clients' access to care or ability to engage in services.

A social work mentor reminded me to apply my theoretical knowledge of the strengths perspective to my own professional growth. As I worked with clients to employ their strengths, utilize their support systems, and take advantage of services to reach their goals, I found that these methods also worked to help me achieve my professional goals. I have used the peer educator model to support other social workers and have committed to the concept of knowledge transfer (ideas, techniques, lessons and learned) to other social workers. I have done this through working in research (through grants on demonstration projects with the Centers for Disease Control and Prevention), presenting at local and national conferences, teaching, field instruction, and supporting the educational goals of my immediate staff.

What do I like about my life as a social worker? It is hard work. It can be rewarding. It is a journey. I have been at the same agency for over 15 years. Each year my job has looked completely different. In regard to professional growth, I am most proud that I have made efforts to change my job by embracing new projects, involving myself with other disciplines, and seeking to mold my job by taking on new responsibilities and giving up others. Because of this, I find that my job looks radically different about every three to five years. I like the quote about a journey answering questions you didn't know to ask because I find myself loving projects that weren't even a part of my job the year before. I love working in the field of HIV/AIDS because HIV is a relatively new disease and the face of AIDS and those who work in the field changes constantly. This creates opportunities and challenges. This also means constant learning and the understanding that I'll never be an expert.

step of the social work intervention. In critical reflection (or reflective practice) the social worker thinks about the helping relationship and the intervention, identifies the learning that has occurred for the social worker as a result of the experience, and considers the way in which this learning will impact future practice (Davies, 2012). Critical reflection helps social workers make future choices about which theoretical approach(s) to take in various circumstances. REFLECT is a mnemonic device that provides helpful reminders to think about when you engage in critical reflection (Davies, 2012):

- **R**elate experience in terms of thoughts, feelings, behaviors, and actions.
- **E**valuate thoughts, feelings, behaviors, and actions and the influencing factors of self and others.
- **F**ormulate the learning need/issue/problem.
- **L**ist strengths and weaknesses of behaviors and actions.
- **E**xplore other strategies and approaches.
- **C**onclude main learning points.
- **T**hink about new understanding and action plan to change practice.

(p. 11)

Taking time to consider the actions you will take or have taken and the theory(ies) that you will use or have used can guide future practice decisions and help you develop practice competence. There are four times in particular during the helping process when it is especially helpful to reflect on your work (Forte, 2014b):

- Before the relationship begins, identify the most relevant evidence-based theories and interventions.
- During the helping process, consider events and/or client actions and the helpfulness of the theoretical approach, and adjust the plan as needed.
- As the helping relationship is progressing toward an end, look to the future to identify any potential obstacles and opportunities that may exist.

■ After the relationship has ended, review the theoretical approaches that were successful or unsuccessful and consider the reasons for each.

(pp. 41–42)

CONCLUSION

This chapter has explored the role of the generalist social worker and the theoretical frameworks that guide and inform generalist social work practice. Applying these theoretical concepts to your practice can be a challenge, particularly because there are so many theories and approaches from which to choose. These constructs provide a basis on which to build your knowledge of effective and ethical social work practice and ways in which the constructs can be applied to enable them to be meaningful in practice interventions.

One chapter in a book provides only enough space to cover a small number of the many available theoretical approaches. This chapter has focused on the most prominent approaches in social work today. As you continue the lifelong process of social work education, you will add other theoretical constructs to your repertoire. For additional information on the social work profession and generalist practice, resources that may be helpful include the CSWE *Educational Policy and Accreditation Standards* (2015) and the NASW *Code of Ethics* (2008).

MAIN POINTS

■ Generalist social work practice provides for assessment and intervention at three levels: individuals and families, groups, and organizations and communities. The generalist social worker employs a variety of skills and plays many roles, including educator, advocate, and mediator.

■ Evidence-based practice provides the social work practitioner with empirically-supported theoretical knowledge, skills, and practice behaviors guide and inform social work assessment and intervention approaches.

■ The person-in-environment perspective views the individual within the context of the environment in which she or he lives. This perspective is the foundation of all social work theoretical approaches.

■ The ecological perspective helps social workers understand the meaning of interactions between client systems and their environments.

■ Building on the ecological model, systems and ecosystems theories help social workers understand and facilitate the change process that occurs for client systems within the context of the larger physical and social environment.

- Strengths-based and empowerment perspectives help the social worker and client work together to identify the client system's strengths and frame goals that will build on those strengths and empower the client system to make positive changes.
- Derived from the strengths perspective, the solution-focused perspective has implications for practice at the micro, mezzo, and macro levels of practice because the social worker has knowledge and skills to help clients reconstruct the ways in which they view their situation to enable them to envision possible solutions.
- Theoretical approaches can be combined at all three levels of generalist practice to develop strategies that include engagement and assessment of the client system, and planning, implementation, and evaluation of the social work intervention.

EXERCISES

1. This exercise relates to the Sanchez family interactive case (www.routledg-esw.com/caseStudies). It focuses on Gloria Sanchez.
   a. Read the following case scenario and identify the challenges and strengths within the client situation. Using the Strengths Form in Exhibit 7.9, link each of those strengths to one or more of the principles of client strength described earlier in the chapter in Quick Guide

EXHIBIT 7.9

Strengths Form

CLIENT CHALLENGES	CLIENT STRENGTHS	PRINCIPLE(S) OF STRENGTHS PERSPECTIVE

#7.1. Lastly, review the scenario to describe the client situation from a deficits perspective.

You are the social worker at Our Lady of Guadalupe Church, which the Sanchez family has attended for years. During a recent church event, you noticed Gloria Sanchez wearing a long-sleeved turtleneck sweater on a particularly warm day. You speculate that she is wearing the turtleneck to cover up bruises. On numerous occasions, you have observed her husband, Leo, speaking to her in an extremely disrespectful and demanding manner. The next time you see her, you ask how things are going and she bursts into tears. She discloses to you that Leo has abused her throughout much of their marriage; she wants to leave him, but knows the teachings of the church oppose divorce. She shares that her sister, Carmen, is aware of the abuse, but, for the present, has agreed not to tell the rest of the family. Carmen is very supportive, but is pushing her to "get help or get out." Gloria is terrified that her parents will learn about the abuse and blame her as they love Leo "like one of their own." Gloria has always felt close to her family and is saddened that she does not see them as often as she would like. She visits them less often than she used to out of fear that they will suspect something is wrong.

b. In part a of this exercise, you identified the strengths in Gloria's situation. Now consider Gloria's situation using a solution-focused approach. With your help, Gloria has identified the following areas of concern: being battered by her husband; thinking of divorce; ensuring that the rest of her family does not learn about the violence; and being concerned that her relationship with her family is becoming distant. From a solution-focused perspective, and drawing on your knowledge of her strengths, consider each of these areas in terms of the solutions that Gloria might aspire to and a behavioral strategy to help her achieve the goal. The solution-focused Form in Exhibit 7.10 will help you organize your ideas.

2. For this exercise, access the Sanchez family interactive case at ww.routledgesw.com/caseStudies and familiarize yourself with situations involving several family members.

    a. Review the case file for Celia Sanchez. Then answer Celia's Critical Thinking Questions.

    b. Review the case file for Alejandro Sanchez. Then answer Alejandro's Critical Thinking Questions.

    c. Locate the Case Study Tools and click on the ecomap icon. Review the ecomap for the Sanchez family. Using the ecomap guide provided in this chapter or on the Sanchez site, create an ecomap for yourself.

EXHIBIT 7.10

Solutions Form

CHALLENGE	STRENGTH/RESOURCE POSSESSED	GLORIA'S GOAL	RESOURCES NEEDED	GOAL OR OBJECTIVE
Violent spouse				
Desire for divorce				
Family learning about the violence				
Losing her relationship with her family				

Provide a narrative analysis of your own ecomap, focusing on your strengths, areas for growth and change, areas in which your energies are focused, and a future perspective on your life.

3. Go to the Riverton interactive case at www.routledgesw.com/caseStudies and review the case information. Begin to develop an intervention:
   a. Describe the system as you perceive it from a strengths-based perspective.
   b. Identify the barriers and challenges to change.
   c. Provide your thoughts on ways in which the Alvadora residents may be empowered to address their concerns about the state of their neighborhood.
4. Research a scholarly article or chapter that describes evidence-based social work practice. When you have gained some familiarity with this concept, go to the RAINN interactive case at www.routledgesw.com/caseStudies and describe the ways in which evidence-based practice techniques are being utilized.
5. To integrate social work theory with practice, go to the Hudson City interactive case at www.routledgesw.com/caseStudies. Using systems theory, the strengths perspective, and the solution-focused model, describe how you would work with an individual or family living through a disaster.

6. Visit the Brickville interactive case at www.routledgesw.com/caseStudies. Click on Assess and Introduction to the Stone family. Familiarize yourself with all the information related to the Stone family and, from an ecological and strengths-based perspective, respond to the three questions at the end of the description. Then reflect in writing on your responses in terms of developing empowerment-focused strategies for the family as individuals and as a whole unit.

FIELDS OF SOCIAL WORK PRACTICE

Source: iStock

Like many students considering a career in social work, Emily was captivated by the range and diversity of employment possibilities. Through her social work classes, Emily learned that a BSW prepares her for generalist social work practice with a variety of persons and settings. The challenge for Emily then became narrowing her practice focus. Emily decided she needed to explore in depth the many and varied opportunities available to her as a BSW generalist social worker. In her investigation of the fields of social work practice, Emily used a number of strategies. She began by reading about fields of practice, using the internet to learn about social work organizations and opportunities, talking to fellow students and faculty at her program, interviewing practicing social workers, and volunteering in a social service setting that provided her with a range of different experiences. Even as she progressed through this exploration, Emily could still see herself working in a number of different areas, but she felt confident that she was more aware of the breadth of opportunities available to her.

C an you relate to Emily's dilemma? Social work is a profession that offers the potential to work in an array of fields. Many social workers are drawn to a particular field of practice because of their life experiences or their interests in a particular setting or population. Have you considered the field or fields of practice that interest you? To get you started in your investigation, Exhibit 8.1 provides a sampling of the many fields of social work practice.

In this chapter, thirteen social workers share their perspectives on the areas of social work in which they practice. These "voices from the field" provide a window into their areas of practice, the training and education required to work in those areas, the potential rewards and challenges, and a perspective on the future of each of those fields of social work practice. Written by the social workers themselves, these narratives are their views based on their own experiences. Though each of these practitioners has the same kind of social work degree, each works with a different population and in a different setting. A social work degree offers a lot of flexibility for working in a variety of settings with different populations throughout your career.

As you will learn in the next three chapters, social work interventions are built on the concept of planned change—a model that encompasses the stages of engagement of the client system, assessment of the client's situation to determine the strengths and barriers related to change, the planning and implementation of an intervention strategy, and the termination and evaluation of the helping relationship. This chapter's voices from the field illustrate the planned change process in action in different areas of social work practice.

Planned change
A process in which the social worker and client system work together to develop and implement mutually agreed-upon goals for enhancing the functioning and well-being of the client system.

EXHIBIT 8.1

Fields of Practice and Practice Settings

FIELD OF PRACTICE	SETTINGS
Mental health services	Community-based mental health centers
	Inpatient-based psychiatric facilities
	Disaster relief programs
	Employee assistance programs
	Private practice
	Hospitals and rehabilitation programs
	Residential facilities
Medical social work	Hospitals and rehabilitation programs
	Community-based health care programs
	Community-based health education programs
Gerontological social work	Community-based service programs
	Hospitals and rehabilitation programs
	Residential facilities
	Adult day care programs
Chemical dependency and addiction treatment	Community-based treatment programs
	Hospital-based treatment programs
	Prevention and education programs
Child welfare services	Family service agencies
	Adoption programs
	Elementary and secondary schools
	Public child welfare agencies
School social work	Elementary and secondary schools
	Alternative school programs
International social work	U.S.-based immigrant and refugee programs
	Non-U.S.-based programs
	Disaster relief programs
	U.S.-based international programs
	Advocacy organizations
Domestic and family violence	Shelter-based programs
	Hospitals
	Legal system programs
	Community-based mental health programs
Criminal justice	Corrections settings
	Legal system programs
Crisis intervention	Disaster relief programs
	Victim assistance programs

Rural social work	Community service programs
	Hospitals and rehabilitation programs
Military social work	Military mental health and family service programs
	Deployment support programs
Community development	Nonprofit and public sector
Community organizing	Community-based programs
Advocacy	Community-based programs
Policy development and analysis	Nonprofit and public sector programs

SOCIAL WORK PRACTICE WITH CHILDREN AND FAMILIES

Social work practice with children and families encompasses a range of practice areas in a diverse array of settings, all focused on child welfare, or ensuring that children are safe and protected from harm (National Association of Social Workers Studies (NASW) Center for Workforce Studies (CWS), 2004). Child welfare includes child protection services, family preservation, foster care, group homes, residential facilities, adoption services, and kinship care programs (NASW CWS, 2004, p. 6). Social workers who practice in this field may work in public and private child welfare agencies, residential care facilities, family service agencies, schools, mental health centers, chemical dependency and addiction treatment programs, agencies that serve persons with disabilities, or health care settings.

Working with children and families is the second largest practice area and is particularly popular with those with BSWs. Twenty-two percent of social workers work with children: 11% work in child welfare and family services, 5% work with adolescents, and 6% work in schools (Whitaker & Arrington, 2008).

Services to children and families may be publicly funded, nonprofit, or for-profit. Nearly half of social workers who work with children and families are employed in a private nonprofit setting, with another 41% working in the public sector, and the remaining 11% in private for-profit organizations (Whitaker & Arrington, 2008). Of those social workers working in the child welfare system, two-thirds provide direct services to children and families (NASW CWS, 2004).

Policy-Practice Considerations with Children and Families

Social workers who specialize in child welfare may work in residential group homes as case managers, childcare workers, and therapists. In public child welfare agencies, social workers investigate referrals about child abuse and neglect; and they work with children and families in the areas of alternative out-of-home care, prevention and adoption services, and family preservation and reunification programs. In private family service agencies, social workers work with children and families on adoption, family preservation and reunification, alternative care, and in-home therapy programs. In agencies that provide services to persons with physical or mental illness, addictions, or disabilities, social workers complete intake assessments, develop and implement treatment plans and follow-up, provide individual and group therapy, and work with the children and/or their parents.

In recent years, greater emphasis has been placed on family preservation—specifically, the prevention of out-of-home placement for children—and on strengthening the family's ability to cope and manage. As social work education emphasizes a strengths-based, systems approach, social workers are well trained to serve as family preservation professionals. Social workers provide therapeutic case management, parenting education, and life skills services to families in both the family's home and in agency settings.

School social work is a related area of growth and opportunity for social workers interested in working with children and their families. In schools, social workers conduct assessments, serve as liaisons between the school and the family, facilitate groups, and participate in interprofessional teams to develop individual educational plans for students. Through one-on-one and family services as well as educational and prevention programs, school social workers also support students at risk for poor academic and social outcomes.

One of the most serious issues confronting social workers who intervene with children and families is child abuse and neglect. Child abuse and neglect are problems. Child abuse occurs when a child is subjected to physical and/or emotional injury, which may include sexual abuse. Child neglect exists when the child's caregiver does not ensure that the child's emotional, physical, nutritional, educational, or shelter needs are being met. Public education and media attention have increased awareness of child abuse and neglect and the reporting process.

Child abuse and neglect Perpetration of physical, emotional, or sexual harm to a child or the inadequate provision of physical, medical, emotional, or educational care to a child.

Most often, school personnel report cases of child abuse and neglect. Other primary reporters include professionals in social service agencies, law enforcement, and health care organizations. Many professionals who work in these settings are legally mandated to report suspected cases of child abuse, neglect, or exploitation. Non-mandated reporters (for example, family, friends, neighbors, or observers) can make anonymous reports and are protected from prosecution as long as they do not file the report with malicious intent.

In 2012, there were 3.4 million reports of suspected child abuse or neglect. 686,000 of those reports were substantiated, and three-quarters (78.3%) of the substantiated cases were cited as neglect (U.S. Department of Health and

Human Services (DHHS), 2012). Affected children are almost evenly divided by gender (the percentage of girls is slightly higher), tend to be less than one year of age, and are most likely to be abused or neglected by a parent, slightly more often the mother. While these numbers are staggering, child abuse, neglect, and fatalities are all decreasing due to increased awareness, treatment, and parenting education (DHHS, 2012).

Even so, the number of children entering the foster care system continues to be extremely high. Of those children found to be abused or neglected, over 405,000 entered the foster care system in 2011, a 23% decrease over the previous decade (DHHS, 2013). Children of color are disproportionately represented in the foster care system. Strides have been made in decreasing the length of time children spend in foster care (in 58% of states), although children with a disability and those over twelve years old are more likely to wait longer for a permanent home (DHHS, 2013). For these reasons, Mitchell and colleagues (2012) recommend that the child welfare system in the 21st century should focus on the primary prevention of child maltreatment through emphases on strengthening the child welfare workforce and the policies that guide regulations, increasing funding for prevention services, and engaging communities in this effort.

Working with a vulnerable population such as children who have been abused or neglected is consistent with the profession's mission, and working with degreed social workers has been shown to improve children's and families' outcomes (NASW, 2013b). For these reasons, NASW's *Standards for Social Work Practice in Child Welfare* (2013b) and the NASW policy statement (NASW, 2012–2014k) provide guidelines for competent practice with children and call for better support for social workers practicing in this area.

Angela (Chierek) Bratcher, BSW, MSW, LCSW, BCBA, LBA, Registered Play Therapist-Supervisor, Great Circle

I earned my bachelor's and master's degrees in social work. I have also completed the requirements to be a licensed clinical social worker and to be certified as a Registered Play Therapist-Supervisor, and I am a licensed Board Certified Behavior Analyst. For five years I worked for the Missouri Children's Division as a Social Service Worker II in a Child Abuse and Neglect unit. I started at Boys & Girls Town of Missouri as a behavior specialist in the Fostering Futures program and later became program manager and therapist for the Fostering Futures program. In 2009, Boys & Girls Town of Missouri merged with Edgewood Children's Center and is now known as Great Circle. As assistant director of community-based services, I helped oversee programs in the department and run the respite program. Currently, I serve as clinical director of day treatment services, overseeing therapists in the day treatment school. I also oversee two community-based programs that provide therapeutic mentoring and therapeutic support services to students in the Ferguson-Florissant School District.

My position as a Social Service Worker II laid the foundation for my career in the social work field. My primary responsibility was to respond to mandated reports of suspected child abuse and neglect and to preventive reports received through the agency's hotline. State laws mandate that any professional who works with children—such as social workers, physicians, teachers, and day care workers—must report suspected child abuse and neglect. Any concerned person may make a preventive report; these often relate to a family's need for services, such as counseling or utility assistance referrals.

In general, child welfare workers are very focused on their essential role in the child protection system; children cannot protect themselves. Using a strengths-based approach, social workers employed in child welfare agencies strive to achieve positive outcomes by emphasizing the strengths of the families with whom they are working. The Child Abuse and Neglect unit and the community as a whole count an emphasis on teamwork as one of their strengths. Social workers support each other by helping provide resources to

assist families and by aiding in the process of placing children in foster care. Child welfare agencies are also placing increased emphasis on implementing community support for children and families. Connecting children and families to their communities provides them with a safety net to protect them in the event of another crisis.

My work was challenging and demanding, as family situations can include everything from substance abuse to the need for parenting, conflict management, or help with appropriate discipline. One of the first challenges for any worker is to involve families with the Children's Division. A family may be angry about the report, which can be an obstacle to their active involvement in the case.

Some issues cannot be addressed by providing services to families in their home. Severe physical and sexual abuse places the child's safety at immediate risk. In these cases, the child or children must either be temporarily placed with a relative with a safety plan, or the court must take the child into protective custody and place her or him in foster care. If a child is temporarily placed with a relative, the allegations are investigated and a decision is made based on evidence compiled during the investigation. If the child is placed into protective custody, there is an initial hearing to determine whether the child will remain in foster care. The foster care case manager and ·the parents develop a service plan to work toward reunification of the parents and child.

Properly supporting and providing services to families is difficult enough without the ongoing challenge of handling typically large caseloads. This requires prioritizing the needs of some families over the needs of other families whose children are considered safe. Attracting and retaining workers with social work education who want to work in the field of child welfare is challenging as well. Not all child welfare agencies require service workers to have a social work degree, but our social work training makes us well suited for the field of child welfare because we are trained to fully focus on the needs of the family.

My experience in child welfare has taught me that children who are placed in foster care often come from environments that lack structure and nurturance. These factors often lead to behavior problems when a child is placed in a foster home. I used my five years of experience in public child welfare to gain employment as a behavior specialist in the Fostering Futures program. In this position, I worked to stabilize a child's placement using behavior management. Children in foster care can have multiple placements in different homes or residential settings. Being placed in multiple settings is often another setback that children in foster care experience. Fostering Futures seeks to prevent multiple placements.

Children referred to Fostering Futures exhibit different behaviors

that may disrupt their foster home placements. These behaviors may include temper tantrums, lying, stealing, talking back, difficulty following household rules, and substance abuse. Each child's behaviors are assessed using information gathered from the foster parent, case manager, and the child, and from the specialist's direct observation. I developed an individualized behavior plan to address the unique needs of each child. This plan guides the implementation of activities that address the child's behaviors through weekly home visits. The activities utilize therapeutic techniques including play therapy and art therapy, which provide non-verbal outlets for feelings.

Through my work with children in foster care, I have discovered that children do want to improve their behavior. Acting-out behaviors are often just an outlet for feelings of anger, loss, and trauma associated with being in foster care. By teaching children alternative strategies for dealing with their feelings, children's behavior eventually improves.

Another factor essential to stabilizing a child's foster care placement is the cooperation of the child's foster parents. Although foster parents are informed about the struggles children in foster care experience, still they are often unprepared to handle the child's behaviors. I educated foster parents to understand the reasons behind those behaviors so that they would be more willing to work with the children instead of asking that the children be removed from their homes. These efforts with foster parents and consistent implementation of interventions can help stabilize the placement. Foster parents have to be flexible and open to trying different techniques to manage a child's behavior instead of believing that one approach will work with every child.

The future of services for children in foster care focuses on stabilization to reduce multiple placements. Improved education for foster parents is needed to help them understand the issues children in foster care face so they can develop strategies to handle those issues. As stipulated in the 1997 Adoption and Safe Families Act, greater emphasis needs to be placed on permanency for children in foster care. Many children still linger in foster care for several years without a permanent living arrangement, which denies them the security of a family.

My experiences as program manager, assistant director, and clinical director illustrate what it takes to provide quality services to children and families while maintaining balanced budgets and ensuring accountability in order to retain program funding. Although not typical social work skills, these abilities are increasingly needed to sustain programs and to keep the funding that enables programs to exist. Additionally, a leadership role requires a social worker to function not only as a clinician providing direct services to families, but also as a motivator and coach for program employees, helping them

to provide quality services that meet client needs and achieve desired program outcomes.

In the respite programs I supervised, my agency works to provide services that will develop more independent living and social skills for children with a developmental disability, including children diagnosed on the autism spectrum. These programs also educate parents, siblings, and family members on how to address problem behavior and cope with their emotions. Without the continued support of these programs, many families would be unable to support their child with a developmental disability in their community, which could result in more out-of-home placements for these children.

In my current position as clinical director, I focus on overseeing therapists in the day treatment school program. Children and youth who are admitted to this program range from those with mental health diagnoses such as bi-polar disorder, autism spectrum diagnoses, or social skills deficits. These children and youth have not succeeded behaviorally in their home school district or alternative school program. For many of them, the day treatment program is their first opportunity to experience what it's like to succeed and feel safe at school. Though the children and youth come from a wide range of backgrounds, including different ethnicities and socioeconomic status, they tend to share a history of trauma. Trauma history can include experiences such as abuse and neglect, witnessing domestic violence, car accidents, house fires, natural disasters, or living in a violent neighborhood. Many children and youth respond behaviorally to these trauma experiences. To address these experiences, all of the therapists at my agency are training in Trauma Focused-Cognitive Behavior Therapy. This specific therapy allows children and youth to cope with their experiences through psycho-education, relaxation and stress management, affective expression, cognitive coping, trauma narrative, in vivo mastery of trauma reminders, conjoint child-parent sessions, and enhancing future safety, which addresses safety concerns that may impede future developmental growth. Offering this therapy in a school setting allows the child or youth to receive trauma therapy on a consistent basis and avoids the barriers that often impede service delivery to families, such as lack of access to qualified therapists, lack of funding, and scheduling difficulties. Trauma therapy teaches children and youth to cope with their trauma experience and to express themselves in healthier ways.

In 2013, Great Circle began collaborating with the Ferguson-Florissant School District to provide programs for their students. This collaboration resulted in two programs that provided therapeutic mentoring and therapeutic student support services. In August 2014, I worked in partnership with the leaders of the school district to assess what staff

and students needed to cope with a recent community crisis. Our consultations resulted in several meetings with school district staff to allow them to express their own feelings and prepare for students returning to school. Twenty-five therapists from Great Circle were present to support students and staff at all the elementary and middle schools on the first day of school. As a key person in this process, I fulfilled the essential role of the social worker, serving others who are in need. This experience allowed me to focus on how to enhance support for students, parents, and school staff, and play a small role in the healing of the community. I think that social workers should always be aware of how they can use their skills outside of the narrow scope of their employed role in an agency. Social work skills can make a difference in communities in need and can help improve society overall.

Being a social worker in the child welfare system can be challenging and demanding, but it can also be rewarding. As a beginning social worker working in children's services, I had a great opportunity to hone my organizational skills and to learn a variety of different intervention strategies. This knowledge provided me with a framework for my continued work with children in foster care and with children with developmental disabilities and mental health needs. It has enabled me to provide interventions that bring more stability to their lives and to the lives of their families.

Source: Jupiter images

GERONTOLOGICAL SOCIAL WORK PRACTICE

Practice with older adults, or gerontological social work, is currently under-going dramatic changes. The "aging tsunami" is considered a demographic imperative at the global level due to the widespread impact of an aging popula-tion on families, employment, education, housing, and, of course, health and mental health services (Hooyman, 2012). With the anticipated increases in the older-adult population as the Baby Boomers reach their senior years and people live longer, the need for more health and social services is increasing. Currently, 13.7% of the U.S. population (one in seven Americans) is age 65 or older (Administration of Aging (AoA), 2013). This number grew by 21% from 2002 to 2012. By 2030, all Baby Boomers will have reached age 65, and the 65 and over cohort will make up nearly one-quarter—the largest segment of any age cohort—of the U.S. population. Less than three 20- to 64-year-old persons will work to support one older adult (through Social Security) (West, Cole, Goodkind, & He, 2014; U.S. Census Bureau, 2014c). Once an individual reaches 65 years of age, she or he can expect to live for 19.2 more years (20.4 years for women and 17.8 years for men) (AoA, 2013). Exhibit 8.2 depicts the "squaring of the age pyramid." Prior to the aging of the Baby Boomer population, the top of the population pyramid (older adults) comprised a rela-tively small percentage of the population. The U.S. is not the only country with an aging population, as 60+-year-olds are the fastest growing segment of the world's population (U.N., 2009). Globally, populations are rates of global

Gerontological social work
Social work practice focused on older adults that can include work at the individual, family, group, organizational, and community level.

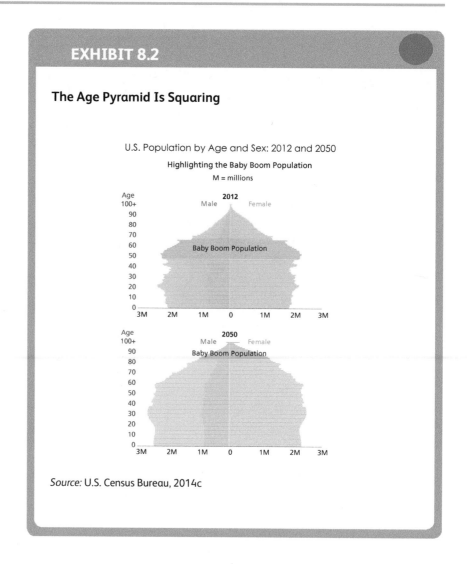

EXHIBIT 8.2

The Age Pyramid Is Squaring

U.S. Population by Age and Sex: 2012 and 2050

Highlighting the Baby Boom Population

M = millions

Source: U.S. Census Bureau, 2014c

aging at the fastest rates in recorded history and are a staggering 1.9%/year in developed countries, where 80% of older adults live, and 3%/year in developing countries (U.N., 2009).

More social workers will be needed to provide services to this population and their family members and caregivers, particularly in the areas of care coordination, case management, mental health services and supports, government program eligibility determination, care-giving support, and counseling (DHHS, 2006, p. 1). Currently, fewer than 10% of social workers identify practice with older adults as their primary field of practice, and only 4% of social workers report having been trained in geriatrics (Eldercare Workforce Alliance, 2011;

Whitaker & Arrington, 2008). However, three-fourths of social workers report working with older clients (55+ years), while one-quarter have caseloads comprised largely of older adults (Center for Health Workforce Studies & Center for Workforce Studies (CHWS/CWS), 2006).

Despite these statistics, only 7% of MSW students and 2.8% of BSW students (5% across all social work students) concentrate their education on gerontological social work practice (Council on Social Work Education (CSWE), 2011). More encouragingly, over one-quarter of students in one survey reported taking an aging-related course as an undergraduate student, and approximately 20% completed a graduate-level aging course (Cummings, Adler, & DeCoster, 2005).

As the over-65 population grows, between 60,000 and 70,000 social workers—or approximately double the number of social workers currently working in gerontological practice—will be needed in a wide range of fields (CSWE/SAGE-SW, 2001). Today, it takes 55,000 social workers to meet the needs of older adults in long-term care; that number will double to 109,000 by 2050 (DHHS, 2006, p. 1). Unsurprisingly, exposure to gerontological issues during their education, positive attitudes toward older adults, and training in gerontological social work skills predict the likelihood of a social worker pursuing employment with older adults (Cummings & Adler, 2007). All social workers need increased awareness and skills for working with issues related to aging.

Policy-Practice Considerations with Older Adults

Recent initiatives have made social work educators aware of the need for increased emphasis on preparing students to work competently with older adults regardless of the social work setting. One such initiative, "Strengthening Aging and Gerontology Education for Social Work" (CSWE/SAGE-SW, 2001), has identified 10 crucial competencies (see Exhibit 8.3) that all social workers must possess in order to work effectively with older adults.

Social workers often work directly with older clients and their families in host settings. A host setting is an organization whose primary mission is to provide services other than social services (for example, health care or education). Such settings include hospitals, rehabilitation programs, residential care facilities such as skilled care and assisted living facilities or senior independent living communities, adult day service programs, senior centers with congregate meal programs, home health agencies, and hospice programs. Gerontological social workers may work in agencies that provide case management services for older adults; investigate elder abuse, neglect, and exploitation; or provide

EXHIBIT 8.3

Social Work Competencies for Practice with Older Adults

1. Assess one's own values and biases regarding aging, death, and dying.
2. Educate self to dispel the major myths about aging.
3. Accept, respect, and recognize the right and need of older adults to make their own choices and decisions about their lives within the context of the law and safety concerns.
4. Understand normal physical, psychological, and social changes in later life.
5. Respect and address cultural, spiritual, and ethnic needs and beliefs of older adults and family members.
6. Examine the diversity of attitudes toward aging, mental illness, and family roles.
7. Understand the influence of aging on family dynamics.
8. Use social work case management skills (such as brokering, advocacy, monitoring, and discharge planning) to link elders and their families to resources and services.
9. Gather information regarding social history, such as social functioning, primary and secondary social supports, social activity level, social skills, financial status, cultural background, and social involvement.
10. Identify ethical and professional boundary issues that commonly arise in work with older adults and their caregivers, such as client self-determination, end-of-life decisions, family conflicts, and guardianship.

Source: CSWE/SAGE-SW, 2001.

supportive services for family members and caregivers. Social workers are also well trained to work in elder-friendly communities (i.e., communities that support older adults by having services, transportation, and living spaces conducive to aging successfully in place), consumer-directed care programs, community-based models for chronic disease management, assistance with life transitions, programs for all-inclusive care for the elderly (PACE), and health promotion and disease prevention programs (Hooyman, 2012). As Hooyman (2012) asserts, "social workers are well-positioned to build intersections of both formal and informal sources of support since an elder-friendly community is more than its physical aspects" (p. 540).

Another important area of practice for gerontological social workers is policy practice. Influencing the development of legislation, policy, and programming for older adults is critical to their enhanced longevity and quality of life. Advocacy is particularly needed to provide funding for research and health and social services, especially for older adults who experience dementia. For example, in 2014, care for persons with Alzheimer's disease and other dementias will cost $214 billion, but only 25% of that amount is spent on researching cures for dementias (Alzheimer's Association, 2014; NIH, 2014).

Carroll Rodriguez, BSW, Alzheimer's Association

In my role as the Vice President and public policy director for a state coalition of Alzheimer's Association chapters, I am charged with mobilizing others in an effort to bring about governmental and legislative changes that will benefit persons with Alzheimer's disease, their families, and their care partners. I work with the three state chapters to coordinate state and national public policy activities for my state.

Alzheimer's Advocates at the Missouri State Capitol for Memory Day

Photo courtesy of Alzheimer's Association, 9370 Olive Boulevard, St. Louis, Missouri. Used by permission. Memory Day 2014.

The route to becoming a state public policy director was not a straight one for me. Upon graduating with my BSW, I worked as a social worker in a skilled care nursing facility and in an adult day program. In these positions, I was responsible for facilitating support groups, working with older adults and their families, and coordinating admissions and care planning. After relocating with my family, I continued my gerontological social work career in community-based services, working as a program supervisor with an area agency on aging. In this position, I supervised senior center programs in rural communities and had the opportunity to open up several new senior centers in never-before served small communities. From there, it was a natural progression for me to work for the Alzheimer's Association, where I started out working in the respite program, in which I coordinated access to these much-needed services to provide a break for caregivers. These varied experiences gave me both valuable skills in working with persons with dementia and their families and insight into the many different facets of care needed to maintain a quality of life for our older-adult population.

In my current position, I work to improve the laws and policies that govern the services provided to persons with Alzheimer's disease and to advance funding for Alzheimer's research. Alzheimer's disease is the most common form of dementia (the terms are often used interchangeably), a progressive, degenerative disease of the brain for which there is no known cure. Alzheimer's disease affects a person's memory, judgment, and ability to reason. More than five million Americans are living with Alzheimer's disease, impacting the 15.5 million family members and friends who serve as their care partners. A person with dementia will live an average of eight years and as many as 20 years after symptoms first appear. As sufferers advance through the disease process, long-term care and support are critical but can exhaust any care partner from time to time.

My experience as a social worker working with older adults prepared me well for working at the policy level. Having direct practice experience with this population in a variety of settings enables me to understand the needs of older adults and their care partners, the gaps in the service delivery system, and the importance of ensuring that policy decision makers are well informed as they enact legislation and make policy.

The Alzheimer's Association chapters are part of the nation's largest voluntary health organization devoted to conquering Alzheimer's disease. Through a network of more than 70 chapters across the country, all those affected by the disease have access to a broad range of programs and services, and can participate in support for research and advocacy. Because the association is so large, we are able to influence state and federal policies for this population.

State public policy and platform development is a three-phase process:

1. *Issue identification.* As the Alzheimer's Association determines the areas for advocacy, we routinely ask the following questions: What are the greatest unmet needs? Where are the gaps in services? How can we build an enhanced long-term care delivery system to meet the growing demands of an aging population? The answers to these questions come from the voices of persons with the disease and their care partners. Through focus groups, surveys, support group visits, and other

means of communication, the coalition that I direct has identified three current areas of greatest need: (a) enhanced access to a continuum of long-term care services; (b) improved quality of care throughout the long-term care continuum; and (c) a cure for Alzheimer's disease.

2. *Development of potential solutions.* Once a policy agenda is established, the next critical task is to develop potential solutions. This process involves coalition building and networking both internally, within the chapter network, and externally, with interested partners. Health care providers, leaders within state agencies, researchers in the field of aging, and families with a vested interest in the issue are examples of partners that can aid in developing viable solutions and achievable goals. Research is needed, both to learn about effective policies being implemented in other states and to gather data to advance proposed solutions.

3. *Creation of public policy platform.* Building on this process, the coalition collaborates with key stakeholders and experts in policy issues related to persons with dementia to outline a public policy platform that includes goals and objectives addressing the areas of focus. Some of the components necessary to advance a public policy include language for proposed legislation; legislative sponsorship;

public hearings; and a broad base of support made up of constituents, professionals, and legislators. Grassroots advocacy is at the core of this process. When you mobilize people that are passionate about an issue, you can accomplish a great deal.

Every year I travel with other advocates to my state capital and to Washington, DC, to talk with the legislature about appropriations for funding research to find a cure for Alzheimer's disease, to study the effects of the disease on individuals and their families, and to develop interventions to enhance their lives. Along with thousands of supporters, I write letters and e-mails and meet with legislators in the capitols and in their home districts. As a result of these ongoing grassroots advocacy efforts, Congress has increased Alzheimer's research funding to approximately $500 million over a 13-year period. Still, this amount is far short of the federal government's commitment to combat diseases such as stroke, heart disease, HIV/AIDS, and breast cancer, which have all seen death rates decline as a result of an increased investment in research.

A current challenge for the families for whom I advocate is that both Medicare and private health insurance fail to address the chronic health care needs of persons with Alzheimer's disease. Medicaid is the program that serves as the safety net for long-term care services. It supports community-based programs as well as nursing home care. Access to Medicaid services has become a primary area of focus for Alzheimer's advocates. Through grassroots efforts, we have worked to maintain and at times expand options, support, and access to home and community services.

A second area of challenge in my current advocacy work is improving the quality of care provided in long-term care settings. More than half of all residents have some form of dementia. My fellow advocates and I drafted and passed legislation in my state that requires all employees caring for persons with dementia to be trained in dementia care.

Working with a coalition of Alzheimer's Association chapters to shape a public policy platform and mobilizing advocates to move that platform forward has required me to call upon a skill set I acquired earning my BSW and serving for 25 years in the field of aging. Through these experiences I have learned the value of listening to others, the importance of negotiation and compromise, and the merits of networking and coalition building. Perhaps most importantly, I have learned that when many voices come together, they can effect change.

At the current rate of diagnosis and population growth, 14 million Baby Boomers will develop Alzheimer's disease by midcentury. Costs for persons with Alzheimer's disease will continue to increase as well. Annual public spending for Medicare and Medicaid is projected to reach $174 billion by 2020; if current policies stay in place, costs of this magnitude will overwhelm our health care system and bankrupt both Medicare and Medicaid. As the Alzheimer's Association succinctly states, "We are facing a race against time." Now more than ever, there is a need for social workers to engage in public policy advocacy in support of persons with Alzheimer's disease and their care partners. To learn more about the National Plan to Address Alzheimer's Disease, visit: http://aspe. hhs.gov/daltcp/napa/natlplan2014. shtml.

SOCIAL WORK PRACTICE WITH PERSONS WITH DISABILITIES

Throughout history, the concept of "disability" has carried many connotations, often negative, but in the last 50 years perceptions have begun to shift. The emergence of the disability rights movement in the 20th century culminated in the passage of the Americans with Disabilities Act (ADA) in 1990. This landmark legislation mandated easier access and less discrimination in employment, telecommunications, public accommodations, and societal services (Mackelprang et al., 2008, p. 38). The ADA has been expanded twice, in 1997 and 2004, to address educational access and equity. There has been great progress with inclusion, and people with disabilities have been integrated into schools and the community. On a global level, disability is now considered a human rights and social justice issue. In 2001, United Nations General Resolution 56/108 addressed the issue of rights for persons with disabilities around the world. This led to passage in 2007 of the Convention on the Rights of Persons with Disabilities, which has now been adopted by 82 countries (Mackelprang, 2012). The recent passage of the Affordable Care Act (ACA), which provides access to health and wellness care for nearly every U.S. citizen and enables those with disabilities to live in their communities, has also significantly impacted persons living with disabilities (Mackelprang, 2013).

According to current estimates, approximately 10% of the world population, or 650 million people, have disabilities. Nineteen percent of U.S. civilians (with non-military-related disabilities), or 56.7 million people, live with a disability (U.S. Census Bureau, 2014a). Among those, a majority (50%) are older adults, and 20% are female. Those who live with a disability tend to live near or in poverty (23%).

Older Adults

Source: iStock/Silvia Jansen

Disabilities occur primarily in the areas of hearing, vision, memory and thinking, and mobility. Most people will experience at least one disability in their lifetime. With the dramatic increases in people being diagnosed with autism spectrum disorder, social workers in a variety of settings are working with more persons experiencing this disability. Recent findings by the Centers for Disease Control and Prevention (2012) indicate that one in 88 children has been diagnosed with an autism spectrum disorder, an increase of 78% since

2008. This increase may be related to better assessment and diagnostic criteria and tools.

Given the significant segments of our population who are impacted by a disability, social workers must develop competent practice knowledge and skills to work effectively with these individuals and their families. In a policy statement, NASW (2012–2014i) calls for social work curricula to include content on the history, culture, research, best practices, and civil rights issues related to disabilities and to include social workers with disabilities in the professional organization (p. 249). Whether or not social workers choose a practice that focuses on people with disabilities, they will likely have a client, a family members of a client, or a co-worker who has a disability.

Policy-Practice Considerations in Working with People Who Have Disabilities

Social workers have a long history of working with and advocating for persons with disabilities. Currently, social workers work with individuals with all types of disabilities (Mackelprang et al., 2008):

- *Neurocognitive disabilities* involve limited capacities of intellect, memory, sensory integration, and thought processing. These conditions exist along a continuum that includes autism, Down syndrome, developmental disabilities, Alzheimer's disease, and sensory integration dysfunctions.
- *Physical disabilities,* which are typically acquired after birth, create limitations in physical function or activity. They include paraplegia and other mobility limitations, speaking, hearing, and vision challenges, and chronic organ system-related disease.
- *Psychiatric disabilities* result from serious and persistent mental illness (e.g., schizophrenia, anxiety, depression, or bipolar disorder).

As societal perceptions about disabilities have evolved over time, the theoretical concepts for working with individuals with disabilities have become more focused. Contemporary thought has understood disability as a "naturally occurring phenomenon that adds to societal diversity" (Mackelprang et al., 2008, p. 40). The problems that persons with disabilities experience can be framed within the context of society and the systems within which the individual lives. While this theoretical framework is consistent with social work values and ethics, and though antidiscrimination and access policies represent significant strides for persons with disabilities, these persons continue to experience housing, health care, and income benefits challenges (Mackelprang et al., 2008).

The type and extent of the disability may inform the practice approach. However, some general assumptions guide the planning and implementation

---

EXHIBIT 8.4

Principles and Practice Guidelines for Working with People Who Have Disabilities

Principles for Social Work:

- Disability as diversity—acknowledge persons with disabilities as equals.
- Accept social workers who are persons with disabilities as contributing to the profession.
- Assume competence—persons with disabilities are competent to be involved in their decision-making and social workers can advocate for access to needed resources.
- Assume equal worth and value—advocate for anti-ableist attitudes and for social inclusion.
- By using person-first and content-specific terms and joining advocacy efforts, demonstrate social work disability competence, view disability culture as interdependent, self-identifying, and eliminate beliefs that people must "overcome" their disabilities.

Practice Guidelines for Social Work:

- Be person-centered, involving the individual in the decision-making process regarding her or his life.
- Incorporate the strengths-based perspective to build on the client's existing strengths and resources.
- Facilitate access and respect in the person's environment.
- Focus on helping the individual and her or his support network cope with any situation that may be challenging the person.

Source: Mackelprang, 2012; Mackelprang et al., 2008.

---

of all social work interventions involving a person with a disability (see Exhibit 8.4). Being a resource for the disability community by redefining ableist attitudes, providing disability-positive role models, advancing disability as a social justice issue, and learning about and respecting the perspectives of persons with disabilities are aspects of competent social work practice with those with disabilities (Mackelprang, 2012). When these behaviors guide the practice intervention, the social worker may engage in crisis intervention, case management, interprofessional collaboration, and advocacy to support the client in maintaining the optimal quality of life.

Mark A. Keeley, MSW, LCSW, St. Louis Arc

For more than three decades, I have worked with individuals who have intellectual and developmental disabilities and their families. My first interaction with people with developmental disabilities occurred when

I volunteered in high school to help with the Special Olympics in order to avoid taking a math test. I succeeded in avoiding the math test and, more importantly, found my calling and career path. On that spring day, I met many wonderful individuals, from teenagers to adults, who were enjoying the thrill of victory and competition. I began speaking with them and asking them about their lives. At that time, many of the individuals were living in institutions and had little or no family involvement. I wondered who took care of them and advocated for their needs if they were not able to do so for themselves. Within two months, I was working full-time with six adults, two women and four men, who had developmental disabilities and had just moved from an institution to a group home. Additionally, I worked in a respite facility on weekends, which gave me exposure to the support needs of families. I subsequently obtained a bachelors and masters in social work, focusing on supporting people with disabilities.

Throughout my career, my primary focus has been taking a holistic approach to addressing the support needs not only of the individual with a disability but also of her or his entire family. When someone is diagnosed with a disability, everyone in the family is impacted in some way. As the person ages, new challenges emerge and those too impact everyone. Addressing the individual and group needs of a family helps to strengthen the family as a unit and each member individually.

From the beginning, the people with disabilities with whom I have worked have taught me a great deal. They have taught me to see them as the unique individuals they are and to see their disabilities as attributes but not as things that define them. People with disabilities rarely want someone to do everything for them, but appreciate it when someone offers support so they may achieve their own goals.

People with disabilities often experience a sense of isolation. When they are infants and toddlers, people with disabilities can easily coexist with their typically developing peers. As they get older, when school and sports become competitive, there is often an unnecessary divide that separates people with disabilities from those without. Inclusion has dramatically increased over the past 30 years, but people with disabilities are still too often left out of many activities. As social workers, we must continue to work towards full inclusion in school, employment, and the community as a whole.

A challenge for most people with disabilities and their families is the Individualized Education Program (IEP) process they go through in school. Any person with a disability requiring additional supports beyond the standard curriculum will have an IEP. Unfortunately, the IEP process is too often focused on a person's deficits, not their strengths. Most people build upon their own interests and strengths, not on their weaknesses. Most people choose a career that suits their strengths and interests, but the

IEP process focuses on the negatives. The social worker can be an advocate for the strengths.

People with disabilities want the same opportunities as anyone wants in life. They want to be able to live independently, away from their parents. They want to go to college, get a job, have a social life, and have friends and someone to love. With the proper supports, people with disabilities can succeed in achieving their goals.

Social workers and other professionals should never let a person's disability or diagnosis be a predictor of what they may or may not be able to achieve. Too often parents hear that their child will never be able to achieve her or his goals. Parents are told their child will never walk, never talk, or never be able to achieve independence. Time and time again, I have seen individuals surpass the limitations professionals set for them. When Michael Wasserman was born with Down syndrome in November 1961, his young mother was told to take him home and enjoy him, but that he would not live to see Christmas. Michael is alive today and has myriad of medals and achievements highlighting his accomplishments. Today, he is a successful and talented artist who raises funds for charities through the sale of his artwork. Michael's mother, Mary has never let professionals limit what he could achieve.

Sometimes we need to be creative in how we support people to achieve their goals. For example, a man who had significant physical and cognitive disabilities wanted to play professional baseball. Given his physical limitations, realistically he would not qualify for a professional team. The people who supported him explored why he wanted to play professional baseball. It became clear that what he was really interested in was being part of a team and wearing a uniform; he really had no interest in actually playing the game. He is now the assistant coach of a little league team and could not be happier.

Parents learning they are about to have or have had a child with a disability face myriad emotions. Expectant parents dream of having the perfect child. When they receive news that their child has a disability, those dreams are shattered, and they go through cognitive coping to achieve a new dream or dreams for their child's future. Young parents face a tremendous sense of isolation when they do not know any other parents who have a child with a disability. They rely on social workers and other professionals to help them navigate the ever-changing maze of services and supports their child needs. Connecting parents with one another helps address their isolation and builds natural supports for families.

Families need to be educated about the services and supports available to them and their family members throughout the life span. The services that exist for infants and toddlers are different from those available to school-aged children. As children become teenagers, parents face not only the typical challenges of teenagers, but also the challenges that may occur as a result of the person's disability. Parents need help to plan for the future of their son or daughter with a disability. Will they go to college, will they live independently or in a residential setting with others, will they have competitive employment or other day supports? Many parents I have talked to intend to always keep their son or daughter at home. They pray for the ability to always care for their family member and that they may have just "one breath more" than their son or daughter. Social workers need to work with families to develop plans that address the long-term support needs and wishes of the individual and family.

When taking a holistic approach to supporting individuals with developmental disabilities and their families, it is important to remember siblings. Siblings bear a large responsibility when they have a brother or sister with a disability. Siblings, like parents, often experience a tremendous feeling of isolation. They may not know anyone else who has a brother or sister with a disability. Siblings of individuals with disabilities often excel in academics, sports, or hobbies in order to get recognition from their parents and other adults. Sibshops, originated by Don Meyer, are support groups for siblings of individuals with disabilities that offer a high energy, fun way for siblings to meet one another and process their feelings and emotions about having a sibling with a disability.

It is important for parents and social workers to consistently give age-appropriate information to

Wasserman Family Photo

Mary, Al, and Michael Wasserman.

Source: Jay O. Fisk, used by permission.

siblings so they understand the needs of their brother or sister and also so they know what the long-term plans are for the care of their sibling. I have heard 6-year-olds talking about how they will be taking care of their brother or sister for the rest of their or their sibling's life. No child should feel that sense of obligation or responsibility. Parents often have plans for their son or daughter with a disability, but they may not always share those plans with her or his siblings.

A holistic approach to supporting people with disabilities and their families provides them with the tools they need to achieve their individual and family goals. Social workers who support people with disabilities and their families need to offer services that address the unique needs of each individual and family while ensuring the services are flexible enough to address the needs of the community as a whole.

SOCIAL WORK PRACTICE WITH MILITARY FAMILY MEMBERS

Social workers have a long history of working with military personnel, veterans, and their family members in a variety of settings. First trained to work with soldiers returning from World War I in 1918, social workers have been present throughout each military action since then, as well as consistently working on the home front and abroad (CSWE, 2010). Social workers practice in combat zones during deployment activities, on military installations in the United States and throughout the world, in veterans' medical centers and service organizations, and in civilian public and private organizations. Social work practitioners who are themselves on active duty and civilian workers employed by the Department of Defense provide these services.

Just like their civilian colleagues, social workers working in military-related settings with individuals and families connected to the armed services provide an array of services, including (CSWE, 2010, p. 2):

- Direct practice, which can include prevention, treatment, and rehabilitative services, particularly related to combat experiences (e.g., traumatic brain injury, posttraumatic stress, depression, substance abuse, combat stress, readjustment issues, intimate partner violence, and polytrauma (i.e., presence of multiple injuries))
- Policy (practice) and administration
- Advocacy
- Development of programs, policies, and procedures to improve clients' quality of life

■   Assistance and treatment for military members and families as they transition from active duty to veteran status

Their duties may include everything from working in the field with service members to assess morale to working with retirees in a medical center intervention (Angelis, 2012). Families are an integral part of most of these interventions.

Policy-Practice Considerations in Military Social Work

The United States is in the midst of the longest military engagement in our history. As a result, social workers in a variety of settings, regardless of their primary areas of practice, work with military-related issues. Veterans of recent deployments experience higher levels of suicide, mental illness, posttraumatic stress disorder, and substance use and abuse than previous cohorts (Larson, Wooten, Adams, & Merrick, 2012). Social workers possess knowledge and skills in outreach, assessment, and intervention that can be instrumental in responding to the needs of this population along the continuum of care (Larson et al., 2012). Just as with many of the other diverse areas of social work practice, it is critical that social work practitioners gain awareness of, and competence in, the culture of the military community. The military and its related institutions have a specialized language, structure, and hierarchy, which become an important part of the service member's identity and which can be difficult to leave behind when she or he separates from the military. This culture is unfamiliar to most civilians. A social worker now working with veterans and a veteran himself, Don McCasland (2014) offers these suggestions for effective engagement with recent veterans seeking help:

■   Hear and listen to the veteran, regardless of your own level of discomfort regarding the information you are hearing or that you need to complete the assessment process.
■   When a veteran displays hyper-vigilance, which may take the form of wariness of perceived threat in public or new situations, allow her or him to gain control of the environment (e.g., select a seat, leave door open, etc.) to help ease anxieties.
■   Recognize that asking for help is contrary to the veteran's training to be strong and independent. Framing the helping relationship as a team effort may enable the veteran to trust the process.
■   Developing cultural sensitivity to the veteran's value system and being flexible and creative will facilitate an effective helping process.

Identifying a need for such expertise, the CSWE has outlined a competency-based framework for military social work. This collaborative project calls for social workers to raise their awareness regarding the issues affecting the nearly three million individuals who have served in current military actions, as well as their families and support networks. Exhibit 8.5 presents some of the CSWE's guidelines for practice in military social work. Additionally, NASW has issued a set of standards for social work practice with service members, veterans, and their families (NASW, 2012a).

Social workers provide services to active duty personnel, veterans, retirees, and the family members of all these groups during peace time, deployments,

---

EXHIBIT 8.5

Practice Guidelines for Military Social Work

Building on the Council on Social Work Education Educational Policy competencies, advanced practice behaviors for social work practice with military members and families include:

Educational Policy 2.1.1
- Engage in lifelong learning, supervision, and consultation to enhance knowledge and skills needed to work effectively with service members, veterans, their families, and their communities.
- Practice self-reflection and continue to address personal biases and stereotypes to build knowledge and dispel myths regarding service members, veterans, their families, and their communities.

Educational Policy 2.1.2
- Demonstrate a professional demeanor that reflects awareness of and respect for military and veteran cultures.
- Recognize boundary and integration issues between military and veteran cultures and social work values and ethics.

Educational Policy 2.1.3
- Employ strategies of ethical reasoning in an environment that may have policy and value conflicts with social work service delivery, personal values, and professional ethics.
- Identify the military culture's emphasis on mission readiness, support of service, honor, and cohesion and how these influence social work service delivery at the micro, mezzo, and macro levels.
- Recognize and manage appropriate professional boundaries within the military and veteran context.

Educational Policy 2.1.4
- Analyze the unique relationships among the client, the family, the military, and various veterans' organizations.
- Use professional judgment to meet the needs of all involved clients.

- Analyze appropriate models of assessment, prevention, intervention, and evaluation within the context of military social work.
- Use appropriate practice models with service members, veterans, their families, and their communities.
- Demonstrate effective oral and written communication using established DoD/VA professional standards and practices.

Educational Policy 2.1.5

- Manage potential conflicts between diverse identities within and among individuals and the military and veterans' organizations.
- Manage potential conflicts between personal feelings/expression and collective/institutional responsibility.
- Recognize the potential risk and protective factors among diverse populations and communities that may be the result of military service.
- Communicate with a culturally responsive approach that includes service members with varying statuses such as active duty/retired, guard/reserves, and combat/garrison.

Educational Policy 2.1.6

- Identify and analyze conflictual responses and potential consequences to conflicts between basic human rights and military life and duty experience.
- Advocate at multiple levels for service parity and reduction of service disparities for the diverse service member populations.
- Identify the needs of military and veteran individuals, families, and communities to civilian providers and workplace management.
- Teach skills to promote self-sufficiency, self-advocacy, and empowerment within the context of practice and culture.

Educational Policy 2.1.7

- Locate, evaluate, and analyze current research literature related to military social work.
- Evaluate research to practice with service members, veterans, families, and their communities.
- Analyze models of assessment, prevention, intervention, and evaluation within the context of military social work.
- Apply different literature and evidence-informed and evidence-based practices in the provision of services across the DoD/VA continuum of care and services.

Educational Policy 2.1.8

- Recognize and assess social support systems and socioeconomic resources specific to service members, veterans, their families, and their communities.
- Recognize the impact of military transitions and stressful life events throughout the family's life course.
- Identify issues related to losses, stressors, changes, and transitions over their life cycle in designing interventions.
- Demonstrate the ability to critically appraise the impact of the social environment on the overall well-being of service members, veterans, their families, and their communities.

Educational Policy 2.1.9

- Communicate effectively with various veterans' service organizations to provide effective social work services and accurate benefits, entitlements, and services information to clients, their family members, and their communities.

- Apply knowledge of the Uniform Code of Military Justice.
- Use social policy analysis as a basis for action and advocacy with the chain of command and within federal agencies.
- Respond to civilian and governmental inquiries (e.g., congressional inquiry).

Educational Policy 2.1.10

- Assess service systems' history, trends, and innovations in social work practice with service members, veterans, their families, and/or their communities.
- Apply knowledge of practice within the military context to the development of evaluations, prevention plans, and treatment strategies.
- Use information technologies and organizational analysis techniques for outreach, planning multiyear projections, for service delivery to service members and the veteran populations as well as to their families and their communities.
- Recognize the unique issues and culture presented by the service member, veteran, and/or family member client.
- Establish a culturally responsive therapeutic relationship that addresses the unique issues associated with confidentiality and reporting requirements within a military context.
- Explain the nature, limits, rights, and responsibilities of the client who seeks services.
- Explain the stigma, risks, and benefits of seeking or not seeking services.
- Engage with military leadership, the unit, veteran service organizations, and/or family members.
- Demonstrate a knowledge base related to risk and protective factors associated with deployment, military service, and other aspects of life and role transitions that service members and veterans experience.
- Demonstrate knowledge related to health and mental health illnesses, injuries, and outcomes for service members, veterans, their families, and their communities.
- Select and modify appropriate multisystemic intervention strategies based on continuous clinical assessment of military or veteran issues.
- Use differential and multiaxial diagnoses that take into consideration signature injuries as well as other military related illnesses and injuries.
- Use empathy, cultural responsiveness, and other interpersonal skills in completing an assessment.
- Assess coping strategies to reinforce and improve adaptation to life situations and transitions while also emphasizing ways of coping with readjustment from military to civilian life.
- Use a range of appropriate clinical and preventive interventions for various injuries, diagnoses, and psychosocial concerns identified in the assessment, including crisis intervention and advocacy strategies as needed.
- Engage clients in ongoing monitoring and evaluation of practice processes and outcomes.
- Demonstrate the capacity to reflect on one's own responses (i.e., affect and world views) that influence the progress in and the completion of treatment.
- Use clinical and program evaluation of the process and/or outcomes to develop best practice interventions and programs for a range of biopsycho-social-spiritual conditions and evaluate their own practice to determine the effectiveness of the applied intervention on military/ veteran issues.

Source: CSWE, 2010.

and following the veteran's time of service. Social workers can help support military-related clients during times of transitions and crises related to military service, but also for non-military-related needs (e.g., health events, end-of-life issues, or school-related problems). While military personnel and families experience the same life issues as others, they face unique challenges, particularly during times of deployment. Having a family member, especially a parent, serving in a combat zone can cause a child physical and emotional stress and behavioral and school-related problems. Providing family-oriented interventions in which parents learn to work with their children through play, for instance, can be an effective strategy for helping children adjust to their parent's deployment (Chawla & Solinas-Saunders, 2011).

Monica M. Matthieu, Ph.D., LCSW, Research Social Worker, Department of Veterans Affairs

In my nearly twenty years as a social worker, I have had the opportunity to work with Veterans and their families in two distinct social work roles—as a direct social work practitioner and as a researcher. My MSW provided me with a strong background in systems and ecological theories, clinical practice models, and therapeutic interventions. Hence, I wanted my first "real" social work job to focus on conducting clinical assessments and providing cognitive behavioral therapy. After attaining my MSW from Tulane University, I accepted a clinical social work position in the Department of Veterans Affairs, Veterans Health Administration, Readjustment Counseling Service's Vet Center program, one of nearly 300 community-based counseling centers across the U.S. (www.vetcenter.va.gov). This amazing job provided me with the opportunity to hone my developing clinical skills with a challenging and often underserved population of veterans and their families who had served in combat operations from World War II to the Persian Gulf, while enhancing my knowledge about social work roles in administration and policy by working for the federal government.

My interest in mental health assessments, trauma-focused treatments, outreach, and community mental health services grew over the five and a half years I delivered therapeutic and psychosocial interventions to aging veterans (and their families) recently returned from the Persian Gulf who were struggling to transition back home and to resume career and/or educational pursuits. At the New Orleans Vet Center, I conducted thousands of assessments with veterans from every major recent military conflict, and led daily individual therapy focused on combat and sexual trauma and weekly group therapy sessions with Vietnam combat veterans. My 200+

caseload was predominately African American and Caucasian combat vets, due in part to the central location of the Vet Center in New Orleans and to our burgeoning fee contract program that covered all of south Louisiana. I provided ongoing therapeutic and psychosocial interventions for clients with serious mental illness (SMI), which were some of my first encounters with suicidal clients. When I was promoted to Clinical Coordinator of the Vet Center, with additional administrative and program development duties, I began in-depth work coordinating care across multiple Veterans Administration (VA) treatment programs for veterans with SMI, a population at great risk of suicide due to their struggles with depression, manic depressive disorder, and schizo-affective disorders.

I was also responsible for assisting with the redesign of outreach programs for Vet Center services, sexual trauma eligibility, and PTSD counseling services to varied veteran populations spanning multiple generations and diverse ethnic communities. My emerging clinical interest and results from the programs we created from the needs assessments we gathered informally from our local communities guided our decisions regarding who and where to target Vet Center outreach efforts. These approaches targeted those veterans at critical developmental or stressful transitional points occurring across the life course, such as returning from war to resume college or retiring from the military. These novel outreach

programs gave me experience in approaching the world of academia and the military, which again revealed the need for multi-system, comprehensive psychosocial and healthcare services for Veterans. Because clinical service delivery was of paramount importance to me, I had relatively little time to devote to evaluating the programs we created, and my skill in integrating program results with clinical outcomes was lacking.

My worldview dramatically expanded when I volunteered to do national disaster response mental health work for the VA. Getting my LCSW and becoming eligible for the disaster mental health (DMH) training with the American Red Cross (ARC) led me to become a DMH volunteer. Prior to being called up for a two-week federal government response to tornados in Oklahoma, I volunteered locally with the ARC during hurricane and flood season. DMH work always involved very brief mental health assessments, jumping in and out of the ARC trucks, providing community resource information, and debriefing ARC volunteers who appeared overextended or were leaving to go home. This initial population-based crisis counseling experience sparked my interest in providing mental health services to stressed and traumatized populations, prevention of PTSD among disaster victims, and the impact of multiple disaster assignments on volunteers. As I returned to clinical practice at the Vet Center, I again struggled with my lack of expertise or skills to evaluate the work I had done or to research the questions I had about delivering disaster response mental health services.

Clinical work was satisfying, yet my desire to contribute to the field of social work more broadly and my own curiosity to learn more about preventing the chronic mental health conditions I treated led me back to school. I left the VA and the New Orleans Vet Center to pursue my Ph.D. in social work at Columbia University, a degree choice that would allow me to focus entirely on prevention and mental health research. A Ph.D. in social work is a program devoted to integrating previous clinical practice experience with advanced research training. By 2004, I completed this challenging doctoral program, focusing on my areas of research and clinical interest topics in suicide prevention, mental health services research, and trauma treatment.

My path to the world of research began here, with my second "real" job as a social work researcher. I joined the faculty at the University of Rochester Medical Center as a Senior Instructor and received postdoctoral training in suicide prevention research at the Center for the Study and Prevention of Suicide. It was in my "post doc" that I returned to what I knew the best, clinical service delivery with veterans. For three years, I studied suicide prevention and conducted research with my mentor on translating the innovative techniques utilized in the suicide prevention program model derived from the U.S. Air Force into other settings such as

in a psychiatry department, in colleges, with VA clinical providers in healthcare settings, and with VA clinical, administrative, and outreach workers in community-based counseling centers (Vet Centers).

I have returned to work part-time at the VA, maintain a full-time faculty position at Saint Louis University, and have completed a number of VA suicide prevention studies in collaboration with the national Vet Center program, Veterans Integrated Healthcare Network 2, the Veterans Benefits Administration, and with community and clinical stakeholders in Missouri. I work as a Research Social Worker at the VA St. Louis Health Care System and serve as a Co-Implementation Research Coordinator for the Mental Health Quality Enhancement Research Initiative (QUERI) for the PTSD and Suicide Prevention Coalitions. Really, my job is to co-facilitate two national-level coalitions comprised of VA clinicians, operations managers, researchers, quality improvement experts, and non-VA academic experts in PTSD and Suicide Prevention for the Mental Health QUERI, the VA's leading implementation science research center focused on mental health. I am also the Director of the VA's Patient Safety Center of Inquiry on Suicide Prevention, a clinical innovation and dissemination center focused on safety planning interventions to help prevent suicide among veterans.

Looking back, I realize how much I have learned about the social work profession and the various roles social workers can play in the lives of veterans and their families. Twenty years later, it feels like my career has come full circle. I have always focused on serving veterans and their families, first as a clinical social worker in direct practice providing trauma therapy, and now as a social work researcher studying how to implement evidence-based practices for suicide prevention and trauma treatment in routine VA care settings. Going forward, I am mentoring the next generation of social work professionals to serve their country, albeit never in uniform, to be professional social workers with a mission-centric career in the Department of Veterans Affairs.

James Allen, Ph.D., MSW, U.S. Army (Retired)

I have been practicing social work for 43 years. For 20 of those years, I served as a social work officer in the U.S. Army. During that time, I was a member of a military family and provided service to other military families. This experience shaped my understanding of how military life impacts families and the most appropriate means of responding to their needs.

The designation "military family" may suggest that these families are significantly different from others. Understanding military families, however, begins by considering the critical dimensions relevant for all families. Communication is among the most important of these dimensions. Effective communication enhances the ability of families to deal appropriately with the challenges they face. Families that communicate effectively are better able to cope with challenges in a healthy manner. The ability of family members to talk and listen creates an environment in which each person feels valued. Being valued, in turn, increases the likelihood that members will actively participate in developing strategies to deal with expected and unexpected challenges. Given the importance of effective communication, it is critical that we assist all families in examining their communication patterns and finding ways to enhance them.

One of the most significant challenges facing military families is the deployment of a family member, particularly to a combat zone. This event typically generates significant feelings on the part of all members of the family and household. Given the role of deployed service members, the family may confront multiple fears. It is particularly important that the social worker help the family acknowledge and address these fears. Openly dealing with these fears is challenging. The social worker has no power to change the situation, but creating an environment in which members feel free to talk about their feelings helps them to deal with the reality in a healthy manner. Open communication also allows family members to talk about necessary strategies to deal with the impact of the deployment.

All families are organized in a certain way. Individual members are assigned particular roles. Military families are no different. In some families, roles are strictly defined. Each member knows her or his role and its associated responsibilities. Rigidly defined roles may enable families to deal with their current situation effectively but may also make it difficult for them to deal with changes, such as the deployment of a family member. Family members may find themselves being called on to assume roles and responsibilities that are new to them.

Trying to address this crisis in a short time frame can be overwhelming. Failure to make the adjustment, however, can further complicate the family's ability to maintain a sense of balance. Working with families to create a more balanced sharing of responsibilities can increase flexibility and prepare them to make the necessary accommodations the absence of a family member requires.

An important dimension associated with roles is that of decision making. There are always decisions to be made. Ideally, families develop patterns that maximize the involvement of all members as appropriate. Creating such an environment when all members are present increases the likelihood that the family will be able to make needed decisions when one or more members is absent. The crisis the deployment of a key decision maker creates disrupts the balance

of the family and produces trauma. With this in mind, families should be invited to examine their decision-making strategies carefully and to consider alternative approaches that will allow them to maintain the needed balance.

Many military families include children. Changes in the family, both anticipated and unanticipated, affect these children profoundly, and they often have difficulty communicating the impact of these events. If parents do not try to draw their children into the conversation, the children's feelings go unaddressed. At times, these feelings become overwhelming and children express them behaviorally. When this happens, children's behavior may be misunderstood. In such situations, social workers can advocate for the children. We can encourage parents to recognize children's feelings and to help them develop ways of encouraging children to share their thoughts and feelings. Creating such opportunities can help reduce tension within the family and enable them to deal more effectively with the demands of the situation.

While similar to nonmilitary families in many respects, it is important that the social worker acknowledge the impact of unique experiences on military families. In particular, the impact of combat deployment on the family must be addressed. The high incidence of PTSD among combat veterans and their families is well documented. The high rate of domestic violence is an area of particular concern. Studies indicate that 80% of service members diagnosed with PTSD have engaged in at least one act of violence. This incidence is fourteen times higher than that found in the general population. One half of these violent acts are considered severe, involving strangulation, stabbing, or shooting. This reality is further complicated by combat veterans' frequent use of alcohol and prescription drugs. Again, usage rates among combat veterans are higher than those among civilians. The impact of domestic violence on all family members cannot be overstated. Those working with military families must, therefore, be knowledgeable about assessing and intervening in domestic violence situations.

As in all social work, it is important to adopt a strengths perspective when working with military families. This perspective focuses on helping families recognize their strengths and resources. It also encourages them to examine ways in which they can use these strengths and resources to confront current and future challenges. Asking families to identify those strategies that have helped them to address challenges in the past is a starting point. Recognizing that they have coped in the past helps to relieve some of the anxiety associated with the current situation.

Social workers can also help families identify resources in the community that can assist them. A sense of community among military families is a major strength. Families tend to come together, both formally and informally, to support one other as they deal with shared challenges. Encouraging families to connect with others can help them overcome a sense of isolation.

While military families may share much in common, each family is unique. From the outset, it is critical to recognize individual differences. With this in mind, social workers can view the family as the "experts" and help them to reflect on their own experience and consider lessons learned that can help them deal with current challenges.

Military families are more like than unlike other families. To work effectively with them, social workers must apply the same theoretical and practice frameworks that we use in working with all families.

SOCIAL WORK PRACTICE WITH IMMIGRANTS AND REFUGEES

The number of current U.S. residents born in other countries exceeded 40 million in 2011 (Pew Research Center Hispanic Trends Project, 2013). They may be in the United States as refugees or asylum seekers; be here on an immigrant, student, business, or extended visa; or live here without documentation (there were approximately 12 million undocumented immigrants in the United States in 2011). Exhibit 8.6 shows where they have come from; in recent years, most immigrants have come from Asia (Walters & Trevelyan, 2011).

EXHIBIT 8.6

Where U.S. Immigrants and Refugees Were Born

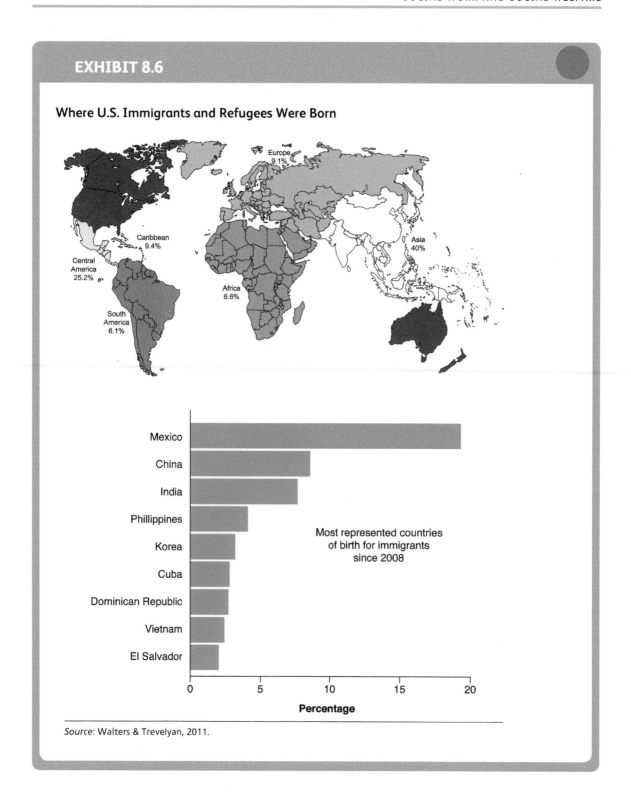

Source: Walters & Trevelyan, 2011.

Policy-Practice Considerations with Immigrants and Refugees

Social workers in the United States have always worked with an array of international issues, including providing services to people who immigrate to this country from their homelands. Social workers work with persons living in countries outside the United States as well as persons living in the United States who were born in other countries. To be a social worker with a global focus you need not work outside the United States. In the area of international adoptions, social workers assist families with applications, conduct home studies, act as liaison to the international adoption organization, and provide post-adoption support services. Social workers also provide services in international emergency and disaster situations and in administering U.S.-based programs that provide services in the international community.

In addition to working with international issues, social workers play a prominent role in working with immigrants and refugees living in the United States. The settlement house movement originally focused on the provision of services to recent immigrants to the United States. Training culturally competent social workers sensitive to the needs of the many and varied populations of persons that are new to this country is a priority for the profession. Nearly one million persons became lawful permanent residents in 2013, with their top three countries of birth being Mexico, China, and India (Monger & Yankay, 2014). Refugee-focused legislation has been in place in the United States since 1948, when nearly a half million post-World War II refugees were admitted (Martin & Yankay, 2012). Such legislation has been amended throughout the decades as refugees' needs are identified. Despite caps being imposed on the numbers of immigrant and originating countries, refugee entry to the United States has consistently grown, with a significant and long-lasting decrease in the period following September 11, 2001 (Martin & Yankay, 2012). Countries from which the largest numbers of refugees are currently beginning their journeys include Burma (30%), Bhutan (27%), and Iraq (17%) (Martin & Yankay, 2012). From another perspective, the U.S. is the most frequent destination in the world for immigrants, and immigrants comprise 13% of the current U.S. population (Pew Research Center Hispanic Trends Project, 2013).

Persons born in other countries span the spectrum of the social work client population, thus requiring U.S.-based social workers in virtually every field of practice to have the knowledge and skills to practice with diverse populations. In direct practice, social workers may work with individuals and families that have immigrated to this country. In policy work, social workers may advocate on behalf of entire communities of persons who have relocated to the United States. Immigration-related policies and practices have long been controversial, particularly in the partisan political arena, which often results in slow or little progress (Lusk, 2013). Immigration policies are often conflicted, thus creating a need for social workers to become the voice for new residents. NASW has called for the federal government to support immigrants and refugees through the enactment of legislation and programming that ensures fair and equitable actions on the part of government agencies (NASW, 2012–2014f). Consider the changing demographic status of children living in immigrant and refugee families, who comprise the fastest-growing segment of the population. These children are at elevated risk of living in poverty and experiencing educational and health care deficits (Society for Research in Child Development, 2008). Social workers are well positioned to advocate for improved and more culturally-focused services for these children and their families. Social workers who work with children of immigrants who may be detained or deported must be culturally-responsive and develop a working knowledge of immigration terms, laws, and policies (Meruvia, 2014).

Suzanne LeLaurin, MSW, LCSW, International Institute

I am a social worker who works with persons who have emigrated from other countries to the United States. I am the senior vice president for programs at an international social services agency and the president of that organization's subsidiary for community development. I oversee several departments that provide a variety of services to immigrants and their families. In the client services department, we provide case management, employment, social work, and counseling services for newly arrived refugees, human trafficking survivors, and other immigrants. The education department is responsible for teaching English to speakers of other languages, as well as computer skills and preparation for citizenship. The economic development department provides microloans to immigrant and refugee entrepreneurs who have difficulty accessing capital from mainstream banks, as well as individual development accounts to help them save towards higher education, start a business, come up with a down-payment for a home, or purchase of a car. The program development and quality assurance department is responsible for continuous quality improvement and staff training on grant requirements.

Social work is a second career for me. After spending over 20 years in the for-profit sector working for a large insurance company, I decided I wanted to work in the nonprofit sector, and chose to get my MSW because I want to help others gain access to needed services and enhance their quality of life. Since completing my MSW, I have obtained my license to practice clinical social work in my state.

In reflecting on my social work practice working with persons born in other countries, I must emphasize the importance of advocacy. The United States is a nation of immigrants, but as a society, we have conflicting views about the importance of immigrants to our country. In the mid-1990s, Congress passed legislation that restricted access for noncitizens who entered the United States legally to certain benefits available to U.S. citizens. Since then, a number of initiatives have sought to ease those restrictions, especially since they were harming some of the most vulnerable persons in our society—seniors who were unable to learn English sufficiently to obtain citizenship and who were increasingly at risk of homelessness as well as despair (which pushed some of them to suicide). Much national debate has centered on how to reform our immigration system. Regardless of one's political persuasion, most see our immigration system as badly broken.

With the terrorist attacks on the United States on 9/11/2001 and the surge of Central American unaccompanied minors across our borders in 2014, many who had welcomed immigrants to our shores shifted their stances once again. Security has tightened for all immigrants attempting to enter the United States. The effects of this heightened security have been most pronounced for refugees—the largest population with which I work. In the wake of 9/11, the number of refugees admitted dropped from almost 70,000 in fiscal year 2001 to fewer than 30,000 in 2002. After 9/11, my agency worked with an advocacy group to accompany our clients to farmers' markets and doctors' appointments, to protect them from shouts of "go home, terrorist" and worse. One of my own staff, a former refugee herself, slept with her clothes on and a stick and her cell phone with her, for fear of intruders. While the impact of 9/11 has now eased somewhat and refugee resettlement is back to the 70,000 level, 2014 saw the explosion of a humanitarian crisis, with tens of thousands of unaccompanied minors crossing our southern border for temporary asylum from Central America. Once again we are faced with deep questions about the role of immigrants in the U.S.

The needs of employers are beginning to counterbalance the political forces seeking to keep immigrants out of the U.S. With the Baby Boom generation aging and U.S. birth rates continuing to decrease, employers and policy experts now recognize that future growth in employment forces will depend on migration into our country. But during the recession of 2008–11, job opportunities were drying up for both American-born and foreign-born residents.

For those social workers interested in working with persons with diverse national origins, there will be many opportunities to provide a variety of social work services for refugees, those who are forced to flee their homelands due to civil unrest, persecution, and violence. These persons are considered "reluctant immigrants," as they did not choose to leave their homelands, but were forced to do so by circumstances beyond their control. Typically, they arrive with little more than the clothes on their backs. This population will continue to need our support in basic necessities (food, clothing, and shelter), learning the English language, employment, adapting to U.S. culture (while hopefully holding on to the richness of their own culture), and mental health services for coming to terms with the horrors of trauma and torture. These needs will also exist for migrant workers who come into the United States intent on making enough money to support their families, and who risk being exploited by unscrupulous employers who would take advantage of their undocumented status. Other immigrants arriving to join family or for employment also may benefit from social work support as they adjust to their new home, learn skills to adapt to a western workplace, navigate our complex health care system, learn how the U.S. education systems work, and adapt in other ways to U.S. culture.

Increasingly, cultural competence training for social workers born in the United States must define cultural diversity based not on traditional black-white-indigenous population categories but on ethnicity. Diversity in U.S. religious communities beyond the dominant Judeo-Christian faiths is growing, and social workers need to be trained to work with this wide variety of religious groups.

Social work services must also adapt to accommodate the needs of individuals who adhere to varying cultural norms. Social workers reflect on their practice. For example, I asked myself: "How do I, as a feminist, react to and serve a conservative Muslim woman who considers it immodest to show any parts of her body other than her hands and face even though her clothing limits her ability to work in the only job I can find for her, a manufacturing position that requires that her clothing not get in the way of machines? How do I work with teenagers and parents experiencing family conflicts in which the teens take the American view that adolescence is a time to "move away" from parents and become independent, while the parents hold to their cultural view that youthful independence brings great shame on the family within their cultural community? How do I counsel an adult woman who considers the idea of putting her aging mother in a skilled nursing facility a shameful rejection of her responsibilities as a dutiful and respectful daughter? Is self-esteem a western construct, or does it apply in a culture that is more collectivist than individualistic, one in which the individual is subordinate to a larger group? As a supervisor, can I see promotion opportunities for my foreign-born employees, even though they come from cultures in which employees would never offer their own ideas, lest they be seen as disrespecting their superiors?"

The great joy—and challenge— of working with persons from diverse national origins is that they help me see the world through a cultural and political lens that, because it is influenced by their own life experiences, cultural norms, and beliefs, is different from my own. I am in awe of the resilience and spirit of refugees who come to this country, prepared to build a whole new life. And I marvel at the entrepreneurial spirit of those who leave the comfort of their homes and families to advance their education or their career. I am challenged to see the world through another person's eyes, and I find myself questioning some of my own deeply held assumptions about my country and culture. The world has gotten so much smaller—and more exciting—for me after working with an international population.

SOCIAL WORK PRACTICE WITH SUBSTANCE ABUSE AND ADDICTION

Substance abuse and addiction treatment has undergone dramatic changes in recent years. Early substance abuse treatment efforts focused primarily on the rehabilitation of persons addicted to alcohol. Treatment came in the form of Alcoholics Anonymous, a model focused on mutual peer support.

Substance use and abuse are widespread in the United States. In 2012, the Substance Abuse and Mental Health Services Administration estimated that over 22 million teens and adults were dependent on alcohol and/or illicit drugs, an increase from the previous year (SAMHSA, 2013b). Of the 22 million Americans who experience an addiction to drugs or alcohol, a mere 10% receive treatment (Open Society Foundations, 2010; SAMHSA, 2013b). Individuals report that they choose not to seek treatment because: they lack appropriate health care coverage (nearly half), they are not ready to seek treatment or believe treatment is unneeded (40%), they lack transportation (10%), or they believe treatment would have a negative impact on their employment or their neighbors/community (17%). In the 1970s, inpatient programs emerged to treat alcoholism and other drug addictions. Because most health insurance companies covered only a small portion of the costs associated with these programs, many were eliminated.

Though inpatient substance abuse treatment often achieves positive results (e.g., improved health and employment and reduced crime), most addiction treatment is provided through outpatient programs. Community-based treatment programs commonly use one of three evidence-based intervention approaches: (1) Primary prevention, including harm reduction, school-based psychoeducational prevention programs, environmental prevention (e.g., public education), and changing social norms (e.g., drug-free zones); (2) Secondary (treatment) interventions, including pharmacotherapy, motivational interviewing, cognitive behavioral therapy, relapse prevention, and family therapy; and (3) Tertiary community-based interventions, including community reinforcement, nonconfrontational motivational strategies, drug courts, and therapeutic communities (i.e., long-term, structured programs that include the 12-step model) (see Matto, 2012). Despite improving treatment options, clients may experience relapse, mental and physical health problems related to the substance abuse, and co-occurring disorders (Begun, 2013).

Policy-Practice Considerations in Substance Abuse and Addiction

A relatively small number of social workers identify substance abuse (also referred to as alcohol, tobacco, and other drugs (ATOD)) as their primary area of practice. Fewer than 5% of NASW members surveyed indicated addictions as their primary practice area (Whitaker & Arrington, 2008). Social workers who work in chemical dependency and addiction treatment programs are typically employed by private for-profit or nonprofit organizations. Due to increased need and coverage for treatment, employment for social workers in this area is expected to increase by approximately 23% in the coming years (U.S. Department of Labor, Bureau of Labor Statistics (BLS), 2014b).

Substance use and abuse and addiction issues frequently overlap with mental illness, domestic violence, and corrections; therefore, social workers in these areas must be able to identify signs of chemical dependency and addiction. So, while only a small percentage of social workers practice exclusively in the field of chemical dependency and addiction treatment, knowledge of addiction prevention and intervention is critical for social workers in virtually every field of practice. NASW's (2013c) *Standards for Social Work Practice with Clients with Substance Use Disorders* (see Exhibit 8.7) provide guidelines for understanding addictions, carrying out appropriate and ethical interventions, and advocating and educating for client systems. These guidelines are grounded in standard social work practices, including listening to the client and getting to know her or his story, goals, resources, and coping strategies, particularly as they relate to the potential for relapse (Littrell, 2011).

Dual diagnosis
Co-occurrence of two disease processes or conditions.

Co-occurring disorders
Co-occurrence of two disease processes.

Dual diagnoses are common in this area of social work practice. Dual diagnosis or co-occurring disorders occur when a person is experiencing two diseases or conditions simultaneously, and the interaction of the two diseases can impede diagnosis and treatment. Chemical dependence often co-occurs with mental illness, and these co-occurrences are increasing, possibly due to increased substance use and/or enhanced awareness of the underlying causes of mental health and substance abuse issues. Approximately 5 % of the U.S. adult population experiences a serious mental illness in a given year, and over one-fourth of those individuals also experience co-occurring substance dependence

EXHIBIT 8.7

Standards for Social Work Practice with Clients with Substance Abuse Disorders

Standard 1. Ethics and Values
Social workers working with clients with substance use disorders shall adhere to the ethics and values of the social work profession and shall use the NASW *Code of Ethics* as a guide to ethical decision making, while understanding the unique aspects of social work practice with clients with substance use disorders and the needs of clients and their families.

Standard 2. Qualifications
Social workers shall meet the provisions for professional practice set by NASW and related state and federal laws while possessing knowledge and understanding basic to the social work profession with regard to professional practice with clients with substance use disorders.

Standard 3. Assessment
Social workers shall conduct ongoing assessments of clients to provide clients with substance use disorders with appropriate diagnoses and treatment plans.

Standard 4. Intervention
Social workers shall be knowledgeable of and incorporate information based on assessment and evidence-informed practices in their interventions.

Standard 5. Decision Making and Practice Evaluation
Social workers shall use data to guide service delivery and to evaluate their practice regularly to improve and expand client services.

Standard 6. Record Keeping
Social workers shall maintain appropriate and accurate data and records that are relevant to planning, implementation, and evaluation of social work services, in accordance with professional ethics and local, state, and federal mandates.

Standard 7. Workload Management
Social workers shall organize their workloads so as to fulfill their responsibilities and clarify their critical roles while providing services to clients with substance use disorders.

Standard 8. Professional Development
Social workers shall pursue continuous enhancement of knowledge and skills to provide the most current, beneficial, and culturally appropriate services to clients with substance use disorders and their families.

Standard 9. Cultural Competence

Social workers shall ensure that all clients and their families are provided with services within a context of cultural understanding and competence.

Standard 10. Interdisciplinary Leadership and Collaboration

Social workers shall provide leadership in developing positive treatment environments, supervision of other professionals, administrative direction, and research and treatment relating to substance use disorders.

Standard 11. Advocacy

Social workers shall engage in advocacy that seeks to ensure that clients with substance use disorders and their families have equal access to the appropriate services in a timely manner.

Standard 12. Collaboration

Social workers shall promote interdisciplinary and interorganizational collaboration to support, enhance, and deliver effective services to clients with substance use disorders and their families.

Source: NASW, 2013a.

or abuse (Substance Abuse and Mental Health Services Administration, 2013a). Because of the increasing presence of these co-occurring conditions, social workers must develop awareness and practice skills in both mental health and addictions treatment. Two federal agencies, Substance Abuse and Mental Health Services Administration and Health Resources and Services Administration, have developed SBIRT (Screening, brief intervention, and referral to treatment), an evidence-based framework that provides a streamlined, effective process by which practitioners can identify substance abuse and match clients with appropriate community-based services (Steenrod, 2014). To read more about SBIRT, visit: www.integration.samhsa.gov/clinical-practice/sbirt.

Jon Hudson, Ph.D., MSW, Chestnut Health Systems, Inc.

I am sharing my experience as a BSW student completing my practicum at Chestnut, a large agency that provides residential treatment for adolescents with chemical dependency issues. At the time, I planned to continue on to complete a master's degree, practice clinical social work, and return to school for a doctorate degree in social work. My practicum experience was very valuable, because clinical social work often involves issues of chemical dependency.

The residential population at my practicum site is separated by gender. Clients range in age from 13 to 17 years and stay an average of 90 days. The program provides clients and their families with education, counseling for substance use and mental health issues, and medication for mental health issues when necessary. Nearly all clients are court-mandated to receive treatment, however, the reasons for their sentences are not always directly related to substance use. More often, clients were arrested for other reasons and discovered to be under the influence of chemical substances at the time of their arrest. In the male unit where I work, most of the boys are from modest socioeconomic backgrounds, and their education has been interrupted as a result of interactions with the criminal justice system and a lack of family support. Programs such as the one at Chestnut provide judges with sentencing alternatives for young people who become entangled in the criminal justice system. The young person's arrest may be an opportunity to introduce her or him to needed treatment and healthy recovery. This type of intervention may interrupt a potential maladaptive pattern of substance use and abuse and prevent future legal entanglements.

I work as a primary counselor, providing treatment to individual residential clients and their families, facilitating group therapy, and working with the other counselors to maintain the daily routine of the unit. The daily routine includes accompanying the male residents as they move between their school classes, between class and recreation (either outdoors or in the gymnasium), and from the dormitory to the cafeteria for meals.

During the assessment process, some of the boys are dually diagnosed with mental illness and chemical dependence. Working with persons who are dually diagnosed presents special treatment challenges as both mental illness and chemical dependence issues must be addressed simultaneously.

For these boys, treatment usually consists of working with both a primary counselor and the staff psychiatrist, who provides medication and medication management. The counselor must balance the three main aspects of the client's case at all times: the clinical diagnoses, the legal issues often connected to the case, and the issues each boy's family must process during his time in treatment.

Clients and their families may be surprised by a dual diagnosis. They may not have been aware of the existence of a mental health issue. They may need help adjusting to the diagnosis and processing their reactions to it. Often boys enter treatment unwillingly, not knowing what to expect from a residential treatment program. A dual diagnoses adds to that stress. That, coupled with withdrawal from substances, may cause decompensation (i.e., inability to maintain emotional stability) immediately following entry into treatment. It can be heartbreaking to see a boy who already feels forced into treatment face a diagnosis of mental illness.

In my short time at Chestnut, I have learned that issues of chemical dependence are multi-dimensional. For example, many substances require longer periods of time than other substances to clear the body's natural chemical systems. This can result in the need for extended periods of time in treatment. Research shows that the amount of time a person is actively engaged in recovery predicts the duration of his or her abstinence from substance use. Also, not all models of substance treatment are based on the same assumptions.

Traditional treatment models are based on the 12 steps of Alcoholics Anonymous, a model that has been effective for millions of people since its inception in the 1930s. The primary goal of these models is complete abstinence. It dictates that, before moving forward with the program, substance users must stop using chemicals and admit that they are chemically dependent and powerless over their substance of choice. While the 12-step model has been effective for many as a *self-help* model, it has been criticized as a *treatment* model because of the requirement that one must stop using substances in order to continue in the recovery process. The expectation that a person stop using substances in order to remain in treatment for substance use, particularly given the admission that users are powerless over their substance of choice, is self-defeating and should not be a requirement to be in treatment.

Client-centered models rooted in harm reduction theory are gaining purchase in chemical dependence treatment in the United States. These models recognize the importance of continued engagement in treatment and encourage clients to prioritize well-defined goals and focus on progress.

A needle exchange program in a city where the incidence of intravenous drug use is high is one example of a harm reduction program. Needle exchanges supply new needles to I.V. drug users free of charge at a central location in exchange for used needles. When needles are exchanged, the programs offer information about drug treatment services, housing and shelter, food, and other daily needs. These programs reduce the incidence of communicable diseases spread by the sharing and reusing of needles. But connecting users with treatment, food, and shelter, these programs also help reduce misdemeanor crime.

Harm reduction treatment does not require total abstinence unless that is the client's goal. For example, a social worker may encourage a client who presents with dependence on both alcohol and cocaine to prioritize the goals of treatment. If the client sees cocaine as the more serious problem and wishes to address only his or her cocaine use, a clinician using a harm reduction approach will recognize the value in the client's view of the problem and build on that strength. Preserving a cooperative, supportive relationship rather than an adversarial one improves the chances that the client will remain actively engaged in treatment longer.

Also, cessation of cocaine use is certainly significant progress in treating a substance use disorder. Cocaine is a dangerous drug, and from a harm reduction perspective, the cessation of cocaine use reduces the risk that the client will become entangled with the criminal justice system.

I decided to become a social worker because I believe in the values of the social work profession. I value social justice, the dignity and worth of the person, a person's right to self-determination, and the importance of human relationships. Through course work and in my practicum I have learned to engage, assess, and intervene with client systems. I have also developed the skill of evaluation through critical thinking. Because I have learned to critically evaluate my practice, I have come to understand that treatment models for chemical dependence vary and are more effective with multidisciplinary teams that include social workers as integral parts of the service delivery.

I have been educated and trained in the social work perspective and its approach to facilitating clients' growth and development. In order to understand a person in the context of my practicum and of the disease they may suffer with, I must endeavor to understand how all of the different aspects of their lives are integrated. In order to practice client-centered clinical social work, I need to know about a client's social, physical, and natural environment, spiritual beliefs, and most importantly, the way she or he perceives the problem that prompted them to seek, be referred to, or mandated for help and how they conceptualize the solution to that problem.

SOCIAL WORK PRACTICE IN CRIMINAL JUSTICE

Criminal justice is a growing area for social work employment. Dating back to the Poor Laws of the 17th century, advocating for and working with those involved with the correctional system has been an area of practice for social workers throughout our entire history (Maschi & Killian, 2011). Criminal justice social work is an area of forensic social work, the practice of social work in areas relating to the law and legal systems, which include the criminal and civil legal systems. Examples of forensic social work include child, older adult, and spouse/partner abuse; child custody; juvenile and adult criminal issues; and corrections.

Forensic social work
Social work practice within the legal system, including the criminal and civil legal systems.

Prompted by media and political attention, there is an increasing focus by society on crime and criminals. While the number of adults in the correctional population (e.g., incarcerated or on probation or parole) declined in 2012 for the fourth consecutive year, almost 7 million persons or one in every 35 adults in the United States is still under the supervision of the justice system (Glaze & Herberman, 2013). Half of the residents of correctional facilities are awaiting trial, and many are persons of color and of low socioeconomic status. More than half of persons who encounter the criminal justice system were under the influence of alcohol or other substances at the time the crime for which they are accused was committed. Because criminal activity is often linked to chronic poverty, substance abuse, mental illness, and lack of impulse control, anti-poverty programs are one area of intervention to help reduce crime (Reamer, 2013a). NASW calls for social workers to be trained as culturally competent, forensic professionals (i.e., those who work in the legal system) who can develop intervention plans to address the client within the criminal justice system who may experience chronic poverty, substance abuse, and/or mental illness (NASW, 2012–2014n).

Policy-Practice Considerations in Criminal Justice

Criminal justice social work practice encompasses a wide range of settings and issues. Social workers in this field of practice may work in adult or juvenile correctional facilities at the local, state, or federal levels; community-based probation and parole agencies; mental health facilities; public defenders' offices; law firms; legal services organizations, juvenile or family court agencies; law enforcement agencies; or programs that respond to issues of domestic and family violence (Rome, 2008). Social workers may also be employed in organizations that serve ex-offenders or re-entrants and their support networks (Wilson, 2010). Though social workers have been involved in social work practice in criminal justice since the 1800s, the number of social workers who currently identify criminal justice as their primary area of practice is small (Rome, 2008; Whitaker & Arrington, 2008). However, because criminal justice social work connects to a wide array of settings, social workers whose primary practice area is mental health, health, or substance abuse and addiction treatment, for example, may work with criminal justice issues.

Due to significant turnover in prisons, the number of individuals re-entering the community upon completion of their sentences is rising. While the numbers of persons incarcerated in general are high, two areas are of particular concern—re-arrest rates and the fact that the rate of incarceration for women has increased almost twice as fast as the rate for men (Wilson, 2010). To address these increases, social workers can advocate that incarcerated and re-entering persons receive holistically focused, evidence-based biopsychosocial services that emphasize rehabilitation (Carr, 2012; Wilson, 2010). Social workers are well suited to address the needs of persons in re-entry who will likely face challenges in terms of limited resources and opportunities particularly in the areas of employment, government assistance, housing, and involvement with the legal and child welfare system (Kubiak & Fedock, 2013).

Because the generalist perspective can "help us grasp individual and environmental factors that are correlated in crime and its prevention," BSW social workers are well suited to criminal justice practice (Reamer, 2013a, p. 119). Social work training prepares practitioners to advocate for much needed financial resources, additional training, particularly in evidence-based practice, and more appropriate policies to serve this population (Reamer, 2013a).

Herbert Bernsen, MSW, St. Louis County Department of Justice Services

I have a master's degree in social work and I am the Director for the St. Louis County Department of Justice Services. The American Jail Association has designated me as a Certified Jail Manager. I began my career in criminal justice social work as an MSW student. I worked as a probation and parole officer and have continued in this field for the past 42 years. I have also served as a superintendent of the maximum and medium security correctional institutions. In my work in corrections, I have learned the importance of collaborating with others in the community whose services overlap with the criminal justice system, and I am actively involved with several community organizations. I serve on the board of an Adult Basic Education program that provides General Educational Development (GED) teachers for inmates, and I am a board member for an organization that provides services to persons with developmental disabilities who encounter the criminal justice system. I am also part of a steering committee for an organization that provides re-entry services for ex-offenders being released to the community.

My department is responsible for the operation of the county jail and the Community Corrections Division. We work with adult men and women, 17 years of age and older, who are charged with crimes ranging from felonies and misdemeanors to county ordinance violations. The maximum capacity of the jail is 1,232 inmates. In 2013, 32,427 persons were booked at the jail, and the average daily population was 1,331 inmates, meaning that on some days we were over capacity. The jail population consists primarily of those inmates awaiting trial, but some inmates are sentenced to the jail for periods up to one year. For sentences exceeding one year, inmates are normally sent to the state prison system operated by the Department of Corrections.

We manage our general population housing area using direct supervision. Correctional officers are stationed inside housing area pods, enabling officers to take a proactive role in controlling inmate behavior and minimizing tension. In the past, we had more traditional linear facilities in which officers made only intermittent observations when they

St. Louis County
Department of Justice
Services

St. Louis County Department of Justice Services
100 South Central Avenue
St. Louis, MO 63105
The St. Louis County Department of Justice Services is responsible for the operation of the St. Louis
county jail and the Division of Community Corrections. The county jail provided 1,232 beds for the
county's minimum, medium, and maximum security inmates. The Division of Community Corrections is
located in a nearby building and is responsible for the operation of the Alternative Community Services
Program, Mental Health Court, and Probation Supervision Unit.

Photographs provided by Hellmuth, Obata, and Kassabaum, Inc.

conducted periodic patrols in front of inmates' cells. We find that assaults against staff and other inmates are significantly reduced in our current direct supervision facility because the officer is inside the living area and she or he can often stop problems early, before they escalate.

Communication is the key skill for officers working with inmates. Most inmates follow the rules because they want to live in a safe and secure environment. We set high expectations for inmate behavior, and this becomes a self-fulfilling prophecy. Inmates prefer to live in an environment in which the officer—and not the toughest inmate—is the leader. If an inmate consistently violates the rules, she or he is moved to an indirect housing unit with reduced privileges and restricted movement.

The most important part of the corrections department mission is to ensure inmate safety and security. As an administrator, I read daily reports and review incident reports. If there are numerous inmate assaults against other inmates or staff, we are not doing our job.

Supervisors must make frequent inspections. Cells and inmate living areas must be routinely searched. If there are homemade weapons, inmates cannot feel safe. We teach inmates the rules and the possible sanctions for violating those rules. They also know that their right to a due process hearing to determine their guilt or innocence is affirmed.

The social worker in the corrections area works as a member of a interprofessional team. She or he is responsible for conducting the initial assessment when an inmate is booked and processed into the jail setting. Often, this assessment involves crisis intervention; the social worker must evaluate the inmate's current emotional state to identify issues such as suicidal ideation and mental illness. The results of this assessment determine in which part of the jail system the inmate will be housed. Social workers also coordinate and participate in educational and treatment programs provided for the inmates. They keep in regular contact with inmates to assess how the inmate is functioning within the jail population and to identify any issues she or he faces from external sources (for example, family or financial). Using this information, the social worker prioritizes inmate needs. She or he serves as a liaison between the inmate and the legal system and between inmates and their employers in work release programs. Social workers are also often involved in the evaluation and supervision of inmates being placed on Electronic Home Detention and Pre-Trial Release Supervision programs. Upon their release from jail, inmates turn to social workers who help ensure that they effectively integrate back into their communities.

One of the challenges of working in criminal justice is the high incidence of mental illness and substance abuse among inmates. In the early 1960s, there was a government effort to deinstitutionalize vast numbers of persons with mental illness and to provide them with community support and housing. Unfortunately, these efforts fell woefully short. As a result, jails often became the place of last resort for persons suffering from mental illness, not all of whom had committed crimes but were arrested for inappropriate behaviors, for example. In St. Louis County, we have certainly needed to hire psychiatrists, psychologists, and social workers to work with persons diagnosed with mental illness inside our jails. Many of those experiencing mental illness do not, however, belong in jail in the first place.

Because I was aware of the inappropriate placement of many persons suffering from mental illness, I led the formation of a mental health task force consisting of community mental health providers and criminal justice agencies. The goal of this task force was to establish a mental health court to divert persons with serious mental health disorders from the criminal justice system to appropriate mental health treatment and services in order to improve their mental health functioning and deter future criminal behavior. To ensure the provision of comprehensive services, we worked closely with the police department to implement their Crisis Intervention Team (CIT) program. In this program, police officers are trained to intervene in situations involving persons with mental illness. Our other partners included an advocacy group, the state mental health agency, a nonprofit mental health agency, and a university social work program along with judges, prosecutors, public defenders, probation officers, and our corrections department at the county jail.

Another challenge social workers face working in criminal justice is the issue of substance abuse. The inmate population includes many persons who use and abuse alcohol and other drugs. My department has made a significant commitment to the treatment of substance abuse through the Choices Substance Abuse Recovery Program. Using a 12-step model, this 90-day treatment empowers male and female participants to choose a lifestyle free of alcohol, other drugs, and criminal behavior. During the past twelve years, the Choices program has served 2,413 of our inmates. Judges have embraced the program, and there has been a waiting list since the program's inception.

Each year, faculty and students at a local university who evaluate the program find that it has positive results. For example, during Years 3–14, 72% of inmates who completed the program resided in their home community without being arrested for a new crime, and 82% successfully remained on probation. By the program's fifteenth year, 97% of participants completed the program successfully.

I have learned that providing educational opportunities helps inmates initiate changes in their lives. Local school districts provide instructors to prepare inmates to take the high school equivalency exam, and inmates have the opportunity to be tested. In 2013, 117 inmates took the GED test, and 74 received their diploma.

The successful operation of our jail and the programs I have described depends in part on volunteers. There are currently over 350 active volunteers at the jail. Volunteers conduct creative writing programs and leadership classes and provide individual counseling, religious services, literacy assistance, substance abuse education, and support groups for substance abusers. The volunteers have a positive influence on the well-being of the inmates both inside and outside of confinement.

Social workers in criminal justice settings grappled with many challenges. Jails and prisons are inundated with inmates with mental health and substance abuse problems. Jails and prisons have the highest rates of suicide in our society. Faced with scarce resources and reduced budgets, these social workers must form partnerships with community leaders and organizations to provide services for inmate populations.

The future criminal justice social work is promising. Myriad opportunities exist for correctional officers, social service staff, medical and mental health staff, and administrators. Innovations in inmate supervision and treatment, public health, technology, and community aftercare are among the areas for growth and development. The vast majority of jail and prison inmates return to their communities. Resources directed toward inmate populations during and after incarceration pay significant dividends to those individuals, their families, and the community.

SOCIAL WORK PRACTICE IN HEALTH CARE SETTINGS

Approximately 31% of social workers practice in health-related settings, and this number is expected to increase by 27% in the coming years (BLS, 2014b). The health care field is one of the fastest growing segments of the job market. The aging of the Baby Boomer population accounts for a significant portion of this growth. With the trend toward short hospital stays, emphasis on out-patient care, and the growth of the older adult population, health care social workers are employed most often in outpatient and residential care facilities (BLS, 2014b).

Policy-Practice Considerations in Health Settings

Social workers who practice in any area of health care social work have the opportunity to practice in a variety of organizations with a wide array of client systems and a range of other professionals. Health care social workers providing services across the lifespan, from neonatal intensive care to skilled nursing facilities, all share a common purpose: to assist individuals and families to function in response to health issues, to prevent social and emotional issues from impacting health, and to address service inadequacies (NASW, 2006–2009). Social workers work in interprofessional teams in inpatient hospitals, outpatient medical clinics, health-specific service, educational and advocacy organizations, residential care facilities, skilled nursing facilities, rehabilitation settings, public health agencies, hospice, home health care, and mental health and substance abuse treatment settings. When working as a member of an interprofessional health care team, the social worker must have a clear understanding of her or his role. A competency-based taxonomy can help the social worker to negotiate and function effectively within the team environment. Maramaldi and colleagues (2014) developed an evidence-based categorization of social work functions on the interprofessional team:

- Rapid risk assessment—use 360 degree screening in which information is gathered from as many persons and sources as possible.
- Assessment—serve as a liaison between the interprofessional team and the patient and family in gathering and interpreting information.
- Intervention—participate with other team members to implement strategies to meet health care goals.
- Referral—facilitate patient/family access to resources within and outside the health care setting.
- Expected outcome—to support facilitation of the expected outcome (i.e., quality care), advocate for patient-focused interventions.

■ Contributions to interdisciplinary team—ensure team's understanding of the social work role.

■ Competencies needed—knowledge and skills needed to provide competent care (p. 542).

Some of these organizations work with individuals across the lifespan, while others are specific to adults, adolescents, or children. Other organizational settings may focus on managing a particular disease such as HIV/AIDS, multiple sclerosis, Alzheimer's disease, or diabetes. A shift is occurring within the health care community toward providing services in the primary care setting which is creating new opportunities for social workers to engage in screening, assessments, and treatment protocols in the outpatient setting, an area in which social workers have not historically been employed (Rock, 2009). In 2009, President Obama allocated $155 million to fund 126 new community health centers, increasing opportunities for social workers to serve the uninsured and underinsured in community settings. The Affordable Care Act has resulted in the development of accountable care organizations (ACOs) and health homes aimed at improving patient outcomes and reducing health care costs. Clinical social workers and care coordinators are integral to these organizations (S. Collins, 2013).

Health Care Setting

Source: iStock/Christopher Futcher

Social work in the health field requires the social worker to have knowledge of the biological, psychological, spiritual, and social aspects of human functioning along with an understanding of the distinct and overlapping roles of all the professionals who provide health care services and the skills to work with them. Health care social work integrates direct practice with individuals and families with an awareness of the impact of policies and the willingness to advocate for patients' needs. In an effort to ensure quality practice, NASW has established *Standards for Social Work Practice in Health Care Settings* (2005), providing guidelines in the areas of ethics, social justice, cultural competence, privacy and confidentiality, theory, interprofessional practice, and documentation. These standards apply to health social workers in all settings.

Whether they are working in an inpatient or outpatient medical setting, social workers perform a number of diverse functions. In hospital or inpatient settings, the social worker is primarily responsible for helping the patient and her or his support network understand and cope with the presenting illness or health event (NASW CWS, 2011b, pp. 1–2). Exhibit 8.8 provides an overview. In a rapidly changing health care system, social workers must continually gain competence in the use of technology and telemedicine (using technology (typically video to connect health care providers with patients and families who live at a distance from the provider), video conferencing, and social media), and new models of health care delivery (e.g., medical homes) (Collins, 2013).

EXHIBIT 8.8

Guidelines for Social Work Practice in Health Care Settings

Social workers practicing in health settings are engaged in:
- Screening and evaluating patients and families.
- Conducting comprehensive psychosocial assessments, including mental health evaluation.
- Helping patients and families understand the admission process, treatment options and the consequences (i.e., role changes, responses to illness and treatment).
- Educating patients and families on the levels of health care, roles of the health care team and strategies for effective communication.
- Facilitating health-related decision-making.
- Engaging in crisis intervention.
- Educating professional staff on patient psychosocial issues and serving as a liaison between staff and patients and families.
- Facilitating patient navigation of the health care system and discharge and continuity planning, including resource management.
- Advocating for patient and family needs, including patient rights.

Source: NASW CWS, 2011b, pp. 1–2.

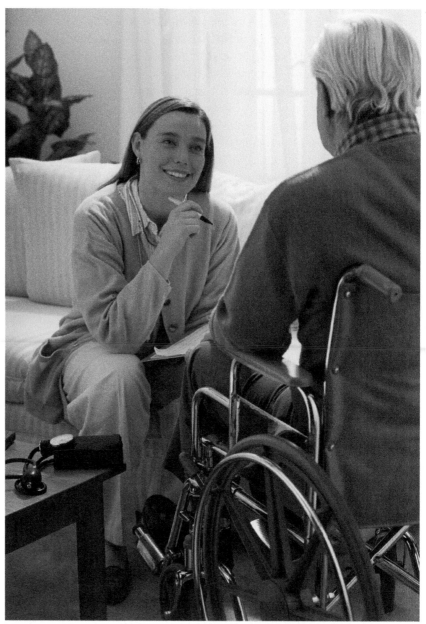

Source: Comstock

Similar to the roles of the social worker in inpatient settings, the social worker who works in the outpatient setting may educate patients and families on health-related issues, conduct assessments of mental health issues, coordinate care management plans and resources, help patients and their support networks navigate the health care system, and engage in advocacy efforts on behalf of patients and families. While not exclusive to outpatient settings, social workers may also counsel patients and families in end-of-life issues, intervene in situations of intimate partner or child/abuse, and develop educational programming specific to health-related issues (Gibelman, 2004; Grobman, 2005; NASW CWS, 2011a).

Lisa Parnell, MSW, LCSW, St. Luke's Hospital

My first job was at Baskin-Robbins Ice Cream Parlor. I was 15 years old and I was very excited about making my own money in the real world. What it didn't take me very long to learn was that working with the public was often fun, but occasionally very stressful. Fortunately, I worked for a very kind couple, who felt that it was important to train each of us thoroughly, and not just to make sure our scoops were the correct size or that we cleaned up the store correctly at closing time each night. What they taught us was far more important. They taught us to respect each customer and listen to them, so we didn't make mistakes and to assure that the customers were pleased with their purchase. These lessons have held up well during my years as a Medical Social Worker at an urban, not for profit hospital.

When I first went to college, I was one of the older students in the class. After high school, I had worked for several years in the restaurant industry, and it wasn't until I was 29 years old that I decided to find a career that would help make our world a better place. I was also looking for a job that didn't make my back and feet hurt so much at the end of the day. My first field of study was in the Business Department. While the classes were interesting and I learned a great deal about the economy, I just couldn't picture myself being satisfied with just trying to make a profit. I had a few elective classes left and my advisor recommended that I take a Social Work class. I knew within the first 15 minutes of the first class that this was the field for me, and I haven't been regretted that decision since.

During my undergraduate studies, I met so many caring professors who were extremely passionate about helping their communities, the underserved, and the world around them. I found myself swept up in their teachings about giving people the tools they need to have a comfortable, stable life, and I began to realize my calling in this field. At that same time, many of my good friends became ill with the AIDS virus and soon began to die. This was a heartbreaking time in my life. My social work studies gave me the hope that I could find a way to give these individuals some comfort and compassion during their final days. It was also during these years that I began to volunteer for an organization that provided food for people living with AIDS. I began to understand what a difference a few caring and compassionate individuals could make in the lives of so many who were suffering.

By the time I began graduate school for an MSW, I had already chosen to work in the health care field. While I felt pulled to help the frail, I was still interested in learning about other social work fields, as I didn't want to miss out on the possibility of finding something that I enjoyed even more. The most fascinating part of my graduate program was the opportunity to participate in practica in such varied settings.

Having already completed BSW practica with an inner city youth sports program and neighborhood stabilization projects, I realized that politics was not my area of interest. Next, I worked with youth in the justice system. The kids were great. I found myself drawn to support and advocate for them, even those who had committed very serious crimes. I just knew that, if given the proper chance, they could lead honest, law abiding lives. Unfortunately, I found myself frustrated by the bureaucracy of the legal system that could be so complex.

In the end I decided to jump into a health setting by signing up for my final practicum with a local hospice organization. At last, I had a feeling of purpose and obtainable goals. Working with the terminally ill and their families was something I felt very passionate about. Granted, this might sound strange to some people, and working in a hospice setting is not for the "faint of heart." This

practicum setting, my field instructor, and my MSW advisor helped me learn how to funnel my passion into giving these patients dignity and choices. All the while, I learned how to separate out my own personal issues in order to mature into a true social work professional.

One day shortly after I started my graduate program, I went to visit a professor who had previously taught in my BSW program. She started telling me about a new research project she was working on, and as luck had it, they needed a graduate student to assist with the study. This part-time position led to my first real social work job after graduation and taught me a great deal about all the necessary, detailed preparation work that goes into every social work organization. Research was fascinating to me because I had never thought too much about the way in which programs were developed. I just assumed that someone came up with a good idea and then figured out how to get the money to start their new program. Obviously, I still had a lot to learn! Spending those years assisting with two extremely important research projects was the best thing that could have happened to me; there is not a day that goes by when I don't think about the statistics involved in running a hospital, and this reminds me of their impact on patient care.

The first research project I worked on involved understanding the impact of caring for individuals suffering from Alzheimer's disease. As a research assistant I called family caregivers to ask them a series of questions related to their own well-being. Listening to these caregivers share their struggles and heartaches taught me to pay attention not only to what they said, but to how they said it and particularly to what they did not say. Often, they seemed to feel guilty for complaining about having to care for their loved ones. While they understood that they were the fortunate ones not to be suffering from such a devastating illness, they still had mixed emotions. Often during my current work with patient's families, I can still hear that same frustration, and I do my best to offer support and express compassion.

My next research position was as the Coordinator for a Mental Health project that followed low-income pregnant women throughout their pregnancies. We collected information on both their mental health and substance abuse issues. We specifically studied women from both urban and rural health clinics, to evaluate potential differences in resources. Our goal was to identify deficiencies in current programs in order to provide improved services in the future. This position had many ups and down; I had never worked so closely with women who had so many obstacles to overcome in their young lives. Before working on this project, I understood that there was a limit to the resources I could help these clients access. I learned that these females had tremendous courage. As I laughed and cried with them, I realized that they had given me more than I could

ever have offered them. I am proud to say that the data we collected in this project has continued to be utilized in ongoing research, which will hopefully make life easier for women in difficult situations in the future.

After completing my part of that research project, I was offered my current position as a medical social worker for a prominent hospital. I have worked there for almost 14 years now, and I continue to learn something new every day. While each social worker at our hospital is assigned to a particular division, we are all cross-trained, and this has helped me stay current on social work policies and practices. We all have experience working in every area of health care including oncology, dialysis, stroke, alcohol and substance abuse, domestic violence, child abuse, psychiatry, infectious disease, respiratory disease, cardiology, women's health (including pregnancy and infant health issues), and other health-related issues. We're very fortunate, as our hospital has a specific Social Work Department, led by an LCSW, who understands our role and supports us in our goal to be advocates for the patients.

My first position in the hospital was in the Rehabilitation Unit, where I worked for eight years. During this time I learned the importance of taking a "team" approach to health care. The majority of our patients had suffered a stroke or other extremely serious health event, which had left their bodies weak and in need of therapy, nursing care, and acute medical treatment. Our Rehab Team consisted of a physiatrist (a doctor who specializes in rehabilitative care), nurses, patient care technicians, a physical therapist (to help patients learn to transfer and ambulate after a serious health incident), an occupational therapist (to help patients learn to perform daily activities such as dressing, bathing, grooming, eating, etc.), a speech therapist, a recreational therapist, a music therapist, a registered dietician, a case manager (to deal with insurance companies), and myself. My goal was to work with this team to create a safe discharge plan that respected the patient's wishes and provided the necessary resources for resuming their lives outside of the hospital.

I used all the skills I had learned throughout my social work education, practicum settings, and prior positions to achieve this goal. My work with each patient began with a psycho-social assessment. It quickly became obvious that the more information I could gather about the patients' prior lives, the more opportunity we would have to help them reach their personal goals for their new lives. I offered supportive counseling to patients and their families in order to help them adjust the changes that resulted from their new medical condition. I then worked with the Rehab Team to determine whether a patient would be well enough to return home when medically stable for discharge or if they would require ongoing care in a skilled rehabilitation facility. Sometimes the patient's condition declined and we helped them make difficult decisions regarding

end-of-life care, either at home or in a nursing facility.

If patients did improve and were able to go directly home, I would help arrange home health care, durable medical equipment, and assistance applying for prescription drug programs, Medicaid insurance (which each state offers for chronically ill patients who meet certain financial guidelines), adult day care programs, or outpatient therapy. If we determined that the patient would benefit from ongoing nursing care and therapy in a skilled setting, I worked with patients and their families to offer choices for this care and to obtain insurance authorization. In addition to these duties, I also facilitated a support group for stroke survivors and their loved ones.

When my hospital decided to build a new Rehabilitation Unit in a building down the street, I was offered the chance to move with them, but decided that I would miss the excitement of the acute hospital setting. An opportunity was available for a Renal Social Worker in the acute hospital setting. When I accepted this position, I used my Rehab skills in a cohesive approach to working with patients suffering from kidney failure. I had much to learn about individuals suffering from chronic renal failure and their ongoing needs outside the hospital. I was fortunate enough to be invited to join the Council of Nephrology Social Workers (CNSW), which meets monthly and offers internet support for its members, so as to effectively meet the ongoing needs of their patients. It was exciting to be a part of this new, larger team and to be able to ask questions of educated professionals.

In addition to working with renal patients, I also work in the Intensive Care Unit, which has offered me the chance to use my counseling skills and to help families make life and death decisions under very stressful conditions. I am also often called upon to handle situations in the Emergency Room, which requires me to think creatively and handle traumatic situations. I have discovered that I do my best in demanding settings. My role in the hospital gives me a sense of accomplishment and pride in my work. I know at the end of the day that my knowledge and empathy skills have helped people in crisis.

As the population of the United States continues to age, there will be multiple opportunities for social workers in the health care field. While I strongly encourage social work students to consider this area for their careers, I would suggest that they pursue practicum opportunities to explore several different settings. The future of medical social work is unlimited, and there will be opportunities not only in hospitals, but also in outpatient clinics, the mental health field, private practice, government agencies, and private industry, which is utilizing increasing numbers of social workers to provide care through employee assistance programs. One of my favorite aspects of being a medical social worker is that every member of our team feels that we should always respect the patient's goals and include them in all decision-making regarding their care. This perspective may differ from the family member's thoughts and insurance company limitations; however, as a team we are able to stay focused and be effective advocates for our patients.

SOCIAL WORK PRACTICE IN MENTAL HEALTH SETTINGS

The social work profession is the largest provider of mental health services in the United States today, accounting for almost half of services. Psychiatrists, psychologists, counselors, psychiatric nurses, and marriage and family therapists make up the other half (see Exhibit 8.9). The federal government recognizes social work as one of the four core mental health professions (Gibelman, 2005). Mental health is the largest area of practice for social workers, with over one-third of social workers reporting it as their primary field of practice and 13% reporting that they work in an outpatient mental health setting (Whitaker & Arrington, 2008). Moreover, social work practice in the area of mental health services is expected to grow by 23% in upcoming years (BLS, 2014b).

After five years of practice as a social worker, the number of social workers who identify mental health as the setting in which they work begins to increase, supporting the idea that, immediately following graduation, social workers

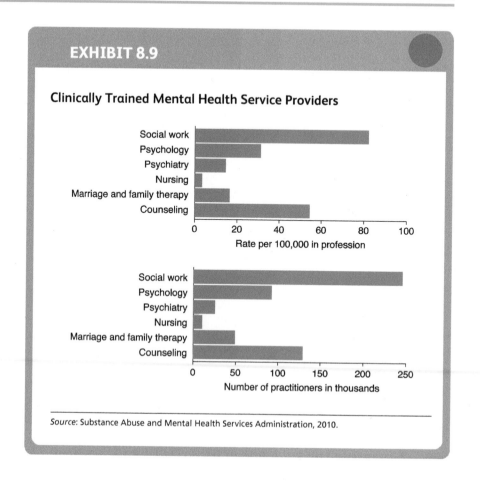

EXHIBIT 8.9

Clinically Trained Mental Health Service Providers

Source: Substance Abuse and Mental Health Services Administration, 2010.

gravitate to employment in the areas of aging, family and children services, and health settings and then shift their focus to the provision of more traditional clinical services after gaining experience. Mental health services are most often provided by social workers with an MSW or Ph.D. These social workers tend to be older, more experienced practitioners. Fewer social workers who are persons of color and of diverse ethnic groups identify themselves as mental health practitioners, indicating a need for greater diversity among mental health care providers (CHWS/CWS, 2006).

Policy-Practice Considerations in Mental Health Settings

Social workers provide mental health services in a variety of settings and geographic locations with diverse client populations. They work with persons from all races, ethnicities, and cultures including children, adolescents, adults of all ages, families, groups, and persons with physical and/or developmental disabilities in correctional facilities, family service or mental health organizations, military and veteran programs, private practice, employee assistance programs, disaster relief programs, crisis intervention programs, and victim assistance programs. Twenty-seven percent of social workers in mental health work in an ambulatory (outpatient) setting, while 15% work in an inpatient facility (BLS, 2014a).

Social workers can provide mental health services in the form of clinical therapy with individuals, families, and groups in both in- and outpatient mental health settings and facilitate support groups related to mental health issues, provide mental health education, and serve as advocates for those persons suffering from mental illness. More social workers providing mental health services are employed in outpatient mental health settings than in inpatient (hospital) settings (Whitaker & Arrington, 2008). The shift of service provision to the outpatient setting is due, in part, to a decreasing availability of "beds" in inpatient psychiatric facilities (SAMHSA, 2013a). The outpatient settings now providing the majority of mental health services include public and nonprofit mental health centers and group and solo private practices located in urban, suburban, and rural locations.

A growing area of mental health practice for social workers is private practice. Seventeen percent of licensed social workers report they are engaged in private or group clinical practice, making this the third-ranked setting in which social workers practice (CHWS/CWS, 2006). One in eight adults in the U.S. receives mental health treatment in any given year, and antidepressant medications are the fastest growing drug prescribed, so competently trained mental health care providers are essential (SAMHSA, 2013b). Nearly every major health insurance provider recognizes the graduate social work degree as appropriate provider of mental health services, thus making clinical practice (private or agency-based) a viable employment option for social workers with MSWs. Social workers in private clinical practice tend to garner the highest salaries within the social work practice community (CHWS/CWS, 2006).

While social workers providing mental health or behavioral health services work with a wide range of clients and client situations, most work primarily in either the community-based outpatient setting or an inpatient psychiatric setting. Exhibit 8.10 provides an overview of social work responsibilities in the community clinic and psychiatric setting.

Social workers in behavioral health services face increases in the numbers of persons experiencing mental health issues, particularly when mental illness co-occurs with another issue (e.g., substance abuse). With an estimated 43.7 (18.6%) million adults and 2.2 (9.1%) million adolescents experiencing mental illness, social workers and other providers of mental health services are in demand (SAMHSA, 2013a). These high numbers of clients seeking treatment

---

EXHIBIT 8.10

Responsibilities for Practice in Mental Health Settings

- Determining service eligibility
- Conducting biopsychosocial (and spiritual) assessments, including identification of psychiatric disorders, physical and emotional functioning, financial stability, safety, substance abuse and addictions, and suicidal or homicidal ideation
- Developing and implementing therapeutic treatment and discharge plans in the form of individual, family, or group interventions
- Providing crisis intervention and case management services
- Engaging in nondirect services on behalf of clients, including advocacy, promotion of mental health services, grant writing, and evaluation

Source: National Association of Social Workers Center for Workforce Studies and Social Work Practice, 2011c, d, p. 1.

---

present several challenges which require specialized training. For example, the increased prevalence of co-occurring disorders (nearly 20% of persons with mental illness) coupled with increases in the number of nonspecialized providers delivering mental health services, the number of psychotropic medications being prescribed (often in lieu of behavioral treatment), and a lack of available emergency and residential treatment facilities mean that practicing as a mental health social worker requires advanced training in mental health, substance abuse treatment, medication use, and crisis intervention (SAMHSA, 2013a). The Affordable Care Act has focused interest on the role social workers can play in coordinating community-based care, prevention, mental and behavioral health services, and substance abuse treatment (Collins, 2013).

Barbara Flory, MSW, LCSW

As a licensed clinical social worker, I was employed in a program for families dealing with domestic violence. I earned an undergraduate degree in human services, a graduate degree in social work from a private university, and a postgraduate certificate in family conflict management from a state university, and I completed family therapy training at a program accredited by the American Association of Marriage and Family Therapy. My combined experience with family therapy and mediation prepared me for the position I held in today's social services environment.

For more than 10 years, I worked for a nonprofit mental health agency in a large metropolitan area. In my capacity as a program manager for a supervised visitation and custody exchange center, I was responsible for all phases of program development, implementation, supervision of staff, and evaluation of program outcomes. The program opened in 1997 to meet the needs of the family court (i.e., the court system that addresses family and juvenile legal issues) and a special needs population of separated, divorced, and never-married families. Three different family court divisions may mandate families to participate in the program: domestic relations (divorce and post-divorce child custody modifications), civil adult and child protection (time-limited protection orders sought by an adult), and juvenile dependency (child abuse and neglect cases resulting from a hotline call to child protection services). In rare cases, families are referred from the criminal child abuse and/or domestic violence dockets (e.g., domestic violence and/or child physical and/or sexual abuse cases that rise to a level at which criminal prosecution is warranted).

In my position with the agency, I acted as liaison between social services and the law, a unique position that required knowledge beyond that which is traditionally a part of social work education.

Typically, a court orders supervised visitation between a noncustodial parent and child when it determines that the parent's behavior threatens the child's safety. Supervised visitation is third-party guided contact between a non-custodial parent and child for the purpose of maintaining or forming a relationship. Service delivery occurs on three levels to (1) ensure the safety of children in cases of alleged abuse; (2) reintroduce parent and child after a prolonged separation; and (3) introduce parent and child when no prior relationship exists. In the context of child abuse and neglect, supervised visitation services have a well-established history as a means to facilitate family reunification, but they are relatively new within the domestic relations arena and are just gaining credibility as an effective intervention in domestic violence cases. Over time, the judiciary has slowly embraced the practice of ordering supervised visitation in domestic violence cases to help ensure the safety of mothers and the children for whom they are responsible.

The population the agency served was largely a violent group that engaged in psychological and/or physical aggression as a way to resolve interpersonal conflict. Approximately 70 percent of the client population had a history of abusive behavior, most often male-on-female intimate partner abuse (i.e. battering); in some instances, children were abuse victims as well. A violent home environment almost ensures diminished overall child well-being. Therefore, the program was structured to meet the unique physical and emotional safety needs of this population.

In order to meet the needs of

Supervised visitation
Third-party guided contact between a non-custodial parent and child for the purpose of maintaining or forming a relationship.

families, the program operated evenings, weekends, and holidays. Weekday and Sunday work hours started at 4:00 p.m., when parents began arriving for supervised visits with their children. The social worker's responsibilities included ensuring children's safety during noncustodial parent/child visitation, teaching parenting skills and age appropriate communication skills, and facilitating attachment and bonding as needed. Modeling and coaching are two important skills that the social workers must possess to be successful in this practice area. Noncustodial parents arrived at the center to pick up their children to spend time with them in an unprotected setting (for example, at home). The center was open on Saturday from 10:00 a.m. to 4:00 p.m., to allow parents scheduling flexibility.

The center served many parents who had untreated, often undiagnosed, mental health disorders that contributed to their violent tendencies. Consequently, safety was paramount, and off-duty police officers helped oversee visits. A no-contact policy was necessary; that is, participating parents did not come face-to-face with each other while at the center or communicate with each other outside the center.

It was encouraging to see that most parents responded well when offered the right circumstance. Unfortunately, sometimes circumstances dictated third-party intervention and court-restricted parental contact to mediate violent behavior. Some parents exhibited levels of anger and distress disproportionate to an event, resulting in violent outbursts. I was often called upon to intervene in situations that, while relatively inconsequential for most parents, represented a crisis for overly stressed parents.

The program that I managed is only one small piece on a continuum of care needed to sustain families experiencing challenges in the modern-day world. The agency in which I worked offered a broad scope of intervention services including individual and family counseling, addictions treatment, workforce development, employee assistance services, suicide prevention, youth mentoring services, teen pregnancy prevention, and in-home geriatrics support services. I am fortunate that my employer valued and supported innovative programming.

Supervised visitation is an emerging field of practice in social services that enjoys both praise and criticism from mental health and legal professionals. Research about the effectiveness of services is limited; my team is among the handful of social workers that have conducted research in this field. As practitioners, in conjunction with a local graduate social work school, we conducted an exploratory study that showed that service can effectively promote noncustodial parent/child safe contact, reducing interparental violence and promoting child well-being (Dunn, Flory, Berg-Weger, & Milstead, 2004; Flory & Berg-Weger, 2003; Flory, Dunn, Berg-Weger, & Milstead, 2001).

Since few social workers conduct research in their practice settings, my research experience and professional publications have resulted in private consulting roles, including judicial training for a national organization and participation in a federal task force charged with developing standards and guidelines for the profession. The task force's commitment to shaping the field to meet public policy expectations added legitimacy to services and helped to ensure the future evolution of the field.

Supervised visitation and safe custody exchange services emerged out of grassroots organizing that will support future programming, albeit at a limited level. Future expansion of services is largely in the hands of family courts faced with shrinking state and federal budgets. There are, however, promising federal legislative efforts to support noncustodial parental access to children. In response to the tendency for many fathers to emotionally and financially withdraw from their children's lives post-divorce, one federal effort has developed state programs focused on maintaining connections between non-custodial fathers and their children. Another federal effort focuses on protecting children from abuse in the unprotected presence of the batterer in cases of domestic violence. Both efforts recognize the benefits of keeping two parents safely involved in children's lives.

It was not until I left this area of practice that I realized just how stressful and debilitating daily exposure to stories of violence and aggressive behaviors were on my own psyche. I learned that education in self-care is essential to support professionals working in this field.

After leaving the domestic violence program, I became involved in the emerging field of collaborative family law. I chose this area of work—often referred to as a "peaceful" divorce process—because it is a stark contrast to the highly antagonistic arena of domestic violence, yet it allows me to continue to work with families in transition. In collaborative divorce the two divorcing parties agree not go to court but to instead engage in a series of meetings with a team of divorce attorneys, mental health professionals, and accountants who work collaboratively to help the parties make fully-informed, carefully considered, settlement decisions consistent with the parties' priorities, goals, needs, and interests. My position in supervised visitation provided me with specialized knowledge about divorce as an emotional process, post-divorce communication issues, child custody parenting plans and schedules, and the effects of divorce on children that prepared me to train and work as a divorce coach and/or child specialist. Specialized knowledge and skills developed in one social work domain are often transferrable to other practice areas.

Currently, I am consulting on a statewide strategic planning effort to improve the state's network of supervised visitation centers. In this capacity, I am writing a policy and procedure manual that completes the state's standards for programming. The goal is to improve the quality of programming by making service delivery more uniform. I am also writing a documentation manual for a hybrid model of case recording/note taking that I developed specifically for the supervised visitation profession.

In retirement, I am using my social work skills as a community volunteer. As a Court Appointed Special Advocate/Guardian ad Litem (CASA/GAL) volunteer, I advocate for abused and neglected children to help ensure that children are placed in a safe, permanent home within the established public policy guidelines in a timely manner. As a GAL, I meet with the parents and foster parents, go on home visits to ensure the child's needs are being met, follow the child's medical and educational progress, and perform other duties deemed appropriate based on case facts. In addition to serving as a GAL, I have been privileged to provide content and skills training to other volunteers at conferences and/or in-service trainings. Volunteers bring few skills to the volunteer arena, and, thus, are very eager to learn. Their appreciation of any training that will help them serve children more effectively is deeply satisfying.

More recently, I have become involved in other areas of volunteerism. The city in which I live is a major hub for sex trafficking. In one volunteer role I am bringing a new nationally acclaimed program to educate and prevent sexual exploitation among youth. *My Life, My Choice* works with girls between the ages of 12 to 17 years to stem the tide of commercial sexual exploitation by harnessing girls' strength, resilience, and outrage. My newfound interest in human trafficking presents an opportunity for me to engage in lifelong learning as it is an area of practice about which I have no prior knowledge or experience. It also allows me to pursue my passion for helping to improve the lives of women and children. Community activism has also emerged as a growing area of interest for me. Using my research skills, I am actively engaged in community development efforts to assess residents' changing needs using community-wide surveys. I am using my background in project management to oversee a major tennis court construction project, proving that there is no end to the applicability of social work skills.

My career has included clinical therapy, parent and divorce coaching, mediation and conflict management, program development and implementation, program administration, staff supervision, research and teaching, system reform, consulting, and volunteerism. The variety of work in which I have engaged represents the depth and breadth of my social work education and the many opportunities an advanced degree in social work affords. As my story shows, the skills and knowledge social workers possess can be used in various ways to benefit the diverse client populations we serve and the communities in which we live.

SOCIAL WORK PRACTICE IN THE PUBLIC HEALTH SETTING

Public health is a societal commitment to individual and population health (Tsay, 2010). It embraces concerns ranging from health education, prevention services, epidemiology, health care delivery, and immunization to environmental and occupational safety and bioterrorism.

The field of public health and the social work profession share a dedication to serving disadvantaged and vulnerable populations. For this reason, social workers have a longstanding history of practicing in public health settings, including local public health departments, clinics, and public health policy organizations. Over 150,000 U.S. social workers are employed in medical and public health settings (Baden, 2010).

The social work focus on public health concerns began in the early 19th century in England (Tsay, 2010). With increased urbanization, environmental and infectious diseases began to affect entire communities. Early public health activists, including Jane Addams, focused their efforts on improving sanitation.

Today public health workers address lifestyle issues (e.g., dietary and nutrition concerns, smoking, substance abuse, and obesity) and environmental issues (e.g., lead paint and chemicals in our environment) that impact health. In developing countries, public health efforts have focused on disease prevention and the promotion of community health (Tsay, 2010).

Each decade, the *Healthy People* initiative (www.Healthypeople.gov) establishes the nation's public health objectives. Those objectives shape program and funding priorities for public health organizations throughout the country. Intended as a 10-year plan, *Healthy People 2020,* issued in 2010, has identified the following goals:

- Attain high-quality, longer lives free of preventable disease, disability, injury, and premature death.
- Achieve health equity, eliminate disparities, and improve the health of all groups.
- Create social and physical environments that promote good health for all.
- Promote quality of life, healthy development, and healthy behaviors across all life stages.

Healthy People 2020 includes new topic areas of special interest to the social work profession: health of older adults; lesbian, gay, bisexual, and transgender health; adolescent health; global health; preparedness; and dementias.

The Centers for Disease Control and Prevention have identified ten essential services for public health in every community. First developed in 1994,

Public health
A commitment by society to individual and population health, including health education, prevention services, epidemiology, health care delivery, and immunization, environmental and occupational safety and bioterrorism.

EXHIBIT 8.11

Responsibilities for Public Health Practice

- Monitoring health status to identify and solve community health problems.
- Diagnosing and investigating health problems and health hazards in the community.
- Informing, educating, and empowering people about health issues.
- Mobilizing community partnerships and acting to identify and solve health problems.
- Developing policies and plans that support individual and community health efforts.
- Enforcing laws and regulations that protect health and ensure safety.
- Linking people to needed personal health services and assuring the provision of health care when otherwise unavailable.
- Assuring competent public and personal health care workforce.
- Evaluating effectiveness, accessibility, and quality of personal and population-based health services.
- Researching for new insights and innovative solutions to health problems.

Source: Centers for Disease Control and Prevention, 2010.

---

these guidelines charge local public health agencies with a range of responsibilities. These mandates share a number of similarities with the mission of the social work profession (see Exhibit 8.11).

Policy-Practice Considerations for Social Work in Public Health Settings

Many factors can significantly influence the health and well-being of an individual and family, including socioeconomic and employment status, ethnicity, access to health care, education, social relationships, neighborhood/housing conditions, and personal behaviors (Collins, 2011, p. 2). A recent report on state funding for public health programs is adamant, however, that one's health and well-being should not be compromised because of inadequate resources for basic preventative health care—in fact, the current generation of children are at risk of becoming the first cohort in our history whose lives may be shorter than their parents' (Trust for America's Health, 2014).

Social workers employed in public health organizations must be aware of the ways in which the fluctuating economy affects their work. For a number of years, underfunding of public health initiatives at the federal, state, and local levels has hampered the ability of public health departments to invest in disease prevention. The Trust for America's Health (2014), a nonprofit, non-partisan advocacy organization focused on promoting health, calls for increased funding, with more emphasis on evidence-based, prevention-focused programs.

Social workers partner effectively with public health professionals at all levels of practice, from working with individuals and families to developing programs and policies to provide guidance to communities and organizations (Collins, 2013). Both the social work profession and the Affordable Care Act place significant emphasis on prevention, putting social workers in a strong position to provide leadership in developing and implementing ACA disease prevention programs. Social work and public health have much in common, including an embrace of both social action and scientific knowledge (Tsay, 2010, p. 1099). In addition, both types of professionals often examine the intersection between the physical and social environments (Tsay, 2010). Finally, its commitment to social justice and expertise in advocating for equitable access to resources, the social work profession is well positioned to be on the forefront of advocacy efforts to increase public health funding.

Chae Li Yong, MSW, MPH

When I entered college, I wanted to help people and thought medical school was the answer. Then I became ill and had to have two surgical procedures along with daily medication to avoid additional procedures. I became disillusioned with the medical field when I realized the difficulty many people face accessing affordable medical care. That many people live in such a prosperous nation and are still forced to choose between food and medicine really troubled me.

When I stumbled into my first health education class, I knew I had found my niche. Health educators improve individual and community health by promoting the adoption of healthy behaviors to the general public. Prevention through education saves money and lives.

As an undergraduate student, I completed an internship focused on communicable disease at a local health department and confirmed that I wanted to be an epidemiologist. My mentor encouraged me to "job shadow" different public health professionals. Some of my diverse activities as an intern included collecting mosquitoes, setting pest traps, finding homes for animals, administering medications to a patient with tuberculosis, and inspecting restaurants and swimming pools. I respected the courage the public health worker showed when closing the pool of an upscale hotel. I admired the compassion of the public health worker who interviewed a prisoner confirmed with a sexually transmitted disease. Being rather naïve, I was amazed at the places we searched for suspected cases of illness. Through those experiences, I came to admire all that public health professionals do to keep the public healthy and safe.

After I completed my undergraduate degree, I worked as a health educator at a local health department. I learned that some local health departments did not perform many of the activities I observed during my internship, largely due to lack of funding. My position was supported through state funding.

As a health educator, I taught numerous target populations, depending on how grant money was allocated. I taught children about injury prevention. I worked with parents regarding child passenger vehicular safety. I collaborated with various populations in smoking prevention and cessation programs. These are just a few examples of the target populations, community groups, and collaborative projects I had the opportunity to work with during my time as a health educator.

After several years working in public health, I returned to school to complete dual graduate degrees in Social Work (MSW) and Public Health (MPH). My premise for attaining the dual degrees was simple. Public health issues often cannot be addressed if accompanying social work issues are too overwhelming. For example, a single mother

struggling to find affordable childcare may not be concerned with a car seat or a bike helmet. A father trying to feed his family may not be concerned about lead abatement or emergency response.

The public's perception of public health is often related to high-profile incidents such as the 2009 H1N1 and national foodborne illness outbreaks. Most people are less aware of the day-to-day operations and accomplishments of those working in public health. These include the following 10 Essential Public Health Services:

1. *Monitoring health status.* If a health-related trend is associated with a specific subset of the population, public health workers might consult social workers to determine the best approach to use with that population. On one occasion, I consulted a social worker about an increase in infant deaths due, in part, to a unique cultural practice.

2. *Diagnosing and investigating health problems.* If an outbreak of a particular disease is associated with a certain practice, public health workers may consult with social workers to determine the most effective approach to gain the cooperation of the persons impacted by the illness. For example, outbreaks of *Salmonella* have occurred in the MSM (men who have sex with men) population. Social workers can suggest strategies for

providing education, prevention, and resource information to this population.

3. *Informing, educating, and empowering individuals about health issues.* Breast cancer awareness is an excellent example of collaborative synergy. Many states fund local health departments' free mammogram programs. Social workers may work in treatment and case management. As a health educator, I regularly sent out press releases to educate the community on breast cancer and related resources in the community, including social service agencies.

4. *Mobilizing community partnerships.* Local health departments regularly assess community needs and create plans based on those needs. They then collaborate with community partners on different projects to improve the quality of life in that community. Several years ago, I was involved in a project focused on improving the morbidity and mortality rates of children who were improperly restrained in a car. The National Highway Traffic Safety Administration offered week-long training that allowed me to become a certified child passenger seat technician. The health department funded and coordinated some of the first technician classes and car seat checks in the U.S. After public health funding for the project ended, community partners—hospitals, police, fire departments, social service agencies, and private businesses—still checked car seats while educating families on proper installation.

5. *Developing policies and plans that support individual and community health efforts.* The Master Settlement Agreement (MSA) of 1998 is a good example. The MSA was a legal settlement between tobacco companies and the Attorneys General of 46 states to recover billions of dollars in costs associated with treating smoking-related illnesses. The percentage of MSA funding allocated for smoking cessation and prevention messages varied by state. Public health and community partners, including social workers at various agencies, competed for state MSA funding to establish partnerships that would prevent the ravages of smoking.

6. *Enforcing laws and regulations that protect health and ensure safety.* Local health departments inspect restaurants looking for potential vectors—which may include infected individuals—in the transmission of disease-causing organisms. In my experience, restaurants voluntarily close at public health's recommendation if their site is associated with a known outbreak. It is in their best interest to cooperate with public health to stop the transmission of illness. However, enforcing regulations can be difficult. If someone in a sensitive

occupation (e.g., food service) is restricted from working for several months because she or he continues to shed an organism such as *Salmonella,* a public health worker might refer the employee to a social worker to help find a different occupation, obtain training, or address the emotional impact of the experience. If religious and/or cultural issues make disease transmission more likely, social workers have the cultural competency skills to work with public health officials to find realistic solutions.

7. *Linking people to needed personal health services and assuring the provision of health care when otherwise unavailable.* With more retailers offering free internet access, an exponential increase of smart phones (e.g., Android, iPhone), and the rising popularity of social media sites, people can easily locate personal health services. This has increased exposure to both reliable and unreliable resources. Due to the latter, one of our greatest public health successes, vaccinations for children, has suffered a major setback. People often choose to believe anecdotal stories spread through the internet, smart phones, and social media possibly because they support the individual's personal beliefs or values, are easier to comply with, or because the individual gets swept up in the fervor. As more Americans refuse to vaccinate

their children, certain vaccine-preventable diseases not seen in large numbers in the U.S. in decades, like whooping cough, are now on the rise.

8. *Assuring a competent public and personal healthcare workforce.* Public health funding is a hotly debated topic among the public and politicians. Many mistakenly believe public health services target only the poor. Over the last few years, cuts to public health budgets at all levels have resulted in the loss of thousands of public health jobs, with many positions being furloughed. This has greatly weakened the overall public health infrastructure. Knowledge gained from experience is invaluable. Due to many public health agencies eliminating or combining positions, key people within the infrastructure are missing the knowledge, confidence, and experience their predecessors gained when public health was better staffed. The shortage of both competent workers and grant funds has forced public health organizations to make tough choices when prioritizing community health issues, putting added stress on private providers.

9. *Evaluating the effectiveness, accessibility, and quality of personal and population-based health services.* The public's lack of trust in government, including public health, is understandable. They hear conflicting

recommendations from both government and private sources, sometimes due to the nuances of public health information and issues despite the clarity (or lack of) of communication. For example, if two people become ill after eating together, and one of the two contacts a public health organization. This individual is adamant that he knows the cause of his illness. The communicable disease investigator asks him additional questions (e.g. his three-day food history, other meals he shared with the other sick person, whether he's been handling animals, etc.) because it usually takes several days to manifest symptoms after exposure to food-borne pathogens. Not understanding the complexity of an investigation, the individual may become frustrated when public health cannot immediately identify the source of an outbreak. The local interview is often the first step of many in identifying national outbreaks.

10. *Researching to find new insights and innovative solutions to health problems.* The Centers for Disease Control and Prevention (CDC) regularly evaluates data collected during national outbreaks to improve the handling of future outbreaks. For example, during an investigation of an intestinal disease, the local investigator identified what he believed to be the probable source of the

outbreak, but had not yet collected specimens from the potential source to confirm. When the investigator contacted the state for assistance, the state employee cited historical data and asked the locals to look for a different exposure. As it turned out, the state's recommendation was correct.

Funding continues to be a challenge for public health as increasing political polarization in the U.S. persists. Politically astute leaders who are knowledgeable about public health issues are needed at the federal, state, and local levels to compete for funds. They need to be adept at running social media campaigns. Political leaders lose credibility and public trust when their recommendations are incorrect or differ from those of neighboring jurisdictions. Hallmark decisions in the public health system are sometimes made based on public opinion rather than scientific literature. Public health does not have the expertise or funding to counter many well-executed social media campaigns. Politicians often side with public opinion despite seeing the scientific evidence because they do not want to offend their constituents.

Social workers in public health care settings often collaborate with other community organizations. For example, I worked on a committee whose goal was to ensure appropriate emergency medical care and disaster preparedness for children. We established a partnership with Telephone

Pioneers, a nonprofit charitable organization consisting primarily of employed and retired telecommunications employees. The Pioneers worked with area schools to identify children in need and provided those children with shoes and socks. The Pioneers solicited local businesses for donations. Members of our committee partnered with the Pioneers to accompany the children as they selected their new shoes and socks.

Social workers in public health must continually update their knowledge and competencies. For example, in my current role as an epidemiologist at a county health department, I regularly have to gain new knowledge and skills, For example, after 9/11, federal funding to prepare for a bioterrorism attack was disseminated to local health departments for the hiring of bioterrorism planners and epidemiologists. To respond to this need, I became a Certified Emergency Response Coordinator and worked with surveillance systems to provide situational awareness.

Public health agencies are tasked with establishing clinics to respond in an emergency and thus conduct exercises to prepare for these clinics. The majority of public health organizations had the opportunity to test those skills during the 2009 H1N1 outbreak. While working in an emergency clinic, public health officials quickly identified area taking a much higher patient load. In order to prevent errors due to fatigue, it was necessary to adjust that load. Because public health had drilled for such emergency clinics, the overall process of implementing 2009 H1N1 clinics went much more smoothly than expected in many jurisdictions.

Public health officials must routinely collect and analyze data for use in decision making. Through communicable disease investigations, public health officials can determine whether there is an outbreak and try to stop the spread of disease. Historical data can tell us when, as in the 2009 influenza epidemic, an outbreak is an anomaly that needs to be addressed.

The future of the public health field is exciting yet uncertain. Most people, including politicians, have difficulty distinguishing between public health (population-driven) and health care (individual-based). It is too early to determine the full implications of health care reform on public health. The debate surrounding government authority at the federal, state, and local level will affect the future of public health.

SOCIAL WORK PRACTICE IN SCHOOL SETTINGS

Social workers have been involved with schools throughout the history of the social work profession. The early settlement houses sent "visiting teachers" out to the homes of immigrant families to *establish a link between home, school, and community,* a mission that aligns with the goals of school social work today.

Unfortunately, the Depression of the 1930s and the rise of psychoanalysis in the helping professions limited the expansion of school social work until the 1960s when the federal government became formally involved in providing funds to support educational achievement for special populations. First, the Title I program provided resources to schools to help improve the reading skills of children from poor neighborhoods. This program is still included in the legislation that has become the massive regular education funding bill, the Elementary and Secondary Education Act (ESEA), known as *No Child Left Behind* during the George W. Bush administrations. ESEA contains many programs that address efforts to combat school failure among students living in poverty. In the mid-1970s, the passage of what is now called the Individuals with Disabilities Education Act (IDEA) provided states with funds for special education programs.

Special Needs

Source: iStock/Christopher Futcher

These federal acts mandate services that include roles for school social workers, and they have precipitated significant growth in the number of school social workers school districts have hired in the last 40 years. During this time, school social work became one of the special practice sections in NASW and was identified as a pupil personnel service in public schools. Social workers were specifically mandated to work in special education, but increasingly they also worked in regular educational settings. In both contexts, school social workers assist children whose difficulties with behavior and/or learning interfere with their ability to succeed in school. In this role, school social workers are at the forefront of efforts to support students at risk for school failure.

School social workers primarily provide individual and group counseling, case management, crisis intervention, support and information for students' families, assessments for special education eligibility and placement, IEP development and review, and collaboration with teachers and community resources, particularly child welfare services. Social work services may also be included in a student's IEP. School social workers play an important role in working at multiple levels of practice. At the individual level, social workers work with children and youth in the assessment and intervention of depression and suicide risk assessment. At the individual, group, and organizational levels, social workers work to address issues related to bullying (including cyberbullying). At the organizational and policy level, social workers advocate for more funding for prevention and education programs, develop programs to address issues of lack of awareness and stigma related to youth mental health issues, and help school staff and students connect in meaningful ways, (Dietsche, 2014). For more information on the issue of bullying, visit: www.stopbullying.gov/.

The School Social Work Association of America (SSWAA) is a national organization representing school social workers. The SSWAA recently developed for the future of school social work (www.sswaa.org). A newer organization, the American Council for School Social Work (ACSSW), focuses on evidenced-based practice for the field (www.acssw.org). Exhibit 8.12 presents the NASW guidelines for school social work practice.

Policy-Practice Considerations in School Social Work

Today, school social work responsibilities can differ across states, across districts, and even between schools in the same district. Depending on the way in which a school district manages special education services, a school social worker may work only in special education, only in regular education, or in both. All school social workers do not work for public school districts. An increasing number work in urban, suburban, and rural parochial or private schools. Some school social workers are employed by public or not-for-profit agencies and are placed in schools as *school-based social workers*. Special schools within districts may operate as *community education centers*, *full-service schools* (schools that provide health, mental health, and social services on site), or *alternative schools* (these may be private or part of a public school district). In the last decade, social workers have increasingly found employment in charter schools. These different educational settings endeavor to improve upon regular public education by specializing in one or more of these curriculum changes: more intensive, individualized teaching methods; emphasis on mental health services; or providing a wider, more meaningful role for parent and community involvement than usually found in regular public school districts.

EXHIBIT 8.12

Guidelines for School Social Work Services

Qualifications: School social workers shall meet the provisions for professional practice set by NASW and their respective state department of education and possess knowledge and understanding basic to the social work profession as well as the local education system.

Assessment: School social workers shall conduct assessments of individuals, families, and systems/organizations (namely, classroom, school, neighborhood, district, state) with the goal of improving student social, emotional, behavioral, and academic outcomes.

Intervention: School social workers shall understand and use evidence- informed practices in their interventions.

Workload Management: School social workers shall organize their workloads to fulfill their responsibilities and clarify their critical roles within the educational mission of the school or district in which they work.

Cultural Competence: School social workers shall ensure that students and their families are provided services within the context of multicultural understanding and competence.

Interdisciplinary Leadership and Collaboration: School social workers shall provide leadership in developing a positive school climate and work collaboratively with school administration, school personnel, family members, and community professionals as appropriate to increase accessibility and effectiveness of services.

Advocacy: School social workers shall engage in advocacy that seeks to ensure that all students have equal access to education and services to enhance their academic progress.

Source: Adapted from National Association of Social Workers (NASW), 2012b.

School social workers have an array of responsibilities, including (NASW CWS, 2010b, p. 1):

- Conducting biopsychosocial assessments.
- Assessing students for substance use/abuse, support systems, physical and emotional functioning, barriers to academic performance, peer issues, suicidal/homicidal ideation, and mental health issues.
- Developing and implementing treatment and discharge plans that support student self-determination.
- Providing direct therapeutic services (e.g., individual, family, and group treatment).
- Providing crisis intervention services and safety assessments.
- Advocating for students' best interests and services.
- Providing case management services (e.g., referrals to community resources and collaboration with other professionals).

■ Providing educational programs for teaching, staff, students, and parents.
■ Conducting home visits.
■ Identifying and resolving ethical issues.
■ Contributing to the multidisciplinary team.

R. Jan Wilson, MSW, Ph.D., LCSW, Saint Louis University School of Social Work

In my years as a school social worker, I have worked for a variety of organizations in which my job responsibilities were associated with schools, often in alternative school settings. I served in an on-grounds school at Youth in Need, a residential shelter that provided education and therapeutic support for adolescents in residential care and for students expelled from local school districts for behavior problems. I provided support services to students at an independent GED program. Though I was employed by a not-for-profit agency, my work was school-based in that I ran a program for teen parents in five school districts and partnered with Parents As Teachers, a program focused on helping parents develop their parenting skills. As part of that program, I worked with the community to start a daycare center for teen mothers.

Any social work job that involves working with children and youth inevitably includes working with a school system. In one role, I provided support services for families of children with disabilities. In this position I worked closely with the special education cooperative to help parents learn to navigate the services system and to teach them strategies for advocating for their children to receive appropriate services for which they were eligible.

School-based social workers tend to have responsibilities for students with mental health issues. Working with these complex and ongoing issues, these social workers stay involved with their clients throughout the entire year—not just during school. Providing services for students and families experiencing mental illness requires the social worker to have a community perspective on social work practice (i.e., viewing the issue within the context of the student and family place within the community, availability of community-based resources, and examining ways in which the community can support the student and family). While social workers working in alternative school settings have a collaborative contracted relationship with the school district in which they are placed, their primary responsibility is the agency where they are employed. The agency may be more focused on social services, while school settings focus on education. Many educational settings only collaborate with one social worker at a time, so it is

Source: Getty Images

important for school-based social workers to be comfortable practicing independently.

School social work provided me with a systemic view of social service and education systems. These two areas comprise a large knowledge base, and I was constantly learning about new information and resources. I worked at all levels of social work practice: micro, mezzo, and macro. As a generalist practitioner in school social work, I had to integrate practice across a wide range of specialties from health to counseling to community organization and program evaluation. I found that I enjoyed the fast pace of school social work. School social work presents a wide range of practice options and requires one to be a life-long learner in order to maintain current expertise in the changing world of students and their families.

SOCIAL WORK PRACTICE IN SMALL COMMUNITIES AND RURAL SETTINGS

In 2010, the U.S. Census Bureau defined small (or rural) communities as those areas of less than 50,000 persons that lie outside of more densely populated areas known as urbanized areas or urban clusters. Social work practice in rural communities is an important area of practice that sometimes goes unnoticed because fewer persons live in rural communities than at any point in U.S. history. The availability of social workers is particularly low in more rural states. For example, the number of licensed social workers per 100,000 persons ranges from a high of 408 (in Maryland, which abuts Washington, D.C.) to a low of 23.7 (in largely rural New Hampshire) (CHWS/CWS, 2006). Early pioneers in rural social work focused on political and policy changes needed to increase the availability of social work services in rural communities, specifically those related to health care, social welfare, and education (Brown, 1933; Mackie, 2011; Martinez-Brawley, 1983).

Small communities in nonmetropolitan areas have a chronic need for generalist social workers with expertise at all levels of practice; however, the Rural Social Work Caucus notes that social work employment opportunities in rural communities are on the rise. A typical social worker in a rural community may be working with individuals and families while at the same time identifying gaps in the delivery system, working with other organizations, and advocating for policy change (Robinson, 2013, p. 98). Mental health in particular is an area in which social workers are needed as they are often the only providers of mental health services in rural areas (Clark, 2003; Gibelman, 2004).

Typically, smaller communities have more BSW social workers than MSWs and doctoral-level social workers. However, despite the small numbers of citizens and lack of services, small communities can have diverse populations. Generalist social workers in these communities are thus well prepared to function at multiple levels and to be knowledgeable about a wider array of issues and resources than may be needed in an urban area where the number of practicing social workers allows for specialization. While practicing in a rural community has many advantages, including a sense of community, recruiting an adequate number of social workers in rural communities may require organizations to consider offering benefits such as loan forgiveness, support for licensure and continuing education, and job security (Phillips, Quinn, & Heitkamp, 2010).

Policy-Practice Considerations in Rural Settings

As generalist social work practice is the method best suited to small and rural areas, social work educators are being called upon to include rural social work practice in social work curricula so that students will understand the sophisticated level of skill and knowledge required for competent rural practice (NASW, 2012–2014m). This focus can help rural social workers conceptualize the possible differences between urban and rural practice and incorporate these differences into the training of other social workers. The Southern Regional Education Board Manpower Education and Training Project's Rural Task Force developed a set of 19 assumptions that includes guidelines for social workers in rural settings (Southern Regional Education Board Manpower Education and Training Project's Rural Task Force, 1998). For example, people living in rural communities are becoming more similar to rather than different from people living in urban areas. The internet and social media have enabled persons in small communities to gain access to people around the world, goods, services, and even some health care. Still inequities persist between life in rural and urban communities, primarily in the areas of economic opportunities, employment, and transportation (Ginsberg, 2014). Although some rural communities may lack even basic services, greater priority is placed by community leadership on services to sustain life than on those to enhance the quality of life. Rural communities have unique characteristics that can include geographically scattered poverty; generational poverty; resistance to formal services and professionals, particularly those who are not members of the community; and more informal service networks.

Practice in small communities can be a uniquely rewarding and challenging opportunity. In addition to their generalist training, social workers who practice in rural communities are required to develop knowledge, skills, and values appropriate for that community. The rural social worker must build on the strengths of community members in the face of oftentimes significant adversity within the community and surrounding region (Robinson, 2013). The social worker may do this by understanding the community's unique aspects and using its customs and traditions as a basis for interventions; respecting the community's culture and values; working within an informal network of services and resources; and developing new resources as needed (Southern Regional Education Board, 1998).

The social worker often plays overlapping roles in a small community. Whereas an urban setting typically offers a social worker anonymity and more formality, in smaller communities, social workers often have not only a history with, but also multiple ties to, persons to whom they provide services. In fact, particularly in rural areas, "social workers' relationships with clients and the community are multi-layered, intertwined, excruciatingly visible, and unbelievably complicated" (Blue & Kutzler, 2014, p. 1). Such complex roles are not impossible in a larger community, but the potential for them is greater in a rural area due to its smaller population. Multiple roles can be both a strength and a liability in the social work relationship. Knowing a person's background, support system, and resources can be an asset in engaging her or him, assessing the situation, and developing and implementing an intervention. On the other hand, having extensive prior knowledge can compromise the social worker's professional objectivity. To practice with competence, social workers must work within the culture and communications patterns of the community and anticipate potential ethical issues (e.g., dual relationships) (Daley, 2010). Understanding that interactions may entail a personal connection and acknowledging how information travels through community networks are key aspects to rural social work practice (Ginsberg, 2011).

Ellen Burkemper, Ph.D., MSW, LCSW, LMFT, RN, School of Social Work

For the last 25 years, I have provided a number of social work professional services in my small, rural community. I have found that social work practice in the small community is varied and requires that I be flexible and able to engage in services at the individual, family, group, and community levels. Through funding from the Department of Health, I participated in a program in which social workers obtain MSWs to provide mental health services through and in rural physicians' offices. Already a registered nurse, I was particularly well suited to this program, as I was familiar with the medical setting and terminology and lived in a rural community.

Upon completing my MSW, I had the opportunity to work in my community's mental health center as the center's coordinator and social work clinician. This practice opportunity brought forth all of my MSW generalist and clinical education and training. I was already knowledgeable about the services available in my community and knew the local physicians and clergy who serve as the primary gatekeepers for referrals for mental health services. I felt this position was a proactive way for me to bring the practice of social work to my community.

My responsibilities in the rural community mental health center included working with individuals, families, groups, organizations, and the community. Some of my practice activities included:

- Providing clinical services (therapy) to individuals and families.
- Working with other agencies to identify and develop community services.
- Representing the center at community meetings and events.
- Organizing fund-raising events.
- Collaborating with other programs involved in the provision of services to persons living with chronic and persistent mental illness.
- Making presentations to community groups on the services provided by the center.
- Serving as a member of the agency's advisory board.
- Writing newspaper articles regarding mental health concerns.

Due to a lack of funding and a need to consolidate services, the center closed after I had worked there for 10 years. The closing might have been a crisis for some people, but I realized that I had gained considerable expertise in clinical and administrative practice. Because of the confidence I had gained as a social worker, I decided to establish a private clinical practice as a solo practitioner. Concurrent with the opening of my private practice, I continued my education, earning a doctoral degree in marriage and family therapy. I also began to work as a trainer and consultant for therapeutic foster parents for child protective services in my county.

The opportunities I have had to provide services in my small community have been rewarding. In small communities, there is a need for mental health services, and social workers are ideally suited to provide these services. As generalists, social workers are trained to engage in all levels of practice, and that versatility enables us to exercise our talents and education. Working in a small community allows me to be more flexible and to perform a range of duties because I am one of a few social services providers in the community.

Working in a small community can present challenges, particularly ethical ones. Rural social workers need to appreciate the special implications of the possible dual relationships that can occur in a small community. My family and I are active in my community, and living and working in a small community means that I am likely to run into clients while grocery shopping, attending weddings, and at church, professional gatherings, or school events. I learned to be careful to keep office work at the office. It is particularly important that client systems knowingly provide informed consent for the social worker to discuss their case with other professionals and that the social worker not discuss cases with friends, family members, or acquaintances. Clients must fully understand the social worker's role

and functions, and the special implications of confidentiality in a small community. I talk with clients about the likelihood that we will encounter one another outside the professional social work setting. I inform clients that should that occur, I will not acknowledge them until they acknowledge me. By placing the decision to communicate in a public setting with clients, I am providing them with the right to self-determination.

Social workers are needed in small communities. Social workers who live and work in the small community have a more complete view of that community than those who drive to the job and return home to other communities. Having been a member of a family in this farming community, my knowledge of the community helps me understand the culture in which client systems live. This insight has provided me with a more efficient understanding of my clients' backgrounds, social environments, and rural ethic. A recent development in my small community is the influx of new residents from the nearby urban area, making us one of the fastest growing areas in the state. Rapid economic growth and increased diversity have been positive for the area and have enabled social workers to help the community to embrace change.

I see small-community social work as a viable field of practice. It offers the opportunity to engage in all levels of practice. In some cases, a benefit of rural practice is the ease of getting tasks accomplished due to the smaller numbers of individuals who need to be consulted. Social workers living and working in small communities are a minority, but rural areas can be an opportunity for employment, and for the expression of professional talents and education.

CONCLUSION

Although vastly different in terms of the settings in which they practice, the populations with whom they work, and the challenges they face, this chapter's "voices from the field" share a number of similarities and common themes. Each of these social workers possesses a social work degree, not a degree in a more specialized field like gerontology, substance abuse treatment, or counseling. Upon completion of the requirements for the social work degree, the social worker is equipped with a set of knowledge, skills, and values that enables her or him to practice at multiple levels with diverse populations in different settings. Specific knowledge of a population and setting is required, but the engagement, assessment, intervention, and evaluation process is common regardless of the targeted client system or setting. Having knowledge of the social work role within a wide range of populations and settings is critical for all social workers.

Another similarity is that each of these social workers emphasizes a strengths-based perspective, regardless of their particular field of practice. Being able to identify the assets and resources a client system or population possesses is essential to being an effective advocate, an ethical practitioner, and a partner with the client system in the change process.

The narratives also provide evidence of the importance of critical thinking as a social work skill. For example, in Jon's narrative on working in chemical dependency and addiction treatment, he describes a traditional treatment modality for substance abuse. Moreover, he voices skepticism regarding the effectiveness of that particular approach for all substance abusers and offers his insights into an alternative framework. Jon's social work training instilled in him the value of questioning and examining his social work practice so that all intervention possibilities can be explored.

All of these social workers' experiences also underscore the importance of advocacy and policy practice. Advocacy is a vital skill, especially when resources are a critical factor and policies are limiting. To provide better access to services, social workers must advocate with legislators on issues such as universal health insurance coverage, equity in mental health benefits, economic reform, and the needs of oppressed groups whose voices are not being heard, for example, older adults, children, persons with disabilities, refugees and immigrants, battered women, and persons in the criminal justice system.

Several of the narratives in this chapter provide insights into social workers' opportunities to build on the practice skills they use with individuals and families in order to move into administrative and management roles. Herb, Suzanne, and Barbara all write how their administrative work is grounded in knowledge of the issues social workers face working with individuals, families, and groups.

Shortages exist in several of the fields of practice described here. More social workers are needed to work with older adults, in substance abuse and addiction treatment, in the child welfare arena, and in small communities. Employment opportunities in the areas of mental health, substance abuse treatment, and marriage and family therapy are expected to grow 23–27% in the next decade (BLS, 2014b). Initiatives have been launched by public and private organizations to increase the number of degreed social workers working in areas such as gerontology and child welfare, but still more initiatives are needed. To gain the experience to respond to these emerging needs, social work students can seek out coursework, field experiences, research opportunities, and service or volunteer experiences in a variety of areas. When social workers gain knowledge and experience with a broad range of populations and settings, they both identify the areas that are the best professional fit for them and help meet the needs of the profession. Using a strengths-based approach, you can assess your strengths and explore professional areas in which those strengths can be assets. To help you in your exploration, check out the information provided in Exhibit 8.13.

MAIN POINTS

- Social workers' range of knowledge and skills should include knowledge of human behavior and biology; the philosophy of other disciplines; awareness of cultures, faith traditions, laws, policies, and social systems; and the ability to work with a diverse population of clients and other professionals.
- A generalist social work degree enables a professional to practice in a variety of different fields over the course of a career, including mental health, chemical dependency, and criminal justice. Within the field, you can work with a variety of client systems at the micro, mezzo, and macro levels.
- In this chapter, thirteen social workers present their experiences in twelve different fields, from working with older adults to working in a rural community, with the goal of sharing the diversity, challenges, and rewards of the social work profession.
- Diverse practice areas share common social work themes. For example, working with older adults and persons with disabilities requires knowledge of both medical and health issues. Working in mental health and child welfare involves interactions with both the legal and health systems.

EXHIBIT 8.13

Activities for Learning About Fields of Practice

Check out social work organizations:

- The website for NASW, located at www.naswdc.org, contains information about the organization and its activities as well as information on specific fields of practice. Be sure to check out NASW's Career Center, located at: http://careers.socialworkers.org/.
- Latino Social Workers Organization, a group for social workers to share experiences regarding education, employment, and the Latino community, located at: www.lswo.org.
- National Association of Black Social Workers, an organization committed to enhancing the quality of life and empowering people of African ancestry through advocacy, human service delivery, and research, is located at: www.nabsw.org.
- North American Puerto Rican and Hispanic Social Workers, a group for social workers and other human service professionals to strengthen, develop, and improve the resources and services that meet the needs of the Puerto Rican and Hispanic communities, located at: www. naprhsw.org.
- Rural Social Work Caucus is an organization focused on issues related to rural social work practice, located at www.ruralsocialwork.org.
- School Social Work Association of America, an organization of social workers working in public and private schools, located at: www.sswaa.org.
- International Federation of Social Workers, a global organization striving for social justice, human rights, and social development, located at: www.ifsw.org.
- Socialworkhelper.com, an international social networking site to provide connections for students and professionals in the helping professionals, located at: www.socialworkhelper. com/index.html.

Read! There is a wealth of social work literature out there. Some possibilities of books for general reference and informational reading include:

Barker, R.L. (2014). *The social work dictionary*. Washington, DC: NASW Press.

Grobman, L.M. (2005a). *Days in the lives of social workers (3rd edition)*. Harrisburg, PA: White Hat Communications.

Grobman, L.M. (2005b). *More days in the lives of social workers*. Harrisburg, PA: White Hat Communications.

Grobman, L.M. (2007). *Days in the lives of gerontological social workers*. Harrisburg, PA: White Hat Communications.

Mizrahi, T. & Davis, L.E. (2008). *Encyclopedia of social work (20th edition)*. Washington, DC & New York, NY: NASW Press and Oxford Press.

National Association of Social Workers. (2012–2014). *Social work speaks. NASW policy statements 2012–2014 (9th edition)*. Washington, DC: NASW Press.

Corcoran, K. & Roberts, A.R. (2015). *Social workers' desk reference (3rd edition)*. New York, NY: Oxford Press.

While the list of social work-related journals is far too extensive to list here, you can check your school's library for a listing or review:

National Association of Social Workers. (2009). *Author's guide to social work journals (5th edition)*. Washington, DC: NASW Press.

Several easily accessible and informative journals include:

BPD Update Online. This online journal is published by The Association of Baccalaureate Social Work Program Directors and is available at http://bpdonline.org.

Journal of Social Work Values and Ethics. Available at www.socialworker.com/jswve, this online journal is dedicated to examining ethical and values issues that impact social work practice, research, and theory development.

The New Social Worker. Published by White Hat Publications, this journal is targeted for social work students and new professionals and is available at: www.socialworker.com.

Social Work. The official publication of the National Association of Social Workers.

Social Work Today. A biweekly magazine for social workers. For free subscription information, go to: www.socialworktoday.com.

For all your social work projects, check into these social work-related databases: www.findarticles.com. A constantly updated, free search engine, articles can be printed in their entirety at no cost.

Information for Practice—http://ifp.nyu.edu/archive. This website provides news and new scholarship from around the world that is relevant for social work practice.

Government documents—www.pueblo.gsa.gov and www.access.gpo.gov.

EXERCISES

1. Use the Sanchez family interactive case (www.routledgesw.com/caseStudies) to get a better sense of some of the practice issues mentioned in this chapter:
    a. Review the case file for Roberto Salazar. Then select Roberto and answer his Critical Thinking Questions.
    b. Review the case file for Carmen Sanchez. Then select Carmen and answer her Critical Thinking Questions.
    c. Review the case file for Gloria Sanchez Quintanilla. Then select Gloria and answer her Critical Thinking Questions.
2. Go to the Carla Washburn interactive case at www.routledgesw.com/caseStudies and read her case file. Develop a list of questions you have about working with older adults. Using the section in this chapter and other sources you can locate, identify the specific gerontological knowledge and skills needed to provide social work services to an older adult.

3. Go to the NASW website at www.naswdc.org/pressroom/features/issue-factsheets.asp. Click on Issue Fact Sheets and read about the various fields of practice discussed in this chapter. Choose three fields that interest you, and reflect on your reasons for being interested in those fields. Develop a list of questions regarding areas in which you would like to have more information, and reflect in writing on possible sources that will provide answers to your questions.

4. With assistance from your instructor, identify a social work student with whom you can conduct an interview regarding her/his primary field of practice interests. Your goal is to gain insight into the reasons that your fellow student has chosen a social work career, the pros and cons of majoring in social work, and the life and academic experiences that she or he perceives to be helpful in pursuing a social work career. Summarize your interview and write a reflection about the information you have learned.

5. With your instructor's assistance, identify a social worker with whom you can conduct an interview regarding her/his primary field of practice. Develop a set of questions to pose to the social work professional, and conduct an interview regarding her or his training, experiences, philosophy, and practice wisdom. Summarize your interview and write a reflection about the information you have learned.

6. You have been given the opportunity to read about various fields of practice in social work. Imagine that you are working in one of these fields. Given your own experience, respond to the following questions. After responding to the questions below, prepare a written reflection on any new insights, thoughts, and/or questions you have.
   a. How might political, economic, and social issues impact your work?
   b. What are the potential "isms" that you might encounter in this field of practice?
   c. How might you adjust to the issues you identified in the previous two questions?

7. Go to the Brickville interactive case at www.routledgesw.com/caseStudies. Review the information about the community and the Stone family. After identifying three areas for potential intervention, use the information in this chapter to create a summary of potential areas for social work involvement.

SOCIAL WORK PRACTICE WITH INDIVIDUALS AND FAMILIES

Individual and family social work practice (micro-level practice)
A method of social practice in which the social worker works with a client system comprised of an individual or family to develop a planned change effort that meets the needs of the individual or family.

Micro social work practice
Working with individuals, couples, and families in direct social work practice toward the goal of planned change *see* individual and family social work practice.

This chapter explores the cornerstone of social work practice: providing services to individuals, couples, and families. Individual and family social work practice, also known as micro social work practice, involves working one-on-one with individuals and families and is the primary focus of most practicing social workers. In individual and family practice, social workers engage, assess, plan, and then terminate and evaluate the social work intervention.

Almost all (96%) social work practitioners spend a portion of their time providing direct services to clients, and over two-thirds report that direct services with individuals and families is their primary practice area, where they spend more than half of their overall work time (Center for Health Workforce Studies & Center for Workforce Studies, 2006; Whitaker & Arrington, 2008). Opportunities for practicing social work with individuals, couples, and families continue to increase. Not surprisingly, a larger proportion of younger and more recently graduated social workers are employed in direct practice areas, while many older, more experienced social workers often move into supervisory, administrative, management, teaching, and research positions.

Practitioners who work with individuals and families continue to work primarily in traditional settings such as health care, mental health, and family services, but they are also found in educational, faith-based, and correctional settings. This chapter focuses on the history and purposes of this level of practice and identifies the skills essential for direct practice with individuals and families. Exhibit 9.1 tells the story of one social worker's career working with individuals and families in a variety of settings.

HISTORICAL PERSPECTIVE ON SOCIAL WORK PRACTICE WITH INDIVIDUALS AND FAMILIES

As you learned in Chapter 2, the history of social work is, in many ways, the history of social work practice with individuals and families. The friendly visitors, outdoor relief, and eventually, the Charity Organization Society movement of the 19th century all served as the forerunners of modern-day social work practice with individuals and families.

The work of these early practitioners evolved into a methodology referred to as social casework. Recall from Chapter 1 that social casework is a method of social work practice in which social workers, through direct contact with the client system, help individuals and families to resolve personal challenges and then work with them to monitor change.

In her 1922 book, *What Is Social Case Work?*, Mary Richmond provided the basis for the teaching and practice of social casework for many decades to come. Richmond proposed that practitioners help individuals adjust to their

EXHIBIT 9.1

Shannon's Story: A Social Work Career Working with Individuals and Families

Shannon Cooper-Sadlo, Ph.D., LCSW, LMFT, has BSW and MSW degrees and has worked in children's residential care, a youth shelter, programs for persons who are chronically mentally ill and homeless, a public mental health facility, an in-patient psychiatric unit, and as a therapist in out- and in-patient substance abuse treatment programs. Here is her story.

I started my career in mental health-related social work as many social workers do, by chance. I originally wanted to work with children, but at the time there were very few jobs in this area of the field. I accepted a position at an agency that provided mental health services for the homeless, where I would be working on the mobile outreach team. During my employment, I realized that this was the right area of social work for me. I enjoyed the fast-paced environment, working in the community rather than in an office, and that no day was ever the same. After completing my MSW with a concentration in community mental health, I had opportunities to work in community support, as a psychiatric social worker at a hospital, and, finally, as a therapist in a community mental health center.

I enjoy working with individuals who are experiencing severe and persistent mental health issues because I am interested in human behavior and relationships. The reason I chose this career in direct service was not to be an observer, but to be a participant in the lives of the people with whom I am honored to work. Hearing their stories of resilience and being a part of their journeys to health continue to motivate me. I am grateful to the clients who have allowed me to share their roads, often finding myself in awe of the fierce spirits that I have met.

The challenges that I experience are often related to access to services and the stigma associated with mental health issues. The lack of appropriate services and resources for persons with mental health issues is frustrating and can be devastating to the clients. I believe the stigma that is still associated with mental illness is an important reason for the difficulties clients face accessing services and for the inadequate funding of mental health services. Current policies are short-sighted, reactionary, and often punitive rather than preventative. Still, the rewards of working in this field outweigh the challenges. Being a part of a recovery story or helping someone achieve goals of stability and health make this job worth all the struggle.

In order to have a career in the mental health field you have to be flexible, adaptable, and maintain a sense of humor. Recognize the limitations of the systems, but always advocate for change. Enjoy the people who have trusted you with their stories and their lives. They are often the most interesting, resilient, and insightful people you will ever have the pleasure to know.

situations by identifying needs, goals, and resources (McNutt & Floersch, 2008). Early social workers were trained in the idea that the social casework approach could be used to help individuals and families resolve problems caused by "deviations from accepted standards of normal social life" (Brieland, 1995, p. 2251). For example, social workers who engaged in casework during this period may have worked with an immigrant family to obtain housing and jobs, helped a widow to obtain financial assistance, or facilitated the adoption of an orphaned child. Social casework continued to be the prevailing model for social work practice well into the 20th century.

This exclusive focus on the individual changed when the social upheaval of the 1960s brought attention to the issues of race, ethnicity, poverty, and human rights (McNutt & Floersch, 2008). This attention prompted social workers to take a broader, more holistic perspective when intervening with client systems. In the 1960s and 1970s, micro practice experienced a number of shifts. The ecological model, which embraced the environmental perspective, gained prominence. The profession began to respond to the demand for research to support and guide practice. Perhaps most significantly, the generalist social work practice model emerged, emphasizing an ecological, systemic, and strengths-based approach to working with individuals, groups, organizations, and communities.

THE PLANNED CHANGE PROCESS IN SOCIAL WORK PRACTICE WITH INDIVIDUALS AND FAMILIES

Change is the purpose of the social worker's involvement with client systems at all levels of practice. Change for the client system involves embracing new attitudes or behaviors. Establishing goals for change is a key component of the social work relationship.

The wide variety of change efforts in which social workers participate in their work with individuals and families includes:

- Beginning or ending a phase of life such as marriage, divorce, parenting, career change, caring for a family member, retirement, or grief.
- Relationship challenges such as issues in friend, romantic, family, marital, parent/child, or employment relationships.
- Life crises such as physical or mental health challenges, violence, natural or economic disasters, or legal situations.
- Substance use, abuse, and addictions (for example: alcohol, drugs, food, gambling, sexual, or spending).

All interventions revolve around **planned change**, a process in which the social worker and client collaborate to plan and then execute a series of actions designed to enhance the client's functioning and well-being. Planned change for interventions with individuals, families, groups, organizations, and communities includes four phases:

1. Engagement
2. Assessment
3. Intervention
4. Evaluation.

See Exhibit 9.2 for a depiction of the planned change model.

Change is a fluid process that involves unexpected starts and stops. Even if the client is able to establish goals for change, work toward achieving those goals may be interrupted when real-life factors intervene. For example, a client seeking employment may be delayed when her or his car breaks down or childcare arrangements fall through. It is the social worker's responsibility to engage in an ongoing assessment of client needs in order to adjust the planned intervention and to monitor and support the change process by helping the individual anticipate and respond to challenges and crises. In addition, social workers should keep in mind the profession's commitment to social justice in all areas of practice. In working with individuals and families, social workers are ethically obligated to help clients seek access to needed resources and to advocate on behalf of clients when organizations, institutions, and services are not responding in a just manner (McLaughlin, 2009).

To facilitate planned change, the social worker must understand the situation from the client's perspective. Some clients want to change something in their lives and feel capable of doing so, whereas others who desire change feel incapable. Still other clients perceive no need for change. The saying "starting where the client is" guides social workers in gaining insight into the client's perception of the problem, its origins, and the desired goal or outcome. The social worker should never make assumptions regarding the client's thoughts, feelings, and values or impose her or his desired goals on the client. Instead, the social worker must understand the client's personal motivation and capacity for change.

Recall from Chapter 7 that the strengths-based perspective is based on the belief that the client is the expert on her or his life, and the social worker's role is to support and empower the client to enhance her or his life function and well-being. Thus the social worker is a collaborator in the planned change process, not the creator or director. Staying true to this social work approach often requires social workers to take stock of their thoughts and feelings about the client's situation, choices, and goals. Social workers must consistently compare the client's goals with their own to ensure that the goals being worked toward are the client's and not those of the social worker. As we all know from

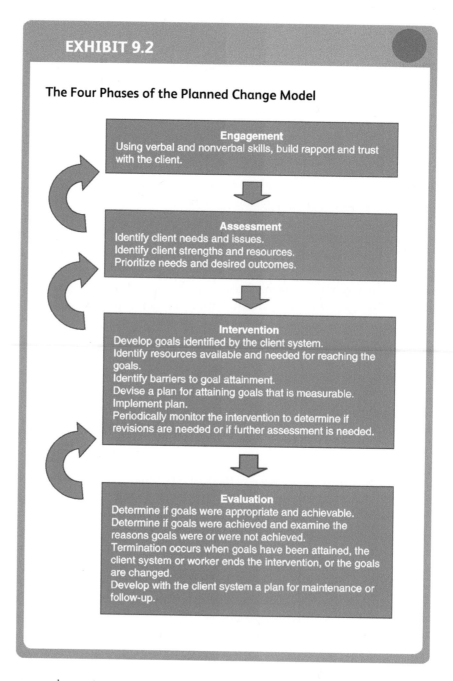

EXHIBIT 9.2

The Four Phases of the Planned Change Model

Engagement
Using verbal and nonverbal skills, build rapport and trust with the client.

Assessment
Identify client needs and issues.
Identify client strengths and resources.
Prioritize needs and desired outcomes.

Intervention
Develop goals identified by the client system.
Identify resources available and needed for reaching the goals.
Identify barriers to goal attainment.
Devise a plan for attaining goals that is measurable.
Implement plan.
Periodically monitor the intervention to determine if revisions are needed or if further assessment is needed.

Evaluation
Determine if goals were appropriate and achievable.
Determine if goals were achieved and examine the reasons goals were or were not achieved.
Termination occurs when goals have been attained, the client system or worker ends the intervention, or the goals are changed.
Develop with the client system a plan for maintenance or follow-up.

personal experience, our motivation is likely to be much higher when the goal we are working toward is one in which we are invested and one that we think has the most possibility for success. Clients are much more likely to be motivated to achieve goals that they themselves determine, desire, and believe in.

The difference in client and social worker goals may be particularly dramatic when working with clients who do not voluntarily seek assistance but who have been forced or even mandated to obtain social services. These clients may want nothing more than to end the professional relationship as soon as possible. Even then, the social worker's responsibility is to "start where the client is" and to identify common ground on which to build a working relationship, which may in turn reduce the client's ambivalent or negative feelings. In some cases, the common ground may be the mutual desire to terminate the relationship.

SKILLS FOR SOCIAL WORK PRACTICE WITH INDIVIDUALS AND FAMILIES

To practice social work with empathy and efficacy, the social worker must possess a repertoire of specialized skills. This section explores beginning social work skills for each of the four phases of the planned change intervention—engagement, assessment, intervention, and evaluation. These basic skills are essential for practice at all levels, and they serve as the foundation for the more advanced skills that social workers develop to address specific situations. To illustrate each of the four areas of the planned change model, follow Emily as she works with a client from engagement through termination and evaluation.

Engagement of Individuals and Families

Though Emily's career has taken her down many paths, the knowledge and skills she has developed for working with individuals and families have proved invaluable in all her practice experiences. She has learned to develop rapport, establish trust, build relationships, conduct interviews, engage clients, perform assessments, and to plan, execute, and evaluate interventions. These skills have formed the foundation of Emily's social work practice, and she has applied them when working with children, families, young adults, and older adult client systems.

While working at a sexual assault response program, Emily responded late one night to a call from a convenience store manager. A woman had come to the store and asked to use the telephone. Her swollen face and bleeding lip suggested that she had been physically assaulted. Recognizing the customer from previous visits to the store, the manager asked if the woman needed help. The woman, Victoria, burst into tears and told the manager she had been attacked as she was entering her apartment by a man she did not know. He dragged her into some bushes, beat and sexually assaulted her, and then left her in the bushes as he fled on foot. Victoria agreed to allow the manager to call Emily's agency, but not the police.

Emily first met Victoria in the store manager's office. As Emily entered the room, she observed Victoria lying on a couch in a fetal position and crying. When Emily moved toward her and said her name, Victoria visibly flinched. Emily recognized that, as a result of the trauma that Victoria had experienced, building trust with Victoria was critical to being able to establish rapport and trust with her.

Emily's first step was to sit down near Victoria, but not so close that Victoria might feel threatened. She told Victoria who she was and that she was there to help in any way that she could. She asked Victoria if she could get her a tissue. Emily spoke slowly and in a warm and soft tone. She leaned forward toward Victoria but made no attempt to touch her.

Emily told Victoria that the manager had informed her that Victoria had been attacked. Emily then suggested that if Victoria was willing and when she was ready, they could go to the hospital so that Victoria could be examined and could call the police to report the assault. Emily was careful not to use graphic, medical, or legal jargon at this point, focusing instead on helping Victoria to feel safe.

Emily sat with Victoria for an hour before Victoria said she was ready to go to the hospital. Emily assured Victoria that she would stay with her through the examination and the police interview. As Victoria rose from the couch, Emily asked for Victoria's permission to physically assist her in getting up and walking to the car. During the trip to the hospital, Emily explained to Victoria what she could expect when they reached the hospital. She continued to speak softly, calmly, and with empathy, assuring Victoria that she was now safe and in control.

In order to conduct a complete and accurate assessment of the client situation, the social worker's first task is to establish a working relationship

Family Work

Source: iStock/Christopher Futcher

of respect, trust, and rapport—three distinct phenomena. When the social worker respects the client, she or he treats the client with esteem and dignity. When the social worker is honest, demonstrates transparency in her or his communications, and follows through as promised, trust will develop in the relationship. The third area, rapport, is the "state of harmony, compatibilities, and empathy that permits mutual understanding and a working relationship between the client and the social worker" (Barker, 2014, p. 355). In the previous description of Emily's initial interactions with Victoria, Emily establishes rapport and builds trust by displaying respect before initiating the formal assessment process.

A component of building rapport is to display empathy for the person with whom you are working. Empathic responses convey compassion for the client's feelings and ideas as she or he is experiencing them at that moment (Barker, 2014). Empathy should not be confused with sympathy, two responses not conducive to helping the client feel empowered to make a change or to building a sense of mutual trust or respect (Gerdes, 2011). Sympathy and pity may instead convey to the client that she or he is not capable of positive change or growth.

Engaging the client is an essential step in building a successful relationship. Engagement is the process of establishing the beginnings of a working relationship with the client for the purposes of eliciting information in an open and sincere manner using both verbal and nonverbal communication. Typically, engagement is achieved through the use of an in-person interview in the home, office, or other setting, via telephone or video, with an individual, couple, family, or group. The interview is "a verbal exchange between one or more clients and one or more social workers in which the social workers involved draw on their knowledge, skills, and techniques to better understand and make judgments as to how to assist a client to enhance her or his psychosocial functioning" (Turner, 2008, p. 30). To ensure that the engagement interview is as successful and meaningful as possible for the client, the social worker must give careful consideration to the details, including using exceptional listening skills, maintaining authenticity, and providing the best possible setting. Is the site physically comfortable? What is the optimal seating arrangement? Is the setting private, confidential, and safe (Turner, 2008)?

To engage the client and build rapport, the social worker should attend to the following aspects of verbal communication:

- Speak at a pace the client can easily follow, particularly with clients whose first language is different from your own or with clients who have a hearing impairment.
- Speak not too loudly, but at a level that the client can easily hear.
- Speak with warmth and empathy.

Engagement
A component of the planned change effort in which the social worker establishes rapport with the client system based on trust and respect.

Interview
A verbal exchange between client and social worker, where the social worker uses his/her skills to better understand and make judgments as to how to assist the client.

- Use language appropriate to the client's culture, ethnicity, and social group, but do not attempt to use language that is unfamiliar to you. If you are uncertain about the appropriate language to use, conduct research prior to the encounter to learn about appropriate language, ask for the client's input regarding appropriate language, and/or review skills appropriate for cultural competence and humility.
- Use language appropriate to the client's educational level.
- Avoid professional jargon that may be unfamiliar to the client, including medical or legal terms or acronyms.
- Use respectful language to refer to individuals and groups, paying particular attention to avoiding language that promotes the "isms."
- Listen patiently, without interrupting, prompting, or interjecting, while the client tells her or his story. Silence on your part can be an effective strategy for enabling clients to speak.
- Avoid "ums," "you knows," and other unnecessary language.
- Provide information that is relevant to the beginning of the relationship, but be cautious about providing too much information or information that is not relevant at this point in the intervention.
- Provide encouragement to allow the client to share information, but take care not to provide inaccurate or false assurances.

Nonverbal communication is as important as verbal communication. Your attending skills can be a critical component of the engagement and rapport-building process. Important nonverbal issues to consider include:

- Ensure that you and the client are both physically on the same level (e.g., both sitting).
- Maintain direct eye contact, when culturally appropriate. When working with a family or small group, maintain equal eye contact with all members of the group. To look at one or some persons more than others can imply a preference or bias and can hamper your ability to establish trust with all members.
- Look at the client while speaking instead of, for example, looking out the window, at forms, or at the client's chart.
- Maintain physical and emotional focus on the client when the client speaks, as opposed to thinking ahead to the next question or comment.
- Avoid distractive behaviors (e.g., playing with pencil/hair, swinging leg, tapping on the desk, checking your phone/computer).
- Directly face the client.
- Lean slightly forward to convey attentiveness.
- Use nonverbal gestures that are typical and comfortable, but ensure that they are not excessive to the point of distraction (e.g., "speaking" with your hands).

■ Demonstrate appropriate facial expressions such as interest, warmth, and varied responses that are appropriate to the client's remarks. Facial expressions should be consistent with words.

As noted earlier, working with clients who have not voluntarily elected to see you requires specialized skills. Strategies that may be helpful in engaging with the involuntary client include (De Jong & Berg, 2013):

■ Assume the client does not want to accept anything that you have to offer.
■ Assume the client has good reasons for what they have chosen to do, think, or feel.
■ Assume the client will be cautious and protective; therefore, your role is to be supportive and not evaluative or judgmental.
■ Listen carefully to the client as she or he may provide information on those areas or people in her or his life that are important (even angry words can be illuminating).
■ When a client displays anger, inquire what the client may have done differently in her or his situation or what could have been different.
■ Ask what the client would like to happen both in her or his life and in the relationship with you.
■ Use relationship-focused questions (as opposed to confrontational or informational), such as "If you had not quit school, what would be different now?"
■ Be respectful when discussing the nonnegotiable aspects of your relationship, and ask for the client's thoughts about them.
■ Ask the client what she or he is willing and able to do about the current situation.
■ Maintain a "not knowing" stance (i.e., ask questions that will enable the client to share her or his thoughts and feelings to strengthen her or his sense of feeling in control).

Having insight into your communication style is critical to the helping process. Exhibit 9.3 provides a checklist of questions you can use to inventory your personal communication style. After answering the questions, identify those areas that may warrant attention in order to enhance your communication style as a social worker.

Assessment of Individuals and Families

Emily stayed with Victoria through the physical examination, the collection of evidence for the rape kit, and the police interview. Because these events took

EXHIBIT 9.3

Checklist of Communication Skills

- Are you more comfortable listening or talking?
- Do you view your role being to give advice or explore options?
- When listening to someone describe a difficulty or challenge, do you feel compelled to offer solutions immediately?
- Do you find it difficult to pay attention when others are talking?
- Do you find that while others are talking, you are thinking of what you are going to say next?
- Do you find that you notice nonverbal communication as well as the verbal message?
- Do you become so consumed with the details of a "story" that you miss the essence of the story?
- Do you have a difficult time listening to a "story" without interjecting your own personal experiences or biases?
- How do you determine if you got the essence of the story?
- Do you find that you are easily distracted when conversing with another person (i.e., watching other activities, thinking of things you have to do later)?
- How do you react to people who have difficulty communicating in a straightforward manner (i.e., non-focused, tangential), are uncommunicative, or hostile?
- Does your speech include "ums," "ers," or "you knows?"
- Do you feel that you communicate in a straightforward manner?
- What is your nonverbal communication style—use of hands and gestures, volume and tempo of your voice, posture?

Source: Updated from Corey & Corey, 1998, p. 69.

several hours, Emily had an opportunity through general conversation (versus formal, structured questioning) to become more familiar with Victoria's situation. She learned that Victoria had moved to the city several years earlier to attend college. She was now a management trainee at a department store in the mall and lived alone in a ground-floor apartment. She was engaged, but her fiancé lived in another state and visited only once a month. Her family was in her hometown several hours away.

By asking questions in a gentle, unobtrusive manner, Emily was able to begin the assessment process. Emily was careful not to ask questions that were not relevant to immediately ensuring Victoria's safety. Emily learned that Victoria's attacker likely knew where she lived and possibly that she lived alone.

She learned that Victoria had friends at school and work, but did not know anyone in her apartment complex, as she had just recently moved there. Victoria admitted that she was terrified to return to her apartment, but she did not want to leave town because of work and school commitments.

Assessment is the professional activity the social worker conducts with the client to provide the basis for understanding the client's situation and planning the social work intervention. The assessment process is ongoing throughout the social worker-client relationship and responds to changes that occur within the client's life situation. With the emergence of evidence-based practice models, assessments have become multi-faceted with a focus on collaboration between the social worker and the client, and on the client strengths, the client's desired outcomes, and the use of qualitative information (Jordan, 2008). In conducting an assessment at any level, the social worker focuses on three main tasks:

1. Using theoretical frameworks to guide the gathering of relevant information and the evaluation of the information to determine its meaning for the client system.
2. Evaluating the level of functioning of the client—with a focus on strengths—as well as the resources available to the entire client system.
3. Working with the client to define and prioritize the issues the intervention will address.

The social worker and the client then begin to develop the intervention, paying specific attention to the client system's desired outcomes and to the resources and strategies appropriate to achieve mutually agreed-upon goals (Logan, Rasheed, & Rasheed, 2008).

In order to develop an accurate assessment and effective intervention plan, the social worker and the client should approach the assessment process from multiple perspectives so that it may capture the complexity of the client's life. The assessment should take into account information gathered from multiple sources, including the client and collaterals (e.g., family members, friends, health and social service providers, and other professionals); archives (e.g., medical, legal, or educational records); direct observation; and standardized measures (O'Hare, 2009). Agencies typically have a uniform assessment format and content (including standardized assessment tools); several considerations that are important to the selection of a standardized measure include (Early & Newsome, 2005):

■ Select an assessment measure that can be used with all clients in a particular situation or program (e.g., family caregiver well-being scale) and an assessment measure that is relevant to the client's current situation (e.g., depression scale).

■ Explain to the client the reason and process for completing the measure.

■ If the client is completing the form, allow adequate time, space, and materials.

■ Be prepared to respond to client questions or requests for clarification.

■ Score the measure, and share the scores and their meaning with the client.

■ Store the measure in the client's record for use in the planning, intervention, and termination/evaluation process. Being able to see evidence of change may be helpful to the client and to the ongoing intervention plan (pp. 390–391).

Interview Practice Skills While an array of diverse methods and sources of information is needed to fully understand the client system, much of the necessary information can be gathered through a client interview; therefore, the next step in the assessment process is for the social worker to consider the types and quality of questions to ask the client. Questions should focus on gathering only information relevant to the situation at hand. They should be grounded in the strengths-based perspective, and they should convey to the client a sense of genuine support and empathy. Follow the interview guidelines below to elicit as much relevant information as possible and to optimize client comfort (Collins & Coleman, 2000; DeJong, 2008):

■ *Ask a balance of open-ended questions and closed-ended questions:*

> ■ Open-ended questions (questions that ask what and how and that ask about feelings) are helpful for gathering information and affirming the client's control of the situation.

> ■ Closed-ended questions and responses (questions that can be answered by yes, no, or short answers) are more directive, provide specific information, suggest specific answers, and allow the social worker to control the interview.

■ *Avoid excessive questioning:* A good rule to follow is to ask no more than two questions in succession without pausing to give yourself and the client time to reflect.

■ *Periodic reflection:* Recapping or paraphrasing the client's response, known as reflection, enables the social worker to clarify her or his understanding of the client's words. Recapping not only makes the client feel validated and understood, but also enables her or him to clarify any misunderstandings or add additional information or detail to the narrative. At the same time, it enables the social worker to consider the information and to plan for future comments and directions for the interview.

Open-ended questions
Eliciting information from a client system through asking questions that address feelings.

Closed-ended questions
Eliciting information from a client system through asking questions that can be answered by "yes", "no", or short answers. *see also* open-ended questions.

Reflection
Recapping or paraphrasing the client's response for the purpose of clarifying the statements made by the client system.

- *Silence:* Not speaking is an important social work skill. Pausing after asking a question enables the client to consider her or his response in a thoughtful manner.
- *Exploring meanings:* Through supportive and non-confrontational questioning, the social worker can delve deeper into client statements to gain insight into the thoughts and feelings behind actions, goals, barriers, or challenges.
- *Reframing:* Clients often present to social workers during challenging periods of their lives and thus have a negative or pessimistic perspective on their situations and are skeptical about any goals or plans to achieve a positive change or resolution. The social worker can "reframe" a client statement to identify possibilities (e.g., "Being laid off when your company is down-sized can now be an opportunity for you to pursue your dream of being a social worker.").
- *Providing information, education, feedback, and suggestions:* Each of these areas can be relevant and necessary to the social work intervention, but, particularly in the beginning of the helping relationship, they should be used sparingly to avoid the appearance that the social worker is the expert on the client's life and is there to direct the intervention.
- *Summarizing:* In addition to periodic re-capping or paraphrasing, the social worker's general summary of the encounter can clarify the discussion and plans for the future, including tasks for the social worker and the client.

For additional guidelines for performing effective assessments, see Exhibit 9.4.

Consider the case of Morgan, a 16-year-old whose mother brought her in because she found evidence of cyber bullying on Morgan's cell phone. Morgan's mother reported finding threatening texts, photos, and tweets from her daughter's classmates, which apparently stem from the fact that Morgan is dating the former boyfriend of one of the classmates who is sending the threats. Morgan did not come to your office willingly and does not want to talk about the incidents. What behaviors would be appropriate when completing an assessment with Morgan? After reviewing the list of assessment behaviors provided in this chapter, determine which of the behaviors could be helpful to a social worker in engaging Morgan and assessing her situation. To learn more about social workers' roles with persons being bullied, visit the NASW Help Starts Here website at: www.helpstartshere.org/kids-and-families/schools-and-communities/tips-for-parents-dealing-with-bullying.html.

Family Assessments When conducting a family assessment, social workers employ the same skill set they use with individuals, but with several additional considerations specific to the challenges family issues present. The family is a system, and when working with a family a social worker is really working with a group. The family assessment provides the social worker and the family with insights regarding patterns of individual behaviors, family functioning, relationships, communication patterns, and dynamics among family members.

EXHIBIT 9.4

Assessment "Don'ts" and "Do's"

ASSESSMENT "DON'TS"	EXAMPLE	ASSESSMENT "DO'S"
Excessive utterances, excessive head nodding	Frequent use of "That's good." "Really?"	Occasional use of these comments can serve as prompters or encouragers.
"Why" questions	"Why did you hit your son?"	"What were you feeling when you struck your son?"
Use of poor grammar (e.g., "that," "it," etc.)	"What did it feel like when it happened?"	"How did you feel when your daughter told you about the abuse?"
Closed questions	"Do you want to tell me what brought you here today?"	"What brought you here today?"
Talking more than clients talk	Social worker does the majority of the talking.	Client does the majority of the talking.
Machine gun questioning—series of "grilling" questions	"Where were you when that happened? How did it feel? What did she say?"	The client's response should guide the next question.
Leading questions	"I'm sure you told him that you would leave him if he didn't stop drinking, didn't you?"	"What did you say to your husband about his drinking?"
Placating	"Now, Mrs. Smith, there is nothing to worry about."	"Mrs. Smith, I will be here to support you through this experience."
Minimizing	"I'm sure you're keeping so busy that you don't really miss him that much."	"Missing a loved one who dies is a normal reaction."

ASSESSMENT "DON'TS"	EXAMPLE	ASSESSMENT "DO'S"
Rescuing	"I'll make sure that you don't get evicted."	"How can I help you with your housing situation?"
Fidgeting	Twirling hair, playing with a pen/pencil, or moving about in the chair.	Movement is a normal action, just not to the point of distraction.
Poor attending skills	Looking out the window, through papers, or responding to a phone.	Focusing on the client during the encounter is essential to the social work relationship.
Giggling at inappropriate times or during silences	Giggling, in general, conveys an unprofessional air and is offensive.	Laughing with the client at appropriate times is supportive.
Use of repetitive words (e.g., "you know," "like," "okay," "uh huh")	"I'm like, you know, happy to set another appointment with you, okay?"	"I will be happy to schedule another appointment with you."
Advice giving	"I definitely think you should have the procedure."	"Let's explore the pros and cons of having the procedure."
Multiple, double-barreled questions	"When did you separate?" "Have you filed for divorce?" (Client may not know which to answer or answer one and leave worker with the wrong impression.)	Ask a question, wait for a response, and continue.
Slouching	Slouching implies a posture that suggests this is a casual relationship and the worker may not be taking the situation seriously.	Sitting upright and leaning slightly forward suggests a professional, interested posture.
Letting the client ramble	Allowing the client to wander off the topic to the point that assessment cannot be completed.	Clients can often provide useful information while talking, but the social worker should monitor.
Mimicking cultural traits or language or client's behaviors	Using language or gestures that are not typical, but done only for the benefit of the client.	Use appropriate language, but do not "experiment" on the client.
Taking sides with the clients	"I know you meant well."	"My role is to be objective and neutral."

ASSESSMENT "DON'TS"	EXAMPLE	ASSESSMENT "DO'S"
Giving false reassurances or agreeing when that is inappropriate or unknown	"I'm sure the doctor will be able to give you good news on your tests."	"If you would like, I can be with you when you get your test results."
Ignoring cues about the client's subjective experiences and only focusing on the objective issues (i.e., getting the form completed)	"Now, what was your annual income last year?" (asked while client is sobbing)	"You seem very upset. Would you like to talk about it?"
Judgmental responses	"I am sure you want to take care of your mother at home instead of putting her in a nursing home."	"Have you thought about your mother's care? Let's discuss the options."
Inappropriate use of humor	"You know how they (fill in the group) can be."	If initiated by the client, the social worker should confront the inappropriate humor.
Premature problem solving	"I've heard enough. Let me tell you what I think."	"I need more information before we can discuss options."
Criticizing or belittling clients or condescending behaviors	"You're not being fair." "You shouldn't worry about that."	"You seemed concerned about that."
Over-reliance on "chit-chat"	Anything beyond the usual greeting and pleasantries is too much casual conversation.	Greeting the client, asking about her/his well-being and responding briefly to her/his inquiries is appropriate.
Overprotecting clients by avoiding clear cues to implicit information	"I think there may be some concern about your son's academic performance." (when, in fact, the son is failing)	"I am concerned that your son's grades are below the level needed for him to pass."
Inappropriate response to information shared by client	With wide eyes, "Wow, you have got to be kidding!"	Empathetically stated, "You must have been surprised."
Communicating displeasure when a client does not appear grateful	"I hope you know how difficult it was to get you an appointment today."	Commenting on a client's lack of gratitude is not appropriate.

Source: Adapted from Collins & Coleman, 2000.

The first step in conducting a family assessment is to determine the composition of the family. This requires the social worker to take a broad view of what makes a family, given that traditional families are becoming increasingly less common. The U.S. Census Bureau reports that of the over 110 million households in the United States, two-thirds are family households and one-third are non-family households. "Family" households (co-residents related by birth, marriage, or adoption) have decreased 15% since 1970, while one-person households and the overall age of persons living in households are on the rise (Vespa, Lewis, & Kreider, 2013). These data suggest that social workers need to rethink traditional definitions of family. Just because a group does not comply with the traditional definition of a family, they may still be functioning like a family. From the perspective of the social work intervention, a family may be more than a biological relationship or living arrangement.

Today the accepted social work definition of family is a group of persons, usually residing together, who acknowledge a sense of responsibility for one another and function as a unit. Social workers routinely intervene with persons of all ages who are gay, lesbian, bisexual, and transgender individuals and couples. They work with persons who share a residence but are not biologically or legally related; blended families that include the children of multiple marriages or relationships; single parents; grandparents rearing grandchildren; multigenerational family units; and with foster households and other kinship relationships. Social workers refer to a client's "family of choice," an inclusive term that enables the client to accurately describe those whom the client considers to be family (Gabrielson & Holston, 2014). With any family, but especially when the composition of a family is complex (e.g., blended or multigenerational families), the ecological perspective may be an effective approach as it encompasses the developmental needs of the members, the ability and functioning of the parent(s), and the family within the context of the internal and external environment (Jack, 2012). Being able to view the family from the perspectives of developmental stages, strengths, and resources can aid the social worker in understanding the family's needs and goals. The ecomap (discussed in Chapter 7) can be a particularly helpful family assessment tool as it can capture the entirety of the family constellation and their individual and collective relationships with each other and the various entities within their world.

When conducting a family assessment, the social worker must determine which family members will participate in the change effort. Several factors influence this decision, including the goals of the persons seeking services, the willingness and availability of family members to participate, and the relationships of the family members with one another. For example, in an adoption process, all family members should be involved, as the addition of a new member will affect everyone, but children need not be involved in an intervention related to their parents' relationship.

Family
A group of persons, usually residing together, who acknowledge a sense of responsibility for one another and function as a unit.

Couples Work

Source: iStock/Alina Solovyova–Vincent

Engaging with each family member can be particularly difficult if one or more members do not voluntarily seek the services of a social worker or have different needs and agendas for the intervention. Involuntary participants may feel anger, resentment, or hostility and may be more willing to participate if they are given the opportunity to voice their feelings. Listening to the concerns of every family member can provide a more complete picture of the family environment and situation and provide insights into the potential strengths and resources available for the social work intervention (Jack, 2012).

As in any assessment, it is particularly crucial when assessing a family system to avoid allowing stereotypes and assumptions about the concept of family to interfere with the social work intervention process. Floyd and Gruber (2011) make the following suggestions for ensuring that preconceptions about the idea of family do not negatively affect family assessments:

- Do not allow your own family experience to define the way in which you perceive family functioning.
- Gain experience with different family constellations and challenges.
- Acknowledge your own biases and stereotypes so that you can reframe your perceptions within the context of the family groups with whom you will work.
- Identify those areas of family crises that will be particularly challenging for you and gain knowledge and skills to work in those areas (pp. 75–76).

Documentation of Social Work Practice with Individuals and Families

A key component of the social work intervention process is the documentation of information. A social worker's documentation is essential in the assessment, planning, and evaluation phases of the helping relationship as it provides the basis for the work. While agencies typically have standardized processes (e.g., formats, language, length, etc.) for collecting and maintaining client records, some basic components of the documentation process are common across organizations and practice areas, including:

- Documentation should be clear and concise.
- All documentation should include the client's identifying information.
- The dates, times, and a description of all contacts related to the client should be documented.
- All psychosocial assessments should be documented.
- Documentation should include service and service monitoring plans.
- Documentation should include a description of the service provided and the outcomes, referrals, and rationale for the actions taken that are being documented.
- Documentation should include written permission to gather or share client-related information with others.

(*NASW Standards for Social Work Case Management*, 2013a, pp. 44–46)

The social worker should complete necessary documentation following each encounter with a client system as well as upon receiving or releasing any client-related information. The NASW *Code of Ethics* (2008) specifically addresses content regarding documentation in Section 3.04 (Social Worker's Ethical Responsibility in Practice Settings):

a. Social workers should take reasonable steps to ensure that documentation in records is accurate and reflects the services provided.
b. Social workers should include sufficient and timely documentation in records to facilitate the delivery of services and to ensure continuity of services provided to clients in the future.
c. Social workers' documentation should protect clients' privacy to the extent that is possible and appropriate and should include only information that is directly relevant to the delivery of services.
d. Social workers should store records following the termination of services to ensure reasonable future access. Records should be maintained for the number of years required by state statutes or relevant contracts.

Documenting social work practice is a learned, specialized writing skill. The writing social workers do when they document client interactions and relevant information differs considerably from the academic writing with which students are familiar. To assess your readiness for practice-focused writing, see Exhibit 9.5.

The engagement and assessment skills described in this section are critical to establishing rapport with each family member and the family unit as a whole while observing the interactions among family members and between family and their external environment.

Intervention with Individuals and Families

Using the information she gathered from Victoria during the assessment process, Emily developed both an immediate and a short-term plan for intervention, with the agreement that Victoria would allow Emily to follow up the next day. With Emily's help, Victoria was able to state that her immediate need was to find a safe place to stay. In response, Emily contacted one of Victoria's friends from work and arranged for Victoria to stay with her. At this point, taking into account the trauma that Victoria had experienced, Emily did not want to overwhelm her with a request to establish long-range goals.

Over the next several weeks, Emily had regular contact with Victoria. Emily told Victoria that she was there to support her through this period, but that their goal would be to eventually phase Emily out of Victoria's life as Victoria recovered and regained emotional strength. Together, they established a list of objectives based on Victoria's priorities. Victoria wanted to return to living independently, to feel safe, and to be able to talk with her family and fiancé about her experience. Emily offered several strategies that could be helpful to Victoria, and they rehearsed the conversations she would have with others.

Working together toward the goals Victoria identified, Emily helped Victoria relocate to a new third-floor apartment. Emily referred Victoria to several services that helped her meet her goals: the community police program for an in-home safety assessment, a support group for survivors of sexual assault, and a clinical social worker to help her address her feelings of guilt and violation and to work with Victoria's family and fiancé.

During the assessment phase, the social worker and the client system engage in the process of identifying needs, issues, strengths, and resources. Once this assessment process is complete, the worker and the client can jointly begin the process of planning and carrying out the intervention. In the intervention, they use the information they've gathered to prioritize the client's needs and mobilize the client's strengths and resources to facilitate the desired change.

EXHIBIT 9.5

Documentation Skills Self-Assessment

Honestly rate yourself on each statement below, with 1 = strongly disagree, 2 = disagree, 3 = agree, and 4 = strongly agree.

_____ 1. I can usually select the best words to express myself.

_____ 2. I can usually write in a focused way.

_____ 3. My writing is usually well organized and logical in sequence.

_____ 4. I am highly skilled at expressing myself in writing.

_____ 5. I am highly skilled at comprehending what I have read.

_____ 6. I have confidence that I know how to write about a client.

_____ 7. I have a good memory for details.

_____ 8. I know the difference between objective and subjective information.

_____ 9. I know the difference between a summary and a **SOAP** note (assessment format that include four categories: Subjective (information provided by client), Objective (information observed or obtained), Assessment (subjective and objective information is combined into a brief description of the client situation and needs), and Plan (specific action steps to be initiated by client and social worker)).

_____ 10. I can tell what is important about a client session and what is not.

_____ 11. I am highly skilled in honing in on what is important in a conversation.

_____ 12. I know the difference between a complete and incomplete sentence.

_____ 13. I know the difference between your and you're.

_____ 14. I know the difference between its and it's.

_____ 15. I know when to use commas, periods, semicolons, and colons.

_____ 16. I understand what is meant by subject and verb agreement.

_____ 17. I know the difference between writing in the first, second, and third person.

_____ Total your score and see where you fall on the following scale:

0–17 Your skills need work and can be improved with hard work and diligence.

18–35 Your skills are fair, but you have plenty of room to improve.

36–53 Your skills are good, with room for improvement.

54–68 Your skills are excellent.

Complete each sentence with a short phrase:

(1) The areas I am most confident about documenting are ....

(2) I think my documentation strengths are ...

(3) I am least confident about documenting ...

(4) The documentation areas in which I think I need the most help are ...

Source: Sidell, 2011, pp. 25–26.

The social work intervention involves two steps:

1. *Planning.* The social worker and the client identify the areas on which the client wants to focus the intervention. Initially, the goals may be broad or seem unattainable. Through discussion, the social worker and the client prioritize and define each goal in specific behavioral and achievable terms. At this point in the intervention, the social worker and the client negotiate and document a mutually agreed upon, clear, measurable, and specific contract.
2. *Implementation.* Once an intervention plan is in place, the next step is to put the plan into action. Reviewing the contract on a regular basis enables the client and the social worker to monitor progress and determine whether the goals and strategies are realistic or if they should be changed or eliminated.

Applying the strengths-based approach to planning and implementation, the social worker recognizes the client as the expert on her or his life and respects the client's right to self-determination in facilitating the change process. Exhibit 9.6 provides guidelines for facilitating the planned change social work intervention.

Developing your own repertoire of practice skills for working with individuals and families is a part of the professional maturation process. The theoretical perspectives you adopt will determine the practice skills that you incorporate into your social work interventions. Chapter 7 introduced two useful approaches to working with individuals and families, Motivational Interviewing and the Solution-focused framework.

Motivational Interviewing (MI) has shown promise as a clinical approach with individuals and families and is built on a framework consistent with the philosophical tenets of the social work profession. MI involves four processes in the change intervention: (1) Engaging; (2) Focusing; (3) Evoking; and (4) Planning (Miller & Rollnick, 2013). See Exhibit 9.7 for descriptions and sample questions that can be incorporated into the MI approach.

Communication skills are essential to building the MI partnership with the client. The following five key communication skills serve as the basis for MI:

- *Asking open questions* empowers the client to share and reflect on her or his concerns in order to direct the change process.
- *Affirming* the client's strengths, worth, resources, ability and motivation to change can serve to validate the client's desires to work on change.
- *Reflective listening* promotes clarification and deepening understanding, which help the client begin the change process.

EXHIBIT 9.6

Steps in Social Work Intervention

ENGAGEMENT

Behaviors

- Substantively and affectively (emotionally) prepare for action by applying knowledge of human behavior and the social environment, person-in-environment, and other multidisciplinary theoretical frameworks to engage with clients
- Use empathy and other interpersonal skills to effectively engage diverse clients
- Develop a mutually agreed-upon focus for the work and desired outcomes

Possible Strategies

- Engage the client in a focused, goal-directed way
- Build rapport with warmth, interest, empathy, and genuineness
- Demonstrate culturally competent communication skills

ASSESSMENT

Behaviors

- Collect, organize, and interpret information from clients
- Apply knowledge of human behavior and the social environment, person-in-environment, and other multidisciplinary theoretical frameworks in the analysis of assessment data from clients
- Develop mutually agreed-upon intervention goals and objectives based on the critical assessment of strengths, needs, and challenges within clients
- Select appropriate intervention strategies based on the assessment, research knowledge, and values and preferences of clients

Possible Strategies

- Allow the client to tell her or his story
- Use assessment tools (e.g., ecomap or culturagram) to gather and organize client information
- Evaluate information
- With the client, prioritize the needs and issues the client has raised and establish clear, achievable goals

INTERVENTION

Behaviors

- Critically choose and implement interventions to achieve practice goals and enhance capacities of clients
- Apply knowledge of human behavior and the social environment, person-in-environment, and other multidisciplinary theoretical frameworks in interventions with clients
- Use interprofessional collaboration as appropriate to achieve beneficial practice outcomes
- Negotiate, mediate, and advocate with and on behalf of diverse clients
- Facilitate transitions and endings that advance mutually agreed-upon goals

Possible Strategies

■ Mobilize client strengths and resources
■ Develop a mutually agreed-upon plan (contract)
■ Reflect on the plan
■ Develop a timeframe for the intervention, identifying respective responsibilities
■ Monitor implementation plan and make changes as needed

EVALUATION AND TERMINATION

Behaviors

■ Select and use appropriate methods for evaluation of outcomes
■ Apply knowledge of human behavior and the social environment, person-in-environment, and other multidisciplinary theoretical frameworks in the evaluation of outcomes
■ Critically analyze, monitor, and evaluate interventions
■ Apply evaluation findings to improve practice effectiveness at the micro level

Possible Strategies

■ Review goals and objectives
■ Develop plan for maintenance and continued contact
■ Express feelings about termination
■ Conduct process and/or outcome evaluation

Sources: Council on Social Work Education, 2015; Logan et al. 2008.

■ *Summarizing* brings together information and ideas the social worker and client have discussed to form an action plan.
■ *Informing and advising* are done only with the client's permission and collaboration and serve to clarify the work being completed.

(Miller & Rollnick, 2013, pp. 33–35)

Using a solution-focused approach with individuals and families, the social worker and client develop a future-oriented and goal-focused stance grounded in practice-based tenets. In essence, the solution-focused practitioner is pragmatic and efficient, yet thoughtful in her or his use of the client's strengths and previous successes. Quick Guide #9.1 provides eight basic tenets for incorporating solution-focused ideology into social work practice.

Solution-focused interventions build on the concepts of those solutions that have worked in the past. Rooted in the work of de Shazer and colleagues (2007), this approach encourages the professional to listen for the client to identify possible solutions, select questions to ask that may lead to a possible solution, and build on the client's words to find solutions (Bavelas et al., 2013). Specifically, a solution-focused intervention involves:

■ a positive, collegial, solution-focused stance;
■ looking for previous solutions;

EXHIBIT 9.7

Motivational Interviewing: Definitions and Sample Questions

Engaging: The process that occurs when the social worker and the client establish a working relationship.

- How comfortable is this person in talking to me?
- How supportive and helpful am I being?
- Do I understand this person's perspective and concerns?
- How comfortable do I feel in this conversation?
- Does this feel like a collaborative partnership?

Focusing: The purpose of the helping relationship is to bring about client change, and the relationship, once established, concentrates on discussing the change the client wants to make.

- What goals for change does this person really have?
- Do I have different aspirations for change for this person?
- Are we working together with a common purpose?
- Does it feel like we are moving together, not in different directions?
- Do I have a clear sense of where we are going?
- Does this feel more like dancing or wrestling?

Evoking: Building on the focused conversation regarding change, evoking occurs when the social worker is able to elicit the client's ideas, thoughts, and feelings about the desired change to empower the client to guide the intervention process.

- What are this person's own reasons for wanting change?
- If the client is reluctant, is that reluctance more about lack of confidence or the level of importance of change?
- What change talk (e.g., references to altering thoughts and behaviors) am I hearing?
- Am I steering too far or too fast in a particular direction?
- Is the righting reflex (i.e., social worker being persuasive) pulling me to be the one arguing for change?

Planning: Once the client becomes focused and has processed her or his feelings about the change, the social worker and client begin planning for both a commitment to change and the way in which the change will occur (plan of action).

- What would be a reasonable next step toward change?
- What would help this person to move forward?
- Am I remembering to evoke rather than prescribe a plan?
- Am I offering needed information or giving advice with the client's permission?
- Am I retaining a sense of quiet curiosity about what will work best for the person?

Source: Miller & Rollnick, 2013, p. 32.

> ## QUICK GUIDE #9.1 TENETS OF SOLUTION-FOCUSED INTERVENTION
>
> ✓ If it isn't broken, don't fix it.
> ✓ If it works, do more of it.
> ✓ If it's not working, do something different.
> ✓ Small steps can lead to big changes.
> ✓ The solution is not necessarily directly related to the problem.
> ✓ The language for solution development is different from the language needed to describe a problem.
> ✓ No problems happen all the time; there are always exceptions that can be utilized.
> ✓ The future is both created and negotiable.
>
> *Source*: de Shazer, Dolan, Korman, Trepper, McCollum, & Berg, 2007, pp. 1–3.

■ looking for exceptions;
■ asking questions as opposed to giving directives or interpretations;
■ focusing questions on the present and the future as opposed to the past;
■ offering compliments and encouragement when solutions are working.

(de Shazer et al., 2007, pp. 4–5)

Consider the following scenario using a solution-focused approach. Eva was referred to your agency for help adjusting to her diagnosis of multiple sclerosis. She has experienced sadness, fear, and dread since learning of this chronic and debilitating illness. Using a solution-focused approach, you convey to Eva that the two of you can collaborate on developing a solution. You might inquire about ways in which she has handled problems or stressors in the past and look for times when she thought problems would occur, but they did not. Your interactions with Eva will primarily take the form of supportive questioning aimed at helping her articulate her goals and develop proposed solutions focused on the future (e.g., "What would your life be like if you were not feeling sad and nervous?").

Regardless of which practice approach you choose to develop a social work intervention, the client must identify the goals of the intervention. The social worker can provide input at appropriate times and in appropriate quantities to ensure that the goals remain those of the client and not those of the social worker. Goals must be clear and achievable—for example, "being a better person" is not a clear or achievable goal, but "spending more time with my children doing fun and healthy activities" is both clear and achievable when the client and social worker develop a step-by-step plan and schedule for creating fun and healthy activities the client can do with her or his children. Specifying the tasks, timeframe, person responsible, and available and needed resources are all aspects of the planning and implementation phases of the intervention.

When working with a client who does not voluntarily seek services, the social worker must be sensitive to the client's misgivings when planning and implementing an intervention. The involuntary client may require more time and specialized strategies to be able to engage in a meaningful way in the planning and implementation processes. It may help to elicit the client's understanding of the situation and to point out the congruency (or lack thereof) between the situation and the client's feelings (Berg, 2008). When a social worker addresses the incongruency, the client's ambivalence may lessen and their motivation for change increase (Berg, 2008). Motivational interviewing (MI) and Solution-focused strategies are well suited to working with involuntary clients. Solution-focused strategies are grounded in the concept that clients have choices about participation and change, and thus collaborating with the client on solutions can be effective (Berg, 2008).

Consider the case of Adam, a 15-year-old adolescent mandated by the family court to work with your agency as the result of a vandalism and theft charge. Not surprisingly, he presents for his first appointment with you in a sullen and uncommunicative manner, stating that he does not want to be there and does not plan to return. Using the MI FRAMES approach highlighted in Chapter 7, you *empathetically* acknowledge his unhappiness about coming to your agency and ask him to tell you his goal (*feedback*). He responds that he just wants this "court thing off [his] back." You share with him your perception of the way in which you can both achieve the goal of him completing the court-ordered sessions, including the non-negotiable items (e.g., must attend and participate in the sessions) (*advising on need for change and noting that he is responsible for change*). You provide him with the *menu of options* for moving forward, and you work with him on those areas he chooses to address. Adam is thus able to voice his ambivalence, understand that he can choose the outcome, and that you will collaborate with him, not direct his actions.

Developing social work interventions with families requires the same skills necessary for intervening with individuals, but is generally more complex. The intervention may encompass the immediate or extended family along with formal and informal support networks. Family group conference (FGC) is a relatively new approach that can be used in situations involving children, adults, or intergenerational families. FGC brings together professionals, client systems, extended family, and others in the client's support networks to discuss and collaborate to determine the optimal way to serve the client (Brodie & Gadling-Cole, 2008). Family group conferencing involves a multi-faceted approach, somewhat similar to convening and facilitating a group intervention. The process of conducting a family group conference includes:

Family group conference (FGC) Convening client, professionals, and extended family to develop intervention plan.

- Identifying the need for a family gathering, receiving a referral from another professional, or receiving a request from a family member.
- Coordinating willingness to participate with scheduling a face-to-face meeting (or alternatively, determining feasibility of using technology (e.g., telephone or videoconferencing) to bring members together).
- In collaboration with the family, establishing an agenda for the meeting.
- Facilitating the meeting, including discussing strengths and concerns, sharing information, allowing the family to meet without professionals present, and a reconvening to discuss plans for moving forward.

(Brodie & Gadling-Cole, 2008)

Consider the following example of an FGC:

The Bennetts are a multi-generational family. The matriarch, Roberta, has custody of Anna, her 14-year-old granddaughter, and of Anna's aunts (Roberta's daughters), Jolene and Julia, who live in the same city. Anna's parents are not able to care for her at this time. Anna's school referred the family because Ava has had a concerning number of absences. As the social worker, you talk with each member of the family individually, compile a summary of your interviews, and then coordinate a meeting that includes Roberta, Anna, Jolene, and Julia. During your interviews you learn that Roberta has been experiencing a health problem and that Anna has been missing school because she has been going with Roberta to medical appointments. Because they use public transportation, the appointments often take much of the day. When the meeting begins, you work with the group to establish an agenda and ground rules for the session. All members share their strengths and concerns. Once all the issues are out in the open, the professionals leave the room and allow the family to discuss options for resolution. When the group re-convenes, the family has devised a plan in which Jolene and Julia will share the responsibility of joining Roberta on her medical visits and of checking in daily to see how Roberta and Anna are doing so that Anna and Roberta can continue to live together but Anna does not have to assume the role of caregiver or miss school. The family and the professionals agree to try the plan and meet again in one month.

The Social Work Contract

A written contract, mutually agreed upon by both the social worker and the client, is another valuable tool in the development and implementation of an intervention. Contracting with a client can help the social worker and client to clarify goals, tasks, and activities, to determine which individual is responsible for each task and activity, and to agree on a timeframe for the intervention. Exhibit 9.8 provides an example of a contract based on Emily's work with

EXHIBIT 9.8

Sample Contract for Client System and Social Worker Intervention Planning

Client Name(s):

Victoria H.

Client System's Description of Issues to be Addressed:

Feel safe
Remain independent

Goals and Tasks:

Goal	Client Tasks/Date	Social Worker Tasks/Date
1. Arrange for safe alternative housing.	Inquire about apartment above ground floor.	Provide referral to community police program.
2. Talk with my family and fiancé about the rape.	Attend survivor support group and meet with therapist.	Provide referral to survivor support group and therapist specializing in rape trauma.
3. Assume control of my life.	Journal daily and share journal with social worker.	Provide support as needed.

Date Contract will be reviewed

3 months from date of contract

I agree with the above stated goals, to complete the contracted tasks, and participate in a review and evaluation of the contract on the specified date.

Victoria

Client

Emily

Social Worker

_____

Date

_____

Date

Victoria that they could use to develop goals and strategies for the planned change effort.

The intervention can be gratifying and fulfilling, but it can also be challenging for both clients and social workers. Changing longstanding or even lifelong behaviors and patterns of interaction is sometimes difficult and even painful for clients. When clients are unable or unwilling to change their lifestyles, social workers may have difficulties or become frustrated. Nevertheless, when social workers and clients commit to mutually agreed-upon goals and agree to make needed adjustments, the intervention can produce a positive outcome.

Evaluation and Termination of Intervention with Individuals and Families

After Emily worked with Victoria for three months, she reminded Victoria that their goal was to terminate the relationship once Victoria felt she no longer needed Emily's support. The two of them took this opportunity to evaluate their work together. As a basis for their evaluation, they reviewed each of the objectives in the contract they had negotiated.

By that time, Victoria had settled into her new apartment. With the community police officer's help, she had taken a number of personal and environmental safety measures. She was regularly attending a sexual assault survivor support group and had seen her clinical social worker three times. She wanted to continue with the support group because she felt they understood her fears, setbacks, and uneasiness in talking about the event with others.

Because the goals they had established were specific and measurable, Emily and Victoria were able to determine that their work together had been a success and that Victoria was ready to terminate her relationship with Emily.

Evaluation Although the intervention phase may seem to be the conclusion of the client-social worker relationship, evaluation and termination of the intervention are equally important. Evaluation is the process by which the social worker and client assess the progress and success of the planned change effort and determine whether it is time to terminate the relationship.

In order for the social worker and the client to conduct a meaningful evaluation, the assessment and intervention phases must have been conducted in a comprehensive, well conceived, and collaborative manner. In turn, these phases can be completed successfully only if the goals and objectives were specific and included clear-cut strategies for measurement. In the *Standards for Social Work Case Management* (2013a), NASW has provided guidelines for incorporating evaluation into social work practice. These guidelines emphasize the need for client input, process, and outcome objectives, self-evaluation, and application of evaluation findings.

Evaluations can occur in two forms:

1. *Process evaluations* focus on the way in which service was delivered to the client within the context of the organization, environment, and the persons facilitating the implementation (Chen, 2006, p. 183). In essence, a process evaluation enables the social worker and client to explore the nature of the client–social worker relationship (e.g., communication and rapport), the way in which the two worked together to plan and implement the intervention, and the tasks and activities completed (Grinnell, Unrau, & Gabor, 2008).

2. *Outcome evaluations*, empirical examinations of the change that has occurred, are typically completed at the termination of the client-social worker relationship (Grinnell et al., 2008). Standardized tools or protocols may be used to measure a behavior or belief at the onset of the intervention compared with its level at the end of the working relationship.

The social worker may want to conduct periodic evaluations throughout the course of the intervention to monitor its progress. If progress is not being made, the social worker and client can refocus the intervention strategy in a direction that is more likely to promote a successful outcome. Developing the contract to identify mutual goals, strengths, and resources; strategies for achieving the goals; and barriers to goal achievement will give the social worker and client a working document for evaluating change throughout the intervention.

In addition to the contract, social workers typically document each encounter with and about the client, recording information such as facts related to the situation, observations, and client activities. Such documentation cannot, under most circumstances, be shared or released without the client's informed consent (written permission granted by the client or the client's legal representative, usually a parent or guardian). Within the evaluation and termination phases of the social work intervention, documentation can serve a variety of purposes: accounting to supervisors, funders, or the legal system; monitoring client progress and accomplishments; and improving the social worker's practice skills (Kagle, 2009). Therefore, documenting is as important to the evaluation process as it is to the assessment and intervention processes.

Although regular, periodic evaluations are helpful, evaluating the intervention at the time agreed upon in the contract is critical. At that time, the social worker and the client can address some fundamental questions: Can the relationship be terminated because the goals have been successfully achieved? If the goals were not achieved, should they be renegotiated? Should the relationship be terminated because it is no longer needed?

Determining whether the intervention facilitated the change the client desired also serves as a way of evaluating the social worker's practice (for example, is the social worker offering appropriate and helpful input?). Using the contract as a basis for evaluation, the social worker and client can scrutinize each aspect of the intervention to determine if the social worker upheld her or his commitment to the client and the change effort, adhered to professional ethical standards, and met the obligations to which she or he contracted. Client satisfaction measures should be interpreted with caution, however, as satisfaction, or lack thereof, does not necessarily determine the success or effectiveness of the intervention.

Agencies that fund social work programs and services have placed increasing importance on evaluating social workers' services as a way to determine funding, staffing, and resource levels. Social workers can no longer just try to "help people;" they must verify that people were helped, and they must identify quantitative and qualitative changes that occurred as a result of the intervention. Within the profession itself, evaluating social work methods and practices enables social work educators to develop curricula that will train new social workers to be effective and efficient.

Termination The official ending of the social worker-client relationship, termination is the goal from the first encounter. Failure to establish termination as the ultimate objective can lead to situations in which the client becomes dependent on the social worker. Individuals and families can come to feel comfortable in their relationships with the social worker and may be reluctant to lose the support and caring the social worker provides. Because the mission of social work is to empower clients to enhance their personal, independent functioning and well-being, social workers are obligated to engage the client, assess the situation, plan and carry out an intervention, evaluate the intervention, and then terminate the planned change relationship.

The social worker who empowers the client to make changes in her or his life and devises a plan for maintaining that change provides a greater service than a worker who creates a relationship in which the client continues to look to the worker for help with each life crisis. Of course, if future events create a real need for assistance, services can, under most circumstances, be resumed.

Termination
A component of the planned change effort in which the social worker ends the planned change relationship.

After completing their evaluation of their work together, Emily and Victoria planned for the termination of their relationship. They agreed to meet one more time. At that meeting, they again reviewed the goals they had established and the progress Victoria had made in meeting her goals. They discussed plans for handling situations in which Victoria felt her safety was being threatened, and they anticipated events such as the anniversary of the rape and her upcoming marriage. Emily offered Victoria the option to contact her in the future if she felt a need to talk or just to let Emily know how she was doing. Emily commended Victoria on her strength in handling this situation, and she told Victoria she appreciated her willingness to work together. Victoria told Emily that she had been a "lifesaver" and that she would forever be grateful to her. She admitted that she would miss Emily and was grateful to know that she could call Emily if she felt a need to talk with her.

Terminations occur for a variety of reasons and in a variety of ways. The social work relationship can be terminated in the following situations:

- The goals are successfully achieved.
- The client withdraws from the relationship because she or he no longer agrees with the plan established within the contract.
- The client is no longer eligible to receive services.
- The social worker feels that the goals cannot be achieved or the client is unwilling to comply with the contract.
- The social worker or agency is no longer the most appropriate service provider for the client.
- The social worker leaves the agency.

Ideally, the concept of termination is introduced at the first social worker-client encounter. It is then built into the intervention, routinely discussed, and carried out in a planned manner. Planned terminations enable the client to enter into the contract and work through the intervention with a clear focus on the desired outcome, knowing that when the specified goals are reached, the planned change relationship will be terminated.

Determining the point at which termination should occur often influences the planning and implementation of the intervention. For example, when working with a person who identifies self-sufficiency as a priority, the social worker can design an intervention aimed toward independent living and economic stability. When the person has secured housing and a regular income, the planned change relationship can then be successfully terminated.

Successful termination of the social work relationship involves:

- Reviewing the goals and objectives included in the contract to determine if these goals have been met, to identify barriers to meeting the goals, and to consider future goals.
- Developing a plan for maintaining change after the relationship has been terminated. This plan must anticipate possible issues, such as the client's response should the crisis reoccur and the skills, resources, and strengths needed to address that response.

■ Discussing continued professional contact between the social worker and the client, and anticipating questions, such as when and under what conditions future contact would be acceptable and what the appropriate parameters would be for that contact.

■ Expressing feelings about ending the relationship. The nature of the social work relationship can be intense and personal, and both the client and the social worker can feel anxious or sad about ending that part of their lives. Therefore, discussing feelings is an important ingredient in a successful termination.

A skillfully facilitated termination can be gratifying for both the client and the social worker. Clients can achieve a sense of closure and, if permitted by agency policy, can be reassured that they can contact the social worker in the future if the need arises. The social worker can benefit from feeling a sense of closure.

Review the case example in Exhibit 9.9 in which the social worker had to be prepared to address multiple issues with a client who has a history of crises, erratic behaviors, and non-compliance with plans and medications.

CONCLUSION

A systematic approach to social work practice with individuals and families involves engagement, assessment, intervention, evaluation, and termination. Although such an approach provides a structure for working with individuals and families, facilitating a planned change is not always straightforward, simple, or without complications.

Working with client systems whose lives may be steeped in crises, unexpected twists and turns, and external pressures requires social workers to be flexible, creative, and patient. Social workers must be willing to renegotiate or delay plans for interventions and to mobilize or develop new resources and supports in order to respond to unanticipated circumstances. Typically, the change process is a fluid one that may require returning to previous steps.

Chapters 10 and 11 explore the process of engagement, assessment, intervention, and evaluation/termination in the context of social work practice with groups, organizations, and communities. Although client systems at the group and community levels are larger, the same basic premise serves as a foundation for the social work intervention. The knowledge and skills needed to build rapport and trust, gather information, develop a planned change effort, and evaluate and terminate the intervention are the same regardless of the size or makeup of the client system. The skills and practice behaviors you have learned for working with individuals and families are the same ones you will

EXHIBIT 9.9

Tammy

Tammy is a 35-year-old Caucasian female seeking services at your community mental health program after her release from a 21-day residential drug/alcohol treatment facility. She lost custody of her 8-year-old son due to her continued substance abuse. She was arrested for driving under the influence with her son in the car. Her son, Jared, is in the temporary care of Tammy's mother. Tammy has a 20-year history of drug and alcohol abuse. She has also been diagnosed with Bipolar Disorder. She was recently prescribed medication by the staff psychiatrist at the residential treatment facility that her insurance does not cover. She has been non-compliant with medication in the past due to its side effects and her drug/alcohol use. She has had brief periods of sobriety but often relapses after a few weeks. Her 21 days in treatment is the longest she has been sober since the birth of her son.

Tammy has never been married and has a difficult relationship with her family of origin. When Tammy was 8 years old, her mother placed her in foster care, citing the child's "out-of-control" behavior. Tammy reports that her mother was physically and emotionally abusive to her and that whenever her mother found a new boyfriend she would leave Tammy with various relatives. Tammy's father is not in her life, and she has few friends and little contact with her mother. She is angered that her mother has custody of her son. Tammy has been involved with her son's father sporadically for the past nine years. Currently, she names him as a source of support.

Tammy is not currently employed, but she receives public assistance (Medicaid, Social Security Disability, and SNAP). She lives with her boyfriend but would like to have her own apartment. She has her high school diploma and is interested in returning to school.

- How might you approach engagement, assessment, and intervention with Tammy?
- What goals might be appropriate (taking into consideration Tammy's history with following through on goals)?
- What are Tammy's strengths and areas for change?
- How would you know when your work with Tammy is complete?

Source: Shannon Cooper-Sadlo, LCSW, LMFT

need when you are planning and implementing social work interventions with groups, organizations, and communities of all sizes and compositions.

This chapter has provided you with the framework from which to expand your social work knowledge and skills. The agency in which you work will determine the specific assessment tools, intervention protocols, and evaluation methods that you will use, but having strong understanding of the change process will enable you to transfer your knowledge and skills to particular settings.

MAIN POINTS

- Direct social work practice with individuals and families is the process of working one-on-one with the client system to identify and assess a need and develop a plan for facilitating a planned change.

- The client's investment in the change process is key to the success of the social work intervention. The social worker collaborates with the client in the planned change process.

- The strengths perspective is essential to identifying the assets and resources the client system possesses and for planning a successful intervention.

- Social workers practicing with individuals and families use a variety of theoretical and practice approaches, skills, and practice behaviors within the context of engagement, assessment, intervention, and evaluation/termination.

- Engagement is the building of respect, rapport, and trust with the client system.

- Assessment includes gathering information about the client system and about the client's perception of her or his strengths, resources, and needs.

- With the client, the social worker plans an intervention that includes determining desired goals, priorities, barriers to change, and strategies for making change.

- Evaluation consists of assessing the progress and/or success of the change process, the effectiveness of the social work intervention, and the readiness to terminate the client-social worker relationship.

- Documentation is a specialized skill integral to the social work assessment, intervention, and evaluation and termination processes.

- The knowledge and skills for intervening effectively with individuals and families are also relevant in social work practice at the group and organizations and community levels of social work practice.

EXERCISES

1. Using the Sanchez family, Carla Washburn, Brickville (Stone Family), or Hudson City interactive case (www.routledgesw.com/caseStudies), complete the following to get a sense of what it is like to participate in a social work relationship from engagement through evaluation.

   a. Locate the Case Study Tools and select Biopsychosocial. Review each of the four perspectives for the Sanchez family, Carla Washburn, Brickville, or Hudson City. Answer each of the questions that appear.

   b. Go to the Intervene tab. Following the prompts, respond to each of the questions that will enable you to define goals and needs, identify tasks for the intervention, complete the timeline, and identify coalitions.

c. Next, go to the Case Study Tools and select the Interaction Matrix. Match a client with the members of the client system by clicking on Plot the Interaction. Identify the issues or barriers that exist between your client and system members.

d. Go to the Evaluate tab. Review the Introduction. Continuing with your selected client, complete the Intervention Evaluation and Closing the Case sections.

e. Provide a written analysis of your experience with developing a social work intervention.

2. Go to the Sanchez interactive case at www.routledgesw.com/caseStudies. Click on the Engage tab, scroll down to Video, click on Video, and scroll down to the video entitled Initial Social Work Interview with Emilia Sanchez. While viewing the video (individually or as a group in class), identify the engagement, assessment, and intervention skills the social worker demonstrates. Reflect in writing on the skills you have observed.

3. This chapter highlights the importance of "starting where the client is." Review this scenario and prepare a response to the questions that follow:

Mr. J. is a 61-year-old male. He was diagnosed with probable Alzheimer's dementia. Mr. J. is experiencing increasing memory problems; he has been unable to find his car in the mall parking lot on three occasions and has begun to lose his possessions (e.g., glasses, keys) on a regular basis. He works as a shipping and receiving foreman for a discount chain store.

Given that the typical course of Alzheimer's disease is 8–10 years from time of diagnosis to death, the physician has recommended that Mr. J. consider early retirement within the next year and that he be evaluated by the Department of Motor Vehicles to determine if it is safe for him to drive. The physician has asked you to follow up with Mr. J. and his family to implement these recommendations.

Mr. J. and his family—which includes his wife and adult son—are adamantly opposed to both recommendations, stating that his forgetfulness is just normal aging and that everyone misplaces small items and gets lost in large parking lots. Where do you begin?

a. Identify the person(s) you consider to be your client(s).

b. Describe the way(s) in which you would start where the client(s) is (are).

c. Reflect on the possible strengths and challenges related to starting where the client(s) is (are) in the scenario you have just read.

4. Write a script, as though it were a play, for a social worker interviewing an individual or family client system. Include in the script the questions that the social worker would ask in an assessment of the individual or family. Insert directions regarding the facial and body language of the social worker and the client system. Include the client system's responses to the social worker. At the close of the script, draw an ecomap of the individual or family system and identify the individual's and family's strengths and areas for growth and change.

5. Personal reflection: Describe a change you have made in your life, how you were able to make the change, why you made it, and the long-term effects of the change on you and those in your environment. Discuss how this experience might impact your work and professional development.

6. As an in-class activity, create a three-person group to complete the following communications and interviewing exercise. Select from the following statements to create a dialogue between a "social worker" and a "client." As the "social worker" and the "client" interact, the "observer" will complete the checklist (Exhibit 9.3) of communication skills she or he notices the "social worker" using. Each person in the group will have the opportunity to role play each of the roles.

    a. "He left me after eighteen years of marriage. I can't believe he'd do a thing like that."

    b. "I'll never be able to face my friends again. I'm beginning to think life isn't worth living."

    c. "I've been trying to raise two boys by myself ever since my husband left. Nobody knows how tough it has been."

    d. "My mother-in-law would drive anyone crazy. She's always trying to tell me I'm not good enough for her 'precious' son."

    e. "My job is really getting to me. The boss makes passes at me—just subtle enough that I feel like I can't report him. There's no way to move to another department or get another job with good benefits. I just have to take it."

    f. "What's so bad about taking a few pills to help me get through the day? Everybody needs something."

    g. "I wouldn't feel so bad if I had someone to talk to. I get so tired of being alone."

7. Complete the Documentation Skills Self-Assessment (Exhibit 9.5). Upon completion, reflect in writing or within a group discussion on your responses and thoughts about the documentation process.

SOCIAL WORK PRACTICE WITH GROUPS

Over time, Emily began to notice that clients staying at a shelter for women who had experienced intimate partner violence shared a common concern regarding parenting. Many of these women voiced their apprehension about the effects of domestic violence on their children.

Emily was unsure how to most effectively address this issue. After talking to co-workers and conducting research, Emily determined three possible strategies for helping her clients with children affected by domestic violence:

1. *Emily could suggest that the Community-wide Domestic Violence Coalition develop a program to address the issue.*
2. *Emily could approach a local clinical social worker about forming a therapy group for women who had experienced intimate partner violence, and parenting skills could be incorporated as a therapeutic goal.*
3. *Emily's agency could form a support group for current and former residents of the shelter that could include a focus on parenting.*

This chapter will explore each of the options Emily proposed, including the one that ended up best addressing Emily's clients' needs.

Working with groups has long been a part of social work practice. In group work or mezzo (meso) practice, the social worker collaborates with multiple clients to develop a planned change effort that meets the needs of the group. Group work can focus on addressing individual issues; the need for information, education, and support; or social problems. The social worker's role in a group can be that of initiator, facilitator, therapist, resource person, consultant, evaluator, or a combination of these roles.

Group practice is built on the concept that change occurs as a result of ongoing, fluid group dynamics and group members' interactions with one another. Thus, social work practice with groups emphasizes group interdependence, interaction, and support as the vehicle for change. It focuses on both the individual and the group as a whole, balancing the needs and autonomy of each (International Association for Social Work with Groups, Inc. (IASWG, Inc.), 2010). The strength of group work is that people can accomplish more as a group than a person can accomplish alone, whether the desired change is on the individual, community, or organizational level.

Multiple helping relationships coexist in a group intervention (IASWG, Inc., 2010). Group members address both their own and other members' individual needs as well as the needs of the group. As scholar Roselle Kurland puts it, "The very act of forming a group is a statement of our belief that every member of the group has something to offer the others, something to give to others, not just to get from them" (2007, p. 12).

While only 18% of social workers identify group work as their primary area of practice (Whitaker & Arrington, 2008), most social workers engage in some form of group practice. The NASW *Code of Ethics* (2008) includes working with groups as one of the ethical principles and key competencies for social work practice. The *Code* charges social workers to strengthen relationships and the well-being of people at all levels of social work practice, including group practice.

This chapter highlights the historical development of group work as a method of social work intervention and the role of group work within generalist social work practice. It explores different types of group work methods and introduces the skills needed to effectively deliver group services.

HISTORICAL PERSPECTIVE ON SOCIAL WORK PRACTICE WITH GROUPS

As with individual and family practice approaches, group work has its roots in England. Emerging in the English post-Industrial Revolution era, group work first took the form of mutual aid groups (Alissi, 2009). Put simply, mutual aid groups are: "people helping one another as they think things through" (Steinberg, 2014, p. 2).

> **Mutual aid groups**
> Where people help one another as they think things through.

In the United States, group methods were initially used by helping professionals as a strategy for working with youth through organized activities (e.g., YMCA/YWCA and organizations for children and youth). Workers in the settlement houses of the late 19th century formed groups to achieve educational and cultural goals. They also embraced group approaches as a means to furthering social action agendas such as improving sanitation in the cities. Volunteers typically facilitated these groups, without the benefit of formal (i.e., governmental) support, as collaborative efforts to engage members in discussion and decision-making (Dominelli, 2008).

Group work for the promotion of recreational and educational activities emerged after World War I. In the 1920s, group work flourished in agency settings to address "recreational, educational, character-building, and community organized group activities" (Alissi, 2009, p. 8). During this decade, with its emphasis on the individual in interventions, groups were often used as an extension of individual casework to engage clients in a therapeutic relationship (Hopps & Lowe, 2008). However, it was not until 1923 that formalized structures or training in group work emerged with the first university-level course on group social work.

By the 1930s and 1940s, professional social workers were conducting group work interventions with hospitalized patients, persons with developmental disabilities and mental illness, and returning World War II veterans.

Source: Corbis.

During the Great Depression of the 1930s, social workers mobilized groups to lobby for workers' rights and to simply help people survive the depression (Alissi, 2009; Toseland & Horton, 2008). Former settlement house and YWCA worker, social work educator, and NASW Pioneer, Grace Coyle first wrote about group processes in the 1930s, emphasizing the effectiveness of group interventions for educating adults and promoting social action, social justice, and social change (Toseland & Horton, 2008, p. 2:299). Other professionals debated whether group work was a recreational activity, a social work method, or a separate profession.

Interest in incorporating group methods into social work practice continued to grow and expand into more settings over the next several decades. During the 1940s, scholars developed formalized knowledge regarding the practice of group work, which helped the approach to gain acceptance as an integrated aspect of clinical practice (Alissi, 2009). In the 1960s, a philosophical shift toward considering social work in a more generic context without specialized methodologies reduced the role of group work practice in the social work profession (Alissi, 2009). In the 1970s, many social workers participated in experimental groups focused on self-improvement as well as social action and advocacy. The women's movement, in particular, created and promoted a variety of group interventions to raise awareness about and promote social and political action related to women's issues so that the "personal became political" (Dominelli, 2008, p. 480).

Over the next 20 years, group work became an integrated part of social work practice at the individual and family, organizational, and community levels. Within the range of group interventions, social workers adopted the roles of broker, teacher/educator, enabler, advocate, mobilizer, mediator, and case manager.

Group social work practice is now recognized as a methodology to achieve the profession's mission to empower, promote well-being, and, in many instances, strive for social justice. Group methods employ a variety of practice approaches and can be applied in a range of settings, with diverse populations, and at the individual, group, and community levels (Garvin & Galinsky, 2008).

All social work students are exposed to group work theory and practice through coursework and field experiences. Quick Guide #10.1 provides an overview of the IASWG standards for group work.

QUICK GUIDE #10.1 STANDARDS FOR SOCIAL WORK PRACTICE WITH GROUPS

I. Core Knowledge and Values
- ✓ Familial, social, political, cultural context of member identity, interactional style, and problem
- ✓ Members are viewed as citizens
- ✓ Members are capable of change and capable of helping one another
- ✓ Attention to the whole person systems perspective used in assessment and intervention
- ✓ Person and environment
- ✓ Bio-psycho-social perspective
- ✓ Member-in-group
- ✓ Group-in-community

II. Competency-based assessment
- ✓ Emphasis on member strengths as well as concerns
- ✓ Mutual aid function
- ✓ Group consists of multiple helping relationships
- ✓ Worker's primary role is one of helping members to help one another
- ✓ Groups characterized by democratic process
- ✓ Members are helped to own the group
- ✓ Equal worth of members and worker
- ✓ Worker is not all powerful "expert"
- ✓ Worker to group and worker to members relationships characterized by egalitarianism and reciprocity

✓ Emphasis on empowerment
✓ Group goals emphasize individual member growth and social change
✓ Group worker promotes individual and group autonomy
✓ Worker's assessment and interventions characterized by flexibility and eclecticism
✓ Small group behavior
✓ Group as an entity separate and distinct from individual members
✓ Phases of group development foster change throughout the life of the group
✓ Recognition of how group process shapes and influences individual member behavior
✓ Groups formed for different purposes and goals
✓ Group type (e.g., education, problem-solving, social action) influences what worker does and how group accomplishes its goals
✓ Monitoring and evaluation of success of group in accomplishing its objectives through observation and measurement of outcomes and/or processes

III. Group Work in the Pre-Group Phase
Tasks:
✓ Identify common needs of potential group members
✓ Plan and conduct outreach, recruitment of members
✓ Secure organizational support and sanction for group, if needed
✓ Address organizational resistance to groups, if needed
✓ Screen and prepare members for group, when appropriate
✓ Secure permission for members' participation, when needed
✓ Develop compositional balance, if appropriate
✓ Select appropriate group type, structure, and size
✓ Establish meeting place, time, etc. that promotes member comfort and cohesion
✓ Develop and articulate verbally and/or in writing a clear statement of group purpose that reflects member needs and, where appropriate, agency mission
✓ Develop and articulate clear statement of worker role that reflects the group's purpose
✓ Use preparatory empathy to tune into members' feelings and reactions to group's beginning
✓ Knowledge Needed:
✓ Organization's mission and function and how this influences nature of group work service
✓ Social and institutional barriers which may impact on the development of group work service
✓ Issues associated with group composition
✓ Human life cycle and its relationship to potential members' needs
✓ Cultural factors and their influence on potential members' lives and their ability to engage in group and relate to others
✓ Types of groups and their relationship to member needs
✓ Specific types of individual and social problems that lead to a need for group

IV. Group Work in the Beginning Phase
Tasks:
✓ Provide clear statement of group (and, if necessary, agency) purpose and worker role

- ✓ Elicit member feedback regarding perception of needs, interests, and problems
- ✓ Encourage members to share concerns and strengths with one another
- ✓ Facilitate connections between members and members and worker
- ✓ Encourage awareness and expression of commonalities among members
- ✓ Monitor group for manifestations of authority theme and, when needed, respond directly
- ✓ Assess impact of cultural differences between members and between members and worker and address directly when needed
- ✓ Assist group in establishing rules and norms that promote change and growth
- ✓ Use of self to develop cohesion among members and comfort with worker
- ✓ Assist members in establishing individual and group goals
- ✓ Clarify link between individual and group goals
- ✓ Help members to establish a beginning contract which provides clarity and direction to their work together
- ✓ Promote individual autonomy and empowerment of members
- ✓ Create and maintain environment of sociocultural safety

Knowledge Needed:
- ✓ Group dynamics in beginning stage of group
- ✓ Causes/manifestations of resistance to change among members and in external environment

V. Group Work in the Middle Phase
Tasks:
- ✓ Point out commonalties among members
- ✓ Reinforce connection between individual needs/problems and group goals
- ✓ Encourage and model supportive, honest feedback between members and between members and worker
- ✓ Use here and now/process illumination to further group's work
- ✓ Help members use role playing, behavioral rehearsal, and other verbal and non-verbal activities to accomplish individual and group goals
- ✓ Monitor norms that govern group's work
- ✓ Assess group's progress towards its goals
- ✓ Re-contract with members, if needed, to assist them in achieving individual and group goals
- ✓ Identify obstacles to work within and outside group's boundaries and deal with directly
- ✓ Clarify and interpret communication patterns between members, between members and the worker, and between the group and others external to the group
- ✓ Identify and highlight member conflict, when needed, and facilitate resolution
- ✓ Summarize sessions

Knowledge Needed:
- ✓ Group dynamics in the middle phase
- ✓ Role theory and its application to members' relationships with one another and with worker
- ✓ Communication theory and its application to verbal and non-verbal interactions within group and between group and others external to group

✓ Member interactions as manifestations of sociocultural forces of race, class, gender, sexual orientation, etc.

✓ Member interactions as manifestations of psychodynamic factors

✓ Purposeful use of verbal and non-verbal activities

VI. Group Work in the Ending Phase

Tasks:

✓ Identify and point out direct and indirect signs of members' reactions to ending

✓ Share worker's ending feelings with members

✓ Assist members in sharing their feelings about endings with one another

✓ Help members identify gains they have made and changes that have resulted from their participation in the group

✓ Assist members in applying new knowledge and skills to their daily lives

✓ Encourage member feedback to worker

✓ Help members honestly reflect on and evaluate their work together

✓ Develop plans for continuation of service or referral of members, as needed

✓ Assess individual member and group progress

✓ Evaluate impact of group experience on individual members and external environment

Knowledge Needed:

✓ Group dynamics in the ending phase

✓ Formal and informal resources which maintain and enhance members' growth

✓ Influence of past losses and separations in lives of members and worker on group's ending

Source: IASWG, 2010.

MODELS OF CHANGE IN SOCIAL WORK PRACTICE WITH GROUPS

Building on the knowledge and skill base established for working with individuals and families, group work practice has evolved into four distinct models with similar theoretical underpinnings. In the 1960s a variety of scholars working together as well as independently developed the first three—respectively emphasizing social goals, remediation or therapy, and reciprocal aid (Alissi, 2009). Each of those first three models is grounded in systems theory and emphasizes a goal-oriented outcome. The fourth is a goal-oriented model based on group tasks (Toseland & Horton, 2008). Each of these four models has multiple uses and distinct characteristics. What all four models have in common, however, is that they employ group effort to bring about change that individual efforts could not achieve. As an example, Emily's experience illustrates that more than one type of intervention may effectively address a given issue.

Social Goals Groups

Social goals groups, or social action groups, aim to facilitate social change at the organizational or community level. These groups are rooted in concepts of social responsibility, social action, democracy, and social justice and strive to change society by improving social structures (Toseland & Horton, 2008). Social goals groups arose from the early work of reformers and social activists and are a key component of social work practice that seeks to achieve social change and social justice within organizations and communities.

Social goals groups
Group intervention approach focused on social action and societal change.

Social workers use social goals groups to accomplish specific tasks, carry out an organization's goals, change a law or policy, or develop a new program. Some such groups focus on community action, with the goal of addressing social problems by changing policies and practices. Identity-based social action groups form around individuals' membership in specific interest groups (e.g., concern for environmental issues) (Dominelli, 2008). In a social change group, a social worker may serve as initiator, facilitator, participant, or consultant. Both professionals and laypersons may lead social action groups. Typically, group goals determine group leadership.

Groups with specific goals may disband once that goal is achieved or if the goal has somehow changed or become irrelevant. Goal-specific groups with an ongoing mission may persist indefinitely.

The following are examples of social action groups:

- *Neighborhood safety groups:* Such groups may hold regular meetings to strategize ways to monitor and improve neighborhood safety. They may be composed of neighborhood residents, social service professionals who work in the neighborhood, and law enforcement personnel. Such groups often continue long-term, but their focus may shift from establishing a plan for safety to maintaining and monitoring the plan and its results. Due to their involvement in the community, social workers are often in a position to identify the need for a neighborhood group; so they may mobilize the group, but not to lead it. Neighborhood residents with an investment in their community are usually most effective as group leaders.

- *Alzheimer's Association advocacy group:* Such a group may form to lobby legislators to introduce and pass legislation requiring mandatory dementia education for long-term residential care workers caring for patients with Alzheimer's disease. This group may be composed of family members of persons experiencing dementia, representatives from the residential long-term care industry, and health and social service professionals. While the group may endure over multiple legislative sessions, the group's success or failure in its efforts to enact the proposed legislation determines longevity of the advocacy group. If its efforts are successful and the legislation is enacted, the group may refocus on work with state agencies to implement and monitor that legislation, or they may redirect their efforts to lobby for other legislation that would protect persons living with dementia. The social worker's employment or personal interest in the issue determines her or his role.

■ *Child welfare workers who are employed by the public and private agencies that monitor the foster care system:* To ensure that children in foster care have timely and permanent residential and educational plans for their futures, such a group might meet regularly to oversee foster care cases in a city, county, or region. Group members might represent multiple professions, such as social work, education, health, and law. This kind of group provides a quality assurance function and could continue to meet indefinitely. The social worker's role in such a group might be as a leader, facilitator, chair, participant, or a combination of these roles.

Faced with a dilemma regarding the best approach for strengthening the parenting skills of women receiving services in the domestic violence program, Emily asked to have the issue placed on the agenda for the monthly meeting of the Community-wide Domestic Violence Coalition. This group of social, health care, and legal service professionals organized to enhance communication among the community's domestic violence services, influence legislation, and train community members to respond effectively to persons experiencing intimate partner violence. Because they had developed programs to address specific partner violence-related needs, Emily thought the group might be able to help her create a parenting program.

Coalition members determined that the provision of direct client services in Emily's proposed program was outside the purview of their mission. They felt that, in order to simplify issues of group leadership, funding, practitioner competence, and the comfort level of potential participants, individual agencies should provide such a service.

Remedial Groups

Remedial groups
Professionally led group intervention focused on a therapeutic goal of enhanced social functioning.

Professionally facilitated remedial groups (a.k.a. therapeutic or treatment groups, group therapy, group psychotherapy, and clinical group work) aim to enhance their members' social functioning. They seek to develop the individual's ability to change her or his behavior and to hone her or his problem solving and coping skills to deal with or eliminate a specific social, emotional, or behavioral issue (Barker, 2014; Toseland & Horton, 2008). The presence of a professional group leader and treatment goals specific to each individual distinguish remedial groups from other groups focused on individual growth and change. Group dynamics—interacting with other group members, hearing their experiences, and strategizing personal attitudinal and behavioral change—help promote change within group members, but group goals are secondary to those of each individual.

Remedial groups were first introduced into clinical practice in the early 20th century, and it was not until mid century that clinically oriented group work became a widely accepted treatment intervention in hospitals, clinics, and rehabilitation settings with a variety of populations (Alissi, 2009, p. 10).

Group Therapy

Source: iStock/Alina Solovyova–Vincent

In a remedial group, a social worker typically functions as a leader or facilitator. Social workers may also serve as co-leaders of certain types of therapy groups, particularly in cases of single-gendered groups, groups that may be confrontational in nature, or groups that may address emotionally sensitive issues. Co-leaders/facilitators provide multiple benefits. In emotionally intense or confrontational groups, multiple perspectives can do a better job meeting members' needs. Leaders can also provide support to each other within and outside of the group.

Therapeutic groups often form when a professional identifies several individuals within a community or an agency's population who share a common issue. Therapeutic groups may meet for a specified number of sessions or weeks, or the duration of the group may be open-ended. They may also be closed or open: Closed groups have a designated group membership that does not change, whereas members may move in and out of an open group as needs arise.

The following are examples of groups that might be formed for the purpose of therapeutically focused group work:

■ *Persons hospitalized for mental health issues:* Social workers working in mental health facilities often conduct group therapy on a daily or weekly basis with patients hospitalized for newly diagnosed, chronic, or persistent mental illness. In these social worker-led groups, the interactions among group members serve to enhance and supplement individual therapy. Such a group is typically open and ongoing, its membership changing with admissions to and discharges from the facility. Group membership may be determined by diagnosis, time and duration of admission, or gender.

■ *Survivors of childhood incest:* Because of the emotional intensity of the issue and survivors' considerable trust problems, a group of persons who are survivors of incest is likely to be single gender. The administrative or clinical staff of an agency may form a survivor group, and it may be either time-limited or ongoing and open or closed. In determining the type and timing of a survivor group, the social worker is sensitive to the nature of the trauma and to individual member's situations.

■ *Male perpetrators of intimate partner violence:* A therapeutic group made up of men whom the social service or legal system has identified as being violent toward their partners may participate in a therapeutic group on a voluntary or an involuntary basis. Involuntary groups, particularly ones in which members have a history of violence, can be challenging to facilitate due to members' hostility and resentment. A group for perpetrators is typically highly structured and focused on behavioral change. Co-facilitators often lead such groups to enable a balanced response to any disputes or angry outbursts. Behaviorally focused groups are typically time-limited and closed in order to enhance the therapist's ability to provide information and promote individual change and group cohesion.

For the mothers at Emily's shelter, Emily determined that the agency was serving a number of clients who shared a common concern. She considered forming a therapy group to respond to their need for parenting information. Emily's BSW did not train her to conduct a therapy group, so she explored the possibility of co-leading a treatment group with a local clinical social worker in private practice.

Emily's idea was that the therapist would offer a weekly therapy group for women who had been abused by their partners. This voluntary, open-ended group would be accessible to women in the community. Emily hoped that the therapist could address the issues involved in parenting children who have also experienced the domestic violence.

Emily partnered with a clinical social worker who agreed that a therapy group was one effective approach for addressing the women's feelings regarding their life experience and that parenting issues would naturally become a part of the discussion. The two social workers agreed that they would not include a formal parenting education curriculum in this group.

Reciprocal Groups

Reciprocal groups—also known as mutual aid, self-help, and support groups—emphasize common goals, interests, and idea exchange as the basis for change. Group members come together out of a shared interest or experience. Personal growth and change occur when group members share those commonalities, exchanging support and information about their shared issue. Receiving support from others who have similar experiences can be validating and empowering for members. Based on a member's needs and personality, support groups can augment individual treatment or can be a stand-alone resource.

Reciprocal groups
Group intervention model that emphasizes common goals, interests, and exchanges.

Reciprocal aid groups differ from therapy groups in several ways. Their leaders can be professional or nonprofessional, individual members do not typically have specific treatment goals, and interventions occur as a result of members' interpersonal relationships. Support groups are typically less formal than therapy groups and are open so that members can move in and out of the group as they feel a need.

While their format is typically less formal, groups that provide mutual support can effectively promote individual and group member change. Using the less structured approach, a range of individual and group dynamics, listed below, characterizes mutual aid groups (Steinberg, 2014).

- Sharing information can help members identify their strengths and ways to share with others.
- The dialectic process establishes expectations that promote the creation of a safe space in which members feel comfortable sharing with others.
- During the initial phase of group development, group members and the group facilitator should discuss expectations and model appropriate behavior to foster the group's capacity to address sensitive topics.
- As the group develops a universal perspective, group members may experience the "all in the same boat phenomenon," and the group process should help members move from an individual perspective to a mutual aid perspective.
- The demonstration of mutual support in the form of empathy (as opposed to sympathy) is important to group bonding and growth.
- The demands of individual members can result in no one person getting

adequate time to deal with his or her personal concerns in an in-depth way; therefore, it is the group facilitator's responsibility to establish and maintain a focus on the group and not the individual.

■ A competent facilitator can encourage individual problem solving by modeling effective strategies for exchanges in which meaningful insights can occur.

■ The group can serve as a safe place for members to rehearse behaviors or conversations they wish to engage in outside the group.

■ Group members may benefit from connecting with others, learning about one's strengths, and discovering ways to share those strengths with others.

The group and the reasons for its origins often determine the social worker's role. A social worker may lead an effort to create a support group to meet a common need among her or his clients. Initially, the social worker may serve as the group's facilitator before eventually turning that role over to the group itself. The group leader's role can be multifaceted. She or he may serve as a mediator between group members, encourage an environment that enables members to work as a group, and facilitate interactions between members to support individuals in meeting their goals (Toseland & Horton, 2008).

The following are examples of self-help, support-focused groups:

■ *Addictions groups:* Alcoholics Anonymous and similar groups are examples of self-help groups in which group members provide leadership. Addictions self-help groups have expanded to include other drugs, food, gambling, and sexual behavior. Social workers can play a leadership role in addictions groups, but in a traditional 12-step model like that of Alcoholics Anonymous, there is no formal or professional leadership. Most addictions-focused groups are open-ended, with members using the group to sustain their recovery process. Members may stop participating when they feel confident in their behavioral change.

■ *Adoption or sibling groups:* Families acquiring new members through adoption, remarriage, or birth may join groups that provide both education about issues such as the adoption or birth and an opportunity for members to identify and share their feelings about the change.

■ *Disease/health condition groups:* Hospital social workers or social workers in organizations that advocate for and educate the public on specific health concerns often facilitate groups for persons experiencing particular health conditions. Some typical conditions for which people form support groups include cancer, multiple sclerosis, stroke, and pregnancy,

■ *Significant-other groups:* Support groups for the families and friends of persons experiencing a particular life event, transition, or health condition have increased in recent years. For example, such groups provide support for the family and friends of persons newly diagnosed with a serious or disabling illness or injury and persons experiencing an addiction.

Investigating the third option in her pursuit of a parenting program, Emily approached the administration of her own agency. Emily described the need she and her fellow social workers had identified among the mothers the agency served and presented the results of her research and consultation. She proposed that the agency offer a psychoeducational group (one that includes both edu-cation and emotional support) to expose clients to parenting education and to enable them to share their concerns and strategize ways to respond to their children's experience with domestic violence. Emily felt a group could have greatest impact on this issue because the women in the group could support one another and because it would allow her to provide information on parenting and complement the individual work she and her co-workers were doing with each woman.

Psychoeducational group
Group work model that emphasizes education and emotional support.

The agency director agreed with Emily's assessment and approved Emily's plan to develop the group and advertise it to her co-workers and former and current residents. Although several potentially viable options for responding to a client need emerged from Emily's ideas and research, she was confident that the support group approach would provide the parenting support and information mothers needed.

Task Groups

A fourth model of group practice, the task group model, brings together fea-tures of the three models described above. Task groups collaborate to solve specific problems or issues, that group members select and agree upon, affect-ing a larger group (Furman, Bender, & Rowan 2014; Toseland & Horton, 2008). Task groups rely on reciprocal respect and information sharing and use a decision-making process to achieve goals. A task group may have a focused goal (like the social goals model), it may seek the return of stability or normal function (like the remediation model), or it may aim to provide mutual support (like the reciprocal model).

Task groups
Group intervention approach that emphasizes specific solutions for a designated group.

Building on a strengths-based foundation, the social worker strives to help members of a task group identify their strengths and potential contributions. The social worker facilitates group communication, consensus, and progress toward agreed-upon goals. While typically structured with a designated leader, agenda, and work plan, task groups can also hold meetings to brainstorm, plan, and resolve conflicts (Furman et al., 2014).

Examples of task groups include:

■ *Individual education plan group:* Along with parents or guardians, school and community staff members meet regularly to discuss the educational progress and social and emotional needs of students who have been identified as having special needs. The social worker brings a systemic and strengths-based perspective to this interprofessional team.

■ *Senior immigrant project task force:* A group of co-workers at a community-based agency that serves older adults wants to provide culturally appropriate services to the growing population of older immigrants that lives in the area. The social worker convenes a group to write and submit to a private foundation a grant proposal for a program for the older adults and their families.

■ *Volunteer appreciation task force:* The volunteer coordinator at a food pantry calls a staff meeting to develop plans to show appreciation for the countless hours the agency's volunteers spend helping the organization collect, sort, and distribute donations.

Facilitating a psychoeducational group was a new experience for Emily, and she was careful to consider the full range of issues related to content and process. To do so she formed a task group to advise her on the development and facilitation of a support group for residents and former residents of the shelter program. In addition to recruiting co-workers with support group experience, she sought out community professionals with expertise in parenting and child development. The group met several times prior to the support group launch to help Emily strategize about recruitment, phases of group work, and content for parenting education. She reconvened the group several times for their input on the group process, needed adjustments, and evaluation.

SKILLS FOR SOCIAL WORK PRACTICE WITH GROUPS

Social work practice with groups builds on many of the same skills social workers use with individuals and families. These levels of practice have five things in common: (1) the systems approach; (2) an understanding of group dynamics; (3) the intervention approach; (4) an understanding of intervention processes; and (5) a commitment to evidence of effectiveness (Garvin & Galinsky, 2008). The skill set required for group practice is not unique to group work; it is the purpose with which those skills are used that is unique to group work (Ephross & Greif, 2009). The skills required for a social work planned change intervention with individuals and families are similar to those utilized at the group level, the difference being that the client system is the group as opposed to an individual. In addition to employing the skills associated with a planned change intervention, the social worker leading groups must also understand group dynamics as well as insights into the world in which group members exist, including both policy and practice approaches and skills (Dominelli, 2008).

Group work skills including engagement, assessment, intervention, and evaluation were introduced in Chapter 9 as part of the planned change process for working with individuals and families. However, at the group level, these phases can be fluid and dynamic, particularly in groups that are open-ended or in which the goal or purpose may change after the group is formed. Monitoring individual and group progress toward goal achievement requires that the social worker be able to move back and forth comfortably between phases of work.

Group work requires sensitivity to group dynamics. Establishing a group for persons with a common cause, need, or agenda can bring challenges. Individual members may not feel a connection with other members, the group may lack cohesion or direction, some members may have "hidden agendas," the group culture and norms may become counterproductive to group process, and the group may focus excessively on individual problem solving (Steinberg, 2014). Moreover, the social worker may attempt to be the sole "helper" in the group instead of activating the power of group members as contributors to the helping process (IASWG, Inc., 2010). Conflict may become a normal part of the group process; a skilled social worker uses that conflict as a part of the intervention itself.

As with all other areas of social work practice, social workers must vigilantly uphold ethical standards in all phases of the group intervention process. Ethical issues that arise in groups may include dilemmas related to sharing information obtained during the group process (i.e., can or should the information be shared with or reported outside the group?), mediating values conflicts among group members, and resolving conflicts between the group process and the sponsoring agency's policy or mission. Social work's standards for ethical practice are the best guide in these situations (Pullen-Sansfaçon, 2011).

Social workers engaged in group practice are ethically bound to be aware of potential issues of social justice such as social inequities, discrimination, power, privilege, oppression, and marginalization—whether among or between group members and those outside the group. As a group facilitator, the social worker must use a multicultural approach in order to address the diversity within the group. The group leader is also responsible for increasing knowledge and awareness of these experiences so group members learn to begin to view their own lives and issues with the context of the larger systems that make up their worlds and thus feel empowered to engage in change (Singh & Salazar, 2011). Framing group members' issues and concerns within the context of social injustice often leads to "courageous conversations" about empowerment (Singh & Salazar, 2011, p. 214). Professionals committed to maintaining a social justice perspective can reflect on the potential impact of personal experiences, challenge the appropriateness of practice interventions, and take action to remedy any identified social inequities (Constantine, Hage, Kindaichi, & Bryant, 2007).

Group leaders can strive to achieve social justice within the group setting by incorporating social justice concepts into the development and maintenance of the group. The Dimensions of Social Justice Model (Ratts, Anthony & Santos, 2010) views social justice both as a goal (i.e., everyone has a right to access resources) and as a process (i.e., groups should be inclusive and affirming) and identifies five dimensions of social justice within the group intervention:

- Naiveté—The group leader and members are unaware of one another's cultural history, including oppression and discrimination, and makeup (e.g., race, ethnicity, gender, sexual orientation, etc.). If the group remains naïve, the oppressive status quo is maintained.
- Multicultural integration—With group leader's assistance, members begin to move outside themselves to understand and relate to others.
- Liberatory critical consciousness—With the group leader's support, members begin to recognize life's injustices and to see issues outside of the individual and in the environment.
- Empowerment—The group leader and group members develop tools for self-advocacy.
- Social justice advocacy—The traditional group work model is extended to advocating with and on behalf of the individual's and group's concerns.

Exhibit 10.1 outlines principles for multicultural and social justice competence for group workers.

Engagement of Groups

At the start of the planned change process, the group is formed and its membership determined. When social workers determine group membership, they may be able to ease potential group conflict and enhance group cohesion and dynamics by forming a group that is optimally configured in terms of goals, member characteristics, and logistical issues. However, social workers do not always have the freedom to determine group membership.

The following factors affect group dynamics and processes.

- Individual and group eligibility criteria (e.g., gender, age, life experience, or situation) and goals determine who may be able to or interested in joining the group.

EXHIBIT 10.1

Multicultural and Social Justice Competence Principles for Group Workers

I. *Awareness of Self and Group Members: As group workers move towards multicultural and social justice advocacy competence they will:*

(1) Demonstrate movement to being increasingly aware of and sensitive to their own multicultural identity and how their race, ethnicity, socio-economic class, age, gender identity and expression, sexual orientation, religion, and spirituality, are impacted by their own experiences and histories.

(2) Demonstrate movement towards being increasingly aware of and sensitive to the multiple dimensions of the multicultural and multi-layered identities of group members.

(3) Demonstrate an awareness of different connecting and communicating styles. Group workers recognize different communication styles related to the various nuances of one's cultural worldviews. They are aware of how myths, stereotypes, and 4 assumptions learned by living in a society that bases one's cultural identity on excluding and devaluing others, impacts group dynamics.

(4) Seek to understand the extent to which general group leadership skills and functions may be appropriate or inappropriate for group work facilitation with multicultural group members.

(5) Recognize obstacles that group members encounter based on lack of opportunities and systems of oppression (e.g., sexism, classism, heterosexism) and gain awareness of how to integrate an advocacy focus into group learning to address these barriers.

(6) Increase awareness and deeper level of understanding through educational, consultative, training and cultural immersion experiences in order to become more fluent with culturally-based practices.

II. *Strategies and Skills: As group workers move towards multicultural and social justice advocacy competence they will incorporate ASGW Best Practice Principles of Planning Performing and Processing.*

(a) Planning involves identifying group needs, goals, determining type of group to be implemented, selecting group leadership and membership, pre-screening and preparing group members, and determining techniques, leadership styles and resources needed. Group workers demonstrating multicultural and social justice competence in group planning will:

1. Develop multiple ways to demonstrate respect for group members' multicultural worldviews, which affect psychosocial functioning and expressions of distress.

2. Develop skills, through language development or familiarity with interpreter use, to actively value bilingualism and sign language and not view another language as an impediment to group work.

3. Seek knowledge and information of members' life experiences, cultural heritage, and sociopolitical background who have endured trauma, violence, and/or other overt forms of oppression.

4. Exhibit understanding of impact of race, ethnicity, culture, gender, sexual identity, different abilities, age, socioeconomic status, other shared cultural experiences and other immutable personal characteristics on personality formation, vocational choices, psychological disorders, physical symptoms, help-seeking behavior(s), and the appropriateness of theoretical approaches to group work.

5.   Model relationship skills to connect with and create connections between multicultural group members while planning, performing, and processing groups.
6.   Recognize group needs and goals, determine type of multicultural and social justice variables in assessments, identify appropriate groups to be implemented, select group leader(s) and members, pre-screen and prepare members, and determine techniques, leadership styles and resources.
7.   Collaboratively decide on group setting, time, structure, and format that best fits the cultural context of group members.
8.   Address communication styles across cultural groups and negotiate conflicts.
9.   Use culturally grounded frameworks and techniques that provide the best fit for group members' cultural context.
10. Adopt roles such as teacher, mentor, ally or advocate, and serve as role model in helping members navigate personal and systemic change.
11. Identify cultural nuances if the focus of the group is not on multicultural issues.
12. Articulate impact of multicultural elements on the group dynamics (e.g., cultural conceptions of time and differences in communication styles due to high context (primarily non-verbal) and low context (primarily verbal) communication.
13. Use culturally appropriate pre-group screening mechanisms to select members based on type, focus, and purpose of the multicultural group.
14. Determine if group membership needs to be expanded or altered to allow for a greater level of connection and support who are isolated due to one or more dimensions of multicultural identity or experience to ensure a framework of support.
15. Refer clients from diverse backgrounds to culturally appropriate groups and group work providers as necessary.
(b) Group workers demonstrating multicultural and social justice competence in group performing and processing will:
1.   Establish group norms to accept, value, and respect cultural differences and allow for open discussion of dynamics related to cultural issues.
2.   Attend to acculturation levels, racial/ethnic and cultural identity, and multiple identities related to gender, age, sexual orientation, disability, immigration status, social class, education level, geographical location, etc.
3.   Attend to intra-cultural differences to avoid stereotyping and labeling.
4.   Demonstrate just and fair leadership; be aware of alliances, identify the impact on alliances, and work toward including multiple perspectives and free expression.
5.   Address overt and covert cultural conflicts. Avoiding and/or ignoring cultural conflicts due to "political correctness," fear of offending members, or discomfort with addressing diversity issues will intensify group conflict and be detrimental to group process. Address underlying cultural conflicts and model ways to address the issues.
6.   Respond to language needs. If interpreters are used, attend to the dynamics that can occur with their presence and the act of interpretation in a group setting. Work with the interpreters and group to keep disruption at a minimum and check with interpreters on impact of group dynamics on them and debrief as needed.
7.   Incorporate traditional and spiritual healing or seek consultation when appropriate. Group members who find solace in culturally-based therapeutic techniques may respond to traditional healing methods that engage the mind-body-spirit connection. Group leaders who are not immersed in the cultural context and/or very familiar with the healing techniques can consult or invite spiritual or cultural leaders.
8.   Use culturally grounded frameworks and techniques as appropriate (e.g., use of storytelling, poetry, music, food, and other culturally and spiritually based practices). When utilizing

western approaches, use techniques and frameworks that fit the cultural context or adapt the approach.

9. Use culturally-appropriate assessment and evaluation tools where the benefits of quantitative, qualitative, or mixed method data collection is carefully considered. Because marginalized groups have often experienced exploitation and/or over-analysis by practitioners and/or researchers, assessment should be used sensitively. Research and evaluation findings should be shared with members to empower and reduce/eradicate barriers imposed by those in position of power.

III. *Social Justice Advocacy: As group workers move toward social justice advocacy competence they will:*

1. Discuss importance and influence of social justice and advocacy issues in a group.
2. Develop awareness of opportunities for activism and community organizing in local, state, national, and international settings and identify ways to provide group worker expertise.
3. Participate in a consciousness-raising group related to issues of social justice.
4. Volunteer with an activist and/or community-organizing group or initiative.
5. Use technology for group-related activism and community-organizing and increase equity through resources and access to group work.
6. Address: (a) Equity with focus on involvement in culture-centered approach; (b) Access, with focus on understanding identity construction based on differences and deficiency model; (c) Participation, with focus on mutuality and authenticity; (d) Wellness, with focus on a culturally defined state of being which integrates mind, body, and spirit to promote a fulfilled life.
7. Be aware of influence of local, state, national, and international policies on workers and members.
8. Know community and government advocacy services and organizations available to workers and members.
9. Initiate discussions and training opportunities to identify influence of personal statuses of privilege and oppression and oppressive systems on workers' and members' lives and make changes related to planning and facilitation and types of groups offered.
10. Write letters to community and government leaders advocating resource equity for members.
11. Address personal statuses of privilege and oppression and oppressive systems that arise in group worker facilitation.
12. Advocate and exercise institutional intervention skills and intervene at an institutional level when working with culturally diverse groups, including applying for funding to recruit more diverse membership or provide amenities such as food, child care, and transportation; working with management and administration in institutionalizing diversity efforts in the organization; or acting as an advocate for a member experiencing discrimination.
13. Expand the "client" to include systems and communities when examining change.

Source: Adapted from Association for Specialists in Group Work (Singh, Merchant, Skudrzyk, Ingene, Hutchins, & Rubel), 2012.

- Logistical issues such as meeting time, location, cost, duration, and accessibility (for example, an open versus closed group).
- Optimal group size is 6–8 members for a therapy group and 15–20 members for a support or educational group. Sizes for social action and task groups are typically determined by the group's chosen issue or theme.

- Some groups thrive on a mixture of personality types, ages, and genders, while other groups need more homogeneity for a successful experience. For example, young children can be in mixed-gender groups, but adolescents may find mixed-gender groups uncomfortable, particularly if issues of sexuality will be discussed.

Exhibit 10.2 provides a thought-provoking list of questions to consider when planning and facilitating any type of group intervention.

It is a good idea to meet with individuals prior to inviting them to join the group, but that may not always be an option. If you are able to screen potential group members, keep these thoughts in mind (Fall, 2013):

- Assess the individual's readiness to participate in the group process.
- Inquire about the person's relationships—even one significant relationship can increase a person's potential for engaging in the group.
- Determine if the person will be a good fit for the goals and make-up of the group. Depending on the goals of the group, a person in the throes of a severe mental health crisis or extreme life situation may not be in a position to meaningfully contribute to the group.

Once the group is formed, the social worker engages members by perceiving them both as individuals and as a client system.

Regardless of the type of group work, every group begins with group formation and first-meeting activities:

- *Making introductions:* Group members have the opportunity to introduce themselves by the name they wish to be called during group meetings and to share any information they feel is relevant to the group experience. Members of social goals and task groups may share their affiliation, particular knowledge, or the expertise that brought them to the group.
- *Explaining the purpose of the group:* The person who convened the group (this may be the group leader) explains why the group has been formed and shares her or his role in and expectations for the group.
- *Establishing group rules, norms, and boundaries:* An important step in engaging group members is to give each person the opportunity to voice her or his feelings about individual and group goals and expectations for the group experience. Enabling all members to contribute to a set of group rules, norms, and boundaries enhances their connection to the leader and to one another, and motivates them to continue with the group's work. For example, group members may choose to establish rules regarding attendance, timeliness, meeting time and location, conflict management, sharing information outside the group, and even responsibility for providing refreshments.

EXHIBIT 10.2

Questions to Consider When Organizing and Running a Group

1. Objectives—before recruitment phase
   1. Why set up a group?
   2. Who is the group for?
   3. What will the group seek to achieve (what problem(s) is it intended to solve)?
2. Group membership—before recruitment phase
   1. Who will join the group?
   2. What will the size of the group be?
3. Group name—during and after recruitment phase
   1. What will the group be called (and who will decide)?
4. Decision-making process—during membership maintenance and power relations processes
   1. How will the group make decisions?
   2. What role will members and leaders play?
5. Group atmosphere—during maintenance and emotional work processes
   1. How will members be made to feel comfortable?
   2. How will individual and group morale be maintained?
   3. How will conflict be handled?
6. Group actions—during maintenance and evaluation processes
   1. Who will organize group activities?
   2. How will group visibility be achieved?
   3. How will the membership be kept on board?
   4. How will success be measured?
   5. Who will evaluate actions and ensure lessons learned for the future?
7. Resources—during maintenance and evaluation processes
   1. What resources does the group have (including networking with other groups)?
   2. How will additional resources be obtained?
   3. Who is responsible for obtaining resources?

Source: Dominelli, 2008, p. 483.

■ *Attending to group members:* Just as attending skills are important for engaging individuals and families, a similar set of practice behaviors is required for developing effective group work skills. Using verbal and nonverbal skills to enhance communication, clarify exchanges, and create an environment in which the person feels safe is somewhat more complex at the group level, however, as the social worker must attend to all group members simultaneously. In addition, group work involves establishing rapport with individual members as well as with the group and then helping members articulate individual and group goals in the hope that the members will find a stimulating and motivational common ground (Steinberg, 2014). During this early phase of group development, social workers should be aware of and sensitive to members' feelings about participating in a group (IASWG, Inc., 2010).

The engagement, or beginning, phase in group practice is critical to building group cohesion and trust. Regardless of the type or structure of the group, individual members need to take risks in sharing thoughts, feelings, and ideas. When a group leader effectively engages group members, they are more likely to feel connected to each other and to the leader and to trust the safety of the group process.

For group members who are mandated or forced to attend, the engagement phase is equally critical but more difficult. The social worker must demonstrate that she or he accepts these group members, regardless of their anger or resistance, particularly during the engagement phase (Levin, 2009).

Once Emily had permission to form a parenting support group for current and former shelter residents, she began gathering information from her co-workers regarding their perceptions of clients' parenting needs. She also obtained input from the clients themselves at one of the weekly house meetings in which staff and current clients discuss house issues. Her idea was favorably received, so she went ahead with the planning. Because of the groups' psychoeducational focus, Emily felt that diversity in age, race, and ethnicity would be an asset. Emily scheduled the group for a time and location that Emily felt best served the clients. She arranged for a volunteer to supervise the group members' children during meetings. Emily created flyers to post around the house and to mail to those former clients whom she knew it was safe to contact. For the client's own safety, social workers cannot always contact women who return to live with their once-violent partners.

During the first session, Emily explained the origins and purpose of the group. She asked each member to introduce herself, to say as much or as little about herself as she wished, and to state one goal she had for herself in joining this group.

Next, Emily and the group developed some general rules related to frequency of sessions, attendance, speaking out of turn, handling conflicts, and sharing information about group members outside the group meeting. Because Emily knew the group members from their stays at the shelter, the first session was comfortable, and the members began to bond with one another.

Assessment of Groups

Following engagement, the next phase of the group process is to assess individuals within the group as well as the group as a whole. Ongoing assessment is particularly important in group practice. Because the group experience involves a variety of individual personalities and life experiences, the group's goals, concerns, and dynamics change constantly.

In group work, the social worker is aware of the interactions among group members and monitors individual and group progress toward goals. Individual and group goals, as well as group structure and dynamics (for example, rules, norms, or membership), are always in flux. With vigilance and flexibility, group members and the social worker can develop plans and interventions that fit the changing needs of individual members and the group as a whole.

Focusing on the following assessment-related issues will help the group process benefit all members:

- *Group development:* The process of establishing group norms, rules, and goals can provide the social worker with information for assessing individual members' communication and interpersonal styles as well as the group's ability to function collectively. To assess and promote group cohesion, the social worker can help members connect to one another as well as to the social worker her-/himself. Helping members identify shared experiences and similarities can aid in this process (IASWG, Inc., 2010). Throughout the group assessment experience, the social worker can raise group members' awareness of their commonalities and their ability to support the goals of individual members and of the group.
- *Group diversity:* As part of the assessment of group development, the social worker should keep in mind how member diversity influences the group building and group work processes (IASWG, Inc., 2010). Group member characteristics that can impact group dynamics include race, ethnicity, gender, cultural background, age, values, and professional affiliations. The group process can increase group members' awareness and understanding of stereotypes and diversity issues.
- *Group members' strengths and resources:* In conducting initial and ongoing assessment of the group and its individual members, the social worker helps both individuals and the group as a whole to identify strengths, resources, and areas for growth and change. Group assessment shifts the emphasis to members of the group, who ask questions, share experiences and insights, and identify resources that are new to other members or the social worker.
- *Balance of personal and group goals:* To assess the balance of personal and group goals, the social worker invites each group member to share her

or his motivation for participating in the group experience and identifies her or his expectations for that participation. The social worker helps members link personal needs to group needs and goals (IASWG, Inc., 2010). Group members can be a resource for identifying the concerns and priorities of other members, thus involving all members of the group in the personal change process. Such a strategy enables the social worker to foster development of individual group member assessment as well as group cohesion. To achieve balance and to involve all members, the worker uses a combination of open- and closed-ended questions and encourages members to question one another.

Despite the fact that Emily knew all of the group members before they joined the group, she needed to assess their current situations and, specifically, their concerns and strengths in the area of parenting children exposed to intimate partner violence. Emily began her assessment of the group members as they introduced themselves, shared their stories, and stated their expectations for the group. This process enabled Emily to learn about the level of violence to which the children had been exposed, the way in which the mothers had handled that exposure, whether the children had been physically abused as well, and children's behaviors that concerned the mother.

In addition to assessing each individual, Emily was able to assess the group as a whole in terms of their strengths as parents and the areas in which they could build on those strengths to enhance their parenting skills. Other factors she thought were important to address included the members' investment in the group process, their ability to bond with and support one another, and the ways in which the members might handle emotional and conflicted situations that could occur within the group.

Intervention with Groups

As with social work interventions at the individual and family practice level, group interventions occur in two phases: planning and implementation. The dual emphasis on individual and group goals is important in both planning and implementation. Even if the group is able to develop a mutually agreed-upon set of goals, individual perceptions of the tasks and activities needed to achieve those goals may vary considerably. In addition, the group may reach consensus on group goals, but individual goals are bound to be as distinct and unique as the group members themselves. Moreover, both individual and group goals may change over the lifetime of the group, requiring periodic review. The social worker is responsible for monitoring the changing balance of issues.

Planning interventions at the group level requires that the social worker help to establish goals and document the agenda for the group experience:

■ *Establishing goals:* The social worker helps the group create goals for the group itself and for the individuals in the group, using specific and measurable tasks and outcomes. The social worker provides input into the development of the goals, weighs the advantages and disadvantages of proposed goals, identifies barriers and available and needed resources, and provides links between individual and group proposals (IASWG, Inc., 2010).

■ *Documenting the agenda for the group experience:* For groups with the general goals of remediation and reciprocity, developing individual and group working agreements helps each participant focus on her or his personal commitment as well as the commitment to the larger group. For social action and task groups, the agreement may take the form of a working statement of the purpose, goals, and activities of the group and a delineation of the roles of individual members. Exhibit 10.3 shows an example of a working agreement or contract, similar to the individual contract in Chapter 9 that can be used in remedial, reciprocal, and social action goals groups.

Documenting the events and activities of each group meeting/session is equally important. For remedial/treatment and reciprocal client groups, the leader's notes should be entered into a file for the individual client as well as a record for the entire group. Members' names and identifying information cannot be included in the group record as that record is a legal document that could be subpoenaed into a court action. In order to protect the member confidentiality, names must be withheld. A summary sheet can be compiled that includes: events of the meeting/session, interventions implemented, problems and issues—including new issues, and future plans (Sidell, 2011).

Once established, individual and group goals are put into action. As they proceed, the social worker and group members engage in ongoing assessment of their individual and collective work to determine whether they should revise any goals.

This implementation stage may provide the greatest challenges for the social worker and group members, as it involves actually changing attitudes and behaviors and completing agreed-upon tasks. The social worker watches for and addresses individual and group issues that can impede the work of the group. Some group dynamics that may impede the implementation process include:

■ *Conflict:* Differences may arise for several reasons, including the varying paces at which group members work toward their contracted goals,

EXHIBIT 10.3

Sample Working Agreement for Individual and Group Intervention Planning

Group Members:

Olivia M.	Tammy R.
Shirley B.	Megan S.
Cynthia W.	Angela G.

Group Goals as Agreed on by All Group Members:

Identify our strengths as mothers

Improve parenting skills

Have a safe place to talk about our experiences

Group Rules and Expectations:

Group will meet weekly; members attend as needed

Members will respect one another's right to speak

All information shared will be confidential

Individual Group Member Goals and Tasks:

Group Member	Goal	Client Tasks/Date	Social Worker Tasks/Date
Olivia	1. Be able to share my situation with others	I will share at least one personal item each meeting	Each meeting, I will support Olivia by asking if she would like to share
	2. Identify my strengths as a parent	I will report at least one positive thing I did during the week as a mother	I will provide information on "parenting without spanking"
	3.		

Date Contract Will Be Reviewed:

8 weeks from today

I agree with the above-stated goals, to complete the contracted tasks, and participate

in a review and evaluation of the contract on the specifi   ed date.

Olivia M.	Emily
Client	Social Worker
Date	Date

differences in individual and group values, and changing individual and group needs. The social worker may often be confronted with member-to-member conflict or member-to-social worker conflict. While conflict typically makes members and leaders uncomfortable, it may mean that the member(s) feel(s) safe enough in the group to open up in that manner (Fall, 2013). The social worker can model conflict resolution by responding directly to the conflict and by involving group members in facilitating a positive outcome.

- *Violation of group rules and norms:* Even if rules are clearly outlined during the group's early development, members may find themselves unable to comply with them or to fulfill expectations. Responsibility for confronting violations falls to the group leader. Asking the group to review previously established rules and to address any infraction empowers the group to act as a unit in determining an appropriate response.

- *Disruptive members:* The group process can suffer when a member creates obstacles to achieving desired goals. Behaviors that impede the group's progress include talking too much or too little, not fulfilling obligations (for example, attendance or tasks), and being overly critical. A group leader minimizes a disruption by monitoring for such behaviors and addressing them either within the group session itself or outside the group meeting. Offering alternative strategies for interacting with the group and modeling appropriate behaviors while in the group are two ways to provide members with options for appropriate interaction.

The established purpose and goals of the group can influence the development and implementation of the intervention. For example, an intervention for an anger management group focused on helping the members learn appropriate skills for handling their anger may be highly structured and formalized, whereas a group for persons recently widowed may be less structured to foster the sharing of feelings and mutual support. Regardless of the type of intervention, the social worker is responsible for building on individual and group strengths, meeting individual and group needs, and focusing on specific and measurable outcomes.

Social workers utilize a range of skills when facilitating a group experience. Consider the social worker who is approached by a group of community residents concerned about the number of teens who "hang out" in community parking lots, often making excess noise, littering, and, on occasion, threatening passers-by. This informal social action group attempted to raise their concern with local law enforcement and were disappointed in the response. They have sought your agency's help because of your successful record developing youth programs.

Agency staff meets with the group to hear their concerns and goals. It quickly becomes apparent that there is a key division within the group. One part of the group wants a law enforcement intervention, while the other would like to offer the teens an alternative location where they can hang out without loitering in public spaces. Emotions are intense on this issue, and the conflicting opinions are turning members against each other.

In this scenario, the social worker employs a number of practice skills: (1) establishing norms and rules for group discussion; (2) clarifying specific individual and group goals; (3) potentially, managing conflict if members become disruptive or violate rules of decorum; (4) identifying strengths and challenges related to each perspective; (5) exploring options for moving forward as one group or as two new groups; and (6) mediating the two groups to determine if they have common ground.

The same practice approaches used in interventions with individuals and families are appropriate for group work. Two approaches highlighted in Chapter 9 for working with individuals and families, motivational interviewing and the solution-focused approach, are also viable options for group interventions.

As noted in earlier chapters, with motivational interviewing (MI)'s client-centered and goal-oriented focus, it is well suited to group work, which is less leader-directed than other social work interventions. MI works well in groups addressing substance abuse and addictions, co-occurring disorders, chronic health problems, weight management, intimate partner violence, and in groups made up of adolescents (Wagner & Ingersoll, 2013). There are several advantages to incorporating MI strategies into a group intervention. MI enables members to connect with others, which can inspire change. MI's client-centered focus provides opportunities to adapt to client's goals and needs. The non-directive nature of goals can be used for groups focused on support, education, and psychological or behavioral changes. When group members engage in the MI process, they explore and broaden their perspectives and, finally, act (Wagner & Ingersoll, 2013).

Interventions that emphasize a solution-focused approach can also be used in the group format. For example, social workers have successfully used a solution-focused approach in group treatment for substance abuse, enabling group members to connect with one another and to use the experiences of others to inform their own choices (NREPP, 2014). The solution-focused approach's attention to the future, to co-constructing alternatives and solutions with the client based on her or his desired goals, to making small initial changes, and assumes that clients have solutions can be incorporated into a group environment in which group members support one another through the co-construction of new behaviors and life changes (Trepper et al., 2013). Group-focused activities and exercises can strengthen the experience for group members in many ways. Activities can be creative and may include artwork (drawing/painting, collage-making, etc.), writing imagery, mindfulness, music, movement, dance, exercise, role-playing, or storytelling (Brown, 2013). These kinds of activities can (Brown, 2013):

- Inspire and challenge group members.
- Give focus to feelings of chaos or anxiety group members may be experiencing.
- Provide a vehicle for the expression of thoughts, emotions, and ideas.
- Clarify perceptions.
- Illuminate the obvious.
- Provide solace, centering, and grounding.
- Enable members to simplify and process complicated or conflicting feelings or values.
- Offer new ways to perceive and relate to people and issues.
- Engender balance and reconnections.

(p. 2)

To learn more about the group work experiences of a social worker who brings artwork into her practice, see Exhibits 10.4 and 10.5.

EXHIBIT 10.4

The "Art" of Group Work

Peg Schwartz, MA, MSW, LCSW, ATR-BC has master's degrees and professional credentials in Social Work and Art Therapy, so it was only natural for her to integrate art into her group experiences. She has identified opportunities to use creative and artistic strategies in all the settings in which she has practiced social work, including residential treatment agencies for children and adolescents, outpatient treatment facilities for sexually abused children, general child/family issues, domestic violence treatment, and private clinical practice.

Peg has incorporated art therapy into groups for child victims of sexual abuse, child witnesses to domestic violence, and adult women survivors of child sexual abuse. She has used art therapy in school-based anger management groups for middle school students. These groups were primarily experiential, using art and play to address feelings, issues, and behaviors as they pertained to managing anger and other difficult feelings. She has also included art in psycho-educational and supportive therapy groups for non-offending parents of sexually abused children and teens.

Peg finds that groups—and art-related activities, in particular—enable clients to express their feelings, fears, and aspirations when words might fail them. For Peg, group work is especially rewarding when treatment groups take on a life of their own, and she can see that the change and growth that occur are happening both because of and in spite of her efforts. Peg recognizes that group work can be challenging when conflict exists within a group and there can be a fine line between a successful and therapeutic experience and one that is disappointing or frustrating for members and facilitators alike.

Peg shares these words for new social workers regarding group work:

The time and effort that you put into preparing for a new group is typically not wasted. Before recruiting clients, be clear about the goals and logistics of the group. Set up a meeting space that affords privacy, accessibility, and the resources that are needed for group activities (i.e. access to a water source and tables or drawing boards for art activities, comfortable seating arranged in a configuration that encourages group interaction, décor that is conducive to the mood you want to create, etc.). When possible, set up individual screening sessions with potential participants to ensure that all are a good fit for the type of group you are leading. Throughout the planning stages and the entire life of the group, effective communication with co-leaders is crucial to creating a successful group experience. Once the group sessions begin, even the most experienced social worker will learn a great deal, because every group has its own unique dynamics and one will always be challenged to stretch and grow in response. Strong group leaders recognize that there are times when it makes sense to modify structure and/or plans in order to meet the needs of the group members.

Using the group's individual and collective goals, Emily proposed that each session have two components: education and support. Each meeting would begin with a "checking-in" period in which the members could share successes or ask for help. The second half of the session would include a presentation by Emily or another professional on a topic specific to parenting children who have experienced trauma. Together, Emily and the group developed a list of possible topics to cover, while acknowledging that they needed to be flexible in case additional topics arose.

Throughout each session, Emily monitored group members' interactions with her and with each other and noted individual growth and change. Emily routinely shared her observations with the group and asked group members to do the same.

Evaluation and Termination of Groups

In the final phase of group work, the social worker collaborates with group members to evaluate the group and to determine whether or not to continue to meet. This segment of group work provides the opportunity for the social worker and the group members to reflect on what they have learned and gained and on how they have changed; to consider the impact of the group experience on members as well as on persons outside the group; and react to the possible ending of the group experience (IASWG, Inc., 2010). Final group meetings are

EXHIBIT 10.5

Building on Strengths: A Powerful Group Intervention

As the lone therapist facilitating a weekly school-based anger management group for middle school students (grades 6–8), I was pleasantly surprised at how eager the five original group members were to meet and how honestly they approached group activities and discussions. Given that all of the students had been identified because of multiple incidents of disruptive behavior including verbal and physical aggression, the group was refreshingly cooperative.

In the third week, however, I was given little warning before a new 7th grader, Brittanie, joined the group. Brittanie came into the session determined to hate everything about it. She refused to participate in the planned activity and spent the entire session pontificating about how "stupid" the group was, how it was a waste of her time, and how pathetic the other kids were if they enjoyed it. One student half-heartedly volunteered that it was better than being in class, but Brittanie quickly shot him down with a derisive expression, and his tentative bravado faded immediately. The other kids immediately took their cues from Brittanie, and we essentially accomplished nothing in that session. The previously open and trusting kids behaved as if they all thought the group was ridiculous and were being forced to participate.

I consulted with the school counselor to find out whether or not I was obligated to keep Brittanie in the group. The counselor explained that each identified student participated in the group by choice of participation, but that if they chose not to participate, there would likely be another consequence (i.e., suspension) for their disruptive behavior. Armed with the approval of the school counselor, I met individually with Brittanie a few days before the next group session. I informed her that I had observed that she was clearly a leader among her peers, whether she realized it or not. I explained that the group members had been working cooperatively together before she attended, but that when the others saw how she looked down on the group, they felt compelled to do the same. Brittanie seemed startled and stated that she did not intend to influence the others, but that she was simply expressing her own feelings and opinions. I solemnly explained that leadership is a quality that sometimes chooses us, whether we like it or not. I told Brittanie that I was willing to work with her, but not at the expense of the rest of the group. I let her know that she had a choice to stay or quit the group and accept the consequences, but that if she chose to stay, she would have to use her leadership skills to help me ensure that the students took the group seriously. Brittanie was ambivalent, and I told her that was okay, and that she should simply come back to the next session if she wanted to do so.

That week when the group met, Brittanie did attend. This time, however, when one of the boys started to complain about the group, Brittanie assertively and politely explained to him that "This lady is here to help us learn, so we should be respectful to her and to one another." The others were momentarily stunned, but within minutes, the group was back to its old self, with Brittanie participating just as openly and cooperatively as the others.

Source: Peg Schwartz.

also a time to discuss ways to apply what group members have learned and to review follow-up plans (including referrals or ongoing treatment, in the case of client-focused groups).

Evaluation at the group level can be more complicated than evaluation with individuals and families. Individual and group goals are evaluated along with the group process itself. In general, strategies for evaluating a group experience evolve from the structure of the group, the goals of the group and its members, and intervention tasks and activities. For example, structured groups benefit from more formalized evaluations, while less structured groups (for example, ongoing support groups) may be able to informally evaluate process and progress on a regular basis.

Evaluation is part of the group process from the time the group is formed, but building evaluation into the ending phase can be empowering for both the group members and the social worker. The social worker and group members identify personal and group changes that have occurred, assess the impact of the group experience on members' lives, and determine whether future intervention is needed (IASWG, Inc., 2010). In the event that individual or group goals have not been achieved, the social worker can use the termination and evaluation phase to help individual members and the group identify positives, reflect on possible reasons the goals were not reached, and develop strategies for continuing to work on the original or new goals (Garvin & Galinsky, 2008).

To capture the complexities of the group experience, a multifaceted plan for conducting a group evaluation might be needed. It could include the following:

- Audio- or videotaping meetings, with group members' informed consent, to enable the social worker to observe group dynamics and her or his intervention skills.
- Obtaining information from group members through needs assessments, measures of attitudes or behaviors, or physical measures before and after the group experience.
- Obtaining group member feedback regarding satisfaction with the group experience and group leadership.
- Reviewing individual and group goals.
- Reviewing processes used to accomplish goals.

Groups that are time-limited or based on a specific goal or activity may terminate as a group at this stage. In open-ended groups, however, termination occurs for individuals as they leave the group. Evaluation in these situations may occur for the individual and still involve members who are not yet leaving the group.

Regardless of the type of group, the social worker facilitates termination using a common set of skills:

■ The social worker and group members share feelings about ending the group experience and leaving the group.
■ The social worker and group members develop plans for maintaining change.
■ Group members discuss their feelings about having contact after termination from the group (for example, returning to the group, having contact outside the group, or having group reunions).

During the beginning phase of the group's work, Emily and group members agreed that the group would meet weekly for eight weeks, and then evaluate the future of the group. To help evaluate their progress, group members completed a standardized parenting questionnaire at the first and eighth sessions to determine how their knowledge and parenting styles had changed. At the eighth session, the group asked that Emily continue the group but open it to other current and former shelter residents.

Through these two evaluation strategies, Emily and the group members were able to assess both individual and group goals and make decisions for the future.

CONCLUSION

Group work can be a powerful experience for both the social worker and for the members of the group. A group can often achieve far more than a person could achieve alone, but a group intervention is not for every person or every situation. An effective social worker uses engagement and assessment skills to determine whether a group intervention is the optimal approach in a given situation.

In group work, the social worker uses the same skills that she or he would use working with individuals: engagement, assessment, intervention, and evaluation. However, in group practice, the social worker must simultaneously build rapport with individual group members and facilitate group cohesiveness, being careful not to focus too much attention on one group member or issue. With a social worker's leadership, group members can provide input into individual and group intervention plans and participate in a group-wide evaluation of the experience. In working with a group, the social worker's skill in viewing strengths from a systemic perspective can be an asset. Susan Boykin, a seasoned social worker, wrote this poem about her experiences leading groups (2014):

Ode to Group Treatment
Social workers do groups
We like to rally the troops
Genuine, authentic, and caring
It is all about the sharing
Groups are powerful and healing
Members openly discuss their feelings
Trust is provided, kindness, and caring
Remember to check to see how all are faring
When all is said and done
Everyone has become one…

MAIN POINTS

■   In group work, the social worker works with a collection of persons to address individual issues, to address a need for information and education, to provide mutual support, or to address social conditions. Following the first course on group methods offered in 1923, group work soon became an established part of the social work educational curriculum.

■   The main group work models are in the areas of social action, individual growth (or remediation), self-help and support (or reciprocal), and tasks. The goal of a social action group is to initiate or change a policy, law, or program. Individual growth groups emphasize clinically oriented treatment for a personal issue or concern. Support groups are mutual aid groups based on a common life experience, and task groups complete a predetermined goal typically focused outside the group members themselves.

■   In the practice of social work with groups, the social worker forms the group, facilitates group meetings, provides resources, and works with the group to develop strategies to meet desired goals.

■   Desired outcomes for the group are based on members' abilities and willingness to be interdependent and to interact with one another for the purpose of achieving stated goals. Although change occurs for individual members of the group, the intervention focuses on the group as a whole.

■   As with social work practice with individuals and families, skills for group work focus on engagement, assessment, intervention, termination, and evaluation.

EXERCISES

1.   Below are descriptions of four groups in which Sanchez family members (www.routledgesw.com/caseStudies) may be participants. Read the

descriptions and, using the group practice models highlighted in this chapter, complete the exercises that follow.

- *Group 1—Grandparents Raising Grandchildren.* Hector and Celia are members of this group. The group meets for a monthly potluck meal, and members share strategies and resources related to rearing grandchildren. A social worker who has custody of her granddaughter organized the group. Occasionally, the group meeting includes a presentation by a professional on a topic of interest to the group (e.g., legal and financial issues and childrearing strategies).

- *Group 2—Women's Group.* Celia Sanchez is a member of a group for persons experiencing depression. Two clinical social workers facilitate the group, which meets weekly for 90 minutes at the mental health center to identify causes and symptoms of depression and to discuss treatment and strategies for coping with depression. The group is composed of eight women who were referred by other mental health professionals and then interviewed by group leaders to determine their appropriateness for the group. Celia and Hector's adoption social worker referred Celia to the group. The adoption social worker noted that Celia had experienced episodic depression throughout her life and was currently reporting depressive symptoms.

- *Group 3—Grandparents for Justice.* Through their involvement with the grandparents group, Celia and Hector became members of a group in their state working to improve state laws that determine the rights of grandparents.

- *Group 4—Grandparents and Grandchildren Together.* During one of the meetings of Grandparents Raising Grandchildren, one grandmother suggested that the group form a special committee to plan social and recreational activities that the grandparents could attend with their grandchildren. While the group unanimously supported the initiative, they were concerned about the cost of activities being prohibitive for some of the families. Several members of the group, including Celia, volunteered to form a committee to organize and raise funds for the activities.

    a. For each group below, identify the group type. Give at least three reasons for your answer.

    Group 1—Grandparents Raising Grandchildren.

    Group 2—Women's Group.

    Group 3—Grandparents for Justice.

    Group 4—Grandparents and Grandchildren Together.

b. After completing exercise 1a, select one of the group scenarios. Using that scenario, identify at least three skills appropriate for each phase of the group process:

- ▪ Engagement
- ▪ Assessment
- ▪ Intervention
- ▪ Evaluation and termination

2. As you read in Exercise 1, Hector and Celia have become involved in a group, Grandparents for Justice, that is working to improve the state laws that dictate the rights of grandparents. Using your knowledge of the phases of the group process, develop a list of strategies that the group might use to develop a plan to focus local and state attention on their issue.

3. Go to the Riverton interactive case at www.routledgesw.com/caseStudies. As a new resident and social worker in the Alvadora neighborhood of Riverton, you have become aware of the neighbors' concerns about public drinking. Using a social goals approach, your task is to convene a group of neighborhood residents who will develop a plan to advocate with city officials to address the problems.

    After familiarizing yourself with the residents of Alvadora, determine the potential strengths and contributions of each one. From a social goals perspective, develop a plan for organizing a group and provide strategies for recruiting members and creating a goal.

4. Go to the Carla Washburn interactive case at www.routledgesw.com/caseStudies. Following the death of her husband, Carla Washburn joined a widows' group at her church. She benefitted from participation in this group, and she was also able to help other widows to adjust. With the loss of her grandson, Mrs. Washburn has once again found herself grieving the loss of a loved one. Respond to the following:
    a. How could a group experience benefit the client in her current grief?
    b. Describe the group model that you would recommend for Mrs. Washburn and, based on the information in this chapter, provide a rationale for your recommendation.
    c. Develop a draft of a contract you would negotiate with Mrs. Washburn if she were to join a group.

5. As a group or in-class exercise, go to the Carla Washburn interactive case at www.routledgesw.com/caseStudies. Click on Engage, scroll down, and click on Video. As you view the video, complete the following questions, and discuss with your group:

    a. What type of group is this according to the four models for group work?

    b. What characteristics define this type of group (group size, purpose, etc.)?

    c. Was this an open or closed membership group? Describe the benefits or disadvantages of this type of group format.

    d. What are the goal(s) of this group (individual or collective)?

    e. Describe the components of the group phases using examples from the video: Pre-Group Phase; Beginning Phase; and Middle Phase.

    f. Group introductions, explanation of group rules, and defining boundaries are all examples of what group skill?

- Introduction
- Attending Behaviors
- Engagement
- Assessment

    g. Redirecting irrelevant conversation (i.e. group members inviting each other over for dinner) is an example of what group skill?

- Engagement
- Planning
- Attending Behaviors
- Assessment

    h. Describe the barriers/conflicts that arose within the group and how they were handled. Did anyone use empathetic communication? If so, was it effective?

    i. Describe how the facilitator fulfilled her role in this group.

    j. What would you change about this group if you were the facilitator (group size, group members, group rules, etc.)?

6. Using the information you have available regarding the Hudson City case located at www.routledgesw.com/caseStudies, develop detailed descriptions of social work group interventions that are appropriate for each of the four group approaches presented in this chapter. Include the goals, purposes, membership, and basic rules for each type of group.

7. As a group or in-class exercise, go to the Brickville interactive case at www.routledgesw.com/caseStudies, click on: Intervention, then Family and Group Intervention, and Start the Intervention. After viewing the video, return to the previous page and respond to and discuss the three questions that follow the family information.

After reading this chapter, you should be able to:

1. Describe social work practice with communities and organizations.
2. Delineate the types of macro-level social work group interventions, including: Geographic (Neighborhood) Community Organizing, Functional Community Organizing, Social, Economic, and Sustainable Community Development, Inclusive Program Development, Social Planning, Coalition-building, Political, Social, and Legislative Action, and Policy Practice.
3. Within the concepts of planned change, operationalize the phases of social work community-level interventions, including engagement, assessment, intervention, and evaluation and termination.
4. Develop beginning competency-based social work practice skills in the areas of developing and conducting interventions with communities and organizations.
5. Apply knowledge of social work skills to case-based examples.

6. Engage with Individuals, Families, Groups, Organizations, and Communities
7. Assess Individuals, Families, Groups, Organizations, and Communities
8. Intervene with Individuals, Families, Groups, Organizations, and Communities
9. Evaluate Practice with Individuals, Families, Groups, Organizations, and Communities

SOCIAL WORK PRACTICE WITH ORGANIZATIONS AND COMMUNITIES, AND POLICY PRACTICE

Source: iStock/photosmash

In her work in a senior homemaker/chore program, Emily helped Marietta, a 78-year-old widow with several physical challenges, to arrange home-based services so that she could continue living independently. One of those services was home health care. However, changes in state policies governing the reimbursement of home health agencies reduced and in some cases terminated the home health services Marietta and a number of the older adults with whom Emily worked were able to receive. Emily started to notice the negative consequences of these new policies. Some older adults had to move in with family members or into residential care facilities.

As both advocate and case manager, Emily compiled case examples detailing the negative effects of these policy changes. With her agency's support, Emily shared her data with a community coalition of agencies and organizations that engage in legislative advocacy on issues related to older adults. The advocacy group used Emily's data in their campaign to gain a legislative sponsor and to write and introduce state-level legislation to increase the reimbursement rates for home health service providers.

Emily then worked with the advocacy group to prepare testimony for a legislative committee. She arranged for family members of home health care recipients to travel to the state capitol and testify before the committee on the negative impact of the cutbacks.

After a 2-year sustained, collaborative effort, the state passed legislation to increase reimbursement for home health services for older adults.

Community-level social work practice
A method of social work practice in which the social worker works with a client system comprised of organizations and communities to develop a planned change effort that meets the needs of the organization or community.

Policy practice
Working to influence the development, implementation, improvement, and evaluation of policies at the organizational, community, state, and national levels that are aimed at creating social justice for those impacted by the policies.

This chapter explores the third level of generalist social work practice, which targets change efforts at the organizational, community, and societal levels. Community-level social work practice, also referred to as macro practice, promotes changes in practices, policies, and legislation that impact groups of people in an organization, community, state, or country, or even globally. Policy practice is an important aspect of macro-level social work that involves the formulation and implementation of social policies within the context of social and economic development (Iatridis, 2008). Although many of the terms and concepts that describe social work practice with organizations and communities are used interchangeably, they are, in fact, distinct practice approaches (Barker, 2014):

- *Community*—a group of individuals (including families and groups) that may share one or more of the following: geographic proximity, values, services, life experiences, faith traditions, and/or institutions.
- *Organizations*—formally structured arrangements of people and resources that are joined to achieve agreed upon goals and objectives.

- *Mission statements*—an organization's attempt to convey the group's goals, directions, vision, purpose, and values and the way in which these are accomplished.
- *Types of organizations*—public, private for-profit, and private nonprofit, sectarian and non-sectarian—social, health, and educational organizations typically operate as:
  - *public* (primary source of funding and administration is local, state, or federal);
  - *private for-profit* (proprietary);
  - *private nonprofit* (funding may come from clients, third parties, public/philanthropic contributions, and government programs with any profit being returned to the organization);
  - *sectarian* (organizations that operate with a religious or faith-based affiliation);
  - *non-sectarian* (organizations that operate without a religious or faith-based affiliation).

Why is it important for social workers to work at the community and organizational level? DeFilippis and Saegert (2012a) remind us that communities are the hubs of societies where educational, health care, housing, and commerce institutions provide for our physical, emotional, social, psychological, and financial needs. These authors also note that communities are critical for our well-being because they do the following:

- Provide the everyday needs of all persons.
- Create institutions that allocate goods and resources.
- Cultivate relationships among people that promote human and cultural development, effective citizenship, and political will (p.6).

Throughout the history of the profession, social workers have initiated macro-level interventions in response to government incentives (e.g., the economic stimulus programs of 2009); significant funding decreases (e.g., Medicaid cuts); or large-scale social movements to address oppression (e.g., the Occupy Movement) (Gibelman, 2004). When policies are punitive or bureaucracies are large and impersonal, the social worker can advocate for clients to facilitate change in the system intended to serve them. Community-level practice promotes quality of life; human rights; advocacy; human social and economic development; service and program planning; service integration; political and social action; and social justice (Weil & Gamble, 2015, pp. 908–909; Weil, Gamble, & Ohmer, 2013). Within this field of practice, social workers' roles as change agents can occur in three separate but related ways:

■ *Social change agents* focus specifically on initiating and facilitating changes aimed at improving individual and community well-being, particularly in the areas of social justice and social programs.

■ *Political change agents* direct their efforts toward changing societal structures and institutions.

■ *Personal change agents* strive to help individuals adapt to societal norms and rules (p. 32).

While 14% of practicing social workers describe their primary practice focus as macro practice, organizational and community practice is often combined with direct practice. In fact, over half (51%) of social workers surveyed reported spending their time in direct services to clients, but the remaining spent time in activities such as administration, management, supervision, consultation, training, planning, teaching, research, project management, policy/legislative development, fund-raising/grant writing, and community organizing (Whitaker & Arrington, 2008, p. 8). From another perspective, Exhibit 11.1 shows the percentage of time that social workers engage in macro practice activities.

Social workers often begin their careers by working with individuals and families and then move into areas that include administration, management, teaching, or research. This career path means that administrators, supervisors, and teachers have insight into the issues and challenges of social work practice with individuals and families.

Although organizational and community-level practice may not be their primary focus, all social workers are ethically and professionally obligated to advocate for social justice. In the National Association of Social Workers (NASW) *Code of Ethics* (2008), four of the six ethical principles emphasize this responsibility. For social work practice at the community level, the *Code* charges social workers with the responsibility:

1. to promote social change "with and on behalf of vulnerable and oppressed individuals and groups" in the areas of poverty, unemployment, discrimination, and other areas of social injustice;

2. to serve both client systems and the larger society and address the needs of organizations and communities as well as individuals, families, and groups; and

3. to practice with integrity within organizations (NASW, 2008). Moreover, Standard 6 of the *Code of Ethics* (NASW, 2008) focuses on social work practice within the broader society in the areas of:
   1. social welfare
   2. public participation through influencing policies and institutions
   3. public emergencies

4. social and political action through working toward equity in access to resources, opportunities, and policies.

Addressing social injustice is considered to be a social work responsibility because social injustice "harms people and limits their opportunities to live as fully human persons with inherent worth and dignity" (Horejsi, 2002, p. 12).

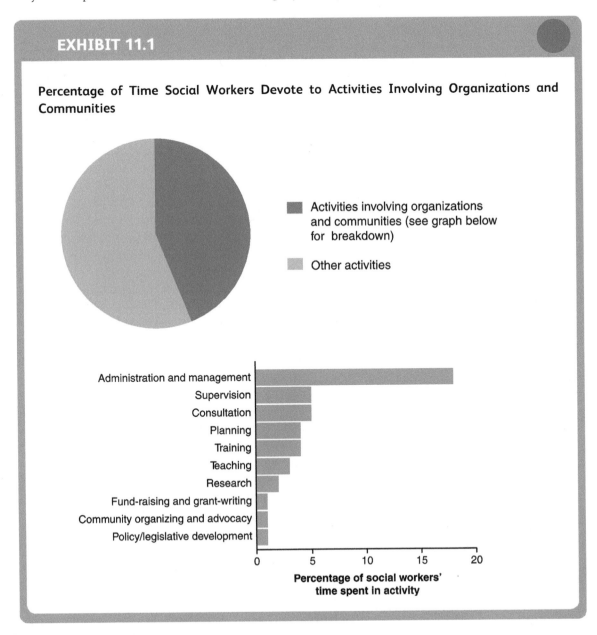

EXHIBIT 11.1

Percentage of Time Social Workers Devote to Activities Involving Organizations and Communities

This chapter begins with a brief overview of policy practice and then reviews the historical development of social work practice with organizations and communities. It examines the models of change used in this level of practice and the skills essential for being an effective practitioner.

A WORD ON GLOBALIZATION AND COMMUNITY PRACTICE

The world of community practice for social workers has become more global, impacting macro-level social work regardless of the country in which social workers practice. As with practice with individuals, families, and groups, macro-level practitioners work domestically with international issues and communities as well as internationally with communities in countries other than their homes of residence. While technology and social networking have enabled the world to become a "smaller" place in terms of communication, collaboration, commerce, and even social work practice, all of which have made international work more accessible and effective, globalization has been the result. Some view globalization in a positive light, citing the way in which it has increased economic and cultural connections, while others view it more negatively, focusing on ways it has damaged economic and social opportunities (Barker, 2014; Mama, 2008). Globalization has created challenges that influence social work practice with communities and organizations, including an increased gap between the individual and national "haves" and "have-nots" (i.e., those persons and countries with adequate resources to meet needs and those who lack resources to meet needs) resulting in increased global poverty, migration, and oppression and decreased governmental support for social programs and power of governmental agencies to influence spending within a country (Reisch, 2013).

Globalization has brought to light the connections between local problems and international developments, but it has also had a range of potentially negative outcomes such as (Reisch, 2013; Weil, Reisch, & Ohmer, 2013):

■ Decreased connections to organized labor occurring at the same time as the growing focus on increasing manufacturing while paying lower wages and jobs moving from developed countries to developing countries (where wages are significantly less and work environments are often unsafe).

■ Decreased interest in reinvestment (unwillingness to raise taxes to support social programs).

■ Increased expectation that not-for-profits/private nonprofits (tax-exempt organizations focused on charitable or educational activities that use any

Not-for-profits/private nonprofits
Tax-exempt organizations focused on charitable or educational activities that use any profits for the organization's activities, and non-governmental organizations (NGOs).

profits for the organization's activities) and non-governmental organizations (NGOs) to fill the gaps in services (Clark, 2012).

◼ Increased racial, religious, and political discrimination.

◼ Exploitation of natural resources due to natural disasters, environmental degradation, and global warming.

◼ Displacement of 50 million people worldwide due to civil wars, drought, poverty, and oppression.

◼ Continued increases in global health problems (e.g., HIV/AIDS and tuberculosis).

Clean Energy

Source: iStock/rrodrick beiler

Social workers around the world are ethically obligated to learn about and stay abreast of current global issues, in general, and those in particular that impact the client systems they serve. The remainder of this chapter provides an overview of models of intervention with communities and organizations and the skill set required to practice macro-level social work. As you review the models and skills, consider not only their domestic but also their international implications.

HISTORICAL PERSPECTIVE ON SOCIAL WORK PRACTICE WITH ORGANIZATIONS AND COMMUNITIES

The origins of social work practice with organizations and communities can be found in the early efforts of the Charity Organization Society (COS) and settlement house movements. While the COS movement focused primarily on individuals and families, COS workers found they also needed to advocate on behalf of their clients. Early settlement house activists organized and advocated at the local and state levels for social, economic, and political change in areas such as urban poverty, housing, child welfare, workers' rights and working conditions, political disenfranchisement (e.g., suffrage), and the environment (Brueggeman, 2013; Fisher, DeFilippis, & Shragge, 2012; Pyles, 2014).

Jane Addams and her colleagues at Hull House were the first to engage in large-scale advocacy efforts. They were concerned about sanitation problems in Chicago. The result was Addams's appointment as sanitation inspector (L. Quam, 2008).

The role of community practice continued to grow throughout the first half of the 20th century. The Great Depression of the 1930s, in particular, focused the country's attention on the need for community-level interventions to address the issues of widespread poverty, unemployment, and hunger. Through the New Deal programs, the federal government assumed responsibility for the development and implementation of community-level interventions for the first time in U.S. history. Such programs as the Civilian Conservation Corps (CCC), Works Progress Administration (WPA), and the Tennessee Valley Authority (TVA) are examples of community development in practice (Hopps & Lowe, 2008).

The social upheaval of the 1960s galvanized social workers into taking a greater role in community organization and advocacy. Social workers of this era advocated for civil rights, employment, the Vietnam War, and welfare rights. Though community organizing and other macro-level interventions had been part of the profession since the beginning, it was not until 1962 that NASW presented a formal definition for this area of practice (Hopps & Lowe, 2008).

Interest in organizational and community change waxed and waned through the 1970s and 1980s; at that time the profession emphasized social work practice with individuals and families. By the 1990s, efforts by social work advocates to promote a reconnection with the original roots of the social work profession created a resurgence of interest in arenas such as political campaigns and advocacy. Following the resurgence of interest in macro-level social work practice, the profession acknowledged the need for competence at multiple levels of intervention, which has contributed to the development of the generalist social work practice model. Practice at the organizational and community level is now considered an integral part of the profession and essential knowledge for all social workers.

Like social workers working at the individual, family, and group levels, social workers practicing at the organizational and community level often face

Protesting Crowd

Source: iStock/ericcrama

funding challenges; however, the profession's commitment to community organization, advocacy, and other organizational and community-level service activities remains strong. The current Council on Social Work Education curriculum guidelines, which state that social workers should be prepared to work with organizations and communities as well as individuals and families and be competent in policy practice to promote effective service delivery, reflect a commitment to ensuring that all social workers have knowledge and skills for organizational and community practice (2015).

MODELS OF CHANGE IN SOCIAL WORK PRACTICE WITH ORGANIZATIONS AND COMMUNITIES

To address social injustices at the organizational or community level, social workers must be ready to work toward positive growth and change within political, social, and economic systems. Community-building then becomes a specifically targeted series of action steps aimed at strengthening, enhancing, and/or supporting community-level goals (e.g., developing affordable housing) (Traynor, 2012). Achieving change within a system is a challenge due to the many and varied persons, policies, agendas, and needs involved. To facilitate system-wide change, social workers need to determine whether the system is ready for a change or if alternatives can be explored. If change is viable, the social worker may focus on identifying the key persons and resources needed to facilitate the change process. As with other levels of practice, the ecological and strengths perspectives can be helpful in framing the social work intervention. Identifying a community's strengths can be a significant step toward meeting the community's self-defined needs and aspirations (Jack, 2012). The strengths perspective, in particular, guides the social worker to meet people literally where they are—in the community—and to identify the strengths and values of the community and where these two areas may be in conflict (Weil & Ohmer, 2013).

The social worker's first step is to define the target community, which may include a physical or geographic environment or a social group or organization. Next, the social worker defines the goal of the change effort. Then the social worker typically works as part of a group or organization to select the most appropriate approach to achieve the desired outcome.

Framed by an increase in multicultural societies, increased demand for human rights, and ongoing social, economic, and political globalization, the models of community organization that have been developed by community activists, scholars, and practitioners to enable social workers to match the community, the goals, and the strategies for intervention include the following (Streeter, Gamble, & Weil, 2008; Weil et al., 2013):

- Geographic (neighborhood) community organizing
- Functional community organizing
- Social, economic, and sustainable community development
- Inclusive program development
- Social planning
- Coalition building
- Political, social, and legislative action
- Policy practice
- Movement for progressive change.

Exhibit 11.2 summarizes these models of change and provides examples of possible interventions to address problems of neighborhood and community safety.

Geographic (Neighborhood) Community Organizing

Geographic community organizing
Aims to improve the economic and social quality of life in a specific neighborhood or other geographic locale, whether in the domestic or international arena.

Overall, geographic or neighborhood community organizing aims to improve the economic and social quality of life in a specific neighborhood or other geographic locale, whether in the domestic or international arena. This approach can be conceptualized as a "process of organizing aggrieved or disadvantaged

EXHIBIT 11.2

Models of Community Action

SOCIAL WORK APPROACH	DEFINITION	EXAMPLE: INTERVENTION FOR IMPROVING NEIGHBORHOOD AND COMMUNITY SAFETY
Geographic-community organizing	Within a specified geographic area that shares a common concern related to a social problem, facilitating the creation or maintenance of a "collective body" to work toward resolution of the shared concern	Organizing a monitoring committee to document instances of vandalism within the neighborhood
Functional-community organizing	Facilitating a change in attitudes or behaviors within a community of shared interests by raising awareness	Providing public information and education about the potential effects on a community if vandalism becomes widespread
Community development	Systematically developing or improving the standard of living or the economic, physical, or social infrastructure within a geographic or interest-based community	Increasing commerce in a community through development of neighborhood watch programs to enhance customer safety
Program development	Providing leadership at the agency level to identify and attain goals, seek and allocate resources, supervise personnel, and oversee service delivery	Helping a group of neighborhood residents to address personal, home, and business safety by facilitating links to the police and fire departments
Social planning	Using a systematic, datadriven, evidence-based process in concert with other experts and professionals to identify a need for social change	In response to community complaints, working with police and community leaders to study crime statistics and trends in the community,

SOCIAL WORK APPROACH	DEFINITION	EXAMPLE: INTERVENTION FOR IMPROVING NEIGHBORHOOD AND COMMUNITY SAFETY
	and conduct an assessment, develop a plan for service delivery, and implement an evaluation	conducting a community needs assessment, and developing a new safety program
Coalition building	Bringing together groups and organizations that are committed to a common cause or concern in order to have a greater impact on decision makers	Coordinating a collaborative effort by organizations that serve older adults to develop a program that educates their clients on safety issues and provides safe escort and transportation services
Political and social action	Building political pressure to resolve a social problem or address a social need at the institutional or policy level, by working to elect candidates who support issues important to a group, organization, or community or advocating for legislation promoting those interests	Supporting candidates who are committed to increasing community policing and safety and providing them with sample legislation or data to support legislation
Movement for progressive change	Undertaking large-scale community, national, and international efforts in order to address social injustices targeting specific populations	Helping advocacy groups across the country to unite in order to address the issue of hate crimes perpetrated on the gay, lesbian, bisexual, and transgender community

Sources: Barker, 2003; Butterfield & Chisanga, 2008; Streeter et al., 2008; Weil & Gamble, 2009.

groups to make demands on the larger community for resources, recognition, or broader social change" (Sites, Chaskin, & Parks, 2012, p. 40). It focuses on building connections among disenfranchised community members, who share the common goal of gaining or regaining power that they perceive to be held by another group, to achieve a desired change (Pyles, 2014). Building trust and networks in-person hopefully leads to the development of social capital and helps community members be more effective collectively than they could be individually (Weil, Gamble & Ohmer, 2013).

Common to most community-building efforts is the concept that a community is complex and dynamic. Growth begins with recognition of the community's existing infrastructure, its many potential collaborations, and its capacity for change (Milligan, 2008).

The process of community organizing has four key elements (Pyles, 2014, pp. 95–99):

1. *Empowerment:* Emboldening people to act for change.
2. *Accountability:* Involving individuals and groups in the organizing effort so they will feel more committed to the cause.
3. *Relationship:* Using the skills of listening and "starting where the client is" to develop a rapport with community members that can evolve over time into a trusting relationship.
4. *Social change:* Facilitating an alternative approach or a solution to a social injustice.

Examples of community organizing social work initiatives include:

- *Organizing for better housing:* Residents of an apartment complex request help from a community-based social services agency to get needed repairs made to their apartment buildings. The landlord has refused to replace inefficient, potentially dangerous heating and cooling equipment, to maintain the exterior of the buildings, or to replace hallway and outdoor lighting. With their assistance, the agency's social worker conducts an on-site assessment of residents' concerns and contacts a local attorney in the housing division of a legal services agency. Together, the legal services attorney and the social worker compile a report and form a team made up of the attorney, the social worker, and representatives from the residents' group. The team presents the report to the landlord, and the landlord promises to make repairs. However, repairs are not made within the promised 6-month period. With the social worker's help, the residents organize a picket outside the landlord's office. The changes are then made promptly.
- *Organizing for improved transportation:* A neighborhood group unites around the desire to extend the public transportation system to their neighborhood to improve access to and from the neighborhood. The social worker begins by convening a gathering of interested stakeholders. The stakeholders make a commitment to advocate for this issue and develop a plan for advocating for expanded transportation services. With the social worker's help, the group conducts a needs assessment, formulates a plan to approach the city government, and implements the campaign. While the plan requires several modifications and compromises, the city government

agrees to conduct a feasibility study—the first step toward reaching their goal.

■ *Organizing for community unity and justice:* Following the August 2014 police-involved shooting of 19-year-old Michael Brown, the residents of Ferguson, Missouri, came together both to call attention to the injustices surrounding the racial representation in the community's governing and law enforcement bodies and to the unity of the community. At this writing, these efforts are evolving, but what has emerged are residents who are committed to building a healthy community. In an effort to address the issues, the Ferguson Commission report released in 2015 identifies four signature priorities for action and justice:

1. Justice for all;
2. Youth at the center;
3. Opportunities to thrive; and
4. Racial equality.

To learn more, review the Report at: http://stlpositivechange.org/.

Functional Community Organizing

In addition to being based on a geographic area, a community can also be interest-based or based in common concerns. These functional communities share commonalities such as ethnicity, values, faith traditions, or socioeconomic groups (Butterfield & Chisanga, 2008). As when organizing a neighborhood, the focus of the change effort in functional community organizing is to identify and raise awareness regarding the need for action, provide education, change attitudes or behaviors, build capacity, and lead an advocacy effort for social justice and change (Weil & Gamble, 2015).

Examples of functional community organizing include:

■ *Students organizing for students:* A group of social work students who have been completing a service learning project in a faith-based after-school program discover that the children are having difficulty getting to the program from their elementary schools. The social work students organize a campaign to help the children's parents advocate for the school district to include the program on its bus route.

■ *Faith-based community organizing for immigrants and refugees:* A group of immigrants and refugees approach the ministerial alliance in their community to request assistance in locating a site where they can hold religious services. The alliance comes together to offer their individual facilities for use on a rotating basis until the group is able to raise funds to secure a permanent location for their services.

▪ *Parents organizing for child safety:* Public health officials have long noted the hazards of lead paint, particularly on the development and health of children who may ingest these chemicals. A group of parents organizes in an effort to draw attention to the lack of testing, monitoring, and eradication of the use of lead paint in their community. Forming a coalition with the public health community, the parents are able to successfully advocate for changes to the municipal codes regarding the use of lead paint in rental housing.

Whether organizing a neighborhood, a community, or a group of individuals united by some other characteristic, the social work organizer strategically and proactively considers the "client's" goals, available and needed resources, the powers of various stakeholders (e.g., politicians, consumers, and the legal system), and strives to implement the best strategy to meet the group's goals and needs (Pyles, 2014). A diverse repertoire of organizing skills, including legislative and legal advocacy, asset-based community development, mobilization for direct action, and negotiation, is essential for effective community organizing (Pyles, 2014).

In response to major changes such as globalization and enhanced technology, community organizing strategies and foci are shifting. New directions for community organizing efforts include environmental justice (e.g., impact of toxic landfills on neighborhoods and communities) and more leader-driven (versus grassroots) campaigns in such areas as addressing the needs of children crossing borders without legal documentation, human trafficking, and other cross-border efforts related to asset-building and micro-financing. Despite new emphases for community organizing, the basis of traditional community organizing which helps us to understand that communities mean different things to different groups continues to serve as the foundation on which to build contemporary community organizing interventions (Sites, Chaskin, & Parks, 2012).

Social, Economic, and Sustainable Community Development

A second area of community-level practice is community development and, like community organizing, community development can and should involve members of the community and professionals committed to community well-being. The goal of the social and economic community development model is to help communities enhance and strengthen their cohesion, capability,

Social and economic community development model
A model to help communities enhance and strengthen their cohesion, capability, and competence, also known as capacity development.

and competence, also known as capacity development (Rothman, 2008). As with community organizing, change efforts in the community development approach can focus on geographic or interest-based groups (Butterfield & Chisanga, 2008). Although developing communities may seem similar to organizing communities, social and economic community development is more focused on creating opportunities for members of the community to engage in civic activities and tends to be less politically focused than community organizing (Traynor, 2012).

Whether working in the local, national, or international arena, social workers engaged in social and economic community development focus on mobilizing community members to confront unmet needs that traditional social and economic systems do not adequately address. This change effort can be directed toward areas such as economic development or community empowerment (Butterfield & Chisanga, 2008). Social and economic community development initiatives involve a change process that occurs within a "participatory, self-governing arena in which residents and stakeholders create services or development activities that remain accountable to this community" (Sites et al., 2012, pp. 40–41).

The social and economic community development model assumes that members of the community have strengths and are invested in changing their environment. To bring about change, community members engage in a cooperative self-help process with one another and with outside individuals and groups. The effectiveness of the change intervention increases as member participation increases. In essence, the client system and the change agent system are the same population.

The best approach for community development is generally a democratic, "bottom-up" approach. Members of the community are called on to define targets for change, assess their needs and resources, and envision and carry out an intervention strategy (Walker, 2010).

The most efficient way to effect change is to use existing networks to build stronger, more effective services and resources and to help individuals, families, and groups in the community gain more control over their lives, communities, and futures (Walker, 2010, p. 195). For example, community development efforts often aim to eliminate poverty (Midgley, 2010). One way to optimize a low-income/low-wealth community's efforts is to seek partnerships with public and for-profit entities to help build the community's assets and economic capacities (Sherraden, 2008, p. 1:382).

The social worker's role in social and economic community development varies. As a professional working in the community and interacting with a range of people and groups, the social worker may be in a unique position to identify a community need that residents or members of the community do not realize is a community-wide problem (e.g., access to affordable housing). In this capacity, the social worker may initiate a social change effort by mobilizing key persons within the community, following the social goals model for group practice described in Chapter 10. The social worker may train a community member to assume a leadership role. In situations in which community members identify the needed change, the social worker helps to facilitate that change. The social worker may also participate in the change effort based on her or his residence in the community or position within an organization. If she has a particular expertise or is a member in the community, the social worker could also act as an outside consultant to the change effort.

Social and economic community development interventions focus on such diverse target areas as employment, training, child care, health care, housing, community enterprise, alleviation of poverty, social exclusion, improvements to physical/environment spaces, improvements to educational and social resources, and development of social capital (Feehan, Feit, & Becker, 2013; Walker, 2010). For instance, NASW has called for social workers to advocate for the environment in general and for those areas of the environment that detrimentally impact disadvantaged communities (NASW, 2012–2014e). The following examples illustrate the scope of community development change efforts:

- *Neighborhood residents concerned about access to health care:* A social worker in a community center learns that residents in a neighborhood largely composed of older adults living on limited incomes are experiencing decreased access to health care. With the help of the agency's neighborhood advisory committee, the social worker conducts a needs assessment to determine the extent of the problem and discovers that many older residents have not seen a physician regularly since the nearby clinic closed several years earlier. The advisory committee approaches the local medical school to propose opening a small free clinic in the agency to serve outpatient needs. The medical school faculty seizes the opportunity to provide a training site for medical students, and a partnership is born.
- *Refugee-owned businesses:* Clients and former clients of a refugee resettlement agency approach social work staff about refugee-owned business owners who are being harassed. In recent months, a number of refugee-owned businesses have been vandalized. With the support of local business owners, the social worker convenes a task force of representatives from the refugee-owned businesses, Chamber of Commerce members, law enforcement personnel, and the community development agency. The task force assesses the neighborhood and finds that the problem is widespread. They agree to address issues of vandalism, security, and community relations. The social worker initially chairs the task force but later works to identify a leader from the refugee business community to assume that role.

■ *Micro-financing of small businesses:* A faith-based organization located in an economically developing Central American country provides low-interest loans to community members, enabling them to start or grow small businesses. The businesses are primarily retail enterprises, owned by women, that target local residents' needs for goods and supplies. The social worker locates potential borrowers, determines eligibility for loans, provides education regarding loan and repayment processes and small business development, and provides services and support during the loan period.

In social and economic community development activities, members of the community are the experts. The social worker's role is to support and assist the community to develop and implement sustainable change to enhance the lives of those in the community. A sustainable community development effort strengthens social equities and the long-term well-being of a community and is rooted in the interconnections with that community, which may include land use, transportation, housing, economic development, and environmental protections (Wheeler, 2012). The multi-faceted goals of sustainable development include promoting equal access to resources, preventing environmental exploitation, and aiding progress toward improved community well-being (Weil et al., 2013).

As with other areas of social work practice, community development interventions are shifting with changes in society to include increases in local, national, and international partnerships and alliances, advocacy coalitions, and use of technology. Even with these changes they will continue to be informed by the foundational concepts of traditional community development (i.e., sense of community values, social regulation, and function) (Sites et al., 2012).

Inclusive Program Development

Program development
The planning and creation of procedures to meet clients' ongoing needs.

Social workers are often well positioned to identify service needs and thus engage in the development of agency or organizational responses. Program development is the planning and creation of procedures to meet clients' ongoing needs (Barker, 2014). Development at the program level can originate in several areas. Social workers working in direct services may identify a need that no organization in the community has yet been able to fill. Current or former recipients of services may also bring attention to the need for a new or expanded service. In essence, the social worker involved in program development serves as a community liaison. Inclusive program development involves community members throughout the change process (Weil, Gamble & Ohmer, 2013).

The social worker's role can be multifaceted. The social worker may draw attention to the need for a service. She or he may then be the one who develops and implements the service. Conversely, the social worker may be approached to aid in the development of a service, to serve as liaison for her or his organization. Social workers can also help develop a program or funding proposal and then advocate for and facilitate that program (Streeter et al., 2008).

Examples in which social workers may engage in program development include the following:

- *Service expansion:* Former recipients of services provided by an urban domestic violence program contact the agency requesting that a satellite office be opened in their rural area. When their own needs assessment determines that the rural community indeed lacks services for women who are survivors of intimate partner violence, the domestic violence program approaches key persons in the community for support and establishes the new program. A social worker working for the shelter may be called on to conduct the needs assessment, develop the program, or manage the satellite program. If the social worker is already a key person in the rural community, her or his support and involvement can help the program gain acceptance.

- *Programming for preschoolers:* A county provides child care and other programs for children up to age 3 and for children 5 and older, but parents of children ages 3–5 must make their own arrangements. A BSW student works with an interagency team to develop a needs assessment and a program proposal that includes a proposal for funding a new program to serve these families (Bollig, 2009).

- *Turning loss into service:* When an MSW student loses her grandmother to complications from Alzheimer's disease, she and her family determine to build something for their community to serve others who experience this disease. Starting with a summer independent study, the student conducts a needs assessment, identifies resources, explores possible sources of community support, and learns the legal requirements for starting her own not-for-profit organization (Nobisch, 2014).

Social Planning

Social planning is an intervention model in which change efforts are aimed at community or policy-level issues. These date-driven, participatory initiatives are considered to be a "technical process of problem-solving focused on substantive social challenges (e.g., delinquency, housing, or mental health) that can be defined and addressed" (Sites et al., 2012, p. 39). Social planning involves working at the institutional and bureaucratic levels to facilitate the desired change at the community and policy levels. Social planning can focus

Social planning
A method of social work practice with organizations and communities in which the planned change efforts are focused on policy or community-wide change.

on community revitalization, service development or refinement, or community-wide service planning (Weil, Gamble & Ohmer, 2013).

Social planning is based on the belief that experts, who are technically proficient and have access to empirical data, are most well suited to orchestrate change. The goal of social planning in the community setting is to incorporate the perspectives and needs of community members into an intervention on behalf of that community that will improve and strengthen it (Weil, Gamble & Ohmer, 2013). Community members may draw attention to the need for change and then seek outside professional expertise. Professionals, outside consultants, and influential decision-makers may also initiate change without any involvement from community members. Those impacted by the planning effort should, however, be involved in the planning itself (Rothman, 2008).

The social worker may participate as a member of a professional team involved in identifying issues, collecting data, analyzing policy, and planning a program to address needs. The social worker is as asset to social planning efforts because she or he brings professional values and knowledge of planned change efforts and training in identification, assessment, resource development and management, and human needs (Sager, 2008).

The following are examples of social planning change efforts:

- *Neighborhood redevelopment*: Municipal officials, concerned about the deterioration of one of the city's historic neighborhoods, conduct a community assessment to determine the extent of decline. Upon determining that the number of businesses, owner-occupied households, and the overall tax base have all drastically decreased, the city's Office of Community and Economic Development applies for federal funding to restore the neighborhood. The funding enables the city to offer tax breaks for new homeowners, low-interest loans for new business owners, and grants for the rehabilitation and beautification of buildings and for the development of social service programs. The social worker may be in a position to gather and analyze data, facilitate the interactions of local officials, publicize the redevelopment effort, review applications, assist with locating and securing funding, and oversee program development.
- *International social work education*: Dramatic social, political, and economic changes in some countries (e.g., former Soviet Union and Haiti) precipitate a need to restructure social service delivery systems. When the expertise to build a social service system does not exist within a country's professional community, in some cases social workers from the United States are called in to assist in the rebuilding effort. The social worker's role in these efforts is to train, facilitate, educate, and consult. The social worker collaborates with other professionals to develop organizational practices, fund-raising mechanisms, and evaluation processes consistent with the new social structure.

◼ *Rural domestic violence services:* Consider the earlier example of the domestic violence agency that established a satellite program in a rural community from a different perspective: while the impetus for change may reside with the former recipients of services, staff of a local hospital might also identify a need and begin the social planning process. In such a situation, hospital staff determine that local services are needed when they notice an increase in the number of women presenting to the emergency room who report being abused by their partners. The nearest domestic violence program is 30 miles away in the county seat. The hospital administrator contacts that program and asks for their help in establishing a satellite program at the hospital. The administrator and shelter director apply for a grant to provide start-up funding for a hospital-based social worker to provide services for women who come to the hospital for abuse-related injuries. Once that program is in place, an advisory group forms and plans to seek long-term funding to keep the program running on a permanent basis.

As with other areas of community practice, social planning is affected by changing societal needs and challenges, creating both opportunities and challenges. Traditional models of social planning can help to maintain focus on social needs, thus providing opportunities to influence the efforts aimed at national and transnational social planning. Conversely, in the current environment of brevity of services, funding sources may view social planning efforts as too long term and those benefitting from social planning may be overlooked (Sites et al., 2012). In essence, those who control funding may view social planning efforts as being too costly when considered over an extended timeframe and those decision-makers will give that factor more weight than they give to the needs of those who would benefit from the effort.

Coalition Building

Coalition development is rooted in the idea that there is "strength in numbers." Coalitions are voluntary collaborative initiatives that unite groups such as agency professionals, client systems, governmental organizations, educational institutions, and legislative groups around a common interest or goal. Coalition building is typically aimed at impacting a large-scale change over a long period of time. It involves influencing the decision-making process and focuses on accessing resources (Streeter et al., 2008).

Coalitions
Collaborations between professional organizations and client systems who share a mutual goal.

The social worker may initiate the building of a coalition or participate as a member of a coalition. With skills in micro-, mezzo-, and macro-level practice, social workers are well positioned to serve in coalition leadership, mediation, and organizing roles (Streeter et al., 2008).

Coalition-building examples may include:

- *Coalition for community development:* This type of intervention is similar to the earlier example of neighborhood redevelopment. In this case, however, a social worker working in an agency in a neighborhood may invite resident associations, social service organizations, and representatives from the faith community to come together as a coalition. The coalition would then advocate for the funding organization to approve the request for neighborhood redevelopment.
- *Coalition for human rights:* A social work student has completed a practicum in a country in which women's rights are being oppressed. She calls on her network of students interested in social justice issues to build a coalition for increasing awareness of the plight of women in these countries. She invites student organizations from across campus to co-sponsor an educational awareness-raising event outside the student center. At the event the coalition provides information on the oppression these women are experiencing, collects signatures on petitions to be sent to legislators, and educates the public about women's needs in that region of the world.
- *Coalition for Residents of Ferguson:* In the days following the death of Michael Brown in Ferguson, Missouri, local social service agencies band together to provide services to community residents. These services include child care, since parents did not feel it was safe for their children to play outside; food and supplies, since the store closest to the neighborhood had been burned down; and crisis intervention services to help residents cope with trauma.

Political, Social, and Legislative Action

Political action
Achieving social change through political campaign, policy, or advocacy support.

Aimed at addressing an institutionalized social injustice or oppression, political action, social action, and legislative action change efforts increase political pressure on decision-makers so that oppressed and disadvantaged groups receive equitable services, resources, and power. These actions are most effective when they are the result of the combined efforts of a group of individuals and organizations, who may establish a political action committee (PAC). Political action strategies can be diverse, but typically include: running for elected office, participating in voter registration and participation, contributing money and/or time, and facilitating citizen initiatives to place referenda on ballots (Mondros, 2013). Effective advocacy groups (Hoefer, 2011):

- Are knowledgeable about and proactive in the policy process.
- Provide timely and policy-related information.

- Build relationships with decision-makers.
- Build coalitions with other interest groups and policy advisors (p. 3).

Social action often involves advocating for rights on behalf of or with a group that does not normally have a strong voice in the decision-making process. Three potential approaches can be used in social action efforts (Ohmer & Brooks, 2013):

- *Conflict or confrontational:* when the persons or groups in power are not interested in compromise, social activists may use strategies to demand accountability and change.
- *Consensus:* when groups seeking change and those in power can find mutual self-interest or common ground, the potential exists for a collaboration to find solutions.
- *Hybrid or combined approach:* depending on the issue and context of the situation, conflict and consensus strategies may be combined, requiring parties to assess the potential for conflict or consensus and all participants to be open to using both methods.

Whether it takes a confrontational, consensus, or combined form, social action requires the change agent to learn about the group that desires the change, promote community awareness about the issue and its implications, and develop a plan for addressing change (Mondros, 2013). Advocacy for policy change and development can occur at the organizational, community, governmental, and legislative levels and may involve a range of activities, from public education campaigns to confrontational meetings and public protests. Social workers also help candidates to get elected to political office or run for political office themselves.

Legislative action focuses on influencing the decisions of state and national elected officials. This form of change can be accomplished most effectively through collaboration and persuasion with considerable voter support, using such strategies as lobbying, mobilizing people and resources, official testimony, demonstrations, and as a last resort, protests (Mondros, 2009; 2013). When engaged in lobbying activities, social activists direct their resources toward the passage of legislation or the election of political candidates who support agendas that would enhance the quality of clients' lives. Mobilizers focus on long-term change efforts, such as fairer treatment for students born in the United States to parents who are not legal residents through the provision of education, public awareness, health care strategies, and improving access to health care. When considering a legislative initiative, be aware of appropriate strategies to employ with your target group and consider the following approaches (Hoefer, 2011, p. 8):

- Develop consensus among issue experts.
- Pursue issues in court.
- Participate in the election of candidates who support the issue.
- Work with legislators on policy formulation.
- Use media outlets to influence public opinion.
- Demonstrate or protest as needed.

When advocating to policy-makers and decision-makers, particularly legislators, an organized, evidence-based strategy is key to success. Policy-makers need well-researched data presented to them by experts or persons with direct experience in the relevant area; the data needs to be derived from credible sources, be easily accessible for them, and be timely and up to date (Borgenschneider & Corbett, 2010). Personal testimonials about individuals' experiences with the issue being discussed (e.g., a person with Alzheimer's disease shares her experience with this devastating illness) are a particularly effective strategy for gaining the attention of decision makers. See Quick Guide 11.1 for strategies to use when advocating with legislators.

The following are examples of political and social action change efforts:

- *Welfare reform:* In the wake of budget cuts that reduce the state's public cash assistance programs, the director of a statewide welfare rights organization forms a coalition of welfare recipients, social service professionals, and the ministerial alliance to engage in a high-profile advocacy effort. Pooling their resources, the coalition mounts an advocacy campaign that uses social media and e-mail along with letters, local visits, and telephone calls to legislators; educational sessions to teach effective lobbying techniques to faith groups; trips to the state capitol to lobby key legislators; and web-, radio-, and television-based public service announcements. A social worker might be involved in any of these activities, either directly or indirectly as a facilitator.

QUICK GUIDE #11.1 GUIDELINES FOR APPROACHING POLICY-MAKERS

1. Aim to inform, not influence.
2. Separate facts from opinions.
3. Supply standards for judging information.
4. Be fair and nonpartisan.
5. Provide private and safe locations for sharing materials.

Source: Adapted from Borgenschneider & Corbett, 2010, p. 251.

■ *Political action:* The PAC for NASW members (PACE—Political Action for Candidate Election) has chapters in every state. On behalf of NASW members, state chapter PACE committees endorse candidates at the local and state level, and the national PACE committee endorses candidates at the national level. PACE endorses candidates based on their platform on issues related to the social work profession. NASW members participate in campaigns, assist with voter registration, and contribute to campaigns.

Regardless of the approach used, political, social, and legislative action strategies share commonalities but must be approached differently in order to be successful. While each of these approaches can occur at multiple levels, must be implemented as a long-term and consistent campaign, and seeks to improve the lives of those in need, the roles of those engaged in the change effort can be dramatically different (Mondros, 2013). For example, when pursuing a change in power and resources (social action), the social worker may take the role of activist and use confrontation, but if the goal is legislative change, the social worker's role would likely be a collaborative and persuasive one (Mondros, 2013).

Policy Practice

Policy practice, which specifically addresses the formulation and implementation of social policies, is a critical area of competence for all social workers, regardless of whether they practice at the individual and family, group, or organization and community level. The concept of what we now refer to as policy practice has been a part of the social work profession since its modern-day inception in the late 19th and early 20th centuries. During the days of the charity organization society and settlement house movements, early social workers engaged in activities to address sanitation and juvenile courts. The profession moved away from policy practice at mid-century, but has recently experienced a renewed interest (Byers, 2014). Policy practice encompasses the identification, definition, and legitimization of a problem, which is then analyzed using the following approach (Ellis, 2008):

■ Gather information about the history and current status of an issue and/or policy.
■ Identify public norms and values regarding the issue.
■ Identify those groups who will support or oppose advocacy efforts.
■ Understand the current system of service delivery.
■ Develop an analysis that examines alternatives, preferred solutions, unintended consequences, and a plan of action.
■ Evaluate outcomes.

A firsthand view of the world in which clients live, a commitment to social justice, and an ethical obligation to serve those in need place social workers in a uniquely appropriate position to become involved in policy practice. Social workers may be the first to recognize a need or a gap in services and can help define, craft, advocate, and implement new policies (Ellis, 2008).

One policy practice strategy is advocacy. Emily's advocacy effort on behalf of her individual client, Marietta, resulted in a policy change, but only because Emily understood the intricacies of the policy, analyzed its impact, and worked with her clients and within the system to effect a change that enhanced her client's well-being. This systematic process highlights one of the many roles that a social worker can play while practicing at the organizational and community level.

Social workers are obligated to develop a working knowledge of social policies and their impact on the populations they serve (Iatridis, 2008). In fact, as one social worker noted, the 2012 closure of Jane Addams's Hull House signaled the need for the social work profession to reinvest in the practice of macro-level policy work (Gale, 2012, p. 19).

Movements for Progressive Change

The social work profession has a long and rich history of participating in and supporting social movements to promote social justice, eliminate oppression and discrimination, and foster opportunities for groups and communities that have previously been unable to access services or rights (e.g., human rights and women and children's rights). Such movements are large-scale and impact change at the national and international level. The women's suffrage and civil rights movements are historical examples of major initiatives that have addressed the need for progressive change. Social workers may be involved in organizing and supporting social movements in either a professional or personal capacity.

The following are examples of current social movements directly relevant to the populations social workers serve or in which social workers are involved:

- *Gay rights movements:* Since the 1960s and 1970s, many in our society have engaged in seeking equal rights for persons who are gay, lesbian, bisexual, and transgender so that those persons can live without discrimination.
- *Immigration rights movements:* Another prominent movement in the United States advocates for the comprehensive reform of immigration laws to expand immigrant rights. Undocumented workers and low-income immigrants have limited resources and are frequently the target of discrimination and unfair labor and financial practices.

■ *Occupy Movement:* The Occupy Movement began in 2011 and quickly spread across the country. Members of this movement focused attention on the need for reforms in U.S. financial issues and promoting greater socioeconomic equality so that they will benefit "the 99%" of the population who are not wealthy and powerful. For more information on current Occupy Movement activities, visit: www.occupytogether.org/.

The profession's commitment to social justice, client and community well-being, and empowerment, give social workers a unique vantage point from which to view movements and the insight and ability to influence social change. Working knowledge of the multiple models of change described here enables the generalist social worker to use the most effective aspects of each for any given intervention. Exhibit 11.3 provides descriptions and examples of community-level interventions that social work students, faculty, and professionals can be involved in to make a difference, while Exhibit 11.4 offers a reflection from one community practice social worker on her experiences developing her expertise.

SKILLS FOR SOCIAL WORK PRACTICE WITH ORGANIZATIONS AND COMMUNITIES

Organizations and communities are made up of persons and groups; the client in organizational and community practice is a group of individuals. For example, the client system may be residents in a neighborhood or community; social service agencies seeking adequate funding; or persons that share a common diagnosis, life event or style, or need. Effective practice with organizations and communities is built on the same skills that are important when working with individuals, families, and groups. Like individual, family, and group work, social work at the organizational and community level may involve engagement, assessment, intervention, and evaluation as methods for structuring social work practice processes and activities.

The role of the social worker in practice with organizations and communities is the same as it is at other levels of practice, but it focuses on a larger client system. At the macro level of social work practice, the social worker may function in one or more of the following ways:

■ *Broker:* The social worker forms connections by building collaborations, coalitions, networks, and partnerships.
■ *Enabler:* Community-level practitioners empower clients and others to participate in change by organizing and coordinating the efforts of individuals and groups committed to a common issue or concern. Many of the tasks

EXHIBIT 11.3

What Students and Faculty Can Do to Influence State Policy

- Get out of your comfort zone.
- Ask your professors for advocacy and policy assignments.
- Identify an issue or problem that you want to change.
- Form a group at work or school to help you advocate.
- Contact your legislators and ask them to help you introduce a bill.
- Develop fact sheets and policy briefs.
- Identify and track a bill in the state legislature that affects your field agency.
- Enter the national contest, State Policy Plus, for a cash prize and commitment.
- Plan a social work "rally day" at the state legislature annually.
- Serve as an intern in the office of a state legislator.
- Visit state senators and representatives personally or as a class and inform them of your concerns on a particular bill.
- Organize a group to prepare testimony at a public hearing or subcommittee.
- Write letters or emails to your state legislators.
- Track state legislation using the internet. Visit www.statepolicy.org.
- Work with your state chapter of NASW in lobbying for its legislative agenda.
- Design a research project analyzing the current impact of state welfare reform.
- Join a coalition or advocacy group and assist them in setting their agenda.
- Organize a forum or luncheon for state legislators, lobbyists, service providers, and clients on a proposed bill or policy.
- Prepare and deliver testimony before a legislative committee.
- Analyze and compare a particular policy or bill among all 50 states or internally.
- Write position papers for candidates who are campaigning for legislative office.
- Volunteer to work in a political campaign to support a candidate.
- Conduct a survey of candidates or legislators on their views about proposed bills or significant issues.
- Persevere and be very determined.

Source: Robert Schneider, Virginia Commonwealth University.

and activities of organizational and community practice involve group meetings, and social workers can use their skills to plan meetings, develop agendas, lead meetings, and facilitate good group dynamics. Because funding sources increasingly require verification that their investment is supporting programs that are having a positive impact, social workers are required to develop and carry out evaluations, analyze findings, and report on those findings to staff, boards of directors, and funders.

EXHIBIT 11.4

"It's Okay Not to Know Everything When You Start Out …"

Jessica Eiland, MSW and President of Northside Community Housing, grew up in Detroit and attended the University of Michigan, where she majored in psychology and had plans to become a biopsychologist. Her minors in Urban and Community Studies and African American Studies, a number of meaningful volunteer and service learning experiences, and the realization that social work encompasses more than clinical work, helped her envision a career in community organizing and development, which led her to obtain an MSW. Her MSW coursework and practicum experiences helped her to refine her areas of interests, each course or experience providing her with insights into the macro-level of social work practice. Her first position with a neighborhood development organization working in community outreach provided her with valuable skills that enabled her to transition to her current position.

In her role as president of an urban neighborhood housing development organization, Jessica oversees the well-being of the residents of 170 housing units owned by the nonprofit agency. In Jessica's day-to-day life, she write grants, helps residents who are working toward buying their homes (residents can purchase their rental home after fifteen years of residence), is responsible for reporting to local, state, and federal agencies, attends and chairs many meetings, and collaborates with other neighborhood organizations to coordinate efforts and projects to improve their overall effectiveness and efficiencies. To accomplish these many and varied tasks, Jessica uses micro-level skills when she is working with residents on home purchases and building relationships with the neighborhood residents and other community partners. She uses mezzo-level skills when she is chairing a meeting and an array of macro skills including community development, analyzing and advocating for policy, financial management, and administration.

In the work Jessica does at the community and organizational level, she is connecting with people and organizations and helping to develop new programs and partnerships. At the same time, she is developing relationships with individuals. No area of practice is without its challenges, and Jessica must deal with limited resources and her inability to respond as she would like to neighborhood residents when they voice their needs in those cases where resources or regulations do not allow her to do so.

As the title of Jessica's profile states: "It's okay to not know everything when you start out. Have people to go to who have experiences and ask a lot of questions!"

■ *Advocate:* Advocates articulate group needs in the form that is most effective with targeted decision-makers (e.g., social media, press releases, letters, public education campaigns, demonstrations, political lobbying, and petitions). Advocates must be willing to take risks and have realistic expectations regarding success. Legislative advocacy requires an array of strategies: providing research and technical information, organizing support, monitoring current issues, education, understanding legislators' biases, having insights into all perspectives on the issues, and presenting those issues in ways legislators can embrace (Reisch, 2015).

■ *Mobilizer:* Social workers may take an active role in writing grant applications and organizing fund-raising campaigns (for example, events, mailings, and telethons). As mobilizers, they may also engage in program development and planning. Organizational and community practice often involves establishing new programs or expanding existing ones, which means identifying the need for a program, conceptualizing and designing the program, securing funding or administrative support, overseeing program operations, and evaluating program outcomes.

■ *Mediator or negotiator:* Through reflective listening, the social worker can help opposing groups establish common ground and a mutually agreed-upon resolution. In the role of mediator, the social worker serves as an unbiased party, while in the role of negotiator the social worker advocates for one side over the other.

■ *Administrator:* Social work administrators oversee program development and operations, budgets, fund-raising, and personnel.

These roles may come into play within each phase of the social work intervention—engagement, assessment, intervention, and termination and evaluation—at the organizational or community level. The following practice behaviors are essential to developing and implementing a community-level intervention (Weil, 2013):

■ Meet with members of the community to discuss community interests, strengths, and needs in order to establish trust and communication.

■ Assess community strengths and needs within the context of the local community.

■ Organize and analyze the data collected and develop a report of the findings.

■ Work with groups to create a vision and goals for proposed change.

■ Gather data related to the issues and goals in order to identify resources and barriers.

■ Develop a working plan that includes a stated purpose and goals for the change.

■ Create work groups to address various areas of the plan.

■ Facilitate the project plan.

■ Implement the project plan.

■ Facilitate formal and informal leadership development and decision-making.

■ Develop an evaluation plan.

■ When external resources are needed to begin or continue the plan, work with the community to procure needed resources.

■ Conduct an evaluation.

■ If desired outcomes are achieved and change is stabilized, shift efforts to next change effort.

As a BSW student, Emily completed a practicum at an urban multiservice community center, where she gained generalist social work experiences working with children in an after-school program, taking applications for a utility assistance program, and co-facilitating an employment skills group with mothers in a welfare-to-work program. To provide Emily with organizational and community experiences, Caroline, Emily's field instructor, invited her to participate in a Neighborhood Advisory Council. This group apprised staff of the community's needs.

During Emily's first meeting with the Neighborhood Advisory Council, a resident council member suggested that neighborhood children and youth needed access to an after-school tutoring program. The council voted to create an ad hoc committee to explore the development of such a program. Together with Caroline, Emily served as co-chair of the ad hoc committee that began to investigate the possibility of adding tutoring to the services the center provided.

Engagement of Organizations and Communities

As the first task as ad hoc chairs, Caroline and Emily identified persons and organizations with an interest in tutoring who could provide support for the program. They scheduled the first meeting at the center (in the room that could house the tutoring program) with representatives from the center's Children and Youth Department, the school district's Office of Administration, the neighborhood council, and neighborhood parents.

At the beginning of the meeting, participants introduced themselves and described their personal or professional role. Caroline explained the reason for forming the ad hoc committee and the purpose of the gathering and then asked each member to share her or his thoughts (or the feelings of the constituency they represented) regarding the need for a tutoring program.

Although the group was generally in agreement on the concept of a tutoring program, some members raised questions about neighborhood residents' support for a tutoring program, the resources needed to mount the program, and staff or volunteers to operate the program. Emily volunteered to conduct a needs assessment and research best practices in tutoring programs and to report back to the committee at next month's meeting.

Organizational and community-level concerns or needs are often addressed by practitioners and policy-makers in a fragmented manner. Relevant parties may not communicate regularly, and key participants may not be involved in the change process. To be effective, social workers must use a systems approach to involve all those persons who can influence or be affected by the change.

As with group work, the first step in engaging the client system is to identify the persons and groups that can contribute knowledge, resources, influence, funding, credibility, or access to other groups or resources. Several different groups may be involved, depending on the type and goal of the organizational or community change effort. For example, a welfare rights coalition (group one) may represent welfare recipients (group two), and front-line workers in the welfare agency may have insight into the needs of the target group (group three). A collaborative group may come together naturally, as in the case of the earlier example of refugee business owners, or one may need to form, as in the case of the neighborhood redevelopment example.

During the engagement phase of an organizational and community change effort, all participants have the opportunity to articulate needs, resources, contributions, and barriers to participation for themselves or for the groups they represent. In addition, each participant contributes to the development of the purpose, goals, decision-making process, and allocation of resources and responsibilities.

A key to sustaining participants' investment in the change process is to ensure that each participant has a clear understanding of the tasks and activities for which she or he is responsible and that individuals are invested in the group's goals. Each participant's contribution is affirmed and valued in the process.

The social work skills of reflective listening, interpretation of both verbal and nonverbal communications, and negotiation can help the group bond around a common concern. As with social work practice at the individual, family, and group levels, social work practice at the community and organizational level requires empathy and rapport-building skills to engage with individuals and groups.

Assessment of Organizations and Communities

In formulating a strengths-based assessment approach, Emily and her field instructor developed the following needs assessment plan for their ad hoc committee:

- *Clarification of purpose: Gauge the interest in and need for a tutoring program and determine the viability of launching and sustaining such a program.*
- *Data collection strategy: To determine neighborhood interest in and need for a tutoring program, develop a multimodal approach to collecting data.*

To ascertain community attitudes regarding a tutoring program, work with a representative from the residents' committee to conduct a door-to-door survey, developed by Emily and approved by the committee, of 50 neighborhood households. Contact the local Board of Education to gather information on existing tutoring resources in the area and on the process for creating a tutoring program built on current resources. Next, contact other tutoring programs and gather information regarding development, staffing, funding, and evaluation. Consult scholarly literature to determine whether a body of research-based literature supports the use of tutoring.

■ *Compilation of data: Compile information from various sources, contact possible volunteer sources, present a written and verbal report to the ad hoc committee highlighting the interest, assets, and potential outcomes for a neighborhood-based tutoring program.*

The assessment process is an essential component of any intervention plan for effecting change within an organization or community. The assessor first identifies the organization or community targeted for change, and then determines whether change is needed, desired, feasible, and sustainable. Insights into the culture of the community, specifically the shared concerns, beliefs, values, and potential conflicts relevant to the community are particularly important. It is then possible to engage the community in a collaborative assessment process (Fuchs, 2008).

Needs assessment for organizations and communities begins with the collection of data and information about the community, its members, available and needed resources, networks and linkages that exist within and outside of the community (Fuchs, 2008). Later in the process the assessor determines goals in order to identify the information to be gathered and the way in which it will be used. The goal-setting phase may be an important aspect of the intervention, particularly when members of the community are invited to help identify the issues and concerns and to participate in the gathering of information (Tropman, 2008). Building alliances with the target group and organizing a core group of supporters can contribute to the change process. With any change effort, however, macro practitioners should be prepared for the possibility of passive or even active resistance, and should incorporate that possibility into the assessment process (Mizrahi, 2015). As with all other phases of macro-level intervention, practitioners conducting community assessments must be mindful of the goal of social justice (Fuchs, 2008).

Now you are ready to actually develop and conduct the assessment. Exhibit 11.5 summarizes the principles for conducting a community-level assessment as well as some of the categories of information to seek, while Exhibit 11.6 provides a list of specific issues to address when communicating the assessment to others.

EXHIBIT 11.5

Guidelines for Conducting Organizational and Community Assessments

GUIDING PRINCIPLES

1. Value participation from diverse constituencies.
2. Use multiple methods (quantitative and qualitative data).
3. Encourage civic participation and technical elements.
4. Keep the assessment realistic.
5. Value asset building.

TYPES OF INFORMATION TO COLLECT

■ Strengths and available resources: Identify the resources and assets possessed by and available to the target group or community.
■ Organizational and community attitudes: Collect input from the key players and others involved in the change process.
■ Barriers to change: Determine the existence of any obstacles to change, such as attitudes, perceptions, funding, political support, space, and participation.
■ Viability of sustaining a change: Determine the organization's or community's ability to maintain a change.
■ Assessment of similar change efforts: Identify organizations and communities that have developed similar programs, policies, or changes. Evaluate the success or failure of those efforts and factors that led to their ending.

Source: Mulroy, 2008, pp. 385–386.

Having a plan for gathering data is critical for organizing, analyzing, and interpreting the data. Data may be gathered using in-person, telephone, or mail surveys; focus groups; official government data; agency records; and in-depth interviews with key stakeholders.

Intervention with Organizations and Communities

Using the data from Emily's needs assessment, the ad hoc committee developed the following plan:

■ *Goal: Develop a plan to establish a tutoring program building on the assets and capacities of the neighborhood residents, and implement it by the start of the next school year.*

EXHIBIT 11.6

Questions to Include in a Community Assessment

When engaging and assessing a community, areas to address include:
(1) What do the people who want change think about the issues?
(2) How do the community and decision-makers view the change agents?
(3) Do change agents have the necessary time, resources, and expertise for the intervention?
(4) What is the make-up of the community—who are the members of the community, what is public opinion regarding the issues, and what is the stance or role of the decision-makers?
(5) Are there viable "insider" strategies (i.e., access to decision-makers)?
(6) Are there viable "outsider" strategies (i.e., no access to decision-makers resulting in the need to take social action) and can the change agent move from being an "outsider" to being an "insider?"
(7) What are the realistic prospects for change?

Source: Mondros, 2013.

- *Objectives: Using information gathered from the Board of Education and other tutoring programs, determine a schedule, curricular plan, budget, and staffing coverage.*
- *Present plan to the ad hoc committee and council for approval.*
- *Publicize the program to neighborhood parents, youth, and school personnel.*

After both the committee and the council approved the plan, Emily and Caroline implemented the intervention by developing a curricular plan for tutoring and a training program for tutors; obtained agency funding for supplies and refreshments; recruited volunteer tutors; advertised the program to parents, youth, and teachers; and prepared the room for the program. Once the program was under way, Emily served as on-site supervisor, and she and Caroline met weekly with volunteer tutors. With permission from students' parents, Emily contacted teachers on a monthly basis to monitor student performance.

Planning and implementation for organizational and community interventions must balance multiple needs, agendas, and resources. The intervention phase of community practice includes the planning, development, and implementation of services, programs, and policies intended to benefit the community as a whole, using strategies appropriate to the community's needs and achievable goals (Reisch, 2008, p. 505). The social worker's role may be to negotiate a plan and intervention between groups whose goals and perceived obligations conflict. Skills for community intervention include the willingness and ability to consistently "listen" to community members, maintain ongoing face-to-face contact with people in their communities, and re-visit their issues and concerns to ensure goals and plans remain viable (Reisch, 2008). Having a realistic understanding of the organizations, policies, and limitations involved in accomplishing goals can help the social worker create viable alternatives for addressing identified needs. Community involvement in intra- and intergroup discussion, collaboration, education, and capacity building from a strengths perspective is key to the success of the intervention (Reisch, 2008). Capacity building requires social workers to get to know the complexities of the communities in which they are working (i.e., people, functioning, social interactions, and conflicts) (Jack, 2012).

The social worker draws on generalist social work skills to help opposing parties to establish a common goal and to compromise on an intervention plan. Goal development means prioritizing needs, articulating overall goals, and attending to the individual wishes of constituent groups. Just as with micro- and mezzo-level interventions, goals must be achievable. Action strategies contain specific objectives aimed at achieving the desired change. Goals, action strategies, and evaluation methods are mutually agreed upon, documented, and shared with all relevant constituencies. As members of the change effort carry out tasks and activities, regular communication and ongoing evaluation help monitor progress.

Practitioners ensure that all groups share equal responsibility for meeting objectives. Although participants may contribute different skills, resources, and influence, all participants have a clear role. Each objective that relates to the overall goal must be specific and measurable so that the change effort can be evaluated.

Evaluation and Termination of Organization and Community Interventions

Emily began the evaluation of the tutoring program with the development of the program plans. The needs assessment yielded information to suggest that a program would fill a void. However, it takes more than simply creating a service to call a plan a success. Maintaining regular contact with the volunteers, students' parents, and teachers provided ongoing input into issues such as student participation, parent and student satisfaction with the program, and student performance at school. Documenting the input from the involved groups enabled Emily and Caroline to report to the council that the tutoring program was meeting a neighborhood need, to recommend continuation, and to make needed adjustments to the program.

Evaluation of organizational and community interventions is continual and complex. Because many interventions are implemented over months or years with a large and varied number of persons and groups, evaluation may need to be compartmentalized and conducted on an ongoing basis.

Evaluation strategies applicable to organizational and community interventions include:

■ Review of the needs assessment and goals to determine whether identified needs and goals have been met.
■ Pre- and post-intervention measures to determine whether and to what extent change occurred.
■ Process evaluation to determine if the intervention is being implemented as planned.

Program outcomes and continuous quality assurance can be evaluated by assessing change-related efforts such as quantity and quality of services provided, revenue generated, altered spending, or behavior change. Gathering information prior to and after the intervention (surveys, interviews, focus groups, etc.) is one way to quantitatively and qualitatively determine if the goals and needs of the community have been met from the perspectives of community members, key stakeholders, and decision-makers.

A form of evaluation that can also provide useful information is the process evaluation. Much like the process evaluation strategies discussed in earlier chapters, process evaluation strategies at the macro level focus on gathering information from stakeholders and reviewing the operational aspects of the intervention. Specific goals include (CDC, 2009):

■ Determining if program activities are being completed as planned.
■ Evaluating the quality of the program's components and implementation strategies.
■ Ascertaining if target group was reached.
■ Reviewing the influence of external factors on program dynamics and goals.

Termination of organizational and community-level change may indicate either the success or the failure of the change effort. In the case of program development, the intervention may be terminated when the program is operational, but then a stabilization effort may begin to sustain the program. In an advocacy effort, termination may occur when a policy is or is not changed, when a law is or is not passed, or when needs change. In these situations, the intervention may shift in response to the change. In other situations, termination is moot because the purpose of the intervention is to facilitate an ongoing change.

CONCLUSION

Social workers can apply their skills from working with individuals, families, and groups to influence large-scale changes in organizations, communities, and society as a whole. Working at the organizational and community level, social workers advocate on behalf of a client, develop a new program, obtain funding, interpret data for program evaluation, or analyze the impact of a new policy on their clients.

Social workers must keep abreast of the policy issues that could affect the lives of those they serve. Working at the organizational and community level often requires vision to see the possibility of large-scale change and patience to traverse the multiple and complex steps needed to achieve the change. Speaking out at a recent panel to discuss the healing process for Ferguson, Missouri, social worker Evan Krauss cautioned his social work audience that "policy does not change people." These words are a reminder that change must come from within people, but policy can be a first step.

Fuchs (2008) offers the following focus for macro-level practitioners:

- Implement practice approaches to emphasize social and economic justice.
- Commit to expanding basic human rights to marginalized groups.
- Promote positive social change for disadvantaged populations through the use of multicultural strategies and coalitions.
- Focus practice on social and economic development to strengthen society through civic and political participation (p. 502).

Specific contemporary issues that warrant attention include the as yet unresolved economic crisis, conflicting political views regarding issues that impact those we serve (e.g., immigration, same-sex marriage, and funding for social programs), impact of globalization on labor, and decreasing financial resources (DeFilippis & Saegert, 2012b).

For additional information on social work advocacy for organizations and communities, check out the following groups and websites:

- Influencing State Policy (www.statepolicy.org), an organization for social work students, faculty, and professionals that provides information on advocacy and current legislation. Includes a comprehensive listing of policy-related resources.

- GovTrack.us, a website designed to track bills in Congress, the voting records of members of Congress, and upcoming meetings, and to subscribe to e-alerts regarding legislative activities.
- Congress.gov, a website that provides information on current and recent legislation, the Congressional Record (official record of Congressional proceedings and debates), and congressional news.
- NASW Legislative Updates (http://cqrcengage.com/socialworkers/home) provides the latest information on the association's advocacy efforts, issues, updates, and political actions. See information on the NASW publication *Social Work Speaks: NASW Policy Statements, 10th edition,* a comprehensive guide to social and political issues affecting the social work profession.
- The States Project, located at www.thestatesproject.org/, an organization that provides non-partisan reports on the states in the United States.
- Association for Community Organization and Social Administration (http://acosa.org), an organization for community organizers, planning activists, administrators, policy practice specialists, students, and faculty.
- International Federation of Social Workers (www.ifsw.org), a global organization striving for social justice, human rights, and social development.
- Alliance for Justice (www.afj.org/), an association of organizations focused on civil rights in the areas of mental health, women, children, consumers, and the environment. This group sponsors the First Monday Campaign, an effort to raise awareness about public policy and advocacy.
- National Budget Simulation, a website that will allow you to see the impact of budget decision-making on the federal budget. To learn more about the budget simulation, go to: http://www.nathannewman.org/nbs/.

MAIN POINTS

- Social work practice with organizations, communities, and public policy involves working toward large-scale change in a practice, policy, program, or law that affects people's lives.
- The social work profession has deep roots in macro-level practice, going back as far as the settlement house workers, whose goal was to improve living conditions for persons in the neighborhoods they served.
- Models for facilitating change within organizations and communities include: geographic (neighborhood) community organizing; functional community organizing; social, economic, and sustainable community development; inclusive program development; social planning; coalition building; political, social, and legislative action policy practice; and movement for progressive change.

■ Development activities bring about change in a specific geographic or functional area; planning focuses on organizing a group of people to facilitate change that may span different groups but affect people experiencing similar life situations; the goal of a social action intervention is to organize people to influence decision-making related to a particular issue.

■ Working with organizations and communities requires the same approaches necessary when working at the other two levels of social work practice: engagement, assessment, intervention, and evaluation.

■ Specific social work skills needed for organizational and community practice include negotiation, fund-raising, collaboration, organization, advocacy, analysis, administration, program planning, and supervision.

EXERCISES

1. In the Sanchez family interactive case (www.routledgesw.com/caseStudies), go to the Engage tab and select "Explore the Town Map."
   a. After familiarizing yourself with the community in which they live, select one Sanchez family member and identify the community resources she or he could access to address her or his need(s). What assets does the community possess to help meet the family's needs?
   b. Staying with the client you selected, return to the Engage tab and complete the Critical Thinking Questions for that family member.

2. You have learned from the Sanchez family case that Hector and Celia have two children with disabilities. They have become involved in a community group that advocates for additional funding for children with disabilities. Based on the information in this chapter, strategize ways in which this group can successfully launch a fund-raising campaign.

3. In the Riverton interactive case (www.routledgesw.com/caseStudies), go to the Engage tab and select the Riverton Town Map.
   a. Using the Town Map, complete the Critical Thinking Questions.
   b. You are now familiar with the many aspects of the community system, including potential partners for developing an intervention to address the issue of public drinking and inappropriate refuse disposal in the Alvadora neighborhood. Because of your professional knowledge and your personal investment, your agency has asked you to establish a task force to "clean up Alvadora."
      i. Identify key stakeholders to invite to join the task force who will be effective in establishing common goals for the area.
      ii. Develop a preliminary and prioritized strategy for the group.

4. Following a disaster, social workers often serve as members of a team that works to rebuild communities. Using the information in the Hudson City

interactive case (www.routledgesw.com/caseStudies) and in this chapter, select five of the areas of social work practice with communities and organizations described in this chapter and explain the roles and activities the social worker would perform at this level of practice.

5. Being able to conduct research and evaluate is key to macro-level social work competency. Go to www.routledgesw.com/caseStudies and select the RAINN interactive case. Familiarize yourself with the aspects of this case and then respond to the Phase III Critical Thinking Questions.

6. To better understand the Brickville community, go to www.routledgesw. com/caseStudies. Click on Assess and review both the Community Sociogram and Community Needs Assessment Matrix and answer the three critical thinking questions included in each of these areas.

7. Because laws impact the lives of everyone in our society, but particularly those persons served by social workers, having an awareness of legislative activity in your state is essential for effective social work practice. Select a state and explore the current legislative activities for that state by going to Influencing State Policy at www.statepolicy.org. Click on Resources, then State Links.

   You might want to investigate current and pending legislation that can impact the client systems with whom social workers work. From within the State Link you have chosen at the website, choose All State-Local Government Servers. Select one legislative issue and prepare a 2-minute presentation on an example of that state's policy and deliver it orally in class. Provide your classmates with a one-page written version of the 2-minute presentation with enough copies for your fellow students and the instructor (Source: R. Schneider, Virginia Commonwealth University, 2002).

8. In this exercise, you will have the opportunity to advocate for an issue that has been written about in a newspaper, periodical, or online publication by writing a commentary. The opinion or comments section is one of the most popular.

   Identify an article from a printed or digital newspaper, periodical, or journal that describes an issue, event, or pending legislation about which you have an opposing view. Post a comment or write a letter to the editor of that publication articulating your point of view.

   Editors tell us the first reason they reject commentaries or "op-eds" is because they are too balanced or only offer facts and figures. A good opinion piece is not a survey of both sides of an issue, but a strong, concise argument.

   The second reason op-eds often are turned down is that writers have failed to grab the reader's attention in the first sentence. Instead they alienate the reader by delaying the point of the piece until the end. Refer to the guidelines in Exhibit 11.7 to advocate more capably for your point of view.

EXHIBIT 11.7

Guidelines for Writing Strong Commentaries

Share your opinion, make a point, keep it clear!
- Respond in a timely manner. An opinion piece is usually only as hot as the news of the day.
- Take a position. Facts and figures are OK to back your case, but don't rely on them. Don't be afraid to offer your opinion.
- Write a compelling first sentence. Summarize your viewpoint and tell the readers why they should care.
- Offer solutions. Don't just address the problem, but discuss ways it can be fixed.
- Write with clarity. Keep your sentences short, simple, and to the point. Use language the average person can understand. Avoid jargon suited only to your expertise.
- Keep it short. Most pieces should not be more than 500–600 words.
- Do not forget the last sentence. Give your ending as much thought as your start. A concise summary is vital.

Source: Adapted from Saint Louis University Marketing and Communications.

THE SOCIAL WORK PROFESSION

Emily has been fortunate to practice social work in a variety of settings with diverse groups of people in a range of different agencies. Her social work degrees have facilitated her career transitions. She values being part of a profession that not only practices empathy and compassion but that also provides her with the knowledge, skills, and values to empower others to enhance their own lives. As Emily's story ends, yours begins.

The social work profession has a long and rich history, but where will it go in the future? Where will the jobs be? What will these jobs pay? What type of preparation will social workers need to be effective in the coming decades? This chapter considers future trends and opportunities for the social work profession, examining the route to becoming a social worker, and, most importantly, helping you to answer the question: Is social work the right career for you?

PROFESSIONAL OUTLOOK FOR SOCIAL WORKERS

Social work does not exist in a vacuum. As much as any profession, social work activity is woven into the very fabric of society. Social work acts and reacts to that which transpires in society.

(Allen-Meares & DeRoos, 1997, p. 384)

In the 21st century, the future looks bright for the social work profession. Employment opportunities are expanding, compensation for social workers is increasing, and more and more society is recognizing the valuable contributions social workers can and do make to the well-being of those they serve. Well into its second century, the profession continues to be a major service profession and an integral part of society.

Employment Trends and Opportunities

The future appears exceptionally promising for social workers. Increases in diversity of all kinds—ethnic, cultural, age, and family structure—will continue to provide expanded opportunities. Projections suggest that social work will have a distinctive focus on the concerns of women, children, older adults, immigrant populations, and military veterans and their families, as these persons continue to be the most vulnerable in our society (U.S. Department of Labor, Bureau of Labor Statistics (BLS), 2014b).

By 2022, increases in social work opportunities are expected in many social work practice areas. For example, social and community service managers will increase 21% (an increase of 27,700 new jobs) and mental health counselors and marriage and family therapist employment will increase 29% (48,200 new jobs). One area of social work employment, corrections, is not expected to grow. Employment opportunities for probation officers and correctional treatment specialists are predicted to decrease by 1% (losing approximately 900 jobs) (BLS, 2014b). This decrease is likely the result of a drop in government spending on social service-related agencies. The BLS projects that the fastest-growing occupations through 2022 will include marriage and family therapists (BLS, 2014b). For social workers interested in working in the area of advocacy, grant writing, and civic organizations, a 14% increase in employment is expected by 2016 (BLS, 2008). Employment prospects are expected to be most competitive in urban areas, but positions in rural communities will also continue to provide significant opportunities for helping professionals, in general, and for those working in the areas of mental health, substance abuse, and rehabilitation, in particular (BLS, 2010a).

Social workers in the United States already number approximately 650,000. This number is expected to reach 811,700 by 2020, an overall growth rate of 19%, with rates of approximately 9–27% depending on area of practice (BLS, 2014b). That is significantly higher than the 11% average growth rate for all careers. Particular areas of growth for social workers include aging, health care, substance abuse treatment, school social work, and mental health services (BLS, 2014b).

The popular press has proclaimed social work, along with other social and public service-related opportunities, to be a career on the rise. Here is a sampling of their reports:

- *U.S. News and World Report* ranks two areas of social work practice on its list of the 100 Best Jobs of 2014: #48—clinical social worker and #76—child/family social worker. Other areas in which social workers' work were also rated on the 100 Best Jobs of 2014 list, including: #76—marriage and family therapist; #86—school counselor; and #97—mental health professional (U.S. News and World Report, 2014).
- CareerCast.com lists social work at #88 on their list of "The Best Jobs of 2014," based on positive employment growth, positive work environments, and lower levels of stress and physical demands when compared with other occupations (CareerCast.com).
- The College Board lists mental health and substance abuse social workers among its Hottest Careers for College Graduates through 2018, with 61,000 jobs expected to be available (Collegeboard.com, 2014).

In addition to increasing opportunities for social work services involving older adults, substance abuse, and mental health, other settings expected to experience growth and employ larger numbers of social workers in the second decade of the 21st century include agencies that provide services in child protection, foster care, adoption, disabilities, human trafficking, veterans services, and homeless services. Social work employment opportunities in the criminal justice system, particularly with adolescents, will continue to grow, as will social work positions within elementary and secondary school systems. Private practice, in which self-employed clinical social workers provide individual, family, and group treatment, will be another growth area for social workers with MSWs.

The funding crises that have plagued the social work profession for much of its history will continue to dictate how much this growth is realized, but the need for social workers will remain. Because our legislators and funding sources will determine whether or not social workers have the resources necessary to meet that need, advocacy will continue to be a critical social work focus.

Areas of Practice The provision of services to families, children, and youth is expected to remain the primary area of practice for social workers. Students enrolled in both BSW and MSW social work programs identify these populations as the largest areas of concentration followed by mental health, school social work, and gerontological social work (CSWE, 2013). Approximately 30% of MSW students and over one-third of social work practitioners report that mental health is their primary area of practice (Whitaker & Arrington, 2008).

With increasing pressure on physicians to prevent or shorten hospitalizations, patients are being returned to their homes with greater needs for in-home health services. Social workers serve as key members of the interprofessional team of health professionals that works with patients discharged from acute care hospital settings and their families. These patients—many of whom are older adults, need home- and community-based care. Private and public funding has been made available to social work educators in recent years to provide students with knowledge, skills, and values so they may work effectively with older adults and their families regardless of the area in which they specialize.

With the privatization of many social service systems, a number of social workers are expected to leave the public and nonprofit sectors to work in for-profit organizations. Privatizing social services shifts administrative responsibility for delivery to a privately owned company that contracts with government agencies and private insurance. Because contract agencies have fewer bureaucratic requirements, they are able to provide services at a lower cost.

Salaries Almost all students want to know what kind of salary they can expect when they choose a social work career. Social work salaries, like many other human service-related and helping careers, have historically lagged behind other professions, but salaries for social workers are improving. In recent years, the profession as a whole has conducted a somewhat successful campaign for higher salaries and better compensation overall. The statistics presented here are broad-based, nationwide salary ranges that differ considerably by region, field of service, educational level, and experience, but they serve as a useful reference point.

The U.S. Department of Labor reports that median annual salaries for all social workers in 2012 ranged from the mid-$30,000s to mid-$50,000s. The median annual salary for all social workers is $54,590 a year (BLS, 2014b). Social workers employed in child, family, and school settings earn $41,530; in medical and public health setting, $49,830; and in mental health and substance abuse treatment services, $39,980. Exhibit 12.1 lists salaries for several categories, as well as the distribution of salaries in 2012 for social workers employed in full-time positions.

Several factors impact social workers' earning potential, including gender, workload, employment sector, years of experience, licensure status, and geographic location. Those social workers who typically earn higher salaries are male, work in an administrative role and have more responsibilities (e.g., supervision and budgeting), are more experienced and educated, are licensed/certified, and work in a military/federal agency (followed by K-12 schools, colleges/universities, and hospitals/medical centers) (NASW/CWS, 2010a). In fact, the Department of Veterans Affairs currently employs 11,000 social workers and trains over 1,000 social work students (http://www. vasocialworkers.org/). Median annual salaries for male social workers are $67,800, while their female counterparts earn $50,000 per year, thought to occur because male social workers more often occupy administrative or management positions which have higher salaries (NASW/CWS, 2011e). Social workers in the United States who possess one or more professional credentials (e.g., licenses or certifications) typically earn $5,000–8,000 more per year than social workers who do not obtain licensure or certification. Geographic location also influences social workers' annual salaries. Social workers in the Pacific region of the U.S. earn the highest salaries, while those in the East South Central (U.S. states in the lower southeastern quadrant) area earn the lowest salaries (NASW/CWS, 2010a). Educational attainment is a factor as well: a 2009 study of social work compensation and benefits reported median annual earnings of $40,000 for social workers at the BSW level, $55,000 for MSW, and $72,000 for doctoral level (NASW/CWS, 2010a). In terms of race and ethnicity, social workers who are Asian/Pacific Islander earn the most, followed by Hispanic/Latino and Native American/Alaskan Native, Black/African American, Multiracial, and White/Caucasian (NASW/CWS, 2011f). Employments rates for social workers with undergraduate and graduate degrees are among the highest for any profession. The unemployment rate for recent BSW graduates is 6.6%, while MSW graduates experience only 2.9% unemployment (Carnevale, Cheah, & Strohl, 2011).

EXHIBIT 12.1

Social Work Salaries

Salaries by specialization:

- Child, Family, and School Social Workers
  - ○ $54,590/year (educational services; state, local, and private)
  - ○ $44,370/year (state and local government; excluding education and hospitals)
  - ○ $36,130/year (health care and social assistance)
  - ○ $35,910/year (religious, grantmaking, civic, professional, and similar organizations)

- Health Care Social Workers
  - ○ $56,290/year (hospitals; state, local, and private)
  - ○ $51,580/year (ambulatory health care services)
  - ○ $43,330/year (nursing and residential care facilities)
  - ○ $38,920/year (social assistance)

- Mental Health and Substance Abuse Treatment Social Workers
  - ○ $47,880/year (hospitals; state, local, and private)
  - ○ $39,840/year (ambulatory healthcare services)
  - ○ $37,170/year (social assistance)
  - ○ $34,950/year (nursing and residential care facilities)

Source: U.S. Department of Labor, Bureau of Labor Statistics, 2012.

Salaries for Social Workers Employed in Full-Time Positions:

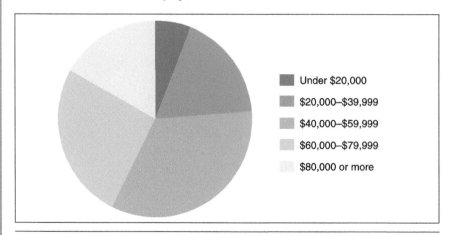

Source: National Association of Social Workers Center for Workforce Studies (2005).

Overall, social work salaries are comparable to those of other helping professions (e.g., elementary and secondary teachers, school counselors, clergy, counselors, and nurses). BSW salaries are on par with nonsocial work counselors in substance abuse and mental health, while MSWs earn salaries comparable to teachers, librarians, nurses, and school counselors (CHWS/CWS, 2006)

Two possible explanations have been offered for the lower salaries earned by social workers:

- *Gender:* Social workers are predominantly women (85% of the total), and women increasingly hold many leadership positions in the field. Professions made up largely of women (for example, nursing and education) routinely receive lower levels of compensation.
- *Economic sector:* The organizations that employ social workers often struggle for financial stability, and thus pay lower salaries.

While these explanations may be valid, they can serve as a call to social workers to engage in more aggressive advocacy for the profession.

Social workers provide much-needed services to a large segment of the population and deserve recognition and compensation for the important work they do. Social workers routinely focus on professional advocacy efforts that will benefit client systems, but to maintain high-quality education and training opportunities social workers also need to advocate for their own salaries and funding. To learn more about median social work salaries across the country, check out the NASW Center for Workforce Studies Salary Calculator at http://workforce.socialworkers.org/calc.asp and information on social work career opportunities at: http://careers.socialworkers.org/.

Despite the challenges noted here, 90% of social workers surveyed report feeling they help their clients to improve their quality of life; more than two-thirds view their salaries as "adequate" to "very adequate;" and the same number perceive they are respected and supported in their work setting (CHWS/CWS, 2006). Additional factors associated with increased job satisfaction include variety of responsibilities and activities and the opportunity to try creative approaches (Smith & Shields, 2013).

Societal Perceptions of the Social Work Profession

Social work is a visible and important profession within our society. Social workers are employed in an increasingly wide range of settings and are being sought to fill needs in the social service delivery system.

In addition to the traditional settings described throughout this book, social workers are entering the political arena. In recent years, over 170 social workers have been elected to political office at the local, state, and national levels. For a listing of social workers in elected office and information on getting involved, visit the NASW Political Action for Candidate Election (PACE) website at http://socialworkers.org/pace. Social workers are called on to use their knowledge and skills to develop state and national policy, and state officials recognize the need to increase the number of social workers.

Social workers must continue to advocate for the profession by educating the public regarding the role it plays in society. They can do this by taking every opportunity to represent the profession favorably in the public eye. For instance, social workers can write letters, make telephone calls, send e-mail messages, blog, and post tweets when social workers are negatively portrayed in the news, on television, and in the movies. They can ensure that when the media highlights social workers, it identifies them as degreed professionals. Conversely, when a person who does not possess a social work degree is identified in the media as a social worker, professional social workers can challenge that label and provide clarification that only those persons who have been awarded social work degrees from CSWE-accredited programs are truly social workers.

PROFESSIONAL SOCIALIZATION

Along with learning the theories and methods of social work practice, becoming a social work professional involves professional socialization. This socialization involves becoming acquainted with the values, norms, and culture of the profession; establishing a professional identity; identifying with the social work profession; feeling comfortable with that self-identity; and understanding the role of social work within the community and society. Being a social worker becomes part of who you are.

You have begun your socialization process by gaining an overview of the profession, experiencing social work through class discussions and exercises, possibly volunteering or completing a service learning experience in a health or social service agency, and, hopefully, by interacting with other social work students and social work practitioners. The linkages you create and pursue to connect coursework and field experiences are critical to your professional socialization (Miller, 2013). In the following sections, we explore additional steps in the professional socialization process.

Social Work Education: Pursuing a Degree

Do you see yourself as a professional social worker? Twenty-two percent of social workers knew before they started college that they wanted to join the profession. For others, the feeling of connection came later in other courses or in their field experience: 45% identified their goals during college and 33% after college (Whitaker, 2008).

Professional identification begins with introspection; you ask yourself, "Is social work the right career for me?" "Do I see myself working in those settings that I have been learning about and doing the work I have been reading about and seeing?"

As you learned in the first chapter of this book, to become a social worker requires a bachelor's or master's degree in social work awarded by a college or university accredited by the Council on Social Work Education (CSWE). In 2015, there were 744 CSWE accredited social work programs—238 MSW and 506 BSW programs. An additional 17 MSW and 15 BSW programs were awaiting word on their accreditation (CSWE, 2015). In 2013, 22,677 MSW degrees were awarded and 17,221 BSWs degrees were granted (CSWE, 2013). In both degree areas, the overwhelming majority of graduates are female (86–88%) and nearly one-half of new social workers are members of an underrepresented ethnic or racial group (CSWE, 2013).

A competency-based social work education at the baccalaureate level is grounded in liberal arts studies and prepares graduates for generalist practice. At the master's level, practitioners are trained for advanced practice in a specific area of concentration.

Due to anticipated retirements of social workers and the growing need for services for a number of populations—older adults and children, in particular—the number of currently practicing social workers is not expected to meet the needs of our society going forward. Societal changes that heighten the need for competently trained social workers include but are not limited to the impact of the Affordable Care Act, the emphasis on reducing the number of children living in out-of-home care arrangements, the need to bridge the health and mental health care service areas, demand for increased interprofessional service delivery teams, and the need for more social workers able to work in the military/veteran and business sectors (Social Work Policy Institute, 2011).

Bachelor of Social Work Social work courses at the BSW level focus on preparing generalist social work practitioners. A brief description of the social work curriculum appears in Exhibit 12.2. As noted in Chapter 1, the CSWE *Educational Policy and Accreditation Standards* (2015) provide competency-based guidelines for BSW and MSW social work curricula, which are summarized in the exhibit, but individual social work programs determine the best model for delivering course-work in their own environment.

Although programs vary considerably, social work majors at the bachelor's level typically take English, communications, human biology, history, mathematics and/or statistics, political science and/or economics, fine arts, sociology and/or anthropology, foreign language, psychology, and philosophy courses. Each of these areas of study is key to becoming an articulate, effective social worker possessing a broad base of knowledge about people, culture, and society. The competent social worker understands the ways in which the human body and mind functions, the role culture plays in our society, the impact of the economy and the political system on the lives of the people social workers serve, and the use of statistical analysis for the purposes of funding and evaluation. Arts and humanities courses provide social work students with an understanding of what motivates human beings.

In addition to general liberal arts courses and required social work courses, social work students complete elective coursework in individual areas of interest. Most BSW programs offer electives, but students can also choose to take electives in other departments. There are a variety of areas you may want to cultivate during your social work training, some of which are listed in Exhibit 12.3.

EXHIBIT 12.2

Council on Social Work Education (CSWE) Guidelines for a Competency-Based Social Work Curriculum

Competency-based education focuses on an outcomes-oriented approach to education with the aim of integrating and applying the competencies in social work practice. Each competency relates to the social work knowledge, values, skills, and cognitive and affective processes that comprise the competency at the generalist level of practice.

- *Demonstrate Ethical and Professional Behavior*—Social workers understand the value base of the profession and its ethical standards, as well as relevant laws and regulations that may impact practice at the micro, mezzo, and macro levels. Social workers: (1) make ethical decisions by applying the standards of the NASW *Code of Ethics* (2008), relevant laws and regulations, models for ethical decision-making, ethical conduct of research, and additional codes of ethics as appropriate to context; (2) use reflection and self-regulation to manage personal values and maintain professionalism in practice situations; (3) demonstrate professional demeanor in behavior; appearance; and oral, written, and electronic communication; (4) use technology ethically and appropriately to facilitate practice outcomes; and (5) use supervision and consultation to guide professional judgment and behavior.
- *Engage Diversity and Difference in Practice*—Social workers understand how diversity and difference characterize and shape the human experience and are critical to the formation of identity and the importance of intersectionality, oppression, poverty, marginalization, and alienation. Social workers: (1) apply and communicate understanding of the importance of

diversity and difference in shaping life experiences in practice at the micro, mezzo, and macro levels; (2) present themselves as learners and engage clients and constituencies as experts of their own experiences; and (3) apply self-awareness and self-regulation to manage the influence of personal biases and values in working with diverse clients and constituencies.

■ *Advance Human Rights and Social, Economic, and Environmental Justice*—Social workers understand that every person has fundamental human rights such as freedom, safety, privacy, an adequate standard of living, health care, and education, the global interconnections of oppression and human rights violations, and are knowledgeable about theories of human need and social justice and strategies to promote social and economic justice and human rights. Social workers: (1) apply their understanding of social, economic, and environmental justice to advocate for human rights at the individual and system levels; and (2) engage in practices that advance social, economic, and environmental justice.

■ *Engage in Practice-informed Research and Research-informed Practice*—Social workers understand quantitative and qualitative research methods and their respective roles in advancing a science of social work and in evaluating their practice, know the principles of logic, scientific inquiry, and culturally informed and ethical approaches to building knowledge, and understand that evidence that informs practice derives from multi-disciplinary sources and multiple ways of knowing and the processes for translating research findings into effective practice. Social workers: (1) use practice experience and theory to inform scientific inquiry and research; (2) apply critical thinking to engage in analysis of quantitative and qualitative research methods and research findings; and (3) use and translate research evidence to inform and improve practice, policy, and service delivery.

■ *Engage in Policy Practice*—Social workers understand that human rights and social justice, as well as social welfare and services, are mediated by policy and its implementation at the federal, state, and local levels and the history and current structures of social policies and services, the role of policy in service delivery, and the role of practice in policy development. Social workers: (1) identify social policy at the local, state, and federal level that impacts well-being, service delivery, and access to social services; (2) assess how social welfare and economic policies impact the delivery of and access to social services; and (3) apply critical thinking to analyze, formulate, and advocate for policies that advance human rights and social, economic, and environmental justice.

■ *Engage with Individuals, Families, Groups, Organizations, and Communities*—Social workers understand that engagement is an ongoing component of the dynamic and interactive process of social work practice with, and on behalf of, diverse individuals, families, groups, organizations, and communities. Social workers: (1) apply knowledge of human behavior and the social environment, person-in-environment, and other multidisciplinary theoretical frameworks to engage with clients and constituencies; and (2) use empathy, reflection, and interpersonal skills to effectively engage diverse clients and constituencies.

■ *Assess Individuals, Families, Groups, Organizations, and Communities*—Social workers understand that assessment is an ongoing component of the dynamic and interactive process of social work practice with, and on behalf of, diverse individuals, families, groups, organizations, and communities. Social workers: (1) collect and organize data, and apply critical thinking to interpret information from clients and constituencies; (2) apply knowledge of human behavior and the social environment, person-in-environment, and other multidisciplinary theoretical frameworks in the analysis of assessment data from clients and constituencies; (3) develop mutually agreed-on intervention goals and objectives based on the critical assessment of strengths, needs, and challenges within clients and constituencies; and (4) select appropriate intervention strategies based on the assessment, research knowledge, and values and preferences of clients and constituencies.

■ *Intervene with Individuals, Families, Groups, Organizations, and Communities*—Social workers understand that intervention is an ongoing component of the dynamic and interactive process of social work practice with, and on behalf of, diverse individuals, families, groups, organizations, and communities. Social workers: (1) critically choose and implement interventions to achieve practice goals and enhance capacities of clients and constituencies; (2) apply knowledge of human behavior and the social environment, person-in-environment, and other multidisciplinary theoretical frameworks in interventions with clients and constituencies; (3) use interprofessional collaboration as appropriate to achieve beneficial practice outcomes; (4) negotiate, mediate, and advocate with and on behalf of diverse clients and constituencies; and (5) facilitate effective transitions and endings that advance mutually agreed-on goals.

■ *Evaluate Practice with Individuals, Families, Groups, Organizations, and Communities*—Social workers understand that evaluation is an ongoing component of the dynamic and interactive process of social work practice with, and on behalf of, diverse individuals, families, groups, organizations and communities. Social workers: (1) select and use appropriate methods for evaluation of outcomes; (2) apply knowledge of human behavior and the social environment, person-in-environment, and other multidisciplinary theoretical frameworks in the evaluation of outcomes; (3) critically analyze, monitor, and evaluate intervention and program processes and outcomes; and (4) apply evaluation findings to improve practice effectiveness at the micro, mezzo, and macro levels.

Source: Adapted from CSWE, 2015. For a complete description of the EPAS, visit: http://cswe.org/Accreditation/ EPASRevision.aspx.

An increasing number of BSW students are finding it helpful to complete a second major or minors, certificates, and/or specializations to prepare them better for the challenging world of social work practice. Maintaining knowledge and skills relevant for contemporary society requires regular, ongoing education. Areas for intervention and employment opportunities are extremely varied and constantly in a state of change.

Master of Social Work At the graduate level, coursework is delineated into two levels: foundation and concentration. Foundation coursework, comparable to the generalist courses completed as part of the BSW degree, consists of social work practice with individuals, families, groups, organizations, communities, and public policy; human behavior and the social environment; social policy; research methods; and field experience. In addition, an understanding and respect for social work values and ethics, diversity, populations at risk, and social and economic justice are typically integrated throughout foundation coursework.

Following the successful completion of the foundation coursework, students select an area of concentration. Each social work program establishes its own areas of specialized study, but the curriculum typically includes advanced

EXHIBIT 12.3

Useful Electives for BSW Students

■ *Courses that focus on critical thinking.* This skill, which is essential for effective social work practice, comes from a broad understanding of the liberal arts. Reading and writing about complex issues helps to hone critical thinking skills.

■ *Social sciences.* Coursework in such areas as economics and domestic and global political environments can enhance your ability to understand various societal systems and to advocate for your clients' and profession's needs.

■ *Legal and financial studies.* An understanding of the legal and financial systems can be invaluable to a practicing social worker. Most fields of social work practice intersect at some point with the legal system. Client systems may encounter the legal system as a victim or as the accused; or when they need guardianship, have end-of-life decisions that require legal intervention, or need legal help with immigration concerns or when they need financial literacy and/or guidance.

■ *Gerontology.* Knowledge of aging and effective practice methods for working with older adults and their families will be essential for social work practice in the coming decades as baby boomers become older adults (CSWE/SAGE-SW, 2001).

■ *Community systems and dynamics.* Knowledge of communities is particularly useful for assessment and intervention at the community level.

■ *Leadership.* In order to guide policy development instead of merely reacting to established policies, social workers need strong leadership skills.

■ *Communication skills.* Public speaking, working with the media, and providing testimony are essential skills for those who want to effectively advocate for social work constituencies.

■ *Applied research skills.* Social workers who intend to conduct agency- or community-based research need the ability to conduct needs assessments and to develop and evaluate programs with measurable outcomes.

■ *Evidence-based practice.* In order to choose the most effective intervention approaches, a social worker needs thorough knowledge of how effective those approaches have proved to be, based on well-designed research.

■ *Sustainability/Environmental Justice.* With increased societal emphasis on preserving natural resources and protecting the environment, coursework in these areas can be helpful to the practicing social worker.

■ *International studies.* Whether a social work student gains proficiency in a second or third language, experiences a study abroad semester or course, or completes a practicum focused on an international population, becoming skilled in working with diverse populations and cultures is essential.

■ *Substance Use and Abuse.* With an increase in co-occurring disorders, social workers in virtually all areas of direct practice can benefit from learning more about the current substances potential clients may be using.

Source: NASW, 2010.

coursework in the areas introduced at the foundation level: practice, human behavior, policy, research, and field experiences. Although concentration areas in MSW programs are wide-ranging, areas of specialization usually include children, youth, and family practice; mental and physical health practice; gerontology; administration; community and policy practice; and social and economic development. Emerging areas of practice that may be offered include services to the military and veteran communities, international services, and services to immigrants and refugees.

Advanced standing
Many schools offer advanced standing into MSW programs to students who have graduated from a CSWE-accredited BSW program.

Many schools offer advanced standing in MSW programs to students who have graduated from a CSWE-accredited BSW program. When awarded advanced standing, the student's BSW coursework may be applied to part or all of the foundation coursework, thus decreasing the total number of credits required for completion of the MSW degree. With advanced standing, students may complete their master's degree in a shorter period of time or take more elective coursework in areas of interest.

Some institutions offer accelerated and "bridge" programs for completing both the BSW and MSW degrees. Accelerated programs typically require the student to complete a joint BSW and MSW degree within a structured plan that is briefer than a standard MSW program. A bridge program typically enables the student to complete three years in another major or institution and begin MSW coursework during the senior year of the undergraduate experience.

MSW students often determine that they would like to gain additional expertise in a specific area of social work practice or a related subject. They can achieve this by specializing or earning certificates within MSW programs. The three most offered certificates MSW programs award are: gerontological social work practice, school social work, and addictions treatment (CSWE, 2013). For those students who elect to develop in-depth knowledge of an area related to social work practice, the dual or joint degree may be an option. CSWE (2013) reports the three top dual degree options are: law, public health, and theology/divinity.

CURRENT ISSUES INFLUENCING SOCIAL WORK TRAINING FOR THE FUTURE

Because social work is a profession that responds to the personal and societal needs and concerns of the times, social work knowledge and education must also reflect current societal changes and needs. For example, in recent years, a struggling economy has created personal financial challenges for a broad array of people, including many who previously were financially stable and those who are considered the working poor. As one social worker notes: "Times like this push people to re-examine their core values, those core values of caring for each other. Those values fit very well with the core values of social work" (Smith, 2009). As we progress through the 21st century, some new opportunities are emerging for social workers.

Some of those opportunities were identified during the historic 2005 Social Work Congress, which was convened to establish the profession's agenda for the next decade (Clark et al., 2006). Building on that congress, over 400 social workers gathered for the 2010 Social Work Congress. They examined the "internal challenges facing the social work profession with a special focus on transferring leadership from established leaders to emerging leaders" (NASW, 2010, p. 1). Of those attending, 30 participants were emerging leaders under the age of 30 years. The gathering established 10 imperatives for the next decade (NASW, 2010), listed in Exhibit 12.4.

This book has addressed a number of these imperatives. What follows is a discussion of issues and opportunities related to a selected sample of the imperatives as well as needs and issues social workers have identified that will impact the profession.

Health Care Social Work Practice As social work becomes more integrated within health care and mental health delivery systems, social workers need to understand the biopsychosocial and spiritual dynamics that impact people's lives. Health care issues affecting the social work profession include the following:

- As our population grows more diverse, social workers will be needed to coordinate health and hospital care to ensure that individuals and families can access health care services and resources (Hoffler, 2012).
- Care coordination among providers was a centerpiece of the 2010 health care reform legislation. Resulting new opportunities for social workers include patient-centered medical homes (multipurpose medical facilities), accountable care organizations (evidence-based health care collaborations), and guided care (patient-centered care for those with chronic conditions) (Fink-Samnick, 2011).
- As the population ages and social workers become more involved in older adult and end-of-life issues, they will need greater understanding of developments in prolonging life, psychopharmacology, and genetic counseling. Knowledge of biochemistry, neuroscience, healthcare ethics, and genetics will be a marketable asset.
- Social workers already play a significant role in the provision of interprofessional physical and mental health and social services to persons across the spectrum of the service delivery system. To prepare for practice in an interprofessional setting, social workers need skills in teamwork, contracting, group process, leadership, and conflict resolution (Abramson, 2009).

EXHIBIT 12.4

Social Work Imperatives for the Next Decade

Business of Social Work

1. Infuse models of sustainable business and management practice in social work education and practice.

Common Objectives

2. Strengthen collaboration across social work organizations, their leaders, and their members for shared advocacy goals.

Education

3. Clarify and articulate the unique skills, scope of practice, and value added of social work to prospective social work students.

Influence

4. Build a data-driven business case that demonstrates the distinctive expertise and the impact and value of social work to industry, policy makers, and the general public.
5. Strengthen the ability of national social work organizations to identify and clearly articulate, with a unified voice, issues of importance to the profession.

Leadership Development

6. Integrate leadership training in social work curricula at all levels.

Recruitment

7. Empirically demonstrate to prospective recruits the value of the social work profession in both social and economic terms.

Retention

8. Ensure the stability of the profession through a strong mentoring program, career ladder, and succession program.
9. Increase the number of grants, scholarships, and debt forgiveness mechanisms for social work students and graduates.

Technology

10. Integrate technologies that serve social work practice and education in an ethical, practical, and responsible manner.

Adopted at 2010 Social Work Congress, April 23, 2010.

Source: NASW, 2010.

■ The Affordable Care Act (ACA) has expanded coverage for behavioral health and addiction treatment; however, there is a shortage of professionals who are appropriately trained to provide services. With the social worker's experience and history in the provision of integrated care, the profession should be on the forefront of developing and delivering new evidence-based services in this area (Lundgren & Krull, 2014).

Gerontological Social Work Practice As baby boomers reach older adulthood, they are changing the face of aging in the United States. Compared with previous generations, as they age they will be healthier, more technologically sophisticated, and better-informed consumers; they will work longer; and they will require more focused, specialized services and care.

To meet the needs of this population, more social workers with specialized expertise in aging are needed. Related opportunities are increasing in a variety of practice areas:

- While social workers are already on the forefront of gerontological services, they will need to take on larger roles as part of interprofessional teams in all geographic areas, but especially in nonurban communities (Whitaker, Weismiller, & Clark, 2006).
- Social workers will be needed particularly in the areas of mental and physical health services.
- Social workers need to be aware of and understand the diverse needs of the older adult population and related emerging issues, including transition from driving a vehicle to driving retirement due to age-related changes; services for LGBTQ older adults, older immigrants, and refugees; older adults living with HIV/AIDS; and aging within prison systems.
- To serve older adults who require alternative living arrangements in retirement, social workers will be needed in residential care facilities, including assisted living, skilled care, and hospice. Social workers can also work to support older adults aging-in-place within their own communities.
- With improvements in medical care and access, older adults of all racial, ethnic, and cultural groups are living longer. Social workers are needed to work with healthy, productive older adults in direct practice, administrative, and policy areas.
- Baccalaureate social workers will be in high demand for direct practice and advocacy roles with older adults who are caregivers and older adults who require the assistance of a caregiver (Williams & Joyner, 2008).

Child Welfare Services The professionalization of child welfare services is at a critical point in the United States. Historically, due to large caseloads and inadequate salaries, child welfare agencies in nearly every state have had difficulty attracting competent, appropriately trained professionals (Whitaker, Weismiller, & Clark, 2006). In addition, the national turnover rate is as high as 90% annually in some regions (U.S. Department of Health and Human Services, Administration for Children and Families, n.d.). High turnover results in less effective and inconsistent services for children and families. Although turnover rates are considerably lower for degreed social workers who work in child welfare, there are not enough licensed social workers trained to provide the range of services for children and families. Thus many states do not require a social work degree for these positions.

More social workers, at both the BSW and MSW level, are needed to work in child welfare services. Social work scholar Briar-Lawson (2012) notes that states should require that degreed social workers be hired for these positions. Employment opportunities for social workers who want to work with children are expected to grow by 43,100 (15%) jobs by 2022 (BLS, 2014b).

Opportunities in this field of practice include:

- Qualified and competent social workers are needed to provide services for children born into poverty (one in every five), abused or neglected (one every 47 seconds), or reared in foster care (101,719) (Children's Defense Fund, 2014).
- Child welfare career possibilities for generalist baccalaureate social workers exist at the micro, mezzo, and macro levels. Social work skills at all levels are useful in public or private agencies in child protective services, family preservation, and foster care. The need for social workers in transitional and independent living for older adolescents, particularly those "aging out" of the foster care system (which occurs at the rate of 23,000/year), is growing (Children's Defense Fund, 2014).
- Student loan forgiveness programs are in place to encourage the development of skilled workers in certain professions. Your state may offer loan forgiveness for social work practitioners in areas such as children and family, health and mental health care, or school social work. To inquire about these opportunities, check your NASW state chapter or your state's department of professional licensing. Information on loan forgiveness programs may also be available at the federal level and in your college or university's student financial services office. For a sampling of some additional resources, see Exhibit 12.5.

Technology and Social Work Practice Social workers need to be able to use the latest information and communication technologies—to provide services, keep records, analyze data for funding and program evaluation, to communicate, and to participate in distance education and service provision. Information and communication technology has enabled social workers to conduct online therapy, support groups, and e-commerce; use avatars to facilitate clinical work with clients; facilitate discussion/chat rooms for clients interested in similar issues; provide long-distance social work education, services, and training; maintain up-to-date knowledge of legislation and policies; and support activism by reaching policy-makers in a matter of seconds around the world. In short, technology has enhanced social workers' abilities to reach

EXHIBIT 12.5

Some Sources of Information about Student Loan Forgiveness Programs

- NASW: www.socialworkers.org/loanforgiveness/default.asp
- The Smart Student Guide to Financial Aid: www.finaid.org
    - Scholarships/Financial Aid for Volunteer Programs: www.finaid.org/scholarships/service.phtml
    - Military Student Aid: www.finaid.org/military/
- Student Aid Center: www.studentloanforgivenessplans.org/index.html
- U.S. Department of Education's Income Contingent Repayment (ICR) Program: https://studentaid.ed.gov/sa/repay-loans/understand/plans/income-driven
- U.S. Department of Education's Public Service Loan Forgiveness: https://studentaid.ed.gov/sa/repay-loans/forgiveness-cancellation/public-service
- National Health Service Corp: nhsc.hrsa.gov/loanrepayment/

more people more often in less time. Technology can create more consistency and continuity in the social work intervention, but must include appropriate content and expectations to protect those involved (Mishna et al., 2014).

As discussed in Chapter 6, social workers are ethically obligated to ensure integrity at all times when using technology (e.g., confidentiality is essential when communicating with or about client systems via cell phone, e-mail, text messaging, or twitter). Websites should be checked to ensure they are credible and secure sources of information. Social media and networking sites (Facebook, LinkedIn, and micro-blogging) present the profession with both opportunity and risk. Facebook, the number one website in the world has over one billion users and continues to grow (Hoffler & Clark, 2012). While these forms of communication enable increased access for both clients and providers, privacy may be virtually impossible to maintain, making informed consent critical (Sfiligoj, 2009), and agencies must monitor content and have strategies for controlling outreach (Hoffler & Clark, 2012).

In an effort to ensure that social workers and client systems have access to and use technology appropriately and ethically, the NASW and the Association of Social Work Boards developed Standards for Technology and Social Work Practice (2005). The standards encompass technology-related issues such as competent, appropriate, legal, and ethical use of technology;

accurate representation of self when using electronic communication technologies; strict adherence to privacy of communication; advocacy for community access to helpful technology; and understanding of the dynamics of electronic communications. While having a set of standards to guide social workers in the ethical use of technology is important, questions continue to loom on the horizon, including: (1) What effect does technology have on social work practice, particularly in the areas of trust and building alliances with clients?; (2) How should threats to privacy, civil liberties, and human rights be addressed without compromising professional credibility?; and (3) What additional ethical standards are needed? (Ley, 2012).

Examples of new and emerging knowledge, skills, and opportunities related to technology include the following:

- Technological enhancements enable social workers to conduct groups and meetings in a virtual environment through telephone/video/web conferencing and internet groups (e.g., chat rooms, bulletin boards, e-mail, and list servs). Social workers must be aware of group dynamics in the absence, in some cases, of verbal and nonverbal communications (Toseland & Horton, 2008).

- Just as traditional records are subject to scrutiny, electronic records (including e-mails, text messages, and online postings) may be used in legal proceedings and insurance determinations. Therefore, social workers must be sensitive to the information included in these forms of communication and ensure they are knowledgeable about the legal restrictions and ramifications regarding electronic communications.

- Opportunities for technological social work interventions exist in online support, advocacy, fund-raising, education, policy development, innovative services, and one-on-one support available for crises (Smith, 2009).

- When facilitating an online support group (OSG), for example, the social worker must develop a unique skill set in order to foster group interaction without the face-to-face contact (Perron & Powell, 2009).

To learn more about one mental health agency's use of technology in work with adolescents, see Exhibit 12.6.

Disaster Response and Crisis Intervention Disaster is defined as an extraordinary natural or human-made event that can bring harm to property and human life. Social workers are increasingly on the scene in times of disaster and crisis to provide support and mental health services. For example, approximately 50% of the volunteers trained by the American Red Cross to provide mental health services in emergency and disaster situations are professional social workers (Dale, 2011).

EXHIBIT 12.6

Bringing Technology to Crisis Intervention

Avatar-assisted therapy is one of the latest technologies being incorporated into social work practice, particularly in mental health services. Built on the concept of digital gaming, avatars are used for the provision of mental health services to individuals and groups for a number of purposes, including socialization, substance abuse treatment, and aftercare. Avatar-assisted interventions can be adapted to most therapeutic approaches.

One agency, Behavioral Health Response (BHR), is offering an innovative approach to avatar assisted crisis intervention programming for youth. The user enters a "community center" where she or he can interact with other youth, participate in group rooms with one or more youth, and have private meetings with substance abuse and behavioral health clinicians and case managers. Sites have clinicians available in avatar form for scheduled appointments, and crisis clinicians will maintain an avatar presence during scheduled shifts. Participant users will have access to BHR clinicians 24/7 via a web chat link placed at kiosks throughout the world. Once a BHR clinician is alerted to a need via web chat, they will quickly be able to join the person in-world. The staff, already trained clinicians who use telephone, video, text, and chat room technology, are trained in the use of the avatar technology.

The target group for this service is 13–19-year-old youth. Users under age 18 can engage only with parental consent. While anonymity is honored, if the professional develops a concern (e.g., suicidal ideation), she or he will work with the user to develop a safety plan. The agency has created a youth advisory council that meets weekly to provide input into the development and ongoing delivery of this service.

■   To learn more about the use of avatar assisted therapy, you can visit an online video interview with the developer of the agency's system, at: https://www.youtube.com/watch?v=Rw-MLglMrrk.
■   Thank you to Danny Gladden for providing information about this innovation.

Social workers' knowledge and skills in crisis intervention make them valuable assets for work with persons traumatized by a disaster or crisis. More social workers are learning to intervene in cases of "disaster syndrome," the series of predictable phases a disaster or crisis survivor experiences including preimpact, impact, postimpact, and disillusionment or long-term impact (Barker, 2014). A specialized skill set is needed as well: knowledge of stress and coping responses; ability to individualize an intervention to the situation and the phase of recovery with sensitivity to specific circumstances; and ability to support other disaster responders (NASW, 2012–2014d).

Here are some examples of disaster and crisis situations in which social workers become involved:

■   Social workers have helped in the aftermath of such natural disasters as deadly tornadoes and hurricanes and manmade crises including the 2014 events in Ferguson, Missouri. They have contributed to the profession's knowledge and skill base regarding disaster and crisis response.
■   Critical skills for working with survivors include listening, anticipating and normalizing reactions and recovery, recognizing resilience, and building on strengths (McPartlin, 2006).
■   Military personnel and their families need social work services. Social workers have accompanied troops in virtually every deployment in recent times and are working with military families on the home front before, during, and after deployment.
■   Because crisis and disaster work can be intense and emotionally challenging, social workers working in this area must vigilantly perform self-care to avoid burnout, also known as compassion fatigue. Self-care strategies include maintaining healthy lifestyle habits (e.g., exercise, nutrition, and sleep), finding time for relaxation, seeking supportive supervision, continuing education regarding disaster responses, and practicing spirituality or meditation (Arrington, 2008; Wharton, 2008).

Compassion fatigue
Also known as burn out, compassion fatigue occurs when professionals experience an extreme emotional response to their work.

International Social Work and Multilingualism With an increased U.S. focus on international and global issues, social workers will continue to play an increasing role both domestically and internationally. Despite its long history, the concept of international social work is a "contested terrain, which is fluid, dynamic, and shifting, as its focus is a global analysis of every-changing sociocultural issue" (Razack, 2012, p. 707). The future of international social work can be conceived within five practice dimensions: (1) outside of one's home country; (2) with immigrants and refugees in one's home country; (3) with international or quasi-governmental organizations; (4) in collaborative or exchange partnerships across borders; and (5) locally, with a focus on the impact on the larger world (i.e., glocalization) (Hugman, Moosa-Mitha, & Moyo, 2013). Social work employment opportunities will continue to grow within the United States in virtually every area of the social service delivery system, particularly in community-based social service agencies, health care facilities, and schools that serve immigrant and refugee populations.

Many social workers are drawn to work outside their country of origin. When working internationally, social work has often taken the form of social workers from developed countries (e.g., North America and Europe) working in developing countries on such issues as poverty, chronic diseases, urbanization, unemployment, inequality, and lack of economic opportunities (Osei-Hwedie & Rankopo, 2012, p. 732). While social workers working internationally may be able to share their knowledge and practice methodologies, they must also build on the strengths and resources within their host country and focus on exchanging ideas and concepts. Within the context of advocacy, social workers must be aware of the ways in which dominance over persons in developing countries has developed and impacted the residents of those countries (Razack, 2012).

As the U.S. population becomes increasingly diverse, social workers who have written and oral proficiency in more than one language are better able to communicate with and advocate for clients. When we think about being bilingual in the United States today, Spanish is typically the first language that comes to mind. However, there is a need for social workers who are fluent in other languages as well, including but not limited to Russian, Bosnian, Chinese, Korean, and American Sign Language.

These are some of the opportunities emerging in the area of international and multicultural social work:

- If you are considering a career in international social work, certain experiences are key. It is helpful to develop internationally focused knowledge and skills through coursework, volunteer/service or paid internships abroad or in immigrant communities, and personal cultural experiences (McLaughlin, 2007).

- Multilanguage fluency and community organization, fund-raising, and clinical skills are useful in this arena (McLaughlin, 2007).
- Opportunities for social workers to assume leadership and administrative roles in international organizations, both in the United States and abroad, continue to grow.
- Maintaining awareness of global issues is critical, regardless of the practice setting. Social workers must be aware of international and global issues that impact every facet of our society and our practice.

Animal-assisted Therapy While not widely used as a therapeutic strategy, animal-assisted therapy (AAT), is gaining acceptance in a variety of settings and with a range of populations. Animals—including dogs, horses, small animals, and birds—have been introduced into residential care facilities, adult and child day care centers, hospitals, schools, hospice programs, clients' homes, prisons, and other settings. Animals have been incorporated into interventions with adults experiencing stress and anxiety, children with behavioral and emotional disorders, persons with dementia, and anger management programs (Dabelko-Schoeny et al., 2014; Geist, 2011). Research regarding the effects of AAT is new but shows promising outcomes including decreased physiological reactions to stress, increases in physical activity, and reduced behavioral problems (Dabelko-Schoeny et al., 2014; Geist, 2011).

Animal-assisted therapy (AAT) Treatment that uses trained animals to enhance physical, social, and emotional well-being.

Animal Assisted Therapy

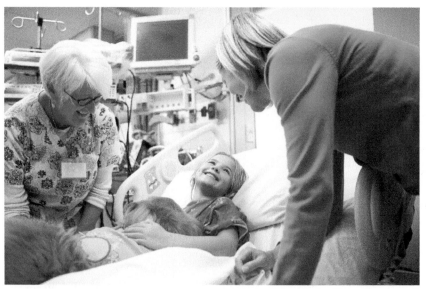

Source: iStock/monkey business images

Financial Social Work Social workers have long been aware of and, in some cases, involved in their clients' financial situations. However, it is only recently that some social workers have undertaken formalized training in financial social work, a "behavioral model that moves clients beyond basic needs with a psychosocial, multidisciplinary approach focused on the thoughts, feelings, and attitudes that determine each person's relationship to and behavior with money" (Wolfsohn, 2012, p. 221).

Financial social work
Area of social work practice focuses on individuals' financial income and expenses.

Regardless of the area in which a social worker practices, a working knowledge of issues related to financial education and management is critical, as many clients with whom social workers engage face financial challenges. A foundation in money management and sound financial decision-making can help clients avoid being taken advantage of by predatory lenders, financial scammers, payday loans, rent-to-own agreements, and co-signing arrangements (Wolfsohn, 2012), all of which may lead to foreclosures, bankruptcy, defaulting on loans, and poor credit scores, endangering their ability to be financially solvent (Wolfsohn, 2012). The social worker can provide financial education, promote financial literacy, and help the client access services (Birkenmaier, Kennedy, Kunz, Sander, & Horwitz, 2013).

As you have learned, there are many ways to practice social work. It is a diverse profession that provides many opportunities for working with individuals, families, groups, communities, and organizations at the local, state, national, and international levels. To learn about the various paths one social worker's career has taken, review Exhibit 12.7.

The Future of Social Work

One of the hallmarks of the social work profession is its ability to adapt to changes in society. While changes are always impacting the social work profession, several changes are currently affecting the future of the profession. The population's aging "tsunami" is affecting society in general as well as the social work profession. With the need for social workers increasing and record numbers of practitioners retiring, recruitment and retention of the next generations of social workers is a critical issue as we approach the third decade of the 21st century.

The Dorothy I Height and Whitney M. Young, Jr. Social Work Reinvestment Initiative is one way in which the social work profession is attempting to address the imminent need for more social workers. Emanating from the 2005 Social Work Congress, NASW first introduced the Social Work Reinvestment Initiative in 2006. The goal of the Initiative is to "secure federal and state investments in professional social work to enhance societal well-being" (www.socialworkreinvestment.org/). The Initiative includes these components (Hoffler, 2012):

EXHIBIT 12.7

"There are Many Ways to Practice Social Work"

Phil Minden's story is a good example of the many professional paths a social worker may take. His social work career has led him from a faith-based community to the non-profit social service sector to city and county government agencies and finally to the for-profit sector. Through all of these experiences, Phil remains steadfastly committed to social work values.

After completing an undergraduate degree in classical languages, Phil served one year in the Jesuit Volunteer Corps in Portland, Oregon, where he worked with the homeless community at St. Vincent DePaul Society. Phil then completed his MSW, focusing on macro-level practice through coursework and practicum experiences at a Diocesan Human Rights Office and a statewide association for social welfare.

Upon graduating with his MSW, Phil worked with a nonprofit community service agency in a socioeconomically disadvantaged urban area, where he gained skills in grant writing for youth, older adult, and housing programs. Phil recognized that it was feasible and profitable for the agency to establish its own nonprofit housing development arm so they did not have to rely on grant funding. Phil's interest in affordable housing was born.

From the nonprofit agency, Phil moved to city government, obtained his real estate and broker's licenses, and worked to develop affordable housing. He then moved to county government, where he began working with developers to facilitate funding and development of affordable housing. Finally, Phil felt he could have the greatest potential impact in the private sector. He obtained an MBA to enable him to understand and advocate for the housing projects he was committed to developing. Phil has now transitioned to the banking industry, where he underwrites mortgages for large-scale affordable rental property developments.

Throughout his career, Phil has maintained a constant presence as a volunteer in the community. He continues to volunteer with the agency where he first worked by writing grants, serving on the board, and advising staff. His beekeeping hobby became the basis for a grant that is funding a project in a low-income neighborhood to teach African American teens entrepreneurial skills through beekeeping. To learn more about this project, go to: http://news.stlpublicradio.org/post/students-find-sweet-opportunity-north-st-louis.

While Phil's career has taken him from grant writing to real estate development to banking, he has consistently worked for social justice to meet the demand for affordable housing which is sorely needed due to the retraction of the federal government to support affordable housing. He has remained committed to continual learning, seeking out educational experiences to better equip himself for new challenges. Phil advises that: "Social workers should be self-starters, take risks, and think outside the boundaries."

- NASW-led state-level reinvestment plans targeting areas relevant to the social work profession including title protection, reimbursement, licensure, public education, and social work education programs.
- Relevant federal legislation that will provide loan forgiveness for social workers, particularly through the Reauthorization of the Higher Education Act of 1965.
- The Social Work Reinvestment Initiative includes two foci: 1) the Social Work Reinvestment Commission, whose goal is to develop "long term research strategies to maximize the ability of the nation's social workers to serve their clients with competence and care" (p. 43), and 2) funding to improve the social work workplace (e.g., increased funding for social work supervision, salaries, decreased caseloads, education and training, and post-doctoral research opportunities, and community-based programs of excellence).

Formed by a group of social work organizations (Association of Baccalaureate Social Work Program Directors, Council on Social Work Education, Group for the Advancement of Doctoral Education, National Association of Deans and Directors of Schools of Social Work, NASW, Society for Social Work and Research, and Social Work Policy Institute),The Action Network for Social Work Education and Research (ANSWER Coalition) seeks to promote the Social Work Reinvestment Act (SWRA) which, to date, has been introduced into three legislative sessions without being passed. In a profession-wide show of unity and strength, over 100,000 social workers have reached out to their legislators to urge their support for the legislation. Efforts continue in the hope of enacting this much-needed legislation. To learn more about the Social Work Reinvestment Initiative, visit: www.socialworkreinvestment. org/.

YOUR CAREER IN SOCIAL WORK

With these insights into some of the societal and social work practice challenges and opportunities that lie on the horizon, turn your attention to your socialization as a social work professional within this context. Exhibit 12.8 provides an array of possible activities that can help you identify further with the social work profession.

Although formal education is an essential part of your professional socialization as a social worker, many informal aspects of your educational experience are equally important to your professional development. The best way to know for sure whether the social work profession is right for you is to gain some experience. Volunteer and service-related activities are valuable opportunities

EXHIBIT 12.8

Activities to Promote Professional Identification

Network
- Through local, state, and national social work organizations, get acquainted with other social workers who have interests similar to your own.
- Join a social work listserv or chat room, or connect with other social workers and social work organizations on twitter for the opportunity to converse with other social work students and faculty.
- Find out if your school has a student social work association or student/faculty special interest groups (for example, social workers interested in working with older adults or a group for students that are gay, lesbian, bisexual, or transgender).
- If you join a group, get involved! There is no better way to get connected than to serve in a leadership position.

Join NASW
- Join as a student member at a discounted rate. You will get a transitional membership rate following graduation. To learn more about student resources, visit: http://www.socialworkers.org/students/default.asp.
- Take advantage of member benefits: a monthly newspaper, *NASW News;* the journal, *Social Work;* and your local chapter newsletter.
- Join one of the Specialty Practice Sections (a member benefit), including aging; alcohol, tobacco, and other drugs; child welfare; health; mental health; poverty and social justice; private practice; and school social work.
- Take advantage of membership in one of the Specialty Practice Sections: participate in the online forums for section members and read the two newsletters per year, with information on the trends, specific activities, and practice updates of interest to members of that section.
- Run for a position as student representative for your NASW chapter or for the national organization.
- Check the NASW website (www.naswdc.org) for a wealth of information on the profession. For example, check out 50 Ways to Use your Social Work Degree at http://50ways.socialworkblog.org/ to read the stories of 50 practitioners, view a video on the profession, learn surprising facts about social work, and even calculate your future salary.
- Connect with NASW through social networking sites, including:
  - Twitter - www.twitter.com/nasw
  - Facebook - www.facebook.com/socialworkers
  - LinkedIn
  - YouTube - www.youtube.com/socialworkers
  - Social Work Blog - www.socialworkblog.org
  - NASW RSS Feeds

Get More Experience
- Continue volunteering at the site where you completed your community service experience for this introductory course.

- Gain a different experience by volunteering at another organization.
- Seek paid employment at an agency. Many social service organizations have part- or full-time positions for students seeking social service experience.

Share Your Experiences with Others

Consider publishing your social work experiences for other social work professionals. Three options include:

- *21st Century Social Justice*—This student-run journal at Fordham University accepts submissions from students from other schools. For more information, visit: http://fordham. bepress.com/swjournal/.
- *The Journal of Baccalaureate Social Work* accepts student submissions provided the topic relates to BSW education or practice. For more information, visit: http://jbsw.msubmit.net/ cgi-bin/main.plex.
- *The New Social Worker* accepts submissions from students related to social work student activities and articles for the magazine. For more information, visit: http://www.socialworker. com/magazine.

for developing insights into the world of social work. As a volunteer in a health, educational, or social service setting you can meet social workers who can share with you the rewards and realities of a social work career.

A group of graduating BSW students provide a helpful perspective when they share their wisdom for optimizing your professionalization during your time as a social work student (Clewes, 2001):

- Be prepared to grow and change. Be open-minded and expect to have your values and beliefs challenged, but do not plan to change anyone but yourself.
- Maximize your learning opportunities; challenge yourself and recognize that every person that comes into your life can teach you something. Venture into areas of learning that are new for you.
- Ask for help when you need it, and see mistakes as learning opportunities.
- Be prepared for your social work program to change you and to provide you with the tools to go out and continue this change.

Your social work training will be a lifelong process; therefore, the list of educational and professional socialization opportunities provided here is just the beginning. Our society is in a constant state of flux, and the knowledge and skills social workers need evolves over the course of a career. As two noted social work scholars eloquently stated (Hopps & Lowe, 2008):

Social work practice in the future will continue to be charged by forces that will forever influence its boundaries. Continuing struggles regarding enhancing social functioning and advancing social justice require that practitioners remain vigilant regarding the needs of both old and new vulnerable populations. The challenge of responding to such problems, however, must be considered in the context of the profession's core mission (p. 59).

CONCLUSION

Is a career in social work for you? Social work is a unique helping profession, dually committed to providing social services to vulnerable groups in our society, such as disaster victims and children who are abused and neglected, and to alleviating social problems through advocacy efforts, such as lobbying for affordable housing policies. Social workers strive to make a difference in a fulfilling profession shaped by the totality of the social worker's life experiences and professional knowledge, skills, and values. You may have already begun the process of identifying with the social work profession in this first social work course and you can revisit that process many times throughout your career.

You are almost at the end of your first social work course. You have been exposed to a wide range of information about the profession and have, hopefully, gained a sense of what a career in social work would entail. Your task now is to determine how your journey will continue. Consider the inspirational theme for NASW Social Work Month 2012 (March is designated annually as Social Work Month) (NASW, 2012c, para 5, lines 1–3):

> *Social Work Matters.* Social Workers fundamentally believe that a nation's strength depends on the ability of the majority of its citizens to lead productive and healthy lives. What drives these professionals? They help people, who are often navigating major life challenges, find hope and new options for achieving their full potential.

MAIN POINTS

- The outlook for the social work profession is promising. Employment trends suggest that social work jobs will expand in areas such as aging, health care, substance abuse treatment, school social work, and mental health services, although provision of mental health services will continue to be the primary area of practice for social work professionals.
- The current median annual salary for social workers is in the mid-$30,000 to mid-$50,000 range.

■ Societal perceptions of the social work profession are improving, but social workers must continue self-advocacy efforts to ensure that such improvements continue.

■ The BSW prepares social workers to function as generalist practitioners. Both BSW and MSW foundation curricula cover a broad spectrum of content including human behavior, social policy, research, and social work practice, all integrated through the field experience.

■ Socialization as a social work professional involves both formal education and informal strategies. If you decide to pursue a social work career, be prepared for a lifelong process of growth and change.

EXERCISES

1. You are now ready to bid farewell to the Sanchez and Stone (Brickville) families. Begin your evaluation and termination by going to the Evaluate tab for either of these interactive cases at www.routledgesw.com/caseStudies.
   a. Review the Evaluation Introduction and complete Task 1 for the entire Sanchez or Stone family case (notebook review).
   b. To conduct an overall review of the Sanchez or Stone family case, complete Task 2, which includes intervention evaluation, case closed, and final thoughts. In the final thoughts section, reflect on the work you have done with the Sanchez or Stone family throughout this course. How would you know that you were effective in your work? For example, would you ask the family to complete a satisfaction survey? Would you review the goals the family set for themselves and measure progress against those goals? If you failed to reach certain goals, how would you respond?

2. You are now familiar with social work interventions at the micro, mezzo, and macro levels. Referring to the community's concerns in the Riverton neighborhood of Alvadora (www.routledgesw.com/caseStudies), identify an issue or challenge and develop an intervention that can be approached from all three levels of social work practice.

3. Social workers practicing in disaster response situations may experience secondary trauma. Review the information presented in this chapter and the Hudson City interactive case (www.routledgesw.com/caseStudies) regarding the impact of crisis intervention on the practitioner, then complete a self-care plan that a social worker working in disaster response could implement, taking into consideration the unpredictability and intensity that is part of disaster response work.

4. Along with completing an introductory social work course and learning about the social work profession, talking with practicing social workers

is an excellent strategy for determining whether social work is the right career for you.

   a. With the help of your instructor for this course or other faculty in the social work program, identify a social work practitioner that you can interview in person at her/his agency. Consider an area of social work that is of interest to you, and select a social worker practicing in that area—for example:

Health/medical	Child welfare	Gerontology
Policy practice	Community organizing	Administration
Advocacy	Mental health	School social work
Law/justice system	Children and families	Adoption
Substance abuse treatment	Domestic violence	Youth

   b. After you have identified a social worker to interview, contact the person by telephone or e-mail to request the interview. Be certain to discuss a convenient time and duration for the interview. Confirm the interview time and location. Before the interview, you may want to e-mail or mail your questions to the interviewee (see Exhibit 12.9 for some suggestions). Remember to send a thank you note after the interview.

   c. Upon completion of the interview, reflect on the information the social worker shared and submit your reflection to your instructor. Summarize the information, but also reflect on your thoughts and reactions to what you have learned. (Exhibit 12.10 offers some suggestions.) You may want to consider audiotaping the interview to help with your reflection paper.

5. Personal reflection: Discuss your current perception of social work. Has your attitude toward or perception of the profession changed since the beginning of the semester? If so, how? How do you see your own future as it relates to the social work profession?

6. Compassion fatigue can affect social workers, but social workers can often mitigate its effects by practicing self-care. Develop a detailed plan of self-care for yourself, and reflect on those strategies that you are currently using and those strategies that would require a lifestyle change.

7. The following exercise provides an opportunity to engage in a planned change intervention:

EXHIBIT 12.9

Sample Questions for Interviewing a Practicing Social Worker

Do not feel limited to these suggestions. Be creative and inquisitive! Ask about the things that matter to you.

- Tell me about your journey into social work. What about social work appealed to you? How did you decide to become a social worker?
- What is your educational background for being a social worker?
- What social work experiences have you had, including volunteer, practicum, and paid experiences?
- How did you determine the area(s) in which you wanted to work?
- Tell me about your current social work position. What are your responsibilities?
- How long have you been employed in this position?
- What do you like/dislike about your job?
- What are the positive aspects of being a social worker?
- What are the negative aspects of being a social worker?
- What suggestions would you offer to someone who is considering a social work career?
- Based on what you now know, what suggestions do you have for courses or field experiences that a social work student might seek out during training?

Lydia Dennyson: A Social Work Planned Change Intervention

This exercise brings together much of the social work knowledge you have gained throughout this course. In order to determine an appropriate intervention plan for the client, you will first need to learn about the aging-related changes she is experiencing and the impact of those changes on her ability to maintain a functional quality of life. You will also need to learn about resources in your community at the individual, family, and organizational level that can be developed or mobilized for the benefit of the client system and about policies that impact older adults and their families.

Background Information Mrs. Dennyson is an 82-year-old woman who lives alone in the home she shared for four decades with her husband, who has been deceased for the past 11 years. She has stayed in the home and, until recently, has been highly functional, active, and productive. At age 66, she retired from her career as a human resources specialist for a large corporation. Her own

---

EXHIBIT 12.10

Sample Questions for Reflecting on an Interview with a Social Worker

- Before the interview, how would you have described or defined social work?
- Did the social worker you interviewed confirm or change your perception of the social work profession?
- What was it about the social worker's job that appealed or did not appeal to you? Can you see yourself working in the area or job of the social worker you interviewed? Why or why not?
- What new information did you learn about social work that you did not previously know?
- Did the social worker discuss how she or he applies the values of the social work profession?
- Did the social worker discuss any ethical conflicts that she/he has encountered? How would you handle similar situations?

---

retirement income combined with her husband's has made her financially comfortable; she is able to travel to visit family, update her home and car, and pursue her cultural and social interests. She has three children, all of whom live several hundred miles away. She sees them a few times a year, but typically only around holidays and on periodic visits to their homes.

Over the past several years, Mrs. Dennyson's vision has deteriorated. Attributing this to "normal" aging, she has not sought specialized medical care. Instead, she has compensated for her visual impairment by developing a strict routine from which she seldom strays, and by generally hiding from family, friends, and her physician that she is becoming less functional. She has limited her driving to daylight, nonpeak hours, stayed close to her home, and used only those routes familiar to her. She only reveals the severity of her impairment when she causes a motor vehicle incident.

During a follow-up appointment, Mrs. Dennyson's physician advises her that her visual condition is degenerative and that it will no longer be safe for her to drive. She informs the physician that, because she has no one to help her, she has no choice but to continue driving. The physician again cautions her against driving.

Over the ensuing months, Mrs. Dennyson discontinues virtually all of her social, volunteer, and religious activities, her travel, and her medical appointments. When her daughter, Janice, comes to visit, she is appalled to see the condition of her mother, the house, and the car. Her usually well-kept mother is disheveled, somewhat confused, and significantly thinner. The previously immaculate house is in disarray, and the car is covered with scratches, dents, and evidence of multiple fender-benders. Upon further inspection, Janice finds multiple unpaid bills, late-payment notices, and large sums of cash hidden throughout the house.

Despite the fact that her mother denies any problems and insists that she will continue living in the home alone, Janice is distraught. She contacts the Senior Services Center and asks for an immediate appointment for her mother. You are the case manager assigned to see Mrs. Dennyson.

The Intervention Your task is to develop a strengths-based intervention plan for Mrs. Dennyson that encompasses engagement, assessment, intervention, and termination/evaluation. You must identify the practice implications for each phase and, ultimately, consider the lessons learned from this experience.

Phase I—Engagement of the client system
    a.   Who is your client?
    b.   How do you engage the client system?
    c.   How do you interact with the nonclient "actors" in this system?

Practice implications for the engagement phase
- What additional information do you need?
- What are the sources of this information?
- What are your initial impressions?
- What knowledge do you need?
- What skills do you need?

Phase II—Assessment
    a.   What are the strengths of the client system?
    b.   What are the goals and needs of the client system?
    c.   What community and family resources are available to meet those goals and needs?
    d.   What are the barriers to meeting those goals and needs?
    e.   What is your assessment of the client system's goals and needs?

Practice implications for the assessment phase
- What knowledge do you need?
- What skills do you need?
- Are you aware of the client system's values?
- What is your ethical obligation in this situation?
- What is your legal obligation in this situation?

■   Who are potential partners in gathering information?
■   How might you manage conflicting goals within the client system?
■   What policies might impact the case?

Phase III—Intervention

a. What is an intervention plan that is realistic and potentially helpful in this situation—for the client, the daughter, and the service delivery system?
b. How does the intervention plan build on the strengths of the client system?
c. Are adequate and viable resources available to fulfill the plan—at the individual, family, organizational, or community levels?
d. What new or different resources are needed to implement the intervention plan?
e. What are the barriers to obtaining those resources?
f. What is an appropriate timeframe for the implementation of this intervention plan?
g. Are the barriers at the individual, family, or community level?
h. What policies impact the situation?

Practice implications for the intervention phase

■   What knowledge do you need?
■   What skills do you need?
■   Who are potential partners in developing and implementing an appropriate intervention plan?
■   Is the intervention plan achievable? Measurable? Ethical?
■   How might you manage situations in which you and others (i.e., clients, co-workers) have conflicting views of the intervention plan?

Phase IV—Termination and Evaluation

a. What constitutes a successful intervention? How will you know when you have completed the intervention?
b. What evaluation process would help you to gauge the success of the intervention?

Practice implications for the termination and evaluation phase

■   What knowledge do you need?
■   What skills do you need?
■   How will you evaluate the intervention?

Lessons Learned

Upon completing the planned change process, consider the following:

a. What information did you realize you already possessed?

b. What information did you realize you needed?

c. What knowledge did you realize you possessed?

d. What knowledge did you realize you needed?

e. What skills did you realize you possessed?

f. What skills did you realize you needed?

g. What are the value and ethical issues related to this scenario?

h. What are the legal implications of this scenario?

i. What is your knowledge of related community resources?

j. What is your awareness of strategies to develop or mobilize needed community resources?

k. What policy information about older adults did you realize you already possess?

l. What policy information about older adults did you realize you need?

Bibliography

Abramson, J. (2009). Interdisciplinary team practice. In A.R. Roberts (Ed.), *Social workers' desk reference* (2nd ed.) (pp. 44–50). New York: Oxford Press.

Adams, M. & Joshi, K.Y. (2013). Religious oppression. In M. Adams, W.J. Blumenfeld, C. Castañeda, H.W. Hackman, M.L. Peters, & X. Zúñiga (Eds.), *Readings for diversity and social justice* (3rd ed.) (pp. 229–237). New York: Routledge.

Administration on Aging (AoA), Administration for Community Living, U.S. Department of Health and Human Services. (2013). A profile of older Americans: 2013. Available at: www.acf.hhs.gov/sites/default/files/cb/cwo08_11_exesum.pdf.

Akin, J. (1998). *100 skills of the professional social worker.* Tallahassee, FL: NASW Florida chapter.

Albelda, R. (2012). Different anti-poverty programs, same single-mother poverty. *Dollars & Sense, 298,* 11–17.

Albelda, R., Folbre, N., & the Center for Popular Economics. (1996). *The war on the poor. A defense manual.* New York: The New Press.

Ali, S. & Hartman, D. (2015). *Migration, incorporation, and change in an interconnected world.* New York: Routledge.

Alissi, A.S. (2009). United States. In A. Gitterman & R. Salmon (Eds.), *Encyclopedia of social work with groups* (pp. 6–13). New York: Routledge.

Allen, K. (2012). What is an ethical dilemma? *The New Social Worker, 19*(2), 4–5.

Allen-Meares, P. (2000). Our professional values and the changing environment. *Journal of Social Work Education, 36*(2), 179–182.

Allen-Meares, P. & DeRoos, Y. (1997). The future of the social work profession. In M. Reisch & E. Gambrill (Eds.), *Social work in the 21st century* (pp. 376–386). Thousand Oaks, CA: Pine Forge Press.

Alzheimer's Association. (2014). 2014 facts and figures. *Alzheimer's and Dementia, 10*(2).

Angelis, T. (2012). Social workers help military families. Available at: www.naswdc.org/pressroom/events/peace/helpFamilies.asp.

Angell, B. (2008). Behavioral theory. In T. Mizrahi & L.E. Davis (Eds.), *Encyclopedia of social work* (20th ed.) (pp. 1:188–192). Washington, DC: NASW Press and Oxford University Press.

Annie E. Casey Foundation. (2011). *The changing child population of the United States: Analysis of data from the 2010 Census.* Baltimore, MD: Annie E. Casey Foundation.

Annie E. Casey Foundation. (2014). *Kids count. 2014 data book. State trends in child well-being.* Baltimore, MD: Annie E. Casey Foundation.

Appleby, G.A. (2011). Dynamics of oppression and discrimination. In G.A. Appleby, E. Colon & J. Hamilton (Eds.), *Diversity, oppression, and social functioning* (3rd ed.) (pp. 61–77). Boston: Allyn & Bacon.

Arrington, P. (2008). *Stress at work: How do social workers cope? NASW membership workforce study*. Washington, DC: NASW.

Association for Specialists in Group Work (Singh, A.A., Merchant, N., Skudrzyk, B., Ingene, D., Hutchins, A.M., & Rubel, D.). (2012). *Multicultural and social justice competence principles for group workers*. Available at: http://asgw.org/pdf/ASGW_MC_SJ_Priniciples_Final_ASGW.pdf.

Association of Baccalaureate Social Work Program Directors. (2007). Definition of social work practice 2007. Available at: http://bpdonline.org/.

Association of Social Work Boards. (2012). *Model social work practice act*. Available at: www.aswb.org/wp-content/uploads/2013/10/Model_law.pdf.

Austin, D.M. (1997). The profession of social work in the second century. In M. Reisch & E. Gambrill (Eds.), *Social work in the 21st century* (pp. 396–407). Thousand Oaks, CA: Pine Forge Press.

Baden, B. (2010). Best careers in 2011: Medical and public health social worker. Available at: http://money.usnews.com/money/careers/articles/2010/12/06/best-careers.

Baldino, R.G. (2000). Wearing multiple hats as a social worker. *The New Social Worker, 7*(2), 25.

Barker, R.L. (2014). *The social work dictionary* (6th ed.). Washington, DC: NASW Press.

Barth, R., Birkenmaier, J., & Berg-Weger, M. (2014). Individual microfinance lending: A study in Gros Morne, Haiti. *Social Development Issues, the Journal of the International Consortium of Social Development, 36*(2), 78–92.

Bassuk, E.L., DeCandia, C.J., Beach, C.A. & Berman, F. (2014). *America's youngest outcasts. A report card on child homelessness*. Waltham, MA: National Center on Family Homelessness. Available at: http://homelesschildrenamerica.org/mediadocs/280.pdf.

Bavelas, J., De Jong, P., Franklin, C., Froerer, A., Gingerich, W., Kim, J., Korman, H., Langer, S., Lee, M.Y., McCollum, E.E., Jordan, S.S., & Trepper, T.S. (2013). *Solution focused therapy treatment manual for working with individuals* (2nd version). Available at: http://SFBT_Revised_Treatment_Manual_2013%20(1).pdf.

Begun, A.L. (2013). Alcohol abuse and dependence: The 7 percent problem. In E.F. Hoffler & E.J. Clark (eds.), *Social work matters. The power of linking policy and practice* (pp. 131–136). Washington, DC: NASW Press.

Bell, L.A. (2013). Theoretical foundations. In M. Adams, W.J. Blumenfeld, C. Castañeda, H.W. Hackman, M.L. Peters, & X. Zúñiga (Eds.), *Readings for diversity and social justice* (3rd ed.), (pp. 21–26). New York: Routledge.

Berg, I.K. (2008). Authoritative settings and involuntary clients. In T. Mizrahi & L.E. Davis (Eds.), *Encyclopedia of social work* (20th ed.) (pp. 1:182–184). Washington, DC: NASW Press and Oxford University Press.

Birkenmaier, J., Kennedy, T., Kunz, J., Sander, R. & Horwitz, S. (2013). The role of social work in financial capability: Shaping curricular approaches. In J.M. Birkenmaier, M. Sherraden & J. Curley (Eds), *Financial capability and asset development. Research, education, policy, and practice* (pp. 278–301). New York: Oxford University Press.

Bishaw, A. (2011). *Areas with concentrated poverty: 2006–2010*. Washington, D.C.: U.S. Census Bureau.

Bishaw, A. & Fontenot, K. (2014). Poverty: 2012 and 2013. Washington, DC: U.S. Census Bureau. Available at: www.census.gov/content/dam/Census/library/publications/2014/acs/acsbr13-01.pdf.

Blank, B.T. (1998). Settlement houses: Old idea in new form builds communities. *The New Social Worker, 5*(3), 4–7.

Blank, B.T. (2006). Racism—the challenge for social workers. *The New Social Worker, 13*(4), 10–13.

Blue, E.T. & Kutzler, A.M. (2014). Ethical guidelines for social work supervisors in rural settings. *Contemporary Rural Social Work, 6,* 1–15.

Blundo, R. (2008). Strengths-based framework. In T. Mizrahi & L.E. Davis (Eds.), *Encyclopedia of social work* (20th ed.) (pp. 4:173–177). Washington, DC: NASW Press and Oxford University Press.

Boes, M. & van Wormer, K. (2015). Social work with lesbian, gay, bisexual, and transgendered clients. In K. Corcoran & A.R. Roberts (Eds.), *Social workers' desk reference* (3rd ed.) (pp. 1027–1032). New York: Oxford Press.

Bollig, K. (2009). Personal communication. April 2, 2009.

Borgenschneider, K. & Corbett, T.J. (2010). *Evidence-based policymaking.* New York: Routledge.

Bowles, D.D. & Hopps, J.G. (2014). The profession's role in meeting its historical mission to serve vulnerable populations. *Advances in Social Work, 15*(1), 1–20.

Boykin, S. (2014). Ode to group treatment. *The New Social Worker.* Available at: www.socialworker.com/extras/creative-work/ode-to-group-treatment/.

Briar-Lawson, K. (2012). From a staffing crisis to the building of a national workforce agency for social work. In E.F. Hoffler & E.J. Clark (eds.), *Social work matters. The power of linking policy and practice* (pp. 53–58). Washington, DC: NASW Press.

Briar-Lawson, K. (2014). Building the social work workforce: Saving lives and families. *Advances in Social Work, 15*(1), 21–33.

Brieland, D. (1995). Social work practice: History and evolution. In R.L. Edwards (Ed.), *Encyclopedia of social work* (19th ed.) (pp. 2247–2257). Washington, DC: NASW Press.

Briggs, D. (2012). Diversity rising: Census shows Mormons, nondenominational churches, Muslims spreading out across U.S. Available at: http://blogs.thearda.com/trend/featured/diversity-rising-census-shows-mormons-nondenominational-churches-muslims-spreading-out-across-u-s/.

Brodie, K. & Gadling-Cole, C. (2008). Family group conferencing with African-American families. In C. Waites (Ed.), *Social work practice with African-American families: An intergenerational perspective* (pp. 123–143). New York: Routledge.

Brown, J. (1933). *The rural community and social casework.* New York: Family Welfare Association of America.

Brown, N.W. (2013). *Creative activities for group therapy.* New York: Routledge.

Brueggeman, W.G. (2013). History and context for community practice in North America. In M. Weil, M. Reisch & M.L. Ohmer (Eds) *The handbook of community practice* (2nd ed.) (pp. 27–47). Thousand Oaks, CA: Sage Publications, Inc.

Buila, S. (2010). The NASW *Code of Ethics* under attack: A manifestation of the culture war within the profession of social work. *Journal of Social Work Values and Ethics, 7*(2), 1–8.

Buss, J.A. (2010). Have the poor gotten poorer? The American experience from 1987–2007. *Journal of Poverty, 14,* 183–196.

Butterfield, A.K.J. & Chisanga, B. (2008). Community development. In T. Mizrahi & L.E. Davis (Eds.), *Encyclopedia of social work* (20th ed.) (pp. 1:375–381). Washington, DC: NASW Press and Oxford University Press.

Byers, K.V. (2014). Reemergence of policy practice: A journey back to our roots. *Advances in Social Work, 15*(1), 34–50.

Calhoun, C.J. (2007). *Sociology in America: A History.* Chicago: University of Chicago Press. CareerCast.com. (2014). The best jobs of 2014. Available at: www.careercast. com/jobs-rated/best-jobs-2014m. (2014).

Carnevale, A.P., Cheah, B. & Strohl, J. (2011). *Hard times: Not all college degrees are created equal.* Georgetown: Georgetown University, Center on Education and the Workforce.

Carr, N. (2012). Criminal and juvenile justice. In M. Gray, Midgley, J. & Webb, S.A. (Eds.), *The SAGE Handbook of Social Work* (pp. 597–612). London: Sage.

Casio, T. (2012). Approaching spirituality as a client strength. In *Transcendent worldviews: Understanding spirituality in practice, Families in Society Practice & Policy Focus* (1).

Castañeda, C. & Zúñiga, X. (2013). Introduction to Section 2: Racism. In M. Adams, W.J. Blumenfeld, C. Castañeda, H.W. Hackman, M.L. Peters, & X. Zúñiga (Eds.), *Readings for diversity and social justice* (3rd ed.), (pp. 57–64). New York: Routledge.

Center for Assessment and Policy Development (n.d.). Racial equality. Available at: www.racialequitytools.org/glossary#racial-equity.

Center for Health Workforce Studies & Center for Workforce Studies. (2006). *Licensed social workers in the US, 2004.* Rensselaer, NY: University of Albany School of Public Health Center for Health Workforce Studies and NASW Center for Workforce Studies.

Center on Budget and Policy Priorities. (2009). *American Recovery and Reinvestment Act of 2009: State-by-State estimates of key provisions Affecting Low- and Moderate-Income Individuals.* Washington, DC: Center on Budget and Policy Priorities.

Center on Budget and Policy Priorities. (2014a). *A quick guide to SNAP eligibility and benefits.* Washington, DC: Center on Budget and Policy Priorities. Available at: www. cbpp.org/files/11-18-08fa.pdf.

Center on Budget and Policy Priorities. (2014b). *Chart Book: The legacy of the Great Recession.* Washington, DC: Center on Budget and Policy Priorities. Available at: www.cbpp.org/cms/index.cfm?fa=view&id=3252.

Center on Budget and Policy Priorities. (2014c). New report highlights need for states to help address income inequality. Washington, DC: Center on Budget and Policy Priorities. Available at: www.offthechartsblog.org/?s=Income+inequality.

Centers for Disease Control and Prevention. (2009). Developing process evaluation questions. *Evaluation Briefs, 4.* Available at: www.cdc.gov/healthyyouth/evaluation/ index.htm.

Centers for Disease Control and Prevention. (2010). *10 Essential Public Health Services.* Available at: www.cdc.gov/nphpsp/essentialServices.html.

Centers for Disease Control and Prevention. (2012). Prevalence of autism spectrum disorders—autism and developmental disabilities monitoring network, United States 2008. *Morbidity and Mortal Weekly Report (MMWR) 61*(3).

Central Intelligence Agency (CIA). (2013–2014). *The World Factbook 2013–14.* Washington, DC: Central Intelligence Agency. Available at: https://www.cia.gov/ library/publications/the-world-factbook/index.html.

Chace, W.M. (1989). The language of action. *Wesleyan LXII* (2), 36.

Chambliss, D.F. & Takacs, C.G. (2014). *How college works.* Boston: Harvard University Press.

Chatterjee, P. & Fauble, M. (2008). Toward a mission-based model for social work: A foundation for practice. *Social Work with Groups, 31*(1), 5–23.

Chawla, N., & Solinas-Saunders, M. (2011). Supporting military parent and child adjustment to deployments and separations with filial therapy. *American Journal of Family Therapy, 39,* 179–192.

Chen, H.T. (2006). *Practice program evaluation: Assessing and improving planning, implementation, and effectiveness.* Thousand Oaks, CA: Sage.

Children's Defense Fund. (2014). *The state of America's children 2014.* Available at: www.childrensdefense.org/child-research-data-publications/data/2014-soac.pdf?utm_source=2014-SOAC-PDF&utm_medium=link&utm_campaign=2014-SOAC.

Chowa, G.A.N., De Vera Masa, R., Sherraden, M., & Weil, M. (2013). Confronting global poverty: Building economic opportunity and social inclusion. In M. Weil, M. Reisch & M.L. Ohmer (Eds). The *handbook of community practice* (2nd ed.) (pp. 607–632). Thousand Oaks, CA: Sage Publications, Inc.

Claiborne, N. (2004). Presence of social workers in nongovernment organizations. *Social Work, 49*(2), 207–218.

Clark, E.J. (2003). The future of social work. In R.A. English (Ed.), *Encyclopedia of social work* (19th ed., 2003 supplement) (pp. 61–70). Washington, DC: NASW Press.

Clark, E.J. (2009). *A broader vision for the social work profession.* Washington, DC: NASW.

Clark, E.J. (2012). The business of social work. In E.F. Hoffler & E.J. Clark (Eds.), *Social work matters. The power of linking policy and practice* (pp. 9–13). Washington, DC: NASW Press.

Clark, E.J., Weismiller, T., Whitaker, T., Waller, G.W., Zlotnik, J.L. & Corbett, B. (2006). *2005 social work congress—final report.* Washington, DC: NASW.

Clark, S. (2007). Social work students' perceptions of poverty. *Journal of Human Behavior in the Social Environment,* 16(1/2), 149–166.

Clewes, R. (2001). Experto credite: New social work graduates share their wisdom. *The New Social Worker,* 8(4), 14–16.

Cohen, C.S., Phillips, M.H. & Hanson, M. (2009). *Strength and diversity in social work with groups.* New York: Routledge.

Colby, I.C. (2008). Social welfare policy as a form of social justice. In Sowers, K.M. & Dulmus, C.N. (Eds). *Comprehensive handbook of social work and social welfare* (pp. 113–126). Hoboken, NJ: John Wiley & Sons, Inc.

Colby, S.L. & Ortman, J.M. (2014). The baby boom cohort in the United States: 2012 to 2060. Population estimates and projections. U.S. Census Bureau Current Population Reports. Available at: www.census.gov/prod/2014pubs/p25-1141.pdf.

Coleman-Jensen, A., Gregory, C. & Singh, A. (2014). Household food security in the United States in 2013. Available at: www.ers.usda.gov/media/1565415/err173.pdf.

Collegeboard.com. (2014). Hottest careers for college graduates. Available at: https://bigfuture.collegeboard.org/explore-careers/careers/hottest-careers-for-college-graduates#graduate.

Collins, D. & Coleman, H. (2000). Eliminating bad habits in the social work interview. *The New Social Worker,* 7(4), 12–15.

Collins, J.M. & Birkenmaier, J. (2013). Building the capacity of social workers to enhance financial capability and asset development. In J.M. Birkenmaier, M. Sherraden, & J. Curley (Eds), *Financial capability and asset development. Research, education, policy, and practice* (pp. 302–322). New York: Oxford University Press.

Collins, P.H. (2013). Toward a new vision. Race, class, gender. In M. Adams, W.J. Blumenfeld, C. Castañeda, H.W. Hackman, M.L. Peters, & X. Zúñiga (Eds), *Readings for diversity and social justice* (3rd ed.), (pp. 606–611). New York: Routledge.

Collins, S. (2011). Healthy People 2020: Social work values in a public health roadmap. *NASW Practice Perspectives, 03,* 1–4.

Collins, S. (2013). Strategies for strengthening health care social work in the health reform era. *NASW Practice Perspectives,* 1–4.

Collins, S. (2014). Social work update on the Affordable Care Act: What impact has the law had on those we serve? *NASW Practice Perspectives,* 1–5.

Colon, E., Appleby, G.A. & Hamilton, J. (2011). Affirmative practice with people who are culturally diverse and oppressed. In G.A. Appleby, E. Colon & J. Hamilton (Eds.), *Diversity, oppression, and social functioning: Person-in-environment assessment and intervention* (3rd ed.) (pp. 259–276). Boston, MA: Allyn & Bacon.

Comartin, E.B. & Gonzáles-Prendes, A.A. (2011). Dissonance between personal and professional values: Resolution of an ethical dilemma. *Journal of Social Work Values and Ethics, 8*(2), 51–54.

Concoran, K. & Roberts, A.R. (2015) *Social workers' desk reference* (3rd ed.). New York: Oxford Press.

Congress, E. (1999). *Social work values and ethics: Identifying and resolving professional dilemmas.* Belmont, CA: Wadsworth.

Congress, E.P. (2015). The culturagram. In K. Corcoran, & A.R. Roberts (Eds.), *Social workers' desk reference* (3rd ed.) (pp. 1011–1018). New York: Oxford University Press.

Congress, E.P., Black, N.P. & Strom-Gottfried, K. (2009). *Teaching social work values and ethics? A curriculum resource.* Alexandria, VA: Council on Social Work Education.

Congressional Budget Office. (2013). A description of the immigrant population—2013 update. Available at: www.cbo/publication/44134.

Constantine, M.G., Hage, S.M., Kindaichi, M.M. & Bryant, R.M. (2007). Social justice and multicultural issues: Implications for the practice and training of counselors and counseling psychologists. *Journal of Counseling and Development, 85*(1), 24–29.

Corbett, B.S. (2008). Distinctive dates in social welfare history. In T. Mizrahi & L.E. Davis (Eds.) *Encyclopedia of social work* (20th ed.) (pp. 4:403–424). Washington, DC: NASW Press and Oxford University Press.

Corcoran, J. (2008). Direct practice. In T. Mizrahi & L.E. Davis (Eds.), *Encyclopedia of social work* (20th ed.) (pp. 2:31–36). Washington, DC: NASW Press and Oxford University Press.

Corey, M.S. & Corey, G. (1998) *Becoming a helper* (3rd ed.). Pacific Grove, CA: Brooks/ Cole Thomson Learning.

Council on Social Work Education. (2009). *Guide to the economic stimulus bill.* Available at: www.cswe.org/NR.

Council on Social Work Education. (2010). *Advanced social work practice in military social work.* Alexandria, VA: Council on Social Work Education. Available at: www.cswe. org/File.aspx?id=42466.

Council on Social Work Education. (2011). *Why recruit students to gerontological social work.* Alexandria, VA: CSWE. Available at: www.cswe.org/File.aspx?id=31797.

Council on Social Work Education. (2008, updated 2012). *Educational policy and accreditation standards.* Washington, DC: Council on Social Work Education.

Council on Social Work Education. (2013). *2013 statistics on social work education in the United States: A summary.* Available at: www.cswe.org/File.aspx?id=74478.

Council on Social Work Education. (2014). *Statistics on social work education in the United States: A summary.* Alexandria, VA: CSWE.

Council on Social Work Education. (2015). *Accreditation.* Available at: www.cswe.org/Accreditation.aspx.

Council on Social Work Education/SAGE-SW. (2001). *Strengthening the impact of social work to improve the quality of life for older adults and their families: Blueprint for the new millennium.* Washington, DC: Council on Social Work Education/SAGE-SW.

Cree, V.E. (2013a). Introduction. In V.E. Cree (Ed.). *Becoming a social worker. Global narratives* (2nd ed.) (pp. 1–9). New York: Routledge.

Cree, V.E. (2013b). Social work: A global profession. In V.E. Cree (Ed.). *Becoming a social worker. Global narratives* (2nd ed.) (pp. 212–217). New York: Routledge.

Crisp, B.R. (2014). *Social work and faith-based organizations.* New York: Routledge.

Crocker, R. (2006). *Mrs. Russell Sage: Women's activism and philanthropy in Gilded Age and Progressive Era America.* Blooming, IN: Indiana University Press.

Cummings, S.M. & Adler, G. (2007). Predictors of social workers employment in gerontological work. *Educational Gerontology, 33,* 925–938.

Cummings, S.M., Adler, G. & DeCoster, V.A. (2005). Factors influencing graduate-social-work students' interests in working with elders. *Educational Gerontology, 31,* 643–544.

Curley, J. & Tebb, S. (2010). Sister Jean Abbott. Bringing healing to victims of trauma worldwide. In A. Lieberman (Ed.), *Women in social work who have changed the world,* (pp. 149–163). Chicago, IL: Lyceum Books, Inc.

D'Aprix, A. S. (2005). Ethical decision-making models: A two-phase study (Doctoral dissertation, Case Western Reserve University).

D'Aprix, A.S., Boynton, L.A., Carver, B. & Urso, C. (2001). When the ideal meets the real: Resolving ethical dilemmas in the real world. *The New Social Worker, 8*(2), 20–23.

Dabelko-Schoeny, H., Phillips, G., Darrough, E., DeAnna, S., Jarden, M., Johnson, D. & Lorch, G. (2014). Equine-assisted interventions for people with dementia. *Anthrozoös, 27*(1), 141–155.

Dale, M. (2011). Building resilience after disaster. *NASW News, 56*(8).

Dale, M.L. (2001). Your summer vacation—or is it? The value of experiential learning as part of the new social worker's career campaign. *The New Social Worker, 8*(1), 4–6.

Daley, M.R. (2010). A conceptual model for rural social work. *Contemporary Rural Social Work, 2,* 1–7.

Daly, M. (2012). Gender and welfare. In M. Gray, Midgley, J. & Webb, S.A. (Eds.), *The SAGE handbook of social work* (pp. 81–93). London: Sage Publications, Ltd.

Daniel, C.L. (2008). From liberal pluralism to critical multiculturalism: The need for a paradigm shift in multicultural education for social work practice in the United States. *Journal of Progressive Human Services, 19*(1), 19–38.

Davies, S. (2012). Embracing reflective practice. *Education for Primary Care, 23*(1), 9–12.

Dedman, D.E. (2014). Connecting with Hull House. *The New Social Worker.* Available at: www.socialworker.com/feature-articles/practice/connecting-with-hull-house/.

DeFilippis, J. & Saegert, S. (2012a). Communities develop. The question is, how? In J. DeFilippis & S. Saegert (Eds), *The community development reader* (2nd ed.) (pp. 1–7). New York: Routledge.

DeFilippis, J. & Saegert, S. (2012b). Concluding thoughts. In J. DeFilippis & S. Saegert (eds)., *The community development reader* (2nd ed.) (pp. 377–382). New York: Routledge.

De Jong, P. (2008). Interviewing. In T. Mizrahi & L.E. Davis (Eds.), *Encyclopedia of social work* (20th ed.) (pp. 2:539–542). Washington, DC: NASW Press and Oxford University Press.

De Jong, P. (2015). Solution-focused therapy. In K. Corcoran & A.R. Roberts (Eds.), *Social workers' desk reference* (3rd ed.) (pp. 268–275). New York: Oxford Press.

De Jong, P. & Berg, I.K. (2013). *Interviewing for solutions* (4th ed.). Belmont, CA: Brooks/ Cole.

De Jong, P. & Cronkright, A. (2011). Learning solution-focused interviewing skills: BSW student voices. *Journal of Teaching in Social Work, 31,* 21–37.

DeNavas-Walt, C. & Proctor, B.D. (2014). *Income and poverty in the United States: 2013. U.S. Census Bureau, current population reports, P60-249.* Washington, DC: U.S. Government Printing Office. Available at: www.census.gov/content/dam/Census/ library/publications/2014/demo/p60-249.pdf.

DeNavas-Walt, C., Proctor, B.D. & Smith, J.C. (2011). *Income, poverty, and health insurance coverage in the United States: 2010. U.S. Census Bureau, current population reports* (pp. 60–239). Washington, DC: U.S. Government Printing Office.

DeNavas-Walt, C., Proctor, B.D. & Smith, J.C. (2013). *Income, poverty, and health insurance coverage in the United States: 2012. U.S. Census Bureau, current population reports.* Washington, DC: U.S. Government Printing Office. Available at: www.census.gov/ prod/2013pubs/p60-245.pdf.

de Shazer, S. (1982). *Patterns of brief family therapy: An ecosystemic approach.* New York: The Guilford Press.

de Shazer, S., Dolan, Y., Korman, Trepper, T., McCollum, E. & Berg, I.K. (2007). *More than miracles: The state of the art of solution-focused therapy.* Binghamton, NY: Haworth Press.

Dietsche, S.I. (2014). Shining a light on the dark side of adolescence: The role of school social workers in protecting youth at-risk. *NASW Practice Perspectives, 1–6.*

Diller, J.V. (2015). *Cultural diversity: A primer for the human services* (5th ed.). Stamford, CT: Cengage Learning.

Dolgoff, R., Loewenberg, F.M. & Harrington, D. (2009). *Ethical decisions for social work practice* (8th ed.). Belmont, CA: Thomson Brooks/Cole.

Dolgoff, R., Loewenberg, F.M. & Harrington, D. (2012). *Ethical decisions for social work. practice* (9th ed.). Belmont, CA: Thomson Brooks/Cole.

Dominelli, L. (2008). Group work: A critical addition to the social work repertoire. In Sowers, K.M. & Dulmus, C.N. (Eds) *Comprehensive handbook of social work and social welfare* (pp. 473–487). Hoboken, NJ: John Wiley & Sons, Inc.

Dominelli, L. (2012). Anti-oppressive practice. In M. Gray, J. Midgley, & S.A. Webb, (Eds.), *The SAGE handbook of social work* (pp. 328–340). London: Sage Publications, Ltd.

Drake, M. (2014). How social workers can change the world. Care2. Available at: www. care2.com/causes/how-social-workers-can-change-the-world.html.

Duggan, M. (2014). *On line harassment.* Washington, DC: Pew Research Center. Available at: www.pewinternet.org/2014/10/22/online-harassment/.

Dunlap, K.M. & Strom-Gottfried, K. (1998). Everyday ethics and values for social workers (part 1 in a series on ethics). *The New Social Worker, 5*(1), 16–18.

Dunn, C. (2002). The importance of cultural competence for social workers. *The New Social Worker, 9*(2), 4–5.

Dunn, J.H., Flory, B.E., Berg-Weger, M. & Milstead, M. (2004). An exploratory study of supervised access and custody exchange services: The children's experience. *Family Court Review, 42*(1), 60–73.

Early, J. & Newsome, W.S. (2005). Measures for assessment and accountability in practice with families from a strengths perspective. In J. Corcoran, *Building strengths and skills: A collaborative approach to working with clients* (pp. 359–393). NY: Oxford University Press.

Eldercare Workforce Alliance. (2011). *Geriatrics workforce shortage: A looming crisis for our families.* Washington, DC. Available at: www.eldercareworkforce.org/research/issue-briefs/research:geriatrics-workforce-shortage-a-looming-crisis-for-our-families/.

Elliott, D. & Segal, U.A. (2012). Immigrants and refugees. In M. Gray, J. Midgley, & S.A. Webb, (Eds.), *The SAGE handbook of social work* (pp.564–578). London: Sage Publications, Ltd.

Ellis, R.A. (2008). Policy practice. In Sowers, K.M. & Dulmus, C.N. (Eds). *Comprehensive handbook of social work and social welfare* (pp. 129–143). Hoboken, NJ: John Wiley & Sons, Inc.

Ephross, P.H., & Greif, G.L. (2009). Group process and group work techniques. In A.R. Roberts & J. Watkins (Eds.), *Social workers' desk reference* (2nd ed.) (pp. 679–685). New York: Oxford University Press.

Fall, K.A. (2013). *Group counseling. Process and technique.* New York: Routledge.

Fass, S., Dinan, K.A., & Aratani, Y. (2009). *Child poverty and intergenerational mobility.* New York: Columbia University: National Center for Children in Poverty.

Federal Bureau of Investigation. (2013). FBI releases 2012 hate crime statistics. Washington, DC: Federal Bureau of Investigation. Available at: www.fbi.gov/about-us/cjis/ucr/hate-crime/2012/resource-pages/summary/summary_final.pdf.

Feeding America. (2012). *Map the meal gap. Child food insecurity 2012.* Chicago, IL: Feeding America. Available at: http://feedingamerica.org/hunger-in-america/hunger-studies/map-the-meal-gap/~/media/Files/a-map-2010/2010-MMG-Child-Executive-Summary-FINAL.ashx?.pdf.

Feeding America. (2014). Child hunger facts. Chicago, IL: Feeding America. Available at: http://feedingamerica.org/hunger-in-america/hunger-facts/child-hunger-facts. aspx.

Feehan, D.M., Feit, M.D. & Becker, C. (2013). Community economic and social development in a changing world. In M. Weil, M. Reisch, & M.L. Ohmer (Eds). The *handbook of community practice* (2nd ed.) (pp. 495–513). Thousand Oaks, CA: Sage Publications, Inc.

Fink-Samnick, E. (2011). Understanding care coordination: Emerging opportunities for social workers. *The New Social Worker, 18*(3), 18–21.

Fisher, R., DeFilippis, J., & Shragge, E. (2012). History matters: Canons, anti-canons, and critical lessons from the past. In J. DeFilippis & S. Saegert (Eds.), *The community development reader* (2nd ed.) (pp. 191–200). New York: Routledge.

Flory, B.E., & Berg-Weger, M. (2003). Children of high conflict custody disputes: Striving for social justice in adult focused litigation. *Social Thought, 22*(2/3). (Also published in Stretch, J.J., Burkemper, E.M., Hutchison, W.J. & Wilson, J. (2003). *Practicing justice* (pp. 205–219). New York: Haworth Press.)

Flory, B.E., Dunn, J., Berg-Weger, M. & Milstead, M. (2001). An exploratory study of supervised access and custody exchange services: The parental experience. *Family and Conciliation Court Review, 39*(4), 469–482.

Floyd, M. & Gruber, K.J. (2011). Baccalaureate student perceptions of challenging family problems: Building bridges to acceptance. *Journal of Teaching in Social Work, 31*, 65–78.

Foppe, J. (2002). *What's Your Excuse? Making the Most of What You Have.* Nashville, TN: Thomas Nelson, Inc.

Forte, J.A. (2014a). *An introduction to using theory in social work practice*. New York: Routledge.

Forte, J.A. (2014b). *Skills for using theory in social work*. New York: Routledge.

Frumkin, M., & Lloyd, G.A. (1995). Social work education. In R.L. Edwards (Ed.), *Encyclopedia of social work* (19th ed.) (pp. 2238–2246). Washington, DC: NASW Press.

Fry, R. (2013). Decline in young adult home acquisition. In R. Fry, *Pew Research Center Young adults after the recession: fewer homes, fewer cars, less debt*. Available at: www.pewsocialtrends.org/files/2013/02/Financial_Milestones_of_Young_Adults_FINAL_2-19.pdf.

Fry, R. (2014). In post-recession era, young adults drive continuing rise in multi-generational living. Pew Research Social & Demographic Trends. Available at: www.pewsocialtrends.org/2014/07/17/in-post-recession-era-young-adults-drive-continuing-rise-in-multi-generational-living/.

Fuchs, D.M. (2008). Assessment of communities. In K.M. Sowers, & C.N. Dulmus, (Eds). *Comprehensive handbook of social work and social welfare* (pp. 488–504). Hoboken, NJ: John Wiley & Sons, Inc.

Furman, J. & Parrott, S. (2007). *A $7.25 minimum wage would be a useful step in helping working families escape poverty*. Washington, DC: Center on Budget and Policy Priorities.

Furman, R., Bender, K. & Rowan, D. (2014). *An experiential approach to group work*. Chicago, IL: Lyceum Books.

Gabrielson, M.L. & Holston, E.C. (2014). Broadening definitions of family for older lesbians: Modifying the Lubben Social Network Scale. *Journal of Gerontological Social Work, 57*, 198–217.

Gale, L. (2012). Lessons from Hull House. *The New Social Worker, 19*(2), 18–19.

Gambino, C.P., Acosta, Y.D. & Grieco, E.M. (2014). English-speaking ability of the foreign-born population in the United States: 2012. American Community Survey Briefs. Available at: www.census.gov/library/publications/2014/acs/acs-26.html.

Gamble, D.N. (2012). Well-being in a globalized world: Does social work know how to make it happen? *Journal of Social Work Education, 48*(4), 669–689.

Gambrill, E. (2012). Behavioural perspectives**.** In M. Gray, J. Midgley, & S.A. Webb, (Eds.), *The SAGE handbook of social work* (pp.143–160). London: Sage Publications, Ltd.

Garran, A.M. & Rozas, L.W. (2013). Culture competence revisited. *Journal of Ethnic & Cultural Diversity in Social Work, 22*, 97–111.

Garvin, C.D., & Galinsky, M.J. (2008). Groups. In T. Mizrahi & L.E. Davis (Eds.), *Encyclopedia of social work* (20th ed.) (pp. 2: 287–298). Washington, DC: NASW Press and Oxford University Press.

Gates, T. (2006). Challenging heterosexism: Six suggestions for social work practice. *The New Social Worker, 13*(3), 4–5.

Geist, T.S. (2011). Conceptual framework for animal assisted therapy. *Child and Adolescent Social Work, 28*, 243–256.

Gerdes, K.E. (2011). Empathy, sympathy, and pity: 21st century definitions and implications for practice and research. *Journal of Social Service Research, 37*, 230–241.

Germain, C. B. (1973). Ecological perspective in case work practice. *Social Casework, 54*(6), 323–330.

Germain, C.B. & Gitterman, A. (1980). *The life model of social work practice*. New York: Columbia University Press.

Germain, C.B. & Gitterman, A. (1995). Ecological perspective. In R.L. Edwards (Ed.), *Encyclopedia of social work* (19th ed.) (pp. 816–824). Washington, DC: NASW Press.

Gibelman, M. (2005). *What social workers do* (2nd ed.). Washington, DC: NASW Press.

Gil, D.G. (2012). Social work, social policy, and welfarism. In M. Gray, J. Midgley, & S.A. Webb, (Eds.), *The SAGE handbook of social work* (pp. 19–32). London: Sage Publications, Ltd.

Ginsberg, L. (2011). Introduction to basic concepts of rural social work. In L. Ginsberg (Ed.), *Social work in rural communities* (5th ed.) (pp. 5–20). Alexandria, VA: CSWE Press.

Ginsberg, L. (2014). The origins and future of rural social work. *Advances in Social Work, 15*(1), 105–116.

Ginsberg, L.H. (2001). *Careers in social work* (2nd ed.). Boston, MA: Allyn & Bacon.

Gitterman, A., & Germain, A. (2008). Ecological framework. In T. Mizrahi & L.E. Davis (Eds.), *Encyclopedia of social work* (20th ed.) (pp. 2:97–102). Washington, DC: NASW Press and Oxford University Press.

Glaze, L.E. & Herberman, E.J. (2013). Correctional population in the United States, 2012 (NCJ 243936). Available at: www.bjs.gov/index.cfm?ty=pbdetail&iid=4843.

Golden, G.K. (2008). White privelege and the mental health profession. *The New Social Worker, 15*(2), 4–5.

Goode, T.D., & Jones, W. (2006). *A definition of linguistic competence.* Washington, DC: Georgetown University National Center for Cultural Competence.

Goodwin, J. (n.d.). Mother's pension. *Encyclopedia of Chicago.* Available at: www.encyclopedia.chicagohistory.org/pages/845.html.

Granich, S. (2012). Duty to warn, duty to protect. *The New Social Worker, 19*(1), 4–7.

Green, G.P., & Haines, A. (2002). *Asset building in community development.* Thousand Oaks, CA: Sage Publications.

Grinnell, R.M., Unrau, Y.A. & Gabor, P. (2008). Program evaluation. In T. Mizrahi & L.E. Davis (Eds.), *Encyclopedia of social work* (20th ed.) (pp. 3:429–434). Washington, DC: NASW Press and Oxford University Press.

Grobman, L.M. (2005a). *Days in the lives of social workers: 54 professionals tell real-life stories from social work practice.* Harrisburg, PA: White Hat Communications.

Grobman, L.M. (2005b). *More days in the lives of social workers.* Harrisburg, PA: White Hat Communications.

Grobman, L.M. (2007). *Days in the lives of gerontological social workers.* Harrisburg, PA: White Hat Communications.

Hagen, J.L., & Lawrence, C.K. (2008). Temporary assistance to needy families. In T. Mizrahi & L.E. Davis (Eds.), *Encyclopedia of social work* (20th ed.) (pp. 4:225–229). Washington, DC: NASW Press and Oxford University Press.

Halabuza, D. (2014). Guidelines for social workers' use of social networking websites. *Journal of Social Work Values & Ethics, 11*(1), 23–32.

Hall, E. & Lindsey, S. (2014). Teaching cultural competence: A closer look at racial and ethnic identity formation. *The New Social Worker, 21*(3), 4–5.

Harriman, K.K. & Blount, C. (2014). The Affordable Care Act and social work field education: A shifting landscape. *Field Educator, 4.1*, 1–4.

Hart-Landsberg, M. (2014). Minimum wage hikes work. *The Society Pages.* Available at: http://thesocietypages.org/socimages/2014/10/09/minimum-wage-hikes-work/.

Hartman, A. (1978). Diagrammatic assessment of family relationships. *Social Casework, 59,* 465–476.

Herman, C. (2014). Economic insecurity among older adults. *(NASW) Practice Perspectives*. Washington, DC: NASW, pp. 1–4.

Hernandez, V.R. (2008). Generalist and advanced generalist practice. In T. Mizrahi & L.E. Davis (Eds.), *Encyclopedia of social work* (20th ed.) (pp. 2: 260–268). Washington, DC: NASW Press and Oxford University Press.

Hernandez Palacio, C.M. (2014). The magnificence of the social work profession. *The New Social Worker*. Available at: www.socialworker.com/extras/creative-work/the-magnificence-of-the-social-work-profession/.

HIPAASpace. (2011). "Social worker" professionals availability ratio by state. Available at: www.hipaaspace.com/Medical.Statistics/Healthcare.Professionals.Availability/Social%20Worker/201112.

History of Social Work. (2009). Available at: www.historyofsocialwork.org.

Hodge, D.R. (2010). Social justice as a unifying theme in social work education: Principles to realize the promise of a new pedagogical model. *Journal of Comparative Social Welfare, 26*(2–3), 201–213.

Hoefer, R. (2011). Highly effective human services interest groups. *Journal of Community Practice*, 9(2), 1–14.

Hoffler, E.F. (2012). Reinvesting in the profession to secure the future. In E.F. Hoffler & E.J. Clark (eds.), *Social work matters. The power of linking policy and practice* (pp. 39–45). Washington, DC: NASW Press.

Hoffler, E.F. & Clark, E.J. (2012). Social media for social workers: An imperative for the profession. In E.F. Hoffler & E.J. Clark (eds.), *Social work matters. The power of linking policy and practice* (pp. 14–19). Washington, DC: NASW Press.

Hoffman, K.S., Lubben, J.E., Ouellette, P.M., Westhuis, D., Shaffer, G.L., Hutchison, E.D., Alvarez, A.R., Biegel, D.E. & Colby, I.C. (2008). Social work education: Overview. In T. Mizrahi & L.E. Davis (Eds.), *Encyclopedia of social work* (20th ed.) (pp. 4:107–137). Washington, DC: NASW Press and Oxford University Press.

Hokayem, C. & Heggeness, M.L. (2014). *Living in near poverty in the United States: 1966-2012. Current Population Reports, P60-248*. U.S. Census Bureau, Washington, DC Available at: www.census.gov/prod/2014pubs/p60-248.pdf.

Hollister, M. (2011). Employment stability in the U.S. labor market: Rhetoric versus reality. *Annual Review of Sociology, 37,* 305–324.

Hooyman, N.R. (2012). Older people. In M. Gray, J. Midgley, & S.A. Webb, (Eds.), *The SAGE handbook of social work* (pp. 531–546). London: Sage Publications, Ltd.

Hopps, J.G., & Collins, P.M. (1995). Social work profession overview. In R.L. Edwards (Ed.), *Encyclopedia of social work* (19th ed.) (pp. 2266–2282). Washington, DC: NASW Press.

Hopps, J.G. & Lowe, T.B. (2008). The scope of social work practice. In Sowers, K.M. & Dulmus, C.N. (eds). *Comprehensive handbook of social work and social welfare* (pp. 37–62). Hoboken, NJ: John Wiley & Sons, Inc.

Hopps, J.G., Lowe, T.B., Stuart, P.H., Weismiller, T., & Whitaker, T. (2008). Social work profession. In T. Mizrahi & L.E. Davis (Eds.) *Encyclopedia of social work* (20th ed.) (pp. 4,138–168). Washington, DC: NASW Press and Oxford University Press.

Horejsi, C.R. (2002). Social and economic justice: The basics. *The New Social Worker,* 9(4), 10–12.

Houtrow, A.J., Larson, K., Olson, L.M., Newacheck, P.W. & Halfon, N. (2014). Changing trends of childhood disability, 2001-2011. *Pediatrics, 134*(3), 530.

Howden, L.M., & Meyer, J.A. (2011). *Age and sex composition: 2010.* Washington, DC: U.S. Census Bureau.

Howe, E. & Hamilton, J. (2011). African Americans: Consequences of discrimination. In G.A. Appleby, E. Colon & J. Hamilton (Eds.), *Diversity, oppression, and social functioning. Person-in-environment assessment and intervention* (3rd ed.) (pp. 78–89). Boston, MA: Allyn & Bacon.

Hugman, R. (2012). Human rights and social justice. In M. Gray, J. Midgley, & S.A. Webb, (Eds.), *The SAGE handbook of social work* (pp. 372–385). London: Sage Publications, Ltd.

Hugman, R., Moosa-Mitha, M., & Moyo, O. (2013). Towards a borderless social work: Reconsidering notions of international social work. *International Social Work, 53*(5), 629–643.

Humes, K.R., Jones, N.A., & Ramirez, R.R. (2011). Overview of race and Hispanic origin: 2010 Census brief no. 2. Available at: www.census.gov/prod/cen2010/briefs/c2010br-02.pdf.

Hunte, S. (2014). Social work professional discovery: Find your niche. *The New Social Worker.* Available at: www.socialworker.com/feature-articles/practice/social-work-professional-discovery-find-your-niche/.

Iatridis, D.S. (2008). Policy practice. In T. Mizrahi & L.E. Davis (Eds.), *Encyclopedia of social work* (20th ed.) (pp. 3:362–368). Washington, DC: NASW Press and Oxford University Press.

International Association for Social Work with Groups, Inc. (2010). *Standards for social work practice with groups.* Available at: www.iaswg.org/Practice_Standards.

International Association of Schools of Social Work (IASSW), International Council on Social Welfare (ICSW), & International Federation of Social Workers (IFSW). (2014). Global agenda for social work and social development: First report–promoting social and economic equalities. *International Social Work, 57*(S4), 3-16. Available at: http://cdn.ifsw.org/assets/ifsw_23031-6.pdf.

International Federation of Social Work. (n.d.). *What we do.* Available at: http://ifsw.org/what-we-do/.

International Federation of Social Work. (2012). *Statement of ethical principles.* Available at: http://ifsw.org/policies/statement-of-ethical-principles/.

International Federation of Social Work & International Association of Schools of Social Work. (2004, updated in 2012). Statement of ethical principles. Available at : http://ifsw.org/policies/statement-of-ethical-principles/.

Institute for Women's Policy Research. (2014). The gender wage gap: 2013. Differences by race and ethnicity. Available at: file:///C:/Users/bergwm/Downloads/C423-wage%20gap%20Sept.%202014.pdf.

Investopedia. (n.d.). Gini Index. Available at: www.investopedia.com/terms/g/gini-index.asp.

Irwin, N., Miller, C.C. & Sanger-Katz, M. (2014, August 19). America's racial divide, charted. *The New York Times.* Available at: htttp://nyti/ms/1o022St.

Jack, G. (2012). Ecological perspective. In M. Gray, J. Midgley, & S.A. Webb, (Eds.), *The SAGE handbook of social work* (pp. 129–142). London: Sage Publications, Ltd.

Jackson, K.F., & Samuels, G.M. (2011). Multiracial competence in social work: Recommendations for culturally attuned work with multiracial people. *Social Work, 56*(3), 235–245.

Jenson, J.M., & Howard, M.O. (2008). Evidence-based practice. In T. Mizrahi & L.E.

Davis (Eds.), *Encyclopedia of social work* (20th ed.) (pp. 2:158–165). Washington, DC: NASW Press and Oxford University Press.

Johnson, A.G. (2013). What can we do? In M. Adams, W.J. Blumenfeld, C. Castañeda, H.W. Hackman, M.L. Peters, & X. Zúñiga (Eds.), *Readings for diversity and social justice* (3rd ed.), (pp. 612–618). New York: Routledge.

Jordan, C. (2008). Assessment. In T. Mizrahi & L.E. Davis (Eds.), *Encyclopedia of social work* (20th ed.) (pp. 1:178–180). Washington, DC: NASW Press and Oxford University Press.

Kagle, J.D. (2009). Record-keeping. In A.R. Roberts & J. Watkins (Eds.), *Social workers' desk reference* (2nd ed.) (pp. 28–32). New York: Oxford University Press.

Kane, M.N. (2008). When I'm 75 years old: Perceptions of social work students. *Social Work in Health Care, 47*(2), 185–213.

Kelly, M.S. (2008). Task-centered practice. In T. Mizrahi & L.E. Davis (Eds.), *Encyclopedia of social work* (20th ed.) (pp. 4:197–199). Washington, DC: NASW Press and Oxford University Press.

Kendall, K.A. (2000). *Social work education: Its origins in Europe.* Alexandria, VA: Council on Social Work Education.

Kincel, B. (2014). The centenarian population: 2007–2011. American Community Survey Briefs. Available at: www.census.gov/prod/2014pubs/acsbr12-18.pdf.

Kindle, P.A. (2006). The inherent value of social work. *The New Social Worker, 13*(4), 17.

King, M.L. Jr. (1963, June 23). Speech at the Great March on Detroit.

Knitter, P.F. (2010). Social work and religious diversity: Problems and possibilities. *Journal of Religion & Spirituality in Social Work, 29*, 256–270.

Kochhar, R. (2014). 10 projections for the global population in 2050. Washington, DC: Pew Research Center. Available at: www.pewresearch.org/author/rkochhar/.

Kohli, H.K., Huber, R., & Faul, A.C. (2010). Historical and theoretical development of culturally competent social work practice. *Journal of Teaching in Social Work, 30,* 252–271.

Kondrat, M.E. (2008). Person-in-environment. In T. Mizrahi & L.E. Davis (Eds.), *Encyclopedia of social work* (20th ed.) (pp. 3:348–354). Washington, DC: NASW Press and Oxford University Press.

Krogstad, J.M. (2014). Number of Latino children caught trying to enter U.S. nearly doubles in less than a year. Washington, DC: Pew Research Center. Available at: www.pewresearch.org/fact-tank/2014/06/10/number-of-latino-children-caught-trying-to-enter-u-s-nearly-doubles-in-less-than-a-year/.

Kubiak, S.P. & Fedock, G. (2013). Policy and practices affecting those involved in the criminal justice system. In E.F. Hoffler & E.J. Clark (Eds.), *Social work matters. The power of linking policy and practice* (pp. 111–117). Washington, DC: NASW Press.

Kurland, R. (2007). Debunking the "blood theory" of social work with groups: Group workers *are* made and not born. *Social Work with Groups, 30*(1), 11–24.

Lalayants, M., Doel, M., & Kachkachishvili, I. (2013). Pedagogy of international social work: A comparative study in the USA, UK, and Georgia. *European Journal of Social Work, 17*(4), 1–20.

Larson, M.J., Wooten, N.R., Adams, R.S. & Merrick, E.L. (2012). Military combat deployments and substance use: Review and future directions. *Journal of Social Work Practice with Addictions, 12*, 6–27.

Lavers, M.K. (2014). Report: LGBT Americans more likely to live in poverty.

Washington Blade. Available at: www.washingtonblade.com/2014/09/29/report-lgbt-americans-likely-live-poverty/.

Leachman, M., & Mai, C. (2011). *New CBO report finds up to 2.4 million people owe their jobs to the Recovery Act.* Washington, DC: Center for Budget and Policy Priorities.

Leachman, M., Williams, E., & Johnson, N. (2011). *Governors are proposing further deep cuts in services, likely harming their economies. Less-harmful alternatives include revenue increases and rainy day funds.* Washington, DC: Center for Budget and Policy Priorities.

Lee, J. & Foreman, K. (2014). *U.S. naturalizations: 2013. Annual flow report.* Department of Homeland Security Office of Immigration Statistics. Available at: www.dhs.gov/sites/default/files/publications/ois_natz_fr_2013.pdf.

Lei, S. (2013). *The unwaged war on deep poverty.* Washington, DC: Urban Institute. Available at: www.urban.org/deeppoverty/.

Leicht, K.T. & Fitzgerald, S.T. (2014). *Middle class meltdown in America. Causes, consequences, and remedies* (2nd ed.). New York: Routledge.

Leighninger, L. (2000). *Creating a new profession: The beginnings of social work education in the United States.* Alexandria, VA: Council on Social Work Education.

Leighninger, L. (2008). The history of social work and social welfare. In Sowers, K.M. & Dulmus, C.N. (eds). *Comprehensive handbook of social work and social welfare* (pp. 1–23). Hoboken, NJ: John Wiley & Sons, Inc.

Lens, V. & Garfinkel, I. (2012). Inequality, social welfare policy, and social work. In E.F. Hoffler & E.J. Clark (eds.), *Social work matters. The power of linking policy and practice* (pp. 191–197). Washington, DC: NASW Press.

Levin, K.G. (2009). Involuntary clients (engagement processes). In A. Gitterman & R. Salmon (Eds.), *Encyclopedia of social work with groups* (pp. 287–290). New York: Routledge.

Ley, T. (2012). New technologies for practice. In M. Gray, J. Midgley, & S.A. Webb, Eds.), *The SAGE handbook of social work* (pp. 677–692). London: Sage Publications, Ltd.

Littrell, J. (2011). How addiction happens, how change happens, and what social workers need to know to be effective facilitators of change. *Journal of Evidence-Based Social Work, 8,* 469–486.

Logan, S.M.L. (2003). Issues of multiculturalism: Multicultural practice, cultural diversity, and competency. In R.A. English (Ed.), *Encyclopedia of social work* (19th ed., 2003 supplement) (pp. 95–105). Washington, DC: NASW Press.

Logan, S.L., Rasheed, M.N. & Rasheed, J.M. (2008). Family. In T. Mizrahi & L.E. Davis (Eds.), *Encyclopedia of social work* (20th ed.) (pp. 2:175–182). Washington, DC: NASW Press and Oxford University Press.

Long, S.K., Karpman, M., Kenney, G.M., Zuckerman, S., Wissoker, D., Shartzer, A., Anderson, N. & Hempstead, K. (2015). Taking stock: Gains in health insurance coverage under the ACA as of March 2015. Washington, D.C.: Urban Institute. Available at: http://hrms.urban.org/briefs/Gains-in-Health-Insurance-Coverage-under-the-ACA-as-of-March-2015.html.

Longres, J.E. (2008). Hopkins, Harry Lloyd (1890–1946). In T. Mizrahi & L.E. Davis (Eds.), *Encyclopedia of social work* (20th ed.) (p. 4:339). Washington, DC: NASW Press and Oxford University Press.

Longres, J.E. (2008b). Richmond, Mary Ellen (1861–1928). In T. Mizrahi & L.E. Davis (Eds.), *Encyclopedia of social work* (20th ed.) (p. 4:368). Washington, DC: NASW Press and Oxford University Press.

Lundgren, L. & Krull, I. (2014). The Affordable Care Act: New opportunities for social work to take leadership in behavioral health and addiction treatment. *Journal of the Society for Social Work and Research, 5*(4), 415–438.

Lusk, M. (2013). Immigration: Linking policy to practice. In E.F. Hoffler & E.J. Clark (eds.), *Social work matters. The power of linking policy and practice* (pp. 203–208). Washington, DC: NASW Press.

Lynch, D. & Vernon, R. (2001). You will need a social worker . . . For free distribution information visit: http://hsmedia.biz.

Mackelprang, R.W. (2012). Disability. In M. Gray, J. Midgley, & S.A. Webb, (Eds.), *The SAGE handbook of social work* (pp. 547–563). London: Sage Publications, Ltd.

Mackelprang, R.W. (2013). If I go to work, I will die: The impact of health policy on disability rights. In E.F. Hoffler & E.J. Clark (Eds.), *Social work matters. The power of linking policy and practice* (pp. 137–142). Washington, DC: NASW Press.

Mackelprang, R.W., Patchner, L.S., DeWeaver, K.L., Clute, M.A., & Sullivan, W.P. (2008). Disability. In T. Mizrahi & L.E. Davis (Eds.), *Encyclopedia of social work* (20th ed.) (pp. 2:36–60). Washington, DC: NASW Press and Oxford University Press.

Mackelprang, R.W., & Salsgiver, R.O. (2009). *Disability: A diversity model approach in human service practice* (2nd ed.). Chicago, IL: Lyceum Books.

Mackie, P.F. (2011). Rural social work recruitment and retention challenges: Why is it difficult to fill rural social work positions?. In L. Ginsberg (Ed.), *Social work in rural communities* (5th ed.) (pp. 141–160). Alexandria, VA: CSWE Press.

Mackun, P., & Wilson, S. (2011). *Population distribution and change: 2000 to 2010.* Washington, DC: U.S. Census Bureau.

Malai, R. (2014). Minors need link to services. *NASW News, 59*(9), 1,4.

Mama, R.S. (2008). Social policy from a global perspective. . In Sowers, K.M. & Dulmus, C.N. (eds). *Comprehensive handbook of social work and social welfare* (pp. 13–19). Hoboken, NJ: John Wiley & Sons, Inc.

Maramaldi, P., Sobran, A., Scheck, L., Cusato, N., Lee, I., White, E., & Cadet, T.J. (2014). Interdisciplinary medical social work: A working taxonomy. *Social Work in Health Care, 53*(6), 532–551.

Marson, S.M., & MacLeod, E.H. (1996). The first social worker. *The New Social Worker, 3*(2), 11.

Martin, D.C. & Yankay, J.E. (2012). *Refugees and asylees: 2013. Annual flow report.* Washington, DC: Department of Homeland Security Office of Immigration Statistics. Available at: www.dhs.gov/xlibrary/assets/statistics/publications/ois_rfa_fr_2011. pdf.

Martin, J. I., & D'Augelli, A. R.. (2012). Timed lives: Cohort and period effects in research on sexual orientation and gender identity. In W. Meezan and J. I. Martin (Eds.), *Handbook of research on gay, lesbian, bisexual, and transgender populations.* New York: Haworth Press.

Martinez-Brawley, E. (1983). *Seven decades of rural social work.* New York: Praeger.

Maschi, T. & Killian, M.L. (2011). The evolution of forensic social work in the United States: Implication for 21st century practice. *Journal of Forensic Social Work, 1,* 8–36.

Mason, S.E. (2012). The Occupy Movement and social justice economics. *Families in Society: The Journal of Contemporary Social Services, 93*(1), 3–4.

Mason, S.E. (2014). Preventing poverty: A call for collaboration. *Families in Society: The Journal of Contemporary Social Services, 95*(4), 223–225.

Massachusetts General Hospital. (n.d.) Social service history. Available at: www. mghpcs.org/socialservice/History.asp.

Matto, H. (2012). Drug and alcohol interventions. In M. Gray, J. Midgley, & S.A. Webb, (Eds.), *The SAGE handbook of social work* (pp. 579–596). London: Sage Publications, Ltd.

McAuliffe, D. (2010). Ethical decision-making. In M. Gray, & S.A. Webb, (Eds), *Ethics and value perspectives in social work (pp. 41–50)*. New York: Palgrave Macmillan.

McAuliffe, D. (2012). Ethical decision making. In M. Gray, J. Midgley, & S.A. Webb, (Eds.), *The SAGE handbook of social work* (pp. 316–327). London: Sage Publications, Ltd.

McCasland, D. (2014). Home from the war: Reflections on Memorial Day. *The New Social Worker, 21*(3), 14–15.

McLaughlin, A. (2007). How to snag a job in international social work. *The New Social Worker, 14*(2), 26–27.

McLaughlin, A.M. (2009). Clinical social workers: Advocates for social justice. *Advances in Social Work, 10*(1), 51–68.

McNutt, J., & Floersch, J. (2008). Social work practice. In T. Mizrahi & L.E. Davis (Eds.), *Encyclopedia of social work* (20th ed.) (pp. 4:138–144). Washington, DC: NASW Press and Oxford University Press.

McPartlin, T.K. (2006). Notes from the Gulf: A social worker reflects on hurricane relief. *The New Social Worker, 13*(1), 18–23.

Meckler, L. (2014, June 26). Americans' generational race gap gets wider. *Wall Street Journal*. Available at: http://online.wsj.com/articles/americans-generational-race-gap-grows-wider-1403755263.

Meruvia, R.T. (2014). Caught in the middle: Supporting families involved with immigration and child welfare systems. *(NASW) Practice Perspectives*. Washington, DC: NASW.

Midgley, J. (2010). Social development. In T. Fitzpatrick, H. Kwon, N. Manning, J. Midgley & G. Pascall (Eds.), *International encyclopedia of social policy* (pp. 1236–1241). London: Routledge.

Midgley, J. (2012). Welfare and social development. In M. Gray, J. Midgley, & S.A. Webb, (Eds.), *The SAGE handbook of social work* (pp. 94–107). London: Sage Publications, Ltd.

Miller, S.E. (2013). Professional socialization: A bridge between the explicit and implicit curricula. *Journal of Social Work Education, 49*, 368–386.

Miller, W. R. & Rollnick, S. (2013). *Motivational interviewing: Helping people change*. New York, NY: Guilford.

Milligan, S.E. (2008). Community building. In T. Mizrahi & L.E. Davis (Eds.), *Encyclopedia of social work* (20th ed.) (pp. 1:371–375). Washington, DC: NASW Press and Oxford University Press.

Minahan, A. (1981). Purpose and objectives of social work revisited. *Social Work, 26*(1), 5–6.

Mindell, C.L. (2007). Religious bigotry and religious minorities. In G.A. Appleby, E. Colon, & J. Hamilton (Eds.), *Diversity, oppression, and social functioning: Person-in-environment assessment and intervention* (2nd ed.) (pp. 226–246). Boston, MA: Allyn & Bacon.

Mishel, L., Bivens, J., Gould, E., & Shierholz, H. (2012). *The state of working America* (12th ed.). Ithaca, NY: Cornell University Press.

Mishna, F., Bogo, M., Root, J. & Fantus, S. (2014). Here to stay: Cyber communication as a complement in social work practice. *Families in Society: The Journal of Contemporary Social Services, 95*(3), 179–186.

Mitchell, L., Walters, R., Thomas, M.L., Denniston, J., McIntosh, H. & Brodowski, M. (2012). The Children's Bureau vision for the future of child welfare. *Journal of Public Child Welfare, 6*, 550–567.

Mizrahi, T. (2015). Community organizing principles and practice guidelines. In K. Corcoran & A.R. Roberts (Eds.), *Social workers' desk reference* (3rd ed.) (pp. 894–906). New York: Oxford University Press.

Mizrahi, T. & Davis, L.E. (2008). *Encyclopedia of social work* (20th ed.). Washington, DC: NASW Press and Oxford University Press.

Mondros, J. (2013). Political, social, and legislative actions. In M. Weil, M. Reisch, & M.L. Ohmer (Eds). *The handbook of community practice* (2nd ed.) (pp. 345–361). Thousand Oaks, CA: Sage Publications, Inc.

Mondros, J.B. (2009). Principles and practice guidelines for social action. In A.R. Roberts & J. Watkins (Eds.), *Social workers' desk reference* (2nd ed.) (pp. 901–906). New York: Oxford University Press.

Monger, R. & Yankay, J. (2014). *U.S. lawful permanent residents: 2013. Annual Flow Report.* Washington, DC: Department of Homeland Security Office of Immigration Statistics. Available at: www.dhs.gov/sites/default/files/publications/ois_lpr_fr_2013.pdf.

Movement Advancement Project (MAP), Family Equality Council (FEC) and Center for American Progress. (2011). All children matter: How legal and social inequalities hurt LGBT families (including two companion reports: *LGBT families of color: Facts at a glance* (2012) and *Obstacles and opportunities: Ensuring health and wellness for LGBT families* (2011). Available at: Available at: http://action.familyequality.org/site/PageS erver?pagename=AllChildren.

Mulroy, E.A. (2008). Community needs assessment. In T. Mizrahi & L.E. Davis (Eds.), *Encyclopedia of social work* (20th ed.) (pp. 1:385–387). Washington, DC: NASW Press and Oxford University Press.

NASW Foundation. (n.d.). NASW Social Work Pioneers. Available at: www.naswfoundation.org/pioneers/default.asp.

National Association of Black Social Workers. (n.d.). *Code of ethics.* Available at: www.nabsw.org/mserver/CodeofEthics.aspx.

National Association of Social Workers. (n.d.) Top ten reasons to be a social worker. Washington, DC:NASW.

National Association of Social Workers. (n.d.a). Definitions. Available at: www.socialworkers.org/practice/intl/definitions.asp.

National Association of Social Workers. (n.d.b). History of the Social Work Code of Ethics. Available at: www.socialworkers.org/nasw/ethics/ethicshistory.asp.

National Association of Social Workers. (n.d.c). *Issue fact sheets. Diversity and cultural competence.* Available at: www.naswdc.org.

National Association of Social Workers. (n.d.d). *Social work profession.* Available at: www.socialworkers.org/pressroom/features/general/profession.asp.

National Association of Social Workers. (n.d.e). *Social work profession and issue fact sheets.* Available at: www.naswdc.org.

National Association of Social Workers. (1973). *Standards for social service manpower.* Washington, DC: NASW.

National Association of Social Workers. (1998). *Milestones in the development of social work and social welfare.* Washington, DC: National Association of Social Workers.

National Association of Social Workers. (2005). *NASW standards for social work practice in health care settings.* Washington, DC: NASW Press.

National Association of Social Workers. (2006–2009). *Health care. Social work speaks: National Association of Social Workers policy statements 2006–2009*. Washington, DC: NASW Press.

National Association of Social Workers. (2007). *Indicators for the achievement of the NASW standards for cultural competence in social work practice*. Washington, DC: NASW.

National Association of Social Workers. (2008). *Code of ethics*. Washington, DC: NASW. Available at: www.naswdc.org

National Association of Social Workers. (2009). *Training curriculum for child welfare services with lesbian, gay, bisexual, transgender, and questioning (LGBTQ) youth in out-of-home care*. Washington, DC: National Association of Social Workers.

National Association of Social Workers. (2009–2012a). *Economic policy. Social work speaks: National Association of Social Workers policy statements 2009–2012*. Washington, DC: NASW Press.

National Association of Social Workers. (2010). *2010 Social Work Congress final report*. Available at: www.socialworkers.org/2010congress/documents/FinalCongress-StudentReport.pdf.

National Association of Social Workers. (2012a). *NASW standards for social work practice with service members, veterans, & their families*. Washington, DC: NASW.

National Association of Social Workers. (2012b). *NASW Standards for school social work services*. Washington, DC: NASW Press.

National Association of Social Workers. (2012c). Social Work Month 2012. Available at: www.socialworkers.org.

National Association of Social Workers. (2012–2014a). *Confidentiality and information utilization. Social work speaks: National Association of Social Workers policy statements 2012–2014* (9th ed.). Washington, DC: NASW Press.

National Association of Social Workers. (2012–2014b). *Cultural and linguistic competence in the social work profession. Social work speaks: National Association of Social Workers policy statements 2012–2014* (9th ed.). Washington, DC: NASW Press.

National Association of Social Workers. (2012c). Social Work Month 2012. Available at www. social workers.org.

National Association of Social Workers. (2012–2014c). *Deprofessionalization and reclassification. Social work speaks: National Association of Social Workers policy statements 2012–2014* (9th ed.). Washington, DC: NASW Press.

National Association of Social Workers. (2012–2014d). *Disasters. Social work speaks: National Association of Social Workers policy statements 2012–2014* (9th ed.). Washington, DC: NASW Press.

National Association of Social Workers. (2012–2014e). *Environment policy. Social work speaks: National Association of Social Workers policy statements 2012–2014* (9th ed.). Washington, DC: NASW Press.

National Association of Social Workers. (2012–2014f). *Immigrant and refugees. Social work speaks: National Association of Social Workers policy statements 2012–2014* (9th ed.). Washington, DC: NASW Press.

National Association of Social Workers. (2012–2014g). *Language and cultural diversity in the United States. Social work speaks: National Association of Social Workers policy statements 2012–2014* (9th ed.). Washington, DC: NASW Press.

National Association of Social Workers. (2012–2014h). *Lesbian, gay, and bisexual issues. Social work speaks: National Association of Social Workers policy statements 2012–2014* (9th ed.). Washington, DC: NASW Press.

National Association of Social Workers. (2012–2014i). *People with disabilities. Social work* speaks: *National Association of Social Workers policy statements 2012–2014* (9th ed.). Washington, DC: NASW Press.

National Association of Social Workers. (2012–2014j). *Poverty and economic justice. Social work speaks: National Association of Social Workers policy statements 2012–2014* (9th ed.). Washington, DC: NASW Press.

National Association of Social Workers. (2012–2014k). *Public child welfare. Social work speaks: National Association of Social Workers policy statements 2012–2014* (9th ed.). Washington, DC: NASW Press.

National Association of Social Workers. (2012–2014l). *Racism. Social work speaks: National Association of Social Workers policy statements 2012–2014* (9th ed.). Washington, DC: NASW Press.

National Association of Social Workers. (2012–2014m). *Social work in the criminal justice system. Social work speaks: National Association of Social Workers policy statements 2012–2014* (9th ed.). Washington, DC: NASW Press.

National Association of Social Workers. (2012–2014n). *Transgender and gender identity issues. Social work speaks: National Association of Social Workers policy statements 2012–2014* (9th ed.). Washington, DC: NASW Press.

National Association of Social Workers. (2012–2014o). *Welfare reform. Social work speaks: National Association of Social Workers policy statements 2012–2014* (9th ed.). Washington, DC: NASW Press.

National Association of Social Workers. (2012–2014p). *Women's issues. Social work speaks: National Association of Social Workers policy statements 2012–2014* (9th ed.). Washington, DC: NASW Press.

National Association of Social Workers. (2013a). *NASW standards for social work case management.* Washington, DC: NASW Press.

National Association of Social Workers. (2013b). *NASW standards for social work practice in child welfare.* Washington, DC: NASW Press.

National Association of Social Workers. (2013c). *NASW standards for social work practice with clients with substance use disorders.* Washington, DC: NASW Press.

National Association of Social Workers. (2013d). *Social workers in Congress.* Available at: www.socialworkers.org/pace/swcongress/2013swcongress.pdf.

National Association of Social Workers. (2014). *Unaccompanied migrant children: Overview & recommendations.* Washington, DC: NASW. Available at: www.social-workblog.org/wp-content/uploads/Unaccompanied-Migrant-Children.pdf.

National Association of Social Workers. (2015). *Ethics 8 series: 8 social media and technology tips for social workers.* Washington, DC: NASW. Available at: https://www.socialworkers.org/nasw/ethics/ethics8series/social_media.asp.

National Association of Social Workers and Association of Social Work Boards. (2005). *NASW and ASWB standards for technology and social work practice.* Washington, DC: NASW Press.

National Association of Social Workers Center for Workforce Studies. (n.d.). Workforce planning. Available at: workforce.socialworkers.org/planning.asp.

National Association of Social Workers Center for Workforce Studies. (2004). *"If you're right for the job, it's the best job in the world." NASW Child Welfare Specialty Section members describe their experiences in child welfare.* Available at: www.socialworkers.org/practice/children/NASWChildWelfareRpt062004.pdf.

National Association of Social Workers Center for Workforce Studies. (2005). *Assuring the sufficiency of a frontline workforce: A national study of licensed social workers.* Washington, DC: NASW.

National Association of Social Workers Center for Workforce Studies. (2007). *More money—less money: Factors associated with the highest and lowest social work salaries.* Washington, DC: National Association of Social Workers.

National Association of Social Workers Center for Workforce Studies. (2010a). *NASW 2009 compensation and benefits study. Summary of key findings.* Washington, DC: National Association of Social Workers. Available at: workforce.socialworkers.org/8-SalarySurvey.pdf

National Association of Social Workers Center for Workforce Studies and Social Work Practice. (2010b). *Social workers in schools (kindergarten through 12th grade). Occupational profile.* Washington, DC: National Association of Social Workers.

National Association of Social Workers Center for Workforce Studies and Social Work Practice. (2011a). *Social workers in health clinics and outpatient health care settings. Occupational profile.* Washington, DC: National Association of Social Workers.

National Association of Social Workers Center for Workforce Studies and Social Work Practice. (2011b). *Social workers in hospital and medical centers. Occupational profile.* Washington, DC: National Association of Social Workers.

National Association of Social Workers Center for Workforce Studies and Social Work Practice. (2011c). *Social workers in mental health clinics and outpatient facilities. Occupational profile.* Washington, DC: National Association of Social Workers.

National Association of Social Workers Center for Workforce Studies and Social Work Practice. (2011d). *Social work salaries by gender. Occupational profile.* Washington, DC: National Association of Social Workers.

National Association of Social Workers Center for Workforce Studies and Social Work Practice. (2011e). *Social work salaries by race & ethnicity. Occupational profile.* Washington, DC: National Association of Social Workers.

National Association of Social Workers Center for Workforce Studies and Social Work Practice. (2011f). *Social work salaries by race & ethnicity. Occupational profile.* Washington, DC: National Association of Social Workers.

National Association of Social Workers Legal Defense Fund. (2011 & 2012). *Social workers and skype—Parts I and II.* Available at: https://www.socialworkers.org/ldf/legal_issue/2011/112011.asp?back=yes.

National Association of Social Workers Office of Ethics and Professional Review (n.d.). *Ethical Decision Making Framework—DECISIONS Approach.* Available at: www.social-workers.org/nasw/ethics/resourcesliterature.asp.

National Association of Social Workers President's Initiative. (2007). *Institutional racism and the social work profession: A call to action.* Washington, DC: NASW Press.

National Conference for Community and Justice—St. Louis Region. (2002). Action continuum: From discrimination to respect. Developed by Roni Branding, St. Louis, MO.

National Conference of State Legislatures. (2014). State minimum wages/2014 minimum wage by state. Available at: www.ncsl.org/research/labor-and-employment/state-minimum-wage-chart.aspx.

National Institutes of Health. (2014). Estimates of funding for various research, condition, and disease categories (RCDC). Available at: http://report.nih.gov/categorical_spending.aspx.

National Law Project. (2012). Federal minimum wage. Available at: www.nelp.org/content/content_issues/category/federal_minimum_wage/.

National Registry of Evidence-Based Programs and Practices (NREPP). (2014). *Solution-focused brief therapy.* Available at: www.nrepp.samhsa.gov/ViewIntervention. aspx?id=281.

Nichols, M.P. (2011). *The essentials of family therapy* (5th ed.). Boston: Allyn & Bacon.

Nicks, D. (2014, August 18). How Ferguson went from middle class to poor in a generation. *Time Magazine.* Available at: http://time.com/3138176/ferguson-demographic-change/.

Nobisch, A. (2014). Personal communication. October 1, 2014.

Noss, A. (2014). *Household income: 2013. American Community Survey* Briefs. Washington, DC: U.S. Census Bureau. Available at: www.census.gov/prod/2013pubs/acsbr12-01. pdf.

Nurius, P.S. & Macy, R.J. (2008). Cognitive-behavioral theory. In K.M. Sowers, & C.N. Dulmus, (Eds). *Comprehensive handbook of social work and social welfare* (pp. 101–133). Hoboken, NJ: John Wiley & Sons, Inc.

Nwosu, C., Batalova, J., & Auclair, G. (2014). *Frequently requested statistics on immigrants and immigration in the United States.* Washington, DC: Migration Policy Institute. Available at: www.migrationpolicy.org/article/frequently-requested-statistics-immigrants-and-immigration-united-states.

O'Hare, T. (2009). *Essential skills of social work practice. Assessment, intervention, and evaluation.* Chicago, IL: Lyceum Books.

Ohmer, M.L. & Brooks, F. (2013). The practice of community organizing: Comparing and contrasting conflict and consensus approaches. In M. Weil, M. Reisch & M.L. Ohmer (Eds). *The handbook of community practice* (2nd ed.) (pp. 233–249). Thousand Oaks, CA: Sage Publications, Inc.

Okun, B.F., Fried, J. & Okun, M.L. (1999). *Understanding diversity: A learning-as-practice primer.* Pacific Grove, CA: Brooks/Cole.

Olson, C.J., Reid, C., Threadgill-Goldson, N., Riffe, H.A., & Ryan, P.A. (2013). Voices from the field: Social workers define and apply social justice. *Journal of Progressive Human Services, 24,* 23–42.

Omi, M. & Winant, H. (2015). *Racial formation in the United States.* New York: Routledge.

Open Society Foundations. (2010). *Defining the addiction treatment gap: Data summary.* New York: Open Society Foundations.

Ortman, J.M., Velkoff, V.A., & Hogan, H. (2014). *An aging nation: The older population in the United States. Current Population Reports, P25-1140.* U.S. Census Bureau, Washington, DC Available at: www.census.gov/content/dam/Census/library/publications/2014/demo/p25-1140.pdf.

Osei-Hwedie, K. & Rankopo, M.J. (2012). Social work in "developing" countries. In M. Gray, J. Midgley, & S.A. Webb, (Eds.), *The SAGE handbook of social work* (pp. 723–739). London: Sage Publications, Ltd.

Paraquad. (n.d.). Words with dignity. Available at: www.paraquad.org.

Parrott, S. (2008). *Recession could cause large increases in poverty and push millions into deep poverty.* Washington, DC: Center on Budget and Policy Priorities.

Parrott, S. (2014). *Commentary: War on Poverty: Large positive impact, but more work remains.* Washington, DC: Center on Budget and Policy Priorities. Available at: www. cbpp.org.

Pawar, M. (2012). Regional perspectives. In K. Lyons, T. Hokenstad, M. Pawar, N. Huegler, & N. Hall (Eds.), *The Sage handbook of international social work,* (pp. 389–392). Thousand Oaks, CA: Sage Publications, Inc.

Peck, S. (1999). Who are we? *The New Social Worker, 6*(1), 4–6.

Peebles-Wilkins, W. (2008). Wells-Barnett, Ida Bell. In T. Mizrahi & L.E. Davis (Eds.), *Encyclopedia of social work* (20th ed.) (pp. 4:385). Washington, DC: NASW Press and Oxford University Press.

Perron, B.E., & Powell, T. J. (2009). Online groups. In A. Gitterman & R. Salmon (Eds.) *Encyclopedia of social work with groups* (pp. 311–314). New York: Routledge.

Pew Research Center for the People & the Press. (2014). Political polarization in the American public. Washington, DC: Pew Research Center. Available at: www.people-press.org/2014/06/12/section-3-political-polarization-and-personal-life/.

Pew Research Center Hispanic Trends Project. (2013). *A nation of immigrants: A portrait of the 40 million, including 11 million unauthorized.* Available at: www.pewhispanic. org./2013/01/29/a-nation-of-immigrants/.

Pew Research Global Attitudes Project. (2014a). Emerging and developing economies much more optimistic than rich countries about the future. Available at: www. pewglobal.org/2014/10/09/emerging-and-developing-economies-much-more-optimistic-than-rich-countries-about-the-future/.

Pew Research Global Attitudes Project. (2014b). Global population estimates by age, 1950-2050. Available at:www.pewglobal.org/2014/01/30/global-population/.

Pew Research Global Attitudes Project. (2014c). Middle Easterners see religious and ethnic hatred as top global threat. Available at: www.pewglobal.org/2014/10/16/middle-easterns-see-religious-and-ethnic-hatred-as-top-global-threat/.

Pew Forum on Religion and Public Life. (2008). U.S. religious landscape survey. Religious affiliation: Diverse and dynamic. Washington, DC: Pew Forum on Religion and Public Life. Available at: http://religions.pewforum.org/pdf/report-religious-landscape-study-full.pdf.

Pew Research Religion and Public Life Project. (2014a). Gay marriage around the world. Available at:www.pewforum.org/2013/12/19/gay-marriage-around-the-world-2013/.

Pew Research Religion and Public Life Project. (2014a). Religious hostilities reach a six-year high. Available at: www.pewforum.org/2014/01/14/religious-hostilities-reach-six-year-high/.

Phillips, A., Quinn, A., & Heitkamp, T. (2010). Who wants to do rural social work? Student perceptions of rural social work practice. *Contemporary Rural Social Work, 2,* 51–65.

Poirier, J. M., Fisher, S. K., Hunt, R. A., & Bearse M. (2013). *A guide for understanding, supporting, and arming LGBTQ12-S children, youth, and families.* Washington, DC: American Institutes for Research. A Guide for Understanding, Supporting, and Affirming LGBTQI2-S Children, Youth, and Families.

Pollard, W.L. (2008). Civil rights. In T. Mizrahi & L.E. Davis (Eds.), *Encyclopedia of social work* (20th ed.) (pp. 1:301–309). Washington, DC: NASW Press and Oxford University Press.

Polowy, C.I., Morgan, S., Bailey, W.D. & Gorenberg, C. (2008). Confidentiality and privileged communication. In T. Mizrahi & L.E. Davis (Eds.), *Encyclopedia of social work* (20th ed.) (pp. 1:408–415). Washington, DC: NASW Press and Oxford University Press.

Preston-Shoot, M. & Höjer, S. (2012). Social work, social justice, and protection: A reflective review. In K. Lyons, T. Hokenstad, M. Pawar, N. Huegler & N. Hall (Eds.), *The Sage handbook of international social work*, (pp. 249–264). Thousand Oaks, CA: Sage Publications, Inc.

ProCon.org. (2015). *Gay marriage. Pros and cons.* Available at: http://gaymarriage. procon.org/view.timeline.php?timeline.

Pullen-Sansfaçon, A. (2011). Ethics and conduct in self-directed groupwork: Some lessons for the development of a more ethical social work practice. *Ethics and Social Welfare, 5*(4), 361–379.

Pyles, L. (2014). *Progressive community organizing: Reflective practice in a globalizing world* (2nd ed.). New York: Routledge.

Quam, J.K. (2008a). Brace, Charles Loring. In T. Mizrahi & L.E. Davis (Eds.), *Encyclopedia of social work* (20th ed.) (pp. 4:325–326). Washington, DC: NASW Press and Oxford University Press.

Quam, J.K. (2008b). Dix, Dorthea Lynde. In T. Mizrahi & L.E. Davis (Eds.), *Encyclopedia of social work* (20th ed.) (p. 4:334). Washington, DC: NASW Press and Oxford University Press.

Quam, J.K. (2008c). Perkins, Frances. In T. Mizrahi & L.E. Davis (Eds.), *Encyclopedia of social work* (20th ed.) (pp. 4:364–365). Washington, DC: NASW Press and Oxford University Press.

Quam, L. (2008). Addams, Jane (1860–1935). In T. Mizrahi & L.E. Davis (Eds.), *Encyclopedia of social work* (20th ed.) (pp. 4:318–319). Washington, DC: NASW Press and Oxford University Press.

Racial Equity Tools. (n.d.) Glossary. Available at: www.racialequitytools.org/ glossary#racism.

Rank, M.R. (2004). *One nation, underprivileged: Why American poverty affects us all.* New York: Oxford University Press.

Rank, M.R. (2006). Toward a new understanding of American poverty. *Journal of Law and Policy, 20*(17), 17–51.

Rank, M.R. (2008). Poverty. In T. Mizrahi & L.E. Davis (Eds.), *Encyclopedia of social work* (20th ed.) (pp. 3:387–395). Washington, DC: NASW Press and Oxford University Press.

Rank, M.R. (2009). Measuring the economic racial divide across the course of American lives. *Race and Social Problems, 1,* 57–66.

Rank, M.R. (2013). Poverty in America is mainstream. *The New York Times Opinionator,* November 2, 2013.

Rank, M.R. (2014). Why poverty and inequality undermine justice in America. In M. Reisch (Ed.), *Routledge international handbook of social justice* (pp. 436–447). New York, NY: Routledge.

Rank, M.R., & Hirschl, T.A. (2001a). The occurrence of poverty across the life cycle: Evidence from the PSID. *Journal of Policy Analysis and Management, 20*(4), 737–755.

Rank, M.R., & Hirschl, T.A. (2001b). Rags or riches? Estimating the probabilities of poverty and affluence across the adult American life span. *Social Science Quarterly, 82*(4), 651–669.

Rank, M.R. & Hirschl, T.A. (2002). Welfare use as a life course event: Toward a new understanding of the U.S. safety net. *Social Work, 47*(3), 237–248.

Rank, M.R. & Hirschl, T.A. (2009). Estimating the risk of food stamp use and impoverishment during childhood. *Archives of Pediatrics and Adolescent Medicine, 163,* 994–999.

Rapp. C.A. & Sullivan, W.P. (2014). The strengths model: Birth to toddlerhood. *Advances in Social Work, 15*(1), 129–142.

Ratts, M.J., Anthony, L. & Santos, K.N.T. (2010). The dimensions of social justice model: Transforming traditional group work into a socially justice framework. *Journal for Specialists in Group Work, 35*(2), 160–168.

Razack, N. (2012). International social work. In M. Gray, J. Midgley, & S.A. Webb, (Eds.), *The SAGE handbook of social work* (pp. 707–722). London: Sage Publications, Ltd.

Reamer, F.G. (2001). *Ethics education in social work.* Alexandria, VA: Council on Social Work Education.

Reamer, F.G. (2006). *Ethical standards in social work.* Washington, DC: NASW Press.

Reamer. F.G. (2008a). Ethics and values. In T. Mizrahi & L.E. Davis (Eds.), *Encyclopedia of social work* (20th ed.) (pp. 2:143–151). Washington, DC: NASW Press and Oxford University Press.

Reamer, F.G. (2008b) Ethical standards in social work: The NASW Code of Ethics. In T. Mizrahi & L.E. Davis (Eds.), *Encyclopedia of social work* (20th ed.) (pp. 4:391–397). Washington, DC: NASW Press and Oxford University Press.

Reamer, F.G. (2009). *The social work ethics casebook: Cases and commentary.* Washington, DC: NASW Press.

Reamer, F.G. (2012). Code of Ethics. In M. Gray, J. Midgley, & S.A. Webb, (Eds.), *The SAGE handbook of social work* (pp. 299–315). London: Sage Publications, Ltd.

Reamer, F.G. (2013a). Reforming criminal justice: From practice to policy. (2013). In E.F. Hoffler & E.J. Clark (Eds.), *Social work matters: The power of linking policy and practice* (pp. 118–122). Washington, DC: NASW Press.

Reamer, F.G. (2013b). *Social work values and ethics* (4th ed.). New York: Columbia University Press.

Reamer, F.G. (2014). The evolution of social work ethics: Bearing witness. *Advances in Social Work, 15*(1), 163–181.

Reamer, F.G. (2015). Ethical issues in social work. In K. Corcoran & A.R. Roberts (Eds.), *Social workers' desk reference* (3rd ed.) (pp. 143–148). New York: Oxford Press.

Recovery Act. (2012). Available at: www.recovery.gov/About/Pages/The_Act.aspx.

Reid, P.N. (1995). Social welfare history. In R.L. Edwards (Ed.), *Encyclopedia of social work* (19th ed.) (pp. 2206–2225). Washington, DC: NASW Press.

Reisch, M. (1997). The political context of social work. In M. Reisch & E. Gambrill (Eds.), *Social work in the 21st century* (pp. 80–92). Thousand Oaks, CA: Pine Forge Press.

Reisch, M. (2000). Social work and politics in the new century. *Social Work, 45*(4), 293–297.

Reisch, M. (2008). Intervention with communities. In K.M. Sowers, & C.N. Dulmus, (Eds). *Comprehensive handbook of social work and social welfare* (pp. 505–529). Hoboken, NJ: John Wiley & Sons, Inc.

Reisch, M. (2013). Community practice challenges in the global economy. In M. Weil, M. Reisch & M.L. Ohmer (Eds.). *The handbook of community practice* (2nd ed.) (pp. 47–73). Thousand Oaks, CA: Sage Publications, Inc.

Reisch, M. (2015). Legislative advocacy to empower oppressed and vulnerable groups. In K. Corcoran & A.R. Roberts (Eds.), *Social workers' desk reference* (3rd ed.) (pp. 920–927). New York: Oxford University Press.

Reisch, M., Ife, J. & Weil, M. (2013). Social justice, human rights, values, and community practice. In M. Weil, M. Reisch & M.L. Ohmer (Eds). *The handbook of community practice* (2nd ed.) (pp. 73–103). Thousand Oaks, CA: Sage Publications, Inc.

Reisch, M., & Jarman-Rohde, L. (2000). The future of social work in the United States: Implications for field education. *Journal of Social Work Education, 36*(2), 201–214.

Responsible Reform for the Middle Class. (2010). Patient Protection and Affordable Care Act. Available at: http://dpc.senate.gov/healthreformbill/health bill04.pdf.

Robinson, D. (2013). Policy and practice in rural social work. In E.F. Hoffler & E.J. Clark (Eds.), *Social work matters. The power of linking policy and practice* (pp. 97–102). Washington, DC: NASW Press.

Rock, B.D. (2009). Social work in health care for the 21st century. In A.R. Roberts (Ed.), *Social workers' desk reference* (2nd ed.) (pp. 10–15). New York: Oxford University Press.

Rome, S.H. (2008). Forensic social work. In T. Mizrahi & L.E. Davis (Eds.), *Encyclopedia of social work* (20th ed.) (pp. 2:221–223). Washington, DC: NASW Press and Oxford University Press.

Rothman, J. (2008). Multi mode of community intervention. In J. Rothman, J. Erlich & J. Tropman (Eds.), *Strategies of community intervention* (7th ed.) (pp. 141–170). Peosta, IA: Eddie Bowers.

Rubin, A. (2014). Evidence-based practice empowers practitioners: A response to Epstein. *Research on Social Work Practice*, 1–3.

Ruffing, K.A., & Horney, J.R. (2011). *Economic downturn and Bush policies continue to drive large projected deficits. Economic recovery measures, financial rescues have only temporary impact.* Washington, DC: Center for Budget and Policy Priorities.

Sager, J.S. (2008). Social planning. In T. Mizrahi & L.E. Davis (Eds.), *Encyclopedia of social work* (20th ed.) (pp. 4:56–61). Washington, DC: NASW Press and Oxford University Press.

Saint Louis University Marketing and Communications. (n.d.). *Guidelines for writing a strong commentary.* St. Louis, MO: Saint Louis University Marketing and Communications.

Saleebey, D. (1996). The strengths perspective in social work practice: Extensions and cautions. *Social Work, 41*(3), 296–305.

Saleebey, D. (2006). *The strengths perspective in social work practice* (4th ed.). Boston, MA: Allyn & Bacon.

Saleebey, D. (2008). The strengths perspective: putting possibility and hope to work in our practice. In K.M. Sowers, & C.N. Dulmus, (Eds) *Comprehensive handbook of social work and social welfare* (pp. 123–142). Hoboken, NJ: John Wiley & Sons, Inc.

Sandoval, D.A., Rank, M.R. & Hirschl, T.A. (2009). The increasing risk of poverty across the American life course. *Demography, 46*(4), 717–737.

Sargent Shriver National Poverty Law Center. (n.d.). Available at: www.povertylaw.org/.

Schlesinger, E.G. & Devore, W. (1995). Ethnic-sensitive practice. In R.L. Edwards (Ed.), *Encyclopedia of social work* (19th ed.) (pp. 902–908). Washington, DC: NASW Press.

Schneider, R. (2002). Influencing "state" policy: Social work arena for the 21st century. *The Social Policy Journal, 1*(1), 113–116.

Schott, L. (2008). *Summary of final TANF rules. Some improvement around the margins.* Washington, DC: Center on Budget and Policy Priorities.

Schott, L. & Pavetti, L. (2011). *Many states cutting TANF benefits harshly despite high unemployment and unprecedented need.* Washington, DC: Center on Budget and Policy Priorities.

Seccombe, K. (1999). *"So you think I drive a Cadillac?" Welfare recipients' perspectives on the system and its reform.* Boston, MA: Allyn & Bacon.

Segal, E.A. (2007). *Social welfare policy and social programs: A values perspective.* Belmont, CA: Thomson Brooks/Cole.

Senkowsky, S. (1996). Social work's religious roots. *The New Social Worker, 3*(2), 10.

Senreich, E. (2013). An inclusive definition of spirituality for social work education and practice. *Journal of Social Work Education, 49,* 548–563.

Sensoy Ö. & DiAngelo, R. (2012). *Is everyone really equal? An introduction to key concepts in social justice education.* New York & London: Teachers College Press.

Sfiligoj, H. (2009). New technology transforming profession, *NASW News, 54*(4), 4.

Shanks, T.R.W. (2012). Helping low-income families obtain economic security: The value of local partnerships. In E.F. Hoffler & E.J. Clark (Eds.), *Social work matters. The power of linking policy and practice* (pp. 209–215). Washington, DC: NASW Press.

Sheafor, B.W. (2014). The professionalization of baccalaureate-level social work. *Advances in Social Work, 15*(1), 196–206.

Sherman, A. (2014). 2009 Recovery Act kept millions out of poverty. Washington, DC: Center on Budget Policy & Priorities. Available at: www.offthechartsblog.org/?s=20 09+Recovery+Act+kept+millions+out+of+poverty.

Sherman, A., Greenstein, R. & Parrott, S. (2008). *Poverty and share of Americans without health insurance were higher in 2007—and median income for working-age households was lower than at bottom of last recession.* Washington, DC: Center for Budget and Policy Priorities.

Sherman, A. & Trisi, D. (2014). *Deep poverty among children worsened in welfare law's first decade.* Washington, DC: Center on Budget and Policy Priorities. Available at: www. cbpp.org/files/7-23-14pov2.pdf.

Sherman, A., Trisi, D. & Broaddus, M. (2014). Poverty fell and health coverage improved in 2013, but economic recovery is slow to reach many: median income rose for families with children but not overall. Washington, DC: Center on Budget and Policy Priorities. Available at: www.cbpp.org/files/9-22-14pov.pdf.

Sherraden, M. (1990). *Assets and the poor: A new American welfare policy.* Armonk, NY: M.E. Sharp.

Sherraden, M.S. (2008). Community economic development. In T. Mizrahi & L.E. Davis (Eds.), *Encyclopedia of social work* (20th ed.) (pp. 1:381–385). Washington, DC: NASW Press and Oxford University Press.

Sherraden, M.S. (2013). Building blocks of financial capability. In J.M. Birkenmaier, M. Sherraden & J. Curley (Eds), *Financial capability and asset development. Research, education, policy, and practice* (pp. 3–43). New York: Oxford University Press.

Sidell, N.L. (2011). *Social work documentation. A guide to strengthening your case recording.* Washington, DC: NASW Press.

Simmons, B.M. (2012). Evidence-based practice, person-in-environment, and clinical social work: Issues of practical concern. *Smith College Studies in Social Work, 82,* 3–18.

Simmons, C.S., Diaz, L., Jackson, V. & Takahashi, R. (2008). NASW cultural competency indicators: A new tool for the social work profession. *Journal of Ethnic and Cultural Diversity in Social Work, 17*(1), 4–20.

Singh, A.A. & Salazar, C.F. (2011). Conclusion: Six considerations for social justice group work. In A.A. Singh & C.F. Salazar (Eds.), *Social justice in group work: Practical interventions for change* (pp. 213–222). London: Routledge.

Sisneros, J., Stakeman, C., Joyner, M.C. & Schmitz, C.L. (2008). *Critical multicultural social work.* Chicago, IL: Lyceum Books, Inc.

Sites, W., Chaskin, R.J., & Parks, V. (2012). Reframing community practice in the 21st century. Multiple traditions, multiple challenges. In J. DeFilippis & S. Saegert (Eds). *The community development reader* (2nd ed.) (pp. 38–47). New York: Routledge.

Smith, C.J. (2009). Hard times steer some toward social work. Available at: http://blog/syracus.com/progress_impact/2009/02.

Smith, J.C. & Medalia, C. (2014). *Health insurance in the United States: 2013. Current Population Reports,* U.S. Department of Commerce, Economics and Statistics Administration. Available at: www.census.gov/content/dam/Census/library/publications/2014/demo/p60-250.pdf.

Smith, D.B. & Shields, J. (2013). Factors related to social service workers' job satisfaction: Revisiting Herzber's motivation to work. *Administration in Social Work, 37,* 189–198.

Social Work Policy Institute. (2011). *Investing in the social work workforce.* Washington, DC: National Association of Social Workers.

Social Work Policy Institute. (2014). *Achieving racial equity: Calling the social work profession to action.* Washington, DC: NASW. Available at: www.socialworkpolicy.org/wp-content/uploads/2014/05/SWPI-Racial-Equity-Report.pdf.

Social Work Reinvestment Initiative. Available at: www.socialworkreinvestment.org.

Society for Research in Child Development. (2008). Children in immigrant families key to America's future. *Social Policy Report Brief, 22*(3), 1–2.

Society for Research in Child Development. (2011a). Reducing prejudice and promoting equity in childhood. *Social Policy Report Brief, 25*(4), 1–2.

Society for Research in Child Development. (2011b). Food insecurity harmful to children's development. *Social Policy Report Brief, 25*(3), 1–2.

Society for Research in Child Development. (2013). Investing in our future: The evidence base on preschool education. Available at: www.srcd.org/sites/default/files/documents/washington/2013_10_16_yoshikawa.pdf.

Southern Regional Education Board Manpower Education and Training Project's Rural Task Force. (1998). Educational assumptions for rural social work. In L. Ginsberg (Ed.), *Social work in rural communities* (3rd ed.) (pp. 23–26). Alexandria, VA: Council on Social Work Education.

Soydan, H. & Palinkas, L.A. (2014). *Evidence-based practice in social work. Development of a new professional culture.* New York: Routledge.

Specht, H. & Courtney, M. (1994). *Unfaithful angels: How social work has abandoned its mission.* New York: The Free Press.

Steenrod, S. (2014). What every social worker needs to know about Screening, Brief Intervention, and Referral to Treatment (SBIRT). *The New Social Worker, 21*(3), 16–17.

Steinberg, D.M. (2014). *A mutual-aid model for social work with groups* (3rd ed.). New York: Routledge.

Stiglitz, J.E. (2014, June 17). Inequality is not inevitable. *The New York Times.* Available at: http://opinionator.blogs.nytimes.com/2014/06/27/inequality-is-not-inevitable/?_php=true&_type=blogs&emc=eta1&_r=0.

Stone, C. (2012). If you think income inequality is high, you should see wealth inequality.Washington, DC: Center on Budget Policy and Priorities. Available at: www.offthechartsblog.org/if-you-think-income-inequality-is-high-you-should-see-wealth-inequality/.

Stone, C. (2014). Illustrating income inequality, part 2: Top earners have outpaced rest since 1979. Washington, DC: Center on Budget Policies and Priorities. Available at: www.offthechartsblog.org/illustrating-income-inequality-part-2-top-earners-have-outpaced-rest-since-1979/.

Stone, C., Shaw, H., Trisi, D. & Sherman, A. (2014). *A guide to statistics on historical trends in income inequality.* Washington, DC: Center for Budget and Policy Priorities. Available at: www.cbpp.org/cms/?fa=view&id=3629.

Stone, C., Trisi, D., Sherman, A., & Debot, B. (2015). *A guide to statistics on historical trends in income inequality.* Washington, DC: Center for Budget and Policy Priorities. Available at: www.cbpp.org/research/poverty-and-inequality/a-guide-to-statistics-on-historical-trends-in-income-inequality.

Streeter, C.L., Gamble, D.N., & Weil, M. (2008). Community. In T. Mizrahi & L.E. Davis (Eds.) *Encyclopedia of social work* (20th ed.) (pp. 1:355–368). Washington, DC: NASW Press and Oxford University Press.

Strom-Gottfried, K. (2015). *Straight talk about professional ethics.* Chicago, Illinois: Lyceum Books.

Strom-Gottfried, K. & Dunlap, K.M. (1998). How to keep boundary issues from compromising your practice (Part 2 in a series on ethics). *The New Social Worker, 5*(2), 10–13.

Strom-Gottfried, K., & Dunlap, K.M. (1999). Unraveling ethical dilemmas. *The New Social Worker, 6*(2), 8–12.

Strom-Gottfried, K., Thomas, M.S. & Anderson, H. (2014). Social work and social media: Reconciling ethical standards and emerging technology. *Journal of Social Work Values & Ethics, 11*(1), 54–65.

Substance Abuse and Mental Health Services Administration. (2012). *Mental health, United States, 2010.* HHS publication no. (SMA) 12-4681. Rockville, MD: Center for Mental Health Services, Substance Abuse and Mental Health Services Administration. Available at: www.samhsa.gov/data/2k12/MHUS2010/MHUS-2010.pdf.

Substance Abuse and Mental Health Services Administration, (2013a). *Results from the 2012 National Survey on Drug Use and Health: Mental Health Findings,* NSDUH Series H-47, HHS Publication No. (SMA) 13-4805. Rockville, MD: Substance Abuse and Mental Health Services Administration. Available at: www.samhsa.gov/data/NSDUH/2k12MH_FindingsandDetTables/2K12MHF/NSDUHmhfr2012.htm#high.

Substance Abuse and Mental Health Services Administration. (2013b). *Results from the 2012 national survey on drug use and health: Summary of national findings.* NSDUH series H-46, HHS publication no. (SMA) 13-4795. Rockville, MD: Substance Abuse and Mental Health Services Administration. Available at: www.samhsa.gov/data/NSDUH/2012SummNatFindDetTables/NationalFindings/NSDUHresults2012.pdf.

Substance Abuse and Mental Health Services Administration. (2014). *Substance use and mental health estimates from the 2013 National Survey on Drug Use and Health: Overview of findings.* Rockville, MD: Substance Abuse and Mental Health Services Administration. Available at: www.samhsa.gov/data/sites/default/files/NSDUH-SR200-RecoveryMonth-2014/NSDUH-SR200-RecoveryMonth-2014.htm.

Sullivan, W. P. (2012). Strengths perspective. In M. Gray, J., Midgley, & S.A. Webb, (Eds.), *The SAGE handbook of social work* (pp. 176–190). London: Sage Publications, Ltd.

Sundar, P., Sylvestre, J., & Bassi, A. (2012). Diversity and social work practice. In M. Gray, J., Midgley, & S.A. Webb, (Eds.), *The SAGE handbook of social work* (pp. 355–371). London: Sage Publications, Ltd.

Syers, M. (2008). Flexner, Abraham (1866–1959). In T. Mizrahi & L.E. Davis (Eds.), *Encyclopedia of social work* (20th ed.) (p. 4:338). Washington, DC: NASW Press and Oxford University Press.

Tapp, K. & Payne, D. (2011). Guidelines for practitioners: A social work perspective on discharging the duty to protect. *Journal of Social Work Values and Ethics, 8*(2), 2-1–2-13.

Tervalon, M. & Murray-García, J. (1998). Cultural humility versus cultural competence: A critical distinction in defining physician training outcomes in multicultural education. *Journal of Health Care for the Poor and Underserved,* 9(2), 117–125.

Terrell, P. (2010). Poverty, War on. In T. Fitzpatrick, H. Kwon, N. Manning, J. Midgley & G. Pascall (Eds.), *International encyclopedia of social policy* (pp. 1061–1063). London: Routledge.

Thyer B.A. (2012). Evidence-based practice and social work. In M. Gray, J. Midgley, & S.A. Webb, (Eds.), *The SAGE handbook of social work* (pp. 408–423). London: Sage Publications, Ltd.

Tiehen, L., Jolliffe, D. & Gundersen, C. (2012). *Alleviating poverty in the United States. The critical role of SNAP benefits.* Washington, DC: U.S. Department of Economic Research Service. Available at: www.ers.usda.gov.

Toseland, R.W. & Horton, H. (2008). Group work. In T. Mizrahi & L.E. Davis (Eds.), *Encyclopedia of social work* (20th ed.) (pp. 2:298–308). Washington, DC: NASW Press and Oxford University Press.

Traynor, B. (2012). Community building: Limitations and promises. In J. DeFilippis & S. Saegert (Eds.), *The community development reader* (2nd ed.) (pp. 209–219). New York: Routledge.

Trepper, T.S., McCollum, E.E., De Jong, P., Korman, H., Gingerich, W. & Franklin, C. (2013). *Solution focused therapy manual for working with individuals.* Available at: www.sfbta.org/research.pdf (Research Committee of the Solution Focused Brief Therapy Association).

Trevithick, P. (2012). Practice Perspectives. In M. Gray, J. Midgley, & S.A. Webb, (Eds.), *The SAGE handbook of social work* (pp. 113–128). London: Sage Publications, Ltd.,

Trisi, D. (2014a). *Income inequality remains at record high, new census figures show.* Washington, DC: Center on Budget Policies and Priorities. Available at: www.offthechartsblog.org/?s=Income+inequality.

Trisi, D. (2014b). *Safety net cut poverty nearly in half last year, new census data show.* Washington, DC: Center on Budget Policy & Priorities. Available at: www.offthechartsblog.org/safety-net-cut-poverty-nearly-in-half-last-year-new-census-data-show/.

Trisi, D. Sherman, A. & Broaddus, M. (2011). *Poverty rate second-highest in 45 years; record numbers lacked health insurance, lived in deep poverty.* Washington, DC: Center for Budget and Policy Priorities.

Tropman, J. (2008). Phases of helping. In J. Rothman, J. Erlich & J. Tropman (Eds.), *Strategies of community intervention* (7th ed.) (pp. 127–133). Peosta, IA: Eddie Bowers.

Trust for America's Health. (2014). *Investing in America's health. A state-by-state look at public health funding and key health facts.* Available at: www.healthyamericans.org/assets/files/TFAH2014-InvestInAmericaExecSum02.pdf

Tsay, J. (2010). Public health. In T. Fitzpatrick, N. Manning, J. Midgley, Kwon, H., & G. Pascall (Eds.), *International encyclopedia of social policy* (pp. 1098–1101). London: Routledge.

Turner, F.J. (2008). Interviewing skills. In Sowers, K.M. & Dulmus, C.N. (Eds.) *Comprehensive handbook of social work and social welfare* (pp. 29–45). Hoboken, NJ: John Wiley & Sons, Inc.

United Nations (2009). World population to exceed 9 billion by 2050. Available at: www.un.org.ezp.slu.edu/esa/population/publications/wpp2008/pressrelease.pdf.

United Nations High Commissioner for Refugees (UNHCR). (2014). *Global trends 2013.* Available at: www.unhcr.org/5399a14f9.html.

Urban Experience in Chicago. (n.d.). Available at: http://uic.edu/jaddams/hull/urbanexp/contents.htm.

Urban Institute. (2014, January 9). Understanding poverty. Available at: www.urban.org/poverty/index.cfm.

U.S. Census Bureau. (2012) Statistical Abstracts. Available at: http://www.census.gov/compendia/statab/2012 edition/html.

U.S. Census Bureau. (2012a). 2012 American Community Survey 1-year data file. Available at: www.census.gov/hhes/samesex/.

U.S. Census Bureau. (2012b). U.S. Census Bureau projections show a slower growing, older, more diverse nation a half century from now. Available at: www.census.gov/newsroom/releases/archives/population/cb12-243.html.

U.S. Census Bureau. (2014a). Anniversary of Americans with Disabilities Act: July 26. Available at: www.census.gov/newsroom/releases/pdf/cb14ff-15_ada.pdf.

U.S. Census Bureau. (2014b). Families below poverty level and below 125 percent of percent of poverty by race and Hispanic origin: 1980 to 2012 (Selected Years). ProQuest Statistical Abstract of the U.S. 2014. Available at: http://statabs.proquest.com/sa/abstract.html?table-no=743&acc-no=C7095-1.13&year=2014&z=DD4EB17F762C1BB5D2534907C7C98EF4B9C1C832.

U.S. Census Bureau. (2014c). Fueled by aging baby boomers, nation's older population to nearly double, Census Bureau Reports. Available at: www.census.gov/newsroom/releases/archives/aging_population/cb14-84.html.

U.S. Census Bureau. (2014d). People below poverty level by selected characteristics: 2012 (By race, sex, age, education, region, and citizenship status) ProQuest Statistical Abstract of the U.S. 2014. Available at: http://statabs.proquest.com/sa/abstract.html?table-no=741&acc-noC7095-1.13&year=2014&z=2B255D10F70090A53873829AB182D31A52B6B811.

U.S. Census Bureau. (2014e). State and county quick facts. Available at: http://quickfacts.census.gov/qfd/states/00000.html.

U.S. Census Bureau. (2014f). U.S. & World Population Clock. Available at: www.census.gov/popclock/.

U.S. Census Bureau (2014g). Resident population projections by sex and age: 2015 To 2050 (Quinquennially, as of July 1) ProQuest Statistical Abstract of the U.S. 2014 Online Edition. Available at: http://statabs.proquest.com/sa/abstract.html?table-no=9&acc-no=C7095-1.1&year=2014&z=CC7ACAA06FB0D0A70E958CEE142E529C0CF1C839.

U.S. Census Bureau Fertility and Family Statistics Branch. (2013). Frequently asked questions about same-sex couple households. Available at: www.census.gov/hhes/samesex/files/SScplfactsheet_final.pdf.

U.S. Census Bureau, International Data Base. (2011). *World population growth rates: 1950–2050.* Washington, DC: U.S. Census Bureau.

U.S. Census Bureau News. (2014). Women's history month: March 2014. Available at: www.census.gov/newsroom/releases/pdf/cb14-ff05_womens_history.pdf.

U.S. Census Bureau Newsroom. (2012). Nearly 1 in 5 people have a disability in the U.S., Census Bureau reports. Available at: www.census.gov/newsroom/releases/archives/miscellaneous/cb12-134.html.

U.S. Census Bureau Newsroom. (2013). Measuring America. More American households rely on government benefit programs. Available at: www.census.gov/how/infograph-ics/government_benefits.html.

U.S. Department of Agriculture Food and Nutrition Service. (2012). Supplemental Nutrition Assistance Program (SNAP) pre-screening eligibility tool Available at: www.foodstamps-step1.usda.gov/fns/.

U.S. Department of Commerce, Bureau of the Census. (2014). *Poverty Thresholds for 2013 by Size of Family and Number of Related Children under 18 Years*. Washington, DC: U.S. Census Bureau.

U.S. Department of Health and Human Services. (2004). Protecting the privacy of patients' health information. Available at: www.hhs.gov/news/facts/privacy.html.

U.S. Department of Health and Human Services. (2006). The supply and demand of professional social workers providing long-term care services: Report to Congress. Available at: http://aspe.hhs.gov/daltcp/reports/2006/Swsupply.htm#ref7.

U.S. Department of Health and Human Services. (2013). Child welfare outcomes 2008–2011. Report to Congress. Available at: www.acf.hhs.gov/sites/default/files/cb/cwo08_11_exesum.pdf.

U.S. Department of Health and Human Services Administration on Aging. (2011). A profile of older Americans: 2011. Available at: www.aoa.gov/AoARoot/Aging_Statistics/Profile/2011/docs/2011profile.pdf.

U.S. Department of Health and Human Services, Administration for Children and Families, Administration on Children, Youth, and Families, Children Bureau. (2012). Child maltreatment 2012. Available at: www.acf.hhs.gov/programs/cb/research-data-technology/statistics-research#can.

U.S. Department of Health and Human Services, Administration for Children and Families (n.d.). Worker turnover. Available at: www.childwelfare.gov/management/workforce/retention/turnover.cfm.

U.S. Department of Health and Human Services Health Resources and Services Administration, Maternal and Child Health Bureau. (2013). *Women's health USA 2013*. Rockville, MD: U.S. Department of Health and Human Services. Available at: www.mchb.hrsa.gov/whusa13/dl/pdf/whusa13.pdf.

U.S. Department of Justice. (2015). Investigation of the Ferguson Police Department. Available at: www.justice.gov.

U.S. Department of Labor. (2008). Career guide to industries, 2008–2009 edition. Advocacy, grantmaking, and civic organizations. Available at: www.bls.gov/oco/cg/cgso54.htm.

U.S. Department of Labor, Bureau of Labor Statistics. (2010a). Career guide to indus-tries, 2010–11 edition, state and local government, except education and health. Available at: www.bls.gov/oco/cg/cgs042.htm.

U.S. Department of Labor, Bureau of Labor Statistics. (2010b). The 2008–18 job outlook in brief. *Occupational Outlook Quarterly*. Available at: www.bls.gov/career-outlook/2010/spring/spring2010ooq.pdf.

U.S. Department of Labor, Bureau of Labor Statistics. (2012). Employment situation summary. Available at: www.bls.gov/news.release/empsit.nr0.htm.

U.S. Department of Labor, Bureau of Labor Statistics. (2013). Fastest growing occupa-tions. Available at: www.bls.gov/emp/ep_table_103.htm.

U.S. Department of Labor, Bureau of Labor Statistics. (2014a). Industry-occupation matrix data, by industry. Available at: www.bls.gov/emp/ep_table_109.htm.

U.S. Department of Labor, Bureau of Labor Statistics. (2014b). Occupational outlook handbook, 2014–15 edition, social workers. Available at www.bls.gov/ooh/community-and-social-service/social-workers.htm.

U.S. Department of Labor, Bureau of Labor Statistics. (2014c). A profile of the working poor, 2012. Washington, DC: U.S. Department of Labor. Available at: www.bls.gov/cps/cpswp2012.pdf.

U.S. Department of State, Bureau of Population, Refugees, and Migration (PRM). (2014). FY13 Refugee Admissions Statistics. Available at: www.state.gov/j/prm/releases/statistics/228666.htm.

U.S. News and World Report (2014). The 100 best jobs. Available at: http://money.usnews.com/careers/best-jobs/rankings/the-100-best-jobs?page=3.

U.S. Social Security Administration. (2013). *Fact sheet, February 7, 2013*. Baltimore, MD: U.S. Social Security Administration.

USA Life Expectancy. (2015). Life expectancy. All races. Available at: www.worldlifeexpectancy.com/usa/life-expectancy.

Valutis, S., Rubin, D. & Bell, M. (2011). Professional socialization and social work values: Who are we teaching? *Social Work Education, First Article,* 1–12.

Van Hook, M.P. (2014). *Social work practice with families: A resiliency-based approach.* Chicago, IL: Lyceum Books.

Van Soest, D. (2008). Oppression. In T. Mizrahi & L.E. Davis (Eds.), *Encyclopedia of social work* (20th ed.) (pp. 3:322–324). Washington, DC: NASW Press and Oxford University Press.

Vaughn, M., Fu, Q., DeLisi, M., Beaver, K., Perron, B. & Howard, M. (2009). Are personality disorders associated with social welfare burden in the United States? Results from the National Epidemiologic Survey on Alcohol and Related Conditions. *The American Journal of Psychiatry, 24,* 709–721.

Vespa, J., Lewis, J.M. & Kreider, R.M. (2013). *America's families and living arrangements: 2012. Current Population Reports, P20-570.* Washington, DC: U.S. Census Bureau, Washington. Available at: www.census.gov/prod/2013pubs/p20-570.pdf.

Wagner, C.C. & Ingersoll, K.S. (2013). *Motivational interviewing in groups.* New York: Guilford Press.

Wagner, E.F. (2008). Motivational interviewing. In T. Mizrahi & L.E. Davis (Eds.), *Encyclopedia of social work* (20th ed.) (pp. 3:273–276). Washington, DC: NASW Press and Oxford University Press.

Walker, A. (2010). Community-based development. In T. Fitzpatrick, H. Kwon, N. Manning, J. Midgley & G. Pascall (Eds.), *International encyclopedia of social policy* (pp. 195–196). London: Routledge.

Walsh, J. (2010). *Theories for direct social work practice* (2nd ed.). Belmont, CA: Wadsworth Cengage Learning.

Walters, N.P. & Trevelyan, E.N. (2011). *The newly arrived foreign-born population of the United States: 2010.* Washington, DC: U.S. Census Bureau.

Walton, S. (1996). Getting real: Mastering the art of helping others. In *America's best graduate schools* (p. 63). Washington, DC: *U.S. News and World Report.*

Wang, W. (2012). *The rise of intermarriage. Rates, characteristics vary by race and gender.* Washington, DC: Pew Research Center. Available at: http://pewresearch.org/pubs/2197/intermarriage-race-ethnicity-asians-whites-hispanics-blacks.

Watkins, J.M. & Holmes, J. (2008). Educating for social work. In Sowers, K.M. & Dulmus, C.N. (Eds.) *Comprehensive handbook of social work and social welfare* (pp. 25–36). Hoboken, NJ: John Wiley & Sons, Inc.

Webb, R. (2013). Advancing health equality through the National Culturally and

Linguistically Appropriate Services (CLAS) Standards. *NASW Practice Perspectives*, 1–3.

Webb, R. (2014). Multiculturalism: Implications for culturally competent social work practice. *NASW Practice Perspectives*, 1–4.

Weil, M. (2013). Community-based social planning: Theory and practice. In M. Weil, M. Reisch & M.L. Ohmer (Eds). The *handbook of community practice* (2nd ed.) (pp. 265–299). Thousand Oaks, CA: Sage Publications, Inc.

Weil, M.O. & Gamble, D.N. (2015). Community practice model for the twenty-first century. In K. Corcoran & A.R. Roberts (Eds.), *Social workers' desk reference* (3rd ed.) (pp. 907–919). New York: Oxford University Press.

Weil, M., Gamble, D.N. & Ohmer, M.L. (2013a). Evolution, models, and the changing context of community practice. In M. Weil, M. Reisch & M.L. Ohmer (Eds). The *handbook of community practice* (2nd ed.) (pp. 167–195). Thousand Oaks, CA: Sage Publications, Inc.

Weil, M. & Ohmer, M.L. (2013). Applying practice theories in community work. In M. Weil, M. Reisch, & M.L. Ohmer (Eds). *The handbook of community practice* (2nd ed.) (pp. 123–163). Thousand Oaks, CA: Sage Publications, Inc.

Weil, M., Reisch, M. & Ohmer, M.L. (2013). Contexts and challenges for 21st century communities. In M. Weil, M. Reisch, & M.L. Ohmer (Eds). *The handbook of community practice* (2nd ed.) (pp. 3–27). Thousand Oaks, CA: Sage Publications, Inc.

West, L.A., Cole, S., Goodkind, D. & He, W. (2014). *65+ in the United States: 2010. Special Studies. Current Population Reports (P23-212)*. Available at: www.census.gov/content/dam/Census/library/publications/2014/demo/p23-212.pdf.

Wharton, T.C. (2008). Compassion fatigue: Being an ethical social worker. *The New Social Worker, 15*(1), 4–7.

Wheeler, S.M. (2012). Sustainability in community development. In J. DeFilippis & S. Saegert (Eds.), *The community development reader* (2nd ed.) (pp. 175–183). New York: Routledge.

Whitaker, T. (2008). *Who wants to be a social worker? Career influences and timing. NASW membership workforce study*. Washington, DC: National Association of Social Workers.

Whitaker, T. & Arrington, P. (2008). *Social workers at work. NASW membership workforce study*. Washington, DC: National Association of Social Workers.

Whitaker, T., Weismiller, T. & Clark, E. (2006). *Assuring the sufficiency of a frontline workforce: A national study of licensed social workers. Special report: Social work services for children and families*. Washington, DC: National Association of Social Workers.

Whitaker, T., Weismiller, T., Clark, E. & Wilson, M. (2006). *Assuring the sufficiency of a frontline workforce: A national study of licensed social workers. Special report: Social work services in health care settings*. Washington, DC: National Association of Social Workers.

White, N. (2011). Personal communication.

Wilkinson, R. & Pickett, K. (2009). *The spirit level: Why equality is better for everyone*. Harmondsworth: Penguin.

Williams, L.D. & Joyner, M. (2008). Baccalaureate social workers. In T. Mizrahi & L.E. Davis (Eds.), *Encyclopedia of social work* (20th ed.) (pp. 3:322–324). Washington, DC: NASW Press and Oxford University Press.

Williams, M. & Smolak, A. (2007). Integrating faith matters in social work education. *Journal of Religion & Spirituality in Social Work, 26*(3), 25–44.

Williamson, J. (2010). Demographic trends. In T. Fitzpatrick, H. Kwon, N. Manning, J.

Midgley & G. Pascall (Eds.), *International encyclopedia of social policy* (pp. 297–300). London: Routledge.

Wilson, M. (2010). *Criminal justice social work in the United States: Adapting to new challenges*. Washington, DC: NASW Center for Workforce Studies.

Wolfsohn, R. (2012). Financial social work. In E.F. Hoffler & E.J. Clark (Eds.), *Social work matters: The power of linking policy and practice* (pp. 219–223). Washington, DC: NASW Press.

Worden, B. (2011). Women and sexist oppression. In G.A. Appleby, E. Colon & J. Hamilton (Eds.), *Diversity, oppression, and social functioning. Person-in-environment assessment and intervention* (3rd ed.) (pp. 90–107). Boston, MA: Allyn & Bacon.

Worldbank Group. (2003). Understanding poverty. Available at: www.worldbank.org/poverty/mission/up1.htm.

World Bank. (2013a). Poverty reduction in practice: How and where we work. Available at: www.worldbank.org/en/news/feature/2013/02/05/poverty-reduction-in-practice.

World Bank. (2013b). Remarkable declines in global poverty, but major challenges remain. Available at: www.worldbank.org/en/news/press-release/2013/04/17/remarkable-declines-in-global-poverty-but-major-challenges-remain.

Young, I.M. (2012). Five faces of oppression. In J. DeFilippis & S. Saegert (Eds)., *The community development reader* (2nd ed.) (pp. 328–337). New York: Routledge.

Glossary/Index

Page numbers in **bold** refer to exhibits

commitment 4, 61

communication: community-level 554; group work 505–6; nonverbal 449–50; skills 244–6, **425**; style 451; verbal 449–50

community 524

community assessments 554–6, **556**, **557**

community-building *see* community-level social work

Community Chests 62

community development **352**, **533**, 537–40, 544. *See also* community-level social work

community education centers 426

community health centers 402

community-level social work practice: a method of social work practice in which the social worker works with a client system comprised of organizations and communities to develop a planned change effort that meets the needs of the organization or community 524–64; advocacy websites 560–1; assessment 554–6, **556**, **557**; coalition building **534**, 543–4; communication 554; community unity and justice 536; conflict 545; consensus 545; empowerment 538; engagement 553–4; evaluation 558–9; functional community organizing **533**, 536–7; funding 531; geographic or neighborhood community organizing 532, **533**, 534–5; and globalization 528–9; goals 525, 537; goal-setting 555; history and development 529–31; housing 535; hybrid or combined approach 545; international social work education: 542; interventions 552–60; leadership 539; models of change 531–2, **533–4**, 534–49; movements for progressive change **534**, 548–9; neighborhood redevelopment 542; organization process 535; policy practice 547–8, **550**; political, social, and legislative action **534**, 544–7, **546**; program development **533**, 540–1; rural domestic violence services 543; skills 537, 549–53, **552**, 560; social and economic community development model **533**, 537–40; social planning **533–4**, 541–3; social worker roles 525–6, 549–52; stakeholders 537, 554; strategies 537, 558; strengths-based perspective 532; target community 532, 554; termination 559–60; time devoted to 526, **527**; transportation 535–6; vision 560

Community Mental Health Center Act 67

community networks 431

community organization: a method of social work that involves working with groups and communities to identify conditions and develop strategies to address community level conditions 14, 535

community practice; practice focused on social change within communities and organizations 174

community sector 21

community service 35

community unity and justice 536

community well-being **160**

compassion fatigue: also known as burn out, compassion fatigue occurs when professionals experience an extreme emotional response to their work 588

compassionate conservatism 71, 117

Comprehensive Employment and Training Act (CETA) 69

conceptual frameworks 79

confidentiality: maintaining client-related information and disclosing only with the permission of the client or the client's guardian 275–8, **277**, **279**, 292, **293**, 294, 509; exceptions 273–4, 277–8; relative 279

conflict of interest 254, 259, 282

NEW DIRECTIONS IN SOCIAL WORK

SERIES EDITOR: ALICE LIEBERMAN, UNIVERSITY OF KANSAS

New Directions in Social Work is an innovative, integrated series offering a uniquely distinctive teaching strategy for generalist courses in the social work curriculum, at both undergraduate and graduate levels. The series integrates 5 texts with custom websites housing interactive cases, companion readings, and a wealth of resources to enrich the teaching and learning experience.

FOURTH EDITION

HUMAN BEHAVIOR IN THE SOCIAL ENVIRONMENT

Perspectives on Development and the Life Course

Anissa Rogers, University of Portland

Hb: 978-1-138-81950-4 ▪ Pb: 978-1-138-81951-1 ▪ eBook: 978-1-315-74439-1

THIRD EDITION

RESEARCH FOR EFFECTIVE SOCIAL WORK PRACTICE

Judy L. Krysik, Arizona State University and
Jerry Finn, University of Washington, Tacoma

Hb: 978-0-415-52100-0 ▪ Pb: 978-0-415-51986-1 ▪ eBook: 978-0-203-07789-0

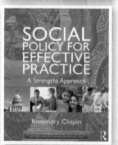

THIRD EDITION

SOCIAL POLICY FOR EFFECTIVE PRACTICE

Rosemary Chapin, University of Kansas

Hb: 978-0-415-51991-5 ▪ Pb: 978-0-415-51992-2 ▪ eBook: 978-0-203-79476-0

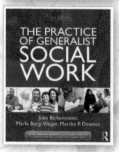

THIRD EDITION

THE PRACTICE OF GENERALIST SOCIAL WORK

Julie Birkenmaier and **Marla Berg-Weger**, both at St. Louis University and **Martha P. Dewees**, University of Vermont

Hb: 978-0-415-51988-5 ▪ Pb: 978-0-415-51989-2 ▪ eBook: 978-0-203-07098-7

Routledge
Taylor & Francis Group

Routledge... think about it
www.routledge.com